INTRODUCTION

In this first edition of *The Irish Almanac and Yearbook of Facts* we have sought to put together a book which comprehensively covers all aspects of life in Ireland, North and South. We have attempted to make available information which is not readily available but which is important to the understanding of modern Ireland.

The Irish Almanac and Yearbook of Facts can be used as a useful reference book by either the serious student/academic or the reader who simply wishes to browse through the book.

In this publication detailed facts and figures are given about the Ireland of today - the population breakdown, the performance of the economy, the latest available statistics on health, education, agriculture, fishing and industry.

There are chapters on key Irish political personalities, Irish writers, historical events of significance, a breakdown of the various religions, details on the counties and cities, geographical superlatives plus an extensive section on sport which not only covers current events and personalities but provides details about Irish sporting heroes of the past.

In addition, there are also sections which provide useful information about Irish embassies abroad, telephone codes, newspaper sales (local/regional/national), radio and t.v. stations and their most popular programmes, as well as coverage of all the main news stories and key events during 1996.

While Ireland is the last island on the European land mass, its isolation on the periphery of western Europe has been almost totally eroded in recent times by the growth in mass communications. Politically, socially, educationally and economically the island has also been influenced by European Union membership. The Ireland of the 1990's is radically different to the Ireland of the 1960's. We have attempted to provide the detail which puts that change into perspective.

In our endeavours we have been helped by numerous people, many of their names appear in the acknowledgments, and by many others who gave of their time and expertise, but who, for a variety of reasons, would prefer to remain anonymous. We extend our thanks to them all. However, a special word of thanks goes to Fr. Kevin O'Doherty, a Donegal man, whose encouragement, inspiration and commitment to the project was very much appreciated by all concerned.

This book has been the culmination of two years of planning and research. Our objective has been to provide a unique publication, a one-stop archive of facts and figures about Ireland in 1996.

While every effort has been made to ensure that all information in this publication is correct at the time of going to press (31st August, 1996), the editors do not accept responsibility for any errors or omissions.

Pat McArt.

ACKNOWLEDGMENTS

The Editors would like to thank the following people and organisations for their much valued assistance in compiling information for this publication: Elaine Duffy, Department of the Taoiseach; Dáil Éireann; Adrienne, Áras an Uachtaráin; Pat Quearney, The Workers Party; Democratic Left; David Landy, The Green Party; Labour Party; Eugene McCartan, Communist Party of Ireland; Philip Hannon, Fianna Fáil; Pat Boland, Sinn Féin; Simon King, Fine Gael; Gerry Cosgrove, Social Democratic & Labour Party; Jim Wilson, Ulster Unionist Council; Christopher Cahoon, Ulster Unionist Party; W. L. McIntyre, Ulster Popular Unionist Party; Pat Costello, South Dublin County Council; Geraldine Murphy, Monaghan County Council; D. Breen, Sligo County Council; J. Cullen, Galway County Council; M. Donnelly, Cavan County Council; C. O'Connell, Limerick County Council; Kevin Boyle, Roscommon County Council; Dolores Whitty, Wexford County Council; A. Moore, Donegal County Council; A. McNicholl, Laois County Council; J. Guckian, Dun Laoghaire - Rathdown County Council; Martin O'Donoighue, Kerry County Council; Sheila Connolly, Offaly County Council; Fergus Galvin, Waterford Corporation; Aida Baragwanath, Dublin Corporation; Thomas McEvoy, Cavan County Enterprise Board; Robert Wilson, Belfast City Council; Claire Lundy, Derry City Council; Tipperary (N.R.) County Council; Tipperary (S.R.) County Council; Mayo County Council; Waterford County Council; Northern Ireland Tourist Office; Dublin Tourist Information Office; Limerick Tourist Information Office; Ireland West Tourism; Cork Kerry Tourism; Niall Brookes, Meteorological Service; M. McDermott, Ordnance Survey; Oscar Merne, Office of Public Works; Department of the Environment; Dermot McLaughlin - Wildlife Officer, Buncrana; Ellen Moore, Northern Ireland Economic Research Centre; John Keating, Teagasc; John McLoughlin, Coillte Teoranta; Kathleen Regan, Department of the Marine; Bernie Rooney, Department of Economic Development (N. I.); Irish Dairy Board; Milk Marketing Board (N.I.); Livestock Marketing Commission (N.I.); Department of Agriculture, Food & Forestry; Forest Service, Department of Agriculture for Northern Ireland; Fisheries Service, Department of Agriculture for Northern Ireland; Bord Iascaigh Mhara; Industrial Development Board (N. I.); Industrial Development Agency; Forbairt; Forfás; Jonathan King, Department of Enterprise & Employment; Brian Masterson, Department of Education; Orla Christie, Higher Education Authority; Gerry McDonnell, National Council for Educational Awards; Department of Education (N. I.); An Chomhairle Leabhrann; University of Ulster; Queens University of Belfast; Limavady College of Further Education; Omagh College of Further Education; Western Education & Library Board; Belfast Education & Library Board; Southern Education & Library Board; South Eastern Education & Library Board; Fergal Goodman, Department of Health; Eastern Health Board; Midland Health Board; Mid-Western Health Board; North Western Health Board; An Bord Altranais; P. J. O'Brien, Burt; Capt. Roger McGrath, Defence Forces; Paul Gorecki, Northern Ireland Economic Council; Anne Jordan, Northern Ireland Statistics & Research Agency; John O'Malley, Central Bank of Ireland; Tony Lynch, Department of Finance; Linda Daly, Irish Banks Information Service; John Keegan, An Post; National Treasury Management Agency; Trustee Savings Bank; Allied Irish Banks; Gary Lynch, National Roads Authority; Shirley Groarke, Department of the Environment; Ann Walsh, Department of the Environment; C. M. Caughey, Driver & Vehicle Licensing Northern Ireland; Trevor Evans, Driver & Vehicle Licensing Northern Ireland; Paul King, Transportation Unit Northern Ireland; Terence Savage, Northern Ireland Transport Holding Company; Conor Faughnan, Automobile Association; Kathy Tease, Automobile Association (N.I.); Córas Iompair Éireann; Bus Éireann; Iarnród Éireann; Mary F. McIntyre Lawlor, Department of Tourism & Trade; Marie Fitzpatrick, Office of Public Works; Elaine Gowan, Central Statistics Office; John Brown, Bord Fáilte; Northern Ireland Tourist Board; Donal Clarke, Bord na Móna; Brian O'Byrne, Department of Energy, Transport & Communications; Eithne Brown, Department of Energy, Transport & Communications; Miriam Farrelly, Bord Gáis Éireann; Janet Hoy, Department of Economic Development; Siobhan Browne, Electricity Supply Board; Sergeant Kenneth Hill, Garda Síochána; Séamus Hanrahan, Department of Justice; Jim Cantwell, Catholic Press & Information Office; Rev. Samuel Hutchinson, Presbyterian Church in Ireland; Stephen Lynas, Presbyterian Church in Ireland; Rev. Brian D. Griffin, Methodist Church in Ireland; Rev. Edmund T. I. Mawhinney, Methodist Church in Ireland; June Howard, Church of Ireland; Pastor William Colville, Baptist Union of Ireland; Gerard Ryan, Dianetics & Scientology; Muhammed O'Curnain, Islamic Foundation of Ireland; Western Buddhist Order; Liz Powell, The Arts Council; Éanna Mac Giolla Ruaidh, Department of Arts, Culture and the Gaeltacht; Dr. Felicity Devlin, National Museum of Ireland; Jacqui Berkeley, Ulster Television; Helena Gaffney, Ulster Television; Fionnuala O'Kelly, Radio Telefís Éireann; Angela Hunter, BBC Northern Ireland; Méabh Ní Chatháin, Bord na Gaeilge; Caitríona Ní Ghriallais, Comhdháil Náisiúnta na Gaeilge; Máire Seosaimhín Breathnach, Údarás na Gaeltachta; Seán Ó Ceallaigh, Gael-Linn; Film Institute of Ireland; National Lottery; Sport Council in Ireland; Sports Council for Northern Ireland; Barry Holohan, Olympic Council of Ireland; Hugh O'Rorke, Irish Federation of Sea Anglers; Gerard Carmody, Irish Rugby Football Union; Eavan Lyons, Irish Rugby Football Union; Veronica Byrne, Irish Amateur Swimming Assoc.; Peadar Casey, Irish Amateur Rowing Union; Seamus Smith, Golfing Union of Ireland; Joe Kirwan, Irish Amateur Boxing Assoc.; Brid Donelan, Tennis Ireland; Eavan Brady, Irish Tug of War Assoc.; Judy Cohen, Irish Women's Cricket Union; Derek Scott, Irish Cricket Union; Zoe Lally, Irish Surfing Assoc.; Irene Johnston, Irish Ladies Hockey Union; Beryl Walsh, Irish Hockey Union; Síle de Bhailís, Cumann Camógaíochta na nGael; Harry Havelin, Motor Cycle Union of Ireland; Jack Watson, Federation of Irish Cyclists; Liam Hennessy, Bord Lúthchleas na hÉireann; Kitty Barlow, Football Assoc. of Ireland; Alex Sinclair, R.I.A.C.; Irish Sailing Association; Lisa Royle, Northern Ireland Blind Sports; Richard Date, Northern Ireland Amateur Fencing Union; Thomas E. Snoddy, Ulster Gliding Club; Michael Murray, Canoe Assoc. of Northern Ireland; Clare White, Irish Triathlon Assoc.; Doreen Miskelly, Irish Women's Indoor Bowling Association; R. McDermott, Irish Indoor Bowling Association; Jim Graves, Northern Ireland Ice Hockey Association; Northern Ireland Women's Football Association; Northern Ireland Karting Association; Seán Ó Pronntaigh, Connacht Council; Tom Ryall, Kilkenny County Board; Pádraig Ó Laoighléis, Wicklow County Board; Damhnaic MacEochaidh, Tyrone County Board; Gerry McGlory, Antrim County Board; Pádraig Óg Nuinsean, Armagh County Board; Padraig Ó Tomhnair, Louth County Board; Cavan County Board; Kildare County Board; Monaghan County Board; Noreen Doherty, Donegal County Board; David Guiney; Neil Russell, Audit Bureau of Circulations; Sean Gordon, Irish Amateur Swimming Assoc.; Staff of Central Library, Derry; Staff of Central Library, Letterkenny; Fr. Seán Ó Gallchóir, Bun a' Leaca; Pearse Callaghan, Killea, Co. Donegal; John McCafferty, Rathfarnham, Dublin.

CONTENTS

Please note the following abbreviations used throughout the 'Contents' and in chapters throughout the book: -
R.O.I. = Republic of Ireland   N.I. = Northern Ireland

TOP TEN NEWS STORIES, 1996................................11

CHRONOLOGY OF 1996..12

WHAT WAS SAID IN 1996 19

POLITICS (Republic of Ireland) ....(22-50)
Introduction 22
Explanatory notes on the President, Parliament
and Government 22
The Office of President of Ireland 22
Explanatory notes on Northern Ireland 22
State Emblems of the R.O.I. 23
R.O.I. Political Parties..23
R.O.I. Political Leaders 25
Irish Politics - The "Family" Tree................................26
R.O.I. General Election Results (1992) 26
R.O.I. By-Election Results since 1992 28
R.O.I. Government System..29
Government of the R.O.I..30
Key to R.O.I. Political Parties.....................................30
Current position of R.O.I.Parties................................30
Dáil Summary (1996) 31
Members of the 27th Dáil...33
Current breakdown Seanad Éireann 35
Members of Seanad Éireann 35
R.O.I. Members of European Parliament.....................36
European Parliament Election Results 37
Constitutional Referenda 1937 - 1996 37
President of Ireland Statistics 38
Biographies of Presidents of Ireland..........................38
Presidential Election Results (1945-1990)..................39
Taoisigh and Tánaistes of Ireland (1922-'96) 40
Biographies of Irish Taoisigh 40
Governments (1922-96)..43

Elections:
All-Ireland General Election (1918)............................49
General Election to Parliament
of Southern Ireland (1921)...49
Dáil Éireann Elections (1922-1992) 49
Votes recorded at Dáil Elections (1948-1992) 50

POLITICS (Northern Ireland) ....(50-58)
N.I. Political Parties..50
N.I. Political Leaders 51
N.I. General Election Results (1992) 52
N.I. By-Election Results since 1992...........................53
Key to N.I. Political Parties 53
Current position of N.I. Parties...................................53

N.I. Members of Parliament 53
Elections:
N.I. Elections to Westminster (1922-1974) 54
N.I. Elections to Westminster (1974 - 1992) 54
Changing state of the Parties (1983-1996).................54
Parliament of Northern Ireland (1921-1973) 54
N.I. Forum Election (1996)..55
N.I. Members of European Parliament 55
N.I. European Parliament Elections (1979-1994) 55
N.I. Prime Minister Statistics.....................................55
Biographies of N.I. Prime Ministers 55
Governments of N.I. (1921-1972) 57

Lord Lieutenants and Chief Secretaries of Ireland 58
Selected Biographies of Political Figures 59

HISTORY ....(61-80)
Chronology of Irish History 61
Historical Movements and Organisations 67
Historical Documents 72
Burial Places of Famous Irish Personalities 74

WHO WAS WHO 75

WHO'S WHO IN IRELAND ....(81-83)

INTERNATIONAL WHO'S WHO and WHO WAS WHO
International Figures with Irish Connections ....(84-85)

GEOGRAPHICAL & ENVIRONMENT................(87-91)
Ireland Geographical and Physical Statistics..............87
Introduction: Island of Ireland - Physical Features.......87
Ireland Area Comparison Table....................................88
Area by Province/Persons per Sq. Km (R.O.I) 88
Ireland: World Time Differences 89
Meteorological Stations 89
Irish Mammals 90
Birds of Ireland...90
List of Extinct and Endangered Irish Birds..................91
Counties of Ireland (Largest to smallest) 91

POPULATION..(92-102)
Typical Irish Person through Eyes of the Census........92
Republic of Ireland Census...93
Northern Ireland Census...93
Overview Irish Census Information (1891-1996) 93
R.O.I. Population
by Province and County (1991-1996) 94
R.O.I. Population by Age-Group (1981-1991) 94

R.O.I.: Males and Females under 40 years-of-age......95
R.O.I. Enumerated by Selected Birthplace 95
Demographic Statistics (R.O.I. & N.I.) 96
R.O.I. Religious Denominations 96
R.O.I. Occupations by Industrial Group 96
R.O.I. Province & County by Religion 97
R.O.I Marriages, Births and Deaths 97
R.O.I. Selected Occupations Statistics 98
N.I. Census Overview (1891-1991) 98
N.I. Overview Religious Denomination 98
N.I. Overview Religious Denominations
by Percentage..99
N.I. Religion by District Area 99
Persons by N.I. District Council area
by Religious Denomination (%) 99
N.I. by Age-Group (1971-1991) 100
Males and Females in N.I. (1971-1991) 100
N.I. Marriages, Births and Deaths (1988-'93) 100
N.I. Occupations by Industrial Group 101
N.I. Selected Occupations 101
Main Irish Towns..101

COUNTIES & CITIES ....(104-110)
Introduction 104
Profiles of Irish Counties and Major Cities 104

BUSINESS, FINANCE AND TRADE..............(111-117)
Republic of Ireland Introduction 111
Northern Ireland Introduction 111
R.O.I. Value and Volume of Exports and Imports 112
Geographical Distribution of R.O.I. Exports 112
Geographical Distribution of R.O.I. Imports 112
Composition of R.O.I. Exports 112
Composition of R.O.I. Imports 112
International Trade Statistics 112
Cross Border Trade - Manufacturing Goods..............112
R.O.I. National Debt Statistics 113
R.O.I. Official External Reserves IR£m 113
R.O.I. Current Account Balance
in IR£m and Percentage of GNP 113
Exchange Rate of R.O.I. Pound 113
Purchasing Power of the Irish Pound 113
Foreign Grant-Aided Investment in R.O.I. 113
Construction Costs in Europe 113
Government Spending in N.I. 114
Macro - Economic Statistics 114
Interest Cost of R.O.I. National Debt 114
R.O.I. Currency Composition of Foreign Debt (%).....114
R.O.I. Public Finance Developments 114
R.O.I. GDP by Sector 114
Government Finance: N.I. 115
N.I. Public Expenditure as Percentage of GDP 115
R.O.I. and N.I. Social Insurance Contributions 115

R.O.I. Banking Statistics 116
R.O.I. Banking Profits 116
R.O.I. Bank Employment/Branches 116
R.O.I. Post Office Statistics 116
N.I. Banking Statistics 117
R.O.I. Tax Table 117
R.O.I. and N.I. Tax Rates 117

INDUSTRY ....(119-142)
Manufacturing
Introduction 119
Top 30 R.O.I. Companies 119
R.O.I. Employment Figures by Industry 120
R.O.I. Industrial Workers Weekly Earnings 120
Average Weekly Earnings of R.O.I.
Industrial Workers by Sector......................................120
Gross Earnings and hours worked
by R.O.I. Industrial Workers......................................120
R.O.I. Average Hourly Earnings Comparison Table ..121
R.O.I. Strikes Statistics 121
Origins of IDA-assisted Overseas
Companies in R.O.I. 121
IDA Supported Jobs in R.O.I. 121
Labour Costs Comparison Table 122
Pay and Tax Rates (R.O.I. & N.I.) 122
Unemployment & Employment Statistics
(R.O.I. & N.I.) 122
Top 30 N.I. Companies 123
N.I. Manufacturing Employment by sector 123
N.I. Gross Weekly Wage and Replacement Rate......123
Examples of Earnings in N.I. 124
N.I. Main Sales Markets..124
Work Stoppages in N.I. 124
N.I. Male Unemployment by Age-Group 124
Unemployment in N.I. 124
N.I. Employment and Training 124
N.I. Unemployment Rates by Qualification and Age..124
Trade Unions in Ireland 125

Agriculture
Introduction 126
Main R.O.I. Agricultural Bodies..................................126
R.O.I. Farms by Size and Number..............................126
R.O.I. Persons in Farming 127
Agriculture in Relation to Population
and Labour Force in R.O.I. 127
R.O.I. Agricultural Wages 127
R.O.I. Gross Agricultural Output 128
R.O.I. Agricultural Production and Exports 128
R.O.I. Selected Prices for Farm Products..................128
R.O.I. Use of land for Agricultural Purposes..............129
Direct Income Subsidies paid in R.O.I. 129
R.O.I. Livestock Figures 130

R.O.I. Cattle and Sheep by Region 130
Chief Crops in R.O.I. 130
R.O.I. Area under Crops and Pasture by Region 131
R.O.I. Dairy Exports by Country 131
R.O.I. Dairy Exports by Product...............................131
R.O.I. Farm Machinery and Equipment 132
N.I. Farms by Number and Area...............................132
N.I. Persons in Farming 132
N.I. Gross Agricultural Output..................................133
Imports of Cattle to N.I. from R.O.I. 133
Average Producer Prices
of Agricultural Products in N.I. 134
N.I. Land under Cultivation 134
N.I. Livestock Figures 135

Fisheries
Introduction 135
Top 20 R.O.I. Ports...136
R.O.I. Aquaculture Output Value 136
R.O.I. Value of Fish Exports 136
Geographic Spread of R.O.I. Export Markets 137
Fishing Quotas..137
Trends in R.O.I. Fish Exports 138
Trends in R.O.I. Fish Imports....................................138
Numbers Engaged in Sea Fishing in R.O.I. 138
R.O.I. Fishing Fleet...138
Liveweight / Estimated Value of landed Fish in N.I....139
Fishing Ports in N.I. 140
Liveweight / Estimated Value
of all landed Fish in N.I. by Port...............................140
Liveweight and Estimated Value
of Fish landed by N.I. Vessels outside N.I. 140

Afforestation
European Forest and Area Resources 141
R.O.I. Afforestation by County 141
N.I. Afforestation 141
N.I. Forest and Area Resources 142

ENERGY ....(143-147)
Introduction: R.O.I. 143
Introduction: N.I. 143
Mining 144
Power Stations in Ireland by Type and Capacity 144
Electricity Expenses in R.O.I. and N.I. 145
ESB Development in R.O.I. 145
ESB Contribution to R.O.I. Economy 145
ESB Network Statistics in R.O.I. 145
ESB Distribution Statistics in R.O.I. 145
ESB and Bord na Mona Employee Numbers 145
R.O.I. Energy Demands...146
R.O.I. Total Fuel Consumption 146
N.I. Energy Industry Employees 146

N.I. Coal Shipments..146
N.I. Energy Consumption by Source 146
Selected N.I. Electricity Statistics 146
Northern Ireland Water Output 146
R.O.I. Petrol Prices 147
N.I. Petrol Prices..147

TOURISM..(148-153)
Introduction 148
Visitors to R.O.I. by Country of Origin......................148
Expenditure by Visitors to R.O.I. 149
Destination and Expenditure by Visitors to R.O.I.......149
Expenditure per Person by Visitors to R.O.I. 149
Accommodation and Social Expenses (R.O.I. & N.I.)149
Visitors to N.I. by Country of Origin 150
Holiday Visitors to N.I. by Country of Origin 150
Expenditure by Visitors to N.I. 151
Visits abroad by R.O.I. Residents (Route of Travel)..151
Visits abroad by R.O.I. Residents
(Reason for Journey) 151
Overseas Visits by R.O.I. Residents..........................151
Heritage Centres in Ireland.......................................152

TRANSPORT...(155-165)
Introduction 155
R.O.I. Bus Transport...155
N.I. Bus Transport...156
R.O.I. Rail Transport...156
N.I. Rail Transport...156
Iarnród Éireann Receipt Statistics 157
Iarnród Éireann Passenger Statistics 157
R.O.I. Shipping and Boat Transport...........................157
N.I. Shipping and Boat Transport 157
Passenger Movement by Sea to and from R.O.I. 157
R.O.I. Airline Statistics 158
N.I. Airline Statistics 158
Air Passenger Movement to and from R.O.I. 158
R.O.I. Cross-Border Passenger Movement 159
R.O.I. Passenger Movement by Sea,
Rail, Road and Air...159
Licensed Vehicles in N.I. 159
Licensed Vehicles in R.O.I. 160
Driving Licenses in R.O.I. 160
Driving Licenses in N.I. 161
R.O.I. Car Registration Index Marks..........................161
N.I. Car Registration Index Marks..............................162
R.O.I. Speed Laws..162
N.I. Speed Laws 162
Minimum Age for Driving by Category in R.O.I. 162
Minimum Age for Driving by Category in N.I...............162
20 Most Popular Cars Licensed in R.O.I. 163
20 Most Popular Cars - N.I. 163
Transport Infrastructure (R.O.I. & N.I.) 163

Cross-Border Connections
and Road Closures in N.I...163
Length of Public Roads in R.O.I. 164
Length of Public Roads in N.I. 164
Transport Costs (R.O.I. & N.I.). 165

RELIGION ....(166-171)
Introduction: Religion in Ireland 166
Introduction: Catholic Church 166
Introduction: Church of Ireland 166
Introduction: Presbyterian Church 166
Introduction: Methodist Church...................................166
Hierarchy of Main Churches in Ireland 167
Boundaries of Catholic Dioceses...............................168
List of all Irish Cardinals...168
Membership of Main Irish Churches 169
Church of Ireland Statistics.......................................169
Presbyterian Church Statistics...................................169
Methodist Church Statistics 169
Catholic Parishes, Churches and Schools.................170
Numbers of Catholic Priests and Religious 170
Applicants and Entrants to Catholic Church 171
Percentage of Irish Catholic Missionaries
by Continent..171
Catholic Church Personnel 171
Nullity of Marriages in the Catholic Church................171
Selected Biographies of Religious Figures 171

EDUCATION ....(172-182)
Introduction 172
Public Libraries in R.O.I. & N.I. 172
Library Stocks in R.O.I. 174
R.O.I. RTC's and Colleges of Further Education 175
Student Enrolment in R.O.I. 176
Student Enrolment in N.I. 177
National Schools Numbers in R.O.I. 177
Secondary School Numbers in R.O.I. 177
Higher Education Student numbers in R.O.I. 178
Stage at which Leavers with no Formal
Qualifications left School in R.O.I. 178
R.O.I. Economic Status of
Second Level School Leavers 178
R.O.I. First Destination of
Sub-Degree Respondents 178
Numbers of Schools and Colleges in R.O.I. 179
Numbers of Schools and Colleges in N.I. 179
Number of National School Teachers in R.O.I. 179
Number of Secondary School Teachers in R.O.I. 180
Numbers Employed in 3rd Level Education in R.O.I. 180
Teachers Employed in Primary, Secondary
and Third Level Education in N.I.................................180
Universities in Ireland: North and South 181
University of Ulster: Student Population 181

University of Ulster: Total Student
Population by Faculty 181
Full time Higher Education Student
numbers in R.O.I. 181
Higher Education Students in R.O.I.
by Field of Study 182
Qualifications of N.I. School Leavers.........................182
University Degrees and Diplomas obtained in N.I. 182

HEALTH...(183-189)
Introduction 183
R.O.I. Health Boards...183
N.I. Health Boards 183
Persons Employed in R.O.I. Health Services 183
Persons Employed in N.I. Health Services 183
Publicly Funded Hospitals in R.O.I. 184
Number of Hospital Beds Available in N.I..................184
Available Hospital Beds by Care Programme.............184
Deaths classified by Cause in R.O.I. 184
Deaths classified by Cause in N.I. 184
Infant Mortality in R.O.I. 185
Infant Mortality in N.I. 185
Numbers Employed in Health Services in R.O.I. 185
Capital Expenditure Allocated in R.O.I.
between Health Boards and Voluntary Bodies 185
Non-Capital Expenditure by Programme in R.O.I. 186
R.O.I. Sources of Funds for
Statutory Non-Capital Health Services 186
Number of Factory Accidents notified in R.O.I. 186
Number of Railway Accidents notified in R.O.I. 186
Fatal Road Accidents in R.O.I. 186
Casualties by Road-User Type in R.O.I. 187
Road Casualties in R.O.I. by Age and Gender.........187
Road Accident Statistics for N.I. 187
List of Hospitals in R.O.I. 187
List of Hospitals in N.I. 189
Psychiatric Patients in R.O.I. 189

LAW AND DEFENCE ....(191-204)
Introduction 191
Constitution of Ireland...191
R.O.I. Court System..192
Judiciary of R.O.I. 192
N.I. Court System 194
Judiciary of N.I...194
Organisation and Location of N.I. Courts...................194
Garda Personnel by Number and Rank 195
Garda Strength by Rank 195
Numbers of Garda Stations in R.O.I. 196
R.U.C. Personnel by Numbers and Rank 196
Numbers of Police Stations in N.I. 196
Strength of Police Force and UDR/RIR 196
Crime Rate per Garda Division in R.O.I. 197

Indictable Offenses Reported in R.O.I. 197
Non-indictable Offenses Reported in R.O.I. 199
Notable Offenses Recorded by N.I. Police 200
Offenses Reported - Known to the Police..................201
R.O.I. Prison Population 201
N.I. Prison Population 202
Deaths / Injuries connected with 'The Troubles' 203
Security Incidents in N.I. 203
R.O.I. Defence Staff Breakdown................................204
Headquarters of Irish Defence Forces.......................204
R.O.I. Defence Personnel 204
R.O.I. Defence Personnel on Overseas Duties 204
R.O.I. Defence Personnel (1960-1994) 204

CULTURE, ARTS AND ENTERTAINMENT....(205-224)
Introduction 205
The Gaeltacht - Irish Speaking Areas........................205
Glossary of Irish Words 206
Irish Speakers and Non-Irish Speakers
in each Province. 207
Irish Speakers in Gaeltacht Areas of R.O.I. 207
Biographies of Famous Irish Writers...........................208
Galleries and Art Centres in Ireland...........................210
Irish Theatres, Theatre Companies
and Receiving Venues in Ireland 211
Major Publishing Houses in Ireland 212
Arts Council Funding in R.O.I. and N.I.......................213
Arts Attendances at Principal Venues
and Festivals in N.I. 213
Irish Nobel Prize Winners 213
Top Five Paintings on Public Display in
the National Gallery of Ireland 213
Television and Radio Broadcasting in Ireland 214
Television Licenses in R.O.I. by Province 214
Television Broadcasting by RTE.................................214
Radio Broadcasting by RTE 214
Television Licenses in N.I. 215
50 Most Popular RTE 1 Programmes.........................215
50 Most Popular Network 2 Programmes...................216
Irish Oscar Winners 217
List of Irish Films (1910-1996) 217
R.O.I. National Lottery Statistics................................222
R.O.I. National Lottery Results...................................222
R.O.I. National Lottery Fund Expenditure..................222
R.O.I. National Lottery Winning Tickets by Prize.......222
Selected Biographies of Arts
and Entertainment Personalities.................................223

MEDIA..(227-246)
Introduction 227
Most Popular Irish Daily Newspapers........................227
Most Popular English Daily Newspapers....................227
Most Popular Sunday Newspapers 228

Most Popular Irish Provincial Newspapers 228
List of all Irish Newspapers.......................................228
National and Local Radio Listenership Ratings 233
National Radio and Television Stations 233
Local Radio Stations..234
List of Periodicals, Magazines and Journals..............235
Irish Copyright Law 245
Selected Biographies of Media Personalities
in Ireland 245

SPORT..(248-285)
General Introduction 248

Olympic Games
Irish Olympic Games Medalists 248
Irish Olympians (1924-1996) 249

Gaelic Games
All-Ireland Senior Hurling Winners (1887-1996) 251
All-Ireland Senior Football Winners (1887-1996).......251
Holders of most All-Ireland Senior Medals
(Hurling and Football) 251
Main G.A.A. Statistics..252
Presidents of the G.A.A. 252
G.A.A. Player's All-Stars 1995 253
1996 All-Ireland Hurling Final Statistics 253
1996 All-Ireland Football Final Statistics...................253
General Secretary
- Director General's of the G.A.A. 253

Soccer
Republic of Ireland Football Team Fact File 254
F.A.I. - Opel International
Soccer Senior Player Awards 254
Top Ten International Scorers 254
F.A.I. Cup Winners 254
League of Ireland Championship Winners.................255
League of Ireland All-Time Top Scorers 255
Current League of Ireland Club Statistics 255
N.I. Irish League Championship Winners 256
N.I. Irish Cup Final Winners.......................................256
N.I. Irish League Football Club Statistics..................257
R.O.I. Bord Gáis F.A.I. Premier Division
Final League Table (1995-96) 257
R.O.I. Bord Gáis F.A.I. First Division
Final League Table (1995-96) 257
N.I. Smirnoff Premier Division
Final League Table (1995-96) 257
N.I. Smirnoff First Division
Final League Table (1995-96) 258

Boxing
Irish Amateur Boxing Statistics 258

Irish Olympic and European Boxing Medalists 258
Irish Amateur Boxing Senior Champions 1996 259

Rugby
International Championship Winners
(Five Nations) 259
Irish Rugby Football Statistics 259
Number of Clubs, Commercial Clubs and Schools....260
Top Ten Most Capped Irish Rugby Players 260

Swimming
Irish Swimming Statistics 260
Womens Individual National Swimming
Champions - Irish Record Holders.............................260
Mens Individual National Swimming
Champions - Irish Record Holders.............................261
Relay: National Swimming Champions
- Irish Record Holders 261

Paralympics
Irish Medal Winners at 1996 Paralympic Games
(Atlanta, USA) 261

Athletics
Irish Athletics Statistics 262
European Championship Medalists 262
World Championship Medalists 262
Current Track and Field Champions 262
Current World Irish Record Holders...........................262

Cycling
Irish Cycling Statistics 263
Irish Cycling Champions 263

Golf
Irish Golfing Statistics 263
Carroll's Irish Open Winners and Venues..................263

Cricket
Irish Cricket Statistics 264
Ladies Cricket 264

Tug-of-War
Tug-of-War Statistics 264

Sailing
Sailing Statistics..265
Presidents Awards..265

Sea-Angling
Sea-Angling Statistics..265
Selected Irish Record Weights
for various Specimen 265

Surfing
Surfing Statistics 265

Fencing
Amateur Fencing Statistics (N.I.) 265

Tennis
Irish Tennis Statistics...266

Hockey
Men's Hockey Statistics...266
Ladies Hockey Statistics..266

Ice Hockey
Ice Hockey Statistics (N.I.)...266

Rowing
Rowing Statistics 266
Irish Rowing World Championship Medalists 267

Motor Sports
RIAC National Rally Champions 267
Analysis of Motor Sports Events (1990-96) 267

Motor Cycling
Motor Cycling Statistics 267
Current Motor Cycle National Champions 267

Camogie
Main Statistics..268

Indoor Bowling
Men's Indoor Bowling Statistics 268
Ladies Indoor Bowling Statistics 268

Selected Sports Stadia in Ireland 268
Membership of Selected Sports in Ireland................269
Sports Organisations in R.O.I 269
Sports Organisations in N.I. 270
Who's Who of Irish Sport 272
Who Was Who of Irish Sport 275

USEFUL INFORMATION................................(287-300)
R.O.I. Passport Requirements....................................287
R.O.I. Diplomatic Representation 287
R.O.I. and N.I. Postal
and Telecommunications Statistics 291
Direct Telephone Codes within R.O.I. & N.I. 292
International Telephone Codes....................................295
Weights, Measures and Formulae..............................295
List of Associations 296

TOP TEN NEWS STORIES, 1996

○► **CEASEFIRE ENDS:** The IRA cease-fire which had held since August 1994 was shattered with the bombing of Canary Wharf in London's Docklands on February 9. Two people were killed, many more injured, and millions of pounds of damage caused. Nine days later on February 18th IRA man Ed O'Brien (21) died when the bomb he was carrying exploded on a bus in Aldwych, London, several people were seriously injured. On June 15 a bomb exploded in a busy shopping area of Manchester injuring over 200 people and causing millions of pounds of damage. The Provisionals also attacked a British Army base at Osnabruck in Germany on June 28. There were no injuries and damage was slight. Since the resumption of violence the IRA have not carried out any attacks in Northern Ireland. The Loyalist paramilitary cease-fire has held.

○► **BEEF SCARE:** After new scientific evidence in Britain suggested a link between BSE and its human equivalent (Creutzfeldt-Jakot Disease (CJD))moves were swiftly made to protect Ireland's £2billion beef industry. Gardaí began a massive border operation on March 25 - an operation which is still continuing - to prevent cattle from Northern Ireland being smuggled into the Republic. It followed the European Commission decision to ban all exports of British beef. Northern farmers had wanted their herds to be considered as Irish rather than British to avoid this ban but this was not possible.

○► **FORUM ELECTIONS:** Elections to the Northern Ireland Forum took place on May 30. On the basis of these results representatives will be sent to All-Party talks. Issues raised at the talks will then be sent to the Forum for debate and ratification. Seats won by the parties were: UUP 30; DUP 24; SDLP 21; Sinn Féin 17; Alliance 7; UK Unionist Party 3; Progressive Unionist Party 2; Ulster Democratic Party 2; Labour 2; and the Northern Ireland Women's Coalition 2.

○► **SIX DIE IN FIRE:** Six members of the Maher family from Portarlington in Co. Laois were tragically killed when flames engulfed their home in the early hours of June 2nd. Mrs Breda Maher (48), her daughters Martina (2), Fiona (5), Joanne (9), and sons Barry (12), and Mark (23) were all killed in the blaze. As the shocked town laid the victims to rest on Wednesday June 5th news came through that another son, 25 year-old Laois footballer Colm had died in St James' Hospital in Dublin where he had been treated for burns.

○► **GARDA MURDERED:** 52 year-old Detective Garda Jerry McCabe was shot dead and his colleague Detective Garda Ben O'Sullivan was shot and wounded in Adare, Co.Limerick on June 7. They were guarding a post office lorry which was carrying £50,000 in cash. Their car was rammed by the raiders who then, using AK47s assault rifles, shot the Gardaí. The IRA were immediately suspected and although that organisation at first denied involvement it eventually did accept responsibility.

○► **STORMONT TALKS:** The multi-party talks got under way at Stormont on June 10 with Sinn Féin refused entry because the IRA had not reinstated its cease-fire. The Taoiseach, John Bruton and the British Prime Minister John Major both addressed the opening session before the combined unionist parties objected to the chairmanship of former US Senator George Mitchell. Mitchell was eventually installed as chairman. The talks went into the summer recess on July 29 and were to recommence on September 9th.

○► **JOURNALIST SHOT DEAD:** Journalist Veronica Guerin was shot dead on the outskirts of Dublin in what appeared to be a 'contract killing' on June 26. 36 year-old Guerin worked with the Sunday Independent and had been subjected to previous attacks. In January of 1995 she was shot in the leg at her home and she was beaten in September of that year. Both were seen as warnings to her to desist in her investigative reporting which was revealing increasingly detailed profiles of Dublin-based crime bosses. The murders of Veronica Guerin and Jerry McCabe precipitated Government moves to introduce more stringent anti-crime measures.

○► **E.U. PRESIDENCY:** Ireland assumed the Presidency of the 15 member European Union on July 1. The Taoiseach John Bruton and the Tanaiste and Minister for Foreign Affairs Dick Spring will play the main roles while other ministers will also have their part to play. Important issues which the Irish presidency will deal with will be the defining of the relationship between currencies which are in and out of the European Monetary Union, and attempting to improve the processes of decision making within the EU following the fiasco of the BSE crisis. Ireland's presidency will end in late December with an Inter-Governmental Conference at Dublin Castle.

○► **DRUMCREE SIEGE:** Sustained street violence was sparked off by the beginning of a stand-off at Drumcree, Portadown, Co Armagh on July 7. The RUC prevented an Orange march from proceeding along the nationalist Garvaghy Road and a four day stand-off ensued. Catholic taxi driver Michael McGoldrick was shot dead by renegade Loyalists on July 8 while roads across Northern Ireland were blocked by protesters sympathetic to the Orangemens cause. Violence gripped Loyalist areas particulary in Belfast. Nationalist areas reacted with fury when the RUC overturned its earlier decision on July 11 and forced the Orange march along the Garvaghy Road battoning nationalist protesters and firing dozens of plastic bullets. Widespread rioting was reported in nationalist areas. In the early hours of July 13 Dermot McShane was killed when he was struck by a British army personnel carrier during street clashes in Derry.

○► **TRIPLE GOLD:** Swimmer Michelle Smith became Ireland's most successful Olympian ever when she won three Gold and one Bronze medal at the Centennial Olympic Games at Atlanta in July . She won gold in the 400m Individual Medley, the 200m Individual Medley, the 400m Freestyle and bronze in the 200m Butterfly breaking her personal best times (which are national records) in each event. Smith received a rapturous welcome in her home village of Rathcoole, Co. Dublin.

11

CHRONOLOGY OF 1996

JANUARY 1, TO AUGUST 31, 1996

03: Share prices rocket - Share prices on the Dublin stock exchange increased in value by £250 million to a combined total value of £16.2 billion, their highest ever level.

07: Body of missing woman found - Missing since December 22nd the body of Marilyn Rynn (40) was found on wasteland near her Blanchardstown home in Co. Dublin. A 32 year-old Dublin man was charged with her rape and murder on August 6.

07: Two die as country is lashed by storms - Two men were drowned, one in Bray, Co. Wicklow and the other in Dublin Bay while many homes and businesses were flooded and the electricity supply disrupted as rivers, particularly in the south-east, burst their banks. **11: Challenge to result of divorce referendum begins** - Des Hanafin, the anti-divorce campaigner, brought a challenge to the result of the November 1995 Divorce referendum to the High Court. He claims the government prejudiced the result by funding part of the "Yes" campaign.

15: O'Donnell murder trial begins - The Central Criminal Court began hearing evidence in the trial of Brendan O'Donnell (21) who is charged with the murders of Imelda Riney (29), her son Liam (3) and Fr Joe Walsh (37) in 1994.

16: Jack Charlton to become honourary Irish citizen - The Government announced that the former manager of the Republic of Ireland soccer team, Jack Charlton would be awarded honourary citizenship.

20: Scotland defeat Ireland - Scotland defeated Ireland in the opening game of the 1996 Five Nations Rugby Championship. The Lansdowne Road score was Scotland 16, Ireland 10.

23: Two elderly farmers murdered - The bodies of Patrick Daly (69) and Tommy Casey (68) were discovered in counties Kerry and Galway. Mr Daly's body was found in a well while Mr Casey's body was found with his hands and feet bound.

23: Budget - 10p was put on the price of a packet of cigarettes, 1p was put on a litre of petrol and diesel while 3.1p was put on a litre of super plus unleaded. PRSI, PAYE and Social Welfare concessions are introduced while relief on mortgage interest was reduced.

24: Third murder in two days - The stabbed body of 44 year-old shop-keeper Mrs. Joyce Quinn was discovered in Kildare.

24: Mitchell Report on Decommissioning released - The International Body on Decommissioning, headed by the US Senator George Mitchell released its report. It accepts that decommissioning of paramilitary weapons will not take place before all-party talks. In the House of Commons John Major proposes elections in Northern Ireland before all-party talks commence causing a rift in Anglo-Irish relations. The plan is opposed by the Irish Government and the SDLP.

30: INLA member shot dead - Gino Gallagher (32), reputedly the INLA chief-of-staff, was shot dead in Belfast. The murder was seen as part of an ongoing INLA feud. His funeral was later marred by clashes between the RUC and mourners.

02: Peace Report - The Forum for Peace and Reconciliation Report has recommended that all-party talks should proceed without delay, with any outcome having to be ratified by the people of Ireland, North and South. It went on to say that all political goals must be achieved by peaceful and democratic methods and that there can be no purely internal settlement.

04: Sea claims four lives - Four men were lost at sea, three off the Waterford coast from their 40 foot trawler "Jenalisa" and one off Connemara in a currach accident.

05: New Irish soccer manager appointed - Mick McCarthy (37), the former "Captain Fantastic" of the Republic of Ireland soccer team, was named as manager of the Irish team in succession of Jack Charlton. He was previously the manager of Millwall.

06: Elderly farmer dies after attack - A Tipperary cattle dealer and farmer died after being shot in the leg by raiders. 74 year-old Daniel Fanning died from loss of blood.

07: Referendum challenge dismissed - The High Court dismissed the challenge to the result of the Divorce referendum.

08: National Radio Licence awarded - A new national radio licence was awarded to the Radio Ireland consortium by the Independent Radio and Television Commission.

08: Dáil row over adviser jobs - Minister for Social Welfare Proinsias de Rossa was accused of misleading the Dáil over the non-advertisement of adviser jobs in his department. The jobs were, in fact, publicised in his party's newsletter.

09: IRA ceasefire ends - The 17 month IRA ceasefire ended with a massive explosion at Canary Wharf in London's docklands. Two people were killed, dozens were injured and millions of pounds worth of damage was caused.

10: Sinn Féin ostracised - Both the British and Irish Governments have suspended ministerial contact with Sinn Féin pending the restoration of the IRA ceasefire.

12: Major pushes for Northern Ireland elections - British Prime Minster John Major said he favoured elections as an avenue to all-party talks in Northern Ireland. He was speaking during a debate in Westminster. His remarks drew immediate opposition from SDLP leader John Hume.

14: Extra soldiers for the North - 500 extra British troops are to be posted to Northern Ireland. The British government announced the deployment in reaction to the ending of the IRA ceasefire.

17: French rout - France defeated Ireland by 45 points to 10 at Parc des Princes, Paris.

17: Bishop Brendan Comiskey home - The Bishop of Ferns, Brendan Comiskey celebrated Mass in

Enniscorthy, his first appearance in public since returning from the US.

18: London hit by second IRA bomb - A massive bomb blast ripped through a double decker bus in the centre of London, killing one man and injuring nine other people. The dead man, 21 year-old Ed O'Brien from Wexford, had been carrying the bomb when it exploded prematurely.

22: Mitchell meets Irish Government - George Mitchell, the US Senator who was chairman of the international body on decommissioning, had a meeting with John Bruton, Dick Spring and Proinsias de Rossa and Nora Owen in Dublin.

22: Heroin seized in Dublin - Gardaí moved in to seize heroin with a street value of £400,000 in Ballyfermot, Dublin following a successful surveillance operation.

24: Loyalist ceasefire intact - Loyalist paramilitary leaders went some way to ease fears of Loyalist attacks on Dublin following the IRA bombing of London. They announced that the Loyalist ceasefire will hold firm as long as the IRA did not target Northern Ireland.

26: DUP save Major's Government - Ian Paisley's DUP party abstained in a House of Commons vote on the arms-to-Iraq Scott Report, and thus saved the Tory government who won by a single vote. The Ulster Unionists voted against the government.

26: FAI Financial shortfall - Mr. Joe Delaney, the treasurer of the Football Association of Ireland confirmed that a shortfall of £110,000 existed in relation to outstanding money from tickets for the 1994 World Cup.

28: Bruton and Major in Summit meeting - The Taoiseach and the British Prime Minister John Major held a summit meeting in London, at which June 10th was announced as the commencement date for all-party talks. The two leaders warned that Sinn Féin's inclusion would hinge on a unequivocal commitment to pursue their aims by political means.

29: Minister berates Larry Goodman - In a hard hitting speech in Dáil Éireann the Minister for Agriculture, Mr. Ivan Yates, lashed out at Mr. Larry Goodman of Goodman International, Ireland's largest beef processor, accusing him of tarnishing the entire Irish beef industry. The minister, speaking under Dáil privilege, stated that he would shed no tears should Goodman withdraw from the Irish beef industry.

MARCH

02: Ireland secure first victory - At Lansdowne Road Ireland defeated Wales by 30 points to 17, their first victory in this year's Five Nations Championship.

03: Sinn Féin march blocked - The RUC prevented a Sinn Féin rally from going into the centre of Lurgan, Co.Armagh.

05: INLA feud continues - Belfast -man John Fennell was beaten to death in a Bundoran caravan park. The murder was part of the continuing INLA feud.

12: Fear of Loyalist backlash - A statement by the combined Loyalist Military Command warning that they were prepared to strike in response to further IRA activity sparked fears that the peace process was in

real danger of completely collapsing. The statement came just hours after the IRA admitted planting another bomb in the English capital, London.

12: Suicide attempt by Brendan O'Donnell - Brendan O'Donnell who is being tried at the Central Criminal Court for the murder of Imelda Riney , her son Liam and Father Joe Walsh, has attempted suicide by strangulation at the Central Mental Hospital.

14: 400 Jobs in jeopardy - Two Dublin companies, Packard Electric and W.R. Jacob, both based in Tallaght, announce that they are seeking almost 400 redundancies between them.

14: Irish success at Cheltenham - Wexford jockey Conor O'Dwyer rode the Cork trained steeplechaser Imperial Call to victory in the Gold Cup at Cheltenham.

15: INLA issue death sentences - Four men, accused of being involved in the murder of former INLA leader, Gino Gallagher, have been handed "death sentences" by the Republican paramilitary group. The INLA feud claimed the life of little Barbara McAlorum (9) as she sat in her home.

15: Waterford woman found dead - 36 year old mother of one Sandra Tobin was found dead in her Waterford home. A local man was later charged with her murder.

16: Twickenham defeat - Ireland were defeated by 28 points to 15 by Triple Crown Winners England at Twickenham.

17: St. Patrick's Day celebrations - Around 350,000 people turned out on the streets of Dublin to watch the parade make its way through the city.

19: Publican murdered in Wicklow - 55 year-old County Wicklow publican, Mr. Thomas Nevin, was murdered in the early hours of the morning during an armed raid by a gang who got away with a substantial sum in cash.

20: Irish Beef declared safe - Following further revelations that eating BSE-infected beef could lead to humans developing brain disorders, the Minister for Agriculture, Ivan Yates stated that Irish beef was safe. **21: Date announced for North elections** - John Major, the British Prime Minister, announced in the House of Commons that elections to elect representatives to all-party talks will take place in Northern Ireland on May 30th. The announcement and the format of the elections was greeted with hostility by both nationalist and unionist politicians.

21: No Irish Ban of British Beef - Despite Belgian and French bans on British beef imports, the Irish Department of Agriculture announced that no ban will be implemented here as to do so would be illegal under European Union guidelines.

24: Egyptians refuse to dock Irish cattle - Egyptian authorities at the port of Alexandria refused to allow a ship carrying in excess of 1,600 Irish cattle permission to dock. The move follows the banning of all European beef by the Egyptians due to the BSE scare in Britain.

23-25: Border operation due to beef scare - A massive Garda and Customs operation continues along the Border in order to ensure no smuggling of cattle from the North or of British origin into the Republic as the BSE scare surrounding British beef intensifies all over Europe.

The Ulster Farmer's Union stated that special consideration should be given to Northern Ireland beef, and that it should not be considered British.

Major Irish supermarket chains took steps to ease public fears by withdrawing all British beef products.

24: New Bishop for Limerick - Dr. Donal Murray, the former Auxiliary Bishop of Dublin, was installed as the new Catholic Bishop of Limerick. Dr. Murray succeeds Jerimiah Newman who had been bishop since 1974.

26: Cattle seized on Border - The operation to prevent the smuggling of British or Northern Ireland animals into the Republic proved successful on the Co. Monaghan border when a consignment of cattle were commandeered.

26: Braveheart strikes gold at the Oscars - The film *Braveheart*, much of which was filmed in Ireland using Irish extras, scooped Best Film and Best Director at the Oscars in Hollywood. Five Oscars in all were awarded to the film, a personal triumph for director and main star Mel Gibson.

26: £71 million in beef fines - Ireland will pay £71 million in fines because of irregularities in the beef industry here. The European Commission reduced the fine from an original £95 million, yet, even allowing for further reductions, the Irish taxpayer will be liable for a bill in the region of £50 million.

28: BSE crisis hits jobs - The BSE scare continues to wreak havoc in the Irish meat industry. More than 500 workers in meat factories in the Republic have been laid off or placed on protective notice, and a further 700 jobs have been lost in the North.

30: Irish cattle finally dock in Egypt - After spending several days on the high seas off the Egyptian port of Alexandria, permission was finally obtained by the Department of Agriculture to unload several thousand Irish cattle in the Egyptian port.

30: Minister O'Higgins admits "mistake" - The involvement of Niall Stokes, chairman of the Independent Radio and Television Commission in a Labour party fundraising function organised by Minister for Arts, Culture and the Gaeltacht was described as a "mistake" by Minister Michael D. O'Higgins. Despite pressure from opposition parties the minister said Mr. Stokes resignation was not necessary.

APRIL

01: Revenge killing in Dublin pub - John Reddan who had stabbed and killed Sean O'Neill in February of last year was himself murdered today. Mr Reddan was shot dead in a Dublin pub by a lone gunman in what is believed to be a revenge attack.

02: O'Donnell sentenced to life - Triple murderer Brendan O'Donnell was sentenced to life imprisonment by the Central Criminal Court. O'Donnell murdered Imelda Riney, her son Liam and Fr Joe Walsh in Clare in 1994.

02: British Government introduce emergency legislation - In an effort to combat IRA attacks in Britain legislation widening the powers of the Prevention of Terrorism Act (making it very similar to the existing legislation in Northern Ireland) was initiated. Despite fears voiced by civil liberties groups the legislation was rushed through parliament with the support of the Labour party.

02: Double killing in Sligo - 37 year old Michael Cawley first stabbed his wife Noleen and then himself. The couple are survived by their five children.

03: Fianna Fáil secure double by election victory - Cecilia Keaveney in Donegal North-East and Brian Lenihan in Dublin West won their respective contests and were duly elected to the 27th Dáil. Mr Lenihan narrowly defeated the independent socialist Joe Higgins while Ms. Keaveney defeated Harry Blaney of Independent Fianna Fail after a recount, the results of which did not come through until the next morning.

08: RUC stop contentious march - The RUC stopped Apprentice Boys from marching down the Nationalist Lower Ormeau Road. Violence followed in Loyalist parts of Belfast accompanied by arrests.

08: Feathered Gale wins National - *Feathered Gale*, third in last year's National, won the Jameson Irish Grand National at Fairyhouse, comfortably beating the favourite *Jodami*.

06-07: Three die in road accidents - three men aged between 17 and 28 died in motor accidents over the Bank Holiday weekend.

10: Irish cattle finally landed in Egypt - 1600 Irish cattle were finally landed at Alexandria after Egypt lifted its ban on Irish beef.

11: McCarthy receives ban - Irish manager Mick McCarthy has received a ten year ban from buying English FA Cup final tickets following revelations that his tickets were sold by touts.

13: Extradition attempt fails - The extradition to Britain of Dublin man Anthony Duncan failed because of incomplete documents. Mr Duncan was re-arrested immediately after his release and charged with IRA membership.

14: 13-year-old found dead in Bundoran - Alison White's body was found in a field near Bundoran, Co. Donegal. Her body had extensive head injuries. A Bundoran man was charged with her murder the following day.

15: Army personnel to remain in Lebanon - Due to the continuing Israeli bombardment of south Lebanon and the accompanying Lebanese exodus north the Army has decided to postpone for a week the return of Irish soldiers serving there with the UN.

15: Woman found dead in Kerry - The body of 39 year old Anne-Marie Duffin was discovered by her sons on returning from school. Mrs Duffin's body had severe neck and head injuries.

15: Supreme Court judges appointed - The President, Mrs Robinson appointed three judges to the Supreme Court. They are Mr Justice Ronan Keane, Mr Justice Kevin Lynch and Mr Justice Frank Murphy.

16: Procedures for Northern elections published - The British Government released the rules and procedures for the Northern elections and subsequent all-party talks. Sinn Féin will not be admitted to the talks without the resumption of the IRA ceasefire. Provision will also be made for greater representation of marginal parties.

17: Explosion in London - The IRA claimed responsibility for the bomb which exploded in central London. There were no casualties.

21: BAFTA award for Irish writers - Television script writers Graham Lenihan and Arthur Mathews won the Best Comedy award at the annual BAFTA awards in London. They won for their comedy series about three priests on an island off the west coast, *Father Ted.*

22: 'Guilty but insane' man should no longer be held - Donegal man John Gallagher (29) who murdered his girlfriend Anne Gillespie and her mother Annie in Sligo in 1988 and was found 'guilty but insane' should not be held any longer at the Central Mental Hospital according to the hospital's director, Dr. Charles Smith. In the director's opinion Gallagher poses no threat to the public should he be released and is no longer ill.

22: Summer hours begin - Extended summer hours in pubs began to-day. 11.30pm is now the official closing time. 'Summer time' continues until Saturday the fifth of October.

24: SDLP and Sinn Féin to contest Northern elections - Sinn Féin and the SDLP announced they will contest the May 30 Northern elections; this had been in some doubt. The SDLP also said they may take their seats at the Northern Ireland Forum. This means that all parties will now contest the elections.

25: Talks without Sinn Féin worthless - Government adviser Fergus Finlay said multi party talks without Sinn Féin would be worthless. His comments were met with a barrage of criticism from Northern Unionists.

27: Young Munster win AIL - Young Munster defeated Limerick rivals Garryowen by 37 points to 12 to win Division 1 of All Ireland Insurance Corporation League.

29: 800 jobs lost - Tallaght is set to lose 800 jobs following the announcement that the Packard plant, which manufactures electrical components, is to close. Workers heard the news from the media.

29: Man jailed for importing drugs - Dublin man Christopher O'Connell (51) was jailed for eight years for trying to import £7million worth of cannabis at Cork in 1991.

MAY

01: Loyalist Ceasefire fears - Roy Magee, the Presbyterian minister who was one of the leading negotiators of the Loyalist ceasefire of 1994, warned that elements of unionism were pushing for a resumption of violence, fearing that the "peace process" was invariably leading to a united Ireland.

01: Nurses reject Government pay deal - Nurses have voted to reject a £40 million deal and are contemplating strike action, weakening the public pay policy of the Government.

02: Ahern criticised on Northern stance - Fianna Fail leader Bertie Ahern was sharply criticised by the Taoiseach, Mr. Bruton, for recent "one-sided" views on Northern Ireland.

05: Derry are NFL Champions - Derry defeated Donegal by 1-16 to 1-9 at Croke Park to retain their Church and General National Football League title.

08: Three women murdered - 49 year old Angela Collins became the third woman to be murdered this week. In unconnected cases 35 year old Martina Halligan in Dublin and 50 year-old Patti Bainbridge in

Laois were murdered earlier in the week. Three men have been charged with the murders.

11: Girl dies at concert - Bernadette O'Brien (17) was crushed to death at the Point Depot. She was attending a rock concert by The Smashing Pumpkins. An inquiry has been announced.

12: Galway and Shelbourne triumph - Galway were crowned National Hurling League Champions after they defeated Tipperary by 2-10 to 2-8 at Limerick while Shelbourne defeated fellow Dubliners St Patrick's Athletic 2-1 in the Harp Lager FAI Cup Final replay at Dalymount Park.

14: IRA prisoner transferred to Portlaoise - Patrick Kelly (43), a convicted IRA man was transferred to Portlaoise gaol. Kelly is seriously ill with skin cancer and was previously transferred from an English jail to Northern Ireland.

14: Monaghan man beaten to death - Patrick Maguire (19) died after being beaten in Monaghan town. Gardaí believe a row developed after a drinking spree. **14: Vigilante Killing** - Josie O'Dwyer (41), a heroin addict was beaten to death by vigilanties in the Dolphin's Barn area of Dublin. Mr O'Dwyer warned people not to touch him as he lay in a pool of blood because he had AIDS.

14: Doubt over bomb convictions - Equipment at a forensic laboratory in Britain was found to be contaminated with traces of Semtex. The find puts the sentences of several men convicted on the strength of forensic results in doubt.

18: Ireland wins the Eurovision (again!) -23 year-old Maynooth student Eimear Quinn won the Eurovision Song Contest for Ireland. Her entry *The Voice* easily won the contest which was held in Oslo, Norway. It was Ireland's fourth victory in five years.

19: Three die in Belfast - William Doherty and David Martin were shot dead by Geoffrey Anderson, an off duty member of the Royal Irish Regiment. Anderson also shot and wounded his girlfriend before he killed himself.

20: Movement on Mitchell principles - Sinn Féin said they were prepared to abide by the Mitchell principles. The British Government replied by reiterating the need for an IRA ceasefire before Sinn Féin could be admitted to multi-party talks.

22: New extradition warrant issued - The British Attorney General has furnished the Irish authorities with a further extradition warrant for Anthony Duncan after it emerged that the original application was mislaid.

23: Prisoner commits suicide in Mountjoy - Carol Ann Daly (21) was found dead in her prison cell. She had hanged herself.This came just a fortnight after a report severely criticised conditions in the jail.

25: INLA feud continues - 37 year old Dessie McCleery was shot dead in Belfast in what appears to be the latest murder in an ongoing INLA feud.

26: 70 year old found dead - The body of Ellen O'Regan was found in her home in Cork. The 70 year old lived alone and Gardaí are treating her death as suspicious.

27: New newspaper launched - A new evening newspaper hit the streets. *The Evening News* printed its first edition to-day.

28: Body found in Dublin - The body of 34 year old

Patricia Murphy was discovered near her home. The dead woman had four children, Gardaí immediately launched a murder inquiry.

28: Mitchell confirmed as talks chairman - George Mitchell was confirmed as chairman of the imminent multi party talks by the British and Irish Governments. His appointment was criticised by Unionist parties.

30: Northern Ireland Forum election - The election to the Northern Ireland forum took place to-day. The turnout was almost 65%. The seats were distributed as follows: Ulster Unionists 30; DUP 24; SDLP 21; Sinn Féin 17; Alliance 7; minor parties shared the other 11 seats.

JUNE

01: Man shot dead in Dublin - A man was shot dead in Ballymun. 42 year old Anthony Lynch was shot in his home by two men.

02: Six die in Co. Laois fire - Six members of the Maher family ranging in age from two to forty-eight died when their Portarlington home was ravaged by fire. A further member, Laois footballer Colm (25) died on Wednesday June 5th as the other members of his family were laid to rest.

04: President begins historic visit - President Robinson began the first official visit by an Irish head of state to Britain. In the course of her four day visit she will meet political leaders including John Major and Queen Elizabeth.

05: Bleak IRA statement - The IRA released a statement all but ruling out an early ceasefire and stating they would not decommission weapons. They also called for negotiations without preconditions.

07: Garda shot dead in Limerick - 52 year-old detective Garda Jerry McCabe was shot dead in Limerick by members of the IRA despite initial claims to the contrary by that organisation. The car in which he was travelling was rammed in the fateful attempted robbery.

09: INLA feud claims another victim - The ongoing INLA feud has claimed its fifth victim, 23 year old Francis Shannon was shot dead in Belfast by a lone gunman.

10: Multi party talks begin - Multi party talks got under way in Belfast with combined Unionist attempts to block the proposed chairmanship of George Mitchell. Sinn Féin were not admitted to the talks - despite being the fourth largest party at the recent elections - because the IRA had not resumed its ceasefire.

11: Ulster Unionists agree to Mitchell - The Ulster Unionist party agreed to the appointment of George Mitchell as chairman of the multi party talks. The decision enraged the DUP and Bob McCartney's United Kingdom Unionist Party who immediately left the chamber protesting.

12: Referendum result upheld - The Supreme Court dismissed the challenge to the Divorce Referendum brought by Des Hanafin. The Government will now move swiftly to initiate legislation in a Divorce Bill.

13: Northern Ireland Forum meets - The Northern Ireland Forum met for the first time to-day under the chairmanship of Catholic Ulster Unionist John Gorman. Sinn Féin did not take their 17 seats.

15: Manchester bomb - An IRA bomb exploded in a busy shopping area of Manchester injuring 200 people. Police said the warning given was insufficient to clear the area. The explosion has put further strain on the Peace Process.

16: New Archbishop enthroned - Walton Empey was enthroned as Church of Ireland Archbishop of Dublin at Christchurch Cathedral. He succeeded Dr Donal Caird.

16: Woman killed in Dublin fire - 26 year-old mother of two Paula Thornton died and her three year old son was seriously injured in an early morning blaze at their Coolock home.

17: Priest pleads guilty to sexual abuse - A Kilkenny parish priest pleaded guilty to the charges of committing sexual offenses against boys he was later sentenced to eight years imprisonment.

18: Casino plan rejected - Plans for an International Conference Centre on the old Phoenix Park racecourse look set to be shelved after the Government refused to give permission for a casino to be included in the development.

19: Divorce Bill published - The Government published the first draft of the Divorce Bill in the Dáil.

20: Drug dealer imprisoned - Tony Felloni received a twenty year prison sentence for possession of heroin. Felloni was known to the Gardaí as a major drug dealer.

20: Bomb-making factory found - Gardaí found a mortar bomb factory and bunker at Clonaslee Co. Laois. The mortars appeared ready for use. Four men were arrested at the scene.

20: Gallagher trial begins - The trial of double murderer John Gallagher began at the High Court. Gallagher was found guilty but insane of the 1988 murders of his girlfriend Anne Gillespie and her mother Annie. The director of the Central mental Hospital has said he can no longer justify holding Gallagher on grounds of mental ill-health.

23: Suicide at St Patrick's institution - Thomas Keane (20) a remand prisoner from Dublin hanged himself in his cell at the institution for young offenders.

24: Kinsale is best kept town - Kinsale, Co. Cork won the inaugural All-Ireland Best Kept Town Award.

26: Veronica Guerin murdered - Journalist Veronica Guerin (36) was shot dead as she waited at traffic lights on the outskirts of Dublin. Her murder is believed to be a 'contract killing'. A huge wave of shock and revulsion swept over the country following the news. She was buried on June 29.

28: British army base in Germany attacked - The IRA launched a mortar bomb attack on the biggest British army base in Germany at Osnabruck. Damage was slight and no injuries were reported.

30: Zagreb wins Derby - A 20/1 outsider won the 1996 Budweiser Irish Derby. Zagreb was the mount of Pat Shanahan and trained by Dermot Weld.

JULY

01: Ireland assumes EU Presidency - Ireland assumed the EU Presidency with a meeting of the European Commissioners at Dublin Castle. Ireland's tenure of Presidency will last until the end of the year.

02: JFK arrives in Dublin - Massive US Navy aircraft

carrier the USS John F Kennedy moored off Dun Laoghaire. 15,000 people visited the ship, while the 5,000 sailors sampled the delights of Dublin.

02: New anti-crime measures announced - In the direct aftermath of the Guerin and McCabe murders the Government announced new measures to combat crime. The measures include the recruitment of 400 new Gardaí, the building of a new remand prison in Dublin, and a special unit is to be set up to target the assets of those involved in crime.

05: Man shot dead in Limerick - 27 year-old John Keane was shot dead in the garden of his home in Limerick. Mr Keane was well known to the Gardaí.

07: Drumcree stand-off begins - Up to 5,000 Orangemen gathered at the Church of Ireland Church at Drumcree, on the outskirts of Portadown, Co. Armagh after the RUC decision not to allow their traditional march along the nationalist Garvaghy Road to proceed. A tense stand-off ensued with 2,000 police blocking the road. Orange sponsored protests brought disruption to many parts of Northern Ireland.

08: Man shot dead in Lurgan - 31 year-old taxi driver Michael McGoldrick was shot dead near Lurgan after collecting a fare. Renegade Loyalists are suspected and the UVF later stood down its 'Portadown unit'.

08: Cruise O'Brien suffers stroke - Erstwhile Irish Government minister and lately member of the United Kingdom Unionist Party Dr Conor Cruise O'Brien suffered a mild stroke.

09: Man killed in Clonmel - 20 year-old David Nugent was tied up and then stabbed and beaten to death in Clonmel, Co. Tipperary.

09: Bórd na Móna MD suspended - Dr Eddie O'Connor was suspended pending further investigation into his pay increases. In a saga which has run since April the board of Bórd na Móna have questioned the details of Dr O'Connor's pay and expenses (said to be worth £1.9million).

09: Law appointments announced - The Government announced the appointment of Diarmuid O'Donovan to the High Court and an additional nine judges to the Circuit Court. Michael Byrne was also appointed Garda Commissioner replacing Patrick Culligan.

11: Orange march proceeds - In the face of a worsening security situation in the North the RUC overturned its earlier decision and forced the Orange march down the Garvaghy Road in Portadown firing plastic bullets and battoning nationalist protesters. The reversal came after four nights of rioting saw families intimidated out of their homes, policemen fired upon, and rioting more violent and widespread than at any time since the 1981 Hunger Strikes.

12: Man dies in Derry - 35 year-old Dermot McShane was killed during riots in Derry city centre. Mr McShane was killed when the hoarding he was sheltering behind was rammed by British army landrover. He was crushed under the hoarding.

13: Blast at Enniskillen hotel - Seventeen people were injured in a bomb explosion at the Killyhelvin Hotel outside Enniskillen, Co. Fermanagh. No-one claimed responsibility for the explosion but the IRA denied involvement.

13: Tipperary youth dies - Denis Mackey (16) died after an altercation in Thurles Co. Tipperary. He

received a blow and was pronounced dead on arrival at hospital.

15: Traveller shot dead - A 35 year-old traveller John McCarthy was shot dead at a halting site near Tallaght. The dead man is survived by his wife and their nine children.

16: Trimble in row over meeting - Ulster Unionist leader David Trimble found himself in trouble after it was revealed that he had met with Billy Wright - who allegedly is the UVF member known as 'King Rat' - on July 10, during the Drumcree stand-off. Mr Trimble has consistently refused to meet with paramilitaries or those with paramilitary connections.

17: Irish shares plummet - £280 million was wiped off the value of Irish shares following a sharp fall on Wall Street. The ISEQ index closed down 48 points at 2,404. The Punt came under pressure the following day when it reached the lowest permitted level within the ERM (Exchange Rate Mechanism).

20-26: Smith wins swimming golds - Dublin woman Michelle Smith became the outstanding swimming star of the Centennial Olympic Games in Atlanta winning the 200m and 400m individual medlies, the 200m freestyle and bronze in the 200m Butterfly. She dismissed allegations that she had taken drugs to enhance her performances, pointing out that the American media made no such allegations when a U.S. swimmer won a medal.

25: Dáil meets for crime debate - The Dáil was reconvened for a special sitting and passed four bills and referred a further two to Dáil committees. The bills are designed to target organised crime.

28-31: O'Sullivan fails in Olympic quest - Ireland's great track hope Sonia O'Sullivan failed in her attempt to capture the Olympic 5,000m and 1,500m titles. An obviously below par O'Sullivan failed to finish in the 5,000m final and did not qualify for the 1,500m final. O'Sullivan told reporters that she had been suffering from a stomach bug and diarrhoea.

29: Multi party talks take break - The multi party talks at Stormont began their summer recess. They are to reconvene on September 9th.

30: Government may appeal High Court decision - The Government may appeal the High Court's decision to award £6.75million in costs (largely legal) arising out of the Beef Tribunal to Larry Goodman.

31: Derry Mayor penalised by council - Unionist Mayor of Derry, Richard Dallas was stripped of the trappings of office following a vote by Derry City Council. The move was taken because Mr Dallas, a member of the Orange Order, took part in the blocking of the Craigavon bridge in the city during the Drumcree stand-off earlier in July.

31: Irish athlete tests positive - 5,000m runner Marie McMahon tested positive for a banned substance in Atlanta. It later emerged that the non performance enhancing drug was ingested through the taking of a throat lozenger. The athlete escaped a ban but got a severe warning.

AUGUST

04: Woman killed in fairground accident - A young mother 25 year-old Marese Egan was killed in a fairground accident in Co. Tipperary. Her four year-old daughter was also injured.

04: Limerick and Wexford to meet in All-Ireland decider- Limerick defeated Antrim by 1-17 to 0-13 and Wexford defeated Galway by 2-13 to 3-7 in the Guinness All-Ireland Senior Hurling Championship semi-finals at Croke Park.

06: Irish Olympians arrive home - Ireland's Olympic squad arrived home in torrential rain. The open topped buses travelled from the airport to the city centre where triple gold-medalist Michelle Smith addressed the rain-soaked crowds.

07: Derry's walls to be closed - In a bid to avert a possibly violent confrontation the Northern Ireland Secretary of State, Sir Patrick Mayhew, ordered the contentious stretch of Derry's walls which overlooks the nationalist Bogside be closed and Apprentice Boys would not be permitted to march along them. In the event the march - on August 10th - passed off relatively peacefully.

09: Contract killing in Limerick - In an apparent 'contract killing' 53 year-old Sean Colbert was shot dead in front of his home in Limerick. Mr Colbert had been shot and wounded in December 1995.

11: Mayo advance - Connacht champions Mayo shocked favourites Kerry defeating them by 2-13 to 1-10 in the Bank of Ireland Senior Football Championship semi-final at Croke Park.

11: McGinley wins in Austria - Dublin golfer Paul McGinley won the Austrian Open by one stroke and £41,600 in prize money. It's McGinley's first tour victory.

12: Tension in Bellaghy - The possibility of violence looms large in the County Derry village of Bellaghy as Loyalist marchers and nationalist protesters face each other in a stand off situation. In the event an agreed compromise defuses the issue after almost 24 hours and both groups disperse peacefully.

13: BSE prompts herd slaughter - The discovery of a cow infected with BSE prompted the immediate slaughtering of a 570 herd in County Cork.

13: Irish actress escapes death - 25-year-old Irish actress, Lisa Hogan, had a miraculous escape when the executive jet on which she was the only passenger crashed through an airport fence onto a busy London motorway. No-one was seriously injured in the accident, including the driver of a van hit by the jet.

14: Biggest ever cocaine find - A cocaine haul, estimated to have a street value of £40 million, was seized by Gardaí and customs officers at Moneypoint in Clare. The seizure - the largest ever cocaine find by Irish authorities - was made on board a Colombian boat, *Front Guilder,* docking coal at the Moneypoint ESB power station.

15: Life for murder of wife and daughter - Dublin publican and former Irish international swimmer, Frank McCann was convicted of murdering his wife Esther and their 18 month-old adopted daughter, Jessica. McCann received two concurrent life sentences for starting the fire which claimed the lives of his wife and daughter.

18: Death of Charles Mitchel - Telefís Éireann's first newsreader, Charles Mitchel, died in Dublin at the age of 76. He had worked with RTE for 23 years up until his retirement in 1984.

19: Drugs seized in Dublin - A Gardaí operation results in the seizure of canabis and cocaine with an estimated street value of £1.5 million in Dublin city.

21 - 22: Rioting in Dublin inner-city - Disturbances broke out in the Summerhill area of Dublin city following a search for drugs. Gardaí and residents clashed for some time before peace was restored.

21 - 25: Japanese fishing fleet off Irish coast - A large contingent of Japanese tuna fishing trawlers play cat and mouse with the Irish Naval service. The Japanese trawlers are suspected of fishing inside the Irish territorial waters, resulting in the apprehending of two vessels by the navy. Tragedy later struck one of the Japanese trawlers, the *Taisei Maru,* when a freon gas leakage killed five senior crewmen.

21: Investment Company under scrutiny - A Dublin based investment firm, Taylor Assets Managers, came under intense scrutiny when it was revealed that investments amounting to more than £1.5 million made by a number of clients were not to hand, including £185,000 invested by the Society of St. Vincent de Paul. Managing director Mr. Tony Taylor is believed to be abroad.

24: Death of Mr. Erskine Childers - Irish diplomat Mr. Erskine Childers died suddenly in Luxembourg during a EU conference. Mr. Childers, (68) was the son of the late President Erskine Childers and is believed to have suffered a heart attack.

27: Taoiseach moves to ease Loyalist tension - Following warnings by Progressive Unionist Party spokesman, Mr. David Ervine, that the Loyalist ceasefire is at breaking point, the Taoiseach, Mr. Bruton, offered to meet loyalist parties in an attempt to defuse the situation.

27: Paralympics team return home - Ireland's hugely successful Paralympic team returned to Ireland, having scooped 10 medals at the Atlanta Games. The team were greeted on their arrival in Dublin by President Mary Robinson and quadruple Olympic medalist Michelle Smith.

28: Loyalist ordered out of North - Portadown loyalist, Mr. Billy Wright, was given 72 hours to leave the North by the Combined Loyalist Military Command, the penalty for refusal being death. Mr. Wright, who has a high profile both in loyalist circles and in the media, said he would defy the order. Mainstream unionist parties pointed out that the death threat placed in jeopardy the continuing participation of fringe loyalist parties such as the PUP and the UDP in the Northern talks process.

29: Growing concern for missing women - Gardaí said they were extremely worried about the safety of two women, Kathleen Keaney of Ballyconneely, Co. Galway and Fiona Pender of Tullamore, Co. Offaly, both missing from their homes for several days.

WHAT WAS SAID IN 1996

"The risk may seem high but the reward is great: a future of peace, equality and prosperity for all the people of Northern Ireland."
From the report of the **International body on arms decommissioning.**

"The idea of elections is being put forward with a view to creating a further hurdle to negotiations rather than with a view to opening the door to them."
Tánaiste **Dick Spring** on the proposed elections in the North.

"The most detested politician in Northern Ireland."
John Taylor, deputy leader of the Ulster Unionist Party on Mr Spring and his reaction to the elections.

"You are a liar."
Fianna Fáil T.D. **Joe Walsh** to Proinsias de Rossa, Minister for Social Welfare, over allegations that the minister misled the Dáil.

"Tá brón orm."
Proinsias de Rossa apologising *as gaeilge* to the Dáil over the appointment of five advisers to jobs which were advertised in his party's newsletter.

"There's no point in playing *Hamlet* without the prince."
Peter Temple-Morris arguing against the exclusion of Gerry Adams and Sinn Féin from the peace process.

"Pedestals are the loneliest places in Ireland, great breeding grounds for present and future alcoholics."
Dr Brendan Comiskey, Bishop of Ferns

"I regret very, very much that the IRA cessation has ended."
Gerry Adams, Leader of Sinn Féin speaking in the US

"I believe that the media have done a service to the church in this regard. The truth can be painful, but it is also healing and liberating."
Cardinal Cahal Daly speaking about the reporting of scandals in the Catholic Church.

"You can't say that an organisation that bombs is committed to peace. But they are still being given a chance - which will probably be a last chance - between now and June 10 to have a genuine ceasefire."
David Trimble reacting to the IRA's Easter message.

"The sooner the shotguns are at the ready and these travelling people are put out of the county the better. They are not our people."
Waterford Fianna Fáil councillor **Paddy Kenneally** on the presence of travellers in Waterford.

".... they won't be worth a penny candle."
Labour party adviser **Fergus Finlay** on multi party talks without Sinn Féin.

"I repudiate it and renounce it."
Gerry Adams on being asked to condemn the Limerick murder of Detective Garda Jerry McCabe.

"I would suspect that the reason why Sinn Féin are not in a position to condemn the murder is there is a debate, a fairly vicious debate raging within the republican movement."
Proinsias de Rossa on why Sinn Féin have not condemned the murder of Garda McCabe.

"The only man who could deal with terror in recent times in this country was Eamon de Valera who put them up against a wall and shot them."
Louth Fine Gael T.D. **Brendan McGahon** speaking after the murder of Garda McCabe.

"It is outrageous that they should try to ask the taxpayer - probably, in some cases the families of victims of the Birmingham bombings - for an additional sum, if indeed any sum at all."
Conservative M.P. **John Carlisle** on attempts by the Birmingham Six to increase the compensation they received for sixteen years of wrongful imprisonment.

"He was a junkie but he did not deserve to die like this."
Caroline Dwyer on the brutal vigilante beating to death of her father, Josie Dwyer.

"When I heard that a drug dealer was dead I did not weep, no more than I wept when I heard the 'General' was dead."
Nell McCafferty on the same murder.

"It's great to be 50."
Legendary footballer **George Best**.

"The onus is on John Major who said the election would provide a direct route to all party talks. He cannot impose an election and then refuse to accept the outcome."
Gerry Adams speaking after his party's strong showing in the Northern elections after which John Major reiterated the need for an IRA ceasefire

before Sinn Féin can be admitted to all party talks.

"This is a disgrace. If we are not giving way one day to the IRA we are giving way the next to Dublin. I am appaled and ashamed that an American, a foreigner, has been chosen for a task which involves a part of the United Kingdom."
Conservative M.P. **Terry Dicks** on the appointment of former US Senator, George Mitchell as chairman of the multi party talks.

"Go on in Conor, age before beauty."
Leader of the Democratic Unionist Party **Rev. Ian Paisley** to Conor Cruise O'Brien on the opening day of multi party talks.

"They are as organically connected as the SS and the Nazi Party."
Economist **Moore McDowell** on the relationship between the IRA and Sinn Féin.

"Sinn Féin is not the IRA. Sinn Féin is not involved in armed struggle. Sinn Féin does not advocate armed struggle."
Gerry Adams on the same relationship.

"It's a nitpicker's paradise in there."
RTE reporter **Charlie Bird** on the multi party talks.

"It is not just Drumcree and Portadown but the majority community in Ulster saying enough is enough."
Grand Master of the Orange Order **Rev Martin Smyth** speaking to protesters at Drumcree following the RUC's decision to re-route their traditional Orange parade away from the nationalist Garvaghy Road.

"This isn't just the Siege of Drumcree, this is a siege of a province, this is a siege of the whole of the United Kingdom."
The **Rev Ian Paisley** speaking at Drumcree.

"Surely to re-route a small number of marches cannot pose a threat to anyone's cultural heritage, unless hatred, intimidation and sectarianism are so deeply ingrained in the traditions of Orangism that to live at peace with one's neighbour is to lose one's identity."
Spokesman for the Lower Ormeau Road Residents Action Group, who oppose Orange marches through their area **Gerard Rice**.

"A state can never yield to the threat of force."
An Taoiseach **John Bruton** on the RUC's overturning of its earlier decision and forcing the Orange Order march along the Garvaghy Road.

"The victory gained by marching down to Garvaghy Road may well prove to be an empty and costly one."
Church of Ireland Archbishop of Dublin **Rt. Rev. Walton Empey** on the same decision.

"Bury your pride with my son."
Father of murdered Lurgan taxi driver Michael McGoldrick appeals for politicians to come together.

"For goodness sake cheer up."
Sir Patrick Mayhew speaking in the aftermath of the worst week of riots in Northern Ireland in years.

"It's not good enough for Sir Patrick Mayhew to say 'For goodness sake, cheer up.' We must say to Sir Patrick 'for goodness sake, clear off.'"
SDLP councillor **Mark Durkan**.

"We're the best geriatric pop show in town."
Paddy Reilly who has joined the 'Dubliners'.

"It's like a dream now. I almost can't believe it."
Michelle Smith after winning her third Olympic Gold medal in five days.

"You can't stop people making accusations but I'm happy with my medals and that's what's important."
Michelle Smith commenting on the allegations about the use of drugs made against her.

"Everything I ever worked for is gone. What can I do now only crawl into a hole and die?"
Donegal farmer **Bob Graham** following the eviction of himself and his family from the country's largest farm, the Grianan Estate, Burt, after a three year legal battle with National Irish Bank.

"I was just the right guy, in the right place, at the right time".
A modest **Gay Byrne** on his success as Ireland's top broadcaster.

"If I have to go to my grave, so be it. I am not afraid. You live and die".
Billy Wright, on a death threat issued against him by the Combined Loyalist Military Command.

"An absolute disgrace"
Alliance Party leader, **John Alderdice**, on DUP M.P. Willie McCrea's decision to appear on a platform with Billy Wright at a rally in Portadown.

"That's it, that's the end."
Sonia O'Sullivan speaking moments after she was eliminated in the first round of the 1,500m at the 1996 Olympic Games in Atlanta.

Moving home?
Need more space?

Talk to the Mortgage Adviser at any AIB Bank branch
or call 1850 412 412.
We'll help you make it a simpler move.

"WARNING
YOUR HOME IS AT RISK IF YOU DO NOT KEEP UP PAYMENTS ON A MORTGAGE OR ANY OTHER LOAN SECURED ON IT."
"THE PAYMENT RATES ON THIS HOUSING LOAN MAY BE ADJUSTED BY THE LENDER FROM TIME TO TIME."
Loan facilities are subject to repayment capacity and financial status, and are not available to people under 18.

AIB
Bank

ASK ABOUT OUR FREE
HOME BUYERS GUIDE

POLITICS

INTRODUCTION

Politically, Ireland is divided in two: the twenty-six "Southern" counties have an independent, sovereign parliament, Dáil Éireann, while the six northern counties are part of the United Kingdom of Great Britain and Northern Ireland under the jurisdiction of Parliament at Westminster. This division, commonly known as partition, occurred in 1920 under the terms of the Government of Ireland Act.

The division of the island has resulted in two very different political landscapes.

In the South after the very bitter Civil War, which followed partition, there emerged two major political parties-Fianna Fáil, which largely commanded the support of those who opposed the signing of the treaty which resulted in partition, and Fine Gael, which gained most of its support from those who believed that signing the Treaty was the best arrangement available at that time. Fianna Fail came to dominate, particularly from the 1930's to the 1960's when they remained in government for lengthy periods. The last twenty-five years have seen a degree of shift in the balance of power with Fianna Fail, while still remaining the largest party, having to go into coalition with other parties to form a Government or being forced into opposition by a coalition of the other Dáil Éireann parties.

In Northern Ireland, the Ulster Unionist party, by far the largest grouping, remained in power from 1921 until the British Government prorogued the Stormont Parliament in 1972. The British Government subsequently introduced direct rule from Westminster by appointing a Secretary of State for Northern Ireland.

Seventeen M.P.'s are returned by the N.I. electorate to the British parliament. All legislation concerning the North is enacted by Westminster.

Explanatory Notes on The President, Parliament and Government

The political system now used in the Republic of Ireland had its genesis in the Constitution of Ireland referendum of 1937 which declared the present Republic of Ireland to be a sovereign, independent, democratic state.

The parliament (the Oireachtas) consists of the President of Ireland (an tUachtarán) and two houses: Dáil Éireann, which is the house of representatives, and Seanad Éireann, which is a senate.

The president is elected by the direct vote of the people every seven years.

Dáil Éireann's 166 members are elected on a system of proportional representation by means of a single transferable vote.

The Seanad has 60 members, eleven of whom are nominated by An Taoiseach (the Prime Minister) and 49 are elected — three by the National University of Ireland, three by the University of Dublin and 43 by panels of candidates established on a vocational basis.

Irish citizens become eligible to vote at the age of 18.

The Office of President of Ireland

The office and function of the President of Ireland are dealt with in Articles 12 and 13 of the Constitution. The current President is Mary Robinson. The President is Head of State only, and although she does not have any executive powers and acts only on the advice and authority of the Government, she does hold a limited number of functions. All bills passed by the Oireachtas (i.e., both Houses of Parliament) are promulgated by her and she may refer bills (excluding money bills) to the Supreme Court to verify their constitutionality.

The President appoints the Taoiseach, on the nomination of Dáil Éireann and appoints Government Ministers on the advice of the Taoiseach.

The Taoiseach also advises her on accepting resignations of ministers, on summoning and dismissing the Dáil, although she has the discretionary power to refuse to dissolve the Dáil. The supreme command of the defence forces is vested in the President who also receives and accredits ambassadors.

Every citizen who is entitled to vote in general elections can also vote in Presidential elections. A Presidential candidate must be an Irish citizen and over the age of thirty-five. The term of office for the President is seven years and the President can be re-elected only once.

Explanatory notes on Northern Ireland

Northern Ireland came into being under the Government of Ireland Act 1920 which marked the partition of Ireland, the twenty six counties gaining independence from Britain while six counties (Antrim, Down, Armagh, Londonderry (popularly called *Derry*), Tyrone and Fermanagh) remained within the United Kingdom. It had its own parliamentary system until 1972 when the Stormont Parliament was prorogued and executive powers were transferred to Westminster which now has ultimate power over Northern Ireland affairs.

The current arrangements for governing are vested in the Secretary of State for Northern Ireland who holds the legislative power in respect of commerce and industry, education, health, agriculture and welfare. These arrangements are reviewed annually.

Northern Ireland sends seventeen members to the House of Commons at Westminster, which is the lower house of the U.K. Parliament. It also sends three members to European Parliament, the United Kingdom of Great Britain and Northern Ireland having joined the European Community on January 1st 1973.

STATE EMBLEMS OF THE REPUBLIC OF IRELAND

Name of State, National Flag, Emblem and National Anthem

Name of State: Article 4 of the 1937 Constitution reads: The name of the State is Éire, or in the English language, Ireland. Previous to this it had been known from Independence as Saorstat Éireann or the Irish Free State. The Republic of Ireland Act of 1948 allows for the state to be described as the "Republic of Ireland", the name remains unaltered from Article 4.

The old Irish form of the name of Éire was Ériu. Ptolemy, a Greek cartographer of the 2nd century A.D. referred to Ireland as Louernia while Julius Caesar refers to Ireland as Hibernia.

The National Flag: Article 7 of the 1937 Constitution reads: The national flag is the tricolour of green, white and orange. The tricolour is rectangular, the width being twice the depth. The colours are "of equal size and vertically disposed, the green being next to the staff, the white in the middle and the orange farthest from the staff as prescribed in Defence Force Regulations.

Thomas Francis Meagher, a member of Daniel O'Connell's Repeal Association, (later a Union Army General during the American Civil War and subsequently Governor of Montana) received the tricolour as a gift from citizens of France (on whose flag the Irish tricolour is no doubt based) in 1848. It flew over the GPO during the 1916 Rising and henceforth became recognised as the national flag. It was the official flag from independence in 1922 until it was enshrined as the national flag in the 1937 Constitution.

The colours are symbolic of the union between older Gaelic and Anglo-Norman Ireland (green) and newer Protestant Planter Ireland (orange) and the white in Meagher's words "signifies a lasting truce between the "Orange" and the "Green".

The Arms of the State: The Arms of the State have no official statue or regulation but the President's official seal of office has an heraldic harp engraved on it. It is also emblazoned on the President's standard as a gold harp on a blue background. The harp is also used by government departments and is engraved on the coinage and depicted on the notes of the state's currency.

The harp is modelled on the fourteenth century 'Brian Boru' harp, displayed in the museum of Trinity College Dublin.

The National Anthem: The National Anthem is 'The Soldier's Song' or *Amhrán na bhFiann*. Peadar Kearney (1883 - 1942) wrote the lyrics and Patrick Heeney (1881-1911) helped him compose the music (although he couldn't read or write music) in 1907. It was first published in the newspaper *Irish Freedom* in 1912 and was adopted by the Irish Volunteers. In 1926 it was formally recognised as the official national anthem displacing the earlier 'God Save Ireland'.

(Source: Department of Foreign Affairs, Dublin)

REPUBLIC OF IRELAND POLITICAL PARTIES

Main Political Parties in the Republic of Ireland

FIANNA FÁIL
13 Upper Mount Street, Dublin 2

Founded in May 1926 by Eamon de Valera, Fianna Fáil ("Solders of Destiny") was originally made up of anti-Treaty Sinn Féin T.D.'s, who first took their seats in the Dáil in1927. De Valera was elected the first President of the party, a position he held until 195°.

Fianna Fáil has had five Taoisigh: Eamon de Valera (re-elected six times); Seán Lemass (re-elected twice); Jack Lynch (re-elected twice), Charles Haughey (re-elected three times) and Albert Reynolds. In government Fianna Fáil drafted the 1937 Constitution, ensured Irish neutrality during World War II, distributed agricultural land, undertook massive housing and social assistance programmes, and oversaw the accession into the EEC. During the Albert Reynolds-led Government the Joint Declaration on peace in Northern Ireland was signed. The party has strong representation in both urban and rural Ireland, and since the 1930's has consistently been the largest party in the Dáil.

The aims of the party, as set out in 1926, and still holding today are: to secure in peace and agreement the unity of Ireland and its people; the development of a distinctive national life in accordance with the diverse traditions and ideals of the Irish people as part of a broad European culture, and to restore and promote the Irish language as a living language of the people; to guarantee religious and civil liberty, and equal rights, equal treatment, and equal opportunities for all the people of Ireland; to develop the resources and wealth of Ireland to their full potential, while making them subservient to the needs and welfare of all the people of Ireland, so as to provide the maximum sustainable employment; to protect the natural environment and heritage of Ireland and to ensure a balance between town and country and between the regions; to promote the family, a wider sense of social responsibility, and to uphold the rule of law in the interests of the welfare and safety of the public; to maintain Ireland's status as a sovereign state, as a full member of the European Union and United Nations, contributing to peace, disarmament and development on the basis of Ireland's independent foreign policy tradition (including military neutrality); and finally to reform the laws and institutions of state, to make them efficient, humane, caring and responsive to the needs of the citizen.

The current party leader is Bertie Ahern, T.D., Chairman of the Parliamentary Party is Dr. Rory O'Hanlon, T.D., and General Secretary is Pat Farrell.

FINE GAEL
51 Upper Mount Street, Dublin 2.

The Fine Gael party was formed in 1933 by the merging of Cumann na nGaedheal, the National Centre Party and the Army Comrades Association (the Blueshirts), with General Éoin O'Duffy (the leader of the A.C.A.) as its first leader.

The party has been in government six times, each time as the major party in coalition. The party has had four Taoisigh: John A. Costello (twice), Liam Cosgrave, Garret FitzGerald (twice) and the current Taoiseach, John Bruton. In government Fine Gael have been instrumental in the Declaration of the Republic of Ireland in 1949, the signing of the Sunningdale Agreement in 1973 and the signing of the Anglo-Irish Agreement in 1985.

The party has a policy of encouraging enterprise through a mixture of state encouragement for private enterprise and direct state involvement. It wants to see decision making devolved to the appropriate level, particularly involving women and young people. The party also promotes fairer opportunities in education, the improvement in social welfare provisions and a greater tax equity. On Northern Ireland the party works for reconciliation and recognises both the Nationalist and Unionist traditions. Fine Gael also commits itself to the development and unification of the European Union.

At the last general election in 1992 Fine Gael won 47 seats, making it the second largest political party in the country.

The current party leader is John Bruton, T.D., Party Chairman is Phil Hogan, T.D., and General Secretary is Jim Miley.

LABOUR
17 Ely Place, Dublin 2

The Labour Party was founded in 1912 at Clonmel by James Connolly, Jim Larkin and William O'Brien as the political wing of the Irish Trade Union Congress. Following the Easter Rising, the party didn't contest the elections of 1918 or 1921 and as such lost a generation of supporters.

In 1943 a split occurred, the Irish Transport and General Workers Union disaffiliated from the party and established the National Labour Party.

The Party has been part of seven coalition governments including the current one which was formed in December 1994. Having won 33 seats its leader, Dick Spring T.D., is Tánaiste and Minister for Foreign Affairs. Labour T.D.s also hold the ministerial portfolios of Finance; Arts, Culture and the Gaeltacht; Environment; Education; and Equality and Law Reform. The party is also represented in Seanad Éireann and the European Parliament. The 33 seats won in the 1992 General Election was the party's highest ever showing in an Irish general election, enabling the party to command a strong position in the present coalition government comprising of Fine Gael, Democratic Left and themselves.

The party also tasted success in the 1990 Presidential Election when their nominated candidate Mary Robinson went on to win and become the first ever female President of Ireland.

The party's socialist principles hope to build a society based on freedom, equality, community and democracy - the four main tenants of socialism. Twelve trade unions, representing 50% of all trade union members in the state are affiliated to the party.

The Party, and in particular its current leader, Dick Spring have played a major role in the current peace process, helping negotiate the Joint Declaration and Framework Document.

Recent leaders of the party have included Frank Cluskey, who stepped down in 1981, succeeded by Michael O'Leary for one year, and Dick Spring has been leader since then.

DEMOCRATIC LEFT
69 Middle Abbey Street, Dublin 1

Democratic Left was founded in 1992 following a split in the Workers Party. Organised both in Northern Ireland and the Republic the party has five T.D.'s and one senator. It is part of the 'rainbow' coalition formed in December 1994 which includes Fine Gael and the Labour Party. Its leader Proinsias de Rossa T.D., is the current Minister for Social Welfare and Pat Rabitte T.D., is a Minister for State.

The party is a modern, democratic, socialist organisation whose main policy document is 'Strategy 2000', published in 1993. Main tenets of their policies include: free access to all levels of education, from pre-schooling to adult education; a commitment to incorporating ecological principles into aspects of economic policy making; the welcoming of moves towards European Union along democratic and not military lines; an ending to the territorial claim on Northern Ireland by the Constitution of the Republic, replacing it by an aspiration for the unity of the people of the island; the complete separation of Church and State; the creation of a new left-led force in Irish politics through co-operation between forces for change such as Labour, the Green party and Democratic Left.

THE GREEN PARTY
5A, Upper Fowes Street, Dublin 2

Founded in 1982 at a public meeting in Dublin, The Green Party experienced a number of title changes until settling on its current title in 1986. Electoral breakthrough occurred in 1989 when Roger Garland became Ireland's first Green T.D. The party currently has two M.E.P.s and one T.D. as well as a number of local government representatives.

The party supports open government, locally based decision making, renewable energy and recycling, neutral peacekeeping in Northern Ireland, workers co-operatives and small business, the wider use of public transport and non-violent direct action. The party opposes the depopulation of the countryside, the control of industry by large national and multi-national companies, nuclear power and weapons, land and property speculation, paramilitary and state violence in Northern Ireland, the exploitation of the Third World, the pollution of air,sea and land, and the exploitation of animals.

The party does not have a leader, rather a co-ordinator of an annually elected Co-ordinating Committee. All positions are rotated each year.

COMMUNIST PARTY OF IRELAND
James Connolly House, 43 East Essex Street, Dublin.

The party was founded in 1921 but was a descendent from James Connolly's Irish Socialist Republican Party of 1896. It aims to bring about a United Secular Socialist Republic and the development of the ideals of James Connolly and the application of those ideals to contemporary Irish society.

The party hopes to establish the common ownership of wealth ensuring harmony between social and economic development with due regard to the protection of the environment. The party is a 32 county organisation striving to secure equality for all people regardless of gender, religion, ethnicity or sexual orientation.

The General Secretary of the party is James Stewart and Chairperson is Eugene McCartan.

THE WORKER'S PARTY
28 Gardiner Place, Dublin 1

The Workers Party is descended from Sinn Féin (founded 1905). A split occurred in 1977 when Sinn Féin The Workers Party was established, and in 1982 the party adopted its current name.

The party is organised throughout the 32 counties along democratic and secular socialist party lines. The aim of the party is the creation, through democratic means, of a single, secular, socialist, unitary Republic on the island of Ireland.

Following a national conference in 1992 six of the seven parliamentary representatives seceded from the party after failing to change the party's constitution and established *Democratic Left*. The Workers Party suffered organisationally and financially but has since recovered somewhat.

Significant past and present figures in the party include Proinsias de Rossa and Tomás MacGiolla respectively. The current party President is Marian Donnelly and the General Secretary is Pat Quearney.

THE PROGRESSIVE DEMOCRATS
25 South Fredrick Street, Dublin 2

The Progressive Democrats were founded in 1985 by Limerick T.D. Desmond O'Malley, following a split in the Fianna Fáil party. Since then the party has been in government on just one occasion, from 1989 to 1991, ironically with Fianna Fáil.

The party sees itself as a modern, liberal party in the wider European context and as such supports movement towards greater political and economic integration between the member states of the European Union. The party also favours positive government action in creating an enterprise society.

The party is currently the second biggest opposition party in the Dáil with eight seats in all. They are also represented in Seanad Éireann. The current party leader is Mary Harney, having succeeded Des O'Malley as party leader in October 1993. She is the first female party leader in the history of the state.

REPUBLIC OF IRELAND POLITICAL LEADERS
Leaders of major Irish political parties, 1922-96

FIANNA FÁIL	
Eamon de Valera	(1926 - 1959)
Seán Lemass	(1959 - 1966)
Jack Lynch	(1966 - 1979)
Charles J. Haughey	(1979 - 1992)
Albert Reynolds	(1992 - 1994)
Bertie Ahern	(1994 -)

CUMANN NA nGAEDHEAL	
William T. Cosgrave	(1922 - 1933)

FINE GAEL	
Eoin O'Duffy	(1933 - 1934)
William T. Cosgrave	(1935 - 1944)
Richard Mulcahy	(1944 - 1959)
James Dillon	(1959 - 1965)
Liam Cosgrave	(1965 - 1977)
Garret FitzGerald	(1977 - 1987)
Alan Dukes	(1987 - 1990)
John Bruton	(1990 -)

CLANN NA POBLACHTA	
Seán MacBride	(1946 - 1957)

LABOUR PARTY	
Thomas Johnson	(1918 - 1927)
T.J. O'Connell	(1927 - 1932)
William Norton	(1932 - 1960)
Brendan Corish	(1960 - 1977)
Frank Cluskey	(1977 - 1981)
Michael O'Leary	(1981 - 1982)
Dick Spring	(1982 -)

PROGRESSIVE DEMOCRATS	
Desmond O'Malley	(1985 - 1993)
Mary Harney	(1993 -)

DEMOCRATIC LEFT	
Proinsias de Rossa	(1992 -)

Irish Politics - The "Family" Tree
Origins of the main Irish Political Parties

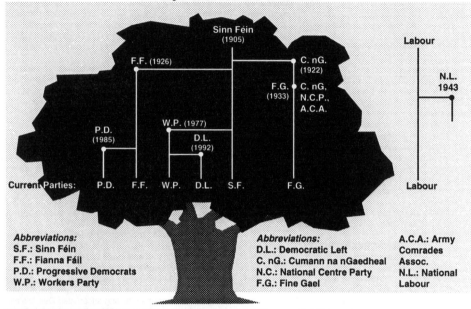

Abbreviations:
S.F.: Sinn Féin
F.F.: Fianna Fáil
P.D.: Progressive Democrats
W.P.: Workers Party

Abbreviations:
D.L.: Democratic Left
C. nG.: Cumann na nGaedheal
N.C.: National Centre Party
F.G.: Fine Gael

A.C.A.: Army
Comrades
Assoc.
N.L.: National
Labour

GENERAL ELECTION RESULTS 1992

The General Election of 25th November 1992 came about following the resignation of the Progressive Democrat ministers from the Fianna Fáil/Progressive Democrat Coalition Government which had been in place from 12th July 1989. The minority Albert Reynolds led Fianna Fail Government were defeated in a vote of confidence on November 5th 1992, thus precipitating a General Election.

Republic of Ireland General Election Results, 25th November 1992

CARLOW - KILKENNY
Seats: 5; Candidates: 9; Electorate: 81,377; Turnout: 69.5%; Quota: 9,294; Elected: Séamus Pattison (Lab) 13,713 - 1st Ct; Liam Aylward (FF) 11,331 - 1 Ct; Philip Hogan (FG) 9,497 - 5 Ct; John Browne (FG) 9,227 - 6 Ct; M.J. Nolan (FF) 8,965 - 6 Ct.

CAVAN - MONAGHAN
Seats: 5; Candidates: 13; Electorate: 79,011; Turnout: 70.73%; Quota: 9,149; Elected: Brendan Smith (FF) 9,162 - 5th Ct; Rory O'Hanlon (FF) 9,767 - 8th Ct; Andrew Boylan (FG) 9,285 - 8th Ct; Seymour Crawford (FG) 8,653 - 8th Ct; Jimmy Leonard (FF) 8,344 - 8th Ct.

CLARE
Seats: 4; Candidates: 11; Electorate: 66,042; Turnout: 68.36%; Quota: 8,922; Elected: Donal Carey (FG) 8,922 - 7th Ct; Tony Kileen (FF) 8,922 - 8th Ct; Moosajee Bhamjee (Lab) 8,985 - 9th Ct; Sile de Valera (FF) 8,825 - 9th Ct.

CORK EAST
Seats: 4; Candidates: 10; Electorate: 58,556; Turnout: 72.02%; Quota: 8,298; Elected: Ned O'Keefe (FF) 8,380 - 1st Ct; Paul Bradford (FG) 9,790 - 7th Ct; Michael Ahern (FF) 8,510 - 7th Ct; John Mulvihill (Lab) 7,830 - 7th Ct.

CORK NORTH CENTRAL
Seats: 5; Candidates: 18; Electorate: 68,479; Turnout: 66.8%; Quota: 7,483; Elected: Gerry O'Sullivan (Lab) 10,008 - 1st Ct; Dan Wallace (FF) 7,670 - 12th Ct; Bernard Allen (FG) 7,730 - 14th Ct; Máirín Quill (PD) 7,363 - 16th Ct; Liam Burke (FG) 5,491 - 16th Ct.

CORK NORTH WEST
Seats: 3; Candidates: 7; Electorate: 44,848; Turnout: 75.6%; Quota: 8,335; Elected: Michael Creed (FG) 10,041 - 4th Ct; Donal Moynihan (FF) 8,425 - 4th Ct; Frank Crowley (FG) 8,263 - 4th Ct.

CORK SOUTH CENTRAL
Seats: 5; Candidates: 18; Electorate: 76,141; Turnout: 71.32%; Quota: 8,933; Elected: Toddy O'Sullivan (Lab) 9,662 - 1st Ct; Michael Martin (FF) 8,971 - 11th Ct; Peter Barry (FG) 9,408 - 15th Ct; Pat Cox (PD) 9,400 - 15th Ct; Bat O'Keefe (Lab) 6,985 - 15th Ct.

CORK SOUTH WEST
Seats: 3; Candidates: 10;

Electorate: 45,769; Turnout: 74.12%; Quota: 8,325; Elected: Joe Walsh (FF) 9,376 - 1st Ct; P.J. Sheehan (FG) 9,222 - 8th Ct; Jim O'Keefe (FG) 8,388 - 8th Ct.

DONEGAL NORTH EAST
Seats: 3; Candidates: 10; Electorate: 46,978; Turnout: 67.63%; Quota: 7,803; Elected: James McDaid (FF) 8,834 - 7th Ct; Paddy Harte (FG) 8,055 - 7th Ct; Neil T. Blaney (Ind. FF) 7,061 - 8th Ct.

DONEGAL SOUTH WEST
Seats: 3; Candidates: 9; Electorate: 48,528; Turnout: 62.84%; Quota: 7,453; Elected: Pat The Cope Gallagher (FF) 7,870 - 1st Ct; Mary Coughlan (FF) 7,624 - 7th Ct; Dinny McGinley (FG) 6,588 - 7th Ct.

DUBLIN CENTRAL
Seats: 4; Candidates: 12; Electorate: 60,391; Turnout: 61.49%; Quota: 7,281; Elected: Bertie Ahern (FF) 11,374 - 1st Ct; Joe Costello (Lab) 7,308 - 1st Ct; Tony Gregory (Ind) 7,667 - 7th Ct; Jim Mitchell (FG) 6,562 - 10th Ct.

DUBLIN NORTH
Seats: 4; Candidates: 10; Electorate: 63,341; Turnout: 69.02%; Quota: 8,636; Elected: Seán Ryan (Lab) 14,693 - 1st Ct; Ray Burke (FF) 8,745 - 1st Ct; Nora Owen (FG) 9,227 - 6th Ct; Trevor Sargent (GP) 8,524 - 8th Ct.

DUBLIN NORTH CENTRAL
Seats: 4; Candidates: 14; Electorate: 64,859; Turnout: 71.72%; Quota: 9,177; Elected: Derek McDowell (Lab) 10,609 - 1st Ct; Richard Bruton (FG) 10,505 - 10th Ct; Seán Haughey (FF) 10,912 -12th Ct; Ivor Callely (FF) 9,632 - 13th Ct.

DUBLIN NORTH-EAST
Seats: 4; Candidates: 14; Electorate: 58,433; Turnout: 69.57%; Quota: 8,003; Elected: Seán Kenny (Lab) 8,873 - 1st Ct; Michael Woods (FF) 8,536 - 9th Ct; Tommy Broughan (Lab) 7,696 - 12th Ct; Liam Fitzgerald (FF) 6,911 - 12th Ct.

DUBLIN NORTH-WEST
Seats: 4; Candidates: 16; Electorate: 58,396; Turnout: 65.36%; Quota: 7,488; Elected:

Róisín Shortall (Lab) 8,634 - 1st Ct; Noel Ahern (FF) 7,609 - 11th Ct; Proinsias De Rossa (DL) 7,704 - 12th Ct; Mary Flaherty (FG) 6,382 - 12th Ct.

DUBLIN SOUTH
Seats: 5; Candidates: 14; Electorate: 85,553; Turnout: 70.41%; Quota: 9,940; Elected: Eithne Fitzgerald (Lab) 17,256 - 1st Ct; Seamus Brennan (FF) 10,001 - 7th Ct; Tom Kitt (FF) 11,005 - 8th Ct; Alan Shatter (FG) 10,685 - 12th Ct; Liz O'Donnell (PD) 8,790 - 12th Ct.

DUBLIN SOUTH-CENTRAL
Seats: 4; Candidates: 14; Electorate: 63,718; Turnout: 64.56%; Quota: 8,049; Elected: Pat Upton (Lab) 11,923 - 1st Ct; Gay Mitchell (FG) 8,730 - 7th Ct; John O'Connell (FF) 8,182 - 12th Ct; Ben Briscoe (FF) 6,526 - 13th Ct.

DUBLIN SOUTH-EAST
Seats: 4; Candidates: 14; Electorate: 69,582; Turnout: 59.23%; Quota: 8,051; Elected: Ruairí Quinn (Lab) 10,381 - 1st Ct; Frances Fitzgerald (FG) 9,718 - 11th Ct; Michael McDowell (PD) 7,752 - 12th Ct; Eoin Ryan (FF) 6,695 - 12th Ct.

DUBLIN SOUTH-WEST
Seats: 5; Candidates: 16; Electorate: 69,922; Turnout: 62.01%; Quota: 7,109; Elected: Mervyn Taylor (Lab) 10,871 - 1st Ct; Chris Flood (FF) 7,856 - 9th Ct; Eamonn Walsh (Lab) 7,167 - 11th Ct; Mary Harney (PD) 7,835 - 13th Ct; Pat Rabbitte (DL) 6,249 - 13th Ct.

DUBLIN WEST
Seats: 4; Candidates: 16; Electorate: 57,955; Turnout: 65.0%; Quota: 7,431; Elected: Joan Burton (Lab) 8,398 - 1st Ct; Brian Lenihan (FF) 8,007 - 13th Ct; Austin Currie (FG) 7,226 - 14th Ct; Liam Lawlor (FF) 6,097 - 14th Ct.

DÚN LAOGHAIRE
Seats: 5; Candidates: 14; Electorate: 87,495; Turnout: 68.63%; Quota: 9,896; Elected: David Andrews (FF) 13,418 - 1st Ct; Niamh Bhreathnach (Lab) 10,074 - 1st Ct; Seán Barrett (FG) 11,590 - 11th Ct; Helen Keogh (PD) 10,038 - 12th Ct; Éamon Gilmore (DL) 9,788 - 12th Ct.

GALWAY EAST
Seats: 3; Candidates: 8; Electorate: 42,672; Turnout: 69.21%; Quota: 7,268; Elected: Michael P. Kitt (FF) 7,571 - 4th Ct; Paul Connaughton (FG) 9,064 - 5th Ct; Noel Treacy (FF) 7,224 - 6th Ct.

GALWAY WEST
Seats: 5; Candidates: 14; Electorate: 79,008; Turnout: 64.60%; Quota: 8,399; Elected: Michael D. Higgins (Lab) 8,910 - 1st Ct; Éamon Ó Cuív (FF) 8,430 - 1st Ct; Pádraic McCormack (FG) 8,508 - 10th Ct; Robbie Molloy (PD) 8,276 - 10th Ct; Máire Geoghegan Quinn (FF) 7,728 - 10th Ct.

KERRY NORTH
Seats: 3; Candidates: 7; Electorate: 48,797; Turnout: 70.36%; Quota: 8,484; Elected: Dick Spring (Lab) 11,515 - 1st Ct; Jimmy Deenihan (FG) 9,665 - 2nd Ct; Denis Foley (FF) 8,698 - 6th Ct.

KERRY SOUTH
Seats: 3; Candidates: 9; Electorate: 44,591; Turnout: 71.37%; Quota: 7,835; Elected: John O'Donoghue (FF) 8,263 - 1st Ct; Breeda Moynihan-Cronin (Lab) 7,843 - 5th Ct; John O'Leary (FF) 7,407 - 6th Ct.

KILDARE
Seats: 5; Candidates: 14; Electorate: 78,069; Turnout: 65.51%; Quota: 8,400; Elected: Emmet Stagg (Lab) 10,656 - 1st Ct; Charlie McCreevy (FF) 10,208 - 1st Ct; Alan Dukes (FG) 10,144 - 11th Ct; Seán Power (FF) 8,527 - 11th Ct; Bernard Durkan (FG) 7,413 - 12th Ct.

LAOIS-OFFALY
Seats: 5; Candidates: 13; Electorate: 77,291; Turnout: 70.41%; Quota: 8,946; Elected: Brian Cowan (FF) 10,117 - 1st Ct; Liam Hyland (FF) 9,246 - 8th Ct; Pat Gallagher (Lab) 9,098 - 10th Ct; Ger Connolly (FF) 9,010 - 10th Ct; Charles Flanagan (FG) 8,468 - 10th Ct.

LIMERICK EAST
Seats: 5; Candidates: 13; Electorate: 71,136; Turnout: 68.98%; Quota: 8,059; Elected: Willie O'Dea (FF) 10,990 - 1st Ct; Desmond O' Malley (PD) 8,304 - 1st Ct; Jim Kemmy (Lab) 8,262 - 1st Ct;

Michael Noonan (FG) 8,627 - 11th Ct; Peadar Clohessy (PD) 6,630 - 12th Ct.

LIMERICK WEST
Seats: 3; **Candidates:** 9; **Electorate:** 44,848; **Turnout:** 72.11%; **Quota:** 7,955; **Elected:** Gerry Collins (FF) 10,913 - 1st Ct; Michael J. Noonan (FF) 7,990 - 7th Ct; Michael Finucane (FG) 7,600 - 7th Ct.

LONGFORD-ROSCOMMON
Seats: 4; **Candidates:** 13; **Electorate:** 60,709; **Turnout:** 75.45%; **Quota:** 9,062; **Elected:** Albert Reynolds (FF) 10,307 - 1st Ct; John Connor (FG) 10,809 - 8th Ct; Tom Foxe (Ind) 9,730 - 9th Ct; Seán Doherty (FF) 7,994 - 9th Ct.

LOUTH
Seats: 4; **Candidates:** 12; **Electorate:** 65,896; **Turnout:** 67.4%; **Quota:** 8,695; **Elected:** Michael Bell (Lab) 9,608 - 1st Ct; Dermot Ahern (FF) 8,707 - 8th Ct; Séamus Kirk (FF) 9,835 - 9th Ct; Brendan McGahon (FG) 8,087 - 9th Ct.

MAYO EAST
Seats: 3; **Candidates:** 6; **Electorate:** 43,449; **Turnout:** 68.40%; **Quota:** 7,325; **Elected:** Jim Higgins (FG) 7,631 - 1st Ct; Tom Moffatt (FF) 7,709 - 3rd Ct; PJ Morley (FF) 7,158 - 3rd Ct.

MAYO WEST
Seats: 3; **Candidates:** 6;

Electorate: 43,472; **Turnout:** 69.12%; **Quota:** 7,415; **Elected:** Pádraig Flynn (FF) 9,629 - 1st Ct; Enda Kenny (FG) 7,656 - 4th Ct; Seamus Hughes (FF) 7,319 - 4th Ct.

MEATH
Seats: 5; **Candidates:** 13; **Electorate:** 78,083; **Turnout:** 66.32%; **Quota:** 8,514; **Elected:** Noel Dempsey (FF) 9,196 - 1st Ct; Brian Fitzgerald (Lab) 8,967 - 1st Ct; John Bruton (FG) 8,584 - 3rd Ct; Mary Wallace (FF) 8,126 - 11th Ct; Colm Hilliard (FF) 8,101 - 11th Ct.

SLIGO-LEITRIM
Seats: 4; **Candidates:** 9; **Electorate:** 60,764; **Turnout:** 71.24%; **Quota:** 8,547; **Elected:** Matt Brennan (FF) 10,332 - 4th Ct; Declan Bree (Lab) 9,107 - 4th Ct; John Ellis (FF) 10,025 - 5th Ct; Ted Nealon (FG) 8,144 - 6th Ct.

TIPPERARY NORTH
Seats: 3; **Candidates:** 6; **Electorate:** 42,754; **Turnout:** 75.53%; **Quota:** 7,957; **Elected:** Michael Smith (FF) 8,156 - 1st Ct; Michael Lowry (FG) 8,330 - 3rd Ct; John Ryan (Lab) 8,112 - 4th Ct.

TIPPERARY SOUTH
Seats: 3; **Candidates:** 9; **Electorate:** 56,800; **Turnout:** 70.78%; **Quota:** 9,918; **Elected:** Theresa Ahern (FG) 10,065 - 3rd Ct; Noel Davern (FF) 10,117 - 5th Ct; Michael Ferris (Lab) 9,727 - 5th Ct; Outgoing Ceann Comhairle Sean Treacy (Ind) returned without

contest.

WATERFORD
Seats: 4; **Candidates:** 11; **Electorate:** 64,037; **Turnout:** 68.18%; **Quota:** 8,598; **Elected:** Brian O'Shea (Lab) 11,235 - 1st Ct; Austin Deasy (FG) 8,634 - 4th Ct; Brendan Kenneally (FF) 8,380 - 7th Ct; Martin Collen (PD) 6,739 - 7th Ct.

WESTMEATH
Seats: 3; **Candidates:** 11; **Electorate:** 46,267; **Turnout:** 67.32%; **Quota:** 7,676; **Elected:** Mary O'Rourke (FF) 7,918 - 7th Ct; Paul McGrath (FG) 7,648 - 9th Ct; Willie Penrose (Lab) 7,321 - 9th Ct.

WEXFORD
Seats: 5; **Candidates:** 10; **Electorate:** 75,886; **Turnout:** 69.76%; **Quota:** 8,696; **Elected:** Brendan Howlin (Lab) 10,338 - 1st Ct; Ivan Yates (FG) 10,716 - 5th Ct; John Brown (FF) 9,233 - 5th Ct; Avril Doyle (FG) 9,303 - 6th Ct; Hugh Byrne (FF) 8,423 - 8th Ct.

WICKLOW
Seats: 5; **Candidates:** 19; **Electorate:** 77,133; **Turnout:** 68.24%; **Quota:** 8,649; **Elected:** Liam Kavanagh (Lab) 11,843 - 1st Ct; Joe Jacob (FF) 8,651 - 11th Ct; Godfrey Timmins (FG) 9,520 - 12th Ct; Liz McManus (DL) 9,162 - 12th Ct; Johnny Fox (Ind) 7,656 - 14th Ct.

BY-ELECTION RESULTS SINCE 1992

DUBLIN SOUTH CENTRAL
(9 June 1994)
Reason for Election: Dr. John O'Connell retired for health reasons; **Candidates:** 11; **Electorate:** 62,283; **Total Poll:** 27,569; **Turnout:** 44.3%; **Quota:** 13,389; **1st Count:** Eric Byrne (DL) 7,445; Michael Mulcahy (FF) 5,642; Brian Hayes (FG) 4,637; Joe Connolly (Lab) 2,643; Cait Keane (PD) 1,881; John Goodwillie (GP) 1,752; Eamonn Gavin (Ind) 972; Michael Park (Ind) 775; Shay Kelly (WP) 595; Martina Gibney (SF) 781; Benny Cooney (Ind) 152; **9th Count:** Eric Byrne (DL) 12,741;

Michael Mulcahy (FF) 8,629; **Elected:** Eric Byrne (DL) without reaching Quota.

MAYO WEST
(9 June 1994)
Reason for Election: P. Flynn resigned to take up EC Commissioner's post; **Candidates:** 5; **Electorate:** 45,318; **Total Poll:** 29,397; **Turnout:** 64.9%; **Quota:** 15,826; **1st Count:** Beverly Cooper-Flynn (FF) 10,967; Michael Ring (FG) 10,390; Paddy McGuinness (Ind) 6,275; Johnny Mee (Lab) 1,103; Jerry Cowley (Ind) 383; **2nd Count:** Michael Ring (FG) 14,063;

Beverly Cooper-Flynn (FF) 13,639; **Elected:** Michael Ring (FG) without reaching Quota.

CORK NORTH CENTRAL
(10 November 1994)
Reason for Election: Death of Gerry O'Sullivan (Lab); **Candidates:** 12; **Electorate:** 70,142; **Total Poll:** 37,778; **Turnout:** 53.9%; **Quota:** 18,675; **1st Count:** Kathleen Lynch (DL) 9,843; Billy Kelleher (FF) 9,528; Colm Burke (FG) 6,035; Lisa O'Sullivan (Lab) 4,003; Jane Power (GP) 1,856; Michael Burns (PD) 1,628; Don O'Leary (SF) 1,304; Jimmy Homan

(WP) 1,082; Con O'Leary (Ind) 1,036; Donie O'Leary (Ind) 445; Gerry Duffy (Ind) 426; Nora Ann Luck (NLP) 162; **8th Count:** Kathleen Lynch (DL) 17,329; Billy Kelleher (FF) 13,730; **Elected:** Kathleen Lynch (DL) without reaching Quota.

CORK SOUTH CENTRAL
(10 November 94)
Reason for Election: Pat Cox (PD) resigned his seat; **Candidates:** 9; **Electorate:** 78,420; **Total Poll:** 42,519; **Turnout:** 54.2%; **Quota:** 21,068; **1st Count:** John Dennehy (FF) 13,316; Hugh Coveney (FG) 13,128; Dan Boyle (GP) 6,677; Brendan Ryan (Ind) 2,618; Joe O'Flynn (Lab) 1,940; Alan Elland (PD) 1,719; Catherine Kelly (CSP) 1,708; Seán McCarthy (WP) 813; Dr. Brian McEnery (NLP) 219; **6th Count:** Hugh Coveney (FG) 19,396; John Dennehy (FF) 17,421; **Elected:** Hugh Coveney (FG) without reaching Quota.

WICKLOW
(29 June 1995)
Reason for Election: Death of Johnny Fox; **Candidates:** 11; **Electorate:** 81, 946; **Total Poll:** 43,830; **Quota:** 21,795; **1st Count:** T. Collins (Lab) 5,064; M. Fox (ind) 11,724; D. Garret (NLP) 104; F. Hayes (WP) 211; T. Honan (FG) 5,503; C. Keddy (Ind) 254; N. Kelly (Ind) 4,556; J. McManus (DL) 2,841; D. Roche (FF) 10,060; E. Singleton (GP) 1,565; J. Tallon (Ind) 80; **8th Count:** M. Fox (Ind) 22,922; D. Roche (FF) 14,895; **Elected:** M. Fox (Ind).

DONEGAL NORTH EAST
(3 April 1996)
Reason for Election: Death of Neil T. Blaney; **Candidates:** 5; **Electorate:** 50,393; **Total Poll:** 30,904; **Turnout:** 61.33%; **Quota:** 15,313; **1st Count:** Cecilia Keaveney (FF) 9,872; Harry Blaney (Ind) 8,943; Jim Sheridan (FG) 5,679; Sean Maloney (Lab) 3,791; Pat Doherty (SF) 2,340; **4th Count:** Cecilia Keaveney (FF) 14,115; Harry Blaney (Ind) 13,077; **Elected:** Cecilia Keaveney (FF) without reaching Quota.

DUBLIN WEST
(3 April 1996)
Reason for Election: Death of Brian Lenihan Snr; **Candidates:** 13; **Electorate:** 65,534; **Total Poll:** 28,636; **Turnout:** 43.70%; **Quota:** 14,206; **1st Count:** Brian Lenihan (FF) 6,995; Joe Higgins (Ind) 6,743; Tom Morissey (FG) 3,728; Tomas MacGiolla (WP) 2,909; John McCann (SF) 1,574; Sheila Terry (PD) 1,314; Paul Gogarty (GP) 1,286; Vincent B. Jackson (Ind) 1,131; Michael O'Donovan (Lab) 1,058; Dr. Gerard Casey (CSP) 768; Sean Lyons (Ind) 514; John O'Halloran (Ind) 369; Benny Cooney (Ind) 21; **11th Count:** Brian Lenihan Jnr (FF) 11,754; Joe Higgins (Ind) 11,384; **Elected:** Brian Lenihan Jnr (FF).

GOVERNMENT

Republic of Ireland Government System

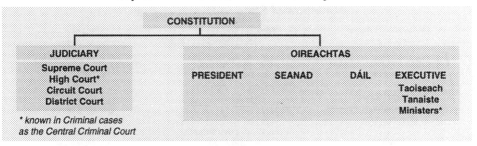

* President appoints Taoiseach on the nomination of the Dáil.
* Taoiseach nominates Ministers, seeks the approval of the Dáil and the President appoints them.
* All 166 members of the Dáil are elected by proportional representation in either a general or by-election.
* The Seanad has 60 members of which eleven are appointees of the Taoiseach, six are elected by graduates of Trinity College Dublin and the National University of Ireland, and forty-three are elected from five panels (representing Culture & Education, Agriculture, Labour, Industry & Commerce and Public Administration). The electorate consists of County Council Members, Corporations of County Boroughs, Members of the outgoing Seanad and Members of the incoming Dáil.
* Judges are appointed by the President on the advice of the Government.
* The Executive acts collectively and is responsible to the Dáil.

* MEMBERS OF THE EXECUTIVE ARE THE MINISTERS FOR:

Defence	Labour	Communications	Industry & Commerce
Foreign Affairs	Energy	Tourism & Transport	Environment
Finance	Social Welfare	Tánaiste	Education
Marine	Justice	Agriculture & Food	The Gaeltacht
		Health	

GOVERNMENT OF THE REPUBLIC OF IRELAND

The Government (appointed December 1994)

TAOISEACH
John Bruton

TÁNAISTE
Minister for Foreign Affairs
Dick Spring

CABINET MINISTERS

Finance Ruairi Quinn	*Education* Niamh Bhreathnach	*Agriculture, Food & Forestry* Ivan Yates
Health Michael Noonan	*Justice* Nora Owen	*Transport, Energy & Communications* Michael Lowry
Equality & Law Reform Mervyn Taylor	*Social Welfare* Proinsias de Rossa	*Defence & the Marine* Sean Barrett
Arts, Culture & the Gaeltacht Michael D. Higgins	*Tourism & Trade* Enda Kenny	
Environment Brendan Howlin	*Enterprise & Employment* Richard Bruton	

ATTORNEY GENERAL (Not a member of the Cabinet)
Dermott Gleeson

Ministers of State (appointed January 1995)

Taoiseach, Defence Jim Higgins	**Tourism and Trade** Toddy O'Sullivan	**Finance** Hugh Coveney
Enterprise and Employment Pat Rabbitte	**European Affairs, Local Development, Taoiseach, Foreign Affairs** Gay Mitchell	**Health, Education, Justice** Austin Currie
Transport, Energy & Communications Emmet Stagg		**Marine** Eamon Gilmore
Health Brian O'Shea	**Education, Environment** Bernard Allen	**Environment** Liz McManus
Enterprise & Employment Eithne Fitzgerald	**Welfare** Bernard Durkan	**Taoiseach, Finance, Transport, Energy and Communications** Avril Doyle
Foreign Affairs, Justice Joan Burton	**Agriculture, Food and Forestry** Jimmy Deenihan	**Taoiseach, Arts, Culture and the Gaeltacht** Donal Carey

Key to Political Parties

FF .... Fianna Fáil	Lab .... Labour
FG .... Fine Gael	PD ....Progressive Democrats
Green ..The Green Party	DL ....Democrat Left
Ind.............Independent	

Current position of Parties

CURRENT POSITION OF THE PARTIES

F.F.	F.G.	LAB.	P.D.s	D.L.	Others
68	47	32	8	6	5

DÁIL SUMMARY (JANUARY - JULY), 1996

TUESDAY JAN 23: The **Misuse of Drugs Bill 1996** amending the Criminal Law at first stage; **Budget 1996** Overview - to increase employment by 31,000; GNP to grow by 5%; inflation will average at about 2.25%; increase of 8% in volume of investment expected; Standard rate of income tax widened; Personal allowance increased; Tax free allowance increased; Corporation tax reduced; From midnight, VAT increased on cigarettes, diesel and petrol; Increase stamp duty on ATM cards; VAT increased on Super Plus unleaded petrol by 3.1p per litre from September 1st 1996.

WEDNESDAY JAN 24: Statements on the **Report of International Body on Decommissioning.**

THURSDAY JAN 25: Expression of sympathy for death of former French President Francois Mitterand.

TUESDAY JAN 30: **Misuse of Drugs Bill 1996** reaches second stage under Private Members' Business; Debate on how funds from National Lottery are distributed.

THURSDAY FEBRUARY 1: Debate on the Campaign & Danger of Ecstacy.

TUESDAY FEBRUARY 6: **Voluntary Health Insurance (Amendment) Bill 1995** and **Dumping at Sea Bill 1995** both had select committee reports; **Commissioners of Public Works (Functions & Powers) Bill 1995** reaches second stage.

WEDNESDAY FEBRUARY 7: Deputy Bobby Molloy suspended from the Dáil; Amendment to **Voluntary Health Insurance Bill 1995** lost; Amendment to the **Dumping at Sea Bill 1995** agreed to; **Commissioners of Public Works (Functions & Powers)1995** both referred to select committees.

THURSDAY FEBRUARY 8: Deputy Tom Kitt suspended from the Dáil.

TUESDAY FEBRUARY 13: **Adoption Bill 1996** at first stage; Report of Select Committee on the **Bovine Diseases (levies) (Amendment) Bill 1995;** Statement on Peace Process condemning the IRA bombing of London on February 9; Statement continued for the duration of the Dáil week.

TUESDAY FEBRUARY 20: **Powers of Attorney Bill 1995** reaches second stage and is referred to select committee; **Protection of Young Persons (Employment) Bill 1996** reaches second stage.

WEDNESDAY FEBRUARY 21: **Domestic Violence Bill 1995** amended; **Bovine Diseases (Levies) (Amendment) Bill 1995** passed; **Protection of Young Persons (Employment) Bill 1996** referred to select committee; **Johnstown Castle Agriculture College (Amendment) Bill 1995** passed.

THURSDAY FEBRUARY 2: Prosecution of **Offences & Punishment of Crimes Bill 1996** at first stage.

TUESDAY FEBRUARY 27: Reports by select committees on **1995 Refugee, Trade Marks** and **Commissioners of Public Works (Functions &**

Powers) Bills; Health (Amendment) Bill 1995 reaches second stage; **Prosecution of Offences and Punishment of Crimes Bill 1996** reaches second stage under Private Members' Business.

WEDNESDAY FEBRUARY 28: **Commissioners of Public Works (Functions & Powers) Bill 1995** passed; **Trade Marks Bill 1995** passed; **Refugee Bill 1995** passed; **Health (Amendment) Bill 1995** referred to select committee; Statements on N.I. Peace Process.

THURSDAY FEBRUARY 29: Dáil visited by a South African Delegation; Further statements on the Peace Process.

TUESDAY MARCH 5: **Criminal Justice (Drug Trafficking) Bill 1996** reaches second stage.

WEDNESDAY MARCH 6: Prohibition of **Anti-Personnel Landmines Bill 1996** at first stage.

THURSDAY MARCH 7: Dáil visited by a Czech Delegation; Statements on the Report on Island Development; **Metrology Bill 1996** reaches second stage.

TUESDAY MARCH 12: Dáil visited by the Governor General Designate of New Zealand, Sir Michael Hardine Boys; Writs issued for Donegal N. East and Dublin West by-elections; **Social Welfare Bill 1996** reaches second stage; **Adoption Bill 1996** at second stage under Private Members' Business.

WEDNESDAY MARCH 13: **Finance Bill 1996** at first stage; **Social Welfare Bill 1996** referred to select committee; **Pensions (Amendment) Bill 1995** reaches second stage.

THURSDAY MARCH 14: **Criminal Justice (Drug Trafficking) Bill 1996** referred to select committee.

TUESDAY MARCH 26: Dáil visited by Albanian and Tanzanian delegations; Statement on BSE and implications for the beef industry; **Criminal Procedure Bill 1995** reaches second stage.

WEDNESDAY MARCH 27: Expression of sympathy following the death of former T.D. (FF) Seán Browne; **Control and Regulation of Horses Bill 1996** at first stage; **Social Welfare Bill 1996** is passed.

THURSDAY MARCH 28: Visit by Finnish, Icelandic and British (Labour party) delegations; Visit by Chinese delegation; Statements on the White Paper on Foreign Policy.

TUESDAY APRIL 2: Statements on Turin European Council which launched the 1996 Inter-governmental Conference.

WEDNESDAY APRIL 3: **Pensions (Amendment) Bill 1995** referred to select committee; The political confidence in the IRTC motion (asking for Stokes' resignation) is lost.

TUESDAY APRIL 16: Expression of sympathy following death of former FG TD Gerry L'Estrange; Introduction of new members of Dáil (Cecilia Keaveney & Brian Lenihan) and their short maiden speeches.

WEDNESDAY APRIL 17: The motion on the Beef Industry Crisis was carried.

THURSDAY APRIL 18: Visit by Tanzanian delegation; **Finance Bill 1996** referred to select committee; Statements on the report of the task force on the travelling community.

WEDNESDAY APRIL 24: **Irish Steel Ltd. Bill 1996** passed; **Metrology Bill 1996** referred to select committee.

THURSDAY APRIL 25: Visit by Singapore delegation.

TUESDAY APRIL 30: Visit by Turkish delegation; Debate on the closing of Packard Electric Plant (Tallaght); Report of select committee on **Finance Bill 1996**; Statement on the **Second Mobile Telephone Licence**; **Civil Service Regulations (Amendment) Bill 1996** at second stage.

WEDNESDAY MAY 1: **Finance Bill 1996** reported on and passed by Dáil.

THURSDAY MAY 2: Visit by Slovenian delegation; **Criminal Justice (Mental Disorder) Bill 1996** at first stage; **Harbours Bill 1995** returned with amendments; **National Standards Authority of Ireland Bill 1996** at second stage.

WEDNESDAY MAY 8: **Electoral (Amendment) Bill 1996** at first stage; Report of select committee on the **Protection of Young Persons (Employment) Bill 1996** and Bill was passed; Visit by Finnish delegation; **Health (Amendment) Bill 1996** at second stage; **Prohibition of Anti-Personnel Landmines Bill 1996** (Private Members' Business) reaches second stage.

THURSDAY MAY 9: Visit of President of Parliamentary Assembly, Sir Dudley Smith MP & Swedish Minister for Foreign Affairs; **Marriages Bill 1996** at first stage; **Waste Management Bill 1995** returns from Seanad & amendments are considered; **National Standards Authority of Ireland Bill 1996** referred to select committee; Private Members' Business - motion against the Establishment of Regional Education Boards (replacing VEC's).

TUESDAY MAY 14: **Gaming & Lotteries (Amendment) Bill 1996** at first stage; **Health (Amendment) Bill 1996** referred to select committee.

WEDNESDAY MAY 15: **Powers of Attorney Bill 1995** has report of select committee and reaches final stages and passed by Dáil; Establishment of regional education boards.

THURSDAY MAY 16: **Criminal Law Bill 1996** reaches second stage.

TUESDAY MAY 21: Report of select committee on **Health (Amendment) Bill 1995**; Motion under Private Members' Business condemning the government's Defence Forces Reform.

WEDNESDAY MAY 22: Minister for Defence amends the Defence Forces Reform motion, commending the government reforms; The amended version was carried.

THURSDAY MAY 23: **Trade Marks Bill 1996** is withdrawn now that the government has produced its own bill; **Transport (Dublin Light Rail) Bill 1996** reaches second stage.

TUESDAY MAY 28: Report of select committee on **Competition (Amendment) Bill 1994**; Private Members' motion calling on government to maintain history and geography as compulsory core subjects up to Junior Certificate.

WEDNESDAY MAY 29: Visit by Norwegian Delegation; **Civil Service Regulations (Amendment) Bill 1996** passed; **Competition (Amendment) Bill 1994** passed; **Control of Horses Bill 1996** at second stage; Minister amends Junior Certificate Curriculum and motion carried.

THURSDAY MAY 30: Visit by John Prescott MP, deputy leader of British Labour Party; **Health (Amendment) Bill 1995** passed by Dáil; Statements on the Beef Industry.

THURSDAY JUNE 6: **Local Government (Planning & Development) Bill 1996** at first stage; **Criminal Laws Bill 1996** referred to select committee; **Garda Síochána Bill 1994** at second stage.

TUESDAY JUNE 11: Report of select committee on **Pensions (Amendment) Bill 1995.**

WEDNESDAY JUNE 12: **Independent Referendum Commission Bill 1996** at first stage; **Pensions (Amendment) Bill 1995** passed; **Garda Síochána Bill 1996** referred to select committee.

TUESDAY JUNE 18: Visit by British delegation; **Transport (Dublin Light Rail) Bill 1996** referred to select committee; **Gaming & Lotteries (Amendment) Bill 1996** reaches second stage under Private Members' Business.

WEDNESDAY JUNE 19: Report of select committee on **Metrology Bill 1996**; **Transnational Information & Consultation of Employees Bill 1996** passed by Dáil.

THURSDAY JUNE 20 1996: **Metrology Bill 1996** passed by Dáil; Statements on the management plan for Burren National Park.

WEDNESDAY JUNE 26: Expression of sympathy following death of former Greek Prime Minister; **Transport (Dublin Light Rail) Bill 1996** passed; Statements on killing of Veronica Guerin; Statements on Florence European Council & Irish Presidency of EU; **Borrowing Powers of Certain Bodies Bill 1996** passed by Dáil; Statements on the Leaving Cert Art Examination Report.

THURSDAY JUNE 27: Visit by Swedish delegation; **Family Law (Divorce) Bill 1996** reaches second stage & is referred to select committee.

TUESDAY JULY 2: Report of select committee on **National Standards Authority of Ireland Bill 1996**; **Criminal justice (Drug Trafficking) Bill 1996** passed by Dáil; **Organised Crime (Restraint & Disposal of Illicit Assets) Bill 1996** reaches second stage & is referred to select committee.

THE 27th DÁIL

Members of the Twenty-Seventh Dáil

The Twenty-Sixth Dáil was dissolved on November 5, 1992 and the General Election subsequently took place on November 25, 1992. The Twenty-Seventh Dáil met for the first time on December 14, 1992.

Ahearn, Theresa: (FG) Ballindoney, Grange, Clonmel, Co. Tipperary; (052) 38142; (Tipperary South).
Ahern, Bertie: (FF) "St. Lukes", 161 Lwr. Drumcondra Road, Dublin 9; (01) 374129; (Dublin Central).
Ahern, Dermot: (FF) Hill Cottage, The Crescent, Blackrock, Co. Louth; (042) 21473; (Louth).
Ahern, Michael: (FF) "Libermann", Barryscourt, Carrigtwohill, Co. Cork; (021) 883592; (Cork East).
Ahern, Noel: (FF) 25 Church Avenue, Drumcondra, Dublin 9; (01) 325911; (Dublin North-West).
Allen, Bernard: (FG) 7 Mount Prospect, Shanakiel, Cork; (021) 303068; (Cork North-Central).
Andrews, David: (FF) 8 Glenart Avenue, Blackrock, Co. Dublin; (01) 6771881; (Dún Laoghaire).
Aylward, Liam: (FF) Aghaviller, Hugginstown, Co. Kilkenny; (056) 68703; (Carlow-Kilkenny).
Barrett, Seán: (FG) "Avondale", 3 Ballinclea Road, Killiney, Co. Dublin; (01) 2852077; (Dún Laoghaire).
Barry, Peter: (FG) Sherwood, Blackrock, Cork; (021) 895444; (Cork South-Central).
Bell, Michael: (Lab) 122 Newfield Estate, Drogheda, Co. Louth; (041) 38573; (Louth).
Bhamjee, Moosajee: (Lab) Kilmorane Heights, Kilrush Road, Ennis, Co. Clare; (065) 29291; (Clare).
Bhreathnach, Niamh: (Lab) 12 Anglessa Avenue, Blackrock, Co. Dublin; (01) 2889321; (Dún Laoghaire).
Boylan, Andrew: (FG) Derrygarra, Butlersbridge, Co. Cavan; (049) 31747 (Cavan-Monaghan).
Bradford, Paul: (FG) Mourneabbey, Mallow, Co. Cork; (022) 29375; (Cork-East).
Bree, Declan: (Lab) 1 High Street, Sligo; (071) 45490; (Sligo-Leitrim).
Brennan, Matt: (FF) Ragoora, Cloonacool, Tubbercurry, Co. Sligo; (071) 85136 (Sligo-Leitrim).
Brennan, Séamus: (FF) 31 Finsbury Park, Churchtown, Dublin 14; (01) 2957171; (Dublin South).
Briscoe, Ben: (FF) Newtown, Celbridge, Co. Kildare; (01) 6288426; (Dublin South-Central).
Broughan, Tommy: (Lab) 23 Riverside Road, Coolock, Dublin 17; (01) 8477634; (Dublin North-East).
Browne, John: (FG) Ballinacarrig, Carlow; (0503) 31579; (Carlow-Kilkenny).
Browne, John: (FF) Kilcannon, Enniscorthy, Co. Wexford; (054) 35046 (Wexford).
Bruton, John: (FG) Cornelstown, Dunboyne, Co.Meath; (01) 8255573; (Meath).
Bruton, Richard: (FG) 210 Griffith Avenue, Drumcondra, Dublin 9; (01) 368185; (Dublin North-Central).
Burke, Liam: (FG) The Grove, Douglas Hall, Cork; (092) 892707; (Cork North-Central).
Burke, Ray: (FF) "Briargate", Malahide Road, Swords, Co. Dublin; (01) 8401734; (Dublin North).
Burton, Joan: (Lab) 81 Old Cabra Road, Dublin 7; (01) 388711; (Dublin West).
Byrne, Eric: (DL) 32 Ashdale Road, Terenure, Dublin 6;

(Dublin South-Central).
Byrne, Hugh: (FF) Air Hill, Fethard-on-Sea, New Ross, Co. Wexford; (051) 97125; (Wexford).
Callely, Ivor: (FF) "Landsdale House", 7 St. Lawrence Road, Clontarf, Dublin 3; (01) 330350; (Dublin North-Central).
Carey, Donal: (FG) 3 Thomond Villas, Clarecastle, Ennis, Co. Clare; (065) 29191; (Clare).
Clohessy, Peadar: (PD) Fanningstown, Crecora, Co. Limerick; (061) 351190; (Limerick East).
Collins, Gerard: (FF) "The Hill", Abbeyfeale, Co. Limerick; (061) 31126 (Limerick West).
Connaughton, Paul: (FG) Mount Bellew, Ballinasloe, Co. Galway; (0905) 79249; (Galway East).
Connolly, Ger: (FF) Bracknagh, Edenderry, Co. Offaly; (0502) 29025; (Laois-Offaly).
Connor, John: (FG) Cloonshanville, Frenchpark, Castlerea, Co. Roscommon; (0907) 70143; (Longford-Roscommon).
Costello, Joe: (Lab) 75 Lower Seán MacDermott Street, Dublin 1; (01) 365698; (Dublin Central).
Coughlan, Mary: (FF) Dromore Lower, Mountcharles, Co. Donegal; (073) 35396; (Donegal South-West).
Coveney, Hugh: (FG) Laharn, Minane Bridge, Co. Cork; (021) 274474; (Cork South-Central).
Cowen, Brian: (FF) 28 Hophill Grove, Tullamore, Co. Offaly; (0506) 52047; (Laois-Offaly).
Crawford, Seymour: (FG) Drumkeen, Aghabog, Monaghan; (047) 54038; (Cavan-Monaghan).
Creed, Michael: (FG) Codrum, Macroom, Co. Cork; (026) 41177; (Cork North-West).
Crowley, Frank: (FG) Strand Street, Kanturk, Co. Cork; (022) 47157; (Cork North-West).
Cullen, Martin: (FF) Abbey House, Ferrybank, Waterford; (051) 51112; (Waterford).
Currie, Austin: (FG) "Tullydraw", Ballyowen Lane, Lucan, Co. Dublin; (01) 6265047; (Dublin West).
Davern, Noel: (FF) Tannersrath, Fethard Road, Clonmel, Co. Tipperary; (052) 22991; (Tipperary South).
Deasy, Austin: (FG) Kilrush, Dungarvan, Co. Waterford; (058) 43003; (Waterford).
Deenihan, Jimmy: (FG) Finuge, Lixnaw, Co. Kerry; (068) 40235; (Kerry North).
Dempsey, Noel: (FF) Knightsbrook, Trim, Co. Meath; (046) 31146; (Meath).
De Rossa, Proinsias: (DL) 39 Pinewood Crescent, Ballymun, Dublin 11; (01) 6764040; (Dublin North-West).
De Valera, Síle: (FF) 6 Riverdale, Tulla Road, Ennis, Co. Clare; (065) 21100; (Clare).
Doherty, Seán: (FF) Coothall, Boyle, Co. Roscommon; (079) 67005; (Longford-Roscommon).
Doyle, Avril: (FG) Kitestown House, Wexford; (053) 42873; (Wexford).
Dukes, Alan M.: (FG) Tullywest, Co. Kildare; (045) 21912; (Kildare).
Durkan, Bernard J.: (FG) Timard, Maynooth, Co. Kildare; (01) 6286063; (Kildare).
Ellis, John: (FF) Fenagh, Ballinamore, Co. Leitrim; (078) 44252; (Sligo-Leitrim).
Ferris, Michael: (Lab) Rosanna, Tipperary; (062)

52265; (Tipperary South).

Finucane, Michael: (FG) Ardnacrohy, Newcastle West, Co. Limerick; (069) 62742; (Limerick West).

Fitzgerald, Brian: (Lab) Warrenstown, Kilcock, Co. Meath; (01) 8251847; (Meath).

Fitzgerald, Eithne: (Lab) 9 Clonard Avenue, Dublin 16; (01) 2955083; (Dublin South).

Fitzgerald, Frances: (FG) 116 Georgian Village, Castleknock, D 15; (01) 8211796; (Dublin South-East).

Fitzgerald, Liam Joseph: (FF) 117 Tonlegee Road, Raheny, Dublin 5; (01) 8470632; (Dublin North-East).

Flaherty, Mary: (FG) 2 Richmond Place, Rathmines, Dublin 6; (01) 976620; (Dublin North-West).

Flanagan, Charles: (FG) 15 Cherrygard, Portlaoise, Co. Laois; (0502) 60707; (Laois-Offaly).

Flood, Chris: (FF) 22 Birchview Lawn, Kilnamanagh, Tallaght, Dublin 24; (01) 518574; (Dublin South-West).

Foley, Denis: (FF) 2 Staughton's Row, Tralee, Co. Kerry; (066) 21174; (Kerry North).

Fox, Mildred: (IND) Calary Lower, Kilmacanogue, Co. Wicklow; (01) 2876386; (Wicklow).

Foxe, Tom: (IND) Athlone Road, Roscommon; (0903) 26507; (Longford-Roscommon).

Gallagher, Pat: (Lab) 5 Unity Hall, Church Street, Tullamore, Co. Offaly; (0506) 52744; (Laois-Offaly).

Gallagher, Pat the Cope: (FF); Dungloe, Co. Donegal; (075) 21364; (Donegal South-West).

Geoghegan-Quinn, Máire: (FF) Woodfield, Cappagh Road, Barna, Co. Galway; (091) 26555; (Galway West).

Gilmore, Eamon: (DL) 24 Corbawn Close, Shankill, Co. Dublin; (01) 2821363 (Dún Laoghaire).

Gregory, Tony: (IND) 5 Sackville Gardens, Ballybough, Dublin 3; (01) 8729910; (Dublin Central).

Harney, Mary: (PD) 11 Serpentine Terrace, Ballsbridge, Dublin 4; (01) 589651; (Dublin South-West).

Harte, Paddy: (FG) The Diamond, Raphoe, Co. Donegal; (074) 45187; (Donegal North-East).

Haughey, Seán: (FF) "Abbeville", Kinsealy, Co. Dublin; (01) 8450111; (Dublin North-Central).

Higgins, Jim: (FG) Devlis, Ballyhaunis, Co. Mayo; (0907) 30052; (Mayo East).

Higgins, Michael D.: (Lab) Letteragh, Circular Road, Galway; (091) 24513; (Galway West).

Hilliard, Colm M.: (FF) Ringlestown, Kilmessan, Navan, Co. Meath; (046) 25236; (Meath).

Hogan, Philip: (FG) 25 The Sycamores, Kilkenny; (056) 61572; (Carlow-Kilkenny).

Howlin, Brendan: (Lab) 7 Upper William Street, Wexford; (053) 24036 (Wexford).

Hughes, Séamus: (FF) Dun Maeve, Newport Road, Westport, Co. Mayo; (098) 26529; (Mayo West).

Hyland, Liam: (FF) Fearagh, Ballacolla, Portlaoise, Co. Laois; (0502) 34051; (Laois-Offaly).

Jacob, Joe: (FF) Leas-Cheann Comhairle; Main Street, Rathdrum, Co. Wicklow; (0404) 46528; (Wicklow).

Kavanagh, Liam: (Lab) Mount Carmel, Convent Road, Wicklow; (0404) 67582; (Wicklow).

Keaveney, Cecilia: (FF) Moville, Co. Donegal; (Donegal North-East).

Kemmy, Jim: (Lab) Mechanic's Institute, Hartstonge Street, Limerick; (061) 312316; (Limerick East).

Kenneally, Brendan: (FF) 38 Viewpoint Park; Waterford; (051) 55964; (Waterford).

Kenny, Enda: (FG) Tucker Street, Castlebar, Co. Mayo; (094) 22299; (Mayo West).

Kenny, Seán: (Lab) 44 Woodbine Road, Raheny,

Dublin 5; (01) 8481806; (Dublin North-East).

Keogh, Helen: (PD) 12 Beechcourt, Killiney, Co. Dublin; (01) 2858433; (Dún Laoghaire).

Killeen, Tony: (FF) Kilnaboy, Corofin, Co. Clare; (065) 27895; (Clare).

Kirk, Séamus: (FF) Rathiddy, Knockbridge, Dundalk, Co. Louth; (042) 31032; (Louth).

Kitt, Michael P.: (FF) Castleblakeney, Ballinasloe, Co. Galway; (0905) 78147; (Galway East).

Kitt, Tom: (FF) 3 Pine Valley Drive, Rathfarnham, Dublin 16; (01) 938200; (Dublin South).

Lawlor, Liam: (FF) Somerton, Lucan, Co. Dublin; (01), 6280507; (Dublin West).

Lenihan, Brian: (FF) Leinster House, Dublin 2; (Dublin West).

Leonard, Jimmy: (FF) Smithboro, Co. Monaghan; (047) 57020; (Cavan-Monaghan).

Lowry, Michael: (FG) Glerreigh, Holycross, Thurles, Co. Tipperary; (0504) 43182; (Tipperary North).

Lynch, Kathleen: (DL) 3 Brookfield Park, The Lough, Cork; (Cork North-Central).

Martin, Micheál: (FF) "Lios Laoi", 16 Silver Manor, Ballinlough, Cork; (021) 295218; (Cork South-Central).

McCormack, Pádraic: (FG) 3 Renmore Park, Galway; (091) 53992; (Galway West).

McCreevy, Charlie: (FF) Straffan Road, Sallins, Co. Kildare; (01) 6621444; (Kildare).

McDaid, James: (FF) 2 Sylvan Park, Letterkenny, Co. Donegal; (074) 21652; (Donegal North-East).

McDowell, Derek: (Lab) 3 Dunluce Road, Clontarf, Dublin 3; (01) 336138; (Dublin North-Central).

McDowell, Michael: (PD) 40 Charleston Road, Dublin 6; (01) 974955; (Dublin South-East).

McGahon, Brendan: (FG) Annaverna, Ravensdale, Co Louth; (042) 32620; (Louth).

McGinley, Dinny: (FG) Bunbeg, Letterkenny, Co Donegal; (075) 31025; (Donegal South-West).

McGrath, Paul: (FG) Carna, Irishtown, Mullingar, Co Westmeath; (044) 40746; (Westmeath).

McManus, Liz: (DL) 1 Martello Terrace, Bray, Co. Wicklow; (01) 2868407; (Wicklow).

Mitchell, Gay: (FG) 192 Upper Rathmines Road; Dublin 6; (01) 903744; (Dublin South-Central).

Mitchell, Jim: (FG) 4 Rathdown Crescent, Terenure, Dublin 6; (01) 6789911; (Dublin Central).

Moffatt, Tom: (FF) Castle Road, Ballina, Co. Mayo (096) 22868; (Mayo East).

Molloy, Robert: (PD) "St. Mary's", Rockbarton, Salthill Co. Galway; (091) 21765; (Galway West).

Morley, P.J.: (FF) Bekan, Claremorris, Co. Mayo; (094), 80217; (Mayo East).

Moynihan, Donal: (FF) Gortnascarty, Ballymakeera, Macroom, Co. Cork; (026) 45019; (Cork North-West).

Moynihan-Cronin, Breeda: (LAB) 10 Muckross Grove Killarney, Co. Kerry; (064) 34993; (Kerry South).

Mulvihill, John: (Lab) Tay Road, Cobh, Co. Cork; (021), 812603; (Cork East).

Nealon, Ted: (FG) 61 Greenfort Estate, Cairns Road Sligo; (071) 61428 (Sligo-Leitrim).

Nolan, M.J.: (FF) Shandon House, Strawhall, Carlow (0503) 31777; (Carlow-Kilkenny).

Noonan, Michael: (FG) 18 Gouldavoher Estate, Fr Russell Road, Limerick; (061) 229350; (Limerick East).

Noonan, Michael J.: (FF) Crean, Bruff, Kilmallock, Co Limerick; (061) 399718; (Limerick West).

Ó Cuív, Eamon: (FF) Corr na Móna, Co. na Gaillimhe

(092) 48021; (Galway West).

O'Dea, Willie: (FF) 2 Glenview Gardens, Farranshore, Co. Limerick; (061) 54488; (Limerick East).

O'Donnell, Liz: (PD) 34 Ormond Road, Rathmines, Dublin 6; (01) 960993; (Dublin South).

O'Donoghue, John: (FF) 14 Main Street, Caherciveen, Co. Kerry; (066) 72413; (Kerry South).

O'Hanlon, Rory: (FF) Carrickmacross, Co. Monaghan; (042) 61530; (Cavan-Monaghan).

O'Keeffe, Batt: (FF) 8 Westcliffe, Ballincollig, Co. Cork; (021) 871393; (Cork South-Central).

O'Keeffe, Jim: (FG) Old Chapel, Bandon, Co. Cork; (023) 41399; (Cork South-West).

O'Keeffe, Ned: (FF) Ballylough, Michelstown, Co. Cork; (022) 25285; (Cork East)

O'Leary, John: (FF) Beechcroft, Killarney, Co. Kerry; (064) 31565; (Kerry South).

O'Malley, Desmond J.: (PD) 2 Sunville House, North Circular Road, Limerick; (01) 6789911; (Limerick East).

O'Rourke, Mary: (FF) Arcadia, Athlone, Co. Westmeath; (0902) 75065; (Westmeath).

O'Shea, Brian: (Lab) 61 Sweetbriar Lawn, Tramore, Co. Waterford; (051) 81913; (Waterford).

Owen, Nora: (FG) 17 Ard na Mara, Malahide, Co. Dublin; (01) 8451041; (Dublin North).

O'Sullivan, Toddy: (Lab) Faranogue, The Lough, Cork; (021) 962788; (Cork South-Central).

Pattison, Seamus: (Lab) 6 Upper New Street, Kilkenny; (056) 21295; (Carlow-Kilkenny).

Penrose, William: (Lab) Ballintine, Ballynacargy, Co. Westmeath; (044) 73264; (Westmeath).

Power, Seán: (FF) Castlekealy, Caragh, Naas, Co. Kildare; (045) 75621; (Kildare).

Quill, Mairín: (PD) 1 Wellesley Terrace, Wellington Road, Cork; (021) 502099; (Cork North-Central).

Quinn, Ruairí: (Lab) 37 Park Court, Sandymount, Dublin 4; (01) 2839563; (Dublin South-East).

Rabbitte, Pat: (DL) 56 Monastery Drive, Clondalkin, Dublin 22; (01) 593191; (Dublin South-West).

Reynolds, Albert: (FF) Mount Carmel House, Dublin Road, Longford; (01) 6689333; (Longford-Roscommon).

Ring, Michael: (FG) The Paddock, Westport, Co. Mayo; (Mayo West).

Ryan, Eoin: (FF) 19 Vavasour Square, Bath Avenue, Sandymount, D 4; (01) 6600082; (Dublin South-East).

Ryan, John: (Lab) 26 St. Patrick's Terrace, Nenagh, Co. Tipperary; (067) 31905; (Tipperary North).

Ryan, Seán: (Lab) 1 Burrow Road, Portrane, Donabate, Co. Dublin; (01) 8436254; (Dublin North).

Sargent, Trevor: (GREEN) 37 Tara Cove, Baile Brigín, Co. Bhaile Átha Cliath; (01) 8412371; (Dublin North).

Shatter, Alan: (FG) 57 Delbrook Manor, Dundrum, Dublin 16; (01) 2983045; (Dublin South).

Sheehan, P.J.: (FG) Main Street, Goleen, Co. Cork; (028) 35236; (Cork South-West).

Shortall, Róisín: (Lab) 12 Iveragh Road, Gaeltacht Park, Whitehall, D 9; (01) 370563; (Dublin North-West).

Smith, Brendan: (FF) Bawnboy, Co. Cavan; (049) 23123; (Cavan-Monaghan).

Smith, Michael: (FF) Lismackin, Roscrea, Co. Tipperary; (0505) 43157; (Tipperary North).

Spring, Dick: (Lab) Cloonanorig, Tralee, Co. Kerry; (066) 25337; (Kerry North).

Stagg, Emmet: (Lab) 736 Lodge Park, Straffan, Co. Kildare; (01) 6272149; (Kildare).

Taylor, Mervyn: (Lab) 4 Spring Field Road, Templeogue, D 6; (01) 904569; (Dublin South-West).

Timmins, Godfrey: (FG) Baltinglass, Co. Wicklow; (0508) 81016; (Wicklow).

Treacy, Noel: (FF) Gurteen, Ballinasloe, Co. Galway; (0905) 77094; (Galway East).

Treacy, Seán: (IND) "Rossa", Heywood Road, Clonmel, Co. Tipperary; (052) 22747; (Tipperary South).

Upton, Pat: (Lab) 1 College Drive, Terenure, Dublin 6; (01) 909653; (Dublin South-Central).

Wallace, Dan: (FF) 13 Killeen's Place, Farranree, Cork; (021) 307465; (Cork North-Central).

Wallace, Mary: (FF) Newtown, Fairyhouse Road, Ratoath, Co. Meath; (01) 8256259; (Meath).

Walsh, Eamon: (Lab) 133 Limekiln Green, Dublin 12; (01) 504772; (Dublin South-West).

Walsh, Joe: (FF) 5 Emmet Square, Clonakilty, Co. Cork; (023) 33575; (Cork South-West).

Woods, Michael J.: (FF) 13 Kilbarrack Grove, Dublin 5; (01) 323357; (Dublin North-East).

Yates, Ivan : (FG) Blackstoops, Enniscorthy, Co. Wexford; (054) 33793; (Wexford)

SEANAD ÉIREANN

Following the dissolution of the Twenty-Sixth Dáil on November 5, 1992 voting was subsequently held for the Seanad Elections, with 60 senators being returned to Seanad Éireann in February 1993.

CURRENT BREAKDOWN - SEANAD ÉIREANN

F.F.	F.G.	LAB.	P.D.s	D.L.	Others
25	17	9	2	1	6

Members of Séanad Éireann

Belton, Louis J.: Kenagh, Co. Longford.

Bohan, Eddie: 18 Orwell Park, Dublin 6.

Burke, Paddy: 161 Knockaphunta, Castlebar, Mayo.

Byrne, Sean: Tubrid, Ballylooby, Cahir, Co. Tipperary.

Calnan, Michael: Kilbarry East, Dunmanway, Co. Cork.

Cassidy, Donie : Church St, Castlepollard, Westmeath.

Cashin, Bill: Kanturk, Co. Cork.

Cosgrave, Liam: 33 Hillside, Dalkey, Co. Dublin.

Cotter, Bill: Rockdaniel Rd, Carrickmacross, Monaghan.

Cregan, Denis (Dino): 7 Elm Grove, Ballinlough, Cork.

D'Arcy, Michael: Annagh, Gorey, Co. Wexford.

Daly, Brendan: Cooraclare, Kilrush, Co. Clare.

Dardis, John: Belmont House, Newbridge, Co. Kildare.

Doyle, Joe: 14 Simmonscourt Tce, Donnybrook, D 4.

Enright, Thomas W.: John's Place, Birr, Co. Offaly.

Fahey, Frank: Kilbeacanty, Gort, Co. Galway.

Farrell, Willie: Grange, Co. Sligo.

Farrelly, John V.: Hurdlestown, Kells, Co. Meath.

Finneran, Michael: Feevagh, Taughmaconnell, Ballinasloe, Co. Roscommon.

Fitzgerald, Tom: Ballinaboola, Dingle, Co. Kerry.
Gallagher, Ann: York St, Castleblayney, Monaghan.
Haughey, Edward: Ballyedmond Castle, Rostrevor, Down.
Hayes, Brian: Leinster House, Kildare Street, Dublin 2.
Henry, Mary: 12 Burlington Road, Dublin 4.
Honan, Cathy: Austen House, Main Street, Portarlington, Laois.
Howard, Michael: One Mile Inn, Ennis, Co. Clare.
Kelleher, Billy: Ballyphilip, White's Cross, Glanmire, Co. Cork.
Kelly, Mary: Maiden Street, Newcastlewest, Co. Limerick.
Kiely, Dan: Doonard, Tarbert, Co. Kerry.
Kiely, Rory: Clooncrippa, Feenagh, Killmalloch, Co. Limerick.
Lanigan, Mick: "St. Judes", Chapel Avenue, Co. Kilkenny.
Lee, Joe: Leinster House, Kildare Street, Dublin 2.
Lydon, Don: Leinster House, Kildare Street, Dublin 2.
McAughtry, Sam: Leinster House, Kildare St, Dublin 2.
McDonagh, Jarlath: Sligo House, Turloughmore, Co. Galway.
McGennis, Marian: 44 Bramley Walk, Bramley Woods, Dublin 15.
McGowan, Paddy: Ballindrait, Lifford, Co. Donegal.
Magner, Pat: Leinster House, Kildare Street, Dublin 2.
Maloney, Sean: 39 McNeely Villas, Letterkenny, Co. Donegal.
Manning, Maurice: 13 Haddington Place, Dublin 4.

Mooney, Paschal: Carrick Road, Drumshanbo, Co. Leitrim.
Mulcahy, Michael: 12 Beechwood Avenue Lower, Ranelagh, Dublin 6.
Mullooly, Brian: Strokestown, Co. Roscommon.
Naughten, Liam: Ardkennan, Drum, Athlone, Co. Roscommon.
Neville, Daniel: Kiltannan, Croagh, Rathkeale, Co. Limerick.
Norris, David: 18 North Great Georges Street, Dublin 1.
O'Kenney, Michael: Gortlandroe, Nenagh, Co. Tipperary.
O'Brien, Francis: Corwillian, Latton, Castleblayney, Co. Monaghan.
O'Sullivan, Jan: 7 Lanahrone Avenue, Corbally, Limerick.
O'Toole, Joe: Kilsallaghan, Co. Dublin.
Ormonde, Ann: Leinster House, Kildare St., Dublin 2.
Quinn, Fergal: Leinster House, Kildare Street, Dublin 2.
Reynolds, Gerry: Main Street, Ballinamore, Co. Leitrim.
Roache, Dick: 2 Herbert Terrace, Herbert Road, Bray, Co. Wicklow.
Ross, Shane P.N.: Leinster House, Kildare St., Dublin 2.
Sherlock, Joe: 20 Blackwater Drive, Mallow, Co. Cork.
Taylor-Quinn, Madeleine: Frances Street, Kilrush, Co. Clare.
Townsend, Jim: Koolholme, Ballybar Upper, Carlow.
Wall, Jack: Castlemitchell, Athy, Co. Kildare.
Wright, G.V.: 58 The Moorings, Malahide, Co. Dublin.

EUROPEAN PARLIAMENT

Republic of Ireland Members of the European Parliament *(by political allegiance)*

The most recent European Parliament elections took place in Ireland, North and South, on June 9, 1994. Of the 15 seats to be filled in the Republic of Ireland, 7 went to Fianna Fáil, 4 went to Fine Gael, 2 went to the Green Party, and 1 each went to the Labour Party and an Independent, Pat Cox. The electorate in Ireland for this fourth European election was 2,631,575 and the turnout was 44 per cent.

In Northern Ireland, three members were returned to the European Parliament; 1 Democratic Unionist, 1 Social Democratic and Labour Party, and 1 Official Unionist.

Fianna Fáil/Union for Europe (EFE)

Gerard Collins TD (Munster), The Hill, Abbeyfeale, Co. Limerick. Tel: (01) 6620068.
Niall Andrews TD (Dublin), 43 Molesworth Street, Dublin 2. Tel: (01) 6794368.
Brian Crowley (Munster),Craigie, Dunmanway Rd., Bandon, Co. Cork. Tel: (021) 395324.
Jim Fitzsimons (Leinster), Ardsion, Dublin Rd., Navan, Co. Meath. Tel: (01) 671 9189.
Pat the Cope Gallagher TD (Connacht-Ulster), Dungloe, Co. Donegal. Tel: (075) 21276.
Liam Hyland TD (Leinster), Fearagh, Ballacolla, Portlaoise, Co. Laois. Tel: (0502) 34051.
Mark Killilea (Connacht - Ulster), Caherhugh House, Belclare, Tuam, Co. Galway. Tel: (093) 55414.

Fine Gael/European People's Party (Christian Democrats) (EPP)

Mary Banotti (Dublin), 43 Molesworth Street, Dublin 2. Tel: (01) 671 0328.
John Cushnahan (Munster), Bedford House, Bedford Rd., Limerick. Tel: (061) 418289.

Alan Gillis (Leinster), Ballyhook House, Grangeecon, Co. Wicklow. Tel: (0508) 81229.
Joe McCartan (Connacht-Ulster), Mullyaster, Newtowngore, Carrick-on-Shannon, Co. Leitrim. Tel: (049) 33395.

Green Party (Greens)

Nuala Ahern (Leinster), La Touche Place, Greystones, Co. Wicklow. Tel: (01) 287 6574.
Patricia McKenna (Dublin), 43 Molesworth Street, Dublin 2. Tel: (01) 661 6833

Labour Party/Party of European Socialists (PES):

Bernie Malone (Dublin), 43 Molesworth Street, Dublin 2. Tel: (01) 676 5988.

Independent/Group of the European Liberal and Reformist Party (EDR):

Pat Cox (Munster), 21 Cook Street, Cork. Tel: (021) 278488.

European Parliament Election Results, 1979 - 1994

Year	Total No. of seats	Turnout %	FF seats	FG seats	LAB seats	WP seats	PD seats	GREEN seats	OTHERS seats
1979	15	63.6	5	4	4	-	-	-	2
1984	15	47.6	8	6	-	-	-	-	1
1989	15	68.3	6	4	1	1	1	-	2
1996	15	44.0	7	4	1	-	-	2	1

CONSTITUTIONAL REFERENDA 1937 - 1996

Date	Issue	Turnout (per cent)	For (per cent)	Against (per cent)	Spoiled (per cent)
July 1, 1937	**Endorse new constitution**	75.8	56.5	43.5	10.0
June 17, 1959	**Introduction of plurality system** *(replacing proportional representation)*	58.4	48.2	51.8	4.0
October 16, 1968	**TD-population ratio**	65.8	39.2	60.8	4.3
October 16, 1968	**Introduction of plurality system** (replacing proportional representation)	65.8	39.2	60.8	4.3
May 10, 1972	**Allow EC membership**	70.9	83.1	16.9	0.8
December 7, 1972	**Lower voting age to 18**	50.7	84.6	15.4	5.2
December 7, 1972	**Abolish 'special position' of the Catholic church**	50.7	84.4	15.6	5.5
July 5, 1979	**Protect adoption system**	28.6	99.0	1.0	2.5
July 5, 1979	**Allow alteration of university representation in Seanad Éireann**	28.6	92.4	7.6	3.9
September 7, 1983	**Prohibit legalisation of abortion**	53.7	66.9	33.1	0.7
June 14, 1984	**Extend voting rights to non-citizens**	47.5	75.4	24.6	3.5
June 26, 1986	**Allow legalisation of divorce**	60.5	36.5	63.5	0.6
May 26, 1987	**Allow signing of Single European Act**	43.9	69.9	30.1	0.5
June 18, 1992	**Allow ratification of the Maastricht Treaty on European Union**	57.3	69.1	30.9	0.5
November 25, 1992	**Restrict availability of abortion**	68.2	34.6	65.4	4.7
November 25, 1992	**Right to travel guarantee**	68.2	62.4	37.6	4.3
November 25, 1992	**Right to information guarantee**	68.1	59.9	40.1	4.3
November 24, 1995	**Right to divorce**	61.94	50.28	49.72	0.3

PRESIDENTS OF IRELAND

Presidents of Ireland Statistics

No.	Name	Politics	Born	In	Inaug.	at age	Died	at age
1	Douglas Hyde	non-political	17 Jan. 1860	Roscommon	25.06.1938	78	12.07.1949	89
2	Sean T. O'Ceallaigh	Fianna Fáil	25 Aug. 1882	Dublin	16.06.1945	63	23.11.1966	84
3	Eamon de Valera	Fianna Fáil	14 Oct. 1882	New York	25.06.1959	77	29.08.1975	93
4	Erskine Childers	Fianna Fáil	11 Dec. 1905	London	25.06.1973	67	17.11.1974	68
5	Cearbhall O'Dálaigh*	non-party	12 Feb. 1911	Wicklow	19.12.1974	63	21.03.1978	67
6	Patrick Hillery	Fianna Fáil	2 May 1923	Clare	03.12.1976	53		
7	Mary Robinson	Labour	21 May 1944	Mayo	03.12.1990	46		

*Resigned as President on 22nd October 1976.

Biographies of the Irish Presidents

DOUGLAS HYDE (1938 - 1945)

Douglas Hyde was born in Frenchpark, Co. Roscommon 17th January, 1860.

The son of a Church of Ireland minister, Dr. Hyde was to the forefront of the cultural revival being co-founder and first President of Conradh na Gaeilge (The Gaelic League) from 1893 to 1915, and first Professor of Modern Irish at University College Dublin in 1909 where he remained until his retirement in 1932. He was also a member of Seanad Éireann from 1925 to 1938.

At the time of his nomination for the Presidency he was the accepted choice of all the political parties although he himself had no political affiliations. He was inaugurated as the first President of Ireland on the 25th June 1938 at the age of 78, and held office until 24th June 1945. He died on the 12th of July, 1949 aged 89.

SEAN T. O' KELLY (1945 - 1959)

Seán T. O'Kelly was born in Dublin on the 25th of August 1882.

A veteran of the 1916 Easter Rising, he was a co-founder of Sinn Féin in 1907 and was Member of Parliament for Dublin from 1918-'21. He was the Ceann Comhairle of the first Dáil. A TD from 1921 until his inauguration to the presidency in 1945, O'Kelly was an opponent of the 1921 Anglo-Irish Treaty, and was subsequently a founding member of Fianna Fáil, holding the posts of Vice-President of the Executive Council 1932-38, Tánaiste 1938-45; Minister for Local Government & Public Health 1932-39; and Minister for Finance 1939-45.

He was inaugurated as President of Ireland on 16th June 1945 aged 63, and was re-elected unopposed for a second term on the 25th June 1952, holding office until 17th June 1959. He died on 23rd November 1966 at the age of 84.

EAMON DE VALERA (1959 - 1973)

Eamon de Valera was born in Manhattan, New York on the 14th October 1882, son of a Spanish immigrant father and Irish immigrant mother.

He was a Commandant in the 1916 Rising and had his death sentence commuted because the British authorities were unsure of his nationality and wanted to avoid an international incident with the United States.

Elected as a Sinn Féin MP for East Clare in July 1917, he was re-elected at each subsequent election until he became President of Ireland in 1959. He was also elected as MP for East Mayo (1918-21), Down (1921-29) and South Down (1933-37). He never took his seat at either Westminister or Stormont.

Mr. de Valera was President of Sinn Féin 1917-26; President of the Irish Volunteers 1917-22; President of the Irish Republic 1919-20; President of Fianna Fáil 1926-59; President of the Executive Council of the Irish Free State 1932-7; President of Council of the League of Nations at its 68th and Special Sessions (September and October 1932); Taoiseach 1937-48, 1951-54 and 1957-59; Minister for External Affairs 1937-48; and Minister for Education 1939-40. He also founded the Fianna Fáil party in 1926, and played a significant part in the drafting of the Constitution of Ireland in 1937.

He was inaugurated as President of Ireland on the 25th June 1959 at the age of 76, and held office until the 24th June 1973 having been re-elected on 1st June 1966. He died on the 29th of August 1975 at the age of 92.

ERSKINE CHILDERS (1973 - 1974)

Erskine Childers was born in London on the 11th of December 1905.

He was first elected to Dáil Éireann in 1938 and held a number of ministerial posts until his inauguration to the Presidency in 1973, including; Post and Telegraphs (1951-54); Lands (1957-59); Transport and Power (1959-69); Post and Telegraphs (1966-69); and Tánaiste and Minister for Health (1969-73).

He was inaugurated as the fourth President of Ireland on the 25th June 1973 aged 67, and held office until his death on 17th November 1974. He is the only President to have died while in office.

CEARBHALL O'DALAIGH (1974 - 1976)

Cearbhall O'Dálaigh was born in Bray, Co. Wicklow on the 12th of February 1911.

Mr. O'Dálaigh had a distinguished legal career, being called to the bar in 1934 and holding the position of Attorney-General on two occasions, 1946-48 and 1951-53. Between 1961 and 1973 he was Chief Justice and President of the Supreme Court, having been a Judge of the Supreme Court since 1953.

Following the death of President Childers in November 1974, Cearbhall O'Dálaigh was appointed unopposed to the Presidency, and was formally inaugurated on the 19th of December 1974 at the age of 63.

When he was presented with an Emergency Powers Bill in September 1976, he refused to sign it and referred it to the Supreme Court to attest its constitutionality. The bill was found to be constitutional and duly passed. However, following comments by Patrick Donegan, Minister for Defence, the President resigned to assert his 'personal integrity' and to 'protect the dignity and independence' of the institution of President on 22 October 1976.

He died on the 21st of March 1978 at the age of 67.

DR. PATRICK HILLERY (1976 - 1990)

Dr. Patrick Hillery was born in Co. Clare on the 2nd of May 1923.

He was a Fianna Fáil T.D. for Clare from 1951 until 1973 and while a member of Dáil Éireann held the following ministerial portfolios: Education (1959-65); Industry and Commerce (1965-66); Labour (1966-69); and Foreign Affairs (1969-72). As Minister for Foreign Affairs he negotiated Ireland's accession to the European Economic Community. He was Ireland's Commissioner to the EEC from 1973 to 1975, he was Vice President of the Commission with special responsibility for Social Affairs from 1973 to 1976.

He was inaugurated as the sixth President of Ireland on the 3rd of December 1976 at the age of 53, and held office until 1990 having been re-elected unopposed on 31st December 1983.

MARY ROBINSON (1990 -)

Mary Robinson was born in Ballina, Co. Mayo on the 21st May 1944. Educated at Trinity College Dublin, she completed her studies at Harvard University in 1968, qualified as a barrister-at-law.

A member of Seanad Éireann from 1969 until 1989, she was Professor of Constitutional and Criminal Law at Trinity College Dublin (1969-75) and Lecturer in European Community Law, also at Trinity from 1975 to 1990.

Although not a member of the Labour party (she resigned in 1985 in protest at the signing of the Anglo-Irish Agreement), Mrs. Robinson was nominated by the party for the Presidency in 1990 and was supported by both the Workers Party and the Green Party. She was elected on the second count defeating Brian Lenihan of Fianna Fáil after a sometimes contentious election campaign.

She was inaugurated as President on the 3rd of December 1990 at the age of 46. She is the first woman and the youngest person ever to hold the office. Her term as President has been punctuated by a number of domestic and overseas visits which have significantly raised the profile of the Irish Presidency.

Presidential Elections, 1945 - 1990

Year	Candidates	Turnout %	1st Count	Transfers	Result	Elected
1945	McCartan, Patrick	63.0	212,834	-212,834	-	
	MacEoin, Seán	-	335,539	+117,886	453,425	
	Ó Ceallaigh, Seán T.	-	537,965	+27,200	565,165	Seán T. Ó Ceallaigh
1959	de Valera, Eamon	58.4	538,003	-	-	Eamon de Valera
	MacEoin, Seán	-	417,536	-	-	
1966	de Valera, Eamon	65.4	558,861	-	-	Eamon de Valera
	O'Higgins, Thomas F.	-	548,144	-	-	
1973	Childers, Erskine	62.2	635,867	-	-	Erskine Childers
	O'Higgins, Thomas F.	-	587,771	-	-	
1990	Currie, Austin	64.1	267,902	-267,902	-	
	Lenihan, Brian	-	694,484	+36,789	731,273	
	Robinson, Mary	-	612,265	+205,565	817,830	Mary Robinson

Note: In 1938, 1952, 1974, 1976 and 1983 no election was necessary as only one candidate was nominated.
The following were the canditates duly appointed: 1938, Douglas Hyde; 1952, Seán T. O'Ceallaigh; 1974, Cearbhall Ó Dálaigh; 1976, Dr. Patrick Hillery; 1983, Dr. Partick Hillery.

TAOISIGH OF IRELAND

Taoisigh and Tánaistes of Ireland, 1922-96

Date	Head of Government	Deputy Head of Government
	President of Executive Council	**Vice-President of Executive Council**
6th Dec. 1922	William T. Cosgrave	Kevin O'Higgins
		Ernest Blythe (10th July 1927)
9th March 1932	Eamon de Valera	Seán T. Ó Ceallaigh
	Taoiseach	**Tánaiste**
29th Dec. 1937	Eamon de Valera	Seán T. Ó Ceallaigh
		Seán Lemass (14th June 1945)
18th Feb. 1948	John A. Costello	William Norton
13th June 1951	Eamon de Valera	Seán Lemass
2nd June 1954	John A. Costello	William Norton
20th Mar. 1957	Eamon de Valera	Seán Lemass
23rd June 1959	Seán Lemass	Seán MacEntee
		Frank Aiken (21st April 1965)
10th Nov. 1966	Jack Lynch	Frank Aiken
		Erskine Childers (2nd July 1969)
14th Mar. 1973	Liam Cosgrave	Brendan Corish
5th July 1977	Jack Lynch	George Colley
11th Dec. 1979	Charles Haughey	George Colley
20th June 1981	Garret FitzGerald	Michael O'Leary
9th Mar. 1982	Charles Haughey	Ray McSharry
14th Dec. 1982	Garret FitzGerald	Dick Spring
		Peter Barry (20th Jan. 1987)
10th March 1987	Charles Haughey	Brian Lenihan
		John Wilson (13th Nov. 1990)
11th Feb. 1992	Albert Reynolds	John Wilson
		Dick Spring (12th Jan. 1993)
		Bertie Ahern (19th Nov. 1994)
15th Dec. 1994	John Bruton	Dick Spring

Biographies of Irish Taoisigh

WILLIAM T. COSGRAVE (1922 - 1932)

William T. Cosgrave T.D. (Cumann na nGaedheal), was President of the Executive Council of the Irish Free State from 6th December 1922 until 9th March 1932. His party had no opposition in the Dáil until Fianna Fáil ended their policy of abstentionism on 11th August 1927.

Born in Dublin in 1880, Cosgrave was a member of the Irish Volunteers and fought in the Easter Rising of 1916. He was first elected as a Sinn Féin T.D. in 1918, and later took the pro-Treaty side following the Anglo-Irish Treaty of 1921. He became leader of Cumann na nGaedheal in March 1923. The party consisted of Sinn Féin T.D.s who accepted the Anglo-Irish Treaty. During his period as Chairman of the Provisional Government (22nd August 1922) and President of the Executive Council he was also Minister for Finance (22nd August 1922 until 21st September 1923); Minister for Defence (19th March 1924 until 20th November 1924); and Minister for Justice (10th July 1927 - 12th October 1927).

Mr. Cosgrave died on the 16th November 1965.

EAMON DE VALERA
(1933 - 1948), (1951 - 1954), (1957 - 1959)

Eamon de Valera T.D., (Fianna Fáil), was Taoiseach from February 1933 until February 1948; June 1951 until June 1954; and from March 1957 until 23rd June 1959 when he became President of Ireland.

As founder and leader of the Fianna Fáil party he contested twelve general elections, winning on eight occasions. Under the Constitution of the Irish Free State the office of Taoiseach was known as 'President of the Executive Council' from 9th March 1932 until 29th December 1937, until the adoption of the Constitution of Ireland (which de Valera had a leading role in drafting) which created the office of Taoiseach.

Mr. de Valera was born in New York on 14th October 1882 and moved to Ireland when he was three years old. While Taoiseach he held the ministerial portfolios of External Affairs (March 1932 - February 1948); Education (September 1939 - June 1940); and Local Government & Public Health 15th - 18th August 1941).

Sentenced to death for his part in the 1916 Easter Rising, he avoided execution because of questions about his nationality, Mr. de Valera went on to become the most influential figure in twentieth century Ireland, holding the position of Taoiseach for longer than anyone else, and became President for two terms - the only person ever to hold both offices.

Eamon de Valera ('Dev') died on the 29th August 1975.

JOHN A. COSTELLO
(1948 - 1951), (1954 - 1957)

John A. Costello T.D. (Fine Gael), was Taoiseach from February 1948 until June 1951 and again from June 1954 until February 1957. Both the administrations he headed were inter-party coalitions consisting of Fine Gael, Labour, Clann na Talmhan, Clann na Poblachta and an independent.

Mr. Costello was born in Dublin in 1891, and went on to become a barrister and was Attorney-General from 9th January 1926 until the 9th March 1932. A member of the Fine Gael opposition during Fianna Fáil's domination of the 1930's and '40's, Mr. Costello was chosen as Taoiseach of the inter-party government of 1948 as the person who could possibly unite the many diverse points of view among the coalition parties. During this period of government he also held the ministerial portfolio of health (following the resignation of Dr. Noel Browne after the controversial 'mother and child' scheme) from 11th April 1951 onwards.

It was Mr. Costello, during a visit to Canada on 7th September 1948, who first declared the intention of Ireland to become a Republic which it duly did on 18th April 1949.

Mr. Costello died on 5th January 1976.

SEAN LEMASS (1959 - 1966)

Seán Lemass T.D. (Fianna Fáil), was Taoiseach from the 23rd June 1959 until he resigned in November 1966. As Taoiseach he was re-elected twice, securing overall majorities on both occasions.

Born in 1899, Lemass first came to prominence as a volunteer in the 1916 Easter Rising, and again during the War of Independence 1919-21. He opposed the Anglo-Irish Treaty and fought with the anti-Treaty forces in the Civil War. He was elected to Dáil Éireann in 1925, but in keeping with Sinn Féin policy did not take his seat. He became secretary of the embryonic Fianna Fáil party, and when they swept into power in March 1932 he immediately took office as Minister for Industry and Commerce until September 1939, and again from 14th August 1941 until 23rd June 1959. He was also Minister for Supplies from 16th September 1939 until 21st July 1945, and Tánaiste from 14th June 1945 until 18th February 1948; 13th June 1951 until 2nd June 1954; and 20th March 1957 until 23rd June 1959.

He is largely credited with the reversal of Irish economic policy away from protectionism towards free trade, a move which helped Ireland later join the European Economic Community in 1973.

Mr. Lemass announced his intention to resign as Taoiseach on November 8th 1966 and was succeeded by Jack Lynch on the 10th of the same month.

Mr. Lemass died five years later on the 11th May 1971.

JACK LYNCH
(1966 - 1973), (1977 - 1979)

Jack Lynch T.D. (Fianna Fáil), was Taoiseach from November 1966 until March 1973 and again from July 1977 until November 1979. During his time as leader of the Fianna Fáil party (1966-1979) he contested three general elections, winning two with overall majorities.

Mr. Lynch was born in Cork city in 1917 and before entering public office had been a barrister. He was first elected a Fianna Fáil T.D. to Dáil Éireann on the 4th February 1948 in his native Cork. He held a number of ministerial posts: Education (March 1957 - June 1959); Industry and Commerce (June 1959 - April 1965); Finance (April 1965- November 1966); Gaeltacht (March 1957 - June 1957).

Mr. Lynch was replaced by Charles Haughey, whom he had earlier dismissed from office in 1970 as leader of Fianna Fáil in November 1979.

In his youth Jack Lynch won six All-Ireland medals in a row (the only man ever to do so) between 1941 and 1946 - five for hurling, and a football medal in 1945.

LIAM COSGRAVE (1973 - 1977)

Liam Cosgrave T.D. (Fine Gael), was Taoiseach from March 1973 until July 1977. During his time as leader of Fine Gael (1965-1977) he contested four general elections and formed a coalition administration with Labour in November 1973.

Mr. Cosgrave was born on 13th April, 1920, the son of William T. Cosgrave, first President of the Executive Council. Before his election to the Dáil on the 23rd June 1943 as Fine Gael T.D. for Dublin County, Mr. Cosgrave was a barrister and Senior Counsel. He was Minister for External Affairs from the 2nd June 1945 until the 12th February 1957.

He succeeded James Dillon as leader of Fine Gael and as Taoiseach signed the Sunningdale Agreement on 9th December 1973, resulting in agreement on the status of Northern Ireland and co-operation between the Irish and British governments.

Following the general election of 1977 and the inter-party government being replaced by Fianna Fáil, Cosgrave was succeeded in the leadership of Fine Gael by Garret FitzGerald.

CHARLES J. HAUGHEY
(1979-1981), (1982), (1987-1992)

Charles J. Haughey T.D., (Fianna Fáil), was Taoiseach from November 1979 until June 1981; February - November 1982; and February 1987 until February 1992. During his time as leader of the Fianna Fáil party he contested five general elections but never secured an overall majority. He led Fianna Fáil into its first coalition government in 1989 along with the

Progressive Democrats.

Mr. Haughey was born in Castlebar, Co. Mayo on the 16th September 1925. A longtime resident of Kinsealy, Co. Dublin, Charles Haughey was always elected T.D. for a Dublin constituency, first winning a seat on the 5th March 1957.

He held the following ministerial offices: Justice (1961-1964); Agriculture and Fisheries (1964-1966); Finance (1966-1970); Health and Social Welfare (1977-1979).

On the 6th May, 1970, following charges of supplying weapons to Northern nationalists, Minister Haughey was dismissed from office by then Taoiseach Jack Lynch and was later arrested on charges of illegal importation of arms for the I.R.A. Following what became known as 'The Arms Trial', Haughey was acquitted in October of the same year.

Mr. Haughey replaced Jack Lynch as leader of Fianna Fáil in November 1979, and continued as leader of the party until his resignation as Taoiseach in February 1992.

DR. GARRET FITZGERALD
(1981 - 1982), (1982 - 1987)

During his time as leader of Fine Gael Dr. Garret FitzGerald T.D. contested five General Elections. He was Taoiseach from 30th June 1981 until 9th March 1982, and again from 24th November 1982 until 10th March 1987. Both administrations formed were Fine Gael/Labour coalitions.

Garret FitzGerald was born in Dublin in February 1926, and prior to winning his first seat he had been a lecturer at University College Dublin. His father, Desmond, was a Cumann na nGaedheal Minister for External Affairs and Defence. Garret FitzGerald was first elected to Dáil Éireann as a member for Dublin South-East on 18th June 1969 having previously been a member of Seanad Éireann (1965-1969). He was Minister of Foreign Affairs (March 1973-July 1977). He had been Fine Gael spokesman on Education and Finance.

As Taoiseach Dr. FitzGerald initiated the New Ireland Forum in 1983 and was a signatory, along with the British Prime Minister, Margaret Thatcher, of the Anglo-Irish Agreement in November 1985 at Hillsborough.

FitzGerald's government lost power in the General Election of February 1987 to the Haughey-led Fianna Fáil, and in March of the same year Dr. FitzGerald was replaced as leader of Fine Gael by Alan Dukes.

ALBERT REYNOLDS (1992 - 1994)

Albert Reynolds T.D. (Fianna Fáil), was Taoiseach from February 1992 until the 15th of December 1994. He was Taoiseach in two administrations, a Fianna Fáil/Progressive Democrat coalition from February 1992 until 25th November 1992 and a Fianna Fáil/Labour coalition from January 1993 until December 1994. During his time as Taoiseach he contested one general

election and his party, Fianna Fáil, won 68 seats.

As Taoiseach, Albert Reynolds played a crucial role in realising the I.R.A. ceasefire of August 1994, following extensive personal negotiations with Sinn Féin leader Gerry Adams and S.D.L.P. leader John Hume, having earlier signed the historic Downing Street Declaration with British Prime Minister John Major in December 1993.

Born in Rooskey, Co. Roscommon in November 1935, Mr. Reynolds has been a long time resident of Longford and was formerly a company director and a dance hall proprietor.

He was first elected to the Dáil as Fianna Fáil member for Longford-Westmeath on the 16th June 1977 and has held his seat ever since. He held the following ministerial posts: Minister for Posts and Telegraphs (1979-1981); Minister for Industry and Energy (March to December 1982), Minister for Industry and Commerce (March 1987 - November 1988); Minister for Finance (November 1988 - February 1992).

He was also the Fianna Fáil spokesman on Energy, and on Industry and Employment during Fianna Fáil's time in opposition. Mr. Reynolds became the fifth leader of Fianna Fáil in February 1992, and was replaced by Bertie Ahern T.D., as leader of that party in November of 1994 following the collapse of the Fianna Fáil/Labour coalition over an extradition controversy.

JOHN BRUTON (1994 -)

John Bruton T.D. (Fine Gael), has been Taoiseach since 15th December 1994, when he led a three party 'rainbow' coalition comprising of Fine Gael, the Labour Party and Democratic Left into power.

Born in Dublin on May 18, 1947 he now resides in Dunboyne, Co. Meath with his wife Finola and their four children. He is a farmer by profession and has also been a barrister at law.

Mr. Bruton was elected to Dáil Éireann as a member of the Fine Gael party in Meath on the 18th June 1969, becoming the youngest member of that, the 19th Dáil. He held various ministries in different administrations, including: Minister for Finance (June 1981-March 1982; February 1986 - March 1987); Minister for Industry, Trade, Commerce and Tourism (December 1983 - February 1986); Minister for Industry and Energy (1982-1983); Minister for Public Service (January - March 1987).

He has also been the Fine Gael spokesman on Industry and Commerce, Education, Agriculture, and Finance during their time in opposition. Deputy Leader of Fine Gael from 1987, he was elected Leader of the party on the 20th November 1990.

Mr. Bruton's coalition government is the first administration to have taken office without the holding of a general election, when they replaced the Fianna Fáil led coalition headed by Albert Reynolds. Much of the focus of the Bruton government, like that of its predecessor, has been on the ongoing efforts to find a permanent solution to the Northern Ireland situation.

GOVERNMENTS OF IRELAND

1922 - 1996

KEY: **(SF)** Sinn Féin; **(CnG)** Cumann na Gaedheal; **(FF)** Fianna Fáil; **(FG)** Fine Gael; **(LAB)** Labour; **(CnP)** Clann na Poblachta; **(CnT)** Clann na Talmhan; **(PD)** Progressive Democrats; **(Ind)** Independent; **(DL)** Democratic Left.

NOTES

Following the General Election of 1918, elected Sinn Féin representatives met for the first time on the 21st January 1919 as the first Dáil Éireann. The new assembly elected a cabinet. The 2nd Dáil met for the first time on the 26th August 1921 and again elected a cabinet. The cabinet was superseded by the Provisional Government in January 1922. The Provisional Government was in turn superseded by the Executive Council in December 1922.

(1) Cathal Brugha was President of the 1st Dáil, January - April 1919.

(2) Eamon de Valera was President of the 1st Dáil, April 1919 - August 1921, and President of the 2nd Dáil from August 1921 - January 1922. De Valera and others who opposed the Anglo-Irish Treaty withdrew from the Dáil in January 1922.

(3) Michael Collins was Chairman of the Provisional Government which came into being after the Dáil ratified the Anglo-Irish Treaty in January 1922. (See note 2).

(4) W.T. Cosgrave became Chairman of the Provisional Government following the assasination of Michael Collins in August 1922.

From December 1922 until December 1937 the office of Prime Minister was known as President of the Executive Council. From December 1937 that position became known as Taoiseach.

MINISTERS FOR FINANCE

Taoiseach	Minister	Appointed
Brugha (1)	Eoin MacNeil (SF)	1919
De Valera (2)	Michael Collins (SF)	1919
Collins (3)	Michael Collins (SF)	1922
Cosgrave (4)	W. T. Cosgrave (CnG)	1922
Cosgrave	Ernest Blythe (CnG)	1923
De Valera	Seán MacEntee (FF)	1932
De Valera	Seán T. O'Kelly (FF)	1939
De Valera	Frank Aiken (FF)	1945
Costello	P.J. McGilligan (FG)	1948
De Valera	Seán MacEntee (FF)	1951
Costello	Gerard Sweetman (FG)	1954
De Valera	James Ryan (FF)	1957
Lemass	James Ryan (FF)	1959
Lemass	Jack Lynch (FF)	1965
Lynch	Charles Haughey (FF)	1966
Lynch	George Colley (FF)	1970
Cosgrave	Richie Ryan (FG)	1973
Lynch	George Colley (FF)	1977

Haughey	Michael O'Kennedy (FF)	1979
Haughey	Gene Fitzgerald (FF)	1981
Haughey	Ray McSharry (FF)	1982
FitzGerald	Alan Dukes (FG)	1982
FitzGerald	John Bruton (FG)	1986
Haughey	Ray McSharry (FF)	1987
Haughey	Albert Reynolds (FF)	1989
Reynolds	Bertie Ahern (FF)	1993
Bruton	Ruairí Quinn (LAB)	1994

MINISTERS FOR JUSTICE (HOME AFFAIRS)*

Taoiseach	Minister	Appointed
Brugha (1)	Michael Collins (SF)	1919
De Valera (2)	Arthur Griffith (SF)	1919
De Valera (2)	Austin Stack (SF)	1921
Collins (3)	Edmond Duggan (SF)	1922
Cosgrave (4)	Kevin O'Higgins (CnG)	1922
Cosgrave	W. T. Cosgrave (CnG)	1927
Cosgrave	J. Fitzgerald Kenny (CnG)	1927
De Valera	James Geoghegan (FF)	1932
De Valera	P. J. Ruttledge (FF)	1933
De Valera	Gerald Boland (FF)	1939
Costello	Seán MacEoin (FG)	1948
Costello	Daniel Morrissey (FG)	1951
De Valera	Gerald Boland (FF)	1951
Costello	James Everitt (LAB)	1954
De Valera	Oscar Traynor (FF)	1957
Lemass	Oscar Traynor (FF)	1959
Lemass	Charles Haughey (FF)	1961
Lemass	Seán Lemass (FF)	1964
Lemass	Brian Lenihan (FF)	1964
Lynch	Brian Lenihan (FF)	1966
Lynch	Mícheál O'Moráin (FF)	1968
Lynch	Desmond O'Malley (FF)	1970
Cosgrave	Patrick Cooney (FG)	1973
Lynch	Gerry Collins (FF)	1977
Haughey	Gerry Collins (FF)	1979
Haughey	Sean Doherty (FF)	1982
FitzGerald	Michael Noonan (FG)	1982
FitzGerald	Alan Dukes (FG)	1986
Haughey	Gerry Collins (FF)	1987
Haughey	Ray Burke (FF)	1989
Reynolds	Pádraig Flynn (FF)	1992
Reynolds	Máire Geoghegan-Quinn (FF)	1993
Bruton	Nora Owen (FG)	1994

*In 1924, the Office of Minister of Home Affairs became known as the Department of Justice.

MINISTERS FOR DEFENCE

Taoiseach	Minister	Appointed
Brugha (1)	Richard Mulcahy (SF)	1919
De Valera (2)	Cathal Brugha (SF)	1919
Cosgrave	Richard Mulcahy (CnG)	1923
Cosgrave	W. T. Cosgrave (CnG)	1924
Cosgrave	Peter Hughes (CnG)	1924
Cosgrave	Desmond Fitzgerald (CnG)	1927
De Valera	Frank Aiken (FF)	1932
De Valera	Oscar Traynor (FF)	1939

Costello	Thomas F. O'Higgins (FG)	1948
Costello	Seán MacEoin (FG)	1951
De Valera	Oscar Traynor (FF)	1951
Costello	Seán MacEoin (FG)	1954
De Valera	Kevin Boland (FF)	1957
Lemass	Kevin Boland (FF)	1959
Lemass	Gerald Bartley (FF)	1961
Lemass	Michael Hilliard (FF)	1965
Lynch	Michael Hilliard (FF)	1966
Lynch	James Gibbons (FF)	1969
Lynch	Jeremiah Cronin (FF)	1970
Cosgrave	Patrick Donegan (FG)	1973
Cosgrave	Liam Cosgrave (FG)	1976
Cosgrave	Oliver J. Flanagan (FG)	1976
Lynch	Bobby Molloy (FF)	1977
Haughey	Pádraig Faulkner (FF)	1979
Haughey	Sylvester Barrett (FF)	1981
Haughey	Patrick Power (FF)	1982
FitzGerald	Patrick Cooney (FG)	1982
FitzGerald	Patrick O'Toole (FG)	1986
Haughey	Michael J. Noonan (FF)	1987
Haughey	Brian Lenihan (FF)	1989
Haughey	Brendan Daly (FF)	1991
Reynolds	John Wilson (FF)	1992
Reynolds	David Andrews (FF)	1993
Bruton	Sean Barrett (FG)	1994

Cosgrave	Richard Mulcahy (CnG)	1927
De Valera	Seán T. O'Kelly (FF)	1932
De Valera	P.J. Ruttledge (FF)	1939
De Valera	Eamon de Valera (FF)	1941
De Valera	Seán MacEntee (FF)	1941
Costello	Timothy J. Murphy (LAB)	1948
Costello	Michael J. Keyes (LAB)	1949
De Valera	Patrick Smith (FF)	1951
Costello	Patrick O'Donnell (FG)	1954
De Valera	Patrick Smith (FF)	1957
De Valera	Neil Blaney (FF)	1957
Lemass	Neil Blaney (FF)	1961
Lynch	Kevin Boland (FF)	1966
Lynch	Bobby Molloy (FF)	1970
Cosgrave	James Tully (LAB)	1973-77

* Not a member of the Executive Council.

In 1924 the office of Local Government became Local Government and Public Health. In 1947 Local Government and Public Health was divided into two ministerial briefs, the Department of Local Government and the Department of Health (see below). The Department of Local Government ceased to exist in 1977, replaced by the new Department of the Environment - see below.

MINISTERS FOR FOREIGN AFFAIRS*

Taoiseach	Minister	Appointed
Brugha (1)	Count Plunkett (SF)	1919
De Valera (2)	Count Plunkett (SF)	1919
De Valera (2)	Arthur Griffiths (SF)	1921
Cosgrave (4)	Desmond Fitzgerald (CnG)	1922
Cosgrave	Kevin O'Higgins (CnG)	1927
Cosgrave	Patrick McGilligan (CnG)	1927
De Valera	Eamon de Valera (FF)	1932
Costello	Seán MacBride (CnP)	1948
De Valera	Frank Aiken (FF)	1951
Costello	Liam Cosgrave (FG)	1954
De Valera	Frank Aiken (FF)	1957
Lemass	Frank Aiken (FF)	1959
Lynch	Frank Aiken (FF)	1966
Lynch	Patrick Hillery (FF)	1969
Lynch	Brian Lenihan (FF)	1973
Cosgrave	Garret FitzGerald (FG)	1973
Lynch	Michael O'Kennedy (FF)	1977
Haughey	Brian Lenihan (FF)	1979
Haughey	Gerry Collins (FF)	1982
FitzGerald	Peter Barry (FG)	1982
Haughey	Brian Lenihan (FF)	1987
Haughey	Gerry Collins (FF)	1989
Reynolds	David Andrews (FF)	1992
Reynolds	Dick Spring (LAB)	1993
Bruton	Dick Spring (LAB)	1994

*Until 1973, the Department of Foreign Affairs was known as the Department of External Affairs.

MINISTERS FOR LOCAL GOVERNMENT

Taoiseach	Minister	Appointed
De Valera (2)	W.T. Cosgrave (SF)	1919
Collins (3)	W.T. Cosgrave (SF)	1922
Cosgrave (4)	Ernest Blythe (CnG)	1922
Cosgrave	James Burke* (CnG)	1923

MINISTERS FOR ENVIRONMENT

Taoiseach	Minister	Appointed
Lynch	Sylvester Barrett (FF)	1977
Haughey	Sylvester Barrett (FF)	1979
Haughey	Ray Burke (FF)	1981
FitzGerald	Dick Spring (LAB)	1982
FitzGerald	Liam Kavanagh (LAB)	1984
FitzGerald	John Boland (FG)	1986
Haughey	Pádraig Flynn (FF)	1987
Reynolds	Michael Smith (FF)	1992
Bruton	Brendan Howlin (LAB)	1994

MINISTERS FOR ECONOMIC AFFAIRS

Taoiseach	Minister	Appointed
De Valera (2)	Robert C. Barton (SF)	1921
Collins (3)	Kevin O'Higgins (SF)	1922
Cosgrave (4)	Joseph McGrath (CnG)	1922

The Department of Economic Affairs merged into the Department of Industry and Commerce on 6th December 1922.

MINISTERS FOR INDUSTRY AND COMMERCE

Taoiseach	Minister	Appointed
De Valera (2)	Eoin MacNeill (SF)	1919
Cosgrave (4)	Joseph McGrath (CnG)	1922
Cosgrave	Patrick McGilligan (CnG)	1924
De Valera	Seán Lemass (FF)	1932
De Valera	Seán MacEntee (FF)	1939
De Valera	Seán Lemass (FF)	1941
Costello	Daniel Morrissey (FG)	1948
Costello	Thomas F. O'Higgins (FG)	1951
De Valera	Seán Lemass (FF)	1951
Costello	William Norton (LAB)	1954
De Valera	Seán Lemass (FF)	1957
Lemass	Jack Lynch (FF)	1959

Lemass ....Patrick Hillery (FF) 1965
Lemass ....George Colley (FF) 1966
Lynch ....................P.J. Lalor (FF) 1970
Cosgrave ....Justin Keating (FG) 1973-77
In 1977, Industry and Commerce became Industry, Commerce and Energy - see below.

MINISTERS FOR INDUSTRY, COMMERCE & ENERGY

Taoiseach	Minister	Appointed
Lynch	Des O'Malley (FF)	1977-79

In 1979, Industry, Commerce and Energy was split into two briefs - The Department of Energy, and the Department of Industry, Commerce and Tourism.

MINISTERS FOR ENERGY

Taoiseach	Minister	Appointed
Haughey	George Colley (FF)	1979-82
FitzGerald	Dick Spring (LAB)	1983
Haughey	Ray Burke (FF)	1987
Haughey	Robert Molloy (PD)	1989-93

Between 1982 and 1983 the Department of Energy was known as the Department of Industry and Energy.

MINISTER FOR INDUSTRY, COMMERCE & TOURISM

Taoiseach	Minister	Appointed
Haughey	Des O'Malley (FF)	1979-82

In 1982 the Department of Industry, Commerce and Tourism was split into two briefs - Industry became part of the Energy portfolio, and a new Department of Trade, Commerce and Tourism was established.

MINISTERS FOR INDUSTRY & ENERGY

Taoiseach	Minister	Appointed
Haughey	Albert Reynolds (FF)	1982
FitzGerald	John Bruton (FG)	1982-83

MINISTERS FOR TRADE, COMMERCE & TOURISM

Taoiseach	Minister	Appointed
Haughey	Des O'Malley (FF)	1982
FitzGerald	Frank Cluskey (LAB)	1982-83

MINISTER FOR INDUSTRY, TRADE, COMMERCE & TOURISM

Taoiseach	Minister	Appointed
FitzGerald	John Bruton (FG)	1984-86

In December 1983 the Department of Industry, Trade, Commerce & Tourism was established. In 1986 the Department of Industry, Trade, Commerce and Tourism was divided into two briefs - the Department of Industry and Commerce, and the Department of Tourism (see below).

MINISTERS FOR INDUSTRY & COMMERCE

Taoiseach	Minister	Appointed
FitzGerald	Michael Noonan (FG)	1986
Haughey	Albert Reynolds (FF)	1987
Haughey	Des O'Malley (PD)	1989
Reynolds	Bertie Ahern (FF)	1993

In 1993 the Department of Enterprise and Employment was established.

MINISTERS FOR ENTERPRISE & EMPLOYMENT

Taoiseach	Minister	Appointed
Reynolds	Ruairí Quinn (LAB)	1993
Bruton	Richard Bruton (FG)	1994

MINISTERS FOR LABOUR

Taoiseach	Minister	Appointed
De Valera (2)	Countess Markievicz (SF)	1919
De Valera (2)	Countess Markievicz (SF)	1921
Collins (3)	Joseph McGrath (CnG)	1922
Cosgrave (4)	Joseph McGrath (CnG)	1922
Lemass	Patrick Hillery (FF)	1966
Lynch	Patrick Hillery (FF)	1966
Lynch	Joseph Brennan (FF)	1969
Cosgrave	Michael O'Leary (LAB)	1973
Lynch	Gene Fitzgerald (FF)	1977
Haughey	Gene Fitzgerald (FF)	1979
Haughey	Thomas Nolan (FF)	1981
Haughey	Gene Fitzgerald (FF)	1982
FitzGerald	Liam Kavanagh (LAB)	1982
FitzGerald	Ruairí Quinn (LAB)	1984
Haughey	Bertie Ahern (FF)	1987
Reynolds	Brian Cowan	1992-93

*The Department of Labour was re-established in 1966, following a lapse of 34 years.

The Department of Equality and Law Reform replaced the Department of Labour in 1993.

MINISTERS FOR AGRICULTURE

Taoiseach	Minister	Appointed
De Valera (2)	Robert C. Barton* (SF)	1919
De Valera (2)	Art O'Connor* (SF)	1921
Collins (3)	Patrick Hogan (SF)	1922
Cosgrave (4)	Patrick Hogan (CnG)	1922
De Valera	James Ryan (FF)	1932
De Valera	Patrick Smith (FF)	1947
Costello	James Dillon (Ind)	1948
De Valera	Thomas Walsh (FF)	1951
Costello	James Dillon (FG)	1954
De Valera	Frank Aiken (FF)	1957
De Valera	Seán Moylan (FF)	1957
De Valera	Patrick Smith (FF)	1957
Lemass	Patrick Smith (FF)	1959
Lemass	Charles J. Haughey (FF)	1964
Lynch	Neil Blaney (FF)	1966
Lynch	James Gibbons (FF)	1970
Cosgrave	Mark Clinton (FG)	1973
Lynch	James Gibbons (FF)	1977
Haughey	Ray MacSharry (FF)	1979
Haughey	Brian Lenihan (FF)	1982

FitzGerald	Austin Deasy (FG)	1982
Haughey	Michael O'Kennedy (FF)	1987
Reynolds	Joe Walsh (FF)	1992
Bruton	Ivan Yates (FG)	1994

* Not a member of the Executive Council.

In 1924 Agriculture became Lands and Agriculture. In 1928 Land and Agriculture reverted to the Department of Agriculture. In July 1965, Fisheries was added to the Agricultural brief, and became known as the Department of Agriculture and Fisheries. In February 1977 Fisheries became a separate department. In January 1993 the Department of Agriculture and Food became known as the Department of Agriculture, Food and Forestry.

MINISTERS FOR THE MARINE

Taoiseach	Minister	Appointed
De Valera (2)	Seán Etchingham* (SF)	1920
Cosgrave	Fionán Lynch* (CnG)	1922
De Valera	P.J. Ruttledge (FF)	1932
De Valera	Joseph Connolly (FF)	1933
Cosgrave	Patrick Donegan (FG)	1977
Lynch	Brian Lenihan (FF)	1977
Haughey	Patrick Power (FF)	1979
Haughey	Brendan Daly (FF)	1982
FitzGerald	Patrick O'Toole (FG)	1982
FitzGerald	Liam Kavanagh (LAB)	1986
Haughey	Brendan Daly (FF)	1987
Haughey	John Wilson (FF)	1989
Reynolds	David Andrews (FF)	1993
Bruton	Sean Barrett (FG)	1994

In 1928 the Department of Fisheries became the Department of Land and Fisheries. In 1934 it became the Department of Lands (see below). In July 1965 Fisheries was attached onto the brief of Agriculture. In February 1977 Fisheries became a separate department. Forestry was incorporated into the brief when in 1979.

In 1987 the Department of Fisheries took on its current guise of Department of the Marine.

* Not a member of the Executive Council.

MINISTERS FOR LANDS

Taoiseach	Minister	Appointed
De Valera	Frank Aiken (FF)	1936
De Valera	Gerald Boland (FF)	1936
De Valera	Thomas Derrig (FF)	1939
De Valera	Séan Moylan (FF)	1943
Costello	Joseph Blowick (CnT)	1948
De Valera	Thomas Derrig (FF)	1951
Costello	Joseph Blowick (CnT)	1954
De Valera	Erskine Childers (FF)	1957
Lemass	Erskine Childers (FF)	1959
Lemass	Mícheál O'Moráin (FF)	1959
Lynch	Mícheál O'Moráin (FF)	1966
Lynch	Pádraig Faulkner (FF)	1968
Lynch	Sean Flanagan (FF)	1969
Cosgrave	Thomas J. Fitzpatrick (FG)	1973
Cosgrave	Patrick Donegan (FG)	1976

MINISTERS FOR EDUCATION

Taoiseach	Minister	Appointed
De Valera (2)	J.J. O'Kelly* (SF)	1921
Collins (3)	Fionán Lynch (SF)	1922
Cosgrave (4)	Eoin MacNeill (CnG)	1922
Cosgrave	John M. O'Sullivan (CnG)	1925
De Valera	Thomas Derrig (FF)	1932
De Valera	Seán T. O'Kelly (FF)	1939
De Valera	Eamon de Valera (FF)	1939
De Valera	Thomas Derrig (FF)	1940
Costello	Richard Mulcahy (FG)	1948
De Valera	Seán Moylan (FF)	1951
Costello	Richard Mulcahy (FG)	1954
De Valera	Jack Lynch (FF)	1957
Lemass	Patrick Hillery (FF)	1959
Lemass	George Colley (FF)	1965
Lemass	Donogh O'Malley (FF)	1966
Lynch	Donogh O'Malley (FF)	1966
Lynch	Jack Lynch (FF)	1968
Lynch	Brian Lenihan (FF)	1968
Lynch	Pádraig Faulkner (FF)	1969
Cosgrave	Dick Burke (FG)	1973
Cosgrave	Peter Barry (FG)	1976
Lynch	John Wilson (FF)	1977
Haughey	John Wilson (FF)	1979
Haughey	Martin O'Donohue (FF)	1982
FitzGerald	Gemma Hussey (FG)	1982
FitzGerald	Patrick Cooney (FG)	1986
Haughey	Mary O'Rourke (FF)	1987
Reynolds	Seamus Brennan (FF)	1992
Reynolds	Niamh Bhreathnach (LAB)	1993
Bruton	Niamh Bhreathnach (LAB)	1994

* Not a member of the Executive Council.

MINISTERS FOR THE GAELTACHT

Taoiseach	Minister	Appointed
De Valera (2)	Séan T. O'Kelly (SF)	1919
Costello	Richard Mulcahy (FG)	1956
Costello	P.J. Lindsay (FG)	1956
De Valera	Jack Lynch (FF)	1957
De Valera	Mícheál O'Moráin (FF)	1957
Lemass	Mícheál O'Moráin (FF)	1959
Lemass	Gerald Bartley (FF)	1959
Lemass	Mícheál O'Moráin (FF)	1961
Lynch	Mícheál O'Moráin (FF)	1966
Lynch	Pádraig Faulkner (FF)	1968
Lynch	George Colley (FF)	1969
Cosgrave	Thomas O'Donnell (FG)	1973
Lynch	Dennis Gallagher (FF)	1977
Haughey	M. Geoghegan-Quinn (FF)	1979
Haughey	Pádraig Flynn (FF)	1982
FitzGerald	Patrick O'Toole (FG)	1982
Haughey	Charles J. Haughey (FF)	1987
Reynolds	John Wilson (FF)	1992
Reynolds	Michael D. Higgins (LAB)	1993
Bruton	Michael D. Higgins (LAB)	1994

De Valera's cabinet of 1919-1921 had a Minister for 'Irish', Sean O'Kelly. In July of 1956 the Department of the Gaeltacht was created.

* In 1993 the Department of the Gaeltacht was reconstituted as the Department of Arts, Culture and the Gaeltacht.

MINISTERS FOR POSTS AND TELEGRAPHS

Taoiseach	Minister	Appointed
Collins (5)	J.J. Walsh (SF)	1922
Cosgrave (6)	J.J. Walsh (CnG)	1922
Cosgrave	Ernest Blythe (CnG)	1927
De Valera	Joseph Connolly (FF)	1932
De Valera	Gerald Boland (FF)	1933
De Valera	Oscar Traynor (FF)	1936
De Valera	Oscar Traynor (FF)	1938
De Valera	Thomas Derrig (FF)	1939
De Valera	P.J. Little (FF)	1939
Costello	James Everett (LAB)	1948
De Valera	Erskine Childers (FF)	1951
Costello	Michael J. Keyes (LAB)	1954
De Valera	Neil Blaney (FF)	1957
De Valera	John Ormonde (FF)	1957
Lemass	Michael Hilliard (FF)	1959
Lemass	Joseph Brennan (FF)	1965
Lynch	Erskine Childers (FF)	1966
Lynch	P.J. Lalor (FF)	1969
Lynch	Gerry Collins (FF)	1970
Cosgrave	Conor Cruise O'Brien (Lab)	1973
Lynch	Pádraig Faulkner (FF)	1977
Haughey	Albert Reynolds (FF)	1979
Haughey	John Wilson (FF)	1982
FitzGerald	Jim Mitchell* (FG)	1982-84

In 1984 the Department of Communications was created.

MINISTERS FOR COMMUNICATIONS

Taoiseach	Minister	Appointed
FitzGerald	Jim Mitchell (FG)	1984
Haughey	Ray Burke (FF)	1987
Haughey	Seamus Brennan (FF)	1991-92

MINISTERS FOR TOURISM, TRANSPORT AND COMMUNICATIONS

Taoiseach	Minister	Appointed
Reynolds	M. Geoghegan-Quinn (FF)	1992-3

In 1993 the Department of Transport, Energy and Communications was created.

MINISTERS FOR TRANSPORT, ENERGY & COMMUNICATIONS

Taoiseach	Minister	Appointed
Reynolds	Brian Cowen (FF)	1993
Bruton	Michael Lowry (FG)	1994

MINISTERS FOR HEALTH

Taoiseach	Minister	Appointed
Cosgrave	James A. Burke* (CnG)	1923
Costello	Noel Browne (Ind)	1948
Costello	John A. Costello (FG)	1951
De Valera	James Ryan (FF)	1951
Costello	Thomas F. O'Higgins (FG)	1954
De Valera	Seán MacEntee (FF)	1957
Lemass	Seán MacEntee (FF)	1959
Lemass	Donogh O'Malley (FF)	1965
Lemass	Séan Flanagan (FF)	1966

Lynch	Séan Flanagan (FF)	1966
Lynch	Erskine Childers (FF)	1969
Cosgrave	Brendan Corish (LAB)	1973
Lynch	Charles J. Haughey (FF)	1977
Haughey	Michael Woods (FF)	1979
FitzGerald	Barry Desmond (LAB))	1982
Haughey	Rory O'Hanlon (FF)	1987
Reynolds	John O'Connell (FF)	1992
Reynolds	Brendan Howlin (LAB)	1993
Bruton	Michael Noonan (FG)	1994

* Not a member of the Executive Council.

From 1924 Health was included under the brief of Local Government and Public Health. In 1947 the Department of Health was established.

MINISTERS FOR SOCIAL WELFARE

Taoiseach	Minister	Appointed
De Valera	James Ryan (FF)	1947
Costello	William Norton (LAB)	1948
De Valera	James Ryan (FF)	1951
Costello	Brendan Corish (LAB)	1954
De Valera	Patrick Smith (FF)	1957
Lemass	Séan MacEntee (FF)	1957
Lemass	Kevin Boland (FF)	1961
Lemass	Joseph Brennan (FF)	1966
Lynch	Kevin Boland (FF)	1969
Lynch	Joseph Brennan (FF)	1970
Cosgrave	Brendan Corish (LAB)	1973
Lynch	Charles J. Haughey (FF)	1977
Haughey	Michael Woods (FF)	1979
FitzGerald	Barry Desmond (LAB)	1982
FitzGerald	Gemma Hussey (FG)	1986
Haughey	Michael Woods (FF)	1987
Reynolds	Charlie McCreevy (FF)	1992
Reynolds	Michael Woods (FF)	1993
Bruton	Proinsias de Rossa (DL)	1994

The Dept. of Social Welfare was established in 1947.

MINISTERS FOR TRANSPORT AND POWER

Taoiseach	Minister	Appointed
Lemass	Erskine Childers (FF)	1959
Lynch	Brian Lenihan (FF)	1969
Lynch	Michael O'Kennedy (FF)	1973
Cosgrave	Peter Barry (FG)	1973
Cosgrave	Thomas Fitzpatrick (FG)	1976
Lynch	Pádraig Faulkner (FF)	1977

The brief of Transport and Power was established in July 1959. In 1977 this was renamed the Department of Tourism and Transport.

MINISTERS FOR TOURISM & TRANSPORT

Taoiseach	Minister	Appointed
Lynch	Pádraig Faulkner (FF)	1977-79
Haughey	John Wilson (FF)	1987
Haughey	Seamus Brennan (FF)	1989-92

MINISTERS FOR TRANSPORT

Taoiseach	Minister	Appointed
Haughey	Albert Reynolds (FF)	1979

Haughey ....John Wilson (FF) 1982
FitzGerald ....Jim Mitchell (FG) 1982-84

MINISTERS FOR TOURISM

Taoiseach	Minister	Appointed
Haughey	George Colley (FF)	1979
FitzGerald	Liam Kavanagh (LAB)	1986-87

Tourism was incorporated into the Department of Industry, Commerce and Tourism in 1979 (see above). It was briefly re-established in 1986, but incorporated again, this time into Tourism and Transport in 1987.

MINISTERS FOR TOURISM & TRADE

Taoiseach	Minister	Appointed
Reynolds	Charlie McCreevy (FF)	1993
Bruton	Enda Kenny (FG)	1994

The Department of Tourism and Trade was established in 1993.

MINISTERS FOR PUBLIC SERVICES

Taoiseach	Minister	Appointed
Cosgrave	Richie Ryan (FG)	1973
Lynch	George Colley (FF)	1977
Haughey	Gene Fitzgerald (FF)	1979
FitzGerald	John Boland (FG)	1982
FitzGerald	Ruairí Quinn (LAB)	1986-87

In November 1973 the Department of the Public Service was created. It was discontinued in January 1987.

MINISTERS FOR ECONOMIC PLANNING AND DEVELOPMENT

Taoiseach	Minister	Appointed
Lynch	Martin O'Donoghue (FF)	1977

The brief of Economic Planning and Development was established in 1977, and abolished in 1979.

ATTORNEY-GENERALS

Taoiseach	Attorney-General	Appointed
Collins (3)	H. Kennedy*	1922
Cosgrave (4)	H. Kennedy*	1922
Cosgrave	J. O'Byrne	1924
Cosgrave	J.A. Costello	1926
de Valera	C.A. Maguire	1932
de Valera	J. Geoghegan	1936
de Valera	P. Lynch	1936
de Valera	K. Haugh	1940
de Valera	K. Dixon	1942
De Valera	C. O'Dalaigh	1946
Costello	C. Lavery	1948
Costello	C.F. Casey	1951
De Valera	C. O'Dalaigh	1951
De Valera	T. Teevan	1953
Costello	P. McGilligan	1954
De Valera	A. O'Caoimh	1957
Lemass	A. O'Caoimh	1959
Lemass	C. Condon	1965
Lynch	C. Condon	1966
Cosgrave	D. Costello	1973
Lynch	A.J. Hederman	1977
Haughey	A.J. Hederman	1979
Haughey	P. Connolly	1982
FitzGerald	P. Sutherland	1982
FitzGerald	J. Rogers	1986
Haughey	J. L. Murray	1987
Reynolds	H. Whelehan	1992
Bruton	D. Gleeson	1994

* In 1922 the post of Attorney-General was known as 'Law Officer'.

Frank Aiken was Minister for Co-ordination of Defensive Measures from September 1939 until June 1945. Sean Lemass was Minister for Supplies from September 1939 until July 1945.

ELECTIONS

All-Ireland General Election, 14th December 1918.

105 seat election. Unionists: 22 seats; Nationalists: 6 seats; Sinn Féin: 73 seats, Labour Unionist: 3 seats; Independent Unionist: 1 seat. Sinn Féin constitute themselves as Dáil Éireann on 21st January 1919.

General Election to Parliament of Southern Ireland, 24th May 1921

128 seat election. Sinn Féin: 124 seats; Independents: 4 seats (Trinity College). No seats contested. The Sinn Féin members abstained from the southern Ireland House of Commons and constituted themselves as the 2nd Dáil on 16th August 1921. They were joined by the Sinn Féin member of the Northern Ireland House of Commons, John O'Mahony of Fermanagh South.

Dáil Éireann Elections, 1922 - 1992

Year of Election	Fianna Fáil	Fine Gael	Labour Party	Farmers Parties	Republican parties	Others	Turnout per cent	Total seats
1922	36	58	17	7	-	10	45.5	128
1923	44	63	14	15	-	17	61..2	153
1927 (1)	44	47	22	11	5	24	68.1	153
1927 (2)	57	62	13	6	-	15	69.0	153
1932	72	57	7	4	-	13	76.5	153
1933	77	48	8	11	-	9	81.3	153
1937	69	48	13	-	-	8	76.2	138
1938	77	45	9	-	-	7	76.7	138
1943	67	32	17	14	-	8	74.2	138
1944	76	30	8	11	-	13	67.7	138
1948	68	31	14	7	10	17	74.2	147
1951	69	40	16	6	2	14	75.3	147
1954	65	50	19	5	3	5	76.4	147
1957	78	40	12	3	5	9	71.3	147
1961	70	47	16	2	1	8	70.6	144
1965	72	47	22	-	1	2	75.1	144
1969	75	50	18	-	-	1	76.9	144
1973	69	54	19	-	-	2	76.6	144
1977	84	43	17	-	-	4	76.3	148
1981	78	65	15	-	2	6	76.2	166
1982 (1)	81	63	15	-	-	7	73.8	166
1982 (2)	75	70	16	-	-	5	72.9	166
1987	81	51	12	-	-	22	73.3	166
1989	77	55	15	-	-	19	68.5	166
1992	68	45	33	-	-	20	67.5	166

Fianna Fáil includes Anti-Treaty Sinn Féin (1922-23).

Fine Gael takes in Pro-Treaty Sinn Féin (1922) and Cumann na nGaedheal (1923-32).

'Farmers' parties takes in the Farmers Party (1922-32), the National Centre Party (1933) and Clann na Talmhan (1943-61).

'Republican' parties takes in Clann na Poblachta (1948-65), and includes Sinn Féin 1927(1) 5 TDs; 1957, 4 TDs) and the National H-Block Committee (1981, 2 TDs).

'Others' take in the National League (1927(1), 8 TDs; 1927(2), 2 TDs), National Labour (1944, 4 TDs; 1948, 5 TDs), the National Progressive Democrats (1961, 2 TDs), Sinn Féin Workers' Party, and the Workers' Party (1981, 1 TD; 1982(1), 3 TDs; 1982(2), 2 TD's; 1987, 4 TDs; 1989, 7 TDs; the Progressive Democrats (1987, 14 TDs; 1989, 6 TDs; 1992, 10 TDs), the Green Party (1989, 1992, 1 TD) and Democratic Left, (1992, 4 TDs). 'Others' also includes smaller groups and independents.

Votes recorded at Dáil Elections 1948 - 1992

Date of Election	Numbers entitled to vote	Votes recorded	Valid votes	Rejected votes	Votes recorded as % of numbers entitled to vote
February 1948	1,800,210	1,336,628	1,323,443	13,185	74.2
May 1951	1,785,144	1,343,616	1,331,724	11,892	75.3
May 1954	1,763,828	1,347,932	1,335,202	12,730	76.4
March 1957	1,738,278	1,238,559	1,227,019	11,540	71.3
October 1961	1,670,860	1,179,738	1,168,404	11,334	70.6
April 1965	1,683,019	1,246,415	1,253,122	11,293	75.1
June 1969	1,753,388	1,334,963	1,318,953	16,010	76.9
February 1973	1,783,604	1,366,474	1,350,537	15,937	76.6
June 1977	2,118,606	1,616,770	1,603,027	13,743	76.3
June 1981	2,275,450	1,734,379	1,718,211	16,168	76.2
February 1982	2,275,450	1,679,500	1,665,133	14,367	73.8
November 1982	2,335,153	1,701,385	1,688,720	12,665	72.9
February 1987	2,445,515	1,793,506	1,777,165	16,341	73.3
June 1989	2,448,810	1,677,592	1,656,813	20,779	68.5
November 1992	2,557,036	1,751,351	1,724,853	26,498	68.5

NORTHERN IRELAND POLITICAL PARTIES

Main Political Parties in Northern Ireland

ULSTER UNIONIST PARTY
3 Glengall Street, Belfast, BT12 5AE.

Founded in 1905 by Edward Carson in response to the perceived threat to the Union by the political advances of the Home Rule movement, the UUP went on to rule Northern Ireland from 1921 to 1972 via the Northern Ireland parliament at Stormont. It remains the largest political party in Northern Ireland, and supports the continuing governance of Northern Ireland from Westminster. The party opposes any arrangement that enables the Irish government to have a say in the internal affairs of Northern Ireland, and accordingly are opposed to all workings and institutions of the Anglo-Irish Agreement. The UUP has been aligned with the British Conservative Party in Westminster over the years, a position exploited fully in recent years as the Conservatives have remained in Government for an extended period. Long time leader James Molyneaux recently stepped down, making way for David Trimble. Well-known figures within the party include MP's John Taylor, Ken Maginnis and Rev. Martin Smyth.

DEMOCRATIC UNIONIST PARTY
296 Albertbridge Road, Belfast BT5 4GX.

Founded in 1971, the DUP is a radical right wing Protestant party, owing its origins to the Ulster Unionist Party. It is fiercely anti-republican, and has in its leader, the Rev. Ian Paisley, perhaps the most controversial party leader in Irish politics, north or south. The DUP has militant tendencies, which it has displayed on more than one occasion on both sides of the border. Its aim is for the continuance of the Union with Great Britain and Unionist domination of the parliamentary institutions. The party has only had the one leader since its foundation, Rev. Paisley, the only European politician this century to found his own church. Well-known figures within the party include Peter Robinson and

Sammy Wilson.

SOCIAL DEMOCRATIC AND LABOUR PARTY
24 Mount Charles, Belfast BT7 1NZ.

Founded in 1970 by members of various nationalist political organisations including the Northern Ireland Labour Party, the Republican Labour party, the Nationalist Party of Northern Ireland, and gelled with leading activists from the civil rights organisation which had made world headlines in 1969, the SDLP is a centrist left nationalist party. Its aspiration is for the future reunification of Ireland, to be achieved through popular consent of the majority of people of Northern Ireland. Over the years the party has gradually moved to the centre of the political spectrum, and is consistently the biggest political voice for the Catholic/nationalist vote in Northern Ireland. Gerry Fitt, leader from 1970, stepped down in 1979, paving the way for John Hume to steer the party through the difficult 1980's and early 1990's. In recent years Hume has been acclaimed world-wide for his pivitol role in negotiating the IRA ceasefire of September 1994. Major figures within the SDLP include Seamus Mallon and Dr. Joe Hendron.

PROVISIONAL SINN FÉIN
51-55 Falls Road, Belfast 12.

Founded in 1905 by Arthur Griffith, Sinn Féin (Ourselves Alone) has a colourful past which can be traced through all the major dates of 20th century Ireland. Following the 1916 Easter Rising the party reorganised under the leadership of Eamon de Valera and won a sweeping victory in the 1918 general election, prompting them to set up Dáil Éireann. Following the War of Independence and the subsequent Anglo-Irish Treaty, Sinn Féin split. Those who supported the Treaty formed the first Cumann na nGaedhal (later Fine Gael) government while those who opposed it continued to call themselves Sinn Féin. In 1926 de Valera founded Fianna Fáil, taking the majority of Sinn Féin with him. Sinn Féin remained a small abstentionist party for decades, emerging as a political force in Northern Ireland in the 1970's, surviving a further split in 1970 which saw the formation of Official Sinn Féin (The Workers' Party). Indeed it is in Northern Ireland that the main focus of Sinn Féin 32-Counties policy lies, and from which it draws most support. It is a republican nationalist party that many commentators have labelled the political wing of the provisional IRA. Its objectives are the achievement of national self-determination and the creation of a secular, socialist republic with a democratic island economy based on the principles of the Proclamation of 1916, the Democratic Programme of 1919 and the beliefs of Tone, Pearse and Connolly. Its leader has been Gerry Adams since 1983. Other figures of note within the party include Martin McGuinness and Mitchel McLaughlin.

ALLIANCE PARTY
88 University Street, Belfast BT7 1HE.
Founded in 1970, the Alliance Party is a non-sectarian moderate party of the centre. It attracts support from both Catholic and Protestant sections of the community but is seen by political commentators as "a moderate centre unionist party". It is vehemently opposed to political violence from either community, and subscribes to power sharing as a means of solving the Northern Ireland stalemate. In 1987 John Cushnahan stepped down as leader, and was replaced by John Alderdice. Other well known figureheads within the party were Phelim O'Neill and Oliver Napier.

UNITED KINGDOM UNIONISTS
Bob McCartney QC *is* the UK Unionist Party. McCartney won the Westminster seat for North Down in a by-election in June 1995, following the death of Popular Unionist MP Sir James Kilfedder. A native of the Shankill Road, McCartney was one of Northern Ireland's top QC's. A member of the UUP, he was expelled from the party in 1987, and his political career seemed to be over, until his re-appearance in June 1995.

PROGRESSIVE UNIONIST PARTY
Established in Belfast in 1978 as the Independent Unionist Group, later becoming the Progressive Unionist Party in 1979. Independent Unionist, Alderman Hugh Smyth was among its founders. The PUP is closely linked with the UVF, and many of the party's leading spokesmen are former loyalist prisoners - Gusty Spence, David Ervine, Billy Hutchinson and Eddie Kinner. The party played a major role in brokering the ceasefire announced by the combined Loyalist Military Command in October 1994. The party is currently represented at the Northern Ireland Forum for Peace and Reconciliation by David Ervine and Hugh Smyth.

ULSTER DEMOCRATIC PARTY
The UDP dates back from December 1989 and was previously known as the Ulster Loyalist Democratic Party (ULDP). The UDP claimed it was an independent political party with no paramilitary links in 1988. The party failed to make any real impact in elections and in 1987 John McMichael, the party's first chairman, was murdered by the IRA in Lisburn. The party is currently represented at the Northern Ireland Forum for Peace and Reconciliation by Gary McMichael and John White, a former loyalist prisoner.

NORTHERN IRELAND POLITICAL LEADERS

Leaders of major Northern Ireland political parties, 1921 - 1996

ULSTER UNIONIST PARTY		PROVISIONAL SINN FÉIN	
Sir James Craig	(1921 - 1940)	Tomás MacGiolla	(1962 - 1970)
John Miller Andrews	(1940 - 1943)	Ruairí O'Brádaigh	(1970 - 1983)
Sir Basil Brooke	(1943 - 1963)	Gerry Adams	(1983 -)
Capt. Terence O'Neill	(1963 - 1969)	**ALLIANCE PARTY**	
Sir James Chichester-Clark	(1969 - 1971)	Phelim O'Neill	(1970 - 1972)
Brian Faulkner	(1971 - 1974)	Oliver Napier	(1972 - 1984)
Harry West	(1974 - 1979)	John Cushnahan	(1984 - 1987)
James Molyneaux	(1979 - 1995)	John Alderdice	(1987 -)
David Trimble	(1995 -)		
		UNITED KINGDOM UNIONISTS	
		Bob McCartney	(1995 -)
DEMOCRATIC UNIONIST PARTY			
Rev. Ian Paisley	(1971 -)	**PROGRESSIVE UNIONIST PARTY**	
		David Irvine	(1994 -)
SOCIAL DEMOCRATIC AND LABOUR PARTY		**ULSTER DEMOCRATIC PARTY**	
Gerry Fitt	(1970 - 1979)	Gary McMichael	(1995 -)
John Hume	(1979 -)		

GENERAL ELECTION RESULTS 1992

Northern Ireland General Election Results, 9th April 1992

ANTRIM EAST
Seats: 1; Candidates: 5; Electorate: 62,864; Turnout: 62.44%; Elected: John Robert (Roy) Beggs (UUP) 16,966; Other Candidates: Nigel Dodds (DUP) 9,544; Seán Neeson (A) 9,132; Myrtle Boal (Con) 3,359; Andrea Palmer (NLP) 250.

ANTRIM NORTH
Seats: 1; Candidates: 6; Electorate: 69,114; Turnout: 65.83%; Elected: Rev. Ian Richard Kyle Paisley (DUP) 23,152; Other Candidates: Joseph Alexander Gatson (UUP) 8,216; Seán Nial Farren (SDLP) 6,512; Gareth Williams (A) 3,442; Thomas Richard Sowler (Con) 2,263; James Kevin McGarry (SF) 1,916.

ANTRIM SOUTH
Seats: 1; Candidates: 5; Electorate: 67,192; Turnout: 62.91%; Elected: Clifford Forsythe (UUP) 29,956; Other Candidates: Séamus Donovan McClelland (SDLP) 5,397; John Blair (A) 5,254; Henry John Cushinan (SF) 1,220; Denis Dino-Martin (Ind RLOFP) 442.

BELFAST EAST
Seats: 1; Candidates: 7; Electorate: 52,869; Turnout: 67.70%; Elected: Peter Robinson (DUP) 18,437; Other Candidates: John Thomas Alderdice (A) 10,650; David Greene (Con) 3,314; Dorothy Dunlop (Ind U) 2,256; Joseph O'Donnell (SF) 679; Joseph Bell (WP) 327; Guy Reddan (NLP) 128.

BELFAST NORTH
Seats: 1; Candidates: 8; Electorate: 55,068; Turnout: 65.22%; Elected: Alfred Cecil Walker (UUP) 17,240; Other Candidates: Alban Maginess (SDLP) 7,615; Patrick McManus (SF) 4,693; Thomas Campbell (A)

2,246; Margaret Redpath (Con) 2,107; Séamus Lynch (NA) 1,386; Margaret Smith (WP) 419; David O'Leary (NLP) 208.

BELFAST SOUTH
Seats: 1; Candidates: 8; Electorate: 52,050; Turnout: 64.52%; Elected: Rev. William Martin Smyth (UUP) 16,336; Other Candidates: Alasdair McDonnell (SDLP) 6,266; John Montgomery (A) 5,054; Leonard Fee (Con) 3,356; Seán Hayes (SF) 1,123; Peter Hadden (Lab & TU) 875; Patrick Lynn (WP) 362; Teresa Mullen (NLP) 212.

BELFAST WEST
Seats: 1; Candidates: 5; Electorate: 54,644; Turnout: 73.15%; Elected: Joseph Gerard Hendron (SDLP) 17,415; Other Candidates: Gerard Adams (SF) 16,826; Fred Cobain (UUP) 4,766; John Terence Lowry (WP) 750; Michael Kennedy (NLP) 213.

DOWN NORTH
Seats: 1; Candidates: 5; Electorate: 68,662; Turnout: 65.47%; Elected: James Alexander Kilfedder (Pop U) 19,305; Other Candidates: Laurence Kennedy (Con) 14,371; Addie Morrow (A) 6,611; Denis Vitty (DUP) 4,414; Andrew Wilmot (NLP) 255.

DOWN SOUTH
Seats: 1; Candidates: 5; Electorate: 76,186; Turnout: 80.82%; Elected: Edward Kevin McGrady (SDLP) 31,523; Other Candidates: Drew Nelson (UUP) 25,181; Seán Fitzpatrick (SF) 1,843; Michael Healy (A) 1,542; Jane MacKenzie-Hill (Con) 1,488.

FERMANAGH & SOUTH TYRONE
Seats: 1; Candidates: 6;

Electorate: 70,253; Turnout: 78.47%; Elected: Kenneth Maginnis (UUP) 26,923; Other Candidates: Thomas Gallagher (SDLP) 12,810; Francis Molloy (SF) 12,604; David Alan Kettyles (Prog Soc) 1,094; Eric Bullick (A) 950; Gerard Cullen (NA) 747.

FOYLE
Seats: 1; Candidates: 6; Electorate: 74,673; Turnout: 69.49%; Elected: John Hume (SDLP) 26,710; Other Candidates: Gregory Lloyd Campbell (DUP) 13,705; James Martin McGuinness (SF) 9,149; Lara McIlroy (A) 1,390; Gordon McKenzie (WP) 514; John Burns (NLP) 422.

LAGAN VALLEY
Seats: 1; Candidates: 6; Electorate: 72,708; Turnout: 67.33%; Elected: James Henry Molyneaux (UUP) 29,772; Other Candidates: Séamus Anthony Close (A) 6,207; Hugh Lewsley (SDLP) 4,626; Timothy Coleridge (Con) 4,423; Patrick Joseph Rice (SF) 3,346; Ann-Marie Lowry (WPO) 582.

LONDONDERRY EAST
Seats: 1; Candidates: 5; Electorate: 75,576; Turnout: 69.38%; Elected: William Ross (UUP) 30,070; Other Candidates: Arthur Doherty (SDLP) 11,843; Pauline Davey-Kennedy (SF) 5,320; Patrick Joseph McGowan (A) 3,613; Alan Edward Elder (Con) 1,589.

MID-ULSTER
Seats: 1; Candidates: 8; Electorate: 69,138; Turnout: 78.34%; Elected: Rev. Robert Thomas William McCrea (DUP) 23,181; Other Candidates: Patrick Denis Haughey (SDLP) 16,994; Barry McElduff (SF) 10,248; John McLoughlin (Ind) 1,996; Anne

Gormley (A) 1,506; Harry Hutchinson (Lab & TU) 89; Thomas Owens (WP) 85; James Anderson (NLP) 64.

NEWRY & ARMAGH

Seats: 1; **Candidates:** 4; **Electorate:** 67,531; **Turnout:** 77.85%; **Elected:** Séamus Frederick Mallon (SDLP) 26,073; **Other Candidates:** James Alexander Speers (UUP) 18,982; Brendan Curran (SF) 6,547; Eileen Bell (A) 972.

STRANGFORD

Seats: 1; **Candidates:** 5; **Electorate:** 68,901; **Turnout:** 65%; **Elected:** John David Taylor (UUP) 19,517; **Other Candidates:** Samuel Wilson (DUP) 10,606; Kieran McCarthy (A) 7,585; Stephen Eyre (Con) 6,782; David Shaw (NLP) 295.

UPPER BANN

Seats: 1; **Candidates:** 6; **Electorate:** 67,460; **Turnout:** 67.42%; **Elected:** William David Trimble (UUP) 26,824; **Other Candidates:** Bríd Rodgers (SDLP) 10,661; Brendan Curran (SF) 2,777; William Ramsay (A) 2,541; Collette Jones (Con) 1,556; Thomas French (WP) 1,120.

BY-ELECTION RESULTS SINCE 1992

NORTH DOWN (15 June 1995)
Reason for Election: Death of Sir James Kilfedder; **Seats:** 1; **Candidates:** 8; **Electorate:** 70,892; **Turnout:** 38.75%; **Elected:** Bob McCartney (UKUP) 10,124; **Other Candidates:** Alan McFarland (UUP) 7,232; Sir Oliver Napier (ALL) 6,970; A. Chambers (Ind. U) 2,170; Stuart Sexton (Con) 583; M. Brookes (Free Lee Clegg) 108; C. Carter (Ulster's Ind. Voice) 101; J. Anderson (NLP) 100.

NORTHERN IRELAND PARTIES

Key to Political Parties in Northern Ireland

UUP	Ulster Unionist Party	**ALL**	Aliance Party
SDLP	Social Democratic and Labour Party	**PUP**	Progressive Unionist Party
DUP	Democratic Unionist Party	**UDP**	Ulster Democratic Party
UKUP	United Kingdom Unionist Party	**NIWC**	Northern Ireland Womens Coalition
SF	Sinn Féin	**LAB**	Labour

CURRENT POSITION OF THE PARTIES

U.U.P. 10	S.D.L.P 4	D.U.P. 2	U.K.U. 1

Northern Ireland Members of Parliament

Northern Ireland is divided into 17 constituencies, each of which return one member to the House of Commons at Westminster, London.

Roy Beggs: (UUP), 9 Carnduff Road, Ballyvernstown, Larne, Co. Antrim BT40 3NJ (Antrim East).

Rev. Dr. Ian Paisley (DUP), 17 Cyprus Avenue, Belfast BT5 5NT (Antrim North).

Clifford Forsythe (UUP), 15 Ballyclare Road, Templepatrick, Ballyclare, Co. Antrim (Antrim South)

Peter Robinson (DUP), 51 Gransha Road, Dundonald, Belfast BT16 OHB (Belfast East).

Cecil Walker (UUP), 1 Wynnland Road, Newtownabbey, Co. Antrim. (Belfast North).

Rev. Martin Smyth (UUP), 6 Mornington, Annadale Avenue, Belfast BT7 3JS (Belfast South)

Dr. Joe Hendron (SDLP), 40 Bristow Park, Belfast BT9 6JT. (Belfast West).

Robert McCartney (UKP). (Down North).

Eddie McGrady (SDLP), Cois-na-Cille, 27 Saul Brae, Downpatrick, Co. Down. (Down South).

Ken Maginnis (UUP), 1 Park Lane, Ballynorthland Demesne, Dungannon, Co. Tyrone. (Fermanagh and South Tyrone).

John Hume (SDLP), 6 West End Park, Derry BT48 9JF (Foyle)

James Molyneaux (UUP), 41 Ballynadrentagh Road, Aldergrove, Crumlin, Co. Antrim BT29 4AR (Lagan Valley).

William Ross (UUP), 89 Teevan Road, Turnmeel, Dungiven, Co. Derry. (Londonderry East).

Rev. William McCrea (UUP), 10 Highfield Road, Magherafelt, Co. Derry BT45 6JD (Mid Ulster)

Seamus Mallon (SDLP), 5 Castleview Road, Markethill, Co. Armagh BT60 1QP (Newry and Armagh)

John Taylor (UUP), Mullinure, Co. Armagh BT61 9EL (Strangford)

David Trimble (UUP), 32 Richmond Court, Lisburn, Co. Antrim. (Upper Bann)

NORTHERN IRELAND ELECTIONS

Northern Ireland Elections to Westminster, 1922 - 1974

Date	No. of seats	U	N	Ind. U	Ind. Lab	Ir. Lab.	S.F.	Rep. Lab	Unity	Prot. U	DUP	VUP
15 Nov. 1922	13	11	2									
06 Dec. 1923	13	11	2									
29 Oct. 1924	13	13										
30 May 1929	13	11	2									
27 Oct. 1931	13	11	2									
14 Nov. 1935	13	11	2									
05 July 1945	13	9	2	1		1						
23 Feb. 1950	12	10	2									
25 Oct. 1951	12	9	2				1					
26 May 1955	12	10					2					
08 Oct. 1959	12	12										
15 Oct. 1964	12	12										
31 Mar. 1966	12	11						1				
18 June 1970	12	8						1	2	1		
28 Feb. 1974	12	7	1*								1	3

* S.D.L.P.

Northern Ireland Elections to Westminster, 1974 - 1992

Date	No. of seats	OUP	DUP	VUP	SDLP	UNITY	Ind. U	Ind. R	SF	Pop. U
10 October 1974	12	6	1	3	1	1				
03 May 1979	12	5	3		1		2	1		
09 June 1983	17	11	3		1				1	1
11 June 1987	17	9	3		3				1	1
09 April 1992	17	9	3		4					1

Key to abbreviations: (U) Unionist, (N) Nationalist, (VUP) Vanguard Unionist Progressive Party, (Pop. U) Ulster Popular Unionist Party.

Changing State of the Parties, 1983 - 1996 (%)

Party	Percentage share of valid vote among major parties								
	General 1983	Euro 1984	General 1987	Local 1989	Euro 1989	General 1992	Local 1993	Euro 1994	Forum 1996
UUP	34	21	38	31	22	35	29	24	24.2
SDLP	18	22	21	21	25	23	22	29	21.4
DUP	20	34	12	18	30	13	17	29	18.8
SF	13	13	11	11	9	10	12	10	15.5
ALLIANCE	8	5	10	7	5	9	7	4	6.5

Parliament of Northern Ireland, 1921 - 1973

Year	No. of seats	U	N	S.F.	Ind. R	Ind. U	NILP	Ind.	Ind. FF	Ind. UA	Soc. Lab	Rep.	CWLP	Ir. Lab.	Rep. Lab.	Ind. A.P.	N.	Lib.	NDP
1921	52	40	6	6															
1925	52	32	10	2		4	3	1											
1929	52	38	11			3													
1933	52	36	9		1	3	2	1											
1938	52	39	8			2	1	1			1								
1945	52	33	10			2	2	2			1		1	1					
1949	52	37	9			2		2			1		1						
1953	52	38	7			1		1			1			1	1	2			
1958	52	37	7				4	1						1	1		1		
1962	52	35	9				4	1						1	1		1		
1965	52	36	9				2	1							2			1	1
1969	52	39	6				2	3							2				

Northern Ireland Forum Election, May 1996

Party	Votes	% of total valid vote	Seats won	Party Representatives
Ulster Unionists	181,829	24.17	30	John Gorman, Anthony Alcock
SDLP	160,786	21.37	21	Jonathon Stephenson, Donita Field
DUP	141,413	18.80	24	Gregory Campbell, Eric Smyth
Sinn Fein	116,377	15.47	17	Luciletta Bhreatnach, Pat Doherty
Alliance Party	49,176	6.54	7	Seamus Close, Eileen Bell
U.K. Unionist Party	27,774	3.69	3	Cedric Wilson, Conor Cruise O'Brien
Progressive Unionists Party	26,082	3.47	2	Hugh Smyth, David Ervine
Ulster Democratic Party	16,715	2.22	2	Gary McMichael, John White
NIWC	7,731	1.03	2	Monica McWilliams, Pearl Sagar
Labour	6,425	0.85	2	Malachi Curran, Hugh Casey
Total No. of seats			110	

Total electorate: 1,166,104. Total poll: 754,296. Turnout 64.69 per cent.
Spoiled votes: 1,908. Total valid poll: 752,388

EUROPEAN PARLIAMENT

Northern Ireland Members of the European Parliament *(by political allegiance)*

Northern Ireland returns three MEP's. The total electorate in the twelve member states (June 1994) was 265.7 million of whom 145 million excercised their eligibility to vote. This accounts for a 56.8 per cent turn out.

Democratic Unionist Party/Independent
Ian Paisley
SDLP/Party of European Socialists
John Hume

Ulster Unionist Party/European People's Party
Jim Nicholson

Northern Ireland European Parliament Elections, 1979 - 1994

Year	Total No. of seats	SDLP seats	OUP seats	DUP seats
1979	3	1	1	1
1984	3	1	1	1
1989	3	1	1	1
1994	3	1	1	1

NORTHERN IRELAND PRIME MINISTERS

Statistics on Northern Ireland Prime Ministers

No.	Name	Politics	Born	in	Appoint.	at age	Died	at age
1	Sir James Craig	UUP	1871	Belfast	June 1921	50	1940	69
2	John M. Andrews	UUP	1871	Co. Down	Nov. 1940	69	1956	85
3	Sir Basil Brooke	UUP	1888	Co. Fermanagh	May 1943	55	1973	85
4	Capt. Terence O'Neill	UUP	1914	London	March 1963	49	1990	76
5	James Chichester-Clark	UUP	1923	Co. Derry	May 1969	46		
6	Brian Faulkner	UUP	1921	Co. Down	March 1971	50	1977	56

Biographies of Northern Ireland Prime Ministers, 1921 - 1972

SIR JAMES CRAIG (1921- 1940)
Sir James Craig was Prime Minister of Northern Ireland from June 1921 until November 1940.

Born in Belfast in 1871, the young Craig became a stockbroker and fought with the British during the Boer War. His leadership qualities were evident from an early age. He was instrumental in representing the Unionist viewpoint which strongly opposed the introduction of Home Rule for Ireland. The Protestant majority in the north rejected any moves for the formation of an Irish state in which they would become a small minority. The Protestants of northern Ireland organised themselves into an armed volunteer group, the UVF (Ulster Volunteer Force) in 1912, led by the leader of the Ulster Unionists, Edward Carson and in which Craig played an important role. The Unionist card worked: Ireland seemed to be on the brink of civil war, and the British Government excluded Ulster from the terms of the Third Home Rule Bill in September 1914.

The UVF later fought in France during the 1st World War under the name of the 36th Ulster Division, with Craig as quartermaster-general of the division.

A leading contributor to the drafting of the Government of Ireland Act in 1920 which provided for subordinate parliaments in Dublin and Belfast, Craig replaced Carson as leader of the Ulster Unionists in February 1921. Following the May 1921 General Election to the parliament of Northern Ireland, the Unionists took 40 of the 52 seats, and when the Northern Ireland House of Commons met for the first time in June of 1921, Craig became the first Prime Minister.

Craig's domination of Northern Ireland politics was total for the next two decades, during which time he presided over the Special Powers Act (April 7, 1922), which give the Northern Ireland authorities virtually unlimited powers of arrest and detention - this was later made permanent in 1933.

Proportional representation was abolished in 1929, and the control of the Unionist majority politically was further enhanced under the direction of Craig by the widespread use of gerrymandering.

On the 24th November 1940, Sir James Craig (Viscount Craigavon) died whist still in office, and was succeeded by James M. Andrews.

JOHN MILLER ANDREWS (1940- 1943)

John Miller Andrews was Prime Minister of Northern Ireland from November 1940, succeeding Sir James Craig, and led the Stormont Government until May 1943.

Born in Cumber, Co. Down in 1871, Andrews was a successful businessman with the family linen-bleaching company, and was also a director of the Belfast Ropeworks. He was returned unopposed as the Unionist M.P. for County Down in every election from 1921 onwards. He held two ministerial portfolios in the Craig cabinet, Minister of Labour from 1921-1937, and Minister for Finance from 1937 until he succeeded Craig in November 1940.

He resigned as Prime Minister on the 28th April 1943, and was succeeded by Sir Basil Brooke.

SIR BASIL BROOKE (1943- 1963)

Sir Basil Brooke was Prime Minister of Northern Ireland from May 1943 until March 1963.

Born in Fermanagh in 1888, Brooke had a military background, and went on to receive the Military Cross and the Croix de Guerre for distinguished service with the British Forces during World War 1.

First elected to the Northern Ireland Senate in 1921, Brooke stepped down shortly after to take over the reins of the Ulster Special Constabulary, and played a leading role in their ongoing fight with the IRA in Northern Ireland.

He was elected Unionist MP for Fermanagh in 1929, and became Minister for Agriculture in Craig's cabinet in 1933. He was also Minister of Commerce and Production from 1941 until he succeeded J.M. Miller in 1943 as Prime Minister. During his two decades in office he fostered strong links between the Northern Ireland government and the Orange Order, of which he was a prominent senior member. In the latter years of his term of office the Northern Ireland authorities had to deal with the IRA border campaign of 1956-62, and nationalist protests at ongoing discrimination.

CAPTAIN TERENCE O'NEILL (1963-1969)

Captain Terence O'Neill was Prime Minister of Northern Ireland from March 1963 until April 1969.

Born in London in 1914, he was the son of the Unionist MP for Mid-Antrim, Arthur O'Neill. The young O'Neill's early years were spent in some privilege in London. He went to school at Eton College in Berkshire where many of England's most illustrious men were educated.

O'Neill opted for a military career and during the Second World War served in the Irish Guards in France, Belgium and the Netherlands. Following the Allied victory O'Neill moved to Northern Ireland in 1945, and the following year was elected unopposed as Unionist MP for Bannside.

He was Parliamentary Secretary in Brooke's government from 1948, and handled the ministerial brief of Finance from 1956 onwards.

Following his succession of Brooke as Prime Minister in 1963, O'Neill proved to be less hardline than any of his three predecessors. He actively sought to improve relations with the Catholic/nationalist community in the province, and with the Irish Republic. In April 1965 he hosted the Irish Taoiseach, Seán Lemass in Belfast, and made a return visit to Dublin on 9th February. O'Neill's policies were vigorously opposed by hardline Unionists.   His position was further complicated in January 1967 with the formation of the Northern Ireland Civil Rights Association, who were demanding an end to discrimination in housing, jobs, in the enforcement of law and order, and the continuance of gerrymandering.

Northern Ireland spiralled into chaos as the Civil Rights campaign which had gained momentum in 1968 and '69 was met with strong opposition from the RUC and a number of right wing politicians. O'Neill responded by conceding to the NICRA's demand for 'one man one vote', but lost the support of three cabinet members - Craig, Faulkner and Morgan. O'Neill himself almost lost his seat to his most bitter critic Ian Paisley in the February 1969 election, and on the 28th of April that year he resigned as Prime Minister.

JAMES CHICHESTER CLARKE (1969-1971)

Major James Chichester Clarke was Prime Minister of Northern Ireland from May 1969 until March 1971.

Born in Castledawson, Co. Derry in 1923, Clarke - like his predecessor and cousin, Terence O'Neill - was educated at Eton College in Berkshire, England. After a career in the British Army, Chichester-Clarke moved into politics in 1960 when he was elected Unionist MP for South Derry, taking the seat vacated by his grandmother, Dehra Parker who had been a Unionist MP since 1921.

Chief Whip of the Unionist Party from 1963 until

1969, Leader of the House from 1966-67, and Minister for Agriculture from 1967 to 1969, Chichester-Clarke was opposed to the attempted reforms of Captain Terence O'Neill and resigned from his cabinet.

When O'Neill resigned in April 1969, Chichester-Clarke replaced him and became Prime Minister during an era of unrivalled tension in Northern Ireland. Rioting and violence exploded across the North, and following extensive trouble in Belfast in early August 1969, Chichester-Clarke requested British Troops in an attempt to stem the situation. His request was granted and on August 15th British troops moved in.

The situation continued to deteriorate, and by 1970 the IRA were becoming established. The first British soldier killed in Belfast on February 6th. Chichester-Clarke was caught in the no-man's land of being unable to control the rapidly worsening situation in Northern Ireland and being unwilling to attempt to make the necessary reforms.

On the 20th March 1970 Chichester-Clarke (Lord Moyola) resigned as Prime Minister.

BRIAN FAULKNER (1971-1972)

Brian Faulkner was Prime Minister of Northern Ireland from March 1971 until March 1972.

Born in Helen's Bay, Co. Down in 1921, Faulkner was educated at St. Columba's College in Dublin. He was involved in Northern Ireland politics from an early age, and when he was elected as the Unionist MP for East Down on 10th February 1949 he became the youngest member of the Northern Ireland parliament.

Chief Whip from 1956, he held the Ministerial portfolio of Home Affairs in Brooke's cabinet, and in 1963 became Minister for Commerce under Terence O'Neill.

Faulkner was deeply opposed to granting concessions of any nature to the Northern Ireland Civil Rights Association, and following attempts at reform by Prime Minister O'Neill he resigned in January 1969

Following his succession of Chichester-Clarke as Prime Minister, Faulkner oversaw the re-introduction of internment without trial in August 1971, and earlier had announced that soldiers could shoot-to-kill on the streets of Northern Ireland on grounds of suspicion alone. During his term of office civil unrest reached unprecedented levels with the emergence of Protestant paramilitaries, particularly the Ulster Defence Assocation and the Ulster Volunteer Force who, enraged at I.R.A. actions, engaged in sectarian killings. On 30th January 1972 Bloody Sunday occurred in Derry city, when British Troops shot dead fourteen people and seriously injured seventeen others resulting in the violence by state and civilian population reaching new levels.

The Northern Ireland government was now coming under increasing pressure from Westminster to concede to power-sharing or direct rule, and on 24th March 1972, following the resignation of Faulkner and his cabinet, direct rule from London was introduced.

Brian Faulkner (Lord Faulkner) died in a riding accident on the 3rd March 1977, aged 56.

GOVERNMENTS OF NORTHERN IRELAND

Northern Ireland Governments, 1921- 1972

MINISTERS FOR AGRICULTURE

Prime Minister	Minister	Appointed
Craig	E. M. Archdale	1921
Craig	Sir B. Brooke	1933
Andrews	Lord Glentoran	1941
Brooke	R. Moore	1943
Brooke	H. W. West	1960
O'Neill	J. Chichester-Clark	1967
Chichester-Clark	P. R. H. O'Neill	1969

MINISTERS FOR COMMERCE

Prime Minister	Minister	Appointed
Craig	J. M. Barbour	1925
Andrews	Sir B. Brooke	1941
Brooke	Sir R. T. Nugent	1943
Brooke	W. V. McCleerey	1949
Brooke	Lord Glentoran	1953
Brooke	J. L. O. Andrews	1961
O'Neill	A. B. D. Faulkner	1963
Chichester-Clark	P. R. H. O'Neill	1969
Chichester-Clark	R. H. Bradford	1969
Faulkner	R. J. Bailie	1971

MINISTERS FOR DEVELOPMENT

Prime Minister	Minister	Appointed
O'Neill	W. Craig	1965
O'Neill	W. K. Fitzsimmons	1966
O'Neill	I. Neill	1968
Chichester-Clark	W. J. Long	1969

Chichester-Clark	A. B. D. Faulkner	1969
Faulkner	R. H. Bradford	1971

MINISTERS FOR COMMUNITY RELATIONS

Prime Minister	Minister	Appointed
Faulkner	D. Bleakley	1971
Faulkner	W. B. McIvor	1971

MINISTERS FOR EDUCATION

Prime Minister	Minister	Appointed
Craig	Lord Londonderry	1921
Craig	Lord Charlemont	1927
Craig	J. H. Robb	1933
Brooke	Rev. R. Corkey	1943
Brooke	S. H. Hall-Thompson	1944
Brooke	H. Midgley	1952
Brooke	W. M. May	1957
Brooke	I. Neill	1962
O'Neill	H. V. Kirk	1964
O'Neill	W. J. Long	1966
O'Neill	W. K. Fitzsimmons	1968
Chichester-Clark	P. R. H. O'Neill	1969
Chichester-Clark	W. J. Long	1969

MINISTERS FOR FINANCE

Prime Minister	Minister	Appointed
Craig	H. M. Pollock	1921
Craig	J. M. Andrews	1937
Andrews	J. M. Barbour	1941

Brooke	J. M. Sinclair	1943
Brooke	W. B. Maginess	1953
Brooke	G. B. Hanna	1956
Brooke	T. O'Neill	1956
O'Neill	J. L. O. Andrews	1963
O'Neill	H. V. Kirk	1965

MINISTERS FOR HEALTH

Prime Minister	Minister	Appointed
Brooke	W. Grant	1944
Brooke	Dame Dehra Parker	1949
Brooke	J. L. O. Andrews	1957
Brooke	W. J. Morgan	1961
O'Neill	W. Craig	1964
O'Neill	W. J. Morgan	1965
Chichester-Clark	R. W. Porter	1969
Chichester-Clark	W. K. Fitzsimmons	1969

MINISTERS FOR HOME AFFAIRS

Prime Minister	Minister	Appointed
Craig	R. D. Bates	1921
Brooke	W. Lowry	1943
Brooke	J. E. Warnock	1944
Brooke	W. B. Maginnes	1945
Brooke	G. B. Hanna	1953
Brooke	T. O'Neill	1956
Brooke	W. W. B. Topping	1956
Brooke	A. B. D. Faulkner	1959
O'Neill	W. Craig	1963
O'Neill	R. W. McConnell	1964
O'Neill	W. Craig	1966
O'Neill	W. J. Long	1968

| Chichester-Clark | R. W. Porter | 1969 |

MINISTERS FOR LABOUR

Prime Minister	Minister	Appointed
Craig	J. M. Andrews	1921
Craig	D. G. Shillington	1937
Craig	J. F. Gordan	1939
Brooke	W. Grant	1943
Brooke	W. B. Maginess	1945
Brooke	H. Midgley	1949
Brooke	I. Neill	1951
Brooke	H. V. Kirk	1962
O'Neil	W. J. Morgan	1964

MINISTERS FOR PUBLIC SECURITY

Prime Minister	Minister	Appointed
Andrews	W. Grant	1941
Andrews	H. Midgley	1942

NORTHERN IRELAND SECRETARIES OF STATE

1972-1973	William Whitelaw
1973-1974	Francis Pym
1974-1977	Merlyn Rees
1977-1979	Roy Mason
1979-1981	Humphrey Atkins
1981-1983	Jim Prior
1983-1985	Douglas Hurd
1985-1989	Tom King
1989-1992	Peter Brooke
1992 -	Patrick Mayhew

LORD LIEUTENANTS & CHIEF SECRETARIES OF IRELAND

Lord Lieutenants 1800 - 1921

1800-1801	Lord Cornwallis
1801-1806	3rd Earl of Hardwicke
1806-1807	6th Earl of Bedford
1807-1813	4th Duke of Richmond
1813-1817	Viscount Whitworth
1817-1821	1st Earl Talbot of Hensol
1821-1828	Richard Colley Wellesley, Marquess
1828-1829	1st Marquess of Anglesey
1829-1830	3rd Duke of Northumberland
1830-1833	1st Marquess of Anglesey
1833-1834	Richard Colley Wellesley
1834-1835	9th Earl of Haddington
1835-1839	2nd Earl of Mulgrave
1839-1841	Chichester Fortescue-Parkinson, Baron Carlingford
1841-1844	Thomas Philip de Gray, 1st Earl
1844-1846	2nd Baron Heytesbury
1846-1847	4th Earl of Bessborough
1847-1852	4th Earl of Clarendon
1852-1853	13th Earl of Eglinton
1853-1855	3rd Earl of St. Germans
1855-1858	7th Earl of Carlisle
1858-1859	13th Earl of Eglinton
1859-1864	7th Earl of Carlisle
1864-1866	John Wodehouse, 1st Earl of Kimberley
1866-1868	1st Duke of Abercorn
1868-1874	John Poyntz Spencer, 5th Earl
1874-1876	1st Duke of Abercorn
1876-1880	7th Duke of Marlborough
1880-1882	7th Earl of Cowper
1882-1885	John Poyntz Spencer, 5th Earl
1885-1886	4th Earl of Carnarvon
1886-1886	1st Marquess of Aberdeen
1886-1889	6th Marquess of Londonderry
1889-1892	3rd Earl of Zetland
1892-1895	1st Marquess of Crewe
1895-1902	5th Earl of Cadogan
1902-1905	2nd Earl of Dudley
1905-1915	1st Marquess of Aberdeen
1915-1918	2nd Baron Wimborne
1918-1921	1st Earl French of Ypres
1921	1st Viscount FitzAlan of Derwent

Chief Secretaries 1800 - 1920

1800-1801	Lord Castlereagh
1801-1802	Charles Abbot
1802-1804	William Wickham
1804-1805	Sir Evan Nepean
1805-1805	Sir Nicholas Vansittart
1805-1806	Charles Lang
1806-1807	William Elliot
1807-1809	Arthur Wellesley
1809-1812	William Wellesley-Pole
1812-1818	Sir Robert Peel

1818-1821	Charles Grant
1821-1827	Henry Goulbourn
1827-1828	William Lamb
1828-1830	Francis Levenson Gower
1830-1830	Sir Henry Hardinge
1830-1833	Lord Stanley
1833-1833	Sir John Cam Hobhouse
1833-1834	Edward John Littleton
1834-1835	Sir Henry Hardinge
1835-1841	Viscount Morpeth
1841-1845	Lord Eliot
1845-1846	Baron Cottosloe
1846-1846	Earl of Lincoln
1846-1847	Henry Labouchere
1847-1852	Sir William Somerville
1852-1853	Lord Naas
1853-1855	Sir John Young
1855-1857	Edward Horsman
1857-1858	Henry A. Herbert
1858-1859	Lord Naas
1859-1861	Edward Cardwell
1861-1865	Sir Robert Peel
1865-1866	Chichester Fortescue-Parkinson
1866-1868	Lord Naas
1868-1868	Lord Winmarleigh
1868-1870	Lord Carlingford
1870-1874	Marquis of Hartington
1874-1878	Sir Michael E. Hicks-Beach
1878-1880	James Lowther
1880-1882	W. E. Forster
1882-1882	Lord Freederick Cavendish
1882-1884	Sir G. O. Trevelyan
1884-1885	Henry Campbell-Bannerman
1885-1886	Sir W. Hart Dyke
1886-1886	W. H. Smith
1886-1886	John Morley
1886-1887	Sir M. E. Hicks-Beach
1887-1891	Arthur J. Balfour
1891-1892	William Lawless Jackson
1892-1895	John Morley
1895-1900	Gerald W. Balfour
1900-1905	George Wyndham
1905-1905	Walter Hume Long
1905-1907	James Bryce
1907-1916	Augustine Birrell
1916-1918	H. E. Dyke
1918-1919	Edward Shortt
1919-1920	Ian McPherson
1920	Sir Hamar Greenwood

SELECTED BIOGRAPHIES OF POLITICAL FIGURES

Adams, Gerry (b. 1948, Belfast). President of Sinn Féin since 1983. Interned in 1970's. Major playmaker in bringing about IRA Ceasefire of August 1994. Noted writer, works include *Falls Memories* and *Cage Eleven*.

Ahearn, Bertie (b. 1951, Dublin). Leader of Fianna Fáil, Ireland's largest political party, since 1994. Member of Dáil Éireann since 1977.

Alderdice, John (b. 1955). Leader of Alliance Party in Northern Ireland since 1987. Awarded life peerage to British House of Lords in August 1996.

Cruise O'Brien, Dr. Conor (b. 1917). Writer and sometime politician. Member of Dáil Éireann from 1969 to 1977. As Minister for Posts and Telegraphs, introduced selective broadcasting ban 'Section 31'. Despite failing to be elected to the Northern Ireland forum, is a member of the UK Unionist Party delegation to the multi-party talks. Published many books including *States of Ireland* (1972) and *To Katanga and Back* (1962). Regular and controversial contributor to *The Sunday Independent*.

de Rossa, Proinnsias (b. 1940, Dublin). Minister for Social Welfare, leader of Democratic Left, formerly leader of Workers Party from which he led 1992 split.

Dukes, Alan (b. 1945). Fine Gael T.D. since 1981. Minister for Agriculture and Finance. Leader of Fine Gael before John Bruton.

Flynn, Pádraig (b. 1939, Mayo). Ireland's Commissioner to the E.U. Holds the Social Affairs Portfolio. Former Fianna Fáil Minister.

Harney, Mary (b. 1953, Galway). Leader of the Progressive Democrats. Former Minister for State. First female leader of an Irish political party.

Hume, John (b. 1937, Derry). Leader of Northern Ireland's Social and Democratic Labour Party. One of the most influential MEP's in Europe. Enjoys respect of Clinton administration in United States. Instrumental figure in bringing about IRA ceasefire of 1994.

Mayhew, Patrick (b. 1929). Secretary of State for Northern Ireland, in office when the IRA Ceasefire came into being. A member of the Conservative Party, has announced his intention to retire at the next election.

McAliskey, Bernadette Devlin (b. 1947, Tyrone). Elected MP for Mid-Ulster at age of 21. Northern Ireland Civil Rights campaigner. Survived Loyalist gun attack.

McGuinness, Martin (b. 1950, Derry). Noted republican leader who played a key role in getting the IRA Ceasefire in August 1994. Was Sinn Féin's chief negotiator in talks with British officials during 1995. Has consistently denied being Chief-of-Staff of IRA.

Paisley, Rev. Ian (b. 1926, Armagh). Leader of the Democratic Unionist Party and Moderator of the Free Presbyterian Church. One of the most controversial politicians in Europe.

Quinn, Ruairí (b. 1946, Dublin). Government Minister. First elected as Labour T.D. in 1977, lost his seat in 1981 but regained it in 1982 and has held it since. Deputy Leader of the Labour Party, and current Minister for Finance.

Spring, Dick (b. 1950, Tralee). Tánaiste. Member of Dáil for Kerry North since 1981. Leader of Labour Party since 1982, current Tánaiste and Minister for Foreign Affairs. Previously held ministerial portfolios of Energy and the Environment. Former Rugby International, played inter-county football and hurling with Kerry.

Sutherland, Peter (b. 1946). Former Attorney General. Accomplished rugby player and one of Ireland's foremost lawyers here and abroad. Attorney General in 1983. Irish Commissioner to EEC in 1984.

Trimble, David (b. 1944). Leader of Ulster Unionist Party since late 1995. Elected MP for Upper Bann in 1990, played a prominent role in Orange Order protests in Drumcree in 1995 and 1996 which resulted in widespread unrest across Northern Ireland.

Set in 300 acres, including 50 acres of Lakes, the Slieve Russell Hotel,
Golf and Country Club offers a unique experience in relaxation and leisure
to our guests.

Enjoy excellent cuisine, professional and friendly service in opulent surroundings.
Our superb leisure facilities include swimming pool, saunas, steamroom, jacuzzi,
fitness suite, tennis, squash, snooker, Hair & Beauty Salon, creche and games room.
For the golfer, our 18 Hole Championship Course ensures a challenging game.
Located just 2 hours drive from Dublin city centre, the Slieve Russell Hotel
offers a haven of comfort and relaxation . . . a place where you will wish to return
again and again.

SLIEVE RUSSELL HOTEL
GOLF & COUNTRY CLUB
BALLYCONNELL, CO. CAVAN

Tel: (049) 26444   Fax: (049) 26511

HISTORY

CHRONOLOGY OF IRISH HISTORY

B.C.

680 B.C. Radiocarbon dating for first inhabited enclosure at Navan Fort (Armagh).

130 - 1000 A.D.

130-180 Map of Ireland appears in Ptolemy's Geography.

297 Irish raids on Roman Britain begin, continue until mid-fifth century.

367 Irish, Picts and Saxons stage major raid on Britain.

431 Palladius the first Bishop arrives in Ireland. Sent by Pope Celestine.

432 St. Patrick's mission.

546 Derry founded by St. Colum Cille.

563 Monastery at Iona founded by St. Colum Cille.

575 Convention of Druim Cett (Co. Derry). Agreement between the Christian Church and the quasi pagan fili, or poets.

670-690 Hagiographical,writings on St. Patrick, combining lives of various missionaries especially Palladius. Part of an attempt (which was successful) of Armagh to establish its primacy as heart of the church in Ireland.

795 First Viking Raids on Ireland, continue until 876.

841 Norse Settlement at Dublin and at Louth.

876 Beginning of 'Forty Years Peace', a respite from Viking Attacks. Ends 916.

914 Large Viking fleet arrives at Waterford marks beginning of second wave of viking attacks.

922 Foundation of Viking Settlement at Limerick.

1001 - 1299 A.D.

1014 Battle of Clontarf; High King of Ireland Brian Bóru (1002-14) defeats Vikings decisively but is killed himself.

1028-36 Building of Christ Church Cathedral, Dublin.

1152 Synod of Kells-Mellifont. Diocesan organisation of Church in Ireland; Four Diocese; Armagh enjoys primacy.

1169 Normans arrive in Ireland, at invitation of Diarmait Mac Murchada, an exiled Leinster King, who is subsequently restored to his throne.

1171 Richard de Clare (Stongbow) succeeds Diarmait Mac Murchada.

1204 Dublin Castle established as centre of Royal Administration in Ireland.

1216 (November) Magna Carta issued for Ireland.

THE 1300's

1315 (May) Edward the Bruce lands at Larne.

1316 (May) Edward the Bruce crowned King of Ireland.

1318 Edward the Bruce killed at Battle of Faughart in 1318.

1348 (August) Black Death first appears at Drogheda and Howth.

1366 (February) Parliament at Kilkenny. Statute of Kilkenny enacted, designed to prohibit assimilation of the Anglo-Irish and the Gaelic Irish.

1395 Richard II defeats Leinster Irish. Most Irish Kings and rebel English submit to him.

THE 1400's

1478 Gearóid Mór Fitzgerald, the eighth Earl of Kildare

becomes Lord Deputy (i.e. King's Representative in Ireland). Holds office until his death in 1513.

1494 Parliament at Drogheda. 'Poynings' Law' enacted. All legislation passed by subsequent Irish Parliaments to be approved by the King. Act not amended until 1782.

THE 1500's

1513 Gearóid Óg Fitzgerald, son of Gearóid Mór, becomes Lord Deputy.

1520-4 Kildare loses the Lord deputyship.

1534 (June) Thomas Fitzgerald, 'Silken Thomas', son of Gearóid Óg and now Lord Deputy rebels. Surrenders August 1535 and is executed February 1537.

1534 Gearóid Óg dies in Tower of London.

1541 (June) Act of Irish Parliament declares Henry VIII as 'King of Ireland'.

1547 Death of Henry VIII; Accession of son Edward VI.

1549 (March) 1st English Act of Uniformity orders use of Book of Common Prayer.

1550-7 Plantation in Laois and Offaly.

1553 Death of Edward VI; Accession of Mary I (daughter of Henry VIII).

1558 Death of Mary I; Accession of Elizabeth I (Last of Tudor Line).

1561 Rebellion of Shane O'Neill, caused by a row over succession to the head of the O'Neill clan. He submits to Elizabeth I in January 1562 and returns to Ulster. Was killed June 1567 by McDonnells of Antrim.

1568-1573 First Desmond Rebellion in Munster.

1579-1583 Second Desmond Rebellion in Munster, accompanied by a revolt in Leinster. Earl of Desmond killed 1583.

1582 (February) Pope Gregory XIII reforms the calendar. 04/10/1582 to be followed by 15/10/1582. Year to begin on 1st January.

1585 (December) Plantation scheme put in place for Munster.

1588 (September) Spanish Armada flounders of Irish Coast; 25 ships wrecked.

1595-1603 Rebellion of Hugh O'Neill, Earl of Tyrone and Red Hugh O'Donnell who enlist Spanish support. Ends March 1603 with Treaty of Mellifont.

THE 1600's

1603 (March) Accession of James I (James VI of Scotland) following death of Elizabeth I.

1607 (September) 'Flight of Earls': Earls of Tyrconnell and Tyrone flee from Lough Swilly. All are charged with treason and their lands are forfeited to the British Crown.

1608-10 Plantation of Ulster: Lands forfeited as a result of the 'Flight of Earls' in counties Armagh, Cavan, Derry, Donegal, Fermanagh and Tyrone.

1608 (April-July) Revolt of Sir Cahir O'Doherty, the Last Irish Chieftain. Sacks Derry. Sir Cahir killed in Donegal, rebellion collapses and lands confiscated.

1632 Compilation of the Annals of the Four Masters begins, completed August 1636.

1641 (October) Rising begins in Ulster continues until 1647.

1649 (August) Oliver Cromwell arrives in Dublin.

1649 (September) Cromwell captures Drogheda. Massacres 2,600 soldiers and townspeople. Cromwell

captures Wexford; massacres 2,000 (October 1649).
1652-3 Cromwellian Land confiscation. Land given to Cromwellian Soldiers.
1660 (May) Charles II proclaimed King In Dublin following restoration of the monarchy in England.
1685 (February) Accession of James II following death of Charles II.
1688 Prince William of Orange and his wife Mary (James II's daughter) invited to take the throne of England.
1689 (April) Siege of Derry: Supporters of William of Orange defy Jacobites (i.e. the followers of James II) who lay siege to the city until July 1689. Jacobites defeated at Newtownbutler, Co. Fermanagh, July 1689.
1690 (July) William III defeats James II at River Boyne. James departs for France; 9th August 1690-30th August 1690 First Siege of Limerick.
1691 (July 12) Jacobites defeated at Aughrim. Second siege of Limerick (September - October 1691).
1691-1703 Williamites begin confiscation of land.
1691 (October 25) Treaty of Limerick marks end of war between William III (William of Orange) and James II.
1691 (December) Penal Law begins. Catholics excluded from Parliament, Public Office, being solicitors, teachers, bearing arms, free worship by Act of the English Parliament. Dissenting Protestants also targeted by the Act but retain their property rights and right to sit in parliament.

THE 1700's

1702 (March) William III dies, succeeded by Anne I.
1714 (August) Anne I dies without an Heir, succeeded by George I, first Hanoverian on British Throne.
1718 (June-July) Ulster Scots (largely Presbyterians) begin significant emigration to New England and other American colonies.
1719 (November) Toleration Act passed for dissenting protestants. Legal Toleration of their religion.
1729 (June) George II accedes to the throne following death of George I.
1737 (September 1) First edition of the Belfast Newsletter.
1751 (May) Act passed for reform of Gregorian Calendar (which we still use today). 02/09/1752 to be followed by 14/09/1752.
1760 (March) Catholic Committee founded in Dublin, consisted of urban Catholic middle class and the remainder of the Catholic Aristocracy and lobbied for some of the Penal Laws to be repealed.
1760 (October) George III accedes to the throne on the death of George II.
1778 (March) Founding of the Volunteer Movement in Belfast. Volunteers lobby for Free Trade, Legislative Independence and relaxation of the Penal Laws. The movement is suppressed March 1793.
1782 (May) Act establishes the Bank of Ireland which opens June 1783.
1782 (June) Ireland gains parliamentary independence. "Grattan's Parliament".
1793 (April) Catholic Relief Act: Culmination of relief acts. Catholics now have Parliamentary franchise, can practice as solicitors, can be teachers, guardians, can intermarry with Protestants but are still debarred from Parliament and the higher offices of State (including Judgeships).
1791 (October) Society of United Irishmen founded in Belfast.

1795 (June 5) Act providing for provision of Catholic seminary at Maynooth (Royal College of St. Patrick opens October 1 1795).
1795 (September) Foundations put in place for the future Orange Order.
1798 (May/June) United Irishmen stage rebellion. French Soldiers land in Kilala, Co. Mayo in August.
1798 (November 3) Wolfe Tone captured off Lough Swilly, and sentenced to death.
1798 (November 12) Wolfe Tone commits suicide.

THE 1800's

1801 (January) Union of Great Britain and Ireland begins. Acts have been put in place in Britain (2nd July 1800) and in Ireland (1st August 1800).
1803 (July 23) Rebellion in Dublin, led by Robert Emmet. Emmet executed 20th September 1803.
1814 British Chief Secretary Robert Peel sets up the 'Peace Preservation Police'.
1823 (May) Catholic Association founded. Its membership included, for the first time, all ranks of Catholics. It was the vehicle which helped O'Connell win Catholic Emancipation.
1828 (June) Daniel O'Connell returned as MP in a Clare by-election. Illegal for a Catholic to take a seat in the House of Commons at Westminster.
1829 (April) Catholic Emancipation granted. A relief act allowing Roman Catholics to enter Parliament, belong to a corporation and eligible to hold the high offices of State.
1830 (June) William IV accedes to the throne on the death of George IV.
1831 Beginning of 'Tithe War'.
1831 (November) Scheme for implementation of nationwide primary schooling.
1837 (June) Victoria accedes to the throne on death of William IV.
1838 (April) Fr. Matthew founded the Total Abstinence Movement (pioneers) with help of a quaker, William Martin.
1839 (January 6) Night of the Big Wind (unprecedented gales).
1840 (April) Daniel O'Connell forms National Association to lobby for Repeal of the Act of Union.
1843 (August) Daniel O'Connell holds monster meeting at Hill of Tara, upwards on 1,000,000 attend. Meeting also held at Trim (March 1843) and one due to be held at Clontarf was prevented by the Government (October 1843).
1845 (September) Arrival of the Potato blight reported. Famine continued until 1848, the worst year being 1847 (Black 47).
1845 (July) Queen's Colleges Act, provision for creation of new Colleges.
1848 (July-August) Young Ireland Rising in Munster (July 29 1848); easily suppressed.
1849 (October) Queen's Colleges at Cork, Belfast and Galway opened.
1850 (August) Irish Tenant League founded. A Tenant Farmers Association. It was the forerunner of the Irish National Party.
1854 (November) Catholic University of Ireland (now UCD) opens.
1856 Phoenix Society (a forerunner of the Fenian Movement) founded at Skibbereen by O'Donovan Rossa.
1858 Irish Republican Brotherhood founded in Dublin.

1859 (March) Fenian Brotherhood founded in New York. Closely linked with IRB.
1859 (March 29) First Edition of the Irish Times.
1860-1861 Major evictions in Mayo and at estates of John George Adair at Derryveagh, Co. Donegal.
1867 (February-March) Fenian Rising in Munster and Dublin. Easily suppressed.
1867 (June) Clann na Gael (United Brotherhood) founded in New York.
1870 (May) Isaac Butt launches the Home Rule Movement.
1870 (August) Gladstone's First Land Act - recognises tenant right.
1871 (January) Disestablishment of the Church of Ireland comes into effect. Act had been passed July 1869.
1871 (October) Fenians invade Canada with view of distracting British attention from Ireland.
1872 (July) Secret Voting introduced.
1877 (March) Charles Stewart Parnell becomes leader of the Home Rule Movement.
1879 (October) Irish National Land League founded. Nationwide association to agitate for land reform. Proscribed October 20 1882.
1879-82 Undeclared 'Land War' ensued. Massive increase in rural crime, especially against landlords and land agents.
1881 (August) Gladstone's second Land Act - Fixing of Rents by independents.
1880 (September 25) 'Boycotting' of land agent Charles Boycott begins in Mayo. Tenants refuse to work the land and ostracise him. Continues until November 26 1880.
1882 (May) Chief Secretary and Ulster Secretary (the principal government officials in Ireland) murdered. Known as 'Phoenix Park Murders'. Their killers were tried and executed (April-June 1883).
1882 (October) Irish National League founded. The banned Land League under a new guise.
1884 (November) Gaelic Athletic Association founded in Thurles.
1885 (May) Irish Loyal and Patriotic Union formed. Aimed to defend the Union.
1885 (August) Ashbourne Act. Loans made available to tenants to purchase land.
1886 (June) First Home Rule Bill - defeated in House of Commons.
1890 (December) Parnell ousted from leadership of Irish Parliamentary party after protracted debates. The citing of Parnell as co-respondent in Captain William O'Shea's petition for divorce was unacceptable to elements within the British Liberal party and members of the Catholic hierarchy. Parnell marries Katherine O'Shea June 25 1891.
1891 (March 10) Irish National Federation founded consisting of anti-Parnellites.
1891 (August) Balfour Act (also establishes Congested Districts Board) - Extension of land purchase scheme.
1891 (October 6) Charles Stewart Parnell dies in Brighton. He is succeeded by John Redmond.
1892 (June) Ulster Convention at Belfast. Delegates vote to oppose moves to Home Rule Parliament.
1893 (July) Gaelic League formed.
1893 (September) Second Home Rule Bill - Passes House of Commons, defeated in House of Lords (September 1893).
1894 (April) Trade Union Congress held for first time.

1899 (May) Irish Literary Theatre founded.
1900 - 1909
1901 (January) Accession of Edward VII on death of Queen Victoria.
1903 (August) Wyndam Land Act. Culmination of a series of Land Acts which started in 1870 and saw the change of land ownership, away from landlordship to tenant proprietorship.
1905 (March) Ulster Unionist Council formed to oppose moves towards Home Rule.
1907 (April) Sinn Féin League founded. An amalgamation of a number of nationalist bodies (Name Sinn Féin adopted September 1908).
1907 (July) Theft of Irish Crown Jewels from Dublin Castle. They have never been recovered.
1908 (August) National University of Ireland instituted by the Irish Universities Act. Gave university status to Queens at Belfast and to the colleges included in the old N.U.I. who were mainly Catholic.
1908 (December) Irish Transport and General Workers Union formed by, among others James Larkin.

1910 - 1919
1910 (February) Sir Edward Carson becomes chairman of the Irish Unionist Party.
1911 (August) Abolishes veto powers enjoyed by House of Lords.
1912 (September 28) Ulster Solemn League and Covenant signed. 218,000 men pledged to use all necessary means to oppose Home Rule in Ireland.
1913 (January) Ulster Volunteer Force founded.
1913 (September 2) The Dublin 'Lock-Out' of workers begins. Continues until Feb 1914.
1913 (November 19) Irish Citizen Army founded to protect the locked out workers.
1913 (November 25) Irish Volunteers founded.
1914 (April) Ulster Volunteers illegally import guns at Larne.
1914 (July) Irish Volunteers illegally import guns at Howth.
1914 (September) Third Home Rule Bill. The Bill was passed but suspended because of the outbreak of W.W. 1 (August 1914).
1914 (September) Irish Volunteers split following being urged by their leader John Redmond to join the war effort. Overwhelming majority follow Redmond.
1915 (December) IRB reorganised and Military Council formed. Plans for a rebellion at an advanced stage.
1916 (April 24) Easter Rising in Dublin. Rebellion put down (April 29 1916) following surrender of rebels.
1916 (May 3) First of the fifteen leaders of Rebellion executed. Executions continue until May 12 1916.
1916 (July) Battle of Somme. Ulster division decimated.
1916 (August 3) Sir Roger Casement hanged for treason for his role in supporting the 1916 Easter Rising.
1918 (November) Universal Suffrage granted. Women granted the vote and the right to sit in Parliament.
1918 (December) An All-Ireland General Election takes place with Sinn Féin winning the majority.
1919 (January 21) Seventy-three Sinn Féin MP's elected at general elections of December 1918 meet at the Mansion House, Dublin, constituting themselves as Dáil Éireann.
1919 (January 21) First encounter of War of Independence, an ambush at Soloheadbeg, Co.

Tipperary. War continues until truce July 9 1921.

1919 (April) Eamon de Valera elected President of Dáil Éireann.

1919 (August) Irish Volunteers, following moves in the Dáil, must now swear allegiance to the Irish Republic. Volunteers now become known as Irish Republican Army.

THE 1920's

1920 (January) First soldiers are recruited into the 'Black and Tans'.

1920 (November 21) "Bloody Sunday": Fourteen secret agents shot dead by IRA. Black and Tans retaliate by firing into the crowd at a Gaelic Football match in Croke Park. Twelve people were killed including one player.

1920 (December 11) Cork city burnt by Black and Tans.

1920 (December 23) Government of Ireland Act. Provides for 2 Home Rule parliaments, one in Dublin, one in Belfast.

1921 (May) General Election to Parliaments in Northern Ireland and Southern Ireland.

1921 (June) Northern Ireland Parliament opened by George V.

1921 (December) Anglo Irish Treaty signed in London. Treaty approved by Dáil Éireann (Jan. 7 1922). Provides for creation of the Irish Free State. Creates split in Sinn Fein Party (Pro and Anti-treaty).

1922 (April) Act establishing the Royal Ulster Constabulary in Northern Ireland.

1922 (June 16) General Election for Irish Parliament with a pro-treaty majority.

1922 (June 28) Civil War breaks out between pro-treaty and anti-treaty IRA.

1922 (August 12) Sinn Féin leader Arthur Griffith dies.

1922 (August 22) Michael Collins, signatory of the Anglo-Irish Treaty and Commander-in-Chief of the forces of the Irish Free State ambushed and killed in Cork.

1922 (October 25) Constitution of Irish Free State approved by Dáil (ratified by British Parliament December 5 1922).

1922 (November 15) Northern Ireland Elections to Westminster, thirteen seats - Unionists winning majority.

1922 (November 17) Irish Free State executes the first of seventy-seven anti-treaty prisoners. Executions of prisoners continue until April 2 1923, including Erskine Childers.

1922 (December 6) William T. Cosgrave elected President of Executive Council, continues until March 1932 as President.

1923 Cumann na Gaedheal in government following a General Election in the Republic of Ireland.

1923 (March) W. T. Cosgrave founds Cumann na nGaedheal. (pro-treaty) (Remains in government until March 1932).

1923 (May) End of Civil War.

1923 (August) Free State Act establishing the Gárda Síochána.

1923 (September) Irish Free State becomes member of the League of Nations.

1923 (December 6) Northern Ireland Elections to Westminster, thirteen seats - Unionists winning majority.

1924 (September) BBC starts broadcasting from Belfast.

1924 (October 29) Northern Ireland Elections to Westminster, thirteen seats - Unionists winning majority.

1925 (July) Act passed by Dáil authorising the Hydro-Electric Scheme at Shannon to create sufficient electrical power for the new State.

1925 (December) British, Northern Irish and Irish Free State Governments revoke powers of Boundary Commission and agree to maintain the existing border between Northern Ireland and the Irish Free State.

1926 (January) 2RN (forerunner of Radio Éireann) begins broadcasting from Dublin.

1926 (May) Fianna Fáil founded by Eamon de Valera.

1927 (June 9) Cumann na nGaedheal remain in government following a Republic of Ireland General Election.

1927 (July) Kevin O'Higgins, Minister for Justice in the Irish Free State assassinated.

1927 (August 11) Eamon de Valera leads Fianna Fáil into Dáil Éireann.

1927 (September) Cumann na nGaedheal remain in government following a Republic of Ireland General Election.

1929 (April) Proportional Representation abolished in Northern Ireland Parliamentary Elections.

1929 (May 30) Northern Ireland Elections to Westminster, thirteen seats - Unionists winning majority.

THE 1930's

1931 (September 5) First edition of the Irish Press.

1931 (October 27) Northern Ireland Elections to Westminster, thirteen seats - Unionists winning majority.

1932 (February) Fianna Fáil in government following a General Election. Eamon de Valera is President of the Executive Council.

1933 Fianna Fáil remain in government following General Election.

1933 (February 22) Eoin O'Duffy dismissed from Gárda Síochána.

1933 (March) Army Comrades Association (Anti-Communist Volunteer Force of National Army Veterans) adopts a blue shirt and black beret as uniform. A.C.A. formed February 1932. A.C.A. changes name to National Guard July 1933 under leadership of Eoin O'Duffy. National Guard proclaimed illegal August 1933.

1933 (September) United Irish Party (Fine Gael), founded from Cumann na nGaedhael, National Centre Party and the National Guard under the Presidency of O'Duffy.

1935 November 14) Northern Ireland Elections to Westminster, thirteen seats - Unionists winning majority.

1936 (June 8) IRA declared an illegal organisation in the Irish Free State. IRA had been declared illegal in Northern Ireland May 23 1922.

1936 (August) Aer Lingus established.

1936 (December) Governor General and all references to the crown removed from the constitution by the External Relations Act. The Act was passed through the Dáil during the abdication of Edward VIII.

1937 Fianna Fáil remain in government following a General Election in the Republic of Ireland.

1937 (December 29) New Constitution of Éire comes into effect. Had been approved by Dáil (June 14 1937) and by referendum (July 1 1937).

1938 Fianna Fáil remain in government following a Republic of Ireland General Election.

1938 (April) Agreement by an Taoiseach Eamon de Valera and the British Prime Minister Neville Chamberlain to end tariff 'war' and return the 'treaty ports' to Éire.

1939 (September) Eamon de Valera declares Éire will

be neutral during the Second World War.

THE 1940's

1941 (April) German air-raids on Belfast, 700 killed.

1941 (May) Germans bomb North Strand in Dublin, 34 killed.

1942 (Jan) American Troops arrive in bases in Northern Ireland.

1943 Fianna Fáil remain in government following a Republic of Ireland General Election.

1944 Fianna Fáil remain in government following a Republic of Ireland General Election.

1944 (December) Córas Iompair Éireann (CIE) set up, taking over from private operators.

1945 (July 5) Northern Ireland Elections to Westminster, thirteen seats - Unionists winning majority.

1946 (June) Bórd na Mona established.

1947 (November) Education Act in Northern Ireland.

1948 (February) Inter-party in government following a General Election in Republic of Ireland.

1949 (April 18) Éire formally declared a republic. The Republic of Ireland Act (December 21 1948) provided this.

THE 1950's

1950 (February 23) Northern Ireland Elections to Westminster, twelve seats - Unionists winning majority.

1951 (April) Minister for Health Dr. Noel Browne resigns over the controversial 'Mother and Child Scheme'.

1951 (May 30) General Election in Republic of Ireland, Fianna Fáil back in power.

1951 (October 25) Northern Ireland Elections to Westminster, twelve seats - Unionists winning majority.

1954 (May 18) Inter-party back in government following a General Election in Republic of Ireland.

1955 (May 26) Northern Ireland Elections to Westminster, twelve seats - Unionists winning majority.

1955 (July) Regular Television service begins in Northern Ireland.

1955 (December) Republic of Ireland affiliated to the United Nations Organisations.

1956 (November) IRA border campaign starts in Northern Ireland. Continues until February 1962.

1957 (March 5) Fianna Fáil remain in government following a General Election in the Republic of Ireland.

1959 (October 8) Northern Ireland Elections to Westminster, twelve seats - Unionists winning majority.

THE 1960's

1961 October 4) Fianna Fáil remain in government following a General Election in the Republic of Ireland.

1961 (December) Inaugural Television Broadcast by Radio Éireann, becomes Radio Telefís Éireann March 8 1966.

1963 (June) President of the U.S. John Fitzgerald Kennedy visits Ireland.

1964 (October 15) Northern Ireland Elections to Westminster, twelve seats - Unionists winning majority.

1965 (January) Seán Lemass, Taoiseach, visits Terence O'Neill, Prime Minister of Northern Ireland at Belfast. O'Neill reciprocated and visits Lemass in Dublin February 1965. These were the first such meetings between Northern and Southern Leaders.

1965 (April 7) Fianna Fail remain in government following a General Election in the Republic of Ireland.

1966 (March) Nelson's Pillar on O'Connell Street, Dublin, destroyed in a bomb blast.

1966 (March 31) Northern Ireland Elections to

Westminster, twelve seats - Unionists winning majority.

1966 (April-May) A Loyalist Parliamentary Organisation, the Ulster Volunteer Force, formed.

1966 (June) Northern Ireland Government declares UVF is an illegal organisation.

1967 (January) Northern Ireland Civil Rights Association formed.

1968 (August) First Civil Rights march held. Coalisland to Dungannon.

1968 (October) Banned Civil Rights march in Derry attacked by R.U.C Two days of rioting follow.

1969 (January) Militant Protestants attack Civil Rights march at Burntollet Bridge, Co. Derry.

1969 (April 28) Terence O'Neill, Northern Ireland Prime Minister, resigns. Succeeded by James Chichester Clark.

1969 (June 18) Fianna Fáil remain in government following a General Election in the Republic of Ireland.

1969 (August 15) British Troops move onto Northern Ireland streets at request of NorthernIreland government, due to the rioting in Derry and Belfast.

1969 (December 18) Act establishing the Ulster Defence Regiment. April 30 1970 'B' Specials disbanded and their duties transferred to the UDR.

THE 1970's

1970 (January 11) Split between 'Officials' and 'Provisionals' at Sinn Féin Conventions.

1970 (May 6) Charles J. Haughey, Minister for Finance, and Neil Blaney, Minister for Agriculture dismissed from Jack Lynch's cabinet. May 28 1970 Arrested on charges of importation of guns illegally for the IRA. October 23 1970 Haughey acquitted. July 2 1970 Blaney discharged.

1970 (June 18) Northern Ireland Elections to Westminster, twelve seats - Unionists winning majority.

1971 (February 6) First British Soldier killed in Northern Ireland.

1971 (August) Ulster Defence Association formed in Belfast. A working class Loyalist Paramilitary Organisation.

1971 (August) Re-introduction of internment without trial in Northern Ireland. Continues until December 1975.

1972 (January 30) 'Bloody Sunday': Thirteen Civilians shot dead by the British Army after taking part in a banned Civil Rights March in Derry. 17 others injured by gun fire, including one who later died.

1972 (February 2) British Embassy burned in Dublin.

1972 (March 24) Direct Rule introduced for Northern Ireland from Westminster.

1972 (July 21) Nineteen people killed in Belfast bombs. (In all, 467 people were killed as a result during the year).

1973 (January) Republic of Ireland becomes member of the European Economic Community along with Britain and Denmark.

1973 (February 28) Coalition parties (Fine Gael/Labour) in government following a General Election in the Republic of Ireland.

1973 (June) Elections to a Northern Ireland Assembly (provided for in an Act of May 3 1973).

1973 (November 22) Ulster Unionists, Alliance and S.D.L.P. agree to a power sharing executive.

1973 (July) Northern Ireland Parliament at Stormont abolished.

1974 (February 28) Northern Ireland Elections to Westminster, twelve seats - Unionists winning majority.

1974 (May 14) Ulster Worker's Council declares a general strike; brings the executive down May 28 1974.

1974 (May) Twenty five killed in Dublin car-bomb explosions. Six killed in Monaghan car-bomb explosions.

1974 (October 10) Northern Ireland Elections to Westminster, twelve seats - Unionists winning majority.

1975 (August 29) Eamon de Valera dies at the age of 92.

1975 (November) Kidnap of Dr. Tiede Herrema ends after 18 days following Kildare house siege.

1976 (July) British Ambassador to the Republic Christopher Ewart-Biggs dies in an IRA land-mine attack in Dublin.

1976 (August 10) 'Peace People' founded by Mairead Corrigan and Betty Williams.

1976 (October 22) President of Ireland, Cearbhall Ó Dálaigh resigns following comments by Minister for Defence Patrick Donegan.

1977 (June) Fianna Fáil back in government after a General Election in the Republic of Ireland.

1979 (January) Oil tanker explodes at Whiddy Island Oil Terminal, killing fifty people.

1979 (March) European Monetary System instituted. Ends parity between Irish Punt and the Sterling Pound.

1979 (May 3) Northern Ireland Elections to Westminster, twelve seats - Unionists winning majority.

1979 (August) Earl Mountbatten dies after IRA explode bomb on his boat near Mullaghmore, Co. Sligo.

1979 (September 29 - October 1) Pope John Paul II visits Ireland. Celebrates public mass at Knock, Drogheda and Dublin, and a private mass at Maynooth.

1979 (December) Charles J. Haughey succeeds Jack Lynch as Taoiseach.

THE 1980's

1981 (February) 48 people killed as fire sweeps through Stardust Ballroom at Artane, Dublin. Over 160 injured.

1981 (March) IRA Hunger Strikes begins with Bobby Sands. He and nine other prisoners die before it was called off (October 1981). Sixty four people were killed in the accompanying disturbances throughout Northern Ireland.

1981 (June) Coalition parties (Fine Gael/Labour) in government following a General Election in the Republic of Ireland.

1982 (February) Fianna Fáil back in government following a General Election in the Republic of Ireland.

1982 (November 24) Coalition parties (Fine Gael/Labour) back in government following a General Election in the Republic of Ireland.

1983 (June 9) Northern Ireland Elections to Westminster, seventeen seats - Unionists winning majority.

1984 (May) Publication of Report of the New Ireland Forum, involving nationalist parties from all of Ireland. Forum met for the first time (May 30 1984).

1985 (October) First Commercial Flight from Knock Airport.

1985 (November) Anglo-Irish Agreement signed, at Hillsborough by Garret FitzGerald and Margaret Thatcher. Passed by Dáil Éireann (November 21 1985) and House of Commons (November 27 1985). Affirming that any change in the status of N.I. would only come about with the consent of the N.I. majority, and establish a British-Irish government Conference.

1987 (February 19) Fianna Fáil back in government following a General Election in the Republic of Ireland.

1987 (June 11) Northern Ireland Elections to Westminster, seventeen seats - Unionists winning majority.

1987 (November) IRA bomb kills eleven people at Remembrance Day Service in Enniskillen.

1988 (March) A week of serious unrest in Northern Ireland follows the S.A.S. killing of three unarmed IRA members in Gibraltar. Three people killed at their funerals in Belfast by loyalist gunman Michael Stone, two British Army men killed at subsequent funerals.

1989 Coalition parties (Fianna Fáil/Progressive Democrats) in government following a General Election in the Republic of Ireland.

1989 (October) Guildford Four, who had been charged with bombings in England, following irregularities by the English police, released.

THE 1990's

1990 (August) Brian Keenan, Irish Hostage in Lebanon released.

1990 (November 7) Mary Robinson elected President of Ireland.

1990 (November) John Bruton succeeds Alan Dukes as Leader of Fine Gael.

1991 (March) The Birmingham Six, who had been charged with planting a bomb which killed 18 people in a Birmingham pub, released, following years of protesting their innocence.

1992 (April 9) Northern Ireland Elections to Westminster, seventeen seats - Unionists winning majority.

1992 (July) ANC Leader, Nelson Mandela visits Ireland and addresses the Dáil.

1992 (November) Coalition parties (Fianna Fáil /Labour) in government following a General Election in the Republic of Ireland.

1993 (December) Downing Street Declaration signed by John Major and Albert Reynolds.

1994 (January) Section 31 broadcasting ban lifted on members of Sinn Féin. On January 31 Gerry Adams arrives in the U.S. for a two-day visit.

1994 (August 30) IRA Ceasefire begins. (ends February 9 1996). Loyalist paramilitary ceasefire follows in Oct. British Prime Minister, John Major, lifts broadcast ban on Sinn Féin.

1994 (November) Albert Reynolds resigns as Taoiseach following scandal over judicial appointment, and his party is replaced in coalition with Labour by John Bruton-led Fine Gael.

1995 (January) Daytime patrols by British troops ended on Belfast streets.

1995 (February) Taoiseach John Bruton and British Prime Minister, John Major, launch Framework Document, detailing frameworks for the future of Northern Ireland. A target of February 1996 eventually set for the beginning of all-party talks in North.

1995 (October) County Derry poet Seamus Heaney awarded 1995 Nobel Prize for Literature.

1995 (November 30 - December 1) President Clinton visits Ireland. Receives rapturous welcome in Dublin, Belfast and Derry. Addresses full sitting of Dáil Éireann.

1995 (December) U.S. Senator George Mitchell appointed to resolve differences over decommissioning of arms in North.

See also *Chronology of 1996*

HISTORICAL MOVEMENTS AND ORGANISATIONS

Ancient Order of Hibernians: Founded 1641. Has been traditionally associated with nationalism and the defence of the Catholic faith. Sometimes described as the Catholic version of the Orange Order. Marches are held annually on the Feast of the Assumption, 15th August.

Apprentice Boys of Derry: Owes its origins to the action of apprentice boys who slammed the gates of Derry shut on the army of King James II at the beginning of the Siege of Derry in 1689. Marches take place annually on August 12 through the city.

Wild Geese: 14,000 Irish Jacobite Soldiers, largely under the command of Patrick Sarsfield, who left Ireland after the Treaty of Limerick (October 1691) and distinguished themselves on European battlefields in the eighteenth century.

Catholic Committee: Founded in March 1760 by Dr. John Curry, Charles O'Connor and Thomas Wyse. Organised the small urban Catholic middle-class and lobbied government for a relaxation of the Penal Laws. Met with considerable success in early 1790's culminating in a Catholic Relief Act in 1793 which repealed many of the Penal Laws.

Whiteboys: First emerged October 1761 in Munster. Generic term for different Catholic secret societies. Violent disturbances were connected with resentment to taxes and changes in farming from arable to dairy as much to sectarianism.

Defenders: Nationalist secret society founded after a skirmish in Armagh, July 1784. Absorbed by the United Irishmen in the 1790's.

Peep o Day Boys: Founded in July 1784 in Armagh. A Protestant Secret Society founded after the same sectarian clash. A further engagement with the Defenders at Loughgall, Co. Armagh led to the formation of the Orange Order.

The Volunteer Movement: Founded in March 1778. An armed corps established to help defend Ireland against French or Spanish invasion. Lobbied for free trade, legislative independence and relaxation of the Penal Laws. Banned in March 1793.

United Irishmen: Founded in October 1791 in Belfast by middle-class radical Presbyterians. Theobald Wolfe Tone was their most famous member. He procured French aid for the United Irishmen Rising of 1798 which tragically turned into a massacre in Wexford. Tone committed suicide rather than face the gallows after his capture.

Orange Order: Founded in September 1795 in County Armagh following serious disturbances between Catholics and Protestants. It celebrates the victory of the Protestant King William over Catholic King James at the Battle of the Boyne in 1690. It is the single largest Protestant organisation in Ireland, with as many as 100,000 members. The Orange Order marches in various centres all over Northern Ireland and in some parts of the South on July 12th each year.

Catholic Association: Founded in May 1823 by Daniel O'Connell. It enlisted the support of the clergy and became a truly national association. In 1826, it succeeded in getting MP's elected in four constituencies who supported Catholic Emancipation. O'Connell stood for election in Clare in 1828 and through efficient organisation he easily defeated the incumbent MP, resulting in the British Government assenting to Catholic Emancipation but disenfranchising many Catholics who had the vote.

Royal Irish Constabulary: The Irish Constabulary was formed in May 1836 and was rewarded with the title 'Royal' in 1867 for quelling the Fenian Rising of 1867. It was an unpopular force because it assisted at evictions throughout the nineteenth century, and because of its role in quelling the violence of the late nineteenth century and early twentieth centuries. It was in fact a police force doing work more suited to an 'Army'. Its members suffered terribly during the War of Independence, many resigning out of fear and disapproval of Black and Tan tactics and many more were dismissed because of their nationalist sympathies. It was disbanded following the Anglo-Irish Treaty of 1921 but its northern members were absorbed into the Royal Ulster Constabulary which was established on June 1st, 1922.

Temperance Movement: Founded in 1838 by Tipperary-born Capuchin Priest, Fr. Theobald Mathew. Disturbed by incidents of widespread drunkenness amongst Irish poor, he began a temperance crusade which reputedly recorded five million pledges in Ireland. Revenue from drink dropped from £1.4 million in 1839 to around £350,000 by 1844 thanks to the campaign.

Repeal Association: Founded in April 1840 by Daniel O'Connell to help his campaign for the repeal of the Union between Great Britain and Ireland and to set up an executive and legislature in Ireland. They organised "monster meetings" throughout 1843, the final one at Clontarf being banned by the Government. The split between O'Connell and some who supported physical force in 1846 signalled the end was nigh. O'Connell died in 1847 and the association petered out.

Young Ireland: Formed in October 1842 by Thomas Davis, Charles Gavin Duffy and John Blake Dillon. They aimed to achieve more than simple repeal, namely an independent Ireland. They broke with O'Connell's Repeal Association in 1846 over his attitude to physical force. In late July 1848 a short-lived Young Ireland Rebellion broke out. It was easily put down. Its leaders were either arrested or they fled the country. 'The Nation', the official newspaper of the movement was first published in October 1842.

Irish Confederation: Founded in January 1847 by the Young Irelanders who had seceded from O'Connell's

Repeal Association. William Smith O'Brien, Charles Gavin Duffy and John Mitchell were prominent members. On July 22 1848 Habeas Corpus was suspended and membership of the confederation declared illegal. Its leaders were arrested and the Young Ireland Rising of July 29, 1848 was a disaster. With this resounding defeat, the Confederation collapsed.

Irish Tenant League: Founded in August 1850 in Dublin by Charles Gavin Duffy and Frederick Lucas. It aimed to improve the Tenant Farmer's lot by securing the "three F's", i.e. Fair rent, Fixity of tenure and Free sale. It was most popular among the larger tenant farmers. It had about forty MP's elected to Westminster in July 1852 who went on to found an independent Irish party in September of that year. The league collapsed in 1855 when Lucas died and Duffy emigrated.

Catholic Defence Association of Great Britain and Ireland: Founded in October 1851 by George Henry Moore and John Sadleir. It was an association designed to highlight Catholic grievances both within Parliament and without. It met with little success.

Phoenix Society: Founded in 1856 in Skibbereen by Jeremiah O'Donovan Rossa. On the surface it was a debating society but it was in fact a revolutionary society and precursor of the Irish Republican Brotherhood.

Irish Republican Brotherhood: Founded on St. Patrick's Day, 1858 in Dublin by James Stephens. It aimed to overthrow the British Rule in Ireland and form an independent Irish Republic. In February and March 1867 they staged a rebellion which was easily put down. The Brotherhood was later to infiltrate such movements as the Land League, the Gaelic Athletic Association, the Gaelic League and even the Irish Parliamentary Party. It was revived in 1904 and its military council organised the 1916 Rising. It was again reorganised (its leaders having been executed) but its influence declined during the War of Independence. It split during the Civil War and dissolved itself in 1924.

Fenian Brotherhood: Founded April 1859 in New York by John O'Mahony. It was the American counterpart of the IRB. They raised funds and procured weapons for the IRB and attacked Britain by raiding Canada in April and June 1867.

Clan na Gael (United Brotherhood): Founded in June 1867 in New York by Jerome J. Collins, a secret organisation recognising the Supreme Council of the IRB as the Government of the Irish Republic. The Clan had an active part in plans for the 1916 Rising, particularly those involving German help.

Amnesty Association: Founded in Dublin in June of 1869 by John Nolan to campaign for the release of Fenians held under harsh conditions in British prisons. The Association met with considerable success in securing the release of a number of Fenians, including leaders such as John Devoy and Jeremiah O'Donovan Rossa. The association also supported the Home Rule party in its early days and was to meet with success in the 1890's in securing further releases, including that of

Thomas J. Clarke, signatory of the 1916 Rising. The movement ceased with Clarke's release, the last of the imprisoned Fenians.

Irish Parliamentary Party: Evolved from the Home Rule League which was established in Dublin by Isaac Butt in May 1870. It was a political party which had the securing of Home Rule as its primary aim but was also concerned with the plight of the Irish Tenant Farmer. Largely ineffective under the leadership of Butt, it met with considerable success, particularly with regard to the land question under the leadership of Charles Stewart Parnell (elected chairman in May 1880). It became the model for subsequent political parties through its creation of a grass roots organisation, a party whip and a party pledge to vote en-bloc. Despite having helped achieve a number of Land Acts and bringing Home Rule to the forefront of the order of business at Westminster, the party split in early June, 1890 following relevations about Parnell's affair with Katherine O'Shea. The party remained divided through the 1890's and was reunited in February 1900 under the leadership of John Redmond. The party remained numerically strong throughout the early 1900's and by 1914 had made Home Rule seem certain, the outbreak of World War 1 put the implementation of Home Rule on hold. However, the rise of Sinn Féin following the 1916 Rising all but wiped out the party. In the general election of 1918 they won only 6 seats (in the last general election before the war in 1910, they had won 70). The party never was a political force again after the formation of Dáil Éireann in 1919 and the Anglo-Irish Treaty of 1921.

Land League of Mayo: Founded in August 1879 at Westport by Michael Davitt and James Daly. It had the securing of the three F's as its aim and it was the organisation on which the Irish National Land League was modelled.

(Irish National) Land League: Founded in October 1879 in Dublin by Michael Davitt and Charles Stewart Parnell. Although ostensibly a peaceful moral force organisation, it enjoyed support from the IRB, the Fenians and Clan na Gael. It aimed the to achieve the three F's and abolish landlordism. It united the country, excluding North-east Ulster, with all classes, religion and political persuasions supporting it. Its primary weapon was the 'boycott'. It helped secure the Land Act of 1881 but was proscribed in October 1881. It was reformed, under the name of the National League, by Parnell in October the following year.

Ladies Land League: Founded 1881 by Anna Parnell, sister of Charles Stewart Parnell. They campaigned against the Landlord system. They were more radical than the Land League itself and were denounced by the hierarchy of the Catholic Church. Parnell disapproved of his sister's rhetoric and cut funds for the Ladies Land League when he was released from prison in May 1882. He suppressed it in August 1882.

Invincibles: Founded 1881. Secret society of hard line terrorists, condemned by Parnell and the Fenians, they assassinated the Chief Secretary and the Under Secretary in what became known as the Phoenix Park murders of May 6, 1882. Five members were later executed for their role in the murders. Organisation disappeared.

National League: Founded October 1882 by Charles Stewart Parnell to replace the banned Land League. It was the 'grass roots' organisation of the Home Rule Party. Its primary aim was Home Rule with Land Reform of secondary importance. It had heavy clerical support. It provided finance and delegates for the Home Rule party in both Ireland or Britain. It too split when the Home Rule party did in 1891 and by the turn of the century it had all but dwindled out.

Gaelic Athletic Association: Founded in Thurles on November 1, 1884 by Michael Cusack and Maurice Davin, under the patronage of the Archbishop of Cashel, Dr. T.W. Croke. The G.A.A.'s primary aim was for the preservation and cultivation of Irish pastimes, such as gaelic football and hurling, which had been slipping into decline due to disorganisation and apathy. The G.A.A. was unashamedly nationalist in policy, banning members from playing foreign games and excluding members of the Crown forces from obtaining membership. The organisation developed gradually, eventually establishing itself in every county in Ireland, administering and providing Gaelic pastimes to vast numbers of Irish people. It remains the single biggest sporting organisation on the island of Ireland.

Irish Loyal and Patriotic Union: Founded May 1885. A political association of Unionist landlords, businessmen and scholars who organised resistance to Home Rule. Contested the general election of November 1885 but made little impact in Southern parts of Ireland. Forerunner of the Irish Unionist Alliance.

Co-operative Movement: Co-operative creameries were first established in 1890 to allow dairy producing farmers to collectively sell their milk.

Congested Districts Board: Established Balfour Land Act of August 1891 as part of the Conservative government's policy of killing Home Rule by kindness. Function was to give aid to 'congested' areas along the western seaboard. Spent its resources on improving the western infrastructure (harbours and roads), aiding the indigenous industries such as fishing and the blossoming cottage industries and modernising methods of farming. Also bought estates and distributed land among the people of the congested areas often through re-location. Dissolved in 1923 by the Free State Government, its functions being taken over by the Land Commission.

Irish Unionist Alliance: Founded 1891 from remnants of the Irish Loyal and Patriotic Union. Aim was to resist Home Rule. Comprised of mainly Southern Unionists, and had close contact and considerable influence with the Conservative Party. (The House of Lords voted against the 2nd Home Rule Bill in 1893.) Became obsolete when Third Home Rule Bill was passed.

Gaelic League (Conradh na Gaeilge): Founded July 1893 by Dr. Douglas Hyde, Eoin MacNeill, and Fr. Eugene O'Growney. Aim was for the revival and preservation of Irish as the spoken language of the

people, leading to the "de-Anglicisation" of Ireland. Although moderately succesful, Hyde resigned from the organisation after 1915 by which time it had taken a political stance.

Irish Agricultural Organisation Society: Founded in April 1894 by Sir Horace Plunkett and Fr. Thomas Finlay to co-ordinate the activities of the nationwide Co-operative Movement.

Irish Socialist Republican Party: Founded in May 1896 in Dublin by James Connolly. It was a precursor to the Communist Party of Ireland (formed November 1921 by Connolly's son). It was a socialist nationalist party but had little support. When Connolly left Ireland for America in 1903 it was renamed and reorganised as the Socialist Party of Ireland.

Irish Literary Theatre: Founded in 1898 by William Butler Yeats. It was a Literary Society which hoped to promote Irish Culture and Customs by staging plays written and set in Ireland. It dissolved in 1904 and was absorbed into the Abbey Theatre.

Cumann na nGaedheal: Founded in October 1900 in Dublin by Arthur Griffith and William Rooney. It was an umbrella group for smaller organisations to help co-ordinate resistance to anglicisation in Ireland. In 1902, it proposed that the Irish Parliamentary Party abstain from Westminster. In 1903, it organised protests against the visit of King Edward VII. The group was absorbed into Sinn Féin in 1907. (*This group should not be confused by the pro-treaty political party Cumann na nGaedheal founded in 1923.*)

National Council: Formed 1903 to oppose royal visit of King Edward VII. Members included leading figures of Cumann na nGaedheal including Arthur Griffith and Major John MacBride. Absorbed into Sinn Féin in 1908.

Ulster Unionist Council: Founded March 1905 in Belfast. A support organisation for the Ulster Unionist Party. Organised the Solemn League and Covenant in 1912, the formation of the Ulster Volunteer Force in 1913, the Larne Gun-running incident of 1914 and appointed a Provisional Government for Ulster in 1913 to take power if Home Rule should come into effect. Played a significant part in the creation of the Northern Ireland state (post 1920).

Dungannon Clubs: Founded 1905 by Denis McCullagh and Bulmer Hobson. Part of the cultural revival, they were republican and non-sectarian and were most widespread in Southern Ulster. Promoted the idea of non-cooperation with the British Army, a programme for economic independence from Britain, and aided in the revival of the Irish Language. Between 1906 and 1908 they became part of Sinn Féin. The Dungannon Clubs were so called in commemoration of the Volunteer Convention at Dungannon in 1782.

Sinn Féin League: Founded in April, 1907 by the amalgamation of Cumann na nGaedheal and the Dungannon Clubs. On October 5th, 1907 the League merged with the National Council and the name Sinn Féin was adopted in September 1908.

Irish Transport and General Workers Union: Founded in January 1909 in Dublin by James Larkin. Originally comprising of dock workers it soon attracted carters and general labourers. Action by the Union resulted in the "Lock Out" (September 1913 - February 1914, when the employers refused to accept the Union's demands). Internal bickering and splits tore at the union from 1923 to 1959 when it united with the Workers' Union of Ireland (which came originally from the ITGWU) to form the Irish Congress of Trade Unions.

Solemn League and Covenant: Signed on September 28,1912 throughout the nine counties of Ulster by Unionists pledging themselves to oppose the Third Home Rule Bill which looked certain to become law. 218,206 men signed the Covenant (women were excluded).

Irish Citizen Army: Founded in November 1913 in Dublin by James Larkin and James Connolly. Its purpose initially was to defend workers during the Lock-Out from attacks by the police. With the end of the Lock-Out, Connolly's attention turned to the creation of a "Workers' Republic". The Citizen Army fought in the 1916 Rising. It also fought in the War of Independence and took the anti-treaty side in the Civil War. It ceased to exist after the Civil War ended in May 1923.

Irish Volunteers: Founded in November 1913 in Dublin by Éoin MacNeill and Bulmer Hobson in response to the emergence of the Ulster Volunteer Force. In September 1914, following a speech by John Redmond, leader of the the the Irish Parliamentary Party, the majority of the Volunteers joined the British Army and fought in World War 1. Those who were left were re-organised and the leadership was heavily infiltrated by the IRB. The Volunteers were manipulated by the IRB and fought in the 1916 Rising. Despite their defeat, they reformed and when the first Dáil met, the Volunteers soon took an oath, swearing allegiance to the Irish Republic and becoming the Irish Republican Army (20th October 1919).

Black and Tans: Enrolments began on January 2nd, 1920. They were a force designed to supplement the Royal Irish Constabulary and recruited from demobilised soldiers in Britain. The uniform was a mixture of military and police uniform. Their reputation stemmed from the vicious reprisals for IRA actions which were inflicted on innocent civilians. Their most infamous exploits include the burning of Balbriggan and Cork City and the killing of eleven spectators and one player at Croke Park on Bloody Sunday, November 21, 1920.

Ulster Special Constabulary: An auxiliary part-time police force established in 1921 to supplement the RUC to defend the infant Northern Ireland state from attack by the IRA. There were 3 grades: 'A', 'B' and 'C'. The 'A' and 'C' specials were not used after the 1920's but the 'B' specials were used in many situations including the civil rights demonstrations in the late 1960's. An exclusively protestant force they often clashed with the marchers. The force was disbanded in April 1970. Many members, however, became members of the new Ulster Defence Regiment.

Irregulars: The name given to members of the IRA who fought the National Army during the Civil War of June 1922 - April 1923. Their leader was Liam Lynch whose death precipitated the truce.

Cumann na nGaedheal: Founded in March 1923 by W.T. Cosgrave. It was a political party whose members supported the Anglo-Irish Treaty of 1921. Cumann na nGaedheal remained in government from its inception until 1932 when Fianna Fáil (who had abstained from the Dáil until August 1927) took power. On September 2nd, 1933 Cumann na nGaedheal merged with the National Centre Party and the National Guard (popularly known as the Blueshirts) to form Fine Gael, with Cosgrave becoming a vice president.

Blueshirts: Formed February 1932 by Edmund Cronin. It was the popular name for members of Army Comrades Association, the Association had adopted a blue shirt and black beret as a distinctive uniform in March 1933. In July 1933 the ACA, now under the leadership of General Éoin O'Duffy, changed its name to the National Guard. It was an anti-communist, quasi-fascist movement consisting mainly of veterans of the Free State Army. It was one of the organisations which merged to become Fine Gael (October 1933) which had O'Duffy as its first president. It declined in the years 1934-6. But in November 1936, O'Duffy led a brigade of Volunteers to fight with General Franco in the Spanish Civil War. They returned in June 1937.

Connolly Column: Formed in December 1936 by Frank Ryan. It was a group of republican volunteers who became members of the Abraham Lincoln Battalion of the 15th International Brigade and fought for the socialists, against Franco, in the Spanish Civil War (1936-9).

Clann na Talmhan (Family of the Land): Founded in Galway in 1938 by Michael Donnellan. A political party which had the aim of improving the lot of the small (principally western) farmer. It was initially successful and in 1948 it entered the Inter-party Government with its leader securing a ministerial portfolio. The number of seats won by the party decreased in each of the seven elections it contested from 1943 so much so that it did not contest any seats in the 1965 general election.

Comhdháil Náisiúnta na Gaeilge (The National Congress of the Irish Language): Formed late-October 1943 as a co-ordinating body for Irish Language organisations including Conradh na Gaelige.

Congress of Irish Unions: Formed April 1945 by William O'Brien who broke away from the ITGWU and the Labour Party because of his disapproval of 'communist tendencies' within those organisations. On February 2nd, 1959, it amalgamated with the Irish Trade Union Congress to form the Irish Congress of Trade Unions.

Clann na Poblachta (Republican Family): Founded in July 1946 by former Chief-of-Staff of the IRA (1936-8) and subsequent Nobel Peace Prize (1976) winner Sean MacBride. A political party with a republican ethos it was part of the Inter-party Government of 1948 holding two ministerial portfolios, one of which, Health, held by Dr. Noel Browne, precipitated the fall of the government in June of 1951 following the controversy which surrounded the Mother and Child scheme put forward by him. Tensions within Clann na Poblachta grew leading to Browne's resignation and the party's number of seats fell sharply in the 1951 election. The party contested 3 further elections but was dissolved in 1965.

Fianna Uladh (Soldiers of Ulster): Formed in 1953 by Liam Kelly, northern republican leader. It was the political wing of Saor Uladh and in cooperation with Clann na Poblachta, Kelly was elected to the Senate in 1954, thus breaking with the traditional republican tactic of not recognising the legitimacy of the Dáil. The party was banned in 1956.

Saor Uladh (Free Ulster): Formed in 1954 in Tyrone by Liam Kelly. It was a splinter group of the IRA who, without IRA approval, attacked police barracks and destroyed bridges. The group continued their campaign until 1959 having been outlawed in 1956.

Northern Ireland Civil Rights Association: Founded in January 1967 in Dungannon. An organisation concerned with the extending of Civil Rights to all the citizens of Northern Ireland. The association was particularly concerned with the allocation of public housing, gerrymandering in nationalist areas and the acceptance by the Northern Ireland Government of the principle of 'one man, one vote' in local elections. The association organised marches as a means of protest but these often led to violent clashes with the RUC. The influence of the association declined as the troubles progressed throughout the 1970's.

People's Democracy: Founded at Queen's University, Belfast in October 1968 by Michael Farrell and Bernadette Devlin among others. It was a socialist organisation which demanded an end to discrimination against Catholics in Northern Ireland, 'one man, one vote' and revoking of the Civil Authorities Special Powers Act. The group was involved in one of the bloodiest encounters of the Civil Rights era when unarmed marchers were attacked by baton wielding Loyalists at Burntollet on January 4th, 1969. Some of its leaders were interned in August 1971 but with the increasing violence of the troubles it became less significant.

'Official' Irish Republican Army: The split in the Irish Republican Army was first reported in late-February 1969. The IRA had, in the late 60's, turned away from violence and applied a Marxist analysis to the Irish situation. The eruption of violence in Northern Ireland in 1969 led the northern command of the IRA to break away becoming the 'Provisionals', while the remaining, mostly southern command, became the 'Officials'. The 'Officials', nicknamed 'stickies' by their northern rivals were led by Tomás MacGiolla and were socialist, bordering on Marxist in policy. Feuds between the Provisionals and Officials soon followed.

"Provisonal" Irish Republican Army : Can be traced to December 1968, following a split in the IRA. Really came into being following the outbreak of violence in

Northern Ireland in 1969 which marked the beginning of 'The Troubles'. For 25 years, until their ceasefire in August 1994, they waged a relentless campaign across Northern Ireland, targeting the main British troops, RUC officers and others they considered to be upholders of the Northern state. This campaign resulted in hundreds of deaths. The IRA campaign has seen conflict in Ireland, north and south, Britain and across Europe. Their political wing, Sinn Féin enjoys much support amongst working class nationalists across Northern Ireland. The Party also enjoys considerable financial support in the United States. The IRA ceasefire of August 1994 has held in Northern Ireland despite a number of bomb attacks in London and Manchester.

Official Sinn Féin: Founded in January 1970 after a split at a Sinn Féin meeting. It was led by Tomás MacGiolla and sought the creation of a democratic socialist republic based of the 1916 Proclamation of Independence. In January 1977, it changed its name to Sinn Féin, the Workers' Party and then to the Workers' Party.

Ulster Defence Regiment: A military force established in 1970 in Northern Ireland following the disbandment of the 'B' specials. The UDR assisted the RUC and the British Army in the campaign against the IRA. It was later merged with the Royal Irish Rangers to become the **Royal Irish Regiment.**

United Ulster Unionist Council: Formed in December 1973 by the Official Unionists, the Democratic Unionist Party and the Vanguard Unionist Party. It was a coalition of loyalist parties which had as its aim the bringing down of Power Sharing Executive of the Assembly of Northern Ireland (which was elected on 28th June, 1973 but did not take office until January 1st, 1974). The council co-operated with the Ulster Workers Council which held a general strike in May of 1974 leading to the collapse of the Executive and the Assembly. The council demanded that the executive be answerable to a majority rule Parliament. But the British Government rejected this. With the dissolving of the Convention in March 1976 the UUUC also collapsed.

Ulster Workers Council: Formed in 1974, it was a Loyalist council established to oppose direct rule (imposed March 1972), the power-sharing Executive of the Assembly of Northern Ireland (established on January 1st, 1974) and the Sunningdale Agreement signed by the British and Irish governments and the power-sharing Executive in December 1973. The council called a general strike on May 14th, 1974 which paralysed Northern Ireland and caused the collapse of the Executive (May 28th, 1974) and the reintroduction of direct rule from Westminster the following day. The strike was called off on the same day.

HISTORICAL DOCUMENTS

Significant Documents in Recent Irish History

Statutes of Kilkenny - Enacted in 1366 by the Irish Parliament meeting at Kilkenny. The Statutes were a number of apartheid-type laws forbidding English settlers assimilating with native Gaelic Irish and their culture. Gaelic laws, customs and language were banned among the Settlers as was marriage between the 'races'. The laws were ultimately ineffectual and were revoked in 1537.

Poynings' Law - Enacted 1 December 1494 and named after the Lord Deputy Sir Edward Poynings. It forbade the Irish parliament to convene without the King's prior permission and all intended legislation had to be approved by him. The law was repealed in 1782.

Compilation of the Annals of the Four Masters - 1632-36. Much of the history of Ireland compiled in book form by religious personnel in Donegal Town. The annals were completed by Michael O'Clery and others on August 10, 1636.

Treaty of Limerick - Signed on 3 October 1691 by the Irish leader Patrick Sarsfield and the Dutch General Ginkel. The Treaty allowed Irish Soldiers their liberty and the freedom to go to France to join other Jacobites. Roman Catholics were to be allowed rights of worship; to retain their property and allowed to practice their professions.

Penal Laws - 1695-1709. The collective name for a series of primarily anti-Catholic but also anti-Dissenter Laws designed to secure the privileged position of members of the Church of Ireland, the established Church, and eradicate the Roman Catholic religion in the country. Presbyterianism was also strongly frowned upon. The laws included restrictions on rights of education, the bearing of arms, the purchase of land, taking a seat in parliament, holding any government office. The Roman Catholic clergy was superseded in 1695. A Toleration Act for Protestant Dissenters was passed in 1719 while Catholics had to wait until late in the century for many of their restrictions to be repealed and 1829 before they could sit in parliament and hold high public office.

Act of Union - 2 July 1800 (came into effect 1st January 1801). This provided for the legislative union of Great Britain and Ireland. The Irish Parliament was abolished and henceforth Irish MP's and Lords sat in the Houses of Parliament at Westminster. The Act also provided for the amalgamation of the Church of Ireland with the Church of England. The Act was superseded by the Anglo-Irish Treaty of 1921.

Roman Catholic Relief Act - 13 April 1829. This Act enabled Roman Catholics to sit in the Houses of Parliament; belong to any corporation; and hold the higher offices of State by replacing the oaths of allegiance, supremacy and abjuration with a new oath, which was possible for Roman Catholics to take.

Irish Church Act - 26 July 1869 (came into effect 1st January 1871). The Act provided for the dissolution of the Churches of England and Ireland, but the main clauses of it provided for the disestablishment of the Church of Ireland (i.e. the dissolution of the legal union of Church and State); confiscated property of the Church of Ireland; discontinued grants to Maynooth College and the Presbyterian Church (although compensation was paid); Ecclesiastical Courts were disbanded; the tithe which was paid by Irish people of all denominations to the Church of Ireland was abolished; and finally, provision was made for tenants on Church of Ireland lands to purchase their holdings.

Land Acts - 1 August 1870 Land Act (Gladstone). This Act attempted to legalise the 'Ulster Custom' of not evicting tenants who were not in arrears and allowing tenants to sub-let their holdings. Also Landlords would in future have to pay compensation for any improvements made by a tenant to his holding. The most significant clause was the 'Bright Clause' which provided tenants with a government loan of 66% of the cost of their holdings to enable them to buy their own farm.

22 August 1881 Land Act (Gladstone). This Act gave tenants the 'Three F's': Fair rents (to be decided by arbitration); Fixity of tenure (tenants who had their rent fully paid could not be evicted); and Free sale (which ensured payment for any improvements paid).

14 August 1885 Land Act (Ashbourne). The Ashbourne Act provided £5m to tenants in the form of a 100% loan to buy out their holdings. The £5m was subsequently increased to £10m.

14 August 1903 Land Act (Wyndham). £83m was provided to tenants to buy out the lands and landlords got a bonus if they sold their entire estate.

Irish Universities Act - 1 August 1908. Provided for the abolishing of the Royal University and the establishing of two new universities namely the National University of Ireland (consisting of University Colleges Cork, Dublin and Galway and other constituent smaller colleges), and the Queen's University of Belfast. The National University of Ireland although officially non-denominational had a significant number of Roman Catholic bishops on its governing body.

Ulster's Solemn League and Covenant - 28 September 1912. This was a promise signed by 218,000 men to oppose Home Rule "using all means necessary; to defend together our place as equal citizens of the United Kingdom; and to refuse to recognise the authority of any Home Rule Parliament that should be set up."

Proclamation of the Irish Republic - Issued on 24 April 1916, it declared the intention of the Irish Volunteers to strike for freedom, and asserts the right of the Irish people to the ownership of a sovereign, independent Irish Republic. The Proclamation guaranteed religious and civil liberties; equal rights and opportunities to all and promised to cherish all the nation's children equally. It was signed by Thomas J. Clarke, Sean MacDiarmada, Thomas McDonagh, P. H. Pearse, Eamonn Ceannt, James Connolly and Joseph Plunkett on behalf of the provisional government. Each of these signatories was executed within three weeks.

Government of Ireland Act - 1920. Passed by the British parliament on 23 December. It proposed to set up two Home Rule parliaments, one in Belfast and one in Dublin. Control of finance and defence would be retained by Westminster. A council of Ireland, comprising of MP's from both parliaments was also proposed. It would have limited powers and would pave the way for an end to partition when both parliaments would assent to it.

Articles of Agreement for a Treaty between Great Britain and Ireland - 6 December 1921, (ratified by Dáil Éireann 7 January 1922). This was signed by the Irish delegation (Arthur Griffith, Michael Collins, Robert Barton, Charles Gavin Duffy and Eamonn Duggan) to the treaty negotiations. It provided for the creation of the Irish Free State, a nation of the British Empire with dominion status. All Members of Parliament in the Irish Free State would be obliged to take an oath of allegiance to the King. Britain retained control over a number of 'treaty ports' and Ireland's coastal defence. Provision was also made for Northern Ireland to opt out of the jurisdiction of the Parliament and Government of the Irish Free State and the establishment of a Boundary Commission to determine (using geographic and economic considerations) a border should Northern Ireland choose to opt out.

Constitution of the Irish Free State - (Saorstát Éireann) approved by Dáil Éireann 25 October 1922. The Irish Free State Constitution Act as passed by the British Parliament on 5 December 1922, ratified both the Constitution and the Anglo-Irish Treaty. It established the Irish Free State as a member of the British Commonwealth of Nations and established the legislature of the new state, the Irish language was recognised as the National language with official recognition of status of the English language, habeas corpus was ensured, freedom to practice religion and expression of opinion was assured as was the right to free elementary education. Articles relating to eligibility to vote and run for public office were also included. The Constitution was superseded by the Constitution of 1937.

External Relations Act - passed on 12 December 1936, during the British abdication crisis of Edward VIII. It removed all reference to the crown from the Irish Free State Constitution and abolished the office of Governor General. The Crown was now recognised only for purposes of external association (e.g. accreditation of diplomats). It made the Irish Free State a Republic in all but name.

Education Act - (Northern Ireland), passed on 27 November 1947. As well as grants towards building and extensions of schools it provided financial assistance to any student, irrespective of denomination or economic background to go to university. Universal secondary schooling was also established.

Republic of Ireland Act - passed on 21 December 1948 but not implemented until 18 April 1949. It repealed the 1936 External Relations Act and declared the 26 Counties a Republic. It took the Republic of Ireland out of the British Commonwealth of Nations.

European Monetary System - established on 13 March 1979. The Republic of Ireland joined, Britain did not, thus ending the one-for-one parity that had existed between the Irish and British pounds since independence. This benefited Irish exporters but was troublesome in border areas where currencies now had to be changed.

Anglo-Irish Agreement - Signed on 15 November 1985 by the Taoiseach, Garret FitzGerald and the British Prime Minister, Margaret Thatcher. The two governments affirmed that any change in the status of Northern Ireland could only come about with the consent of a majority of people of Northern Ireland and should the occasion arise that a majority wanted a United Ireland that they would pass necessary legislation to give effect to that wish. The Agreement also established an Anglo-Irish Inter-governmental Conference which was to deal with political, security and legal matters and the promotion of cross border co-operation. The British government accepted the right of the Irish government to make contributions to the conference (and would therefore have some role in the running of Northern Ireland).

Downing Street Declaration - Signed on 15 December 1993 by Albert Reynolds T. D. and John Major M. P. on behalf of the Irish and British Governments respectively. Main Points:

(Article 4) - The British Government has "no selfish strategic or economic interest in Northern Ireland" and will uphold the democratic wishes of the majority of the people in Northern Ireland should they prefer supporting the Union or a United Ireland.

(Article 5) - The Irish Government accepts that the right of self-determination by the people of Ireland as a whole must be achieved and exercised with and subject to the consent and agreement of a majority of the people of Northern Ireland.

(Article 7) - Taoiseach recognises elements within the Irish Constitution cause resentment to Northern Unionists and confirms that as part of an overall settlement, the Irish Government will put forward and support proposals for change to the Constitution which would reflect the principle of consent in Northern Ireland.

(Article 10) - Both Governments confirm that parties with a democratic mandate and a commitment to exclusively peaceful methods can participate fully in democratic politics and dialogue.

(Article 11) - Provides for the establishment of a Forum for Peace and Reconciliation.

Framework Document - (A New Framework for Agreement). Signed on 22 February 1995 by John Major and John Bruton. In its fifty-eight paragraphs, it sets out a framework agreed by the British and Irish governments to assist discussion and negotiation between the Parties of Northern Ireland.

It has as its guiding principles that agreement must be pursued and achieved using exclusively 'Democratic, Peaceful Means" and that new political arrangements must respect and protect the 'Rights and Identities of Both Traditions in Ireland' and that both communities in Northern Ireland must be afforded 'Parity of Esteem and Treatment'. (Paragraph 10).

The governments aim to establish 'interlocking and mutually supportive institutions on three levels:

(a) Structures within Northern Ireland where elected representatives will 'exercise shared administrative and legislative control' over mutually agreed matters. (Paragraph 13).

(b) North/South Institutions which will have a 'Clear Institutional Identity and Purpose' (Paragraph 25). The Body's functions will fall into three main categories, namely Consultative, Harmonising and Executive. A 'Parliamentary Forum' will be established and will be made up of members from the Oireachtas and from the New Northern Political Institutions. (Paragraph 36).

(c) New East/West structures to enhance relations between the two governments who envisage a new agreement reflecting the 'Totality of relationships between the two Islands' (Paragraph 39). Under this new agreement a 'Standing Inter-governmental Conference' will be established and maintained (Paragraph 40), providing a 'Continuing Institutional Expression for the Irish Governments recognised concern and role in relation to Northern Ireland' (Paragraph 42).

The British government accepts the right of the Irish People to exercise their right of self-determination without external impediment. While the Irish government recognises that that right is subject to the agreement and consent of a majority of the people of Northern Ireland. (Paragraph 16).

The British government pledges that it will not stand in the way of a sovereign united Ireland, if that is the Democratic wish of a majority in Northern Ireland (Paragraph 20). While the Irish government pledges to introduce and support proposals for changes to the Irish Constitution which will reflect the principle of consent in Northern Ireland by removing the claim of territorial Jurisdiction over Northern Ireland contrary to the will of a majority there. The existing birthright of everyone born on the Island to be part of the Irish nation will be maintained (paragraph 21).

The 'Document concludes that the issues it raises should be examined in negotiations with 'Democratically mandated parties in Northern Ireland which abide exclusively by peaceful means" (paragraph 54). And that the outcome of those negotiations will be ratified through referendums, North and South. (paragraph 55).

BURIAL PLACES OF FAMOUS IRISH PERSONALITIES

Name	Description	Died	Burial place
St Patrick,	Irish Patron Saint	490	Downpatrick
St. Bridgid	Irish Saint	525	Downpatrick
St. Colmcille	Irish Saint	597	Iona, Scotland
Brian Boru	High King of Ireland	23.04.1014	Armagh
Strongbow	Norman invader	1176	Christchurch Cathedral, Dublin
Theobald Wolfe Tone	Revolutionary leader	19.11.1798	Bodenstown, Co. Kildare
Lord Edward Fitzgerald	Revolutionary leader	19.05.1798	St Werburgh's Church, Dublin
Daniel O'Connell	'The Great Liberator'	15.05.1847	Glasnevin Cemetery, Dublin
Charles Stewart Parnell	Irish Parliamentary leader	06.10.1891	Glasnevin Cemetery, Dublin
Padraig Pearse	Leader of 1916 Rebellion	03.05.1916	Arbour Hill
James Connolly	Leader of 1916 Rebellion	12.05.1916	Arbour Hill
John Redmond	Irish Parliamentarian	06.03.1918	Wexford
Michael Collins	Militant revolutionary leader	22.08.1922	Glasnevin Cemetery, Dublin
Countess Constance Markievicz	Revolutionary	15.07.1927	Glasnevin Cemetery, Dublin
Kevin O'Higgins	Minister of the Irish Free State	10.12.1927	Glasnevin Cemetery, Dublin
Sir Edward Carson	Unionist leader	22.10.1935	St Anne's Cathedral, Belfast
William Butler Yeats	Poet	28.01.1939	Drumcliffe, Co. Sligo
Sir James Craig	Longtime Northern Ireland P.M.	24.11.1940	Stormont, Belfast
Douglas Hyde	First President of Ireland	12.07.1949	Portahard
Eamon de Valera	Former Taoiseach and President	29.08.1975	Glasnevin Cemetery, Dublin
Christy Ring	Legendary Hurler	02.03.1979	Cloyne, Co. Cork
Bobby Sands	Leader of Republican hunger strike	05.05.1981	Milltown Cemetery, Belfast

WHO WAS WHO

Significant Persons in Irish History

Andrews, Eamon (1922-1987). Broadcaster, was All-Ireland Amateur Boxing Champion before becoming involved in television. Joined BBC and presented many shows including 'The Eamon Andrews Show', 'What's My Line' and "This is Your Life'.

Andrews, John Miller (1871-1956). Born in Down. Prime Minister from 1940 to 1943. Elected unopposed in every election from 1921. County Grand master of the Orange Institution in his native Down.

Andrews, Thomas (1813-1885). Established the composition of ozone.

Alexander, Frances Cecil (Mrs) (1818-1895) Born in Wicklow. Hymn -writer, most famous being "Once in Royal David's City." Died in Derry.

Alexander, Harold R. (1891-1969) Born Tyrone. Distinguished himself in both World Wars with the British Army. Was later Governor-General of Canada (1946-1952). Died near London.

Bacon, Sir Francis (1909-1992). Born in Dublin. Famous Painter.

Balfe, Michael (1808-70). Born in Dublin. Opera composer and violinist. Wrote many operas including 'The Bohemian Girl', (1843) and the music to La Scala's ballet, La Perouse.

Barnardo, Thomas J. (1845-1905) Born in Dublin. Founder of 'Dr. Barnardo's Homes' for orphans. Died in England.

Barry, Kevin (1902-1920) Born Dublin. Executed for his part in an IRA raid which killed six British soldiers. Died in Mountjoy Prison. Subject of popular ballad.

Barton, Robert. Born in Fermanagh. Wrote the music for 'Waltzing Matilda", generally regarded as the unofficial national anthem of Australia.

Beaufort, Francis (1774-1857). Born in Meath. Devised Beaufort Scale which measures the velocity and force of winds.

Bianconi, Charles (1786-1875) Born north Italy. Came to Ireland at age of 15. Started a car service operation in Tipperary in 1815. Became a wealthy roadcar service operator in the south and west of Ireland. Died in Cashel.

Blackburn, Helen (1842-1903) Born Kerry. Influential figure in the Women's Suffrage movement in Victorian England. Died in London.

Blaney, Neil T. (1922-1995) Born Donegal. Former Fianna Fáil Minister. Dismissed from Cabinet by Taoiseach Jack Lynch in 1970, and later expelled from that party. He remained a TD and leader of Independent Fianna Fáil until his death in 1995.

Blythe, Ernest (1889-1975) Born Antrim. Member of the IRB and Dáil T.D. from 1918. Blythe accepted the Anglo-Irish Treaty in 1921 and became a government minister (only Northern Protestant to become a Minister in a Dublin government). Life long upholder of the Irish language. Died in Dublin.

Boru, Brian (941-1014) High King of Ireland (from 999). Died in 1014 at the Battle of Clontarf although his army were victorious in defeating the Norsemen. Buried in Armagh.

Boycott, Captain Charles Cunningham (1832-1897). Gave the verb 'boycott' to the English Language. In 1873, tenants of the Mayo estate, where he was a land agent, protested at his refusal to reduce rents by refusing to work the land, leaving crops in the soil.

Boyle, Robert (1627-91). Born in Waterford. Father of Chemistry. Pioneer of changing chemistry from alchemy to experimental science. Boyle's Law (Volume of a gas is inversely proportional to its pressure at constant temperature).

Bracken, Thomas. Irish born poet who wrote the National Anthem of New Zealand - "God Save New Zealand".

Brendan, St. (c. 484-578). Born in Kerry. 'Brendan the Navigator'. Believed to have discovered America between 535 and 553.

Brigid, St. Born Louth, mid 5th century. Patron saint who founded religious house in Kildare. Her feast day is February 1st, marked by the construction of crosses made from rushes throughout Ireland. Died c. 525.

Brooke, Sir Basil, also Lord Brookeborough. (1888-1973). Born in Fermanagh. Prime Minister from 1943 to 1963. A World War One veteran. Member of Northern Ireland Senate in 1921. As Prime Minister, had no official contacts with trade unionists or Roman Catholics.

Bull, Lucien (1876-1972). Born in Dublin. Invented electrocardiograph in 1908.

Butt, Isaac (1813-1879). Born in Donegal. Leader of the Irish Parliamentary Party at Westminster from 1871 until his death in Dublin in 1879.

Callan, Fr. Nicholas (1799-1864). Born in Dundalk. Invented the induction coil (fore-runner of modern transformer).

Carey, James (1845-1883). Born in Dublin. Member of 'The Invincibles' who assassinated the Chief Secretary and the Under Secretary in the Phoenix Park in May 1882. Carey himself was shot dead by a member of 'The Invincibles' in South Africa in 1883 after he had turned informer and five of his colleagues had been executed.

Carson, Edward (1854-1935). Born in Dublin. A barrister, Carson successfully prosecuted the homosexual writer Oscar Wilde in 1895. He became Leader of the Irish Unionists in 1910. In 1913, he led 218,000 Ulster Unionists in the signing of the Solemn League and Covenant. A member of the British Cabinet during World War 1. Died in Kent in 1935.

Casement, Sir Roger (1864-1916). Born in Dublin. Knighted in 1911 for his work with the British Colonial Service. Attempted to solicit German aid for the 1916

Rising. He secured arms which were scuttled in the 'Aud'. Casement himself was captured at Banna Strand, Co. Kerry. Hanged in 1916 after being tried for treason in London. His body was re-interred in Dublin in 1965.

Childers, Erskine Hamilton 1905-1974). Born in London. President of Ireland from 1973 to 1974. Was a Fianna Fáil T.D. for thirty five years holding various ministries during that time.

Childers, Robert Erskine (1870-1922). Born in London. Author of the first spy novel 'The Riddle of the Sands' (1903). Heavily involved in the Howth gun-running of 1914, he served with distinction in the British Navy during World War 1. Was elected to Dáil Éireann in 1919. Executed by Free State Forces in Dublin in 1922.

Clarke, Austin (1896-1974). Born in Dublin. Acclaimed poet, novelist and dramatist. A lecturer of English at UCD from 1917, he moved to London in 1921 and wrote for The Times, amongst other mainstream newspapers. His 1932 debut novel The Bright Temptation was banned in Ireland until 1954. Returning to Ireland in 1937, he produced plays at the Peacock Theatre and the Abbey, broadcast weekly on Radio Éireann and published numerous works of poetry, fiction and drama. Died in Dublin.

Collins, Michael (1890-1922). Born in Cork. Escaped death sentence for his involvement in Easter Rising. Elected to first Dáil and held ministries for Home Affairs and Finance. Was president of Supreme Council of the Irish Republican Brotherhood and had his own elite group of assassins, known as the 'squad'. Following the truce in 1921, he became a leading member of the Irish negotiating team which signed the Anglo-Irish Treaty of 6 December 1921. In the ensuing Civil War he was ambushed and shot dead at Béal na mBláth on 22 August 1922.

Colmcille, St. (521-597). Born in Donegal. Patron Saint. Founded monasteries at Derry and Kells among others. Founded the monastery at Iona in 563 spreading christianity throughout Scotland and northern England. Died in Iona in 597.

Connell, Jim (c.1850-1929). Born in Meath. Wrote the famous socialist song 'The Red Flag'.

Connolly, James (1868-1916). Born in Edinburgh. Revolutionary socialist. Founded the 'Citizens Army' in 1913 to defend workers during the Dublin lockout. He joined the IRB in 1915 and was Commanding Officer in the GPO during the Easter Rising. Executed by Firing Squad at Kilmainham Jail on 12 May 1916, sitting in a chair because of wounds sustained during Easter Rising.

Cooke, Henry (1788-1868). Born in Co. Derry. Presbyterian leader in Ireland. Ordained in 1808, he went onto become the leading Protestant spokesman of his generation, vigorously opposing Daniel O'Connell's campaign for the repeal of the Union. Died in Belfast.

Conway, William (1913-1977). Archbishop of Armagh and Primate of All Ireland from September 1963, having previously been Professor of Moral Theology and Canon Law at St. Patrick's College Maynooth. Created Cardinal in February 1965. Died in Armagh in 1977.

Cosgrave, William T. (1880-1965). Born in Dublin. First President of the Executive Council of the Irish Free State from 1923 to 1932. Fought in the 1916 Rising. Supported the 1921 Anglo-Irish Treaty and was a founding member of Fine Gael.

Costello, John A. (1891-1976). Born in Dublin. Taoiseach from 1948 to 1951 and from 1954 to 1957 of an Inter Party government. Attorney General from 1926 to 1932. In 1948 repealed External Relations Act which paved the way for the Free State to become a Republic.

Craig, Sir James, also Lord Craigavon (1871-1940). Born in Belfast. Prime Minister from 1921 to 1940. Veteran of the Boer War and World War One. Abolished the PR electoral voting system in 1929.

Croke, Thomas W. (1824-1902). Born in Cork. Archbishop of Cashel from 1875 and Patron of the Gaelic Athletic Association who named their Jones' Road headquarters after him. Died in Cashel in 1902.

Cullen, Paul (1803-1878). Born in Kildare. Ireland's first Cardinal. Archbishop of Armagh from 1850-52. Archbishop of Dublin from 1852. Founded Catholic University in 1854 and Clonliffe College, Dublin in 1859. Primate of All-Ireland from June 1866 until his death. Died in Dublin 1878.

Cusack, Cyril (1910-1993). Theatre and Film Actor, Writer. Joined Abbey Theatre in 1932 and went on to become one of Ireland's most acclaimed actors. Oscar nominated in 1952. His most memorable film roles include 'The Blue Veil', 'Day of the Jackal' and much remembered for the television series 'Strumpet City'.

Cusack, Michael (1847-1906). Born in Clare. Founding member of the GAA in 1884, a stand is named after him in Croke Park. Died in Dublin 1906.

D'Alton, John (1883-1963). Born in Mayo. Archbishop of Armagh and Primate of All Ireland from 1946, was created Cardinal in 1953. Died in Dublin in 1963.

Davis, Thomas (1814-1845). Born in Cork. Young Irelander and founding member of its newspaper 'The Nation'. A noted poet, he wrote 'A Nation Once Again' and 'The West's Asleep'. Died in 1845.

Davitt, Michael (1846-1906). Born in Mayo. Founding member of the Irish National Land League in 1879. He had been imprisoned in England as a Fenian in 1870, but released in 1877. Died in Dublin in 1906.

De Valera, Eamon (1882-1975). Born in New York. President of Ireland from 1959 to 1973. Taoiseach from 1933 to 1954 and from 1957 to 1959. Played a major part in the 1916 Rising. Opposed 1921 Treaty. Founded Fianna Fáil party in 1926. President of the Assembly of the League of Nations in 1938, largely drafted the 1937 Constitution.

Devoy, John (1842-1928). Born in Kildare. Spent most of his life in America where he was an influential figure of Clann na Gael. Died in the United States in 1928.

Dill, Sir John (1881-1944). Born in Armagh. Field Marshall in the British Army. Fought in World War 1 and the Boer War, he was Chief Adviser to the British government on military matters for a period in World War II. Died in Washington in 1944.

Dowland, John (1562-1626). Born in Dublin. Composer and lutenist to Royal Courts at Copenhagen and London. Wrote three volumes of 'Books of Songs or Ayres'.

Dunlop, John (1840-1921). Born in Ayrshire, Scotland. Moved to Belfast as a child. Invented neumatic tyre. Patented in 1888.

Emmet, Robert (1778-1803). Born in Dublin. A United Irishman, he led a Rebellion in Dublin in 1803. He was captured and found guilty of treason. Before he was hanged he gave his famous oration from the dock. Died in Dublin in 1803.

Faulkner, Arthur Brian Deane, also Lord Faulkner of Downpatrick. (1921-1977). Born in Down. Prime Minister from 1971 to 1972. He had also resigned from Terence O'Neill's cabinet because of reform. Introduced internment without trial in August 1971. Was last Northern Ireland Prime Minister.

Ferguson, Harry (1884-1960). Born in County Down. Invented hydraulically controlled plough. Set up Ferguson Factory in 1947, merged with Massey in 1958.

Field, John (1782-1837). Born in Dublin. Composer of seven concerts and four sonatas and pioneer of the nocturne in 1814 which influenced composers in later years. He resided for most of his life in Russia; he is buried in Moscow.

Fitzgerald, Lord Edward (1763-1798). Born in Kildare. Played a leading role in the United Irishmen Rising of 1798 having previously served in the British Army. Died in Dublin in 1798 from a gunshot wound.

Fitzgerald, Lord Thomas (1513-1537). Born in Kildare. ('Silken Thomas)'. Lord Deputy who instigated a Rising in 1534 but surrendered in 1535 after having his pardon guaranteed. In 1537 he was hanged, drawn and quartered at the Tower of London.

Fitzmaurice, Colonel James C. (1898-1965). Born in Dublin. Made first east-west transatlantic crossing by air in April 1928 from Baldonnel, Co. Dublin to Greenly Island, Newfoundland. Two Germans, Captain Kohl and Baron von Hünefeld accompanied him.

Fowke, Francis (1823-1865). Born in Antrim. Designed the Royal Albert Hall in London and the National Gallery of Ireland in Dublin.

French, Percy (1854-1920). Born in Roscommon. Singer-Songwriter who penned the memorable songs 'The Mountains of Mourne' and 'Are ye Right There Michael?'.

Gallagher, Patrick 'The Cope' (1873-1964). Born in Donegal. Set up a Co-operative Society in his native Dungloe and was an influential figure within the Irish Agricultural Organisation Society. Died in Donegal in 1964.

Gandon, James (1743-1823). Born in London.

Architect who designed some of the finest buildings in nineteenth century Dublin, including the Custom House, the Four Courts and Kings Inn. Died in Dublin in 1823.

Grattan, Henry (1746-1820). Born in Dublin. Parliamentarian who lobbied for and successfully gained a measure of Legislative Independence from Westminster. 'Grattan's Parliament' came into being in 1782. The Parliament voted itself out of existence in accepting the Act of Union in 1801.

Griffith, Arthur (1871-1922). Born Dublin, a founding member of Sinn Féin in 1905 and elected to the first Dáil in 1918. The chief negotiator along with Michael Collins in the Irish delegation which signed the Anglo-Irish treaty in 1921. He was president of the second Dáil from January until August 1922 when he died suddenly.

Guinness, Arthur (1725-1803). Born Kildare, founded the Guinness brewery at St James' Gate in 1759.

Halpin, Captain Robert Charles (1836-1894). Born in Wicklow. Laid first transatlantic cable (completed 1866) Valentia to Newfoundland.

Healy, Cahir (1877-1970). Born Donegal, nationalist representative at Stormont from 1925-65 for Fermanagh South and MP for Fermanagh and South Tyrone 1950-55 at Westminster.

Hennessy, Richard (1720-1800). Born Cork, fought with Irish regiments on continental Europe. Founded the Hennessy Brandy distillery in 1763.

Henry, Paul (1876-1958). Born Belfast, landscape painter who favoured using charcoal and oil.

Hoban, James (c.1762-1831). Born in Kilkenny. Designed the White House at Washington.

Hone, Evie (1894-1955). Born Dublin, stained glass artist who overcame poor health to create many masterful stained glass windows.

Horan, Monsignor James (d. 1986). Legendary Parish Priest at Knock, Co. Mayo. Built the basilica there which accomodates 10,000 people. Hosted Pope John Paul II in Knock during his 1979 visit. Was the motivator and providor of the financially succesful Knock International Airport whichs serves the west of Ireland.

Hussey, Thomas (1741-1803). Born Meath, noted for his diplomatic skills in the service of George III in continental Europe. First president of Maynooth College and later Bishop of Waterford and Lismore.

Hyde, Douglas (1860-1949). Born in Roscommon. First President of Ireland from 1937 to 1945 and co-founder of the Gaelic League in 1893.

Ingram, Rex (1893-1950). Born Dublin, film director in Hollywood in the 1920s his most famous films were 'The Four Horsemen of the Apocalypse' and 'Under Crimson skies'.

Jervas, Charles (c. 1675-1739). Born in Offaly. Member of the Courts of George I and II of England. He was the official portrait artist.

Joyce, James - see *Famous Irish Writers*

Kavanagh, Patrick - see *Famous Irish Writers*

Kearney, Peadar (1883-1942). Born Dublin, wrote

the words for the national anthem 'Amhrán na bhFiann'.

Kennedy, Jimmy (1902-1984). Born in Tyrone. Wrote 'The Hokey Cokey', 'South of the Border, Down Mexico Way', 'Red Sails in the Sunset', and 'The Teddy Bears Picnic'.

Lane, Hugh (1875-1915). Born Cork, art collector whose spurned offer of paintings to the Dublin Municipal Gallery is recalled in Yeats's poem 'September 1913'. Lane was drowned when the Lusitania was torpedoed in 1915.

Lavery, Sir John (1856-1941). Born Belfast, painter whose work is internationally famous. Famous paintings include a portrait of his wife Hazel, and Michael Collins lying in state.

Lemass, Seán (1899-1971). Taoiseach from 1959 to 1966 of successive Fianna Fáil governments. Fought in the 1916 Rising. Opposed Anglo-Irish Treaty and was founder member of Fianna Fáil party in 1926. He was a Fianna Fáil T.D. from 1925 to 1966 holding various ministries. Credited with increasing industrialisation in Ireland.

Le Mesurier McClure, Robert John (1807-73). Born in Wexford. Discovered the North-west Passage (i.e. the link between the Pacific and Atlantic via the Arctic Ocean).

Lundy, Robert Governor of Derry when King James and his army lay siege to the city in 1689. Was removed from office by the citizens of Derry when he suggested surrender to the besiegers. Lundy escaped but was later imprisoned in the Tower of London. His effigy is burned annually at celebrations commemorating the relief of the siege.

McAuley, Catherine (1778-1841). Born Dublin, nun who founded the Sisters of Mercy in 1831. The Sisters of Mercy have been responsible for educating hundreds of thousands of Irish students. Her portrait is on the current five pound note.

MacBride, John (1865-1916). Born Mayo he fought in the Boer War against the British. He fought in the 1916 Rising and was executed on May 5 1916.

MacBride, Maud Gonne (1865-1953). Born in Aldershot, England. Founded Inghinidhe na hÉireann (revolutionary society) in 1908. Married John MacBride (who was executed for his part in the 1916 Rising) in 1903.

MacBride, Séan (b. 1904). Educated in Dublin and Paris. Fought in the War of Independence under Michael Collins, opposed the Treaty, took part in Civil War. Chief-of-Staff of IRA in 1936. Leader of Clann na Poblachta (1946-57). First elected to Dáil in 1947. Won Nobel Peace Prize in 1974.

McCormack, John (1884-1945). Born in Athlone, Co. Westmeath. Ireland's most famous tenor ever. He became a Papal Count and enchanted audiences, especially in the United States with his concerts.

McCormack, Liam One of Ireland's leading modern church architects. His churches in the north west of Ireland and in England won him international recognition. Died in Donegal, 1996

McCracken, Henry Joy (1767-1798). Born Belfast, Presbyterian founding member of the United Irishmen. He led the 1798 rising in Antrim and was hanged on July 17, 1798.

MacDiarmada, Seán (1884-1916). Born Leitrim credited with the reorganisation of the IRB in the early 1900s. Signatory of the Proclamation of the Republic he was executed for his role in the 1916 Rising.

MacDonagh, Thomas (1878-1916). Born Tipperary, a poet who believed in the need for a blood sacrifice to revitalise nationalist Ireland. A member of the IRB he signed the Proclamation of the Republic and was executed for his part in the 1916 Rising.

MacEoin, Seán (1893-1973). Born Longford the most successful guerrilla leader in the War of Independence he supported the Treaty and became Chief of Staff of the Free State army. He was later a Government Minister in two Coalition Governments.

MacHale, John (1791-1881). Born Mayo, Archbishop of Tuam from 1834 until his death. An outspoken nationalist he enthusiastically backed Catholic Emancipation, Repeal of the Union and Land Reform.

McKenzie, John (1648-1696). Born Tyrone, Presbyterian minister who survived the Siege of Derry and published his account of it in 1690, 'Narrative of the Siege of Londonderry'.

MacLiammoir, Micheal (1899-1978) Born Cork. Playwright, actor and writer. Actor from childhood, widely considered one of ablest Irish actors of all time. Toured his one man show *The Importance of Being Oscar* all over the world. Died 1978.

MacMurrough, Diarmuid (1110-1171). King of Leinster from c.1126 he courted help from Henry II of England to regain his Kingdom. Richard deClare (Stongbow) arrived in Ireland in 1170 and helped MacMurrough recapture Dublin. Stongbow succeeded MacMurrough as King of Leinster.

McManus, Seamus (1869-1960) Born Donegal. Novelist, poet and historian. Became a teacher and, at the age of 19, principal of his old school at Glencoagh. Contributed articles to local newspapers and became a celebrated folk-lore collector. Moved to the United States in 1889 and achieved considerable success with his stories, novels, poetry and sketches. His autobiography, *The Rocky Road to Dublin* was published in 1938. Died in New York.

McNally, Ray (1925-1989) Born in Donegal. First stage appearance in 1942 and went on to become accomplished film actor. Starred in 'Cal' 'The Mission' and 'My Left Foot'.

McQuaid, John Charles (1895-1973). Born Cavan, Archbishop of Dublin from 1940 was widely perceived as one of the most influential and conservative members of the Catholic hierarchy.

MacSwiney, Terence (1879-1920). Born Cork a prominent member of the Irish Volunteers he was elected Mayor of Cork in 1920 but arrested later that year. He immediately went on hunger-strike and died in Brixton prison after being force-fed. His protest had lasted 74 days.

Mallet, Robert (1810-1881). Born in Dublin. Pioneer of Seismology (the study and measurement of earthquakes).

Markievicz , Countess Constance (1868-1927). Born in London. First woman to be elected to the British parliament in December 1918. She was sentenced to death but reprieved for her part in the 1916 Rising. She was Minister for Labour in the First Dáil.

Matthew, Fr Theobald (1790-1856). Born Tipperary, formed a temperance society in 1838, a forerunner of the current Pioneer Total Abstinence Association.

Meagher, Thomas Francis (1823-1867). Born Waterford deported to Van Diemen's land for his part in the abortive Rising of 1848 he escaped and went to the United States where he became a General in the Union Army in the American Civil War and later Governor of Montana.

Moore, Thomas (1779-1852) Born Dublin. Poet and socialite, most notably in London. Published many works, including his *Irish Melodies* between 1807 and 1834. Died Sloperton.

Mulcahy, Richard (1886-1971). Born Waterford, Chief of Staff of the IRA from 1917 and elected to the first Dáil in 1918. He supported the 1921 Treaty and served as a Minister in successive Cumman na Gaedheal Governments in the 20s and 30s and in Coalition Governments in the 40s and 50s.

Murphy, Fr. John (1753-1798). Born Wexford. Leader of Rising of 1798. Led the rebellion against British, taking the towns of Enniscorthy, Wexford and Ferns. Captured by the British following defeats at Arklow and Vinegar Hill, and hanged.

Murphy, William Martin (1844-1919). Born Cork, founded Independent Newspapers in 1905 and led the employers against the workers in the 1913 Lockout.

O'Casey, Sean - *see Famous Irish Writers*

O'Ceallaigh, Sean T. (1882-1966). Born in Dublin. President of Ireland from 1945 to 1959. Founding member of Sinn Féin in 1905 and Fianna Fáil in 1926. Held various ministries in Fianna Fáil administrations.

Ó'Cléirigh, Mícheál - *see Famous Irish Writers*

O'Connell, Daniel (1775-1847). Born in Kerry. 'The Liberator'. Founded the Catholic Association in 1823. Lobbied for and won Catholic emancipation. In May 1828, he was elected illegally as an MP becoming first Catholic MP. Tried to have the Act of Union repealed but failed.

O'Dálaigh, Cearbhall (1911-1978). Born in Wicklow. President of Ireland from 1974 to 1976. Was Attorney General from 1946 to 1948 and from 1951 to 1953 and Chief Justice and President of the Supreme Court from 1961-1973. Resigned as President 22 October 1976.

O'Dea, Jimmy (1899-1965). Born Dublin, famous entertainer and actor. He starred in the film 'Darby O'Gill

and the Little People' and in many stage shows.

O'Doherty, Cahir (1587-1608). Born Donegal, the last Irish Chieftain. He was killed in 1608 after first sacking both Derry and Strabane.

O'Donnell, Peadar - *see Famous Irish Writers*

O'Donnell, Red Hugh (1571-1602). Born Donegal, Chief of the O'Donnell Clan he allied himself with Hugh O'Neill and they met with great initial success in the nine-years war. O'Donnell was poisoned in Spain in 1602 where he was soliciting further Spanish aid.

O'Duffy, Eoin (1892-1944). Born Monaghan he supported the Anglo-Irish Treaty and in 1922 became the first Commissioner of the new police force. De Valera sacked him in 1933. O'Duffy went on to lead the quasi-fascist Blueshirts and later Fine Gael. He resigned as leader of Fine Gael in 1934 and in 1936 led an Irish Brigade in support of General Franco in the Spanish Civil War.

O'Growney, Fr Eugene (1863-1899). Born Meath, a key figure in the revival of the Irish language in the last century he was vice-president of the Gaelic League from 1893 and Professor of Irish at Maynooth College 1891-96.

Ó'Fiaich, Tomás (1923-90). Born Armagh, Professor of Modern History (1959-74) at Maynooth College and President of Maynooth before being ordained Archbishop of Armagh in 1977 and created Cardinal in 1979.

O'Higgins, Kevin (1892-1927). Born Laois, elected to the first Dáil in 1918, he supported the Anglo-Irish Treaty in 1921. As Minister for Justice he ruthlessly dealt with opponents of the Treaty. 77 prisoners were executed by the Government during the Civil War. He was assassinated in July 1927.

Ó hUiginn, Tadhg Dall (1550-91). Born Sligo, Bardic poet who dedicated his poems to the Gaelic lords in his surrounding area.

O'Malley, Donogh (1921-68) Born Limerick, TD from 1954 until his death and influential Government Minister under Lemass and Lynch. Introduced free post-primary education in 1966.

O'Malley, Grace (1530-1600). Born Mayo, also known as Gráinne Mhaol legendary sixteenth century pirate queen operating off the west coast.

O'Neill, Hugh (1550-1616). Born Tyrone, Chief of O'Neill Clan from 1595 he and Red Hugh O'Donnell engaged the English in the nine-years war culminating in his surrender and the Treaty of Mellifont in 1603. After having large tracts of land taken from him he and other Gaelic Chiefs fled in 'The Flight of the Earls' in 1607.

O'Neill, Owen Roe (1590-1649). Nephew of Hugh, he sailed from Spain in 1642 and became leader of the Ulster forces who were rebelling in support of Charles I and his struggle in the English Civil War. He led his troops to many victories, notably at Benburb in 1646.

O'Neill, Phelim (1604-1653). Leader of the 1641 Rising, he was executed for that role in 1653.

O'Neill, Captain Terence (1914-1990). Born in

London. Northern Ireland Prime Minister from 1963 to 1969. A veteran of World War One. Made moves of reconciliation with Roman Catholics in Six Counties and with the Republic. His reforms didn't go far enough for the Civil Rights Movement and too far for Unionists. He resigned in May 1969.

O'Nolan, Brian (1911-1966). Born Tyrone he was a journalist, humourist, and novelist who used the pseudonyms Flann O'Brien and Myles na gCopaleen.

Ó'Riada, Seán (1931-71). Born Cork his work as a composer awakened a new interest in traditional music in the 60s. Best remembered for the music score in the 1959 documentary 'Mise Éire'.

O'Shea, Katharine (1845-1921). Born Essex, the mistress of Charles Stewart Parnell she married him in 1891 after he had been ousted from the leadership of the Irish Parliamentary Party.

O'Shea, Captain William (1840-1905). Born Dublin, the first husband of Katharine O'Shea he cited Parnell as co-respondent in his divorce from her thus precipitating Parnell's political fall. He had been a Home Rule MP for Clare 1880-5 and Galway 1885-6.

Parnell, Anna (1852-1911). Born Wicklow, founded the Ladies Land League in 1881 and was decidedly more radical than her brother Charles.

Parnell, Charles Stewart (1846-1891). Born in Wicklow. Known as 'the Uncrowned King of Ireland'. Became Leader of the Home Rule party in 1879. Lobbied successfully for Land Reform in House of Commons. Successfully governed public opinion in favour of Home Rule. In 1890 was cited as co-respondent in the divorce suit of Captain William O'Shea. Was voted out of leadership by his party. Married Katherine O'Shea in June 1891. He died in Brighton in October 1891.

Parsons, Charles (1884-1931). Born in County Offaly. Invented turbine for use in ships.

Patrick, St. Missionary bishop who came to Ireland in 432 to help the spread of Christianity. Patrick is the foremost of our three patron saints and his feast day is March 17.

Pearse, Pádraig (1879-1916). Born Dublin, founded the all-Irish Scoil Éanna in 1908 and was heavily involved in the Gaelic League. Pearse joined the IRB in 1913 and was Commander in Chief in the 1916 Rising. He was also President of the Irish Republic and a signatory of the Proclamation of the Republic. Pearse was executed on May 3 1916.

Plunkett, Joseph Mary (1887-1916). Born Dublin, poet and chief military strategist for the rebels in the 1916 Rising and signatory of the Proclamation of the Republic. He was executed on May 4 1916.

Plunkett, Saint Oliver (1625-1681). Born Meath, Archbishop of Armagh from 1669. Hanged, drawn and quartered following spurious charges of involvement in a 'Popish Plot'. Canonised in 1975.

Redmond, John (1856-1918). Born Wexford, an MP from 1881 until his death, he led the Parnellite faction of the Home Rule Party from 1890 and the whole

party when the two factions re-united in 1900. Influential in the gaining of the 1912 Home Rule Bill. He called on the Irish Volunteers to join the British war effort in 1914, almost 200,000 did.

Rice, Edmund (1762-1844). Born Kilkenny, founded his first school in 1803 in what was to be the beginning of the Christian Brothers. Pope Pius VII officially recognised the Christian Brothers in 1820 and Brother Ignatius as he was then known became Superior-General.

Ring, Christy - see Who Was Who Irish Sport

Ryan, Frank (1902-44). Born Limerick, fought on the Republican side in the Civil War. In 1936 he led 200 Irish volunteers to Spain to fight in the 15th International Brigade against Franco. Captured in 1938 he was released to Germany in 1940. He died in Berlin in 1944.

Sarsfield, Patrick Born Dublin, leader of the Irish forces at the Siege of Limerick in 1691. Led 12,000 of his troops to France following the Treaty. He was wounded and died in battle in 1693.

Shanahan, Joseph (1871-1943) Born Tipperary, missionary in Nigeria from 1902 and ordained bishop there in 1920. Died in Kenya in 1943.

Sullivan, Sir Arthur (1842-1900). Born in London. The composing half of the comic opera duo Gilbert & Sullivan. Wrote many comic operas including 'The Mikado', (1885) and 'HMS Pinafore', (1878) but also some serious works such as the opera 'Ivanhoe', (1886). His parents were both Irish.

Swift, Jonathan - see Famous Irish Writers.

Tandy, James Napper (1740-1803) Born Dublin, founding member of the United Irishmen in 1791 he was in Paris in 1798 and enlisted French help. His small force never landed on the mainland but he was captured, tried and sentenced to death in 1798. He was however released following pressure from Napoleon. He returned to France on his release in 1802.

Thompson, William/Lord Kelvin (1824-1907). Born in Belfast. Professor of Natural History at University of Glasgow. A leading scientist of Nineteenth Century . Main achievement was discovery of 2nd Law of Thermodynamics (Kelvin absolute scale of temperature).

Tone, Theobald Wolfe (1763-1798). Born in Dublin. Founding member of United Irishmen in 1791. Enlisted French help for 1798 Rising. Captured at Buncrana, sentenced to be hanged but cheated the gallows by inexpertly slitting his throat.

Yeats, Jack Butler (1871-1957). Born in London. The National Gallery in Dublin houses many of his paintings. Brother of the poet William Butler Yeats. His works are inspired by the people and events of early twentieth century Ireland.

Yeats, William Butler - see Famous Irish Writers

Walker, Rev George (1618-1690) Born Tyrone, Protestant minister who was joint governor of Derry during the siege (April - July 1689). He was appointed bishop of Derry following the siege and was killed in battle in 1690.

WHO'S WHO IN IRELAND

Adams, Gerry President of *Sinn Féin.*

Ahern, T.D., Bertie Leader of *Fianna Fáil.*

Alderdice, Lord John Leader of the *Alliance Party.*

Allen, Very Rev. Dr. David Henry Moderator of the Presbyterian Church in Ireland.

Best, George Former Northern Ireland International footballer.

Best, Rev. Kenneth President of the Methodist Church in Ireland.

Bonner, Packie International footballer.

Bono (Hewson, Paul) Singer with *U2.*

Boothman, Jack President of the *Gaelic Athletic Association.*

Boylan, Sean Meath gaelic football team-manager.

Brady, Archbishop Sean Catholic Primate and Archbishop of Armagh.

Brannagh, Kenneth Actor and director.

Bruton, T.D., John Taoiseach and leader of *Fine Gael.*

Byrne, Gay Television and radio presenter.

Byrne, Patrick Garda Commissioner.

Canavan, Peter Tyrone Gaelic footballer.

Casey, Bishop Eamon Former Bishop of Galway.

Cassells, Pat General Secretary *Irish Congress of Trade Unions.*

Clifford, Archbishop Dermot Catholic Archbishop of Cashel

Connell, Archbishop Desmond Catholic Archbishop of Dublin.

Corrigan, Mairead Founder member of the *Peace People* and Nobel Peace Prize winner.

Cosgrave, Dr. Art President of University College Dublin.

Cosgrave, Liam Former Taoiseach.

Costello, Paul Clothes designer.

Coulter, Phil Composer, song writer.

Daly, Cardinal Cahal Former Archbishop of Armagh.

Dana (Brown, Rosemary) Singer.

de Courcy Ireland, Dr. John Writer, campaigner on maritime issues.

Doherty, Moya Promoter of *Riverdance.*

Doolin, Lelia Chairperson of *Irish Film Council.*

Dunlop, Rev. Dr. John Former Moderator of Presbyterian Church in Ireland.

Eames, Archbishop Robert Church of Ireland Primate and Archbishop of Armagh.

Empey, Reg Former Lord Mayor of Belfast.

Empey, Archbishop Walton Church of Ireland Archbishop of Dublin.

Ervine, David Spokesman for *Progressive Unionist Party.*

Faul, Mgr. Denis Northern Ireland human rights activist.

Finn, Vincent Director General of *RTE.*

FitzGerald, Dr. Garrett Former Taoiseach.

Flanagan, Ronnie RUC Chief Constable.

Fricker, Brenda Actress.

Friel, Brian Playwright.

Gagesby, Douglas Journalist, former Editor of *Irish Times.*

Geldoff, Bob Rock star, founder of *Live Aid.*

Goan, Cathal Ceannasaí (Head) of *Teilifís na Gaeilge.*

Goodman, Larry Businessman.

Greevy, Bernadette Singer.

Griffin, Liam Former Wexford Hurling team manager.

Hamilton, The Hon. Mr. Justice Liam Chief Justice, Republic of Ireland Supreme Court.

Hanifin, Des Anti-Divorce Campaigner.

Harney, T.D., Mary Leader of the *Progressive Democrats.*

Haughey, Charles Former Taoiseach.

Heeney, Seamus Poet, Nobel Prize-winner for literature.

Heffernan, Margaret Businesswoman., Director of *Dunnes Stores.*

Hillary, Patrick Former President of Ireland.

Hume, M.P., M.E.P., John Leader of *SDLP.*

Hurley, S.J., Rev Michael Founder of Irish School of Ecumenics, and Columbanus Ecumenical Community.

Hutchinson, Billy Spokesman for the *Ulster Democratic Unionist Party.*

Jennings, Pat Former Northern Ireland International footballer.

Jordan, Neil Film Director, writer.

Keenan, Brian Former Beruit hostage, writer.

Kelly, Sean Cyclist.

Lee, Senator Joseph Historian.

Logan, Johnny Three-times *Eurovision Song Contest* winner.

Lord Moyola (Clarke, James Chichester) Former Northern Ireland Prime Minister.

Loughery, Patrick Head of BBC Northern Ireland.

Lynch, Jack Former Taoiseach.

MacAonghusa, Proinsias Author. Ex-Uachtarán (President) of *Conradh na Gaeilge.*

Magee, Rev. Roy Presbyterian minister, negotiator in Loyalist Ceasefire, 1994.

Maguire, Sean Traditional fiddler.

Mallon, M.P., Seamus Deputy leader of the *SDLP.*

Marcus, David Editor and writer.

McAliskey, Bernadette Devlin Civil Rights activist.

McBride, Willie John Former International rugby player.

McCarter, Willie Industrialist, Chairman *International Fund for Ireland.*

McCurtain, O.P., Sr. Margaret Historian, religious writer.

McDonagh, Rev. Enda Theologian.

McGuinness, Martin Spokesman for *Sinn Féin.*

McGuinness, Paul Financier, Manager of *U2* rock group.

McKenna, Sr. Breige Spiritual healing writer.

McMahon, Lt. Gen. Gerry Chief of Staff, Republic of Ireland Defence Forces.

McSharry, Ray Former European Commissioner and former Minister of Finance.

Mhac a' tSaoi, Máire Irish language poet.

Molyneaux, Sir James Former leader of the *Ulster Unionist Party.*

Moloney, Paddy Uillean piper, leader of *The Chieftains.*

Murray, Mgr. Raymond Northern Ireland human rights activist.

Neary, Archbishop Michael Catholic Archbishop of Tuam.

Neeson, Liam Actor.

Ní Dhomhnaill, Nuala Irish language poet.

O'Brien, Dr. Conor Cruise Author and critic.

O'Brien, Edna Writer.

O'Brien, Vincent Racehorse trainer.

Ó Cearúlláin, Gearóid Uachtarán (President) of *Conradh na Gaeilge.*

O'Connell, Mick Former Kerry gaelic footballer.

O'Connor Snr., Christy Golfer.

O'Connor, John Pianist.

O'Donnell, Daniel Singer.

Ó Gallchóir, Pól Ceannaire (Head) of *Raidío na Gaeltachta.*

O'Hehir, Michael Former sporting broadcaster.

O'Móráin, Donall Founder *Gael Linn*, former *RTE* Chairman.

Ó Muircheartaigh, Mícheál Gaelic Games broadcaster. Cathaoirleach (Chairman) of *Bord na Gaeilge.*

Ó Muirchú, Labhras President of *Comhaltas Ceoltóirí Éireann.*

O'Reilly, Dr. Tony Businessman.

Ó Sé, Seán Traditional Singer.

Ó Searcaigh, Cathal Irish language poet.

Ó Súilleabháin, Mícheál Composer.

O'Sullivan, Sonia Athlete.

Paisley, M.P., M.E.P., Rev. Dr. Ian Leader of the *DUP* and Moderator of Free Presbyterian Church.

Peters, Mary Olympic gold medalist.

Potter, Maureen Comedienne.

Quinn, Patricia Director of Arts Council.

Quinn, Peter Financier, former President of *Gaelic Athletic Association.*

Quinn, T.D., Ruairí Minister for Finance.

Reid, Rev. Alex Catholic priest, involved in IRA Ceasefire, 1994.

Reynolds, Albert Former Taoiseach.

Robinson, Mrs. Mary President of Ireland.

Robinson, M.P., Peter Deputy leader of the *DUP.*

Roche, Stephen Cyclist.

Rodgers, Bríd Spokesperson for *SDLP.*

Rodgers, Patsy Dan King of Tory Island (Rí Thoraí), naive painter.

Ryan, Dr. Tony Businessman.

Sheridan, Jim Film Director.

Smith, Michelle Olympic Swimming Champion.

Smurfit, Michael Businessman.

Smurfit, Norma Patron of community enterprise.

Smyth, Desmond Chief Executive *UTV.*

Spence, Gusty Spokesman for *Combined Loyalist Command.*

Spring, T.D., Dick Tanaiste and Minister for Foreign Affairs.

Stephenson, Sam Architect.

Stokes, Niall Journalist. Chairman of IRTC.

Sutherland, Peter Former European Commissioner, former Irish Attorney-General.

Taylor, M.P., John Deputy leader of the *Ulster Unionist Party.*

Treacy, Philip Milliner.

Trimble, David Leader of the *Ulster Unionist Party.*

Whelehan, Harry Former Attorney General.

Whitaker, Ken Former senior civil servant. Author of *Programme for Economic Expansion.*

Williams, Betty Founder member of the *Peace People* and a Nobel Peace Prize winner.

INTERNATIONAL WHO'S WHO & WHO WAS WHO

International Figures with Irish Connections

AMERICA

Commodore John Barry (b. Wexford, 1745). "Father of the American Navy". Supervised progress of the US Navy after War of Independence until his death. Died   1803.

Henry Knox (b. Derry, 1750). First Commander-in-Chief of the American Army. Secretary of War 1785 - 97. Died 1806.

William Penn (b. Cork, 1644). Has the state of Pennsylvania (Penn's Woods) named after him. Died 1718.

Joseph Raymond McCarthy (b. 1908). Orchestrated Anti-Communist witchhunts in 1950's America (McCarthyism). His mother, Bridge Tierney was born in Ireland. Died 1957.

American Declaration was hand written by Charles Thomson, first printed by John Dunlop (Tyrone) and signed by James Smith (Dublin), George Taylor and Matthew Thornton (both from Derry).

20 OF AMERICAS 42 PRESIDENTS CLAIM VARYING DEGREES OF IRISH DESCENT

John Adams 2nd President. (1791-1801). Ulster Descent.

James Monroe 5th President. (1816-1820). Derry Descent.

John Quincy Adams 6th President (1825-1829). Son of John Adams, 2nd President.

Andrew Jackson 7th President. (1829-1837). His father was born in Co. Antrim, his mother was also Irish.

James Knox Polk 11th President. (1845-1849). Descendant of a Scots planter who received land in the Ulster Plantation in Derry.

James Buchanan 15th President. (1857-1861). His father James Snr. was born in Ramelton, Co. Donegal

Andrew Johnson 17th President. (1865-1869). Both parents were of Ulster Descent.

Ulysses S. Grant 18th President. (1865-1877). Had ancestral roots in Tyrone.

Chester Alan Arthur 21st President. (1881-1885). Son of Rev. William Arthur from Ballymena, Co. Antrim.

Grover Cleveland 22nd and 24th President. (1885-9 and 1893-7). His mother was of Ulster Descent.

William McKinlay 25th President. (1897-1901). His grandfather was born in Co. Antrim.

William Howard Taft 27th President. (1909-1913). His father married into an Irish family.

Woodrow Wilson 28th President. (1913-1921). His grandfather was from Strabane, his grandmother was from Sion Mills, both Co. Tyrone.

Warren Gamaliel Harding 29th President. (1921-1923). His family intermarried with Irish families.

Herbert Clark Hoover 31st President. (1929-1933). His grandmother was born in Ireland.

Harry S. Truman - 33rd President. (1945-1953). His maternal grandmother was Irish.

John Fitzgerald Kennedy 35th President. (1961-1963). His great-grandfather was born in Wexford. Only Roman Catholic President of the United States.

Richard Milhous Nixon 37th President. (1969-1974). His mother 's family had Kildare ancestry and his father's family had roots in Laois.

Ronald Reagan 40th President. (1980-1988). His paternal great-grandparents came from Ballyporeen, Co. Tipperary.

William J. Clinton 42nd and current President. (1992-). His maternal great-grandparents came from Co. Fermanagh. Seeking second term in office.

CANADA

Sir Francis Hincks - (b. 1807). Prime Minister of Canada from 1851 to 1854. Subsequently, was Governor of the British Colonies of Barbados, the Windward Islands and British Guiana. Died 1885.

Arthur Meighen - Prime Minister from 1920 to 1921. Grandson of a Derry man.

Lieutenant-Colonel George French - (b. 1841, Roscommon.). Founded the Royal Canadian Mounted Police ("Mounties") in 1873.

Brian Mulroney - (b. 1939, Canada). Prime Minister from 1984 to 1992. Ancestors came from Carlow.

SOUTH AMERICA

Ambrosio O'Higgins (b. 1720, Meath). Governor of Chile from 1787. Viceroy of Peru from 1795 to 1801. He was working for the Spanish on both occasions. Died 1801.

Bernardo O'Higgins (b. 1778). Son of Ambrosio, considered as the father of Chilean Independence. Defeated Spanish in 1817 and became first President of Chile. Also founded the Chilean Navy. Died 1842.

Thomas Charles Wright (b. 1799, Drogheda). British Navy veteran. Founded the Navy of Ecuador when it won independence in 1830.   Died 1868.

William Brown (b. 1777, Mayo). British Navy veteran. Founded the Argentine Navy in 1813 helping Argentina shake of the burden of Spanish Rule.   Died 1857.

Peter Campbell (b. Tipperary). Founded Uruguayan Navy in 1814. Died in 1832.

SPAIN

Richard Wall (b. Waterford, 1694). Spanish Secretary of State (i.e. Chief Minister to the King) from 1754 to 1764. Died 1778.

Leopoldo O'Donnell (b. 1809). Governor General of Cuba (for Spain) and Spanish Prime Minister in 1850's and 1860's. Died 1867.

Moran, Patrick (b. 1830, Carlow). Became Australia's first Cardinal in 1885. Died 1911.

BRITAIN

Sir William Petty (b. 1737, Dublin). Prime Minister of Britain from 1782 to 1783. Was the 2nd Earl of Shelburne. Died 1805.

George Canning (b. 1770, Dublin.). Prime Minister in 1827. He died in office. Was unpopular because of his pursuit of Catholic Emancipation. Died 1827.

Arthur Wellesley (b. 1769, Dublin). Prime Minister from 1828 to 1830. 1st Duke of Wellington. Had been Field Marshal and Commander-in-Chief of British Army defeating Napoleon more than once (including at Waterloo in 1815). Passed the law enabling Catholic Emancipation in 1829. Died 1852.

Sir Robert Peel (b. 1788, England). Prime Minister from 1834 to 1835 and from 1841 to 1846. Chief Secretary in Ireland from 1812 to 1818. M.P. for Cashel in 1809. Set up the "Peace Preservation Police" (the Peelers) in 1814. It became the Royal Irish Constabulary (RIC) in 1867. It was the world's first organised Police Force. In 1829, the London Metropolitan Police Force was set up. Died 1850.

Sir Henry John Temple (b. 1784, England). Prime Minister from 1855 to to 1858 and from 1859 to 1865. Came from an Anglo-Irish Family and was 3rd Viscount of Palmerston.

Andrew Bonar Law (b. 1858, Kingston, Canada). Prime Minister from 1922 to 1923. Was a hardline Unionist (reflecting his Ulster Presbyterian roots) in his approach to the Irish situation at the time of his premiership. Died 1923.

Stanley Baldwin (b. 1867, England). Prime Minister from 1923 to 1924, 1924 to 1929 and from 1935 to 1937. Great-grandfather came from County Fermanagh. Died 1947.

James Callaghan (b. 1912). Labour Prime Minister from 1976 to 1979. Great-grandfather left Ireland during the Famine.

AUSTRALIA

James Henry Scullin (b. 1876, Victoria). Prime Minister 1929 to 1931. His father was Irish. Died 1953.

Joseph A. Lyons (b. 1879, Tasmania). Prime Minister from 1931 to 1939. His family was Irish. Died 1939.

John Joseph Ambrose Curtin (b. 1885, Victoria). His father was from Cork. He mobilised Australian Forces to deter Japanese Invasion. Died 1945.

Joseph Benedict Chifley (b. 1885, New South Wales). Prime Minister from 1945 to 1949. His mother was born in Ireland as was his paternal grandfather. Died 1951.

Paul Keating (b. Sydney). Prime Minister from 1991 until 1996. Great-grandfather was from County Galway. Wanted Australia to withdraw from the British Commonwealth and become a Republic by 2000, but was defeated in recent Australian General Election.

NEW ZEALAND

John Ballance (b.1839, Antrim). Prime Minister from 1891 to 1893. Supported notion of Woman's Suffrage which came into being in 1893 in New Zealand, the first country in the world where this happened. Died 1893.

William Ferguson Massey (b. 1856, Derry). Led New Zealand through World War One and was Signatory of the 1919 Treaty of Versailles. Died 1925

Michael Joseph Savage (b. 1872, Australia). Prime Minister from 1935 to 1940. Born in Australia of Irish Parents. Died 1940.

Brendan Bolger (b. 1935, Taranki). Current Prime Minister from 1990. Both parents came from Wexford.

Captain William Hobson (b. 1793, Waterford). Britain's first Consul & Governor of New Zealand from 1839. Died 1872.

ISRAEL

Chaim Herzog - (b. 1918, Belfast). President of Israel from 1983 to 1993. World War Two veteran (with British Army). Joined Israeli Defence Force and became first Military Governor of West Bank.

FRANCE

Patrick Maurice, Counte de MacMahon (b. 1808, France). Grandfather was born in Limerick. President of third French Republic from 1873 to 1879. Died 1893.

Henry James Clarke (b. 1765, France). Both parents Irish. Was Minister of War to Napoleon Bonaparte from 1807 to 1814. Died 1818.

Charles de Gaulle (b. 1890, France). President of France from 1958 to 1969. His maternal ancestors were MacCartan of Donegal who left after the Williamite Wars. Died 1970.

REST OF EUROPE:

Count Peter Lacy (b. 1678, Limerick). Governor of modern day Latvia from 1728 to 1751 and was field-marshal in the Russian Army. Died 1751.

Count George de Browne (b. 1698, Limerick). Governor of Latvia in late eighteenth century and was field-marshal in Russian Army. Died 1792.

SOUTH AFRICA

Asmal, Kadar Abdul (b. 1934, South Africa). Was educated for a time at Trinity College Dublin. Lectured extensively in Ireland from 1962 onwards. Deeply involved in Campaigns against Apartheid, Chairman of Irish Anti-Apartheid Movement since 60's. Now a Minister in the Mandela Government in South Africa.

AUSTINS

IRELAND'S
most friendly
DEPARTMENT STORE

The Diamond, Derry.

GEOGRAPHICAL AND ENVIRONMENT

IRISH GEOGRAPHICAL AND PHYSICAL STATISTICS

Ireland......................Total area ....32,593 sq. miles
Republic of Ireland ....Total area ....27,137 sq. miles
Republic of Ireland ....Land...26,401 sq. miles
Republic of Ireland ....Water..736 sq. miles
Northern Ireland ....Total area...5,456 sq. miles
Northern Ireland ....Land...5,156 sq. miles
Northern Ireland ....Water...300 sq. miles
Greatest length ....North to south.....................................302 miles (486 km)
Greatest width ....East to west..171 miles (275 km)
Total coastline.....................Ireland ....1970.5 miles (3,152 km)
Total coastline.....................Republic of Ireland ....1,737 miles
Total coastline.....................Northern Ireland ....232 miles
Highest point ....Carrantuohill, Co. Kerry 3,414ft (1024.2m)
Lowest point .... No point in Ireland is below sea-level
Largest island...Aran Islands, Galway
Longest river ....The Shannon (rises in Cavan, meets Atlantic in Limerick)....224 miles (358km)
Largest lake ....Lough Neagh, N. Ireland ....149.61 sq. miles (95,748 acres)
Highest waterfall ....Powerscourt, Co. Wicklow 350ft (106m)
Highest cliff ....Croaghan, Achill Island, Co. Mayo 2192ft (668m)
Longest stalactite ....Pollan Ionain, Co. Clare ....20ft 4" (6.2m)
Deepest cave ....Carrowmore Cavern , Co. Sligo 459ft (140m)
Highest temperature recorded ....Kilkenny Castle (26 June 1887)...................92oF/33.3oC
Lowest temperature recorded ....Omagh, (Edenfel) Co. Tyrone (23 January 1881) 2.92oF/-19.4oC
Heaviest rainfall ....Orra Beg, North Antrim (1 August 1980) ....3.82in (97mm) in 45 min
Driest year recorded 1887
Longest drought recorded ....Co. Limerick ....3 April to 10 May 1938 (37 days)
Heaviest snowfall ....January 1917
Highest windspeed ....Kilkeel, Co. Down (January 1974) ....108 knots
Northernmost point ....Malin Head, Co. Donegal
Northernmost town/village ....(Town) Carndonagh, Co. Donegal........................(Village) Malin, Co. Donegal
Southernmost point ....Mizen Head, Co. Cork
Southernmost town/village.................(Town) Skibbereen, Co. Cork....................(Village) Baltimore, Co. Cork
Easternmost point ....Wicklow Head, Co. Wicklow
Easternmost town ....Wicklow Town, Co. Wicklow
Westernmost point ....Dunmore Head, (Slea Head) Co. Kerry
Westernmost town/village..................(Town) Dingle, Co. Kerry....................(Village) Ballyferriter, Co. Kerry
Largest county ....Cork
Smallest county ....Louth
Biggest dam ....Poulaphuca Reservoir, Co. Wicklow
Tallest building ....County Hall, Cork (Cork Corporation)
Tallest structure ....Pigeon House chimneys, Dublin 681ft 2in (207.08m)
Longest bridge span ....Barrow Railway Bridge

INTRODUCTION

The Island of Ireland - Physical Features

The island of Ireland, located in the Atlantic ocean, west of Great Britain and extreme north-west of the continent of Europe, lies between latitude 51.5 and 55.5 degrees north and longitude 5.5 and 10.5 degrees west.

The island consists of a large central plateau, the elevation of which is generally less than 150m above sea level, ringed almost entirely by coastal highlands which vary considerably in geological structure. To the south, the mountain ridges consist of old red sandstone separated by deep limestone river valleys. The mountains of Donegal, Mayo and Galway are geologically dominated by granite, as are those in

counties Down and Wicklow. Almost 5 per cent of the island's total area is between 300 and 600m above sea level, ensuring sparse plant life. The north-east of the island is predominantly covered by a basalt plateau, while the central plain is largely covered with glacial deposits of sand and clay. The central plain also contains numerous areas of bog, most notably the Bog of Allen, and is interspersed with lakes.

Geologists state that the Irish terrain marked by "ice-smoothed rock, mountain lakes, glacial valleys and deposits of sand, gravel and clay" point to at least two great glaciations of the island. They also state that

87

Ireland was separated from mainland Europe following the last Ice Age. Ireland is also separated from the island of Britain by the Irish Sea, the distances between the two islands ranging from 11 to 120 miles apart at its closest and farthest points.

CLIMATE: The climate of Ireland is influenced by the warm waters of the Gulf Stream, with the result that the climate is temperate. The relatively small size of the island and the prevailing south-west winds ensure a uniform temperature over the whole country.

Irish winters are generally mild while the summers are generally cool. The coldest months of the year are usually January and February, with temperatures averaging between 4°C and 7°C. During the winter months snow does occur from time to time but is normally not severe and is shortlived, generally lasting for only a few days at a time. May and June are the sunniest months, averaging 5-7 hours of sunshine per day. July and August are the warmest summer months, averaging between 14°C and 16°C. The minimum length of day occurs in late December, around 7 to 7.5 hours, and the longest occurs in late June and ranges between 16.5 and 17.5 hours between sunrise and sunset. Rainfall, carried in from the Atlantic by prevailing west winds, is well distributed all over the island, however the west generally has a greater annual rainfall than the east thanks to its proximity to the Atlantic Ocean and because it is much more mountainous. In low lying areas the average annual rainfall is between 800 and 1200mm (31" to 47"), and in mountainous areas as much as 2000mm (79") per annum is not unusual.

IRELAND AREA COMPARISON TABLE

The total land area of the island of Ireland is 32,595 sq. miles while, for example, Australia has 2,966,200 sq. miles. Consequently, Ireland would fit into Australia more than 91 times. A comparison table indicates the country's size in relation to the land area of selected countries throughout the world.

(All figures are approximations).

(+ = Number of times greater. - Number of times smaller.)

Country	Area	Comparison
Argentina:	1,073,518 sq. miles	+ 33
Australia:	2,966,200 sq. miles	+ 91
Austria:	32,378 sq. miles	1
Brazil:	3,286,500 sq. miles	+ 100
Canada:	3,849,674 sq. miles	+ 118
China:	3,696,100 sq. miles	+ 113
Greenland:	840,000 sq. miles	+ 26
Egypt:	385,229 sq. miles	+ 12
Ethiopia:	437,794 sq. miles	+ 13
France:	210,026 sq. miles	+ 6
Germany:	137,823 sq. miles	+ 4
India:	1,222,243 sq. miles	+ 37
Iraq:	167,975 sq. miles	+ 5
Indonesia:	741,052 sq. miles	+ 23
Iran:	632,457 sq. miles	+ 19
Israel:	7,992 sq. miles	- 4
Italy:	116,334 sq. miles	+ 4
Japan:	145,850 sq. miles	+ 4
Kenya:	224,961 sq. miles	+ 7
Libya:	678,400 sq. miles	+ 21
Luxembourg:	999 sq. miles	- 33
Mexico:	756,066 sq. miles	+ 23
Monaco:	0.75 sq. miles	- 32,594
Netherlands:	16,033 sq. miles	- 2
New Zealand:	104,454 sq. miles	+ 3
Norway:	125,050 sq. miles	+ 4
Pakistan:	339,697 sq. miles	+10
Peru:	496,225 sq. miles	+ 15
Philippines:	115,860 sq. miles	+ 4
Poland:	120,728 sq. miles	+ 4
Portugal:	35,574 sq. miles	+ 1
Russia*:	6,592,800 sq. miles	+ 202
Saudi Arabia:	865,000 sq. miles	+ 27
South Africa:	472,281 sq. miles	+ 14
Spain:	194,898 sq. miles	+ 6
Sweden:	173,732 sq. miles	+ 5
Switzerland:	15,940 sq. miles	- 2
Syria:	71,498 sq. miles	+ 2
Thailand:	198,115 sq. miles	+ 6
U.K.:	94,251 sq. miles	+ 3
U.S.A.:	3,679,192 sq. miles	+ 113
Venezuela:	352,144 sq. miles	+ 11
Vietnam:	127,246 sq. miles	+ 4
Zimbabwe:	150,872 sq. miles	+ 5

* [Prior to 1992]

Area by province and persons per square kilometre in Republic of Ireland

Province	Total area (hectares)	Selected lakes, rivers and tideways (hectares)	Land and other waters (hectares)	Persons per square kilometre
Rep. of Ire.	7,028,510	139,054	6,889,456	51
Leinster	1,979,432	16,097	1,963,335	95
Munster	2,468,874	56,136	2,412,738	42
Connacht	1,771,342	59,170	1,712,172	25
Ulster*	808,862	7,651	801,211	29

* Cavan, Donegal and Monaghan

IRELAND: WORLD TIME DIFFERENCES

Hours Plus or minus GMT

The 0 degree meridian has been established as the reference line for setting time. This line runs through Greenwich in London, known as GMT, or, Greenwich Mean Time. Because of Ireland's proximity to London, it shares the same time zone as Britain. The times listed below should be added to standard time in Ireland to ascertain various world time differences in relation to Ireland.

Accra (Ghana)	00.00	Karachi (Pakistan	+05.00
Adelaide (Australia)	+09.30	Lagos (Nigeria)	+01.00
Alexandria (Egypt)	+02.00	Lima (Peru)	-05.00
Amsterdam (Holland)	+01.00	Lisbon (Portugal)	00.00
Athens (Greece)	+02.00	Liverpool (England)	00.00
Baghdad (Iraq)	+03.00	London (England)	00.00
Bangkok (Thailand)	+07.00	Los Angeles (United States)	-08.00
Beijing (China)	+08.00	Madrid (Spain)	+01.00
Berlin (Germany)	+01.00	Malta	+01.00
Bombay (India)	+05.30	Manchester (England)	00.00
Brussels (Belgium)	+01.00	Melbourne (Australia)	+10.00
Buenos Aires (Argentina)	-03.00	Montevideo (Urrguay)	-03.00
Cairo (Egypt)	+02.00	Montreal (Canada)	-05.00
Calcutta (India)	+05.30	Moscow (Russia)	+03.00
Calgary (Canada)	-07.00	Nairobi (Kenya)	+03.00
Cape Town (South Africa)	+02.00	New York (United States)	-05.00
Cardiff (Wales)	00.00	Oslo (Norway)	+01.00
Chicago (United States)	-06.00	Paris (France)	+01.00
Christchurch (New Zealand)	+12.00	Perth (Western Australia)	+08.00
Colombo (Sri Lanka)	+05.30	Rangoon (Burma)	+06.30
Copenhagen (Denmark)	+01.00	Rio de Janeiro (Brazil)	-03.00
Delhi (India)	+05.30	Rome (Italy)	+01.00
Detroit (United States)	-05.00	San Francisco (United States)	-08.00
Durban (South Africa)	+02.00	Singapore (Malaysia)	+08.00
Glasgow (Scotland)	00.00	Stockholm (Sweden)	+01.00
Gibraltar (Spain)	+01.00	Sydney (Australia)	+10.00
Halifax (Canada)	-04.00	Tehran (Iran)	+03.30
Helsinki (Finland)	+02.00	Tokyo (Canada)	+09.00
Hong Kong	+08.00	Toronto (Canada)	-05.00
Honolulu (Hawaii)	-10.00	Vancouver (Canada)	-08.00
Houston (United States)	-06.00	Wellington (New Zealand)	+12.00
Istanbul (Turkey)	+02.00	Winnipeg (Canada)	-06.00
Jakarta (Indonesia)	+07.00	Zurich (Switzerland)	+01.00

METEOROLOGICAL STATIONS

Irish Meteorological Synoptic Stations

The Irish Meteorological Service has 15 synoptic stations throughout the country, manned on a 24 hour basis, and the main function of which is to maintain a continuous watch on the weather and to make detailed reports every hour on the hour. These reports provide the basis for all advice and information supplied to the general public regarding the 'weather forecast' and to the various specialised interests.

Station	Date established	County	Station	Date established	County
Valentia Observatory	1866	Kerry	Casement Aerodrome	1943	Kildare
Birr	1872	Offaly	Clones	1950	Monaghan
Roche's Point	1876	Waterford	Belmullet	1956	Mayo
Malin Head	1885	Donegal	Rosslare	1956	Wexford
Shannon Airport	1938	Clare	Kilkenny	1957	Kilkenny
Dublin Airport	1939	Dublin	Cork Airport	1961	Cork
Claremorris	1943	Mayo	Galway	1978	Galway
Mullingar	1943	Westmeath			

IRISH MAMMALS

Red Deer...(Cervus elaphus)	Irish Hare .... (Lepus timidus hibernicus)
Fallow Deer ....(Dama dama)	Pigmy Shrew ....(Sorex minutus)
Japanese Sika Deer ....(Cervus nippon)	Hedgehog ....(Erinaceus europaeus)
Pine Marten ....(Martes martes)	Grey Squirrel ....(Sciurus carolinensis)
Otter ....(Lutra lutra)	Red Squirrel ....(Sciurus vulgaris)
American Mink .... (Mustela vision)	Bank Vole .... (Clethrionomys glareolus)
Badger ....(Meles meles)	Field Mouse ....(Apodemus sylvaticus)
Irish Stoat ....(Mustela erminea hibernica)	Rat .... (Rattus norvegicus)
Fox ....(Vulpes vulpes)	Feral Goat ....(Capra hircus)
Rabbit ....(Oryctolagus cuniculus)	Bat ....(Rhinolophus hipposideros)

BIRDS OF IRELAND

Arctic Skua
Arctic Tern
Avocet
Barnacle Goose
Barn Owl
Bar-tailed Godwit
Bean Goose
Bewick's Swan
Bittern
Blackbird
Blackcap
Black Gullemot
Black-headed Gull
Black-necked Grebe
Black-tailed Godwit
Black-throated Diver
Blue Tit
Brambling
Brent Goose
Bullfinch
Buzzard
Canada Goose
Carrion Crow
Chaffinch
Chiffchaff
Chough
Cirl Bunting
Coal Tit
Collared Dove
Common Gull
Common Sandpiper
Common Scoter
Common Tern
Corncrake
Coot
Cormorant
Corn Bunting
Crossbil
Cuckoo
Curlew
Dipper
Dunlin
Dunnock
Egyptian Goose
Eider
Feral Pigeon
Fieldfare
Firecrest

Fulmar
Gadwall
Gannet
Garden Warbler
Glaucous Gull
Goldcrest
Goldeneye
Golden Pheasant
Golden Plover
Goldfinch
Goosander
Goshawk
Grasshopper Warbler
Great Black-backed Gull
Great Crested Grebe
Great North Diver
Great Skua
Great Tit
Greenfinch
Green Sandpiper
Greenshank
Grey Heron
Grey-leg Goose
Grey Phalarope
Grey Plover
Grey Wagtail
Gullemot
Hen Harrier
Herring Gull
Hooded Crow
House Martin
House Sparrow
Hybrid Carr / Hood
Iceland Gull
Jackdaw
Jack Snipe
Jay
Kestral
Kingfisher
Kittiwake
Knot
Lapwing
Lesser Black-backed Gull
Linnet
Little Auk
Little Grebe
Little Gull
Little Stint

Little Tern
Long-Eared Owl
Long-Tailed Duck
Long-Tailed Tit
Magpie
Mallard
Mandarin
Manx Shearwater
Meadow Pipit
Mediterranean Gull
Merlin
Misile Thrush
Moorhen
Mute Swan
Nightjar
Oystercatcher
Partridge
Peregrine
Pheasant
Pied Wagtail
Pink-footed Goose
Pintail
Pochard
Pomarine Skua
Puffin
Purple Sandpiper
Raven
Razorbill
Red-breasted Merg
Red Grouse
Red-leg Partridge
Red-necked Grabe
Red-necked Phalarope
Redpoll
Redshank
Red-throated Diver
Redwing
Reed Bunting
Ringed Plover
Ringneck Parakeet
Ring Ouzel
Robin
Rock Dove
Rock Pipit
Rook
Roseate Tern
Ruff
Sanderling

Sand Martin
Sandwich Tern
Scaup
Sedge Warbler
Shag
Shelduck
Shore Lark
Short-eared Owl
Shovelar
Siskin
Skylark
Slavonian Grebe
Smew
Snipe
Snow Bunting
Song Thrush
Sparrow Hawk
Spotted Flycatcher
Spotted Redshank
Starling
Stock Dove
Stonechat
Storm Petrel
Swallow
Swift
Teal
Treecreeper
Tree Sparrow
Tufted Duck
Turnstone
Turtle Dove
Twite
Velvet Scoter
Water Rail
Waxwing
Wheatear
Whimbrel
Whinchat
White-fronted Goose
Whitethroat
Whooper Swan
Wigeon
Willow Warbler
Woodcock
Woodpigeon
Wren
Yellowhammer

LIST OF ENDANGERED AND EXTINCT IRISH BIRDS

INDETERMINATE
Barn Owl .... (Tyto alba)
Tree Sparrow .... (Passer montanus)
Twite ....(Carduelis flavirostris)

RARE
Bearded Tit...................................... (Panurus biarmicus)
Black-necked Grebe...................... (Podiceps nigricollis)
Black-tailed Godwit .... (Limosa limosa)
Gadwall... (Anas strepera)
Garganey ....(Anas querquedula)
Goosander .... (Mergus merganser)
Greenshank .... (Tringa nebularia)
Merlin .... (Falco columbarius)
Pintail .... (Anas acuta)
Pochard... (Aythya ferina)
Red-throated Diver............................. (Gavia stellata)
Ring Ouzel .... (Turdus torquatus)
Short-eared Owl .... (Asio flammeus)
Shoveler ....(Anas clypeata)
Wood Warbler.......................... (Phylloscopus sibilatrix)

VULNERABLE
Dunlin .... (Calidris alpina)
Golden Plover .... (Pluvialis apricaria)
Little Tern .... (sterna albifrons)

ENDANGERED
Common Scoter ....(Melanitta nigra)
Corn Bunting..................................... (Miliaria calandra)
Corncrake .... (Crex crex)
Grey Partridge....................................... (Perdix perdix)
Hen Harrier... (Circus cyaneus)
Nightjar .... (Caprimulgus europaeus)
Red-necked Phalarope .... (Phalaropus lobatus)
Roseate Tern .... (Sterna dougallii)

EXTINCT
Bittern... (Botaurus stellaris)
Capercaillie ....(Tetrao urogallus)
Golden Eagle................................. (Aquila chrysaetos)
Marsh Harrier .... (Circus aeruginosus)
White-tailed Eagle .... (Haliaeetus albicilla)
Woodlark.. (Lullula arborea)

COUNTIES OF IRELAND, LARGEST TO SMALLEST
Ranked by size, 1-32

Size No.	County
1	Cork
2	Galway
3	Mayo
4	Donegal
5	Kerry
6	Tipperary
7	Clare
8	Tyrone
9	Antrim
10	Limerick
11	Roscommon
12	Down
13	Wexford
14	Meath
15	Derry
16	Kilkenny
17	Wicklow
18	Offaly
19	Cavan
20	Waterford
21	Sligo
22	Westmeath
23	Laois
24	Kildare
25	Fermanagh

Size No.	County
26	Leitrim
27	Dublin
28	Monaghan
29	Armagh
30	Longford
31	Carlow
32	Louth

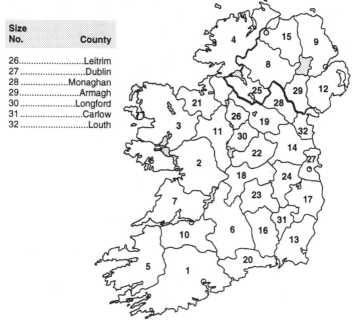

POPULATION

A TYPICAL IRISH PERSON THROUGH THE EYES OF THE CENSUS (Based on statistics from 1991 Census) By **Damian Dowds**

POPULATION

According to the 1991 Census carried out both North and South of the border in April, our island has a population of 5,103,555 with 3,525,719 of us living in the twenty-six counties of the Republic. 53.4% of us are under 25 while only 10.4% of us are aged 65 or older. Females outnumber males, but only just. There are under 60,000 more females than males, a difference of 1.2%.

HOUSEHOLD

We live in 1,579,506 housing units of which 77% are owner occupied with 43% of owner occupied houses in the Republic having mortgage or loan repayments. Figures are more readily available for the Republic where an average of 2.6 people live per household. In houses with an average of 4.74 rooms. Almost 99% of houses have piped running water while 72.3% of these draw their water from public mains (others draw from either local authority or private sources). 98% of household units have sanitary (i.e. toilet) facilities.

LABOUR

2,149,200 of us, or 42% of the island's population make up our labour force. 63% of the workforce (or 1,354,265) are male. As of December 1994, 372,383 (or 17.33% of the workforce) were unemployed with Northern Ireland's workers faring better, 12.3% of them were unemployed while 20% of the Republic's workforce was unemployed. The manufacturing industries provide the biggest number of jobs 388,783 or almost 22% of all those in employment. Other major areas of employment are Professional Services (16.4%), Commerce (13.7%) and Agriculture (10.3%). While the loneliest job in Northern Ireland are the four men (no women) involved in the extraction and preparation of metalliferous ores. There are only four cattle testers and milk inspectors in the Republic.

WHERE WE LIVE

In 1992, it was estimated that 56% of the population of the Republic were urban dwellers. While figures show that every square kilometre of the island would have 60.4 persons, if the population was equally distributed, this is not the case as Leinster, with its 1,860,949 inhabitants has a population density of 95 persons per square kilometre. Connacht with its 423,031 inhabitants is decidedly less congested with only 25 persons per square kilometre.

CITIES

Our five largest cities are (in descending order) Dublin, Belfast, Cork, Derry and Limerick. Unsurprisingly, Dublin is the island's most populous county with 1,025,304 people while Leitrim has the smallest county population with only 25,031 inhabitants.

EDUCATION

For the academic year 1993/1994, 26.9% of us (or 1,349,770) were in full-time education reflecting the youth of our population. 710,723 children attended 4,477 primary schools while 523,713 students attended 1052 secondary schools across the 32 counties. 115,334 (or 2.3% of the population) attended various third-level institutions. Just over 24% of all persons over 15 in the Republic have completed Secondary schooling with the gender breakdown as follows: around 30% of females over 15 and 22.9% of males over 15. In 1996, 59,000 students sat the Leaving Certificate while 68,062 sat the Junior Certificate. Third level institutions awarded 14,383 Primary Degrees and 4,355 Post-graduate Degrees throughout the 32 counties.

LANGUAGE

According to the 1991 Republic of Ireland Census, 32.5% (or 1,095,830 persons) of the 3 years plus population claimed the ability to speak Irish (their level of competence is not clearly defined). 79,000 people in Northern Ireland claim to be able to read, write and speak Irish fluently while a further 63,000 claim to have some knowledge of the language.

RELIGION

The 1991 Census has quite detailed information on our religious persuasions. 75.12% of us on the island are Roman Catholic, 7.1% of us belong to the Church of Ireland, while 6.86% of us are Presbyterians. 3.88% of us preferred not to state our religion while 2.46% professed to having no religion at all. In the Republic 3,228,372 persons or 91.565 % of the population is Roman Catholic with only 2.35% (82,840 persons) belonging to the Church of Ireland and less the 0.7% members of different Protestant denominations. In Northern Ireland, Roman Catholicism is also the largest single denomination with 605,639 persons or 38.4% of the population. Presbyterians with 21.4% (or 336,891 persons) is the second most numerous denomination with the 279,280 members of the Church of Ireland making up 17.7% of the population.

DRIVING FORCE

There were, as of December 1994 1,798,224 vehicles on our roads with 1,453,782 of these being private cars. There is no shortage of drivers amongst us with 2,591,281 licences held throughout the Island.

VOTING

In April 1995, there were 2,646,214 people eligible to vote in elections to Dáil Éireann and at the 1992 November General Election 68.5% of those eligible to vote exercised their democratic right. 754,296 people turned out to vote in the Forum Elections in Northern Ireland in May 1996, with 1,166,104 entitled to register a vote.

The Republic of Ireland Census

The Census figures in the Republic relate to the de facto population - that is, the numbers of persons actually in the state on the night the census is taken. Visitors to the state are included in the census as well as those visitors in residence, while usual residents who are absent from the state are excluded. The intercensal change in population reflects vital events (e.g. births and deaths) and all movement into and out of the state.

Vital Statistics: In the 1986-1991 intercensal period the excess of births over deaths was 119,200 while statistics abstracted from the census indicated a population decrease of 14,900 which implied a net outward migration of 134,200 people. Since 1980 there has been a noticeable decline in the birth rate. In that year there were 74,400 births registered and the natural increase was 41,400. In 1994 the number of births registered was 47,929, compared with 49,456 in 1993. The death rate in 1994 was 8.6 per 1,000 population, the actual number of deaths registered for the year being 30,744. The marriage rate is also in decline, 21,800 in 1980 decreasing to 16,297 in 1994.

The most recent census carried out in the Republic of Ireland took place on April 28th, 1996.

The Northern Ireland Census

The Northern Ireland Census is enumerated somewhat differently than that of the Republic. The actual population is calculated as being the number of people usually resident in Northern Ireland excluding visitors but including those who were stated as being usually resident in the North, irrespective of whether or not they were at their usual address on Census night. This resulted in a population of 1,577,836. However, the population enumerated on the actual census night of April 21, 1991 was 1,569,971.

Vital Statistics: There were 530,369 private dwellings enumerated which contained an average of 3.0 persons per household. In 1981, there were 456,348 enumerated private households containing an average of 3.2 persons per household. The 1991 figures indicated that 7.3% of the population did not answer the voluntary question on religion. This compared with 18.5 in 1981. Only 3.8% said they had no religion. In 1991 26% of the population were aged under 16 years while at the other end of the age spectrum there were 15% of persons at pensionable age (65 years-men, 60 years-women) while 5.2% was aged 75 or over. 72.7% of males and 45.2% were economically active, with, of these, 81% of males and 89.2% of females in employment with 19.0% of males and 10.8% of females out of employment.

Other statistics of note were that 22.6% of the population, i.e. 119,980, live alone while in 4.8% of Northern Ireland households there was more than one person per room. 62.3% of households are owner-occupied with 29.4% were in accommodation rented from a local or public authority. 64.5% of households had one or more cars available.

In education, 65% of all persons aged over 16 had no formal education qualification, 35.1% had some form of academic qualification and 6.5% had a qualification at degree level or higher.

REPUBLIC OF IRELAND CENSUS STATISTICS

Overview Irish Census Information 1891-1996

Year	Total Population Persons	Births registered	Deaths registered	Marriages registered	Natural increase	Change in population	Estimated net migration	Intercensal period
1891*	3,468,694	835,072	639,073	145,976	195,999	-401,326	-597,325	1881-91
1901*	3,221,823	737,934	588,391	148,134	149,543	-246,871	-396,414	1891-01
1911*	3,139,688	713,709	534,305	153,674	179,404	-82,135	-261,539	1901-11
1926	2,971,992	968,742	731,409	230,525	237,333	-167,696	-405,029	1911-26
1936	2,968,420	583,502	420,323	136,699	163,179	-3,572	-166,751	1926-36
1946	2,955,107	602,095	428,297	159,426	173,798	-13,313	-187,111	1936-46
1951	2,960,593	392,270	201,295	80,868	127,975	+5,486	-122,489	1946-51
1956	2,898,264	312,517	178,083	79,541	134,434	-62,329	-196,763	1951-56
1961	2,818,341	302,816	170,736	76,669	132,080	-79,923	-212,003	1956-61
1966	2,884,002	312,709	166,443	80,754	146,266	+65,661	-80,605	1961-66
1971	2,978,248	312,796	164,644	95,662	148,152	+94,246	-53,906	1966-71
1979	3,368,217	548,413	267,378	171,705	281,035	+389,969	+108,934	1971-79
1981	3,443,405	146,224	65,991	42,728	80,233	+75,188	-5,045	1979-81
1986	3,540,643	333,457	164,336	95,648	169,121	+97,238	-71,883	1981-86
1991	3,525,719	277,546	158,300	90,692	119,246	-14,924	-134,170	1986-91
1996	3,621,035	(Remaining Figures not yet available from Census 1996)						1991-96

(* includes Northern Ireland counties)

Republic of Ireland Population: Province and County, 1991-1996

Province and County	1991			1996			Change 91-96	
	Persons	Males	Females	Persons	Males	Females	Actual	%
TOTAL	3,525,719	1,753,418	1,772,301	3,621,035	1,797,596	1,823,439	95,316	2.7
LEINSTER	1,860,949	913,849	947,100	1,921,835	943,212	978,623	60,886	3.3
Carlow	40,942	20,785	20,157	41,616	21,090	20,526	674	1.6
Dublin	1,025,304	492,432	532,872	1,056,666	508,145	548,521	31,362	3.1
Kildare	122,656	62,207	60,449	134,881	67,958	66,923	12,225	10.0
Kilkenny	73,635	37,447	36,188	75,155	38,059	37,096	1,520	2.1
Laois	52,314	26,904	25,410	52,798	27,122	25,676	484	0.9
Longford	30,296	15,542	14,754	30,138	15,478	14,660	-158	-0.5
Louth	90,724	44,823	45,901	92,163	45,660	46,503	1,439	1.6
Meath	105,370	53,291	52,079	109,371	55,119	54,252	4,001	3.8
Offaly	58,494	29,892	28,602	59,080	29,962	29,118	586	1.0
Westmeath	61,880	31,006	30,874	63,236	31,536	31,700	1,356	2.2
Wexford	102,069	51,444	50,625	104,314	52,413	51,901	2,245	2.2
Wicklow	97,265	48,076	49,189	102,417	50,670	51,747	5,152	5.3
MUNSTER	1,009,533	507,095	502,438	1,033,045	517,752	515,293	23,512	2.3
Clare	90,918	46,367	44,551	93,914	47,730	46,184	2,996	3.3
Cork	410,369	204,542	205,827	420,346	209,159	211,187	9,977	2.4
Kerry	121,894	61,932	59,962	125,863	63,655	62,208	3,969	3.3
Limerick	161,956	81,094	80,862	165,017	82,528	82,489	3,061	1.9
Tipperary, N.R.	57,854	29,355	28,499	57,944	29,212	28,732	90	0.2
Tipperary, S.R.	74,918	38,067	36,851	75,364	38,235	37,129	446	0.6
Waterford	91,624	45,738	45,886	94,597	47,233	47,364	2,973	3.2
CONNACHT	423,031	214,131	208,900	432,551	218,013	214,538	9,520	2.3
Galway	180,364	91,005	89,359	188,598	94,424	94,174	8,234	4.6
Leitrim	25,301	13,203	12,098	25,032	13,015	12,017	-269	-1.1
Mayo	110,713	55,981	54,732	111,395	56,297	55,098	682	0.6
Roscommon	51,897	26,694	25,203	51,881	26,639	25,242	-16	0.0
Sligo	54,756	27,248	27,508	55,645	27,638	28,007	889	1.6
ULSTER (part of)	232,206	118,343	113,863	233,604	118,619	114,985	1,398	0.6
Cavan	52,796	27,314	25,482	52,903	27,263	25,640	107	0.2
Donegal	128,117	64,817	63,300	129,435	65,233	64,202	1,318	1.0
Monaghan	51,293	26,212	25,081	51,266	26,123	25,143	-27	-0.1

Republic of Ireland population classified by age-group

Persons	1981	1986	1991
0 - 4 years	353,004	324,078	273,743
5 - 9 years	349,487	350,650	318,503
10 - 14 years	341,238	349,973	348,328
15 - 19 years	326,429	331,100	335,026
20 - 24 years	276,127	286,424	266,572
25 - 29 years	246,053	258,439	246,321
30 - 34 years	231,958	242,689	249,071
35 - 39 years	193,829	229,740	237,889
40 - 44 years	165,924	191,751	225,683
45 - 49 years	151,850	161,740	187,762
50 - 54 years	149,680	147,511	156,806
55 - 59 years	149,606	142,215	142,549
60 - 64 years	139,266	139,978	134,566
65 - 69 years	133,919	129,498	130,752
70 -74 years	103,138	110,996	109,325
75 - 79 years	68,451	75,519	84,082
80 - 84 years	40,462	42,884	49,301
85 plus years	22,984	25,458	29,440
Total	3,443,405	3,540,643	3,525,719

Republic of Ireland: Males & Females under 40 years of age

Total number of males	Total number of females
1986: 1,769,690	1986: 1,770,953
1991: 1,753,418	1991: 1,772,301
1996:......Figures not available from Census 1996	1996:......Figures not available from Census 1996

1986: 1.2 million Rep. of Ire. males and 1.16 million Rep. of Ire. females were under 40 years of age.
1991: 1.15 million Rep. of Ire. males and 1.12 Rep. of Ire. females were under 40 years of age.

Republic of Ireland: Persons enumerated in each county classified by selected birthplace

(1991)		Birthplace							
		Rep. of Ireland							
Place of Enumeration	Total Persons	County of Enum.	Other county	N. Ire.	England & Wales	Scotland	France	Germany	USA
STATE	3,525,719	2,626,053	670,941	35,986	126,487	11,378	4,512	5,792	14,533
LEINSTER	1,860,949	1,321,587	421,031	20,396	62,559	4,747	1,839	2,593	6,425
Carlow	40,942	27,619	11,561	129	1,271	50	11	35	74
Dublin	1,025,304	787,914	166,181	12,121	33,965	3,082	1,383	1,677	4,457
Kildare	122,656	59,273	56,220	1,058	4,289	274	122	107	334
Kilkenny	73,635	54,928	15,181	280	2,462	87	53	108	156
Laois	52,314	38,032	12,338	189	1,408	61	12	13	74
Longford	30,296	20,823	7,975	166	1,048	62	6	9	115
Louth	90,724	71,345	12,594	3,351	2,456	218	32	56	211
Meath	105,370	52,707	46,630	1,166	3,588	262	41	67	249
Offaly	58,494	42,070	14,098	188	1,631	85	14	55	108
Westmeath	61,880	39,399	19,223	386	2,064	108	26	93	216
Wexford	102,069	83,290	13,632	334	3,842	127	49	150	137
Wicklow	97,265	44,187	45,398	1,028	4,535	331	100	223	294
MUNSTER	1,009,533	800,070	151,259	3,991	37,818	1,363	1,460	2,084	4,477
Clare	90,918	57,934	26,034	820	3,968	146	185	350	674
Cork	410,369	348,721	38,565	1,486	14,804	600	638	685	1,632
Kerry	121,894	96,302	17,036	395	5,454	141	281	580	938
Limerick	161,956	126,792	26,740	592	5,478	198	181	235	702
Tipp. N.R.	57,854	45,014	10,459	176	1,702	54	34	51	142
Tipp. S.R.	74,918	57,165	14,124	188	2,680	76	63	89	169
Waterford	91,624	68,142	18,301	334	3,732	148	78	94	220
CONNACHT	423,031	322,091	71,573	2,587	18,499	1,069	1,121	895	2,741
Galway	180,364	138,771	28,211	973	7,955	357	761	347	1,527
Leitrim	25,301	18,020	5,625	328	862	79	9	168	125
Mayo	110,713	89,242	13,718	452	5,549	389	221	162	605
Roscommon	51,897	36,378	12,827	217	1,968	48	11	96	189
Sligo	54,756	39,680	11,192	617	2,147	196	119	122	295
ULSTER*	232,206	182,305	27,078	9,012	7,611	4,199	92	220	890
Cavan	52,796	41,039	8,785	922	1,455	119	24	72	224
Donegal	128,117	103,443	9,399	5,496	4,712	3,851	56	130	530
Monaghan	51,293	37,823	8,894	2,594	1,444	229	12	18	136

* Cavan, Donegal and Monaghan only

Demographic Statistics: Republic of Ireland and Northern Ireland

	Republic of Ireland	Northern Ireland
Population:	3,525,719	1,577,836
Aged 19 & under	36%	32.5%
Aged 20 - 39	28%	29%
Aged 40 - 64	24%	26%
Aged over 65	11%	13%
Birth Rate: *	15	16.5
Death Rate: *	8.9	9.5
Marriage Rate: *	4.8	5.8
Marital Status:		
Single	56	49
Married	39	42
Remarried	—	1
Widowed	5	6
Divorced	—	2
Distribution of Population: **	29%	52%
Average number of children (per family):	2.08	2.14
Numbers receiving full-time education (1993):	976,000	388,633
Primary school pupils	54%	50%
Post-primary school pupils	37%	38%
Third level students	9%	11%

* Based on per 1,000 of population
* Based on Dublin and Belfast areas for the Republic of Ireland and Northern Ireland respectively.

Religious Denominations in Republic of Ireland

Year	Total Persons	R.C.	C.O.I	Prot.	Presb.	Meth.	Jewish	Other	No Religion	Not Stated
1881	3,870,020	3,465,332	317,576	--	56,498	17,660	394	-	12,560	-
1891	3,468,694	3,099,003	286,804	--	51,469	18,513	1,506	-	11,399	-
1901	3,221,823	2,878,271	264,264	--	46,714	17,872	3,006	-	11,696	-
1911	3,139,688	2,812,509	249,535	--	45,486	16,440	3,805	-	11,913	-
1926	2,971,992	2,751,269	164,215	--	32,429	10,663	3,686	-	9,730	-
1936	2,968,420	2,773,920	145,030	--	28,067	9,649	3,749	-	8,005	-
1946	2,955,107	2,786,033	124,829	--	23,870	8,355	3,907	-	8,113	-
1961	2,818,341	2,673,473	104,016	--	18,953	6,676	3,255	5,236	1,107	5,625
1971	2,978,248	2,795,666	97,739	--	16,052	5,646	2,633	6,248	7,616	46,648
1981	3,443,405	3,204,476	95,366	--	14,255	5,790	2,127	10,843	39,572	70,976
1991*	3,525,719	3,228,327	82,840	--	13,199	5,037	1,581	45,090*	66,270	83,375

* Includes 6,347 persons whose denominations was described as "Protestants".
This denomination was included "Church of Ireland" in previous censuses.

Republic of Ireland Occupations by Industrial Group, 1991

Industrial group	Persons	Males	Females
Agriculture, forestry, fishing	158,208	142,255	15,953
Mining, quarrying and turf production	6,015	5,568	447
Manufacturing industries	218,725	152,609	66,116
Electricity, gas and water supply	11,948	10,269	1,679
Building and construction	76,625	72,687	3,938
Commerce	173,385	106,131	67,254
Wholesale distribution	41,988	31,383	10,605
Retail distribution	131,397	74,748	56,649
Insurance, finance and business services	61,915	31,302	30,613
Transport, communication and storage	69,397	55,422	13,975
Public administration and defence	75,541	52,158	23,383
Professional services	196,903	71,317	125,586
Personal services	71,161	25,927	45,234
Other industries	29,257	18,303	10,954
Total	**1,149,080**	**743,948**	**405,132**

R.O.I Persons by province and county, by religious denomination, 1991

Province & County	Total Persons	R.C.	C.O.I	Prot.	Presb.	Meth.	Jewish	Other	No Religion	Not Stated
TOTAL	3,525,719	3,228,327	82,840	6,347	13,199	5,037	1,581	38,743	66,270	83,375
CONNACHT	423,031	397,848	5,321	516	333	286	21	3,208	5,392	10,106
Galway	180,364	168,640	1,358	228	81	76	16	1,772	3,191	5,002
Leitrim	25,301	23,682	721	41	17	61	-	80	217	482
Mayo	110,713	105,839	817	116	101	27	2	601	929	2,281
Roscommon	51,897	50,204	358	28	13	21	2	221	333	717
Sligo	54,756	49,483	2,067	103	121	101	1	534	722	1,624
LEINSTER	1,860,949	1,685,334	50,912	3,391	3,799	2,815	1,439	24,829	43,843	44,587
Carlow	40,942	37,767	1,747	42	15	25	5	262	343	736
Dublin	1,025,304	911,454	26,169	2,157	2,716	1,895	1,383	17,571	33,269	28,690
Kildare	122,656	113,828	2,923	147	153	102	9	1,212	1,859	2,423
Kilkenny	73,635	68,699	1,586	74	143	56	2	599	822	1,694
Laois	52,314	48,461	2,417	41	38	94	1	312	256	694
Longford	30,296	28,645	705	24	46	37	-	161	163	515
Louth	90,724	85,770	939	49	137	20	5	907	974	1,923
Meath	105,370	98,766	1,926	133	142	42	2	797	1,236	2,326
Offaly	58,494	55,172	1,604	52	39	142	1	279	323	882
Westmeath	61,880	58,508	1,059	80	32	38	-	401	528	1,234
Wexford	102,069	94,832	3,287	169	81	77	8	554	1,052	2,009
Wicklow	97,265	83,432	6,550	423	257	287	23	1,814	3,018	1,461
MUNSTER	1,009,533	941,675	15,758	1,385	548	1,185	111	9,192	15,402	24,277
Clare	90,918	84,847	699	72	55	43	12	861	1,778	2,551
Cork	410,369	379,011	8,864	792	240	690	57	4,291	7,567	8,857
Kerry	121,894	114,253	1,415	173	46	34	17	920	1,696	3,340
Limerick	161,956	152,364	1,409	158	86	210	15	1,365	2,084	4,265
Tipp. N.R.	57,854	54,552	1,411	44	25	133	-	353	374	962
Tipp. S.R.	74,918	71,055	721	57	27	14	1	532	700	1,811
Waterford	91,624	85,593	1,239	89	69	61	9	870	1,203	2,491
ULSTER *(part of)*	232,206	203,470	10,849	1,055	8,519	751	10	1,514	1,633	4,405
Cavan	52,796	46,703	3,622	160	710	94	1	240	291	975
Donegal	128,117	111,427	5,602	555	5,412	603	8	866	1,029	2,615
Monaghan	51,293	45,340	1,625	340	2,397	54	1	408	313	815

Marriages, Births and Deaths in Republic of Ireland

Description	1989	1990	1991*	1992*	1993*	1994*
Marriages	18,174	17,838	17,441	16,109	15,728	16,297
Births						
Male	26,754	27,559	27,122	26,567	25,449	24,744
Female	25,264	25,485	25,596	24,990	24,007	23,185
Total	**52,018**	**53,044**	**52,718**	**51,557**	**49,456**	**47,929**
Births within marriage:	45,347	45,277	43,806	42,258	39,792	38,479
Births outside marriage:	6,671	7,767	8,912	9,299	9,664	9,450
Births outside marriage as a percentage of total births:	12.8	14.6	16.9	18.0	19.5	19.7
Deaths.						
Male	17,058	16,828	16,603	16,491	16,783	16,219
Female	15,053	14,542	14,702	14,457	14,873	14,525
Total	**32,111**	**31,370**	**31,305**	**30,948**	**31,656**	**30,744**
Natural increase	19,907	21,674	21,413	20,609	17,800	17,185
Rates per 1000 of est. population						
Marriages	5.2	5.1	5.0	4.5	4.4	4.6
Births	14.8	15.1	15.0	14.5	13.9	13.4
Deaths	9.1	9.0	8.9	8.7	8.9	8.6

*Latest statistics available

Statistics on selected occupations in Republic of Ireland (1991)

Description	Males	Females
Religion	5,053	3,431
Primary education	5,968	18,827
Secondary education	8,267	13,223
Vocational education	4,100	4,977
University education	6,349	4,854
Health Boards, hospitals etc.	6,415	23,794
Dentistry	879	1,181
Veterinary surgery	958	523
Accountancy	6,842	4,792
Legal services	3,703	6,647
Banking and finance	12,517	16,230
Garda Síochána	10,146	705
Defence	11,605	297
Forestry	2,222	76
Fishing	2,669	226
Plumbing and domestic heating	4,414	143
Painting and decorating	5,233	390
Hotels	6,324	9,245
Hairdressing, beauty parlours and saunas	1,387	8,559
Turf production	2,586	170
Beverages	4,945	1,245
Tobacco	755	485
Air transport	5,795	2,785
Railway transport	5,036	589
Road passenger transport	9,753	917
Road freight transport	10,015	744
Postal, telegraph and radio communications	16,401	5,037
Theatres and broadcasting	3,450	1,769
Bookmaking	957	1,144

NORTHERN IRELAND STATISTICS

Overview Northern Ireland Census Information 1891 - 1991

Total Population

Year	Persons	Births registered	Deaths registered	Natural increase	Change in population	Estimated net migration	Intercensal period
1891	1,236,056	312,249	240,339	71,910	68,760	140,670	1881-1891
1901	1,236,952	314,795	246,161	68,634	+896	67,738	1891-1901
1911	1,250,531	309,502	230,506	78,996	+13,579	65,417	1901-1911
1926	1,256,561	431,148	317,545	113,603	+6,030	107,573	1911-1926
1937	1,279,745	280,641	199,806	80,835	+23,184	57,651	1926-1937
1951	1,370,921	402,187	243,744	158,443	+91,176	67,267	1937-1951
1961	1,425,042	298,808	152,459	146,349	+54,121	92,228	1951-1961
1966	1,484,775	182,489	85,055	97,434	+59,733	37,701	1961-1966
1971	1,536,065	148,706	72,578	76,128	+51,290	24,838	1966-1971
1981*	1,532,196	274,786	167,232	107,554	-3,869	111,423	1971-1981
1991	1,577,836	273,227	158,167	115,060	+45,640	69,420	1981-1991

* During the Republican Hunger Strikes of 1981 a substantial number of households were not enumerated. These were subsequently estimated at approximately 44,500.

Overview Northern Ireland Religious Denominations

Year	Total Persons	R.C.	C.O.I	Breth.	Presb.	Meth.	Bapt.	Cong.	Unitn.	Other	None	Not Stated
1961	1,425,042	497,547	344,800	16,847	413,113	71,865	13,765	9,838	5,613	23,236	0	28,418
1971	1,519,640	477,919	334,318	16,480	405,719	71,235	16,563	10,072	3,975	40,848	0	142,511
1981	1,481,959	414,532	281,472	12,158	339,818	58,731	16,375	8,265	3,373	72,651	0	274,584
1991	1,577,836	605,639	279,280	12,446	336,891	59,517	19,484	8,176	3,213	79,129	59,234	114,827

Overview Northern Ireland Religious Denominations by percentage

Year	Total Persons	R.C.	C.O.I	Breth.	Presb.	Meth.	Bapt.	Cong.	Unitn.	Other	None	Not Stated
1961	1,425,042	34.9%	24.2%	1.2%	29.0%	5.0%	1.0%	0.7%	0.4%	1.6%	0	2.0%
1971	1,519,640	31.4%	22.0%	1.1%	26.7%	4.7%	1.1%	0.7%	0.3%	2.7%	0	9.3%
1981	1,481,959	28.0%	19.0%	0.8%	22.9%	4.0%	1.1%	0.6%	0.2%	4.9%	0	18.5%
1991	1,577,836	38.4%	17.7%	0.8%	21.4%	3.8%	1.2%	0.5%	0.2%	5.0%	3.7%	7.3%

Persons in each N.I. District Council area by religious denomination, 1991

District Council area	Total	Male	Female	R.C.	Presb.	C.O.I	Meth.	Other	None	Not stated
TOTAL	1,577,836	769,071	808,765	605,639	336,891	279,280	59,517	122,448	59,234	114,827
Antrim	44,516	22,135	22,381	14,117	13,614	6,384	786	3,600	2,025	3,990
Ards	64,764	31,527	33,237	7,341	25,219	12,137	3,386	7,069	3,904	5,708
Armagh	51,817	25,741	26,076	23,518	8,627	10,604	1,236	3,964	825	3,043
Ballymena	56,641	27,830	28,811	10,392	26,067	6,869	1,442	6,115	1,845	3,911
Ballymoney	24,198	12,022	12,176	7,311	9,411	3,151	123	2,184	524	1,494
Banbridge	33,482	16,568	16,914	9,256	9,608	6,362	624	3,977	929	2,726
Belfast	279,237	130,820	148,417	108,954	47,743	50,242	14,667	20,113	14,756	22,762
Carrickfergus	32,750	15,871	16,879	2,269	10,166	7,698	3,162	4,390	2,476	2,589
Castlereagh	60,799	28,946	31,853	5,743	17,445	14,638	5,323	8,481	3,797	5,372
Coleraine	50,438	24,369	26,069	11,323	15,946	12,550	784	4,214	2,104	3,517
Cookstown	31,082	15,503	15,579	16,522	4,779	5,288	331	2,131	382	1,649
Craigavon	74,986	36,511	38,475	30,060	7,718	18,666	3,904	7,190	1,955	5,493
Derry	95,371	46,708	48,663	66,260	10,539	8,503	853	2,629	1,353	5,234
Down	58,008	28,835	29,173	32,507	9,025	6,183	559	3,454	1,658	4,622
Dungannon	45,248	22,556	22,872	25,299	5,822	8,245	912	2,416	384	2,350
Fermanagh	54,033	27,095	26,938	29,657	1,549	14,283	2,724	2,534	745	2,541
Larne	29,419	14,318	15,101	6,510	11,136	4,083	1,107	2,771	1,291	2,521
Limavady	29,567	15,042	14,525	15,281	5,683	4,699	203	1,035	512	2,154
Lisburn	99,458	48,653	50,805	26,786	20,980	26,286	4,095	9,154	4,780	7,377
Magherafelt	36,293	18,177	18,116	21,377	5,466	4,372	165	2,632	313	1,968
Moyle	14,789	7,355	7,434	7,723	2,766	2,587	29	452	254	978
Newry & Mourne	82,943	41,307	41,636	59,555	8,890	3,861	314	3,376	947	6,000
Newtownabbey	74,035	35,760	38,275	9,635	23,610	14,976	6,437	8,125	4,476	6,776
North Down	71,832	34,284	37,548	6,435	23,658	16,591	5,077	7,500	6,140	6,431
Omagh	45,809	23,022	22,787	29,469	5,141	5,766	785	1,910	570	2,168
Strabane	36,141	18,116	18,025	22,339	6,283	4,256	489	1,032	289	1,453

Persons by N.I. District Council area by religious denomination, 1991 (%)

District Council area	Total	R.C.	Presb.	C.O.I	Meth.	Other	None	Not stated
TOTAL	1,577,836	605,639	336,891	279,280	59,517	122,448	59,234	114,827
		%	%	%	%	%	%	%
Antrim	44,516	31.7	30.6	14.3	1.8	8.1	4.5	9.0
Ards	64,764	11.4	38.9	18.8	5.2	10.9	6.0	8.8
Armagh	51,817	45.4	16.6	20.5	2.4	7.6	1.6	5.9
Ballymena	56,641	18.4	46.0	12.1	2.5	10.8	3.3	6.9
Ballymoney	24,198	30.2	38.9	13.0	0.5	9.0	2.2	6.2
Banbridge	33,482	27.6	28.7	19.0	1.9	11.9	2.8	8.1
Belfast	279,237	39.0	17.1	18.0	5.3	7.2	5.3	8.1
Carrickfergus	32,750	6.9	31.0	23.5	9.7	13.4	7.6	7.9
Castlereagh	60,799	9.4	28.7	24.1	8.8	14.0	6.2	8.8
Coleraine	50,438	22.4	31.6	24.9	1.5	8.4	4.2	7.0
Cookstown	31,082	53.1	15.4	17.0	1.1	6.9	1.2	5.3

District Council area	Total	R.C.	Presb.	C.O.I	Meth.	Other	None	Not stated
Craigavon	74,986	40.1	10.3	24.9	5.2	9.6	2.6	7.3
Derry	95,371	69.5	11.0	8.9	0.9	2.8	1.4	5.5
Down	58,008	56.0	15.5	10.7	1.0	5.9	2.9	8.0
Dungannon	45,248	55.7	12.8	18.1	2.0	5.3	0.9	5.2
Fermanagh	54,033	54.9	2.9	26.4	5.0	4.7	1.4	4.7
Larne	29,419	22.1	37.8	13.9	3.8	9.4	4.4	8.6
Limavady	29,567	51.7	19.2	15.9	0.7	3.5	1.7	7.3
Lisburn	99,458	27.0	21.1	26.4	4.1	9.2	4.8	7.4
Magherafelt	36,293	58.9	15.1	12.0	0.4	7.3	0.9	5.4
Moyle	14,789	52.2	18.7	17.5	0.2	3.1	1.7	6.6
Newry & Mourne	82,943	71.8	10.7	4.7	0.4	4.1	1.1	7.2
Newtownabbey	74,035	13.0	31.9	20.2	8.7	11.0	6.0	9.2
North Down	71,832	9.0	32.9	23.1	7.1	10.4	8.5	9.0
Omagh	45,809	64.3	11.2	12.6	1.7	4.2	1.3	4.7
Strabane	36,141	61.8	17.4	11.8	1.3	2.9	0.8	4.0

Northern Ireland population classified by Age-group, 1971-1991

Persons	1971 000	1981 000	1991 000
0 - 4 years	156.2	130.8	128.2
5 - 9 years	157.1	134.2	129.1
10 - 14 years	143.6	148.9	127.8
15 - 19 years	126.3	144.5	127.6
20 - 24 years	114.9	122.3	126.1
25 - 34 years	188.6	198.7	235.8
35 - 44 years	166.7	173.7	197.2
45- 54 years	166.0	152.1	166.4
55 - 64 years	150.5	143.1	140.4
65 - 74 years	108.1	116.2	117.1
75 and over	57.8	67.8	82.0
Total	1536.1	1532.1	1577.7

Total numbers of males and females in Northern Ireland, 1971-1991

Total number of males		Total number of females	
1971:	754,700	1971:	781,400
1981:	749,400	1981:	782,700
1991:	769,100	1991:	808,600

Northern Ireland Marriages, Births and Deaths, 1988-1993

Description	1988	1989	1990	1991	1992	1993
Marriages	9,961	10,019	9,588	9,221	9,392	9,045
Births	32,231	30,492	31,471	31,571	31,175	30,368
Births outside marriage:	16.1%	16.9%	18.8%	20.2%	21.9%	21.9%
Deaths	15,813	15,844	15,426	15,096	14,988	15,633
Rates per 1000 of est. population	%	%	%	%	%	%
Marriages	6.3	6.3	6.0	5.8	5.8	5.5
Births	17.6	16.5	16.7	16.5	15.9	15.3
Deaths	10.0	10.0	9.7	9.5	9.3	9.6

N. Ireland occupations classified by industrial group - Census of 1991

Industrial group	Persons	Males	Females
Agriculture, forestry, fishing	23,962	22,274	1,688
Mining & Ores	9,147	7,566	1,581
Manufacturing industries	60,174	33,992	26,182
Food, drink & tobacco	*18,142*	*12,201*	*5,941*
Textiles, clothing, footwear and leather	*24,035*	*7,877*	*16,158*
Wood and wood products	*6,819*	*6,102*	*717*
Paper, paper products, printing and publishing	*6,198*	*4,026*	*2,172*
Rubber and plastic products	*4,344*	*3,417*	*927*
Other manufacturing	*636*	*369*	*267*
Energy and water industries	7,180	6,120	1,060
Building and construction	41,079	38,489	2,590
Commerce			
Banking, insurance, finance, business services and leasing	40,075	21,200	18,875
Transport and communications	24,484	19,604	4,880
Distribution, hotels and catering	103,228	55,273	47,955
Metal, engineering and vehicle industries	32,929	26,451	6,478
Government employment/training scheme	13,245	8,649	4,596
Others	9,243	6,074	3,169
Total	**574,950**	**329,400**	**245,550**

Northern Ireland statistics on selected occupations - Census of 1991

Description	Males	Females
Sales personnel	16,381	25,738
Managers and administrators *(private and public industry)*	62,372	19,898
Teaching professionals	10,266	16.577
Legal professionals	1,334	454
Architects, townplanners and surveyors	1,402	134
Computer analysts and programmers	1,307	429
Health professionals	3,457	1,684
Literary, artistic and sports professionals	2,817	1,265
Armed forces	8,546	842
Security and protective services	14,647	1,414

MAIN IRISH TOWNS

Irish cities and towns with a population of 3,000 or over, 1991

REPUBLIC OF IRELAND

Town (County)	Population
Greater Dublin	915,516
Cork County Borough	174,400
Limerick County Borough	75,436
Galway County Borough	50,853
Waterford County Borough	41,853
Dundalk (Louth)	30,061
Bray (Wicklow)	26,953
Drogheda (Louth)	24,656
Sligo	17,964
Tralee (Kerry)	17,862
Swords (Dublin)	17,705
Kilkenny	17,669
Ennis (Clare)	16,058
Clonmel (Tipperary)	15,562
Wexford	15,393
Athlone (Westmeath)	15,358
Carlow	14,027
Lucan (Dublin)	13,574
Leixlip (Kildare)	13,194
Malahide (Dublin)	12,088
Newbridge (Kildare)	12,069
Mullingar (Westmeath)	11,867
Navan (Meath)	11,706
Naas (Kildare)	11,141
Greystones (Wicklow)	10,778
Letterkenny (Donegal)	10,726
Killarney (Kerry)	9,950
Celbridge (Kildare)	9,629
Tullamore (Offaly)	9,430

Portmarnock (Dublin)	9,173
Portlaoise (Laois)	8,360
Cobh (Cork)	8,219
Ballina (Mayo)	8,167
Arklow (Wicklow)	7,987
Shannon (Clare)	7,920
Balbriggan (Dublin)	7,724
Enniscorthy (Wexford)	7,655
Castlebar (Mayo)	7,648
Mallow (Cork)	7,521
Skerries (Dublin)	7,032
Thurles (Tipperary)	6,955
Dungarvan (Waterford)	6,920
Longford	6,824
Carrigaline (Cork)	6,482
Wicklow	6,215
New Ross (Wexford)	6,079
Tramore (Waterford)	6,064
Maynooth (Kildare)	6,027
Midleton (Cork)	5,951
Monaghan	5,946
Ballinasloe (Galway)	5,892
Youghal (Cork)	5,828
Nenagh (Tipperary)	5,825
Tuam (Galway)	5,540
Cavan	5,254
Athy (Kildare)	5,204
Carrick on Suir (Tipperary)	5,143
Tipperary	4,963
Rush (Dublin)	4,839
Bandon (Cork)	4,741
Fermoy (Cork)	4,462
Ashbourne (Meath)	4,411
Buncrana (Donegal)	4,388
Roscrea (Tipperary)	4,231
Kildare	4,196
Trim (Meath)	4,185
Birr (Offaly)	4,056
Gorey (Wexford)	3,840
Edenderry (Offaly)	3,742
Westport (Mayo)	3,688
Newcastle (Limerick)	3,612
Passage West (Cork)	3,606
Ardee (Louth)	3,604
Listowel (Kerry)	3,597
Ceannanus Mor (Meath)	3,539
Roscommon	3,427
Laytown-Bettystown-Mornington (Meath)	3,360
Carrickmacross (Monaghan)	3,341
Loughrea (Galway)	3,271
Portarlington (Laois)	3,211
Mitchelstown (Cork)	3,090

Mountmellick (Laois)	3,003

NORTHERN IRELAND

Town (County)	Population
Belfast (Antrim)	279,237
Derry	72,334
Newtownabbey (Antrim)	57,103
Bangor (Down)	52,437
Lisburn (Antrim)	42,110
Ballymena (Antrim)	28,717
Newtownards (Down)	24,301
Newry (Down)	22,975
Carrickfergus (Antrim)	22,885
Lurgan (Armagh)	21,905
Portadown (Armagh)	21,299
Antrim	20,878
Coleraine (Derry)	20,721
Larne (Antrim)	17,575
Omagh (Tyrone)	17,280
Armagh	14,640
Dundonald (Down)	12,943
Dunmurry (Antrim)	12,771
Banbridge (Down)	12,529
Strabane (Tyrone)	11,981
Enniskillen (Fermanagh)	11,436
Limavady (Derry)	10,764
Cookstown (Tyrone)	10,472
Downpatrick (Down)	10,257
Dungannon (Tyrone)	9,420
Holywood (Down)	9,252
Craigavon (Armagh)	9,201
Comber (Down)	8,516
Ballymoney (Antrim)	8,242
Ballyclare (Antrim)	7,761
Newcastle (Down)	7,214
Magherafelt (Derry)	7,143
Portstewart (Derry)	6,459
Kilkeel (Down)	6,123
Portrush (Derry)	5,703
Warrenpoint (Down)	5,637
Ballynahinch (Down)	5,196
Greenisland (Antrim)	4,967
Donaghadee (Down)	4,799
Randalstown (Antrim)	4,290
Carryduff	4,270
Ballycastle (Antrim)	4,005
Coalisland (Tyrone)	3,802
Whitehead (Antrim)	3,761
Dromore (Down)	3,708
Maghera (Derry)	3,631
Bessbrook (Armagh)	3,147

PLAN-A-HOME

ARCHITECTS & SURVEYORS
HOUSE DESIGN SPECIALISTS

SURVEYING

CONSTRUCTION COST

DESIGN

SPECIFICATIONS

ADVICE & CONSULTANCY

SUPERVISION

PLANNING

LITIGATION

Offices:
**Plan-A-Home Associates: 23 South Bank, Crosses Green, Cork
Tel: 021 319655/6   Fax: 021-319657**

**Plan-A-Home: Offices 8B, The Courtyard, Lr. Main Street, Letterkenny,
Co. Donegal.   Tel.: 074-27844   Fax: 074 27841**

COUNTIES AND CITIES

Ireland has thirty-two counties, twenty-six in the Republic and six in Northern Ireland. There are six major cities in Ireland - Dublin, Belfast, Cork, Derry, Galway and Limerick. In a country with a population of 5.1 million, this means that roughly one-third of the population lives in quite confined urban landscapes while the remaining two-thirds live in the wide open spaces of a frequently underpopulated rural Ireland.

In the South, one-third of the entire population of the 26 counties lives in Dublin. It has meant a total concentration of resources and services being located, or only available, there - Dáil Éireann, major hospitals, the higher courts, national media, national sporting venues etc. By contrast, large counties like Donegal, Galway, Mayo and Kerry are largely dependent on tourism and fishing for their economic well-being.

Northern Ireland has a much more even spread of population. While Belfast is, by far, the largest city there are major population centres in Derry, Ballymena, Coleraine, Dungannon, Craigavon and Omagh. However, there is a significant imbalance in the industrial development between the east and west of the River Bann, the former being largely industrialised while the latter has remained largely agriculture based.

By and large, the east coast of Ireland, North and South, is the most populated, has the most industry and is the most economically well-off. The west coast, from Donegal to Kerry, has been relatively under-developed industrially with much dependence on local resources such as fishing and agriculture. However, the western seaboard counties are expected to benefit most from tourism in the years ahead.

PROFILE OF IRISH COUNTIES AND MAJOR CITIES

ANTRIM
(Province of Ulster)
Aontroim: Solitary Farm. **Main Towns:** Ballymena, Ballycastle, Belfast, Carrickfergus, Lisburn and Newtownabbey. **Radio Stations:** Cool FM. **Newspapers:** Antrim Guardian; Ballymena Guardian; Carrickfergus Advertiser; East Belfast Herald & Post; South Belfast Herald & Post; North & Newtownabbey Herald & Post; North Down Herald & Post; Lisburn Echo and the Ulster Star. **Major Tourist Attractions:** Giant's Causeway; Causeway Safari Park; Carrick-a-Rede Rope Bridge, Ballycastle; Ould Lammas Fair, Ballycastle; Dunluce Castle; and Portrush seaside resort. **Area:** 1,118sq miles.

BELFAST CITY
Description: Belfast city is situated in County Antrim and is the capital city of Northern Ireland. It is an industrial and historical city accommodating some of Northern Ireland's leading employers. A university city, it is a major shopping region for the six counties. It is also the city that provides transport terminals such as Belfast International and City Airports and Belfast Car Ferry Harbour. **Tourist Attractions:** Ulster Museum, Botanic Gardens; City Hall; Linen Hall Library, near City Hall; Botanic Gardens; Belfast Zoo; Belfast Port Harbour.

LOCAL GOVERNMENT:
City Council: City Hall, Belfast BT1 5GS. **Lord Mayor:** Councillor Alasdair McDonnell. **Council Members:** 51, covering nine areas. **Council meetings:** 24-26 Committee or sub-committee meetings per month.

ARMAGH
(Province of Ulster)
Ard Mhacha: Height/Plain of Macha. **Main Towns:** Armagh, Portadown, Lurgan and Keady. **Newspapers:** Armagh Observer; Craigavon Echo; Lurgan Mail; Portadown Times; Ulster Gazette & Armagh Standard and the Lurgan & Portadown Examiner. **Major Tourist Attractions:** Armagh Planetarium; both Armagh Cathedrals; Eamhain Macha; Maghery Country Park and Mullaghbawn Folk Museum. **Area:** 484 sq miles.

CARLOW
(Province of Leinster)
Ceatharlach: Quadruple Lake. **County Town:** Carlow. **Main Towns:** Carlow, Tullow. **Radio Station:** Carlow Kildare Radio. **Newspapers:** The Nationalist & Leinster Times. **Major Tourist Attractions:** Altamont Gardens, Tullow; Carlow Castle; Browne's Hill Dolmen, Carlow; Cathedral of the Assumption, Carlow; and the County Museum in Carlow Town Hall. **Area:** 346sq miles. **Population:** 40,946.

LOCAL GOVERNMENT:
County Council: County Offices, Carlow. **County Manager:** Matt O'Connor. **County Councillors:** 21. **Council Meetings:** First Monday in each month (excluding August). **Rateable Valuation:** £225,986.50. **County Rate:** £33.33. **Urban District Council :** 1 (Carlow). **Town Commissioners:** 1 (Muinebheag).

CAVAN
(Province of Ulster)
An Cabhán: Hollow. **County Town:** Cavan. **Main Towns:** Belturbet, Cavan, Cootehill. **Newspapers:** The Anglo-Celt. **Major Tourist Attractions:** Lough Gowna; Dún na Rí, National Forest Park, Kingscourt; Drumlane Abbey, Belturbet; and the Folk Museum, Cornafaen. **Area:** 730sq miles. **Population:** 52,796.

LOCAL GOVERNMENT:
County Council: Courthouse, Co. Cavan. **County Manager:** B. Johnston. **County Councillors:** 25. **Council Meetings:** Second Tuesday of each month. **Rateable Valuation:** £378,535. **County Rate:** £30.48. **Urban District Council:** 1 (Cavan). **Town**

Commissioners: 2 (Belturbet & Cootehill).

CLARE
(Province of Munster)
An Clár: Plain. **County Town:** Ennis. **Main Towns:** Ennis, Kilkee, Kilrush and Killaloe. **Radio Station:** Clare FM. **Newspapers:** Clare Champion. **Major Tourist Attractions:** The Burren; The Cliffs of Moher; Bunratty Castle and Folk Park; Ennis Abbey; Craggaunowen Castle; and Clare Abbey, Clarecastle. **Area:** 1,262sq miles. **Population:** 90,918.

LOCAL GOVERNMENT:
County Council: New Road, Ennis, Co. Clare. **County Manager:** William Moloney. **County Councillors:** 32. **Council Meetings:** Second Monday of each month. **Rateable Valuation:** £489,748.70. **County Rate :** £35.29. **Urban District Councils:** 2 (Ennis & Kilrush). **Town Commissioners:** 2 (Kilkee & Shannon).

CORK
(Province of Munster)
Corcaigh: Marshy Place. **County Town:** Cork. **Main Towns:** Bantry, Clonakilty, Cobh, Cork, Fermoy, Kinsale, Mallow, Mitchelstown, Skibbereen and Youghal. **Radio Stations:** 96 FM and 103 FM. **Newspapers:** The Southern Star. **Major Tourist Attractions:** Blarney Castle; Bantry House; Castle Gardens, Timoleague; St. Colman's Cathedral, Cobh; Kinsale, Gourmet capital of Ireland; Desmond Castle, Kinsale; Youghal Tourist Trail (incorporating the old town walls); the Church of St. Mary, Youghal; and Mizen Head. **Area:** 2,878sq miles. **Population:** 412,623 (incl. Cork City).

LOCAL GOVERNMENT:
County Council: County Hall, Carrigrohane Road, Cork. **County Manager:** Noel Dillon. **County Councillors:** 48. **Council Meetings:** Second and Fourth Monday of each month. **Rateable Valuation (County) -** £2,155,568.75. **County Rates:** North £39.60; South £39.60; West £39.60. **Urban District Councils:** 9 (Clonakilty, Cobh, Fermoy, Kinsale, Macroom, Mallow, Midleton, Skibbereen & Youghal). **Town Commissioners:** 3 (Bandon, Bantry & Passage West).

CORK CITY
Description: Cork city is situated by the River Lee, in the extreme south of the country. It is the third largest city in Ireland. A university city, accommodating many diverse industries and attracting tourists annually to engage in its rich history and heritage. **Biggest Tourist Attractions:** Fota Wildlife Park; Cork City Gaol; Fitzgerald's Park & Museum, University College. **City Corporation:** City Hall, Cork. **Lord Mayor:** Councillor Joe O'Callaghan. **City Manager:** Jack Higgins. **City Councillors:** 31. **Council Meetings:** Second and fourth Monday of each month. **Rateable Valuation (gross):** £1,173,154.80. **Municipal Rate:** £39.24.

DERRY
(Province of Ulster)
Doire: Oak Grove. **Main Towns:** Derry, Coleraine, Limavady, Maghera, Magherafelt, Portstewart and Dungiven. **Radio Stations:** BBC Radio Foyle, Q102FM. **Newspapers:** Derry Journal; Coleraine Chronicle; Londonderry/Limavady Chronicle; Northern Constitution; and the North West Echo. **Major Tourist Attractions:** Magilligan Strand; Portstewart seaside resort; Mussenden Temple. **Area:** 801sq miles.

DERRY CITY
Description: Derry city is situated by the banks of the River Foyle. A University city, it is steeped in history and culture, famous for its past and the seventeenth century walls which surround it. Alternatively known as Londonderry. **Biggest Tourist Attractions:** The Orchard Gallery; The Walls of Derry; The Tower Museum; The Craft Village; The Guildhall.

LOCAL GOVERNMENT:
City Council: Council Offices, 98 Strand Road, Derry BT48 7NN. **Mayor:** Richard Dallas. **Council Members:** 30, serving in wards, covering five electoral areas. **Council Meetings:** 30 council meetings and 60 Standing Committee meetings each year.

DONEGAL
(Province of Ulster)
Dún na nGall: Fort of the Foreigners. **County Capital:** Lifford. **Main Towns:** Letterkenny, Buncrana, Donegal, Ballyshannon, Ballybofey , Bundoran. **Radio Stations:** Highland Radio, North West Radio and Raidió na Gaeltachta. **Newspapers:** Donegal Peoples Press; Donegal Democrat; Derry People and Donegal News; Derry Journal. **Major Tourist Attractions:** Grianan of Aileach; Glenveagh National Park; Lough Derg; Errigal Mountain; The Poison Glen. **Area:** 1,876 sq. miles. **Population:** 128,117.

LOCAL GOVERNMENT:
County Council: County House, Lifford, Co. Donegal. **County Manager:** Michael McLoone. **County Councillors:** 29. **Council Meetings:** Last Monday in each month (except August & December). 11 County Council Meetings held annually. **Rateable Valuation:** £573,304.55. **County Rates:** £43.05. **Urban District Councils:** 3 (Buncrana, Bundoran & Letterkenny). **Town Commissioners:** 1 (Ballyshannon).

DOWN
(Province of Ulster)
An Dún: Fort. **Main Towns:** Newry, Newtownards, Downpatrick, Banbridge, Bangor, Holywood, Warrenpoint, Newcastle and Kilkeel. **Radio Stations:** Downtown Radio. **Newspapers:** Banbridge Chronicle; County Down Spectator; Down Recorder; The Leader;

Mourne Observer; The Newry Reporter; Newtownards Spectator; and The Outlook. **Major Tourist Attractions:** Bangor Castle; Jordan's Castle, Ardglass; Slieve Donard; Dromore High Cross; and Castlewellan Forest Park. **Area:** 945sq miles.

DUBLIN
(Province of Leinster)
Átha Cliath: Black pool (Dubh Linn).
Dublin is divided into four County Council areas namely: Dun Laoghaire - Rathdown, Fingal, South Dublin and Dublin Corporation.

SOUTH DUBLIN
Area: 223 sq miles. **Population:** 210,000. **Main Towns:** Clondalkin, Lucan and Tallaght. **Major Tourist Attractions:** Round Tower, Clondalkin; Sean Walsh Memorial Park, Tallaght; Griffeen Valley Linear Park, Lucan; the Liffey Valley; and the Dublin mountains. **Local Government - County Council:** P.O. Box 4122, Town Centre, Tallaght, Dublin 24. **County Manager:** John Fitzgerald. **County Councillors:** 26. **Council Meetings:** Average number of 29 Council Meetings and 59 Committee Meetings held each year. **Rateable Valuation:** £1,742,101.65.

DUN LAOGHAIRE - RATHDOWN:
Area: 49 sq miles. **Population:** 185,410. **Main Towns:** Dun Laoghaire, Monkstown, Rathfarnham, Sandy cove and Sandyford. **Major Tourist Attractions:** The Joyce Tower, Sandycove; The Maritime Museum, Dun Laoghaire; Fernhill Gardens Sandyford; Killiney Hill and Bay; Marlay Park, Rathfarnham; and Leopardstown Racecourse. **Local Government - County Councils:** Town Hall, Dún Laoghaire, Co. Dublin. **County Manager:** Kevin O'Sullivan. **County Councillors:** 28. **County Meetings:** Average of 100 council meetings annually. **Rateable Valuation** - £2,022,088.10.

FINGAL
Area: 174 sq miles. **Population:** 152,726. **Main Towns:** Balbriggan, Malahide, Skerries and Swords. **Major Tourist Attractions:** Malahide Castle and Gardens; Swords Castle and Round Tower; Fourknocks Megalithic Tomb, Balbriggan; Ardgilligan Demense, Skerries; Lusk Round Tower; and St.Doulagh's Church, Portmarnock. **Local Government - County Council:** P.O. Box 174, 46-49 Upper O'Connell Street, Dublin 1. **County Manager:** David Byrne. **County Councillors:** 24. **Rateable Valuation:** £1,376,213.35. **Town Commissioners:**1 (Balbriggan).

DUBLIN CITY
Description: Dublin city is the capital city of the Republic of Ireland and is the largest city in Ireland. It accommodates many industries including most Government and Civil Service offices, and is rich in culture and heritage. **Tourist Attractions:** Dublin Writer's Museum; Trinity College Library; Dublin Castle; Phoenix Park Visitors Centre; Kilmainham Gaol; Dublin Zoo; National Museum of Ireland; National Gallery of Ireland; Garden of Remembrance. **Population:** 478,389. **Local Government - City Corporation:** Wood Quay, Dublin 8. **Lord Mayor:**

Alderman Seán Dublin Bay Rockall Loftus. **City Manager:** F. J. Feely. **City Councillors:** 52. **Council Meetings:** First Monday of each month. **Rateable Valuation:** £5,798,663.45. **Municipal Rate:** £34.10.

FERMANAGH
(Province of Ulster)
Fear Manach: Men of Manach.
Main Towns: Enniskillen, Irvinestown, Lisnaskea and Roslea. **Newspapers:** Fermanagh Herald, Fermanagh News. **Major Tourist Attractions:** Devenish Island, Lough-Erne; Enniskillen Castle; Florencecourt Forest Park; Castle Archdale Country Park; the Marble Arch Caves; the Erne - Shannon waterway. **Area:** 647sq miles.

GALWAY
(Province of Connacht)
Gailimh: Stoney River.
County Capital: Galway.
Main Towns: Ballinasloe, Galway, Loughrea and Tuam. **Radio Stations:** Galway Bay FM and Raidió na Gaeltachta. **Newspapers:** The Connacht Sentinel, The Connacht Tribune, Galway Advertiser and the Tuam Herald. **Major Tourist Attractions:** Eyre Square and the Spanish Arch in Galway City; the Aran Islands; Lough Corrib; Connemara National Park; Portumna Forest Park; Thoor Ballylee, Aughrim Museum. **Area:** 2,349sq miles. **Population:** 180,304 (incl. Galway City).

LOCAL GOVERNMENT:
County Council: County Buildings, Prospect Hill, Co. Galway. **County Manager:** Donal O'Donoghue. **County Councillors:** 30. **Council Meetings:** Fourth Monday and second Friday in each month. **Rateable Valuation:** £758,812.30. **County Rate:** £27.69. **Urban District Council:** 1 (Ballinasloe). **Town Commissioners:** 2 (Loughrea & Tuam).

GALWAY CITY
Description: Galway, a university city, is the urban focal point of the West of Ireland and is rich in arts and culture. **Tourist Attractions:** Ó Conaire Monument; Galway Cathedral; Royal Tara China Visitors Centre; Galway Irish Crystal Heritage Centre; University College Galway. **Local Government - City Corporation:** City Hall, College Road, Co. Galway. **Mayor:** Councillor M. G. Ó hUiginn. **City Manager:** J. Gavin. **City Councillors:** 15. **Council Meetings:** First and third Monday of each month. **Rateable Valuation:** £486,367.30. **Municipal Rate:** £35.73.

KERRY
(Province of Munster)
Ciarraí: Ciar's People.
County Town: Tralee.
Main Towns: Dingle, Tralee, Ballybunion, Cahirceveen, Kenmare, Killarney, Listowel. **Radio Stations:** Radio Kerry. **Newspapers:** The Kerryman/The Corkman and Kerry's

Eye. **Major Tourist Attractions:** Ring of Kerry; the Blasket Islands; the Lakes of Killarney; Muckross House and Gardens; O'Connell Museum, Derrynane House, Caherdaniel; Tralee Aqua Dome; and Ardfert Cathedral. **Area:** 1,815sq miles. **Population:** 121,894.

LOCAL GOVERNMENT:
County Council: Áras an Chontae, Tralee, Co. Kerry. **County Manager:** D. P. d'Arcy. **County Councillors:** 27. **Council meetings:** Third Monday in each month. **Rateable Valuation:**£588,322.00. **County Rate:** £42.63. **Urban District Councils:** 3 (Killarney, Listowel & Tralee).

KILDARE
(Province of Leinster)
Cill Dara: Church of the Oak Tree. **County Town:** Naas. **Main Towns:** Athy, Celbridge, Droichead Nua, Kildare, Leixlip, Maynooth and Naas. **Newspapers:** The Liffey Champion and The Kildare Nationalist. **Major Tourist Attractions:** The National Stud and Japanese Gardens, Kildare; St Patrick's College Maynooth; Maynooth Castle; Barberstown Castle; the Curragh Racecourse; St. Brigid's Cathedral, Kildare; and Moone High Cross, Athy. **Area:** 654sq miles. **Population:** 122,656.

LOCAL GOVERNMENT:
County Council: St. Mary's, Naas, Co. Kildare. **County Manager:** F. W. Kavanagh. **County Councillors:** 25. **Council Meetings:** Last Monday of each month. **Rateable Valuation:** £786,333.60. **County Rate:** 35.50. **Urban District Councils:** 2 (Athy & Naas). **Town Commissioners:** 2 (Newbridge & Leixlip).

KILKENNY
(Province of Leinster)
Cill Chainnigh: Church of Cainneach. **County Town:** Kilkenny. **Main Towns:** Castletown, Callan, Graiguenamanagh, Kilkenny and Thomastown. **Radio Stations:** Radio Kilkenny. **Newspapers:** The Kilkenny People. **Major Tourist Attractions:** Kilkenny Castle; Jerpoint Abbey, Thomastown; Dunmore Cave; Rothe House, Kilkenny; Shee Alms House, Kilkenny; St. Canice's Cathedral and St. Canice's Well, Kilkenny. **Area:** 796sq miles. **Population:** 73,613.

LOCAL GOVERNMENT:
County Council: County Hall, John Street, Co. Kilkenny. **County Manager:** P. J. Donnelly. **County Councillors:** 26. **Council Meetings:** Third Monday of each month except August. **Rateable Valuation:** County £251,078.62; City £67,866.60. **County Rate:** £25.18. **Borough:** 1 (Kilkenny).

LAOIS
(Province of Leinster)
Laois: Laeight's Tribe. **County Town:** Portlaoise. **Main Towns:** Abbeyleix, Portarlington and Portlaoise. **Newspapers:** Leinster Express. **Major Tourist Attractions:** Stradbally Steam Museum, Portlaoise; Rock of Dunamase, Portlaoise;Abbeyleix Woodland Garden's; and Emo Court (Gardens), Portarlington. **Area:** 664sq miles. **Population:** 52,325.

LOCAL GOVERNMENT:
County Council: County Hall, Portlaoise, Co. Laois. **County Manager:** N. Bradley. **County Councillors:** 25. **Council Meetings:** Last Monday of each month. **Rateable Valuation:** £384,258.80. **County Rate:** £30.38. **Town Commissioners:** 2 (Portlaoise & Mountmellick).

LEITRIM
(Province of Connacht)
Liatroim: Grey Ridge. **County Capital:** Carrick-on-Shannon. **Main Towns:** Carrick-on-Shannon, Drumshambo and Manorhamilton. **Newspapers:** Leitrim Observer. **Major Tourist Attractions:** Boating on the Shannon; Lough Rinn House, Mohill; Glencar Waterfall; Fenagh Abbey and Hamilton Castle, Manorhamilton. **Area:** 614sq miles. **Population:** 25,297.

LOCAL GOVERNMENT:
County Council: Governor House, Carrick-on-Shannon, Co. Leitrim. **County Manager:** Patrick Fahey. **County Councillors:** 22. **Council Meetings:** Second Monday in each month. **Rateable Valuation:** £184,855. **County Rate:** £34.94.

LIMERICK
(Province of Munster)
Luimneach: Bare spot. **County Town:** Limerick. **Main Towns:** Abbeyfeale, Kilmallock, Newcastle West and Rathkeale. **Radio Stations:** Radio Limerick, 95 FM. **Newspapers:** Limerick Leader and the Limerick Chronicle. **Major Tourist Attractions:** Askeaton Castle; Castle Matrix, Rathkeale; Glin Castle; Franciscan Friary, Adare; Heritage Centre, Adare; Barnagh Gap and Lough Gur. **Area:** 1,064sq miles. **Population:** 161,856 (incl. Limerick City).

LOCAL GOVERNMENT:
County Council: P.O. Box 53, County Buildings, 79-84 O'Connell Street, Limerick. **County Manager:** M. Deigan. **County Councillors:** 28. **Council Meetings:** Fourth Friday of each month. Average of 21 Council Meetings each year. **Rateable Valuation (County):** £959,709.40. **County Rate:** £32.47.

LIMERICK CITY
Description: Limerick, a University city is situated by the banks of the river Shannon, and is the fifth largest city in Ireland. Provides a seat of trade through its many shops and industries. It is also a city steeped in culture and tradition giving way to its many galleries and theatres and also providing some charming historical sites. **Tourist Attractions:** King John's Castle; St. Mary's Cathedral; Arthurs Quay; Limerick City Gallery of Art. **Local Government - City Corporation:** City

Hall, Limerick. **Mayor:** Jim Kemmy TD. **City Manager:** F. O'Neill. **City Councillors:** 17. **Council Meetings:** Second Monday of each month. **Rateable Valuation (City)** - £457,232.95. **Municipal Rate:** £46.86.

LONGFORD
(Province of Leinster)
Longfort: Fortified Place. **County Town:** Longford. **Main Towns:** Ballymahon, Edgeworthstown, Granard and Longford. **Radio Station:** Shannonside / Northern Sound. **Newspapers:** The Longford Leader and the Longford News. **Major Tourist Attractions:** St. Mel's Cathedral, Longford; County Museum, Longford; Edgeworthstown House; and Incherlaun Monastery. **Area:** 403sq miles. **Population:** 31,496.

LOCAL GOVERNMENT:
County Councils: Longford. **County Manager:** M. Killeen. **Council Meetings:** 21. **Council Meetings:** Third Monday of each month except August. **Rateable Valuation:** £204,124.55. **County Rate:** £39.00. **Urban District Council:** 1 (Longford). **Town Commissioners:** 1 (Granard).

LOUTH
(Province of Leinster)
Lú: River Lud or Hollow. **County Town:** Dundalk. **Main Towns:** Ardee, Drogheda and Dundalk. **Radio Station:** LM FM. **Newspapers:** The Argus, The Dundalk Democrat and The Drogheda Independent. **Major Tourist Attractions:** Ardee Castle; Round Tower at Monasterboice; Mellifont Abbey; Cuchulainn's Stone near Dundalk; and the Cooley Peninsula. **Area:** 318sq miles. **Population:** 90,724.

LOCAL GOVERNMENT:
County Council: County Offices, Dundalk, Co. Louth. **County Manager:** John Quinlivan. **County Councillors:** 26 County Councillors. **Council Meetings:** Third Monday of every month. **Rateable Valuation:** £309,818.25. **County Rate:** £30.25. **Urban District Council:** 1 (Dundalk). **Borough:** Drogheda.

MAYO
(Province of Connacht)
Maigh Eo: Plain of the Yews. **County Capital:** Castlebar. **Main Towns:** Ballina, Ballyhaunis, Ballinrobe, Castlebar, Charlestown and Claremorris. **Radio Stations:** Mid & North West Radio. **Newspapers:** Connacht Telegraph, Mayo News and The Western People. **Major Tourist Attractions:** Westport House and Country Estate; Ceide Fields; Foxford Woolen Mills; Ballintober Abbey; Cong Abbey; Clare Island in Clew Bay and Loughs Mask and Carra. **Area:** 2,159sq miles. **Population:** 110,713.

LOCAL GOVERNMENT:
County Council: Áras an Chontae, Castlebar, Co. Mayo. **County Manager:** D. Mahon. **County**

Councillors: 31. **Council Meetings:** Second Monday of each month except August, and fourth Monday of each month in Committee. **Rateable valuation** - £554,430.60. **County Rate:** £40.87. **Urban District Councils:** 3 (Ballina, Castlebar & Westport).

MEATH
(Province of Leinster)
An Mhí: The Middle. **County Town:** Navan. **Main Towns:** Athboy, Bettystown & Laytown, Kells Navan, Slane and Trim. **Newspapers:** The Meath Topic and The Meath Chronicle and Cavan & Westmeath Chronicle. **Major Tourist Attractions:** Newgrange; Bective Abbey, Navan; the Hill of Tara; the river Boyne; Trim Castle; the Round Tower at Kells; Gormanstown Castle; Donaghmore Round Tower; and the Yellow Steeple, Trim. **Area:** 905sq miles. **Population:** 105,370.

LOCAL GOVERNMENT:
County Council: County Hall, Navan, Co. Meath. **County Manager:** Roibeárd Ó Ceallaigh. **County Councillors:** 29. **Council Meetings:** First Monday of each month. **Rateable valuation:** £854,346. **Urban District Councils:** 3 (Kells, Navan & Trim).

MONAGHAN
(Province of Ulster)
Muineachán: Place of the Shrubs. **County Capital:** Monaghan **Main Towns:** Monaghan, Carrickmacross, Clones and Castleblaney. **Radio Stations:** Shannonside/ Northern Sound. **Newspapers:** The Northern Standard. **Major Tourist Attractions:** Patrick Kavanagh Literary Resource Centre, Inniskeen; Lough Muckno Leisure Park, Castleblaney; Castle Leslie, Glaslough and St Patrick's Cathedral, Monaghan. **Area:** 500sq miles. **Population:** 58,494.

LOCAL GOVERNMENT:
County Council: County Offices, Monaghan. **County Manager:** Joseph O. Gavin. **County Councillors:** 20. **Council meetings:** First Monday of each month, average of 12 meetings annually. **Rateable valuation:** £337,665.96. **County Rate:** £32.04. **Urban District Councils:** 4 (Carrickmacross, Castleblayney, Clones & Monaghan). **Town Commissioners** - 1 (Ballybay).

OFFALY
(Province of Leinster)
Uíbh Fhailí: Failghe's People. **County Town:** Tullamore. **Main Towns:** Banagher, Birr, Edenderry, Ferbane and Tullamore. **Radio Station:** Radio 3. **Newspapers:** The Offaly Topic; the Offaly Express and the Tullamore Tribune. **Major Tourist Attractions:** Birr Castle & Demense; Cloghan Castle; Clonmacnoise; Slieve Bloom Display Centre, Birr; and the Clonmacnoise and West Offaly Railway. **Area:** 771sq miles. **Population:** 58,494.

LOCAL GOVERNMENT: **County Council:**

Courthouse, Tullamore, Co. Offaly. **County Manager:** S. P. MacCarthy. **County Councillors:** 21. **Council Meetings:** Third Monday of each month except August. **Rateable Valuation:** £356,673. **County Rate:** £28.35. **Urban District Councils:** 2 (Birr & Tullamore). **Town Commissioners:** 1 (Edenderry).

ROSCOMMON
(Province of Connacht)
Ros Comáin: Comán's Grove/Wood. **County Capital:** Roscommon. **Main Towns:** Boyle, Castlerea, Roscommon, Stroketown. **Newspapers:** Roscommon Champion and the Roscommon Herald. **Major Tourist Attractions:** Clonalis House, Castlerea; Lough Key Forest Park; Boyle Abbey; Roscommon Castle; and Famine Museum, Strokestown House. **Area:** 984sq miles. **Population:** 54,592.

LOCAL GOVERNMENT:
County Council: Courthouse, Roscommon. **County Manager:** Edward J. Sheehy. **County Councillors:** 26. **Council meetings:** Fourth Monday in each month, Average of 22 meetings per year. January to November; third Monday in December. **Rateable Valuation:** £440,689. **Town Commissioners:** 1 (Boyle).

SLIGO
(Province of Connacht)
Sligeach: Shelly River. **County Capital:** Sligo. **Main Towns:** Sligo, Grange, Tubbercurry and Ballymote. **Newspapers:** Sligo Champion and Sligo Weekender. **Major Tourist Attractions:** Lough Gill; Benbulben; Yeats's grave at Drumcliff; Lissadel Demense. **Area:** 709sq miles. **Population:** 54,756.

LOCAL GOVERNMENT:
County Council: Riverside, Sligo. **County Manager:** J. J. Stewart. **County Councillors:** 25 County Councillors. **Rateable Valuation:** £275,638.75. **Rate -** £33.51. **Borough -** 1 (Sligo).

TIPPERARY
(Province of Munster)
Tiobraid Árann: Ára's Well or Ára'a Wood. **County Towns:** Nenagh (North Riding) and Clonmel (South Riding). **Main Towns:** Cahir, Carrick-on-Suir, Cashel,Clonmel, Nenagh, Rocrea, Templemore, Thurles and Tipperary. **Radio Stations:** Tipp FM and Tipperary Mid-West Radio. **Newspapers:** Nationalist Newspaper, the Nenagh Guardian and the Tipperary Star. **Major Tourist Attractions:** Town Hall, Clonmel; Cahir Castle; the Rock of Cashel; Fethard Castle; Cashel Folk Park; Holycross Abbey, Thurles; Devil's Bit Mountain;St. Cronan's Abbey; Barna Castle; and Nenagh Castle. **Area:** 1647sq miles. **Population:** 132,747.

LOCAL GOVERNMENT: **County Council:** Tipperary

(NR), Courthouse, Nenagh, Co. Tipperary. **County Manager:** John McGinley. **County Councillors:** 21. **Council Meetings:** Fourth Friday in each month. **Rateable Valuation:** £468,945. **County Rate:** £33.21. **Urban District Councils:** 3 (Nenagh, Templemore & Thurles).

LOCAL GOVERNMENT:
County Council: Tipperary (SR), Áras an Chontae, Emmet Street, Clonmel. **County Manager:** Vacant. **County Councillors:** 26. **Council Meetings:** First Monday in each month. **Rateable Valuation:** £472,067.30. **County Rate:** £30.43. **Borough:** 1 (Clonmel). **Urban District Councils:** 3 (Carrick-on-Suir, Cashel & Tipperary).

TYRONE
(Province of Ulster)
Tír Eoghain: Territory of Eoghan. **Main Towns:** Omagh, Strabane, Cookstown, Dungannon, Coalisland and Castlederg. **Newspapers:** The Democrat; Dungannon Observer; Dungannon Observer; Dungannon News & Tyrone Courier; Mid-Ulster Observer; Strabane Chronicle; Strabane Weekly News; The Tyrone Constitution; Ulster Farmer and the Ulster Herald. **Major Tourist Attractions:** Gortin Glen Forest Park; Benburb Valley Park; Ulster American Folk Park; Ulster History Park; Castlederg Visitors Centre and the Altmore Open Farm. **Area:** 1,211sq miles.

WATERFORD
(Province of Munster)
Port Láirge: Inlet of Water. **County Town:** Waterford. **Main Towns:** Dungarvan, Tramore and Waterford. **Radio Stations:** WLR FM. **Newspapers:** Munster Express; Dungarvan Leader & Southern Democrat; Dungarvan Observer & Munster Industrial Advocate and the Waterford News & Star. **Major Tourist Attractions:** Town Hall, Clonmel; Cahir Castle; the Rock of Cashel; Fethard Castle; Cashel Folk Park; Holycross Abbey, Thurles; Devil's Bit Mountain;St. Cronan's Abbey; Barna Castle and Nenagh Castle. **Area:** 713sq miles. **Population:** 91,624 (incl. Waterford City).

LOCAL GOVERNMENT:
County Council: Davitt's Quay, Dungarvan, Co. Waterford. **County Manager:** D. Connolly. **County Councillors:** 23 County Councillors. **Council Meetings:** Second Monday in each month, average of 12 monthly meetings, 4 quarterly meetings and other special meetings. **Rateable Valuation (County):** £376,220. **County Rate:** £35.18. **Urban District Councils:** 1 (Dungarvan). **Town Commissioners:** 2 (Lismore & Tramore).

WATERFORD CITY
Description: Waterford city is situated to the south east of Ireland. It is a historical city that provides glorious surroundings and accommodates industries such as Waterford Crystal which proves to be a popular favourite with citizens and tourists alike.

Tourist Attractions: Reginald's Tower; Heritage Museum, Greyfriars; City Hall; Christ Church Cathedral; Cathedral of the Holy Trinity; Municipal Library. **City Corporation:** City Hall, Waterford. **Mayor:** Councillor Maurice Cummins. **City Manager:** T. O'Sullivan. **City Councillors:** 15, 10,000 acres covered. **Council Meetings:** Second Monday in each month; Average of 32 meetings per year. **Rateable Valuation:** £348,013. **Municipal Rate -** £36.77.

WESTMEATH
(Province of Leinster)
An Iarmhí: Middle-west. **County Town:** Mullingar. **Main Towns:** Athlone, Moate and Mullingar. **Newspapers:** Athlone Topic, The Westmeath Topic and The Westmeath Examiner. **Major Tourist Attractions:** Tullynally Castle, Castlepollard; Athlone Castle; St Fechin's Church, Castlepollard; Delvin Castle; Uisneach Hill, Mullingar; and St. Munna's Church, Mullingar. **Area:** 692sq miles. **Population:** 61,182.

LOCAL GOVERNMENT:
County Council: Mullingar, Co. Westmeath. **County Manager:** J. Taaffe. **County Councillors:** 23. **Council Meetings:** Last Monday of each month. **Rateable Valuation:** £512,960.40. **County Rate:** £28.52. **Urban District Council:** 1 (Athlone). **Town Commissioners:** 1 (Mullingar).

WEXFORD
(Province of Leinster)
Loch Garman: Inlet by the Sea-Washed Bank. **County Town:** Wexford. **Main Towns:** Bunclody, Enniscorthy, Gorey and New Ross. **Radio Stations:** South-East Radio. **Newspapers:** The Echo, The Wexford Echo, The Gorey Echo, New Ross Echo, The Guardian, The New Ross Standard and The People. **Major Tourist Attractions:** Courtown Harbour, Gorey; Ferns Castle; Enniscorthy Castle; St. Aidans Cathedral, Enniscorthy; St. Mary's Abbey, New Ross; Westgate Tower, Wexford; Johnstown Castle; and Duncannon Fort. **Area:** 909sq miles. **Population:** 102,045.

LOCAL GOVERNMENT:
County Council: County Hall, Spawell Road, Wexford. **County Manager:** Seamus Dooley. **County Councillors:** 21. **Council Meetings:** Second Monday of each month. **Rateable Valuation:£** 583,433.60. **County Rate:** £35.32. **Borough:** 1 (Wexford). **Urban District Councils:** 2 (Enniscorthy & New Ross). **Town Commissioners:** 1 (Gorey).

WICKLOW
(Province of Leinster)
Cill Mhantáin: Ancient Meadow of the Vikings. **County Town:** Wicklow. **Main Towns:** Arklow, Bray, Greystones and Wicklow. **Radio Station:** East Coast Radio. **Newspapers:** The Bray People and the Wicklow People. **Major Tourist Attractions:** Powerscourt Gardens and Powerscourt Waterfall, Enniskerry; Glendalough; Baltinglass Abbey; Black Castle, Wicklow and the Vale of Avoca. **Area:** 782sq miles. **Population:** 97,265.

LOCAL GOVERNMENT:
County Council: County Buildings, Wicklow. **County Manager:** Blaise Treacy. **County Councillors:** 24. **Council Meetings:** First and second Mondays of each month. **Rateable Valuation:** £711,086.15. **County Rate:** £36.03. **Urban District Councils:** 3 (Arklow, Bray & Wicklow). **Town Commissioners:** 1 (Greystones).

BUSINESS, FINANCE AND TRADE

INTRODUCTION

Republic of Ireland

The Republic of Ireland's economic performance in recent years has been impressive. In 1995 the growth rate was the highest in Europe; Gross Domestic Product was three times the OECD average; inflation was consistently low; the numbers at work continued to increase; while the balance of payments surplus reached a record seven per cent.

There has been a fundamental change in the nature of the Republic's economic development in recent years. In 1960 the Gross Domestic Product was £8,313m. which was broken down as follows - agriculture 25%, industry 30%, services 45%. By 1994 the GDP was running at £30,831m. but agriculture was down to 9 per cent, industry increased by 8 per cent to 38%, while services also increased by eight per cent to 53%.

These statistics indicate a significant shift in the traditional lifestyle of the people of the Republic, a marked increase in the numbers moving away from the land to seek jobs in the industrial and services sectors. By and large this has meant better pay, shorter hours and a overall increase in economic prosperity. All the main economic Standard of Living Indicators - spending on cars, telephones, education, televisions etc - show the Republic closing the gap in living standards with other E.U. countries.

However, despite the sustained growth the net emigration figure shows that well over a quarter of a million people have left the country over the past thirty-five years. While some have left by choice, many have been forced to leave through lack of employment. Indeed, despite the relatively high level of emigration, the Republic still has a high unemployment rate, 12.9%, as compared to the E.U. average of 11%.

Northern Ireland

The situation in Northern Ireland is much less clear. A number of factors have played a part in confusing the picture - inter-communal violence, a worldwide decline in the old traditional industries, and the North's economic dependency on the British economy. In addition, as part of Britain it has not received the same E.C. support as the Republic because of the different criteria applied to assess the economic needs of both countries. Further complication is that the Troubles have actually created employment, particularly in the security and public sector areas.

During the period 1968 to 1986, manufacturing jobs in Northern Ireland declined from 172,000 to 105,000. By contrast, the Republic saw an increase, during the same period, from 196,000 to 224,000. The New Ireland Forum's Economic Report indicated that the total economic cost of violence up to 1982 was in excess of £1.63 billion while an independent economic research study in 1987 estimated that violence had cost 40,000 jobs from 1971 to 1983.

According to a British Government paper of 1993, Northern Ireland was by far the most economically disadvantaged area of the U.K. and was one of the least prosperous regions in the E.C.

Northern Ireland annually receives a subvention from the British Exchequer. For the year 1994/1995 this amounted to £7.6 billion which did not include a further £90m. allocated to the Department of Agriculture and Fisheries.

Unemployment in N.I. has always been higher than in the rest of the U.K. - in August 1993 it was 14.6% compared with 10.5% for the U.K as a whole - while by 1991 public sector employment reached almost 40 percent of the total workforce (175,000 people employed) compared with just over 20% in 1960. It is estimated that 35,000 of the new jobs have been created by the Troubles

The upside of economic integration with Britain is the substantial economic subvention; the downside is the difficulty and lack of autonomy of local policy makers to develop and pursue a cohesive and consistent policy.

EXPORTS AND IMPORTS

Republic of Ireland Value & volume of exports and imports, 1985-1994*

Value at current prices (£m)			Volume Index (1985 = 100)			
			Exports		Imports	
Imports	Exports	Trade balance	Volume	%Change	Volume	%Change
1985.........9,428.2..........9,743.0.............314.8			.....65.2	...............6.5	................72.3	...............3.3
1990.......12,468.8.......14,336.7..........1,867.9			.....100.0	...............8.6	................100.0	...............7.0
1994.......17,157.5.......22,748.1..........5,590.5			.....153.2	...............15.2	................126.9	...............12.3

Geographical Distribution of Rep. of Ire. Exports, 1994

	%
U.K.	28.0
Other EU	41.0
Other non EU	17.0
U.S.	11.0
Japan	3.0

Geographical Distribution of Imports, 1994

	%
U.K.	36.0
Other EU	20.0
Other non EU	21.0
U.S.	18.0
Japan	5.0

Composition of R.O.I. Exports, 1994

(as % of total exports)	1990 %	1994 %
Food, drink & tobacco	22	21
Basic materials and fuels	4	3
Manufactured goods	70	71
Other	4	2
Unclassified	0	3
Total	**100%**	**100%**

Composition of Imports, 1994

(as % of total imports)	1990 %	1994 %
Food, drink & tobacco	10	9
Basic materials	3	3
Fuels	6	4
Manufactured goods	78	75
Other	3	2
Unclassified	—	7
Total	**100%**	**100%**

International Trade Statistics, 1993

	Republic of Ireland	Northern Ireland	Percentage Change (1992-93)
Imports	£14,796 m	—	12%
Exports	£19,671 m	—	18%
Imports from N. I.	£419.2 m	—	-10.5%
Exports to N. I.	£707.9 m	—	-14%

Cross Border Trade - Manufacturing Goods (IR£'000)

Goods	South-North Trade	North-South Trade	Total Trade
Meat & meat preparations	85,962	47,748	133,710
Cereals & cereal preparations	38,954	14,439	53,393
Dairy products	55,053	28,406	83,459
Other food & food preparations	88,002	38,956	126,958
Beverages	44,617	30,143	74,760
Chemicals	32,960	14,974	47,934
Clothing	54,131	20,253	74,384
Crude materials	29,559	10,949	40,508
Data processing machines & parts	13,329	3,822	17,151
Electrical machinery	8,517	5,004	13,521
Fertilisers	6,145	32,117	38,262
Furniture	19,800	5,565	25,365
Industrial machinery	31,670	15,103	46,773
Metals	35,902	12,185	48,087
Non-metallic mineral	24,063	23,605	47,668
Paper & Paperboard	19,669	31,384	98,987
Pharmaceuticals	3,747	1,595	5,342
Road vehicles	43,278	10,922	54,200
Textiles	30,296	31,339	61,635
Miscellaneous	21,157	45,637	66,794
Total Trade	825,053	468,168	1,293,221

FINANCE

Republic of Ireland National Debt Statistics, 1977-1995 (£m)

	1977	1987	1990	1995
Domestic debt	3,190	14,001	16,235	19,647
Foreign debt	1,039	9,693	8,848	10,563
TOTAL NATIONAL DEBT	**4,229**	**23,694**	**25,083**	**30,211**
National Debt as % GNP	75.2	125.0	104.3	90.0
EBR	545	1,786	462	627
General Government Debt		24,636	26,600	32,710
General Debt as % GDP		116.9	97.8	85.4

Republic of Ireland Official External Reserves IR£m

1990	2,891.7	1992	2,112.8	1994	4,041.3
1991	3,256.0	1993	4,277.9	1995	5,424.0

Rep. of Ire. Current Account Balance in IR£m and Percentage of GNP

	IR£m	% GNP
1990	371	0.2
1991	925	3.6
1992	1,447	5.4
1993	2,139	7.6
1994	2,046	6.7
1995	2,675	7.9

Exchange Rate of Republic of Ireland IR£, 1980-1994

	US dollar	Sterling	DM	ECU	Index
1980	2.06	0.89	3.73	1.48	74.0
1985	1.07	0.82	3.11	1.40	62.4
1990	1.66	0.93	2.67	1.30	68.3
1994	1.43	0.98	2.42	1.26	66.17

Purchasing power of the IR£, 1922-1994

1922	100															
1935	121	100														
1945	64	53	100													
1955	46	38	72	100												
1965	33	27	51	71	100											
1975	14	11	21	30	41	100										
1985	4	3	6	9	12	29	100									
1988	4	3	6	8	11	27	91	100								
1989	3	3	5	8	11	25	88	96	100							
1990	3	3	5	7	10	25	85	93	97	100						
1991	3	3	5	7	10	24	82	90	94	97	100					
1992	3	3	5	7	10	23	80	87	91	94	97	100				
1993	3	3	5	7	9	23	79	86	90	93	96	99	100			
1994	3	3	5	7	9	22	77	84	88	91	93	96	98	100		

Foreign Grant-Aided Investment in Rep. of Ire. 1995

Source	%
United States	79
United Kingdom	4
Rest of Europe	4
Germany	3
Others	10
Total	**IR£ 229.3m**

Construction Costs in Europe (1994)

Country	Warehouse (Index)	Offices (Index)
U.K. (Base index)	100	100
Germany	276	179
France	127	141
Italy	137	134
Spain	91	59
REPUBLIC OF IRELAND	**117**	**89**
NORTHERN IRELAND	**75**	**75**

Government Spending in Northern Ireland

The UK Subvention to Northern Ireland

Year	Amount (£m)	% of Public Spending
1969-1970	73	16
1978-1979	945	43
1981-1982	1,024	32
1984-1985	1,413	35
1987-1988	1,554	32
1990-1991	1,975	34
1993-1994	3,390	51

Macro-Economic Statistics (1993)

	Republic of Ireland (£IR)	Northern Ireland * (£Stg)
GNP	£28,563 m	—
GDP	£32,290 m	£12,360 m

* The Northern Ireland GDP figure given is provisional, and no GNP figures exist.

Interest cost of Republic of Ireland National Debt, 1990-1994

Year	IR£ Million
1990	2,109
1991	2,132
1992	2,106
1993	2,076
1994	2,029

Currency Composition of Foreign Debt (%) (Republic of Ireland)

	1990 %	1995 %		1990 %	1995 %
US$	18.7	20.2	Dutch Guilder	5.9	3.2
Deutschemark	35.9	19.6	French Franc	1.4	13.1
Swiss Franc	22.0	15.5	Belgian/Lux Franc	0.2	0.5
Yen	7.6	5.5	Other	0.0	0.2
ECU	6.7	7.2			
Sterling	1.5	15.0	TOTAL	100%	100%

Republic of Ireland Public Finance Developments, 1991-1996

	1991	1992	1993	1994	1995	1996
Current Budget Deficit						
IR£ Million	298	446	379	-15	362	82
Percentage of GDP	1.1	1.5	1.2	-	0.9	0.19
Exchequer Borrowing Requirement (Current and Capital)						
IR£ Million	499	713	690	672	627	729
Percentage of GDP	1.8	2.4	2.1	1.9	1.5	1.8
Public Sector Borrowing Requirement						
IR£ Million	762	910	862	782	826	836
Percentage of GDP	2.9	2.9	2.7	2.2	2.6	2.0

Note: 1996 figures are the Budget Target

The 1996 Budget targets as a percentage of GDP were:- current budget deficit 0.19%; Public Sector Borrowing Requirement 2.0%; General Government Deficit 2.6% and Exchequer Borrowing Requirement 1.8%.

Republic of Ireland GDP by Sector (1994)

Sector	%
Industry	38
Other Services	31
Distribution, Transport and Communications	16
Agriculture, Forestry and Fishing	9
Public Administration and Defence	6

Government Finance: Northern Ireland 1993-1994

	(£m)
Law, order and protective services	929
Agriculture, fisheries and forestry	255
Economic development	420
Environment	647
Education	1,252
Health and personal social services	1,335
Social security	2,101
Other public services	64
Euro regional funded expenditure	82
Total	**7,086**

Northern Ireland Gross Domestic Product

Gross Domestic Product 1993	12,360,000
GDP per head	7,574

Personal Income 1992

Total personal disposable income	10,878,000
Personal disposable income per head	6,755

Public Expenditure as percentage of GDP, Northern Ireland 1983-1994

Year	Northern Ireland %	United Kingdom %
1983-84	70.5	44.8
1987-88	62.3	40.5
1990-91	56.7	39.0
1993-94	60.6	43.5

SOCIAL INSURANCE

Social Insurance Contributions

Weekly Earnings	Employer	Employee
Republic of Ireland: *		
£0 - 231	9%	
Over £231 & under 25,800 p.a.	12.2%	
Over £25,800 p.a.	0%	
£30 - 60		Nil
£60.01 - 178		First £50: nil, balance: 5.5%
£178.01 - 231		First £50: 2.25%, balance:7.75%
Over £231 p.w. & under £21,500 p.a.		First £50: 2.25%, balance: 7.75%
Over £231 p.w. & over £21,500 p.a.		First £50: 2.25%, balance: 2.25%
Northern Ireland: *		
Below £59	0%	0
£59 - 104.99	3%	2% of £59+
£105 -149.99	5%	10% of earnings
£150 - 204.99	7%	Between £59 and £440
£205 - 440	10.2%	
Over £440	10.2%	

* Pay related social insurance (PRSI) and National insurance (NI) applies to Republic of Ireland and Northern Ireland respectively.

BANKING AND POST OFFICES

Republic of Ireland Banking Statistics

	1991	1992	1993	1994	1995
Number of bank employees	20,200	21,500	22,300	22,400	23,100
Number of current accounts	1.68m	1.75m	1.83m	1.90m	2.20m
Number of deposit/savings accounts	5.09m	5.24m	5.24m	4.71m	4.72m
Number of ATM cards in circulation	1.2m	1.5m	2.1m	2.0m	1.7m
Number of credit cards in circulation	0.76m	0.84m	1.0m	1.1m	1.3m
Number of ATM transactions	44m	51m	64m	74m	90m
Number of cheques issued	148m	151m	164m	159m	Not available
Number of credit card transactions	18m	19m	26m	30m	37m
Value of ATM transactions	2.0b	2.4b	2.5b	3.2b	3.7b
Value of cheques issued	250b	264b	323b	342b	Not available
Value of credit card transactions	0.8b	0.8b	1.1b	1.3b	1.8b
Number of direct debits	24m	33m	31m	32m	Not available
Value of direct debits	14b	11b	34b	36b	Not available
Number of credit transfers	45m	44m	71m	73m	Not available
Value of credit transfers	43b	50b	290b	302b	Not available

Republic of Ireland Banking Profits

1994	Total after-Tax Profits (£m)	Total average Assets (£m)	Return on Average Assets
Clearing Banks	537	47,333	1.1%
Main Building Societies	80	8,621	0.9%

Irish Banking employment/branches as compared to Europe 1996

Country	Population (m)	No. of banks	No. of Branches	No. of Employees
Ireland	3,571	46	1,022	22,400
Austria	8,031	56	732	16,732
Denmark	5,206	120	2,245	44,685
France	57,930	427	10,428	199,600
Germany	81,690	331	7,571	219,200
Italy	57,190	315	20,580	328,167
Spain	39,150	165	17,469	150,624

Republic of Ireland: Post Offices

	1991	1992	1993	1994	1995
Mail:					
Letter Post: Items delivered (million)	494.1	483.5	518.1	551.7	559.8
Pieces of Mail per Capita	140.2	137.2	146.9	156.5	158.8
System Size:					
No. of Delivery Points (million)	1.144	1.144	1.178	1.208	1.232
Post Office Network:					
Company Post Offices	95	95	95	95	96
Sub Post Offices	1,928	1,907	1,876	1,854	1,838
Total: Post Office Network	2,023	2,002	1,971	1,949	1,934
Other Company Premises	29	36	38	38	40
No. of Postal Motor Vehicles	2,020	2,020	2,147	2,208	2,214
Personnel:					
Headquarters	455	477	487	481	484
Savings Services	202	215	211	204	190
Remittance Services	74	71	75	71	68
Inspection	40	35	35	38	45
Postmen / Postwomen	4,267	4,264	4,323	4,058	4,066
Postal Sorters	552	539	530	648	766
Post Office Clerks	1,253	1,210	1,165	1,125	1,154
Other Grades	765	771	827	765	737
Temporary	—	598	879	711	515
Total: Personnel	7,608	8,180	8,532	8,101	8,025
Postmasters: Engaged as Agents	1,928	1,907	1,876	1,854	1,838

Northern Ireland Banking Statistics

Bank	Head Office	No. of Branches agencies/ sub-offices	Authorised capital	Issued capital	£ million Paid Up capital
Northern Bank Ltd	Belfast	117	100	88	88
Ulster Bank Ltd	Belfast	108	150	105	105
Bank of Ireland	Dublin	48	1,073	491	491
First Trust Bank (AIB Group)	Belfast	83	20	20	20

TAX

Republic of Ireland Tax Table (1996 - 1997)

Income Tax
Rates (from 6 April 1996)

	Single	Married
27% on first	IR£9,400	£IR18,800

48% on balance

Main Allowances

	IR£
Single Person	2,650
Married Person	5,300
Widow (er)	3,150
PAYE Allowance	800
Child Allowance (Incapacitated)	700
Dependent Relative Allowance	110
Age 65 or over (single)	200
Age 65 or over (married)	400

Reliefs

VHI - Relief for 1996/97 is available at 27% for the premium paid in 1995/96.

Mortgage Interest - 80% of interest paid less IR£l00 for single & widowed, IR£200 for married.
The maximum relief is:

Single	Married	Widowed
IR£1,900	IR£3,800	IR£2,780

Special rules applies to first time buyers. For 1996/97 relief is at an effective rate of 32.25% for 48% taxpayers.

PRSI & Levies
Employer - 12% on first IR£26,800 (8.5% if earning less than IR£13,000)
Employee - 5.5% on first IR£22,300 (IR£80 weekly earnings exempt - max. IR£4,160 p.a).
Self Employed - 5% on first IR£22,300 (first IR£l,040 of annual earnings exempt).
Levies - employees and self employed are subject to 2.25% levies on all income - no limit.

Corporation Tax
Standard Rate* 38%
Manufacturing Rate 10%
* A rate of 30% applies to the first IR£50,000 of taxable income. For groups the rate applies to the first IR£50,000 of group taxable income.

Capital Gains Tax

	Single	Married
Annual Exemption	IR£1,000	IR£2,000
Rate*	40%	

* A rate of 27% applies to disposals of shares in certain unquoted Irish companies.

Residential Property Tax (1.5%)
Market Value Exemption Limit at 5th April 1996 IR£101,000. 10% reduction in tax per dependent child. Income Exemption Limit IR£30,100.

Capital Acquisitions Tax
(Class Thresholds to 31st December 1996)

Relationship to Disponer.	IR£
Child, minor child of deceased child	182,550
Other blood relatives	24,340
None of the above	12,170

Rates of Tax	Inheritance	Gift
Threshold amount	Nil	Nil
Next IR£10,000	20%	15%
Next IR£30,000	30%	22.5%
Balance	40%	30%

Probate Tax
Probate Tax is levied at a rate of 2% on estates with a value if over IR£10,650 (from 1st January 1996).

Tax Rates Republic of Ireland and Northern Ireland

Tax Rates:	Republic of Ireland (£IR)	Northern Ireland (£Stg)
Allowances	Single: £2,500	Single: £3,525
	Married couple: £5,000	Married couple: £1,720

HASSON & COMPANY
S O L I C I T O R S

39/41 CLARENDON STREET
LONDONDERRY BT48 7ER
TELEPHONE 01504 - 266818
FAX 01504 - 267780

———— @ ————

Providing Quality Legal
Services for Generations.

INDUSTRY

INTRODUCTION

The Republic of Ireland's economic growth rate has been remarkable in recent years. One of the major factors in this growth has been American investment: in 1995, out of 114 projects brought on stream by the Industrial Development Authority 62 originated in the States. In Northern Ireland there are 45 American companies operating, employing in the region of 9,000.

Another of the key elements in the Republic's superb growth - Gross Domestic Product increased by an average of 5.05% between 1987 and 1995, by far the highest in the E.C. - was the remarkable rise in exports which increased from £6.2bn in 1981 to almost £22bn. in 1994. This was achieved by an increase of almost 85% in productivity between 1987 and 1994. In addition, after a considerable period of employment decline, in the two year period ending April 1995 almost 90,000 jobs were created, of which two-thirds were in the private sector.

In Northern Ireland total employment rose by 8,550 during 1995 with 730 new jobs in manufacturing employment and an increase of 8,000 in service sector jobs. Goods manufactured in the North and sold to the export markets increased by £462m. to £2.6billion in 1994/1995 -a growth rate of 21%. Sales to the Republic also showed a remarkable increase, growing from £437m. in 1991/'92 to £632m. in 1994/'95 - an increase of 45%. This makes the Republic of Ireland the North's single most important export market.

An estimated 72,000 manufacturing jobs rely on sales outside N.I. The food, drink and tobacco sector is the largest manufacturing industry in the North, accounting for 34% of sales, 27% of external sales and 23% of exports in 1994/1995.

There is little doubt the "Troubles" in Northern Ireland have created difficulties for industry. By 1986 the number of manufacturing jobs had declined from 172,000 to 105,000. However, additional complicatory factors are that a high proportion of the North's manufacturing base has been concentrated in declining industries, such as textiles, leather and footwear while, economically, N.I. is only a small component of the much larger U.K. economy and therefore does not have direct "hands-on" control of the macro-economic levers of power such as fiscal, monetary and exchange policies. It is also worth noting that of the 23,000 jobs promoted by the Industrial Development Board between 1982 and 1988 only 40% were in place at the end of that period.

MANUFACTURING (REPUBLIC OF IRELAND)

Top 30 Companies in the Republic of Ireland

Rank	Company	Nature of Business	Stock Market Value (£ m)	Estimated Turnover (£ m)	Number of employees in Ireland
1	Smurfit Group	Paper / Packaging	1,938	1,317	2,000
2	Allied Irish Bank	Banking	1,728	1,240	9,250
3	Bank of Ireland	Banking	1,385	983	9,316
4	CRH plc	Building Materials	1,203	1,427	2,500
5	Elan Corporation	Healthcare	677	107	500
6	Irish Life	Assurance	555	697	1,609
7	Kerry Group plc	Food	552	880	3,250
8	Waterford Wedgewood	Crystal and Fine China	404	319	1,441
9	Independent Newspapers	Publishing	343	174	1,186
10	Greencore Group	Food	337	404	1,928
11	Fyffes plc	Fruit Distributor	327	611	559
12	Woodchester Investments	Financial Services	252	93	369
13	Irish Permanent	Financial Services	230	86	11,000
14	Avonmore Foods plc	Dairy/Food Products	213	1,129	3,300
15	Waterford Foods plc	Dairy/Food Products	178	694	1,514
16	DCC plc	Industrial Holding Co.	140	336	1,200
17	Anglo Irish Bank	Banking	135	37	173
18	Lyons Irish Holdings	Tea/Coffee	126	26	172
19	IWP International	Household Products	117	121	210
20	Aran Energy plc	Oil/Gas	115	64	17
21	James Crean plc	Industrial Holding Co.	114	245	111
22	Irish Continental Group	Ferry Operator	106	109	1,100
23	Clondalkin Group	Print/Packaging	105	153	530
24	Fitzwilton	Industrial Holding Co.	101	306	415
25	Golden Vale plc	Dairy/Food Products	99	423	741
26	IAWS Group	Agribusiness (Feeds/Food)	98	480	821
27	Hibernian Group	Insurance	98	143	602
28	Barlo Group	Radiators/Plastic Products	76	97	400
29	Tullow Oil	Oil and Gas	73	3	23
30	Flogas plc	L.P.G.	69	46	102

Republic of Ireland Employment Figures classified by Industry

Industry (1991)	Males	Females	Total
Agriculture, Fishing and forestry	142,255	15,953	158,208
Mining,quarrying and turf production	5,568	447	6,015
Manufacturing industries	152,609	66,116	218,725
Electricity, gas and water supply	10,269	1,679	11,948
Building and construction	72,687	3,938	76,625
Commerce	106,131	67,254	173,385
Insurance, finance, business services	31,302	30,613	61,915
Transport, communications, storage	55,422	13,975	69,397
Public Administration and defence	52,158	23,383	75,541
Professional services	71,317	125,586	196,903
Personal services	25,927	45,234	71,161
Other industries/industries not stated	18,303	10,954	29,257
Total: All Industries	**743,948**	**405,132**	**1,149,080**

Republic of Ireland Industrial Workers Weekly Earnings, 1986-1994

Year	Average weekly earnings (£)	Increase on previous year (%)	Increase on previous year in weekly earnings (%)
1986	189.28	7.6	3.6
1987	198.11	4.7	1.5
1988	208.33	5.2	3.0
1989	216.40	3.9	- 0.2
1990	225.16	4.0	0.6
1991	235.23	4.5	1.3
1992	244.27	3.8	0.8
1993	258.00	5.6	4.0
1994 *	261.28	4.3	2.6

* Provisional figures after first quarter

Average weekly earnings of industrial workers in Rep. of. Ire. by sector

Industry	1991 (£)	1992 (£)	1993 (£)	1994 (£)
Total: All Industries	**235.82**	**245.34**	**261.84**	**264.42**
Clothing, Footwear and Leather	129.71	136.19	143.69	150.15
Chemicals	299.71	319.15	332.41	343.82
Drink and Tobacco	367.78	380.49	388.07	404.47
Electricity, Gas and Water	301.61	314.56	366.75	362.05
Food	223.17	224.61	242.95	243.26
Manufacturing Industries	229.08	238.86	252.51	255.96
Metals and Engineering	222.69	234.15	243.05	249.32
Mining, Quarrying and Turf	340.92	333.78	377.26	383.58
Miscellaneous Industries (rubber/plastic, etc.)	221.70	235.36	244.42	253.56
Non Metallic Mineral Products	289.36	295.37	309.88	317.32
Paper and Printing	284.88	293.03	314.24	307.67
Textile Industry	187.66	195.14	210.89	207.96
Timber and Wooden Furniture	182.05	191.67	215.61	204.35
Transportable Goods Industries	232.02	241.17	255.75	259.12

Gross earnings and hours worked by Industrial Workers in Rep. of Ireland

Year	Averages Earnings per hour	Earnings per week	Hours worked per week
1989	£5.08	£210.98	41.5
1990	£5.31	£219.11	41.2
1991	£5.61	£228.72	40.8
1992	£5.87	£237.92	40.5
1993	£6.21	£250.70	40.3
1994	£6.32	£258.03	40.8

Republic of Ireland Average Hourly Earnings Comparison Table, 1987-1994

Year	UK	Germany	France	Italy	USA	Japan	Ireland
1987	100.00	100.00	100.00	100.00	100.00	100.00	100.00
1988	114.80	103.10	102.70	104.90	102.60	113.70	104.30
1989	123.00	106.40	107.20	116.70	113.60	117.80	108.20
1990	127.40	111.90	114.40	125.60	103.20	102.50	114.40
1991	140.60	117.40	118.60	135.50	110.30	118.30	120.80
1992	139.90	131.10	125.10	138.20	111.00	121.10	127.40
1993	135.40	142.90	132.00	124.10	127.20	153.40	128.30
1994	139.70	149.10	134.60	124.60	129.70	167.00	133.90

Indices are in common currency terms.

Republic of Ireland Strikes: Number and Days Lost, 1986-1994

Year	(Strikes) Total no.	Total days lost	Official No.	days lost	Unofficial No.	days lost	Public Sector No.	days lost	Private Sector No.	days lost
1986	100	315,500	62	295,500	38	20,500	35	246,000	65	69,500
1987	76	260,000	54	235,000	22	25,000	30	148,500	46	111,500
1988	72	130,000	46	123,500	26	6,500	24	69,000	48	61,000
1989	41	41,400	28	29,800	13	11,600	14	8,000	27	33,400
1990	51	203,700	35	196,900	16	6,800	19	6,500	32	197,200
1991	52	82,900	39	73,600	13	9,300	31	55,000	21	27,900
1992	41	189,600	30	186,800	11	2,800	15	52,100	26	137,600
1993	48	65,000	39	60,200	9	4,800	19	43,100	29	29,900
1994	32	24,000	27	20,200	5	3,800	11	6,000	21	18,000

Origins of IDA assisted overseas Companies in Republic of Ireland

Country of origin	Number
United States	364
Germany	117
United Kingdom	115
Rest of Europe	219
Japan	34
Rest of the World	37
Total	**886**

IDA Supported Jobs in the Republic of Ireland, 1994 and 1995

62 out of the 114 IDA projects in 1995 originated in the United States, making the US by far the most important market for Ireland.

Superlatives	1994	1995
Total New Jobs filled	9,804	11,517
First Time Jobs filled	8,348	10,166
Net Change	5,095	6,557
Job Losses	4,699	4,960
Total Full-time employment IDA companies	82,895	89,452
Total temporary - contract employment	8,483	11,034
Total number of IDA companies	889	940
Total IDA Grants paid	£73 m	£93 m
Average cost-per-job sustained over 7 years	£13,106	£12,048

Labour Costs Comparison table

(Rate £1 = $1.50)	$	£
Germany	$25.56	£17.04
Switzerland	$22.66	£15.11
Belgium	$21.38	£14.25
Norway	$20.20	£13.47
Netherlands	$20.16	£13.44
Japan	$19.20	£12.80
Denmark	$19.12	£12.74
Sweden	$17.91	£11.94
United States	$16.79	£11.19
Finland	$16.56	£11.04
France	$16.31	£10.87
Italy	$15.97	£10.65
Britain	$12.82	£8.55
REPUBLIC OF IRELAND	$11.80	£7.87
Spain	$11.53	£7.67
NORTHERN IRELAND	$10.26	£6.84
Portugal	$4.60	£3.07

PAY & TAX RATES

Pay and Tax Rates in Republic of Ireland and Northern Ireland

	(£IR) Republic of Ireland	(£stg) Northern Ireland
Pay Rates:		
Industrial workers: *		
Female	£188..81	£161.70
Male	£207.31	£249.30
Public Service: **		
Lowest grade	£7,833 - £11,636	£6,928 - £9,826
Highest grade	£62,774	£82,415
Primary teacher	£13,315 - £24,995	£11,883 - £20,145
Political Representatives: Local councils	expense allowance	expense allowance
Parliamentary Representatives:		
Taoiseach / Prime Minister	£89,573	£76,234
Government Minister	£71,343	£63,047
Minister of State / Junior Minister	£51,532	£44,611

Tax Rate:
Bands of taxable income: *** ....Standard rate (27%): £8,900 ....Lower Rate (20%): £0 - £3,200
Higher Rate (48%): on balance ......Basic Rate (25%): £3,204 - £24,300
Higher rate (40%): over £24,300

* based on average gross earnings, ** based on selected pay scales, *** tax bands for married couples are based on a unit (a single persons tax bands doubled) in the Republic of Ireland.

Unemployment & Employment Statistics

	Republic of Ireland	Northern Ireland
Unemployment rate:		
Live register (Jan. 1995)	14.3%	12.3%
Employment rate (1993):		
Manufacturing	27%	24%
Services	37%	38%
Agriculture	12%	6%
Public Sector	24%	32%

MANUFACTURING (NORTHERN IRELAND)

Top 30 Northern Ireland Companies

Rank	Company	Nature of Business	Turnover (£ Million)	Net Worth (£ Million)	Employees
1	N. Ireland Electricity	Electricity Service	498	343	2,931
2	Short Brothers	Aircraft Manufacturers	353	194	8,752
3	Glen Electric Ltd	Domestic Heating	268	26	2,927
4	Milk Marketing Board	Dairy/Milk Products	267	28	804
5	F.A. Wellworth	Supermarkets	259	62	4,561
6	Stewarts Supermarkets	Supermarkets	251	36	3,633
7	Dunnes Stores (Bangor)	Supermarkets	189	35	2,556
8	F.G. Wilson Eng.	Electricity Generators	166	54	1,026
9	J & J Haslett	Grocery Wholesale	158	15	1,200
10	Moy Park Ltd	Poultry Products	152	6	2,485
11	Charles Hurst Ltd	Vehicle Distributors	151	5	534
12	Crazy Prices	Supermarkets	135	18	1,645
13	Nigen Ltd	Electricity Supply	134	36	488
14	John Henderson Ltd	Grocery Wholesale	126	8	423
15	Northern Telecom	Telecom Sales/Services	49	31	1,375
16	Maxol Oil Ltd	Oil/Petroleum Distributors.	107	11	110
17	Desmond & Sons Ltd	Clothing Manufacturers	92	23	2,640
18	Irish Bonding Co. Ltd	Wine/Spirits Wholesaler	88	10	256
19	Nacco Materials Hd.	Forklift Manufacturer	84	9	490
20	John Hogg & Co. Ltd	Fuel/Oil	77	10	1,030
21	Belfast Co-Op	Supermarket Proprietors	77	- 5	1,009
22	Harland & Wolff	Shipbuilding	72	- 22	1,426
23	Mivan Ltd	Construction	69	7	2,608
24	Cawoods (NI)	Fuel Distributors	69	12	279
25	Arthur Guinness (NI)	Beer Distributors	69	3	193
26	Daewoo Electrics	Video Recorder Manufacturers	67	10	407
27	Dairy Produce Packers	Cheese Manufacturers	66	8	266
28	Leckpatrick Dairies	Dairy/Food Processing	64	8	292
29	Alchem Plc	Pharmaceuticals	64	5	180
30	Foyle Meats Ltd	Meat Processors	63	7	187

Northern Ireland Manufacturing Employment by sector

Sector	1986	1994
Food, Drink and Tobacco	20,000	19,500
Textiles and Clothing	27,860	25,670
Electrical & Electronic Engineering	7,310	10,000
Transport, Vehicles & Mechanical Engineering	24,550	20,640
Chemical Industry & Fibres	3,430	4,540
Paper, Printing & Publishing	5,540	6,290
Timber & Rubber	9,180	10,460
Others	5,730	6,630
Total	**103,600**	**103,730**

Gross Weekly Wage at which replacement rate approaches 75% for selected household types (1993-1994) in Northern Ireland

Household Type	Gross Wage (£)	Replacement Rate
Single person (no dependents)	£120	72.1
Single person (one child under 11)	£110	70.2
Couple (no dependents)	£160	72.0
Couple (two children under 11)	£174	79.1
Couple (two children under 11 & two 11-15)	£174	80.5

Examples of Earnings in Northern Ireland

Group	25% earned less than (£)	50% earned less than (£)
Manual (men)	£175.40	£222.00
Manual (women)	£122.20	£146.80
Non-manual (men)	£253.80	£366.40
Non-manual (women)	£169.70	£227.20

Main Northern Ireland Sales Markets

Market	1991/92 £m	1992/93 £m	1993/94 £m	1994/95
Republic of Ireland	437	498	544	632
Britain	2,388	2,422	2,514	2,599
Rest of European Union	786	879	916	1,099
Rest of World	561	603	715	906
Total	4,172	4,402	4,689	5,236

Work Stoppages in Northern Ireland

Industrial disputes (1993)

Number of disputes - stoppages	7
Number of days lost	15,723

Male Unemployment by Age-Group in Northern Ireland

Total Males unemployed and Males unemployed for 3 or more years by age (1995)

	Age Group 20-29	30-39	40-49	50-59	All 20-59
Number unemployed 3 or more years	4,061	7,944	7,029	5,298	24,332
Total number unemployed	21,892	18,175	12,667	9,641	62,375
% by age group unemployed 3 + years	18.6	43.7	55.5	55.0	39.0
Share of 3 + year unemployed by age group	16.7	32.6	28.9	21.8	100

Unemployment in N.I. (1996)

Unemployment in travel-to-work areas

Area	Percentage Unemployed
Ballymena	7.6%
Belfast	10.0%
Coleraine	12.8%
Cookstown	15.2%
Craigavon	9.3%
Dungannon	13.2 %
Enniskillen	12.4%
Derry	15.6%
Magherafelt	12.3%
Newry	16.2%
Omagh	11.9%
Strabane	17.8%
All Northern Ireland	10.9%

N.I. Employment / Training (1995)

Numbers involved in Employment and Training

Programme	Total numbers
Trainees on Adult Courses	150
Future Managers training	450
Adults in Enterprise Ulster (trainees)	1,250
Adults in Enterprise Ulster (employees)	200
Action for Community Employment	7,700
Job Training Programme	100
Employment Support (for the disabled)	600
Community Work Programme	550
Jobskills	13,850
Youth Training Programme	4,200
Total (Numbers Involved)	29,050

Northern Ireland Unemployment Rates by qualification and age (1981-1993)

	25-34 Qualification Yes	No	35-54 Qualification Yes	No
1981	6.6	27.5	5.4	15.4
1984	13.9	26.7	3.5	18.4
1989	8.9	35.4	7.5	18.1
1991	9.8	29.8	8.6	20.3
1993	13.4	30.4	9.1	20.8

TRADE UNIONS IN IRELAND

Trade Union Information

The Irish Congress of Trade Unions is the central authority for the trade union movement in Ireland. The main function of the ICTU is to co-ordinate the work of trade unions operating in Ireland. In all 66 unions are affiliated to the ICTU (the overall membership is 677,560), 49 of which are based in the Republic. The ATGWU (Amalgamated Transport and General Workers' Union) and SIPTU (Services Industrial Professional Technical Union) account for 44% of the total membership in the Republic. Twenty nine of the unions affiliated to the ICTU have their head-quarters in Northern Ireland and in Britain.

Irish Congress of Trade Unions
19 Raglan Road, Ballsbridge, D.4.
Tel: (01) 668 0641
Northern Ireland Office:
3 Wellington Park, Belfast BT9 6DJ
Tel: (0801232) 681726
General Secretary: P. Cassells.

AFFILIATED UNIONS
Amalgamated Engineering and Electrical Union: Hayes Court, West Common Rd., Bromley, Kent.
Amalgamated Transport and General Workers' Union: Transport Hse, Smith Sq, London.
Association of First Division Civil Servants: 2 Caxton Street, London.
Association of Higher Civil Servants: 4 Warner's Lane, Dartmouth Road, Dublin 6.
Association of Irish Traditional Musicians: 32 Cearnóg Belgrave, Monkstown, Co. Dublin.
Association of Secondary Teachers, Ireland: ASTI House, Winetavern Street, Dublin 8.
Association of University Teachers: United House, 9 Pembridge Road, London.
Automobile, General Engineering and Mechanical Operatives Union: 22 North Frederick Street, Dublin 1.
Bakery and Food Workers' Amalgamated Union: 37 Lower Gardiner Street, Dublin 1.
British Actors Equity Association: Guild Hse., Upper St. Martin's Lane, London.
Building and Allied Trades Union: Arus Hibernia, Blessington St., D.7
Chartered Society of Physiotherapy: Royal Victoria Hospital, Grosvenor Road, Belfast.
Civil Service Alliance: Four Courts, Dublin 7.
Civil and Public Services Association: 160 Falcon Road, London.
Civil and Public Services Union: 72 Lower Leeson Street, Dublin 2.
Communications Managers' Association: Hughes House, Ruscombe Road, Twyford, Reading, Berkshire.
Communications Managers' Union: 577 North Circular Rd., D.1
Communication Workers' Union: Aras Ghaibréil, 575 North Circular Road, Dublin 1.
Communication Workers' Union: CWU House, Crescent Lane, London.
Cork Operative Butchers' Society: 55 North Main Street, Cork.
ESB Officers' Association: 43 East James's Plc., Lower Baggot St., D.2.
Federated Union of Government Employees: 32 Parnell Sq., D.1.
Fire Brigades' Union: Bradley House, 68 Coombe Road, Kingston-upon-Thames, Surrey .
General Municipal Boilermakers: 22-23 Worple Road, London.
Graphical, Paper and Media Union: 63-67 Bronham Road, Bedford .
Guinness Staff Association: St. James's Gate, Dublin 8.
Irish Municipal, Public and Civil Trade Union: Nerney's Court, Dublin 1.
Inland Revenue Staff Federation: Douglas Houghton House, 231 Vauxhall Bridge Road, London.
Institution of Professionals, Managers and Specialists: 75-79 York Road, London.
Irish Airline Pilots' Association: Corballis Park, Dublin Airport, Dublin.
Irish Bank Officials' Association: 93 St. Stephen's Green, Dublin 2.
Irish Federation of Musicians and Associated Professions: 63 Lower Gardiner Street, Dublin 1.
Irish Federation of University Teachers: 11 Merrion Sq., Dublin 2.
Irish Medical Organisation: 10 Fitzwilliam Place, Dublin 2.
Irish National Teachers' Organisation: 32 Parnell Square, Dublin 1.
Irish Nurses' Organisation: 11 Fitzwilliam Place, Dublin 2.
Irish Print Union: 35 Lower Gardiner Street, Dublin 1.
Irish Veterinary Union: 32 Kenilworth Square, Dublin 6.
MANDATE: 9 Cavendish Row, D1.

Marine, Port and General Workers' Union: 14 Gardiner Place, Dublin 1.
Manufacturing Science Finance: 64-66 Wandsworth Common, Northside, London .
National Association of Probation Officers: 3-4 Chivalry Road, Battersea, London.
National Association of Teachers in Further and Higher Education: 27 Britannia Street, London.
National League of the Blind of Ireland: 21 Hill Street, Dublin 1.
National Union of Civil and Public Servants: New Bridgewater House, 5-30 Great Suffolk Street, London.
National Union of Insurance Workers: 27 Old Gloucester Street, London.
National Union of Journalists: Acorn House, 314-321 Gray's Inn Road, London.
National Union of Knitwear, Footwear and Apparel Trades: 55 New Walk, Leicester.
National Union of Rail, Maritime and Transport Workers: Unity House, Euston Road, London.
National Union of Sheet Metal Workers of Ireland: 6 Gardiner Row, Dublin 1.
North of Ireland Bakers, Confectioners and Allied Workers' Union: 80 High Street, Belfast.
Northern Ireland Musicians' Association: 3rd Floor, Unit 4, Fortwilliam Business Park, Dargan Rd., Belfast.
Northern Ireland Public Service Alliance: 54 Wellington Park, Belfast
Operative Plasterers and Allied Trades Society of Ireland: Arus Hibernia, 13 Blessington Street, Dublin 7.
Prison Officers' Association: Millmount Hse, Upper Drumcondra Road, Dublin 9.
Public Service Executive Union: 30 Merrion Square, Dublin 2.
Sales, Marketing and Administrative Union of Ireland: 37 Lower Gardiner Street, Dublin 1.
Seamen's Union of Ireland: 61 North Strand Road, Dublin 3.

Services Industrial Professional Technical Union: Liberty Hall, D. 1.
Teachers' Union of Ireland: 73 Orwell Road, Rathgar, Dublin 6.
Technical, Engineering and Electrical Union: 5 Cavendish Row, Dublin 1.

Transport Salaried Staffs' Association: Walken House, 10 Melton Street, Euston, London.
Union of Construction, Allied Trades and Technicians: Abbeyville Rd., Clapham, London .
Union of Shop, Distributive and

Allied Workers: 188 Wilmslow Road, Fallowfield, Manchester.
UNISON: 1 Mabledon Place, London.
Veterinary Officers' Association: 4 Warner's Lane, Dartmouth Road, Dublin 6.

AGRICULTURE

Introduction

1996 was not a good year for Irish agriculture. While primarily a British problem, farmers in Ireland were badly hit by the BSE scare which resulted in a ban on British beef throughout most of Europe. The knock-on effect on the Irish Beef Industry is incalculable, estimates putting losses to Irish farmers in the hundreds of millions.

Apart from the more recent beef problems, agriculture in Ireland has been undergoing radical changes in the last thirty years, but particularly since Ireland and Britain entered the E.C.

In the Republic in 1960 agriculture was a £2bn. industry, providing a quarter of the country's £8.3 bn Gross Domestic Product. By 1994, the GDP had risen to almost £31bn, but by this time agriculture had slipped from 25 per cent of GDP to 9 per cent.

This has resulted in major demographic and social changes in Irish society. The movement away from the land to the urban environment in search of manufacturing or service jobs has radically changed the lifestyles of much of the population. This lifestyle was exchanged for shorter hours, indoor working, and an industrial wage which was, generally, considerably higher than that which could be achieved from farming. This resulted in workers having a much larger disposable income which, in turn, boosted other sectors of the economy.

Most full time farmers now work much larger holdings than would have been the norm up until the 1960's, the average farm size now being in excess of 100 acres.

In Northern Ireland the impact was similar though agriculture remains an important industry giving employment to almost 60,000 people and worth in excess of £1bn annually to the economy. An Agriculture Census earlier this year indicate a 4 per cent increase in the acreage under cereals, a drop in other crops with potatoes down by 3 per cent, a rise of 4 per cent in cattle, poultry numbers were up by 12 per cent on 1995, while there was a one per cent decrease in the number of persons in the agriculture labour force in June 1996.

Main Agricultural Bodies in Republic of Ireland

TEAGASC - the Agriculture and Food Development Authority - is the national body with responsibility for providing advisory, training, research and development services geared to the Irish Agriculture and Food Industry. Many of Teagasc's activities are co-funded by the EU. Integrated research, advisory and training services are provided through eight research centres, 15 colleges, 40 local training centres and some 100 advisory offices. The organisation's activities are managed by six Directors of Operation, reporting directly to the National Director.

AN BORD GLAS - the Horticultural Development Board - is the state body established by the Government to develop, promote and assist in the production, marketing and consumption of horticultural produce. It carries out the following services: implements plans for the overall development of horticulture; provides marketing information such as price and packaging; assists with promotions, customer introduction; helps with test marketing of new crops or market outlets; assists with quality monitoring; promotes hygiene in the

industry.

AN BORD BIA - the Irish Food Board, which was established in 1994, has responsibility for the market development and promotion of Irish Food and Livestock. The general services of the organisation includes: surveying, investigating and developing markets and potential markets for food; collecting and disseminating market intelligence and providing information and advice in relation to supply and demand and market trends and trade opportunities in food; conducting and/or providing reviews, surveys, symposia, analyses and studies in relation to trade in, and markets and potential markets for food; providing publicity, advertising and promotional campaigns for the purpose of encouraging the increased consumption of food; establishing, equipping and operating exhibitions, show rooms, information bureaux and similar establishments for the purpose of encouraging increased consumption of food; publishing and distributing magazines, journals and reports; operating quality assurance schemes.

Number of farms by size of farm in Republic of Ireland

Hectares	1980	1985	1987	1991
		(000)		
1 - 10	69.3	70.0	67.8	41.8
10 - 20	67.7	63.8	63.3	48.3
20 - 30	36.3	36.9	36.7	31.0
30 - 50	30.3	29.9	26.6	28.4
Above 50	19.7	19.6	19.5	19.6
Total	**223.3**	**220.2**	**213.9**	**169.1**

Persons, Males and Females in Farming in Republic of Ireland

(1991)	Persons	Males	Females
Agricultural and forestry workers & fishing	165,112	149,430	15,682

Farmers

Farmers (Horse, Pig or Poultry)	270	224	46
Under 10 acres	18	16	2
10 and under 15 acres	6	3	3
15 and under 30 acres	10	8	2
30 and under 40 acres	4	3	1
40 and under 50 acres	5	4	1
50 and under 70 acres	9	9	0
70 and under 100 acres	5	3	2
100 and under 150 acres	15	13	2
150 and under 200 acres	3	2	1
200 acres and over	47	41	6
Area not stated	148	122	26
Other Farmers	111,559	104,751	6,808
Under 10 acres	1,541	1,400	141
10 and under 15 acres	2,847	2,604	243
15 and under 30 acres	13,674	12,506	1,168
30 and under 40 acres	12,937	12,017	920
40 and under 50 acres	12,670	11,808	862
50 and under 70 acres	20,883	19,755	1,128
70 and under 100 acres	18,250	17,356	894
100 and under 150 acres	14,297	13,610	687
150 and under 200 acres	5,262	5,005	257
200 acres and over	4,415	4,180	235
Area not stated	4,783	4,510	273

Farmers' sons (in law) and daughters (in law) assisting on farms	11,322	11,257	65
Farmers' other relatives assisting on farm	9,643	3,527	6,116
Farm Managers	1,248	1,152	96
Agricultural Labourers	14,445	13,610	835
Other Agricultural Workers	3,616	3,037	579

Agriculture in relation to population and labour force in Republic of Ireland

	1992 (000)	1993 (000)	1994 (000)
Total population	3,549	3,563	3,571
Total labour force	1,360	1,375	1,397
Total at work	1,139	1,146	1,176
Agriculture, forestry & fishing	153	144	140
Industry	318	312	328
Services	668	690	708
Agriculture	148	139	135
Agriculture as % of total at work	13.0	12.1	11.5

Agricultural Wages in Republic of Ireland

	1990	1991	1992	1993	1994	1995
Leinster	121.70	121.70	126.70	131.49	137.24	139.98
Munster	121.82	121.82	126.82	131.49	137.24	139.98
Connacht	121.61	121.61	126.61	131.49	137.24	139.98
Donegal/Cavan/Monaghan	121.61	121.61	126.61	131.49	137.24	139.98
Ireland	121.73	121.73	126.73	131.49	137.24	139.98

Republic of Ireland Gross Agricultural Output (IR £m)

	1987	1992	1993	1994
Cattle	1,057	1,267	1,349	1,282
Milk and Dairy Products	982	1,078	1,145	1,154
Pigs	144	221	199	200
Poultry and Eggs	111	134	125	134
Sheep and Lambs	128	153	170	169
Horses	68	49	68	63
Wool and Other Products	9	6	7	10
Total Livestock & Products	**2,498**	**2,908**	**3,061**	**3,013**
Barley	106	104	74	58
Wheat	32	72	48	36
Sugar Beet	59	57	51	60
Potatoes	59	56	47	79
Fresh Vegetables	62	93	99	108
Other Crops / Fruit	20	38	39	40
Turf	35	36	31	24
Total Crops and Turf	**373**	**456**	**389**	**405**
Gross Agricultural Output	2,872	3,364	3,450	3,418
Inputs of Materials & Services	1,179	1,380	1,442	1,562
G.A. Product at Market Prices	1,692	1,984	2,008	1,856
Subsidies less Levies	491	361	381	638
G.A. Product at Factor Cost	1,810	2,345	2,389	2,494
Depreciation (-)	292	347	349	358
Wages & Land Annuities (-)	130	181	183	179
Income from Self-Employment & Other	1,386	1,816	1,858	1,956

Republic of Ireland Agricultural Production and Exports

	1987 (IR£m)	1992 (IR£m)	1993 (IR£m)
Beef	590.1	615.4	730.6
Live Cattle	115.7	67.1	97.4
Dairy Products	725.1	1,242.5	980.6
Pigs, Pork & Bacon	61.3	144.5	126.7
Sheep, Mutton & Lamb	59.3	134.5	136.5
Horses & Horsemeat	48.3	39.9	43.6
Food Preparations	640.6	893.7	1,239.8
Other Agricultural Exports	453.6	615.9	579.9
Total Agricultural Exports	**2694**	**3,753.6**	**3,935.1**
Total Exports	**10,723.5**	**16,628.8**	**19,781.7**

Agriculture & Food as % of Total: **1987** - 25.1%; **1992** - 22.6%; **1993** - 19.9%

Selected Prices for Farm Products in Republic of Ireland, 1987-1994

Product	Unit	1987	1992	1993	1994
				(IR£/Unit)	
Wheat	Tonne	121.7	111.7	111.6	96.1
Feed Barley	Tonne	106.0	104.6	96.6	89.0
Malting Barley	Tonne	115.2	121.4	112.3	95.1
Potatoes	Tonne	69.0	86.0	173	196
Sugar Beet	Tonne	36.7	42.0	46.4	44.6
Creamery Milk	Litre	0.176	0.203	0.219	0.218
Bullocks (450-499 kg)	100 kg	124.0	118.1	127.9	131.0
Heifers (350-399 kg)	100 kg	108.0	108.7	118.5	122.3
Pigs (25-34 kg)	Head	30.9	31.2	25.3	27.1
Sheep (40-49 kg)	Head	51.5	38.0	42.6	46.3

Use of Land for Agricultural Purposes, Republic of Ireland 1992-1994

Description	1992 (000 ha)	1993 (000 ha)	1994 (000 ha)
Wheat	90.6	79.2	74.1
Oats	20.1	20.2	20.9
Barley	184.4	180.8	169.7
Other Cereals	5.2	4.7	5.3
Total Cereals	**300.3**	**285.0**	**270.0**
Beans and Peas	2.7	6.1	5.6
Oilseed Rape	5.9	3.4	6.4
Potatoes	22.1	21.6	21.4
Turnips	5.5	5.2	5.6
Sugar Beet	31.3	32.2	35.4
Fodder Beet	11.0	10.9	9.8
Kale & Field Cabbage	1.9	1.8	1.8
Vegetables for Sale	4.3	4.6	4.8
Fruit including Apples	1.7	1.6	1.7
Nurseries, Bulbs & Flowers	1.1	1.0	1.3
Other Crops	5.3	30.5	36.6
Total Non-Cereal Crops	**92.6**	**118.9**	**130.3**
Silage	813.7	872.3	917.4
Hay	415.1	425.9	410.1
Pasture	2,195.6	2,202.5	2,201.3
Crops and Grassland	**3,817.3**	**3,904.7**	**3,929.1**
Rough Grazing	595.9	499.7	461.5
Total Area Farmed	**4,413.2**	**4,404.3**	**4,390.7**
Total Area	**6,890**	**6,890**	**6,890**

Direct Income Payments (Subsidies) 1990-1994, Republic of Ireland

Payments	1990 IR£ m	1991 IR£ m	1992 IR£ m	1993 IR£ m	1994 IR£ m
Cattle headage	49.9	57.7	81.1	54.3	93.7
Beef cow	9.5	7.4	16.5	10.6	19.0
Suckler cow	54.5	43.8	65.7	60.3	89.9
Special beef premium	39.5	32.5	51.8	68.9	122.9
Calf premium	11.5	0.1			
Deseasonalisation				9.0	15.7
Sheep headage	16.5	16.7	19.9	19.3	20.8
Ewe premium	140.3	122.6	114.4	127.8	117.7
Extensification premium					47.5
Total Headage/Aid	321.7	277.8	349.4	350.2	528.2
Bovine TB Eradication	19.9	19.7	17.9	17.2	14.2
Exchange rate guarantee	0.9	0.9	0.8	1.0	0.1
Milk cessation/buyout	9.7	7.8	7.9	20.5	15.7
Milk quota suspension	20.1	17.3	14.6		
Arable aid payments				45.0	66.0
Forestry Premium					1.0
REPS					1.2
Other	10.4	13.9	18.4	12.3	9.3
Total payments	**382.7**	**337.4**	**408.9**	**446.1**	**669.7**

1994 figures are estimations

Numbers of Livestock in Republic of Ireland, 1987-1994

Livestock (000)	1987	1992	1993	1994
Total cattle	6,544.7	6,975.7	7,026.6	7,064.5
Total pigs	999.0	1,385.8	1,521.6	1,530.4
Total sheep	5,595.1	8,908.5	8,647.3	8,433.4
Total horses and ponies	59.3	65.1	66.2	67.0
Total poultry	9,822.6	12,039.2	12,900.0	14,615.8
Total deer		12.5	15.2	15.0

Cattle and Sheep by Region (000) in Republic of Ireland

Description (1994)	Border	Mid-East & Dublin	Midland	Mid-West	South-East	South-West	West	Ireland Total
Bulls	4.3	2.5	2.6	6.9	7.0	10.5	2.8	36.6
Cows (Total)	324.8	169.2	189.9	357.6	396.2	556.9	297.9	2,292.4
- Dairy	132.9	96.5	84.5	219.0	265.4	417.8	75.9	1,292.1
- Other	191.9	72.7	105.3	138.6	130.7	139.1	222.0	1,000.3
Heifers in Calf	32.0	25.7	25.0	45.4	58.4	81.4	27.6	295.7
- Dairy	17.9	17.5	14.8	31.5	43.4	65.1	12.2	202.3
- Other	14.1	8.2	10.2	13.9	15.0	16.4	15.5	93.4
Other Cattle								
- 2 Years Up	134.3	159.6	162.7	140.0	186.6	141.6	173.1	1,097.9
- Male	90.7	113.4	111.6	99.0	134.5	88.8	124.5	762.6
- Female	43.7	46.2	51.0	41.0	52.1	52.8	48.6	335.4
- 1 to 2 Years	204.7	143.5	200.6	212.7	315.8	272.2	254.4	1,603.9
- Male	119.3	86.1	109.2	132.8	197.4	162.8	158.8	966.3
- Female	85.4	57.4	91.4	80.0	118.5	109.4	95.6	637.6
- Under 1 Year	242.9	124.0	170.6	257.5	324.2	367.0	251.7	1,738.0
- Male	121.4	63.7	85.5	133.9	175.6	183.5	136.5	966.3
- Female	121.5	60.3	85.1	123.6	148.7	183.5	115.2	837.9
Total cattle	943.1	624.5	751.4	1,020.2	1,288.2	1,429.6	1,007.6	7,064.5
Rams	20.5	17.7	10.6	5.5	23.4	14.6	27.1	119.4
Ewes	751.0	700.1	348.4	190.6	892.0	639.9	1,130.9	4,653.0
Other Sheep	563.9	565.1	276.7	152.5	768.9	408.6	925.3	3,661.0
Total Sheep	1,335.4	1,282.9	635.8	348.6	1,684.4	1,063.1	2,083.2	8,433.4

Border: Cavan, Donegal, Leitrim, Louth, Monaghan, Sligo. **Midland:** Laois, Longford, Offaly, Westmeath.
South-East: Carlow, Kilkenny, Tipperary (S.R.), Waterford, Wexford. **West:** Galway, Mayo, Roscommon.
Mid-East & Dublin: Kildare, Meath, Wicklow, Dublin.
Mid-West: Clare, Limerick, Tipperary (N. R.). **South-West:** Cork, Kerry.

Chief Republic of Ireland Crops

Crop	Year	Area (000 hectares)	Yield (tonnes per hectare)	Total produce (000 tonnes)
Wheat	1994	74.1	7.7	572
Oats	1994	20.9	6.1	128
Barley	1994	169.7	5.4	910
Beans and Peas	1994	5.6	4.5	25
Oilseed Rape	1994	6.4	2.6	17
Potatoes	1994	21.4	27.6	589
Sugar Beet	1994	35.4	39.3	1390
Turnips	1994	5.6	53.1	296
Fodder Beet	1994	9.8	59	579
Kale and Field Cabbage	1994	1.8	44.5	81

Area under Crops and Pasture by Region in Republic of Ireland

(1994) Description	Border	Mid East & Dublin	Midland	Mid West	South East	South West	West	Ireland
Wheat	6.6	34.3	3.7	0.5	19.0	9.8	0.1	74.1
Oats	1.8	5.9	1.0	0.4	6.6	4.0	1.3	20.9
Barley	15.2	30.4	21.4	8.3	61.9	29.5	3.2	169.7
Other Cereals	0.2	0.8	0.5	0.4	2.1	1.3	0.0	5.3
Total Cereals	**23.8**	**71.3**	**26.6**	**9.5**	**89.6**	**44.6**	**4.6**	**270.0**
Beans and Peas	0.4	1.5	0.8	0.1	1.8	1.0	0.0	5.6
Oilseed Rape	1.6	3.9	0.2	0.1	0.5	0.2	0.0	6.4
Potatoes	4.7	8.2	0.8	0.6	2.9	3.1	1.1	21.4
Turnips	0.2	1.2	0.6	0.3	1.7	0.9	0.8	5.6
Sugar Beet	0.0	2.7	3.9	1.1	16.0	11.2	0.5	35.4
Fodder Beet	0.3	1.3	1.5	0.4	3.7	2.5	0.2	9.8
Kale / Cabbage	0.0	0.3	0.1	0.1	0.4	0.7	0.1	1.8
Vegetables	0.1	2.1	0.4	0.1	0.7	1.2	0.2	4.8
Fruit	0.1	0.5	0.0	0.0	0.9	0.1	0.0	1.7
Nurseries etc.	0.0	0.4	0.1	0.1	0.5	0.1	0.1	1.3
Other Crops	3.4	12.1	3.2	0.9	10.2	6.0	0.8	36.6
Total Crops	**34.7**	**105.4**	**38.1**	**13.2**	**128.9**	**71.6**	**8.4**	**400.3**
Silage	122.0	74.7	91.1	135.6	161.8	203.7	128.5	917.4
Hay	68.3	40.2	43.7	59.1	67.3	54.7	76.7	410.1
Pasture	348.6	221.0	236.0	293.6	342.5	360.7	399.0	2,201.3
Crops & Pasture	**573.6**	**441.3**	**408.9**	**501.5**	**700.4**	**690.7**	**612.7**	**3,929.1**
Rough Grazing	104.6	24.7	19.9	44.9	30.1	130.2	107.0	461.5
Area Farmed	**678.3**	**466.0**	**428.8**	**546.4**	**730.6**	**820.9**	**719.7**	**4,390.7**

Border: *Cavan, Donegal, Leitrim, Louth, Monaghan, Sligo.* **Mid-East & Dublin:** *Kildare, Meath, Wicklow, Dublin.* **Midland:** *Laois, Longford, Offaly, Westmeath .* **Mid-West:** *Clare, Limerick, Tipperary (N.R.) .* **South-East:** *Carlow, Kilkenny, Tipperary (S.R.). Waterford, Wexford.* **South-West:** *Cork, Kerry.* **West:** *Galway, Mayo, Roscommon.*

Republic of Ireland Dairy Exports by Country

Country/Area	(1994) %
Africa	6.7
Central & South America	6.9
North America	14.7
Middle & Far East	9.5
Britain	21.4
European Union countries (excluding Britain)	39.7
Other European countries	1.1

Republic of Ireland Dairy Exports by Product, 1992-1994

Payments	Exports			Value		
	1992 (Tonnes)	1993 (Tonnes)	1994 (Tonnes)	1992 (£IR'000)	1993 (£IR'000)	1994 (£IR'000)
Skimmed Milk Powder	248,881	122,419	79,689	365,000	207,000	134,000
Butter	172,364	98,923	96,206	415,000	254,000	272,000
Cream Liquors	45,836	58,818	42,330	183,000	241,000	187,000
Chocolate Crumb	62,578	57,642	36,153	74,000	65,000	73,000
Cheese	97,910	73,945	89,099	231,000	200,000	199,000
Animal Feed	6,319	2,258	4,724	6,000	3,000	3,000
Cream	1,701	1,151	706	3,000	2,000	2,000
Butter Oil	8,079	12,429	14,036	22,000	31,000	35,000
Whole Milk Powder	33,189	27,656	31,090	68,000	84,000	84,000
Casein and Caseinates	39,290	31,374	30,596	189,000	161,000	132,000
Others				236,000	305,000	297,000
Totals	**716,147**	**486,615**	**424,629**	**1,792,420**	**1,551,893**	**1,416,200**

Republic of Ireland Farm Machinery and Equipment

Description	Number of Farms	Number of Machines
Tractors		
Less than 35 hp	27,287	27,931
35 - 51 hp	53,991	57,021
51 - 80 hp	43,588	52,677
80 + hp	14,370	20,120
Total	**139,236**	**157,749**
Machinery		
Ploughs	39,912	41,002
Power driven harrows	14,299	15,048
Other cultivators	24,433	28,069
Corn drills	3,968	4,034
Fertiliser distributors	72,390	73,145
Slurry spreaders	21,567	21,992
Farm manure spreaders	25,938	26,282
Rotary mowers	37,086	37,413
Other mowers	30,137	30,264
Round balers	4,284	4,384
Other balers	17,269	17,393
Forage harvesters (all)		11,398
Combine harvesters	4,069	4,305
Milking parlours	24,755	24,819
Other milking machines	21,559	21,608
Feeding wagons	908	961
Silage grabs	18,994	19,175

Number and Area of Farms by Area in Northern Ireland, 1994

Size Group (Hectares)	Farms by Total Area		Farms by Area of Crops and Grass	
	Farms	Hectares	Farms	Hectares
Total	28,404	1,006,467	28,404	811,134
Nil			752	
0.1 - 9.9	5,240	32,743	6,249	39,100
10.0 - 19.9	6,951	101,824	7,349	106,701
20.0 - 29.9	4,837	118,750	4,667	113,906
30.0 - 49.9	5,476	211,614	4,933	189,723
50.0 - 99.9	4,417	299,404	3,564	238,379
100.0 - 199.9	1,229	160,882	819	104,518
200.0 +	254	81,250	71	18,808

Persons, Males and Females in Farming Occupation (Northern Ireland)

Description	1990	1991	1992	1993	1994
Total Agricultural Labour Force	**61,035**	**59,812**	**59,129**	**59,624**	**59,607**
Farmers/directors/ partners: Full Time	22,721	22,307	22,215	21,275	21,180
Farmers/directors/ partners: Part Time	13,581	13,684	14,009	13,133	14,197
Farmers/directors/ partners: **Total**	**36,302**	**35,991**	**36,224**	**34,408**	**35,377**
Farmers spouses, partners /directors	**4,741**	**4,562**	**3,908**	**5,790**	**5,489**
Other Family Members - Full Time	3,020	2,874	2,664	2,075	1,887
Other Family Members - Part Time	4,734	4,624	4,620	4,686	4,335
Other Family Members - Casual / Seasonal	2,883	2,794	2,878	3,358	3,402
Other Family Members - **Total** (including spouses)	**15,378**	**14,854**	**14,070**	**15,909**	**15,113**
Total Farmers and Family Workers	**51,680**	**50,845**	**50,294**	**50,317**	**50,490**
Hired workers - Full Time	2,052	2,009	1,934	1,895	1,849
Hired workers - Part Time	1,391	1,338	1,271	1,275	1,250
Hired workers - Casual / Seasonal	5,912	5,620	5,630	6,137	6,018
Hired workers - **Total**	**9,355**	**8,967**	**8,835**	**9,307**	**9,117**

Northern Ireland Gross Agricultural Output

Description	Unit (Quantity)	Produce sold off Farms			
		Quantity		Value £ million	
		1993	1994	1993	1994
Livestock / Products:					
- Finished Cattle & Calves	000 head	481	502	329.1	412
- Finished Sheep & Lambs	000 head	1654	1501	105.6	90.8
- Finished Pigs	000 head	1207	1249	79.8	82.4
- Poultry	000 tonnes (d.w.t.)	99.8	104.5	74.4	77.2
- Eggs for Consumption and Hatching	m. doz	74	75.6	35.5	35.4
- Wool	tonnes	3625	3700	2.4	2.9
- Milk	m. litres	1309	1376	281.1	289.2
Other Livestock / Products		0	0	7.4	9.3
Total Value				**915.3**	**999.2**

Northern Ireland Gross Agricultural Output

Description	Produce Sold off Farms			
	Tonnes (000)		Value £ million	
	1993	1994	1993	1994
Field Crops:				
-Potatoes	231	179.1	14.9	22.3
- Barley	61.5	61.5	10.5	10.6
- Wheat	30.6	30.9	4.4	4.5
- Oats	3.7	4.2	0.6	0.8
- Other Crops	13.4	14.4	1.4	1.3
TOTAL Field Crops	340.2	290.1	31.8	39.4
Horticultural Products:				
- Fruit	51.6	36	7.8	4.9
- Vegetables	33.5	39.8	5.6	6
- Mushrooms	14.3	14.8	16.6	16.3
- Flowers	0	0	8	8.1
Total Value			**38**	**35.3**

Imports of Cattle to Northern Ireland from the Republic of Ireland

Year (per 100 head)	Stores	Finished Cattle	Others (incl. cows)	Total
1987/88	92.2	62.7	3.7	158.6
1988/89	77.9	75.8	1.3	155.0
1989/90	48.1	67.6	7.3	123.0
1990/91	39.7	50.9	1.2	91.8
1991/92	31.4	43.7	1.0	76.1
1992/93	22.0	29.0	1.4	52.3
1993/94	13.4	28.7	1.5	43.7
1994/95	7.3	8.4	1.8	17.5

Average Producer Prices of Agricultural Products in Northern Ireland

	1991	1992	1993	1994	£ per unit Avg. 1991-1994
Finished steers, heifers and young bulls (head)	602	602	674	699	644.25
Finished steers, heifers and young bulls (kg dwt)	1.95	1.98	2.24	2.23	2.1
Calves slaughtered or exported (head)	143	156	158	161	154.5
Culled cows and bulls (head)	329	381	511	461	420.5
Culled cows and bulls (kg dwt)	1.18	1.39	1.80	1.65	1.51
Store cattle exported (head)	523	383	434	442	445.5
Finished sheep and lambs (head)	33.28	32.48	38.01	41.49	36.32
Finished sheep and lambs (kg dwt)	1.70	1.64	1.95	2.04	1.83
Culled ewes and rams (head)	13.69	15.11	18.35	18.43	16.4
Finished clean pigs (head)	64.00	71.07	65.75	65.65	66.62
Finished clean pigs (kg dwt)	0.96	1.06	0.96	0.95	0.98
Culled sows and boars (head)	90.83	116.58	87.48	97.07	97.99
Wool (kg)	0.81	0.78	0.66	0.80	0.76
Milk (litre)	0.18	0.19	0.22	0.21	0.2
Eggs for consumption (dozen)	0.40	0.38	0.43	0.40	0.4
Broilers (kg lwt)	0.58	0.57	0.57	0.56	0.57
Potatoes (tonne): Ware maincrop	77.10	77.92	62.46	119.80	84.32
Potatoes (tonne): Seed	101.09	107.46	84.78	155.98	112.58
Barley (tonne)	114.73	118.22	124.40	112.48	117.46
Wheat (tonne)	121.69	124.75	125.27	114.35	121.52
Mushrooms (tonne)	1,098	1,120	1,161	1,100	1,119.75
Apples (tonne)	122.73	129.36	136.57	113.85	125.63

Northern Ireland Land under Cultivation

(1,000 Hectare)	1991	1992	1993	1994	1995	Average 1991-95
Oats	3	2	2	2	3	2.4
Wheat	6	7	7	7	6	6.6
Winter Barley	5	5	6	6	7	5.8
Spring Barley	33	32	32	28	26	30.2
Mixed corn	—	—	—	—	—	—
Oilseed rape	1	1	1	1	—	0.8
Potatoes	11	11	9	8	9	9.6
Other field crops	5	5	6	7	6	5.8
Total agricultural crops	63	63	63	58	57	60.8
Fruit	2	2	2	2	2	2.0
Vegetables	1	2	1	1	1	1.2
Other horticulture crops	—	—	—	—	—	—
Total horticulture crops	3	4	3	3	3	3.2
Grass						
Under 5 years old	184	179	192	189	188	186.4
Over 5 years old	582	582	584	585	591	584.8
Total grass	766	760	777	774	778	771.0
Total crops and grasses	832	827	843	835	839	835.2
Rough grazing	190	182	180	179	174	181.0
Woods and plantations	13	13	12	12	12	12.4
Other land	29	29	22	21	19	24.0
Total Area	1,063	1,052	1,056	1,048	1,043	1052.4

Livestock Figures in Northern Ireland

Description	1990	1991	1992	1993	1994
Cattle					
Dairy Cows - in milk	257.2	253.2	249.5	250.5	254.9
Dairy Cows - in calf	20.4	20.9	19.9	18.9	19.4
Total Dairy Cows	**277.6**	**274.1**	**269.4**	**269.3**	**274.2**
Dairy Heifers in Calf	39.2	40.2	45.9	49.0	50.3
Beef Cows - in milk	207.9	220.3	227.6	234.8	236.9
Beef Cows - in calf	34.7	37.2	39.1	43.0	41.6
Total Beef Cows	**242.5**	**257.5**	**266.7**	**277.8**	**278.5**
Beef Heifers in Calf	31.1	27.4	30.3	32.9	29.0
Total Cows	**520.2**	**531.6**	**536.1**	**547.2**	**552.7**
Total Heifers in Calf	70.3	67.6	76.3	81.8	79.3
Bulls for Service	12.4	12.7	12.9	13.2	13.6
Other Cattle - over 2 Years	165.8	150.2	149.9	139.3	137.4
Other Cattle - 1 - 2 Years	347.7	360.0	370.7	364.5	366.0
Other Cattle - under 1 year	409.8	429.9	429.8	431.7	431.8
Total Cattle	**1,526.2**	**1,552.0**	**1,575.7**	**1,577.8**	**1,580.8**
Sheep					
Breeding Ewes	1182.0	1212.2	1237.8	1244.9	1218.3
Other Sheep	1352.1	1380.1	1418.7	1366.2	1312.5
Total Sheep	**2534.1**	**2592.3**	**2656.5**	**2611.1**	**2530.8**
Pigs					
Sows and Gilts	58.9	59.2	59.1	59.9	57.8
Other Pigs	532.6	529.8	529.1	534.4	504.5
Total Pigs	**591.5**	**598.0**	**588.2**	**594.3**	**562.3**
Poultry					
Laying Birds	2887.7	2761.0	3131.5	3120.5	3195.4
Growing Pullets	836.0	946.0	928.4	1087.2	1071.3
Breeding flock	913.2	964.2	922.5	1205.3	1353.0
Table fowl	5498.8	6341.8	6967.9	7577.6	7595.7
Total ordinary fowl	10135.8	11013.0	11950.3	12990.6	13215.5
Turkey, Geese & Ducks	341.4	293.4	352.0	390.5	427.5
Total Poultry	**10,477.2**	**11,306.4**	**12,302.3**	**13,381.2**	**13,643.0**
Horses	7.7	7.8	8.4	9.8	10.4
Goats	8.8	7.4	6.5	5.7	5.0

FISHERIES

INTRODUCTION

BIM is the state agency primarily responsible for overall development of the seafish and aquaculture industry in the Republic of Ireland. BIM provides an extensive range of financial, educational, resource development, technical training and marketing services to the production through to the processing and marketing sectors of the fishing industry. The main varieties of sea fish landed in Irish ports are herring, whiting, cod, mackerel, plaice, skate, haddock and ray. In 1994 the total volume and value of exports of Irish fish products amounted to 285,098 tonnes valued at IR£195m, including landings by Irish fishing vessels at foreign ports. When landings at foreign ports are excluded, Irish fish exports in 1994 amounted to 248,453 tonnes valued at IR£185.3m. According to the latest figures available (1992) approximately 7,700 fulltime and occasional Irish fishermen engage in sea fishing.

Fishing in Northern Ireland is also of major importance, particularly to the seaboard communities along the coast of Antrim and Down. In 1994, 20.2m. tonnes was landed at N.I. ports worth an estimated £17.6m. In addition, N.I. vessels landed in the region of 8,000 tonnes of fish at ports outside the North, these being valued at £4.6m.

Kilkeel, in Co. Down, is the busiest harbour in the North, 7.5m. tonnes being landed there in 1994. Portavogie is the second largest with 6,119 tonnes.

The largest port by far, however, in Ireland is Killybegs in Co. Donegal where, in 1995, 143 million tonnes of fish were land at a value of £23m.

Top 20 Republic of Ireland Ports of 1995, listed by value

No.	Port	Live weight (tonnes)	Landed weight (tonnes)	Value £IR
1	Killybegs	143,671.51	143,300.50	22,803,039.44
2	Castletownbere	22,054.55	21,280.22	9,974,212.63
3	Dunmore East	9,990.33	9,356.63	6,771,165.92
4	Dingle	5,714.68	5,159.30	5,834,865.35
5	Rossaveal	7,417.19	6,821.81	5,482,522.45
6	Howth	7,856.47	6,848.59	5,022,718.10
7	Greencastle	4,719.58	4,433.77	4,577,970.81
8	Rathmullan	46,517.01	46,517.01	3,763,982.25
9	Union Hall	2,019.30	1,830.34	2,395,424.70
10	Baltimore	2,505.94	2,366.83	2,011,726.58
11	Skerries	1,502.84	764.90	1,758,750.30
12	Moville	1,297.37	1,297.37	1,701.020.00
13	Wexford	3,676.76	3,676.76	1,661,315.00
14	Valentia	1,009.14	897.94	1,554,022.15
15	Kinsale	1,279.75	1,134.20	1,518,813.21
16	Schull	911.81	805.36	1,164,039.13
17	Cobh	5,878.68	5,858.99	1,124,355.94
18	Burtonport	1,042.70	984.84	1,005,385.91
19	Duncannon/St. Helens	649.39	584.28	102,032.30
20	Clogherhead	696.12	414.34	894,888.60

Republic of Ireland Aquaculture Output Value, 1984 - 1994

Year	£'000	Tonnes
1984	5,923	15,322
1985	6,222	11,964
1986	7,790	12,828
1987	15,275	18,626
1988	24,885	18,327
1989	27,599	21,090
1990	29,900	26,560
1991	39,316	27,699
1992	40,600	28,600
1993	50,315	30,154
1994 (estimated)	48,512	28,612

Value of Republic of Ireland Fish Exports, 1994

	£m	%
France	46.8	25.3
Spain	38.4	20.7
Other Non-European Union	21.8	11.8
Britain	18.8	10.2
Germany	17.0	9.2
Japan	12.3	6.6
Italy	8.8	4.7
Russia	8.2	4.4
Northern Ireland	5.6	3.0
Netherlands	4.3	2.3
Other European Union	3.3	1.8
Total	**185.3m**	**100%**

Geographic Spread of Republic of Ireland Export Markets, 1987-1994

	1987 £'000	1994 £'000	% Change 1987/94	% Market Share for 1994
France	31,043	46,844	+51	26.0
Britain	13,966	15,213	+9	8.5
Germany	11,404	17,033	+49	9.5
Northern Ireland	7,271	4,887	-33	2.7
Spain	8,993	38,393	+327	21.3
Netherlands	6,704	4,307	-36	2.4
Belgium/Luxembourg	2,003	1,616	-19	1.0
Italy	1,779	8,761	+392	4.9
Denmark	802	1,085	+35	0.6
Greece	146	422	+189	0.2
Portugal	64	195	+205	0.1
Total European Union	**84,175**	**138,756**	**+65**	**77.2**
Japan	18,343	12,284	+33	6.8
Other Non-European Union	21,422	28,807	+34	16.0
Total Non European Union	**39,765**	**41,091**	**+3**	**22.8**
TOTAL FISH EXPORTS	**123,940**	**179,847**	**+45**	**100%**

Fishing Quotas
(European Union Member States' shares of 1996 TACs)

SUMMARY in TONNES

	IRE	BEL	DEN	GER	FRA	HOL	UK	SPAIN	POR	SWE	FIN	Not alloc.	Total tonnes
Cod	8,065	5,235	92,960	40,980	26,780	13,780	68,080	11,500	2,390	40,225	2,260	250	312,535
Saithe	4,410	80	4,600	12,445	43,325	120	14,670	-	-	630	-	-	80,280
Haddock	3,440	1,100	12,740	4,520	14,250	710	86,920	-	-	1,200	-	-	124,880
Hake	1,580	300	2,460	120	27,040	250	5,470	20,090	2,690	110	-	-	60,110
Herring	53,120	7,790	128,520	137,700	29,930	69,990	102,790	-	-	203,190	126,610	-	859,640
Mackerel	52,700	400	10,645	16,230	11,970	24,340	146,130	24,750	5,110	3,610	-	-	295,885
Plaice	3,170	6,565	29,580	4,890	6,295	32,870	27,270	120	120	950	-	-	111,140
Whiting	15,890	1,975	11,270	1,930	32,870	4,365	41,890	2,800	2,640	440	-	-	116,160
Sprat	-	1,560	79,480	28,790	2,340	2,340	7,800	-	-	87,470	23,220	164,670	397,670
Sole	660	4,455	2,765	1,645	8,955	18,155	2,940	770	1,245	70	-	-	41,660
Monkfish	2,650	2,490	-	590	23,480	580	6,890	13,060	2,160	-	-	100	52,000
Megrims	3,770	510	-	-	10,330	-	4,340	13,010	180	-	-	-	32,040
Nephrops	8,655	795	4,345	20	12,195	410	33,015	3,400	1,875	1,270	-	-	65,980
Pollack	1,300	470	-	-	13,550	-	3,020	1,640	20	-	-	100	20,100
Bl. Whiting	-	-	-	-	-	-	-	74,000	14,000	-	-	113,500	201,500
Horse Mack.	-	-	-	-	500	-	-	72,270	43,230	-	-	314,000	430,000

SUMMARY %

	IRE	BEL	DEN	GER	FRA	HOL	BRIT	SPAIN	POR	SWE	FIN	Not alloc.	Total tonnes
Cod	2.58	1.67	29.74	13.11	8.56	4.40	21.78	3.67	0.76	12.87	0.72	0.07	100.00
Saithe	5.49	0.09	5.72	15.50	53.96	0.14	18.27	-	-	0.78	-	-	100.00
Haddock	2.75	0.88	10.20	3.61	11.41	0.56	69.60	-	-	0.96	-	-	100.00
Hake	2.62	0.49	4.09	0.19	44.98	0.41	9.09	33.42	4.47	0.18	-	-	100.00
Herring	6.17	0.90	14.95	16.01	3.48	8.14	11.95	-	-	23.63	14.72	-	100.00
Mackerel	17.81	0.13	3.59	5.48	4.04	8.22	49.38	8.36	1.72	1.22	-	-	100.00
Plaice	2.85	5.90	26.61	4.39	5.66	28.95	24.53	0.10	0.10	0.85	-	-	100.00
Whiting	13.67	1.70	9.70	1.66	28.29	3.75	36.06	2.41	2.27	0.37	-	-	100.00
Sprat	-	0.39	19.98	7.23	0.58	0.58	1.96	-	-	21.99	5.83	41.40	100.00
Sole	1.58	10.69	6.63	3.94	21.49	43.57	7.05	1.84	2.98	0.16	-	-	100.00
Monkfish	5.09	4.78	-	1.13	45.15	1.11	13.25	25.11	4.15	-	-	0.19	100.00
Megrims	11.76	1.59	-	-	32.24	-	13.54	40.60	0.56	-	-	-	100.00
Nephrops	13.13	1.20	6.59	0.03	18.50	0.62	50.10	5.16	2.84	1.92	-	-	100.00
Pollack	6.46	2.33	-	-	67.41	-	15.02	8.15	0.09	-	-	0.49	100.00
Bl. Whiting	-	-	-	-	-	-	-	36.72	6.94	-	-	56.32	100.00
Horse Mack.	-	-	-	-	0.11	-	-	16.80	10.05	-	-	73.02	100.00

Trends in Republic of Ireland Fish Exports, 1990-1994

Product	Unit	1990	1991	1992	1993	1994
Fish Fresh/Chilled/Frozen	Tonnes	135,381	137,583	151,663	184,843	205,281
	£'000	91,008	108,004	111,466	113,259	120,594
Fresh Dried/Salted/Smoked	Tonnes	8,714	8,013	6,382	7,598	5,608
	£'000	11,791	11,279	10,436	10,866	8,502
Shellfish Fresh/Chilled/Frozen	Tonnes	22,847	25,372	20,000	12,925	14,430
	£'000	46,262	49,297	44,686	33,575	38,029
Fish Prepared/Preserved	Tonnes	1,719	4,118	5,481	4,631	5,057
	£'000	3,117	6,460	8,922	7,777	9,092
Shellfish Prepared/Preserved	Tonnes	22	85	60	-	2,182
	£'000	58	218	163	-	3,630
Subtotal	Tonnes	168,683	175,171	183,586	209,997	232,558
	£'000	152,236	175,258	175,673	165,477	179,847
Fish Meal/Oil etc.	Tonnes	9,732	18,587	22,404	16,621	15,895
	£'000	2,765	4,195	4,356	4,581	5,468
Totals	Tonnes	178,415	193,758	205,990	226,618	248,453
	£'000	155,001	179,453	180,029	170,058	185,315

Trends in Republic of Ireland Fish Imports, 1990-1994

Product	Unit	1990	1991	1992	1993	1994
Fish Fresh/Chilled/Frozen	Tonnes	29,347	20,393	21,519	8,445	9,253
	£'000	18,164	16,732	14,847	10,354	12,658
Fresh Dried/Salted/Smoked	Tonnes	1,215	1,070	760	970	999
	£'000	3,329	2,620	1,771	1,983	1,896
Shellfish Fresh/Chilled/Frozen	Tonnes	3,395	3,614	2,679	1,752	2,489
	£'000	8,308	8,469	7,199	5,851	6,414
Fish Prepared/Preserved	Tonnes	8,864	9,545	11,972	10,513	8,590
	£'000	22,041	23,393	24,137	23,474	18,781
Shellfish Prepared/Preserved	Tonnes	241	255	231	-	771
	£'000	875	874	613	-	1,409
Subtotal	Tonnes	43,062	34,877	37,161	21,680	22,102
	£'000	52,717	52,088	48,567	41,662	41,158
Fish Meal/Oil etc.	Tonnes	23,239	23,393	20,861	20,192	39,675
	£'000	8,031	8,998	8,055	7,601	11,746
Totals	Tonnes	66,301	58,270	58,022	41,872	61,777
	£'000	60,748	61,086	56,622	49,263	52,904

Numbers engaged in Sea Fishing in Republic of Ireland

Fishermen	1988	1989	1990	1991	1992
Full-time	3,590	3,380	3,350	3,380	3,280
Part-time	4,235	4,520	4,560	4,530	4,420
Total	7,825	7,900	7,910	7,910	7,700

Republic of Ireland Fishing Fleet

Category	No. of Boats
Pelagic	21
Beamer	6
Polyvalent	1,195
Aquaculture	133

The Irish fishing fleet consists mainly of inshore and mid-water vessels, generally engaging in fishing for periods of three to four days or less.

Liveweight and Estimated Value of Landed Fish in Northern Ireland

Species	1990 tonnes	1990 £000	1991 tonnes	1991 £000	1992 tonnes	1992 £000	1993 tonnes	1993 £000	1994 tonnes	1994 £000
Pelagic:										
Herring	4,231	421	3,862	399	4,038	404	3,634	345	3,453	360
Mackerel	2,427	290	1,040	168	19	4	227	19	524	56
Horse Mackerel	—	—	176	17	224	21	386	33	119	12
Demersal:										
Blue ling	—	—	—	—	20	14	—	—	7	9
Brill	22	54	24	56	30	70	27	66	17	50
Catfish	—	—	—	—	1	1	2	1	—	—
Cod	3,446	4,084	2,553	3,192	2,809	3,489	2,769	2,996	2,055	2,406
Conger Eel	169	43	270	98	220	111	183	98	248	172
Dabs	—	—	—	—	1	0	1	—	2	2
Dogfish	702	417	746	486	803	611	967	616	1,338	928
Forked Beard	—	—	—	—	9	5	4	7	2	1
Frost fish	—	—	—	—	57	23	3	2	13	12
Grenadier	—	—	—	—	122	97	19	20	7	4
Gurnard	11	4	17	4	9	2	6	2	6	2
Haddock	211	211	256	254	285	211	327	179	373	309
Hake	1,366	2,808	1,293	3,262	1,013	2,501	836	2,285	584	1,785
Halibut	—	—	—	—	—	1	—	—	—	1
John Dory	—	—	—	—	1	1	—	—	—	—
Ling	60	36	69	42	91	52	88	51	98	60
Megrims	5	3	34	25	59	38	51	59	43	49
Monk / Angler	426	551	268	426	398	553	435	679	272	402
Orange Roughey	—	—	—	—	3	3	5	14	—	—
Plaice	283	208	264	219	183	144	113	72	212	144
Pollack	127	102	186	160	100	91	101	71	152	129
Ray or Skate	135	80	172	98	109	61	89	54	101	71
Redfish	—	—	—	—	1	—	—	—	—	—
Roe	97	99	47	31	65	94	44	51	37	27
Saithe	578	232	446	198	439	192	360	150	394	183
Shark	—	—	—	—	—	—	3	7	8	6
Soles	81	214	70	190	65	169	45	129	54	195
Sturgeon	—	—	—	—	—	—	—	—	—	—
Torsk	—	—	—	—	5	3	—	—	—	—
Turbot	28	116	16	70	22	89	29	114	21	100
Whiting	3,999	2,199	3,279	1,481	3,196	1,431	3,385	1,016	3,533	1,397
Witches	79	35	70	44	86	61	85	59	84	63
Mixed Demersal	250	140	216	149	239	127	184	95	198	106
Total wet fish:	18,733	12,347	15,374	11,069	14,722	10,674	14,409	9,290	13,955	9,041
Shellfish:										
Crabs	407	235	568	320	221	206	463	250	333	196
Escallops	260	412	230	383	246	357	319	410	244	295
Queen Escallops	79	31	191	86	98	36	94	40	19	15
Lobsters	18	112	11	76	24	180	16	138	14	129
Mussels	260	27	1,810	191	2,110	216	624	76	1	—
Nephrops	5,606	7,859	6,039	7,573	5,156	5,784	5,467	6,952	5,920	8,038
Periwinkles	175	72	156	58	113	36	114	40	94	47
Squids	74	71	36	49	90	125	71	103	111	192
Whelks	—	—	—	—	82	27	26	8	188	56
Total Shellfish:	6,879	8,819	9,041	8,736	8,140	6,967	7,194	8,017	6,924	8,968
Total Weight & value of all fish	25,612	21,166	24,415	19,805	22,862	17,641	21,603	17,307	20,879	18,009

Fishing Ports in Northern Ireland

Port	County	Port	County
Glenarm	Antrim	Portstewart	Derry
Whitehead	Antrim	Kilkeel *	Down
Islandmagee	Antrim	Annalong	Down
Whiterock	Antrim	Newcastle	Down
Antrim	Antrim	Dundrum	Down
Portrush	Antrim	Ardglass *	Down
Portballintrae	Antrim	Portavogie *	Down
Ballintoy	Antrim	Newry / Warrenpoint	Down
Carrickfergus	Antrim	Portaferry	Down
Belfast	Antrim	Ballywalter	Down
Ballycastle	Antrim	Bangor	Down
Rathlin Island	Antrim	Donaghadee	Down
Carnlough	Antrim	Down	Down
Larne	Antrim	Strangford	Down
Dunseverick	Antrim	Killyleagh	Down
Waterfoot	Antrim	Killough	Down
Cushendall	Antrim	Groomsport	Down
Cushendun	Antrim	Ringhaddy	Down
Coleraine	Derry	Ballyhalbert	Down
Derry *	Derry	Ballydorn	Down

* Major Ports

Liveweight and Estimated Value of all Landed Fish by Port in N. Ireland

Total landings at:	1990	1991	1992	1993	1994
Ardglass: Tonnes	4,730	4,337	5,085	6,017	5,845
£ 000	2,434	2,312	2,298	2,638	2,960
Kilkeel: Tonnes	10,199	10,258	8,898	7,753	7,588
£ 000	10,150	9,551	7,916	7,088	7,368
Portavogie: Tonnes	6,527	5,985	5,635	5,919	6,119
£ 000	7,331	7,030	6,106	5,742	6,312
Other N.I. Ports: Tonnes	4,156	3,835	3,244	1,914	1,327
£ 000	1,251	912	1,321	1,839	1,369
Total all ports: Tonnes	25,612	24,415	22,862	21,603	20,879
£ 000	21,166	19,805	17,641	17,307	18,009
Total landings by NI vessels in NI ports:					
Tonnes	23,006	23,160	22,018	21,103	20,225
£ 000	20,529	19,356	16,987	16,543	17,589

Liveweight and Estimated Value of Fish landed by Northern Ireland Vessels outside Northern Ireland

	1990	1991	1992	1993	1994
Scotland:					
Tonnes	9,644	4,365	3,892	2,340	1,683
£ 000	1,506	899	1,036	1,127	973
England & Wales:					
Tonnes	2,614	3,357	1,420	3,217	3,190
£ 000	1,491	1,778	1,025	1,500	1,137
Isle of Man:					
Tonnes	542	629	807	773	716
£ 000	105	108	149	114	125
Other Countries:					
Tonnes	6,656	8,612	2,687	2,563	2,366
£ 000	986	2,122	1,609	2,333	2,410
Total:					
Tonnes	19,456	16,963	8,806	8,893	7,955
£ 000	4,088	4,907	3,819	5,074	4,645

AFFORESTATION

European Forest and Area Resources

Country	Total area (1000ha)	Total wooded area (per cent)	Agricultural area in use 1989/1993 (per cent)	Other land area (per cent)	Total inland water (per cent)
REP. OF IRELAND	6,889	7.6	64.5	25.9	2.0
Austria	8,386	46.2	41.6	10.5	1.6
Belgium	3,052	22.1	44.1	32.9	0.9
Britain	24,408	10.1	67.6	21.0	1.3
Denmark	4.3	10.3	64.6	23.9	1.1
Finland	33,814	68.9	9.0	12.2	9.9
France	54,920	29.6	51.3	17.8	1.3
Germany	35,697	30.1	47.8	20.0	2.2
Greece	13,199	43.6	27.7	26.6	2.1
Italy	30,128	29.1	49.6	21.3	-
Luxembourg	259	34.4	48.9	16.3	0.4
The Netherlands	3,733	9.2	53.9	27.8	9.1
Portugal	8,892	34.9	45.0	17.4	2.7
Spain	50,478	27.2	48.6	23.1	1.1
Sweden	45,100	62.1	8.1	20.3	9.5
Totals	**323,255**	**36.5**	**40.1**	**-**	**-**

Afforestation in Republic of Ireland by County (Hectares) 1993 - 1995

County	1993 Coillte Afforestation	1993 Private Sector Afforestation	1994 Coillte Afforestation	1994 Private Sector Afforestation	1995 Coillte Afforestation	1995 Private Sector Afforestation
Carlow	55.5	92.9	83.0	82.6	38.1	87.06
Cavan	186.6	172.7	312.1	131.38	304.1	330.8
Clare	696.9	1000.6	346.6	1008.3	414.3	1439.6
Cork	859.8	801.4	737.9	973.2	530.4	1422.8
Donegal	732.2	844.8	582.1	1310.3	856.5	2544.3
Dublin	0	46.3	10.40	52.45	0	189.58
Galway	816.89	510.90	995.92	519.09	909.63	739.99
Kerry	225.7	884.4	280.5	1444.6	217.34	1857.2
Kildare	34.1	157.1	46.3	70.4	20.9	323.1
Kilkenny	232.8	373.4	56.5	440.03	97.30	454.4
Laois	136.7	321.8	159.9	529.8	40.4	447.63
Leitrim	177.0	521.9	212.3	206.5	418.5	430.74
Limerick	179.7	166.4	310.02	392.6	357.4	550.79
Longford	43.0	104.3	136.8	177.6	70.4	136.9
Louth	0	18.65	0	0	0	11.17
Mayo	369.8	549.5	387.04	1306.2	281.6	967.2
Meath	5.9	88.7	24.3	337.7	0	288.1
Monaghan	6.0	31.7	72.4	26.38	5.6	60.2
Offaly	197.9	372.0	113.6	533.8	51.48	685.3
Roscommon	333.03	246.4	417.5	592.7	402.1	494.6
Sligo	442.41	207.3	192.0	333.3	296.0	542.73
Tipperary	208.0	535.7	487.59	893.5	347.3	1122.9
Waterford	234.9	287.4	175.7	301.5	127.55	422.4
Westmeath	201.8	292.7	128.7	279.7	40.8	973.6
Wexford	75.9	175.6	60.1	248.3	64.0	282.4
Wicklow	165.8	366.1	170.0	564.0	225.1	536.7
	6,633.76	**9,170.81**	**6,499.18**	**12,836.73**	**6,117.16**	**17,343.24**

Afforestation in Northern Ireland (Hectares) 1995

	Derry	Antrim	Down/Armagh	Tyrone	Fermanagh	Forest Service Total
Total area	11,827	13,708	8,462	15,745	25,744	75,486
Forested area	9,875	11,305	6,994	13,199	19,614	60,987

Northern Ireland Forest and Area Resources

	1990/1991	1991/1992	1992/1993	1993/1994	1994/1995
Forested area (000 ha):					
State	60	60	61	61	61
Private	15	16	16	17	18
All forested areas:	75	76	77	78	79
Annual planting area (ha):					
State	1,046	907	869	816	826
Private	638	479	911	928	624
All plant areas:	1,684	1,386	1,780	1,744	1,450
Timber production from state forests:					
Volume (000 m3)	184	188	200	222	222
Value (£ 000)	3,641	2,996	3,022	3,340	5,900
Employees (number):					
State forest service	506	493	492	469	446

ENERGY

INTRODUCTION

Republic of Ireland

Ireland's traditional energy source has been the turf or peat bogs which have, for many generations, provided supplies of heating fuel for large sections of the Irish population, particularly in rural Ireland. It is estimated that about 17 per cent of the land mass of the island of Ireland is comprised of peat much of which was left untouched for centuries.

With the establishment of **Bord na Mona (the Peat Development Board)** in 1946, peat production became a major industry. Now it is a hi-tech business, with Ireland's unique expertise in peat production and technology being in frequent demand worldwide.

Bord na Mona employs in excess of 2,200 workers, produces more than 4 million tonnes of peat per year, 3 million of which goes to provide 12 per cent of Ireland's electricity requirement.

Peat moss and other peat by-products have been developed and the Board exports its produce to 26 countries worldwide. For instance, 90 per cent of the horticulture division's produce is sold abroad. Its engineers and technologists have been responsible for the development of a number of major innovations in peat production and bog machinery which has brought the company international recognition.

The Electricity Supply Board (ESB) was established in 1927 with the responsibility to both produce and distribute electricity throughout the country. It now has 1.2 million customers, spread over 26,000 square miles, consuming 16.5 million units annually. It employs 10,000 people.

It is the main supplier of domestic energy in the Republic. Domestic demand represents about 40 per cent of production, the rest going to industry and commercial establishments. The ESB has ten turf burning electricity generating stations which are unique to Ireland.

The other main native source of energy is natural gas. Offshore exploration began in 1970, and the first find, and still the most significant, was discovered at Kinsale just a year later. In 1989 a smaller gas field was found in Ballycotton.

Bord Gais Éireann (Irish Gas Board) was established in 1976 by the Government with the remit to provide natural gas for domestic use. It's first task was to provide a pipeline to take the gas from Kinsale Head and provide the facilities onshore for its distribution. In the early years the gas was available in the Cork area only but in 1982 a 220 kilometre pipeline was constructed to bring supplies to Dublin.

By the end of 1995 the distribution network totalled 4,771kms, an increase of 357 on 1994. With a turnover of £238million for the year, growth was 6% on the previous year.

With known domestic reserves of natural gas decreasing Bord Gais built, in 1993, a 295kms. "Internconnector" pipeline from Loughshinny in north County Dublin to the North Sea gas field at Moffat, in Scotland. This has a dual purpose: if supplies run out in Ireland gas can be imported; if new fields are discovered here, the interconnector can be used for export purposes. The interconnector cost £265m.

Northern Ireland

Unlike the Republic or Britain, Northern Ireland has no supply of natural gas. It is almost totally dependent on imported coal and oil for its energy needs, particularly oil.

NIE is the sole supplier and distributor of electricity to the North's 1.5m. people. Indeed, the fuel requirement for the generation of that electricity is also totally dependent on imported fuels, oil (70%), coal (30%).

There are extensive lignite reserves but these have not been commercially developed yet. And despite considerable exploration, no worthwhile quantities of oil or natural gas have been discovered which would be commercially exploitable.

Coal still dominates the household energy market, almost 70 per cent using either bituminous or smokeless for home heating

Key developments in the north in recent years are: NIE has been privatised; NIE and Scottish Power have signed an agreement for the supply of electricity through an inter-connector between Scotland and N.I. and British Gas has agreed to purchase Ballylumpford Power station and convert it to gas firing. This would open up the opportunity to make the supply of gas more widespread.

143

MINING

Ireland is in first place in world lists in terms of tonnes of zinc discovered per square kilometre. It is ranked number two for lead. The total value of mineral production and value-added processing contributed well over one billion U.S. dollars to the Irish economy in 1995.

100m. U.S. dollars were earned from non-ferrous metal ores, 45m. dollars for gypsum and gypsum based products, $60m. from the sand, gravel and aggregate industry, $220m. from the cement industry, $37.5m. for magnesia and $7.5m. from the dimension stone industry.

The value of products from non resource-based processing included US $250m. for alumina and in excess of US$300 for industrial diamonds.The contribution to the national economy is estimated at 22% of turnover.

The vast majority of Irish mining produce is exported.

Ireland currently produces more than 3% of world zinc mine production and more than 2% of world lead mine production. These figures are expected to double within the next few years as a number of new mines come on stream.

In 1970 the largest zinc mine in Europe was discovered at Navan, in Co. Westmeath. This 70 Mt. orebody mine was brought into production in 1977. In 1995 its output was 2.6 Mt. and the long term future of the mine is secure at 38.24 Mt.

At Kingscourt, Co. Cavan there are substantial reserves of gypsum. Gypsum Industries Ltd. have an output of approximately 350,000 tonnes from their opencast mine there.

Rock Aggegate: In 1995 crushed rock production was more than 25 Mt. of which 1.2 Mt. was produced for export from a deep water coastal quarry in Co. Cork. Reserves are in excess of 100 Mt.

Recent exploration has indicated the presence of bedrock gold in a number of geological terrains. Gold deposits were discovered in 1982 at Curraghinalt in Co. Tyrone. Since then there have been a significant number of discoveries but no major deposits located

Ireland has a widely varied geological framework that includes a number of mineral "provinces" which contain a wide selection of base and precious metals as well as industrial mineral deposits. In fact, Ireland is now internationally known as a major base metal territory with a number of major finds over the past twenty five years.

The country's mining industry is expected to grow more rapidly in the coming years as many of the metals discovered, particularly zinc, are relatively high grade, are found in shallow locations, and have simple metallurgy which means that costs, compared to excavating minerals in deeper locations, are well below average international costs.

While mining has occurred in Ireland over many centuries, mining on a large industrial scale is less than thirty years in existence.

POWER STATIONS

Irish Power Stations by type and capacity

Name	Type	Capacity (MW)
REPUBLIC OF IRELAND		
Shannonbridge	Milled Peat	125
Ferbane	Milled Peat	90
Lanesboro	Milled Peat	85
Rhode	Milled Peat	80
Bellacoric	Milled Peat	40
Cahirciveen	Sod Peat	5
Gweedore	Sod Peat	5
Turlough Hill	Hydro	292
Liffey-Poulaphouca	Hydro	38
Ardnacrusha	Hydro	86
Erne	Hydro	65
Clady	Hydro	4
Lee-Inniscarra	Hydro	27
Moneypoint	Coal	915
Tarbert	Oil	620
Great Island	Oil	240
Aghada	Gas/Oil	525
Poolbeg	Gas/Oil	510
North Wall	Gas/Oil	104
Marina	Gas	115
NORTHERN IRELAND		
Ballylumford	Fuel Oil/Gas Oil	1080
Belfast West	Coal	240
Kilroot	Fuel Oil/Coal or Gas Oil	600 or 410
Coolkeeragh	Fuel Oil/Gas Oil	420

ENERGY STATISTICS

Electricity Expenses

based on a single unit of electricity	Republic of Ireland	Northern Ireland
Electricity:		
Large Industry	4.71p	4.72p
Small Commercial		9.66p
Domestic	7.65p	9.70p
Industrial	8.04p	5.68p

ESB Development in the Republic of Ireland, 1930-1994

Year	Units sold to Customers Millions	Revenue £000	Average price per unit	Customers Total
1929-30	43.2	478	1.108	48,606
1939-40	318.6	1,946	0.612	172,545
1949-50	626.1	4,774	0.763	310,639
1959-60	1692.2	14,724	0.871	610,946
1969-70	4,411.6	39,400	0.892	786.500
1979-80	8560.3	300,024	3.505	1,043,428
1985-86	9,787.8	757,172	7.736	1,194,765
1990	11,768.0	756,074	6.425	1,278,870
1991	12,370.1	785,205	6.348	1,302,061
1992	13,103.9	826,464	6.307	1,326,547
1993	13,438.7	842,416	6.269	1,348,196
1994	14,024.9	874,879	6.238	1,375,975

ESB Contribution to the Republic of Ireland Economy

	1990 £m	1991 £m	1992 £m	1993 £m	1994 £m
Fuel: Natural Gas, peat, coal	141	132	124	129	137
Irish suppliers of goods and services	175	185	182	189	218
Rates	27	29	31	32	34
Payroll costs, incl. capital projects	235	258	284	301	306
Interest paid to stockholders and lenders	26	25	25	24	22
Total	604	629	646	675	717

ESB Network Statistics in the Republic of Ireland

Network statistics	Installed in 1994	In service at December 31st 1994
Overhead lines (Km)	678	80,302
Underground cables (Km)	175	3,757
Substations: Number	3,022	158,130
Substations: Capacity (MVA)	389	14,423

ESB Distribution Statistics in the Republic of Ireland

Distribution Statistics	1990	1991	1992	1993	1994
New Houses connected	19,482	19,594	21,624	20,864	26,552
Transformer capacity (KVA)	140,755	250,289	471,930	447,821	389,384
Networks installed (Km)	653	965	1,019	1,025	853
Capital expenditure (£'000)	62,420	69,581	84,105	105,758	89,700

Number of employees in ESB and Bord na Mona in the Republic of Ireland

ESB	1990	1991	1992	1993	1994
Number of employees	10,490	10,096	10,340	10,322	10,070
Bord na Mona					
Number of employees	2,694	2,673	2,387	2,297	2,270

Republic of Ireland's Energy Demands

Energy sources	(Estimated for 1995)	%
Oil		49
Natural gas		19
Coal		18
Peat		12
Hydro-Renewables		2

Republic of Ireland's Total Fuel Consumption (1000TOE)*

Year	Coal	Peat	Briquettes	Oil	Nat. Gas	Other	Electricity	Total
1990	847	586	171	3,875	576	109	1,032	7,196
1991	874	478	172	4,015	649	111	1,083	7,383
1992	504	496	163	4,263	689	111	1,145	7,371
1993	518	457	169	4,296	711	111	1,156	7,417

The common unit chosen for measuring energy usage is TOE - Ton of Oil Equivalent.

NORTHERN IRELAND ENERGY STATISTICS

Northern Ireland Energy Industry Employees, 1991

	Males	Females	Total persons
Overall energy and water supply	6,120	1,060	7,180
Water supply	1,236	59	1,295
Production and distribution of electricity, gas and other forms of energy	4,705	989	5,694

Shipments of Coal into Northern Ireland

(per 1000 tonne)	1990	1991	1992	1993	1994
Domestic	1,228	1,303	1,154	1,082	1,211
Industrial	140	191	170	147	190
Electricity	946	1,035	1,134	1,256	1,225
Totals	**2,314**	**2,529**	**2,458**	**2,485**	**2,626**

Northern Ireland Energy Consumption by source

(by million therms)	1990	1991	1992	1993	1994
Coal	388	422	374	349.6	398
Electricity	197.9	201	-	216.3	221
Petroleum	437	449	467	528.1	550
Totals	**1,022.9**	**1,072**	**-**	**1,094**	**1,169**

Selected Northern Ireland Electricity Statistics

	1989/90	1990/91	1991/92	1992/93	1993/94
Total units generated (000)	6750.1	6983.7	7129.6		
Sales to all customers (units)	5,667	5,884	5,997	6,214	6,412
Electricity sales revenue (millions)	347.5	380.0	402.4	418.3	
Total consumers	598,651	605,520	615,133	624,200	633,647

Northern Ireland Water Output

	1990	1991	1992	1993	1994
Total water supplied (million litres per day)	681.0	682.9	670.1	667	682
Supply per capita (litres per person per day)	430	429	416	409	419

PETROL PRICES

Republic of Ireland: Average Price of Petrol Yearly 1987-1995 (IR£)

Year	Premium Leaded	Regular Leaded	Unleaded Petrol
1987	58.87	57.93	0
1988	58.19	57.06	0
1989	61.49	60.57	61.71
1990	63.02	59.92	60.90
1991	62.26	0	59.89
1992	59.04	0	58.27
1993	59.43	0	56.57
1994	59.77	0	56.03
1995	60.57	0	56.34

Northern Ireland: Average Price of Petrol Yearly 1987-1995 (Stg.)

Year	4 star	Super Unleaded	Unleaded	2 star	Derv
1987	37.90	0	0	37.07	34.58
1988	37.38	0	0	36.58	33.99
1989	40.39	0	38.29	39.73	36.18
1990	44.87	0	42.03	0	40.48
1991	48.48	47.31	45.07	0	43.82
1992	50.28	48.38	46.07	0	45.01
1993	54.12	52.91	49.44	0	49.20
1994	56.87	55.98	51.58	0	51.53
1995	60.01	59.03	54.17	0	54.34

TOURISM

INTRODUCTION

According to the World Tourism Organisation, by the year 2000 tourism will be the number one contributor to Gross Domestic Product in the European Union. In the Republic of Ireland, tourism currently contributes in the region of 13% of GDP but, subject to both peace in Northern Ireland and substantial investment in the industry, it is expected to increase to 15 per cent of GDP by the year 2,000.

Between1980 and1994 Irish earnings from tourism increased by an annual average of 10%.

Revenue from tourism, both overseas and domestic, was in the region of £2.3bn. in 1995.

By far the most notable trend in Irish tourism is the rise in numbers from Continental Europe which have increased by more than seven per cent, from 19.3% in 1980 to 26.9% in 1994. Britain still remains the main market with 55.4%, though this has declined from 61 7% in 1980. The North American market has also shown a slight decline in the same period from 15.2% to 13.4%

In Northern Ireland, tourism in 1994 increased to £183m. and was confidently expected to increase dramatically if political stability could be maintained. As in the Republic, the main market for the North is the British visitor who provided £93m. in 1994.

In a 1993 report, prepared shortly after the Downing St. Declaration, the Northern Ireland Tourist Board indicated that, subject to a permanent peace, the tourism industry would create 25,000 jobs within five years of peace breaking out with a growth of one million visitors per annum - both developments subject to the investment of £250m. in the industry .

REPUBLIC OF IRELAND TOURISM STATISTICS

Visitors to Republic of Ireland by country of origin

Number (rounded to nearest 100)	1988	1993	1994	1995
Britain	1,508,000	1,857,000	2,038,000	2,285,000
Continental Europe	408,000	945,000	988,000	1,101,000
- Germany	113,000	265,000	269,000	319,000
- France	111,000	242,000	231,000	234,000
- Italy	21,000	116,000	121,000	112,000
- Netherlands	38,000	69,000	80,000	94,000
- Belgium / Luxembourg	20,000	41,000	41,000	53,000
- Spain	34,000	57,000	59,000	67,000
- Denmark	14,000	17,000	19,000	22,000
- Norway / Sweden	12,000	32,000	33,000	46,000
- Switzerland	24,000	40,000	62,000	62,000
- Other Europe	21,000	66,000	73,000	93,000
North America	419,000	422,000	494,000	641,000
- USA	385,000	377,000	449,000	587,000
- Canada	34,000	45,000	45,000	54,000
Rest of World	90,000	124,000	159,000	204,000
Total Overseas	2,425,000	3,348,000	3,679,000	4,231,000
Northern Ireland	582,000	540,000	630,000	590,000
Total Out-of-State	3,007,000	3,888,000	4,309,000	4,821,000
Domestic Trips	4,161,000	7,930,000	7,405,000	7,093,000

Expenditure by visitors to Republic of Ireland

Revenue (£m)	1988	1993	1994	1995
Britain	267.0	375.1	451.9	501.2
Mainland Europe	123.7	401.6	371.6	413.7
- Germany	35.9	117.3	110.4	122.4
- France	31.0	91.5	74.4	83.8
- Italy	6.9	51.1	46.3	42.4
- Rest of Europe	49.9	145.8	132.0	165.1
North America	165.5	182.1	213.4	275.0
Other Overseas	37.6	54.7	77.2	96.5
Total Overseas	593.8	1,013.5	1,114.1	1,286.4
Northern Ireland	46.1	69.0	80.5	80.6
Excursionist Revenue	15.1	7.5	7.4	8.0
Carrier Receipts	186.0	277.0	296.0	302.0
Total Foreign Exchange Earnings	841.0	1,367.0	1,498.0	1,677.0
Domestic Trips	311.1	639.3	678.3	625.2

Destination and Expenditure by visitors to Republic of Ireland, 1995

Numbers (000's) Revenue (£m)Tourists	Overseas Ireland	Northern	Domestic	Excursionist	Total
Dublin	2,134	130	1,068		3,332
	418.5	15.4	85.5	5.9	525.3
Midlands-East	732	60	898		1,690
	130.5	7.7	72.5	0.6	211.3
South-East	883	70	1,220		2,173
	121.7	13.9	114.6		250.2
South-West	1,217	70	1,199		2,486
	232.3	10.8	110.8		353.9
Mid-West	836	40	843		1,719
	313.5	3.4	73.5		208.4
West	952	100	1,331		2,383
	157.2	12.1	117.3		286.6
North-West	552	200	570		1,322
	94.7	17.3	51.0	1.5	164.5
Total Revenue	1,468.4	80.6	625.2	8.0	2,000.2

Expenditure per person by visitors to Republic of Ireland

%	Total	Britain	North America	Mainland Europe
Bed and Board	24	21	25	27
Other Food and Drink	30	33	28	29
Sightseeing / Entertainment	7	9	6	6
Transport in Ireland	12	9	12	16
Shopping	19	18	24	16
Miscellaneous	8	11	5	7

Accommodation and Social Expenses

	Republic of Ireland	Northern Ireland
Accommodation: One night stay *		
4 / 5 Star Hotel	£70 - £110	£65 - £70
2 Star Hotel	£25 - £40	£30 - £40
Dinner (Michelin Guide Restaurant)	£25 - £30 **	£21.50 ***

*Based on a person sharing. ** Includes 15% service charge. ***Excludes service charge.

NORTHERN IRELAND TOURISM STATISTICS

All Visitors to Northern Ireland by country of origin

Country of Origin	Total 1995	Total 1994	% Change
Great Britain	810,000	708,000	14%
- England and Wales	603,000	538,000	12%
- Scotland	207,000	170,000	22%
Republic of Ireland	470,000	390,000	21%
Europe	109,000	87,000	25%
- France	19,000	14,000	36%
- Germany	32,000	28,000	14%
- Holland	8,000	8,000	0%
- Italy	9,000	9,000	0%
- Other Europe	41,000	28,000	46%
North America	118,000	77,000	53%
- USA	83,000	54,000	54%
- Canada	35,000	23,000	52%
Australia/New Zealand	32,000	20,000	60%
Elsewhere	18,000	12,000	50%
Total	1,557,000	1,294,000	20 %

Data has been rounded to the nearest 100.

Holiday visitors to Northern Ireland by country of origin

Country of Origin	Holiday 1995	Holiday 1994	% Change
Britain	112,000	66,000	70%
- England and Wales	68,000	41,000	66%
- Scotland	44,000	25,000	76%
Republic of Ireland	210,000	125,000	68%
Europe	57,000	44,000	30%
- France	11,000	7,000	57%
- Germany	20,000	19,000	5%
- Holland	3,000	2,000	50%
- Italy	6,000	5,000	20%
- Other Europe	16,000	11,000	45%
North America	60,000	29,000	107%
- USA	47,000	22,000	114%
- Canada	13,000	7,000	86%
Australia / New Zealand	20,000	9,000	122%
Elsewhere	3,000	3,000	0%
Total	461,000	276,000	67 %

Data has been rounded to the nearest 100.

Expenditure by visitors to Northern Ireland

(£ million)	1993	1994
Great Britain	92	93
Republic of Ireland	30	34
North America	20	22
Europe	17	17
Elsewhere	14	17
Total	173	183

(000's)	1993	1994
Domestic visitors		
Long Holidays	235	220
Short Holidays	440	430
Total Home Holidays	675	650

(£ million)	1993	1994
Domestic Expenditure		
Long Holidays	34	34
Short Holidays	21	25
Total Home Holidays	55	59

IRISH TOURISTS ABROAD

Visits abroad by Republic of Ireland Residents (Route of travel)

Estimated expenditure (including international fares), classified by Route of Travel and Total Net International Tourism and Travel Expenditure.

Estimated Expenditure £ million	1989	1990	1991	1992	1993	1994	1995
Total Expenditure (including international fares)	866	868	880	984	1,019	1,274	1,497
Route of Travel							
Air Cross - Channel	331	358	337	367	369	531	621
Sea Cross - Channel	109	113	138	136	151	156	169
Continental European	288	248	246	301	309	362	468
Transatlantic	88	97	103	116	126	150	155
All Overseas Routes	816	816	824	920	955	1,199	1,414
Cross Border (1)	50	51	56	64	64	75	83
Passenger fare payments by Irish visitors abroad to Irish carriers	168	167	181	187	185	202	230 (3)
Total net international tourism and travel expenditure (2)	698	701	699	797	834	1,072	1,267 (3)

(1) Estimates are for tourist expenditure only.
(2) Total expenditure (incl. international fares) less passenger fare payments by Irish visitors abroad to Irish Carriers.
(3) Provisional.

Visits abroad by Republic of Ireland Residents (Reason for Journey)

Estimated Expenditure (including International Fares), classified by Reason for Journey.

Estimated Expenditure £ million	1989	1990	1991	1992	1993	1994	1995
Total Expenditure (including international fares)	816	816	824	920	955	1,199	1,414
Reason for Journey							
Business	189	184	192	194	208	276	326
Tourist	349	339	354	436	428	529	655
Visit Relatives	200	209	199	208	218	266	256
Other	77	83	79	83	100	128	176

Overseas Visits by Republic of Ireland Residents

Estimated Average Length of Stay (nights), classified by Route of Travel and Reason for Journey.

Length of Stay (Nights)	1989	1990	1991	1992	1993	1994 (1)	1995
All Overseas Visits	10.3	10.3	9.6	9.6	9.3	10.0	10.0
Route of Travel							
Air Cross - Channel	9.0	9.1	8.4	8.2	8.3	9.1	9.3
Sea Cross - Channel	10.2	10.0	8.6	8.7	8.3	7.6	8.1
Continental European	10.4	11.2	11.0	11.6	9.9	11.5	11.3
Transatlantic	21.1	18.3	16.8	14.6	18.4	19.7	17.2
Reason for Journey							
Business	6.5	6.4	6.3	6.0	6.4	7.3	6.9
Tourist	10.5	11.3	10.3	10.2	9.5	10.3	10.0
Visit Relatives	10.7	10.1	10.0	9.7	9.9	10.3	10.3
Other	17.0	15.7	11.8	13.3	12.3	13.2	14.7

(1) Revised.

HERITAGE CENTRES IN IRELAND

Listed Alphabetically

CO. ANTRIM

Antrim Castle Gardens, Massereene Demesne, Antrim.
Antrim Round Tower, Steeple Park, Antrim.
Bonamargy Friary, near Ballycastle.
Botanic Gardens, Stranmillis Road, Belfast.
Carnfunnock Country Park, near Larne.
Carrickfergus Castle, Carrickfergus.
Cave Hill Heritage Centre, Belfast Castle.
Colin Glen Woodland Park, Stewartstown Rd., Belfast.
Dunluce Castle, near Portrush.
Dunluce Centre, Portrush.
Giants Causeway, Co. Antrim.
Glenariff Forest Park, Ballymena/Waterfoot Road.
Lagan Valley Regional Park, Hillsborough Rd., Lisburn
Larne Historical Centre, Old Carnegie Library, Larne.
Larne Interpretive Centre, Narrow Guage Road, Larne.
Malone House, Barnett Pk., Upper Malone Rd., Belfast.
Rathlin Island Bird Sanctuary, Rathlin.
Sir Thomas & Lady Dixon Park, Malone Rd., Belfast.
Talnotry Cottage Bird Garden, Crumlin Rd., Crumlin.

CO. ARMAGH

Armagh Planetarium, Collage Hill, Armagh.
Gosford Forest Park, Markethill.
Lough Neagh Discovery Centre, Oxford Island.
Maghery Country Park, near Dungannon.
Navan Centre (Emain Macha), near Armagh City.
Palace Stables Heritage Centre, Friary Road, Armagh.
Peatlands Park, near Dungannon.
Slieve Gullion Forest Park, near Newry.
St. Patrick's Trian, 40 English Street, Armagh.

CO. CLARE

Dromore Wood, Ruan, Ennis.
Ennis Friary, Ennis Town.
Scattery Island Centre, Merchants Quay, Kilrush.

CO. CORK

Charles Fort, Kinsale.
Desmond Castle, Cork Street, Kinsale.
Doneraile Wildlife Park, Doneraile.
Ilnacullin, (Garinish Island), Glengarriff.

COUNTY DERRY

Downhill Castle, Mussendun Road, Castlerock.
Earhart Centre & Wildlife Sanctuary, Ballyarnet, Derry.
Knockcloghrim Windmill, near Maghera.
Martello Tower, Magilligan Point.
Mountsandel Fort, near Coleraine.
Roe Valley Country Park, Limavady, Derry.
Sampson Tower, near Limavady.
Springhill, near Moneymore.
The Walls of Derry, Derry city.

CO. DONEGAL

Donegal Castle, Donegal.
Glebe House and Gallery, Churchill, Letterkenny.
Glenveagh National Park, Churchill, Letterkenny.
Newmills Corn and Flax Mills, Letterkenny.
Grianan Ailigh Centre, Burt, Inishowen.

COUNTY DOWN

Annalong Corn Mill, Marine Park, Annalong.
Ballycopeland Windmill, near Millisle.
Burren Heritage Centre, Burren, Warrenpoint.
Butterfly House, Seaforde Nursery, Seaforde.
Castle Espie, 78 Ballydrain Road, Comber.
Castlewellan Forest Park, Main Street, Castlewellan.
Clough Castle, Clough Village.
Crawfordsburn Country Park, near Helen's Bay.
Delamont Country Park, near Killyleagh.
Dundrum Castle, Dundrum Village.
Exploris, Castle Street, Portaferry.
Greencastle, near Kilkeel.
Grey Abbey, Greyabbey Village.
Hillsborough Fort, Hillsborough.
Inch Abbey, near Downpatrick.
Jordan's Castle, Ardglass.
Mount Stewart House & Gardens, near Newtownards.
Murlough National Nature Reserve, near Dundrum.
Nendrum Monastic Site, Mahee Island, Comber.
North Down Heritage Centre, Castle Pk. Ave., Bangor.
Rowallane Gardens, near Saintfield.
Scarva Visitor Centre, Main Street, Scarva.
Somme Heritage Centre, Newtownards.
Tollymore Forest Park, Tullybrannigan Rd., Newcastle.
Ulster Wildlife Centre, Killyleagh Rd, Crossgar.

CO. DUBLIN

Casino, Marino, Dublin 3.
Dublin Castle, Dame Street, Dublin 2.
Garden of Remembrance, Parnell Sq. East, Dublin 1.
Iveagh Gardens, Clonmel Street, Dublin 2.
Kilmainham Gaol, Inchicore Road, Dublin 8.
Lusk Heritage Centre, Lusk, Co. Dublin.
National Botanic Gardens, Glasnevin, Dublin 9.
Pearse Museum, (St. Enda's), Rathfarnham, Dublin 16.
Phoenix Park Visitor Centre, Dublin 8.
Rathfarnham Castle, Rathfarnham, Dublin 14.
St. Mary's Abbey, Off Capel Street, Dublin 1.
St. Stephen's Green, Dublin 2.
War Memorial Gardens, Islandbridge, Dublin 8.
Waterways Visitor Centre, Grand Canal Qy., Dublin 2.

COUNTY FERMANAGH

Carrothers Family Heritage Museum, Tamlaght.
Castle Archdale Country Park, near Kesh.
Castle Balfour, Main Street, Lisnaskea.
Castle Coole, near Enniskillen.
Enniskillen Castle, Castle Barracks, Enniskillen.
Florence Court, near Enniskillen.
Florencecourt Forest Park, near Enniskillen.
Forthill Park & Cole Monument, Enniskillen.
Lough Navar Forest, near Derrygonnelly.
Marble Arch Caves, near Enniskillen.
Monea Castle, near Enniskillen.
Roslea Heritage Centre, Monaghan Road, Roslea.
Tully Castle, near Derrygonnelly.

CO. GALWAY

Athenry Castle, Athenry.
Aughnanure Castle, Oughterard.
Connemara National Park, Letterfrack.
Portumna Castle, Portumna.

Teach an Phiarsaigh (Pearse's Cottage), Ros Muc.

CO. KERRY
Ardfert Cathedral, Ardfert.
Derrynane House, National Historic Park, Caherdaniel.
Ionad an Bhlascaoid Mhóir, Tralee.
Muckross House, Killarney National Park.
Muckross Friary, Killarney.
Ross Castle, Killarney.

CO. KILDARE
Castletown, Celbridge.

CO. KILKENNY
Dunmore Cave, Ballyfoyle.
Jerpoint Abbey, Thomastown.
Kilkenny Castle, National Historic Park, Kilkenny City.

CO. LAOIS
Emo Court, Emo.
Heywood Gardens, Ballinakill.

CO. LEITRIM
Parke's Castle, Fivemile Bourne.

CO. LIMERICK
Desmond Castle, Newcastlewest.

CO. LONGFORD
Corlea Trackway Visitor Centre, Kenagh.

CO. LOUTH
Old Mellifont Abbey, Collon.

CO. MAYO
Céide Fields, Ballycastle.

CO. MEATH
Hill of Tara, near Navan.
Knowth, near Slane.
Newgrange, near Slane.

CO. OFFALY
Clonmacnoise, Shannonbridge.

CO. ROSCOMMON
Boyle Abbey, Boyle Town.

CO. SLIGO
Carrowmore Megalithic Cemetery, Carrowmore.
Sligo Abbey, Sligo Town.

CO. TIPPERARY
Cahir Castle, Cahir.
Ormond Castle, Carrick-on-Suir.
Rock of Cashel, Cashel.
Roscrea Heritage Centre, Roscrea.
Swiss Cottage, Cahir.

COUNTY TYRONE
An Creagán Visitor Centre, Creggan.
Ardboe Cross, near Cookstown.
Beaghmore Circles, between Cookstown & Gortin.
Benburb Valley Heritage Centre, Benburb.
Benburb Valley Park,10 Main Street, Benburb.
Castlederg Visitor Centre, Castlederg.
Corn Mill Heritage Centre, Lineside, Coalisland.
Donaghmore Heritage Centre, Donaghmore.
Drum Manor Forest Park, near Cookstown.
Fivemiletown Display Centre, Fivemiletown.
Gortin Glen Forest Park, near Omagh.
Grant Ancestral House, Dergina, Ballygawley.
Newtownstewart Gateway Centre, Newtownstewart.
Parkanaur Forest Park, near Dungannon.
Sperrin Heritage Centre, Cranagh, Gortin.
Tullaghoge Fort, near Cookstown.
Ulster American Folk Park, Castletown, near Omagh.
Ulster History Park, Cullion, near Omagh.
Wilson Ancestral Home, Dergalt, Strabane.

CO. WEXFORD
Ballyhack Castle, Ballyhack.
John F. Kennedy Arboretum, New Ross.
Wexford Wildfowl Reserve, North Slob, Wexford.

CO. WICKLOW
Dwyer-McAllister Cottage, Derrynamuck.
Glendalough Visitor Centre, Glendalough.
Wicklow Mountains National Park, Glendalough.

Tom MAGEE

COMMERCIAL
ESTATE - AGENTS

Sales * Lettings

* Acquisitions * Rent Reviews *

* Property Management *

LISMORE HOUSE
23 CHURCH STREET
PORTADOWN
CRAIGAVON BT62 3LN

TELEPHONE 0762 350888
FACSIMILE 0762 350904

TRANSPORT

INTRODUCTION

As Ireland is the last remaining country in the E.C. without direct access to continental Europe - Britain has now achieved a " land link" through the opening of the channel tunnel - the development of transport facilities and infrastructure has become a major priority. Northern Ireland is well served by two major ports, Belfast and Larne, which provide not only high standard passenger services but also fast and efficient freight movement to Britain.

In the Republic there have been major developments at Dublin and Waterford ports, and it is planned to spend in the region of £95m. within the next three years on commercial seaports.

In trade terms, Belfast is the busiest port on the island with not only Northern Ireland firms using its facilities but also many from the Republic, particularly exporters from the Border counties.

As most of Republic's recent economic growth has been export led the development of ports and shipping, which freights out 76% of the Republic's external trade, this has taken on an added importance to the national economy.

Air facilities have improved immensely also in recent years. There are three major international airports in the Republic and one in the North. In addition, there have been significant developments at Cork, Knock, Belfast city and City of Derry airports. The island's multi-million pound tourism industry has benefited enormously from these developments and, according to leading economists and business chiefs, comprehensive air services which provide frequent and efficient access to international airline connections are not only essential for the continued development of this sector but are vital to offset any trading disadvantage Ireland might suffer due to its peripherality.

According to the Republic of Ireland Government's own "Operational Plan for Transport 1994-1999" £2.6bn. will be invested in the transport system: £1,099m. on primary roads, £556m. on non national roads, £356mon public transport, £275m on mainline rail, and £225m. on airports.

In the Republic, Coras Iompair Éireann (CIE), a semi-state body, provides public transport though other than in the main cities the service is not particularly comprehensive. In the North, the main provider of public road transport is Ulsterbus with its sister company, Citybus, providing the service in Belfast.

PUBLIC TRANSPORT

Republic of Ireland: Bus Transport

Coras Iompair Éireann (CIE) - Irish Transport System, provides public transport in Ireland. Two of the three subsidiary companies owned by CIE operate bus services in Ireland (the other subsidiary company providing rail services) - Bus Éireann and Bus Átha Cliath.

Bus Éireann (Irish Bus) - provides the National Bus service outside the Dublin area. It operates a network of inter-urban bus services, bus services throughout the country, and city services in Cork, Limerick, Waterford and Galway. Bus Éireann caters for over 60 million passengers annually.

Bus Átha Cliath (Dublin Bus) - operates the Dublin City bus services. It operates over 160 million passenger journeys annually and covers an area of 1,000 sq km of the Dublin area.

Bus Éireann Fleet Statistics:

Double Deck Buses	37
Single Deck Buses	1,355
Mini-buses	39
Tour Coaches	21
Total: Fleet	**1,452**

Statistics of Provincial City Bus Operators:

Cork:

Number of Routes	16
Number of Stops	600
Kms. per vehicle per year	65,300
Passengers per day	30,000
Number of Buses	42

Limerick:

Number of Routes	11
Number of Stops	270
Kms. per vehicle per year	31,000
Passengers per day	10,500
Number of Buses	18

Galway:

Number of Routes	8
Number of Stops	185
Kms. per vehicle per year	64,700
Passengers per day	7,000
Number of Buses	12

Waterford:

Number of Routes	4
Number of Stops	90
Kms. per vehicle per year	26,100
Passengers per day	1,600
Number of Buses	4

Northern Ireland: Bus Transport

Ulsterbus and Citybus - provide provincial and Belfast City bus services respectively. Citybus operates principally within the boundaries of the Belfast City Council area. However, the actual built-up urban area extends far beyond these boundaries, and both companies cater for bus transportation requirements in this larger urban area. Ulsterbus operates the city services in Derry City. It also operates internal services in virtually every other town in Northern ireland, together with inter-urban express services and rural services.

Citybus Statistics (1994/1995)

Kilometres operated: 12,075,000
Passenger journeys:......................................26,700,000
Bus routes:..100 (approx)
Bus miles:..7,500,000

Passenger receipts:................................£17,813,000m
Bus Fleet: 286
Average age of buses:.......................................8.8 years
Number of staff:...741

Ulsterbus Statistics (1994/1995)

Kilometres operated: 60,214,000
Passenger journeys:......................................55,500,000
Bus routes:..300 (approx)
Bus miles:..37,400,000
Passenger receipts:................................£55,112,000m
Bus Fleet: 1,202
Average age of buses:.......................................7.9 years
Number of staff:...2,213
Bus Stations: 25

Republic of Ireland: Rail Transport

Coras Iompair Éireann (CIE) - Irish Transport System, provides rail services throughout Ireland through its subsidiary company - Iarnród Éireann.

Iarnród Éireann (Irish Rail) - operates rail services around Ireland and into Northern Ireland. It consists of 1,900 route kilometres. It operates passenger and freight services, including DART. Iarnród Éireann carries 26 million passengers annually.

Dublin Area Rapid Transit (DART) - provides a passenger service between Dublin City and Dun Laoghaire and to coastal parts of Co. Wicklow. It consists of 38km of track using electric motive power.

Rail Statistics (1994)
Length of Railway Lines:
Lines owned by Board......................................1,872 km
Other Lines...72 km
Total: ....**1,944 km**

Motive Power:
Diesel Locomotives...112
Electric Motive Units..80
Total: **192**

Rail Service Vehicles:
Ballast Wagons, Tool Vans etc 157

Rail Passenger Vehicles:
Passenger Carriages / Railcars 251
Luggage Vans etc. 50
Total: **301**

Rail Freight Vehicles:
Flat Trucks 965
Specialised wagons etc. 930
Total: **1,895**

Rail Freight Containers:
Covered Containers 1,224
Other Containers...177
Total: **1,401**

Northern Ireland: Rail Transport

Northern Ireland Railways (NIR) - operate all internal public passenger railway services within Northern Ireland, and also operate a joint service with Iarnród Éireann on the Dublin to Belfast Route. The railway links Belfast with Larne Harbour, Carrickfergus, Bangor, Portadown, Ballymena, Coleraine, Portrush, Derry City and intermediate stations and halts.

Rail Statistics:
Kilometres Operated 1994/1995: 211,876,000
Passenger Journeys:......................................6,144,000

Railway Stations: (principle) 17
Halts 41
Passenger receipts:................................£8,736,000m
Number of staff:..788
Rail Network (km):
Double Track 152
Single Track 204
Rolling Stock:
Locomotives 9
Railcars (multiple units) 30
Total Passenger Vehicles (1996) 120

Iarnród Éireann Receipt Statistics, 1994 and 1995*

	1994 Receipts	1995 Receipts *
Passengers, Parcels, Mail etc.	£61,663,000	£66,317,000
Freight Trains	£18,877,000	£17,973,000
Totals	£80,540,000	£84,290,000

Iarnród Éireann Passenger Statistics, 1994 and 1995*

	1994 (000)	1995 * (000)
Number of passengers carried	25,810	27,120

* Provisional figures.

SHIPPING AND PASSENGER BOAT STATISTICS

Republic of Ireland

Boat Transport

Rosslare, Dun Laoghaire, Cork and Dublin are the country's passenger / car ferry ports. Other smaller harbours are located throughout the country dealing in bulk cargoes. There are a number of car ferries currently operating services from Ireland.

Irish Ferries - operate daily services to Britain on the Dublin-Holyhead Route and Rosslare-Pembroke Route. An Irish Ferries Superferry also operates on the Dublin-Holyhead Route. Irish Ferries also operate services to France, connecting Rosslare and Cork with Le Harve and Cherbourg.

Stena Sealink - operates daily services to Britain on the Dun Laoghaire-Holyhead Route and the Rosslare-Fishguard Route. A Stena Sealink High Speed Ferry also operates on the Dun Laoghaire-Holyhead Route.

Brittany Ferries - operate weekly services from Cork to Roscoff between March and October, and from May to September they link Cork with St. Malo.

Swansea Cork Ferries - operate a daily service from Cork to Swansea between March and January.

Shipping

The process of shipping and cargo handling have progressed dramatically in recent times and Irish ports have developed their facilities in accordance, as Irelands external trade depends on shipping for 76% of its trade.

Dublin and Cork are Irelands multi-modal ports, dealing with all cargoes with Waterford Harbour becoming the most up-to-date Lo/Lo handling port in Ireland.

The Irish registered shipping fleet (100 gross tons and over) comprised 79 ships totalling 161,786 gross tons at 30 June, 1994.

Northern Ireland

Boat Transport

Belfast and Larne Harbours are Northern Ireland's passenger / car ferry ports. Other sea ports operate shipping lines out of Northern Ireland. There are three car ferries currently operating services from Northern Ireland. They are:

Belfast Car Ferries - Operates daily services on the Larne to Stranraer Route.

P & O Ferries - Operates daily services on the Larne to Cairnryan Route. A new Jet Liner Service also operates on this route.

Sealink - Operate daily services on the Belfast to Stranraer Route. A new High Speed Ferry also operates on this route.

Shipping

Over 80 international shipping lines operate out of Northern Ireland's five commercial seaports. 90 % of Northern Ireland's total trade, and almost 50 % of the Republic of Ireland's freight traffic, leaves through Northern Ireland's ports. There are 150 sailings weekly to Britain, including regular sailings to ports in the USA, Continental Europe and the rest of the world. 5,500 ships carrying 11 million tonnes of cargo leave Belfast Port each year. Over 55 % of Northern Ireland's seaborne trade is shipped through Belfast Port, which is the busiest port in the Island of Ireland.

Passenger Movement by Sea to and from Rep. of Ireland, 1990-1995

Year	Britain		Other Places		Total	
	Outward	Inward	Outward	Inward	Outward	Inward
1990	1,419,000	1,445,000	197,000	198,000	1,617,000	1,643,000
1991	1,556,000	1,573,000	193,000	191,000	1,749,000	1,765,000
1992	1,579,000	1,581,000	193,000	191,000	1,772,000	1,772,000
1993	1,717,000	1,739,000	192,000	189,000	1,909,000	1,928,000
1994	1,807,000	1,815,000	191,000	189,000	1,998,000	2,004,000
1995	1,950,000	1,938,000	181,000	176,000	2,131,000	2,114,000

AIRLINE STATISTICS

Republic of Ireland

International Airports

The three international airports - Cork, Dublin and Shannon, caters for over 8 million passengers and 94,000 tonnes of freight annually. These airports are managed by Aer Rianta. Aer Rianta International, a subsidiary company of Aer Rianta, manages a number of airports abroad. Dublin International Airport, the busiest, caters for over 6 million passengers and over 65,000 tonnes of freight annually.

Aer Lingus

Aer Lingus is the State Airline. The airline operates flights to 27 cities in the United Kingdom, Europe and North America. Aer Lingus caters for over 4 million passengers and 45,000 tonnes of freight annually.

Other Airlines

A number of other airlines operate flights to and from Ireland, these include CityJet, Ryanair and Translift Airways. Various passenger, freight and helicopter services are operated within the country using the network of Regional airports - Donegal, Galway, Kerry, Knock, Sligo and Waterford.

Flight Times from Dublin:

Destination	via	Travelling Time
Amsterdam		1 hr 30 mins
Berlin	Amsterdam	2 hrs 50 mins
Birmingham		1 hr
Boston		7 hrs
Brussels		1 hr 30 mins
Chicago		8 hrs 20 mins
Copenhagen		2 hrs 5 mins
Edinburgh		1 hr
Frankfurt		2 hrs
Glasgow		1 hr
Hamburg		2 hrs
London (Heathrow)		1 hr 10 mins
London (Stansted)		1 hr 15 mins
Leeds		1 hr
Madrid		2 hrs 35 mins
Manchester		1 hour
Milan		2 hrs 35 mins
Munich	Amsterdam	3 hrs
New York		7 hrs 30 mins
Paris		1 hr 35 mins
Rome		3 hrs
Zurich		2 hrs 10 mins
Sydney	Amsterdam	17 hrs 30 mins
Hong Kong	London	15 hrs
Los Angeles	Chicago	14 hrs 35 mins

Northern Ireland

International Airports Belfast International Airport, situated 13 miles north-west of the city, operates a direct service to 40 major UK and European destinations with onward connections to worldwide centres. It is the second largest freight airport in the UK, outside London. Belfast City Airport, 5 minutes from Belfast City, provides fast connections to most major UK Cities including London. In the north-west of Northern Ireland, the City of Derry Airport has been modernised and provides a wide choice of destinations.

Airlines There are currently 24 scheduled flights daily between Belfast and London, due to competing airlines. Easy access to and transfer at London (and other major UK airports) means that most European destinations can be easily reached.

Freight Services For air freight, 8 International Air Transport Authority (IATA) agents in Northern Ireland

act on behalf of all airlines and offer competitive rates to customers requiring direct consolidated or charter freight. Specialist airlines offer air freight services from both Belfast International and Belfast City Airports. The main passenger airlines also operates freight services, with transport costs and times being very competitive.

Selected Flight Times from Belfast

Destination	via	Travelling Time
Amsterdam		1 hr 30 mins
Brussels	London	4 hrs
Frankfurt	Birmingham	3 hrs
Geneva	Manchester	4 hrs
Madrid	London	4 hrs 30 mins
Rome	London	5 hrs
New York		7 hrs
Hong Kong	London	15 hrs
Tokyo	London	14 hrs

Air Passenger Movement to and from Rep. of Ireland, 1990-1995

Year	Dublin Airport (000) Outward	Inward	Cork Airport (000) Outward	Inward	Shannon Airport (000) Outward	Inward	In Transit	Total* (000) Outward	Inward
1990	2,399	2,362	253	252	543	520	417	3,337	3,270
1991	2,301	2,274	234	237	480	456	462	3,114	3,062
1992	2,548	2,524	253	258	569	537	415	3,441	3,388
1993	2,645	2,621	276	277	586	571	403	3,569	3,530
1994	3,219	3,176	314	313	554	536	301	4,170	4,107
1995	3,737	3,670	388	385	596	579	240	4,824	4,736

* includes: Connaught, Waterford Regional, Galway, Carrickfin and Kerry County Airports. Sligo Airport included from June 1990.

Republic of Ireland Cross-Border Passenger Movement, 1990-1995

	Rail		Road omnibus scheduled services		Total rail and road omnibus scheduled services	
Year	Outward	Inward	Outward	Inward	Outward	Inward
1990	180,000	189,000	309,000	305,000	489,000	494,000
1991	226,000	238,000	386,000	387,000	612,000	625,000
1992	227,000	243,000	418,000	412,000	645,000	655,000
1993	255,000	280,000	417,000	412,000	671,000	692,000
1994	306,000	337,000	411,000	407,000	717,000	744,000
1995	377,000	415,000	430,000	427,000	807,000	842,000

Rep. of Ireland Passenger Movement by sea, rail, road and air (by route)

		(000's)		Routes to / from				(000's)	
		Britain		Northern Ireland		Other Places		Total	
Mode	Year	Outwards	Inwards	Outwards	Inwards	Outwards	Inwards	Outwards	Inwards
Sea	1992	1,579	1,581	—	—	193	191	1,772	1,772
	1993	1,717	1,739	—	—	192	189	1,909	1,928
	1994	1,807	1,815	—	—	191	189	1,998	2,004
Rail	1992	—	—	227	243	—	—	227	243
	1993	—	—	255	280	—	—	255	280
	1994	—	—	306	337	—	—	306	337
Road	1992	—	—	418	412	—	—	418	412
	1993	—	—	417	412	—	—	417	412
	1994	—	—	411	407	—	—	411	407
Air	1992	2,183	2,147	—	—	1,258	1,241	3,441	3,388
	1993	2,211	2,178	—	—	1,358	1,352	3,569	3,530
	1994	2,600	2,552	—	—	1,570	1,555	4,170	4,107
Total	1992	3,763	3,728	645	655	1,450	1,432	5,858	5,815
	1993	3,929	3,917	671	692	1,550	1,541	6,150	6,150
	1994	4,407	4,367	717	744	1,761	1,744	6,885	6,854

PRIVATE AND COMMERCIAL VEHICLES

Licensed vehicles in Northern Ireland, 1990-1994

Type of Vehicle	1990	1991	1992	1993	1994
New Registrations:					
Cycles	2,343	2,218	1,993	1,885	1,943
Motor-hackneys, omni-buses, tramcars etc.	608	620	551	466	1,143
Agricultural tractors and engines	1,611	1,177	1,184	1,658	1,558
Goods Vehicles	8,972	8,892	8,707	9,061	9,576
Private cars	69,091	63,739	62,777	65,360	70,765
Exempt from duty	2,510	2,336	2,463	4,550	6,423
TOTAL:	**85,135**	**78,982**	**77,675**	**82,980**	**91,408**
Current Vehicle & Driving Licences:					
Cycles	10,167	9,684	9,023	8,634	8,775
Motor-hackneys, omni- buses, tramcars etc.	2,786	2,887	2,744	2,679	3,078
Agricultural tractors and engines	8,021	7,199	6,892	7,201	7,317
Goods Vehicles	21,153	18,901	19,601	20,074	20,714
Private cars	481,090	498,471	516,194	515,185	514,760
Other	19,897	21,176	23,858	32,552	41,307
TOTAL:	**543,114**	**558,318**	**578,312**	**586,325**	**595,951**
Current Driving Licences:	874,000	912,000	947,000	978,000	1,005,000

Licensed vehicles in the Republic of Ireland (1994)

Licensing Authority	Private cars	Goods Vehicles	Tractors	Motor cycles	Exempt vehicles (1)	Public Service Vehicles	Other classes (2)	Overall Total
County Councils:								
Carlow	11,133	1,874	1,516	391	70	93	147	15,224
Cavan	14,134	2,526	2,583	285	73	173	96	19,870
Clare	25,173	3,279	3,232	422	97	251	139	32,593
Cork (3)	119,896	19,199	8,784	3,518	816	1,194	1,360	154,767
Donegal	28,119	4,724	3,667	372	153	493	755	38,283
Galway	46,488	6,728	4,582	859	321	575	337	59,890
Kerry	34,428	3,849	6,033	914	166	342	441	46,173
Kildare	34,901	4,979	1,691	843	209	373	266	43,262
Kilkenny	20,188	3,398	3,583	700	110	237	239	28,455
Laois	13,745	2,178	2,316	233	82	136	160	18,850
Leitrim	6,486	1,095	1,194	187	36	78	40	9,116
Limerick	32,518	4,496	3,536	724	163	265	348	42,050
Longford	7,950	1,267	1,220	159	34	75	51	10,756
Louth	20,773	4,302	855	469	144	259	186	26,988
Mayo	27,388	3,981	4,343	518	188	282	192	36,892
Meath	29,510	4,734	2,010	610	140	215	194	37,413
Monaghan	12,709	3,062	2,098	221	76	113	120	18,399
Offaly	14,555	1,985	2,157	537	59	180	271	19,744
Roscommon	14,160	2,215	2,289	177	88	94	62	19,085
Sligo	14,737	2,610	2,030	342	82	163	127	20,091
Tipperary N.R.	16,677	2,761	2,513	310	82	107	154	22,604
Tipperary S.R.	21,129	3,298	2,590	672	131	179	202	28,201
Waterford	13,738	1,864	2,035	625	71	95	218	18,646
Westmeath	16,656	2,734	1,528	362	86	213	107	21,686
Wexford	27,705	4,703	3,616	1,002	115	214	430	37,785
Wicklow	26,525	3,705	1,425	835	146	214	261	33,111
County Boroughs:								
Dublin (3)	266,169	29,999	1,113	6,651	4,195	4,909	2,127	315,613
Limerick	10,755	2,349	35	355	51	230	71	13,866
Waterford	10,657	1,915	72	339	68	158	101	13,310
TOTAL:	**939,022**	**135,809**	**74,646**	**23,632**	**8,052**	**11,910**	**9,202**	**1,202,273**

(1) Includes Government owned, Diplomatic, Invalid, Fire Brigade Vehicles & Ambulance.
(2) Includes School Buses, Mobile Machines, Fork Lifts, Excavators, Dumpers, Hearses, Vintage & Veteran Vehicles.
(3) City & County.

Current Driving Licenses (Republic of Ireland), 1994

Licensing Authority	Provisional Licenses	Annual Licenses	Triennial Licenses	10 Year Licenses	Total No. of Driver Licences
County Councils:					
Carlow	5,066	117	2,932	9,995	18,110
Cavan	5,429	125	3,938	15,330	24,822
Clare	9,001	219	6,304	26,578	42,102
*Cork	43,870	953	24,608	123,604	193,035
Donegal	11,865	248	8,426	35,786	56,325
*Galway	18,982	298	10,984	51,752	82,016
Kerry	14,095	276	8,299	36,788	59,448
Kildare	14,179	216	6,707	36,088	57,190
Kilkenny	8,303	222	5,526	21,467	35,518
Laois	5,230	121	4,067	14,454	23,872
Leitrim	2,307	60	2,189	7,482	12,038
Limerick	11,856	272	7,052	33,859	53,039
Longford	3,133	85	2,323	8,368	13,909
Louth	9,272	140	5,968	23,146	38,526

Licensing Authority	Provisional Licenses	Annual Licenses	Triennial Licenses	10 Year Licenses	Total No. of Driver Licences
Mayo	10,727	276	5,481	30,747	47,231
Meath	11,535	165	6,742	31,438	49,880
Monaghan	5,675	129	4,656	14,950	25,410
Offaly	5,862	146	3,965	15,405	25,378
Roscommon	5,155	144	3,989	15,652	24,940
Sligo	5,211	109	3,971	16,008	25,299
Tipperary N.R.	6,133	116	4,355	17,905	28,509
Tipperary S.R.	8,284	184	6,136	20,790	35,394
Waterford	4,966	103	3,337	14,189	22,595
Westmeath	6,494	148	4,407	17,908	28,957
Wexford	11,503	450	7,269	29,183	48,405
Wicklow	11,010	201	5,856	27,931	44,998
County Borough:					
Dublin (city and county)	102,441	1,811	58,664	271,785	434,681
Limerick Corp.	5,120	60	2,600	10,487	18,267
Waterford Corp.	4,046	56	2,524	9,761	16,387
TOTAL:	**366,750**	**7,450**	**223,255**	**988,826**	**1,586,281**

Current Driving Licenses (Northern Ireland), March 1996

Type of License (excluding Taxi Licenses)	Total
Provisional	130,000
Full	933,000
TOTAL:	**1,063,000**

Car Registration Index Marks (Republic of Ireland)

Index Mark	From Jan. 1987	County	The Authorised Officer County Council Offices
C;	CW	Carlow	Athy Road, Carlow.
ID;	CN	Cavan	Courthouse, Cavan.
IE;	CE	Clare	Courthouse, Ennis.
IF; PI; ZB; ZF; ZK; ZT;	C	Cork	Carrigrohane Road, Cork.
IH; ZP;	DL	Donegal	County Building, Lifford.
IM; ZM;	G	Galway	County Building, Galway.
IN; ZX;	KY	Kerry	Moyderwell, Tralee.
IO; ZW;	KE	Kildare	Friary Road, Naas.
IP;	KK	Kilkenny	John's Green, Kilkenny.
CI;	LS	Laois	County Hall, Portlaoise.
IT;	LM	Leitrim	Priest's Lane, Carrick-on-Shannon.
IU; IV;	LK	Limerick	O'Connell Street, Limerick.
IX;	LD	Longford	Great Water Street, Longford.
IY; ZY;	LH	Louth	The Crescent, Dundalk.
IS; IZ;	MO	Mayo	Courthouse, Castlebar.
AI; ZN;	MH	Meath	County Hall, Navan.
BI;	MN	Monaghan	North Road, Monaghan.
IR;	OY	Offaly	O'Connor Square, Tullamore.
DI;	RN	Roscommon	Abbey Street, Roscommon.
EI;	SO	Sligo	Cleveragh Road, Sligo.
FI;	TN	Tipperary, NR	Kickham Street, Nenagh.
GI; HI;	TS	Tipperary, SR	Emmet Street, Clonmel.
KI;	WD	Waterford	Courthouse, Dungarvan.
LI;	WH	Westmeath	County Buildings, Mullingar.
MI; ZR;	WX	Wexford	County Hall, Wexford.
NI;	WW	Wicklow	County Buildings, Wicklow.
TI;	L	Limerick	City Hall, Merchant's Quay, Limerick.
WI;	W	Waterford	6-8 Lombard Street, Waterford.
IK; RI; SI; YI; Z; ZA; ZC; ZD; ZE; ZG; ZH; ZI; ZJ; ZL; ZO; ZS; ZU; ZV;	D	Dublin	River House, Chancery St., Dublin 7.

Car Registration Index Marks (Northern Ireland)

Index Mark	County
IA; DZ; KZ; RZ	Antrim
IB; LZ;	Armagh
IJ; BZ; JZ; SZ	Down
IL	Fermanagh
IW; NZ; YZ	Derry
JI; HZ; VZ	Tyrone
OI; XI; AZ; CZ; EZ; FZ; GZ; MZ; OZ; PZ; TZ; UZ; WZ	City of Belfast
UI	City of Derry

Issued by: Dept. of the Environment for Northern Ireland, The Vehicle Licensing Central Office,
County Hall, Castlerock Road, Coleraine, Co. Derry BT51 3HS

SPEED LAWS / DRIVING LICENSES

Republic of Ireland Speed Laws

Type of Vehicles	MPH Built-up Areas	MPH Elsewhere	MPH Motorways
Cars (includes light goods vehicles & motorcycles)	30	60	70
Single Deck Buses - not carrying standing passengers	30	50	
Single Deck Buses - carrying standing passengers	30	40	
Double Deck Buses	30	40	
Goods Vehicles (including Articulated vehicles) - gross vehicle weight in excess of 3,500 Kgs	30	50	
Any vehicle drawing another	30	50	

Northern Ireland Speed Laws

Type of Vehicles	MPH Built-up Areas	MPH Elsewhere Single Carriage	MPH Elsewhere Dual Carriage	MPH Motorways
Cars (including car derived vans & motorcycles	30	60	70	70
Cars towing caravans or trailers (including car derived vans & motorcycles	30	50	60	60
Buses and Coaches (not exceeding 12 metres in overall length)	30	50	60	70
Goods vehicles (not exceeding 7.5 tonnes maximum laden weight)	30	50	60	70*
Goods vehicles (exceeding 7.5 tonnes maximum laden weight)	30	40	50	60

* 60 if articulated or towing a trailer

Minimum Age for Driving (Republic of Ireland)

Description of Vehicle	Categories	Minimum Ages for driving/riding
Motorcycles	A, A1	18, 16
Cars	B, EB	17
Trucks	C, EC, C1, EC1	18
Buses	D, ED	21
Minibuses	D1, ED1	21
Work Vehicles/Tractors	W	16

Minimum Age for Driving (Northern Ireland)

Description of Vehicle	Categories	Minimum Ages for driving/riding
Motorcycles	A,	17
Moped	P	16
Cars	B, B1	17
Trucks	C+E, C, C1	21,18
Buses	D, D1	21
Other Vehicles/Tractors	F, G, H, B1, K	16

IRELAND'S MOST POPULAR CARS

20 Most Popular Cars Licensed - Republic of Ireland (1994)

Make	Total
Ford	168,489
Toyota	143,306
Opel	102,847
Nissan	102,050
Volkswagen	68,752
Renault	48,578
Peugeot	36,270
Fiat	34,414
Mazda	33,701
Mitsubishi	23,677
Honda	19,077
Volvo	17,874
Leyland	13,256
Citroen	12,996
Daihatsu	12,316
Rover	11,485
Mercedes	11,440
Vauxhall	11,047
BMW	10,061
Audi	9,401

20 Most Popular Cars - Northern Ireland (1994)

Make & Model	Total
Ford Fiesta	38,532
Ford Escort	27,195
Vauxhall Cavaliar	26,109
Vauxhall Nova	23,569
Vauxhall Astra	19,102
Austin / Rover Metro	16,093
Ford Sierra / Sapphire	14,971
Peugeot 300 Series	12,875
Peugeot 205	12,450
Rover 200 Series	12,117
Volkswagen Polo	11,438
Volkswagon Golf	10,773
Toyota Corolla	10,499
Peugeot 400 Series	9,599
Renault 19	8,754
Ford Orion	8,409
Renault 5	7,443
Toyota Carina	7,387
Ford Transit	7,032
Nissan Sunny	6,870

TRANSPORT INFRASTRUCTURE - ROADS

Transport Infrastructure in Republic of Ireland and Northern Ireland

	Road surface per km2	Road surface per 1,000 inhabitants	Composite indicator	Rail lines per km2	Rail lines per 1,000 inhabitants	Composite indicator
Average of EC	100	100	100	100	100	100
Northern Ireland	95	122	109	45	56	51
Republic of Ireland	76	211	144	51	145	98
Greece	23	45	34	34	65	49
Portugal	42	58	50	63	87	78
Spain	23	43	33	51	97	74

Cross Border Connections, road closures in Northern Ireland, 1993

Classification	Number	Number closed for Security
Roads: Class A	22	1
Roads: Class B	14	5
Roads: Unclassified	141	55
Subtotal	177	61
Tracks / lanes	48	31
Non-road features	4	—
Total	**229**	92

Note: Following the IRA Ceasefire of August 1994 many cross border road closures were removed.

Length of Public Roads (Kms) in the Republic of Ireland

Authority	National	Regional	Local	Total
County Councils:				
Carlow	78	143	998	1,219
Cavan	126	417	2,469	3,012
Clare	236	610	3,381	4,228
Cork	498	1,264	10,369	12,131
Donegal	305	650	5,553	6,508
Dun Laoghaire /Rathdown	20	140	486	646
Fingal	48	189	796	1,033
Galway	430	735	5,442	6,607
Kerry	430	460	3,954	4,844
Kildare	142	390	1,763	2,295
Kilkenny	216	313	2,591	3,120
Laois	161	252	1,859	2,272
Leitrim	55	318	1,857	2,230
Limerick	191	446	2,898	3,535
Longford	96	151	1,321	1,568
Louth	124	181	1,120	1,424
Mayo	401	590	5,367	6,359
Meath	199	471	2,489	3,159
Monaghan	105	288	2,050	2,443
Offaly	140	295	1,589	2,024
Roscommon	246	332	3,358	3,936
South Dublin	49	100	540	689
Sligo	156	214	2,323	2,693
Tipperary (N.R.)	164	357	2,272	2,793
Tipperary (S.R.)	158	422	2,390	2,970
Waterford	105	330	2,128	2,563
Westmeath	180	217	1,732	2,129
Wexford	163	444	2,760	3,367
Wicklow	93	394	1,591	2,079
Borough Corporations:				
Cork	23	38	324	386
Dublin	42	169	966	1,177
Galway	18	31	163	212
Limerick	18	18	145	180
Waterford	8	24	123	154
TOTALS:	**5,426**	**11,393**	**79,166**	**95,984**

Length of Public Roads (Kms) in Northern Ireland

Divisions/Council Areas	Class I Motorway km	Class I Dual Carriage km	Class I Single Carriage km	Class II km	Class III km	Unclass- ified km	Total (1996) km
Ballymena Division							
Antrim	20.92	5.61	78.31	80.39	186.59	419.69	791.51
Ballymena	8.05	9.53	87.51	129.25	194.13	538.94	967.40
Carrickfergus	—	1.35	15.50	30.27	18.66	128.78	194.56
Larne	—	5.88	70.05	74.26	96.85	219.08	466.12
Magherafelt	—	—	99.17	95.05	169.68	542.54	906.45
Total: Ballymena Div.	28.97	22.37	350.55	409.22	665.92	1849.02	3326.94
Belfast Division:							
Belfast City	10.85	13.95	80.16	44.19	22.64	670.80	842.58
Castlereagh	—	8.23	25.75	7.77	39.90	233.92	315.57
Newtownabbey	15.02	2.72	32.40	66.25	68.37	285.61	470.37
Total: Belfast Div.	25.87	24.90	138.31	118.21	130.91	1190.33	1628.51
Coleraine Division:							
Ballymoney	—	—	32.00	115.41	110.61	278.24	536.26
Coleraine	—	3.30	111.75	125.92	120.05	477.50	838.50
Limavady	—	—	74.01	102.18	92.09	355.58	623.86
Derry	—	8.92	63.37	66.57	139.14	549.57	827.57

Moyle	—	—	81.50	105.46	112.92	198.25	498.13
Total: Coleraine Div.	0.00	12.21	362.62	515.54	574.81	1,859.14	3,324.33

Craigavon Division:

Armagh	—	—	130.60	201.30	329.98	1,030.41	1,692.28
Banbridge	—	20.72	50.70	95.23	224.73	591.30	982.68
Craigavon	23.86	4.35	56.96	99.51	136.49	449.78	770.95
Newry / Mourne	—	11.77	150.43	168.66	339.14	998.72	1,668.70
Total: Craigavon Div.	23.86	36.83	388.69	564.68	1,030.34	3070.21	5,114.61

Downpatrick Division:

Ards	-	9.50	124.36	29.14	141.11	407.36	711.47
Down	-	-	157.60	105.32	226.19	600.84	1089.95
Lisburn	19.32	9.59	72.15	168.78	206.53	651.74	1128.11
North Down	-	22.50	8.64	28.41	34.42	226.20	320.17
Total: Downpatrick Div.	19.32	41.59	362.74	331.65	608.25	1886.14	3249.71

Omagh Division:

Cookstown	-	3.83	37.87	141.42	191.70	512.67	887.49
Dungannon	12.70	1.80	118.18	161.48	333.89	895.62	1523.66
Fermanagh	-	-	222.87	224.42	444.74	1156.03	2048.06
Omagh	-	-	88.96	220.45	412.60	1121.73	1843.73
Strabane	-	-	36.55	165.48	316.79	816.32	1335.15
Total: Omagh Div.	12.70	5.63	504.43	913.25	1699.72	4502.37	7638.09

GRAND TOTAL: 110.71 / 143.54 / 2107.34 / 2852.56 / 4709.94 / 14357.21 / 24,281.29

Transport Costs - Republic of Ireland and Northern Ireland

	Republic of Ireland	Northern Ireland
Flights	from Dublin	from Belfast
to London (business rate)	£236	£216
to Brussels (business rate)	£622	£310
to London (cheap rate)	£65	£100
to Brussels (cheap rate)	£179	£99

RELIGION

INTRODUCTION

Religion in Ireland

The total population of Ireland, North and South, is just over 5.1 million, and of this 3.8 million is Catholic. The Catholic church's over-whelming numerical superiority can be ascertained by comparison with the other main churches on the island - 382,000 in the Church of Ireland, 350,000 in the Presbyterian Church, and 64,000 in the Methodist Church.

The Catholic Church has played a significant, often controversial, role in Irish life, particularly in the Irish Republic. Its priests, nuns and christian brothers have been to the forefront of education, many nuns have been involved in the caring professions (e.g. nursing) while the church's hierarchy has been influential in promulgating the church's teaching in regard to a wide range of social and religious issues.

But Ireland has a growing religious plurality with many new churches being established. The liberal democratic nature of Southern Irish society, which has evolved in recent years, has resulted in much more widespread tolerance of religious diversity

The Jewish community is one of the older religious denominations in Ireland but recent years have witnessed growth in Islam, Buddhism, The Society of Friends ("Quakers") and the Church of Scientology.

Despite a slight decline in recent times, Ireland still has the highest number of regular church-goers in Western Europe.

THE CATHOLIC CHURCH

Armagh is the ecclesiastical capital of the Irish Catholic Church, and it is there that the Primate of All-Ireland, usually a Cardinal, resides. The church has four ecclesiastical provinces - Armagh, Dublin, Cashel and Tuam - each with its own Archbishop.

The church has 26 dioceses, approximately 1,360 parishes and about 4,000 Catholic priests. There are in the region of 20,000 people active in the religious life in Ireland while Irish Catholic missionary priests and nuns are active in more than 80 countries across the globe.

THE CHURCH OF IRELAND

The Church of Ireland is a self-governing church within the worldwide Anglican Communion of Churches. It is led by the Archbishop of Armagh , who is Primate of All-Ireland, and the Archbishop of Dublin, who is Primate of Ireland. The Church of Ireland was disestablished in 1871 when it ceased to be the State Church.

When it was disestablished, the Church adopted a Constitution which gave it government by Synod. The General Synod is its supreme legislative authority, and clergy and laity from all dioceses have representation at its meetings. The clergy have 216 representatives while the laity have 432, representatives for both being elected for three year terms by diocesan synods.

Like the Catholic church, the Church of Ireland is deeply involved in education and has its own schools in both parts of Ireland.

There are twelve dioceses in the Church of Ireland. Of its 382,000 members, approximately 75 per cent live in Northern Ireland.

THE PRESBYTERIAN CHURCH

The Presbyterian Church in Ireland has as its chief representative a Moderator, elected at a General Assembly of the Church, who serves for one year only.

This Assembly, which meets annually, makes the rules of the church and decides policy. There are 562 congregations in Ireland and each is entitled to representation at that Assembly.

There are twenty one regions of the Presbyterian Church, each known as a Presbytery. In addition, there are five regional Synods.

The Presbyterian Church believes in the authority of the scriptures in regard to Christian living. It is a Protestant Church in the Reformed Tradition.

The role of the laity is particularly recognised with "elders" being elected by each congregation to actively participate in the affairs of the church.

In the Republic the majority are to be found along the border counties of Donegal, Monaghan and Cavan, and also in Dublin city. In the North more than half of the church's total membership lives within 15 miles of the centre of Belfast. There are approx. 390 ministers and around 30 ordained assistant-ministers, 40 other ministers in special work and almost 150 retired from active duty. The ministry was opened to women in 1972.

THE METHODIST CHURCH

The Methodist Church in Ireland is a democratic church with authority invested in its annual conference whose president is elected for one year only. The church is divided into eight Districts each of which has at its head a chairman who while elected annually can serve up to six years. There are also 77 Circuits, that is groups of congregations throughout the country, North and South, who work together.

The Methodist Church has its foundations in the teachings of the evangelic preacher, John Wesley, who visited Ireland on several occasions in the 18th century. It is a self-governing church but it does have close links with the Methodist Church in Britain.

CHURCH HIERARCHY IN IRELAND

Catholic Bishops of Ireland

The Catholic Church in Ireland is divided into four provinces which are named after the four arch-dioceses - Armagh, Cashel, Dublin and Tuam.

PROVINCE OF ARMAGH

Diocese of Armagh: His Eminence, Cardinal Cahal Daly, Primate of All Ireland and Archbishop of Armagh. Most Rev. Séan Brady, Coadjutor Archbishop of Armagh.
Diocese of Meath: Most Rev. M. Smith.
Diocese of Ardagh and Clonmacnois (Longford): Most Rev. C. O'Reilly.
Diocese of Clogher (Monaghan): Most Rev. J Duffy.
Diocese of Derry: Most Rev. Seamus Hegarty, Most Rev. Francis Lagan, Auxiliary Bishop.
Diocese of Down and Connor: Most Rev. P. Walsh, Auxiliary Bishop Most Rev. A. Farquhar, Auxiliary Bishop Most Rev. M. Dallat
Diocese of Dromore (Down): Most Rev. F.G. Brooks
Diocese of Kilmore (Cavan): Most Rev. F. McKiernan
Diocese of Raphoe (Donegal): Most Rev. Philip Boyce

PROVINCE OF DUBLIN

Diocese of Dublin: His Grace, Most Rev. Desmond Connell, Archbishop of Dublin. Most Rev. E. Walsh. Most Rev. J. Moriarty, Auxiliary Bishop. Most Rev. F. O'Ceallaigh, Auxiliary Bishop.
Diocese of Ferns (Wexford): Most Rev. Brendan Comiskey.
Diocese of Kildare and Leighlin (Carlow): Most Rev. L. Ryan.
Diocese of Ossory (Kilkenny): Most Rev. L. Forristal.

PROVINCE OF CASHEL

Diocese of Cashel and Emly: His Grace, Most Rev. Dermot Clifford.
Diocese of Cloyne (Cork): Most Rev. J. Magee
Diocese of Cork and Ross: Most Rev. M. Murphy. Most Rev. J. Buckley, Auxiliary Bishop.
Diocese of Kerry: Most Rev. William Murphy.
Diocese of Killaloe (Clare): Most Rev. Willie Walsh.
Diocese of Waterford and Lismore: Most Rev. William Lee.
Diocese of Limerick: Most Rev. Donal Murray.

PROVINCE OF TUAM

Diocese of Tuam: His Grace, Most Rev. Michael Neary, Archbishop.
Diocese of Achonry (Roscommon): Most Rev. T. Flynn.
Diocese of Clonfert (Galway): Most Rev. J. Kirby.
Diocese of Elphin (Sligo): Most Rev. C. Jones.
Diocese of Galway and Kilmacduagh: Most Rev. J. McLoughlin (also Apostolic Administrator of Kilfenora - Galway).
Diocese of Killala (Mayo): Most Rev. T. Finnegan.

PAPAL NUNCIO

His Excellency Most Rev. Dr. Luciano Storero: Born 1926 in Italy, ordained priest June 1949, ordained Titular Archbishop of Tigimma in 1970, and appointed Apostolic Nuncio to Ireland on 15th November 1995.

Church of Ireland Bishops of Ireland

There are 12 dioceses in the Church of Ireland divided into two provinces, Armagh and Dublin.

PROVINCE OF ARMAGH

Diocese of Armagh: Most Rev. Robin Eames, Archbishop of Armagh and Primate of All Ireland.
Diocese of Clogher: Right Rev. Brian Hannon.
Diocese of Derry and Raphoe: Right Rev. James Mehaffey.
Diocese of Down and Dromore: Right Rev. Gordon McMullan.
Diocese of Connor: Right Rev. J.E. Moore.
Diocese of Kilmore, Elphin and Ardagh (Cavan): Right Rev. M.H.G. Mayes.
Diocese of Tuam, Killala and Achonry: Right Rev. J.R.W. Neill.

PROVINCE OF DUBLIN

Diocese of Dublin: Most Rev. Donald Caird, Archbishop of Dublin and Primate of Ireland.
Diocese of Meath and Kildare: Right Rev. W.N.F. Empey.
Diocese of Cashel, Waterford, Lismore, Ossory, Ferns and Leighlin: Right Rev. N.V. Willoughby.
Diocese of Cork, Cloyne and Ross: Right Rev. R.A. Warke.
Diocese of Limerick, Ardfert, Aghadoe, Killaloe, Kilfenora, Clonfert, Kilmacduagh and Emily: Right Rev. E.F. Darling.

Presbyterian Church Hierarchy

The Church of Ireland has 5 Regional Synods.

General Assembly Moderator: Rt. Rev. Dr. John Ross.
Synod of Armagh and Down: (Including the Presbyteries of Ards, Armagh, Down, Dromore, Iveagh and Newry) Moderator: Rev. D.M. Scott.
Synod of Ballymena & Coleraine: (Including the Presbyteries of Ballymena, Carrickfergus, Coleraine, Route and Templepatrick) Moderator: Rev. Douglas Armstrong.
Synod of Belfast: (Including the Presbyteries of North Belfast, Belfast South and East Belfast) Moderator: Rev. Henry Gray.
Synod of Derry and Omagh: (Including the Presbyteries of Derry and Strabane, Foyle, Omagh and Tyrone) Moderator: Rev. Arthur O'Neill.
Synod of Dublin: the Presbyteries of Donegal, Dublin & Munster and Monaghan) Moderator: Rev. J.H. Hanson.

Methodist Church Hierarchy

In Ireland the Methodist Church is divided into 8 district synods, each headed by a chairman.

President: Rev. C.G. Walpole
CHAIRMEN OF DISTRICTS
Belfast District: Rev. D.J. Kerr.
Down District: Rev. Dr. K.A. Wilson.
Dublin District: Rev. B.D. Griffin.
Enniskillen and Sligo District: Rev. I.D. Henderson.
Londonderry District: Rev. P.A. Good.
Midlands and Southern District: Rev. J.W. Dowse.
North East District: Rev. Dr. T. McKnight.
Portadown District: Rev. P. Kingston.

Boundaries of Catholic Dioceses

PROVINCE OF ARMAGH

Armagh:
Most of Louth and Armagh; part of Tyrone and Derry; small part of Meath.

Meath:
Most of Meath and Westmeath; part of Offaly; small parts of Cavan, Longford, Louth, Dublin.

Ardagh & Clonmacnois:
Most of Longford; parts of Leitrim and Offaly; small parts of Westmeath, Roscommon, Cavan, Sligo.

Clogher:
Monaghan; most of Fermanagh; part of Tyrone; small parts of Donegal, Louth and Cavan.

Derry:
Most of Derry; parts of Tyrone and Donegal.

Down and Connor:
Almost all of Antrim; part of Down; small part of Derry.

Dromore:
Part of Down; small parts of Armagh and Antrim.

Kilmore:
Most of Cavan; parts of Leitrim and Fermanagh; small parts of Meath and Sligo.

Raphoe:
Most of Donegal.

PROVINCE OF DUBLIN

Dublin:
Almost the whole of Dublin; most of Wicklow; part of Kildare; small parts of Carlow, Wexford and Laois.

Ferns:
Almost all of Wexford; part of Wicklow.

Kildare & Leighlin:
Almost all of Carlow; parts of Kildare, Laois, Offaly, Kilkenny, Wicklow; small part of Wexford.

Ossory:
Most of Kilkenny; part of Laois; small part of Offaly.

PROVINCE OF CASHEL

Cashel and Emly:
Parts of Tipperary and Limerick.

Cloyne:
Part of Cork.

Cork and Ross:
Cork City and part of Cork county.

Kerry:
All of Kerry, except Kilmurrity, and part of Cork.

Killaloe:
Most of Clare; parts of Tipperary, Offaly, Galway, small parts of Limerick and Laois.

Waterford and Lismore:
Waterford; part of Tipperary; small part of Cork.

Limerick:
Most of Limerick; parts of Clare; small parts of Kerry.

PROVINCE OF TUAM

Tuam:
Parts of Galway, Mayo and small parts of Roscommon.

Achonry:
Parts of Roscommon, Mayo and Sligo.

Clonfert:
Part of Galway; small parts of Roscommon and Offaly.

Elphin:
Most of Roscommon, parts of Sligo and Galway.

Galway and Kilmacduagh:
Parts of Galway and Clare; small part of Cork.

Killala:
Parts of Mayo and Sligo.

CARDINALS OF IRELAND

List of all Irish Cardinals

1866 was the first year Ireland received a residential cardinal, and in the 130 years since nine Irish diocesan bishops have been elected Primate of All-Ireland.

Paul Cullen : Born in 1803, ordained Archbishop of Armagh in 1850 and created Cardinal by Pope Pius IX on 22nd June 1866, died 1878.

Edward McCabe: Born in 1816, ordained Bishop of Gadara and appointed Auxiliary Archbishop of Dublin in 1877, appointed Archbishop of Dublin in 1879 and created Cardinal by Pope Leo XIII on 27th March 1882, died 1885.

Michael Logue: Born in 1840, ordained Bishop of Raphoe in 1879, appointed Archbishop of Armagh in 1887 and created Cardinal by Pope Leo XIII on 16th January 1893, died 1924.

Patrick O'Donnell: Born in 1856, ordained Bishop of Raphoe in 1888, appointed Archbishop of Armagh in 1924 and created Cardinal by Pope Pius XI on 14th December 1925, died 1927.

Joseph McRory: Born 1861, ordained Bishop of Down and Connor in 1915, appointed Archbishop of Armagh in 1928 and created Cardinal by Pope Pius XI on the 12th December 1929, died 1945.

John D'Alton: Born 1882, ordained Bishop of Binda and appointed Co-adjutor to Bishop of Meath in 1942, appointed Bishop of Meath in 1943, appointed Archbishop of Armagh in 1946 and created Cardinal by Pope Pius XII on 12th January 1953, died 1963.

William Conway: Born 1913, ordained Bishop of Neve and appointed Auxiliary Archbishop of Armagh in 1958, appointed Archbishop of Armagh in 1963, created Cardinal by Pope Paul VI on 22nd February 1965, died 1977.

Tomás Ó Fiaich: Born 1923, ordained Archbishop of Armagh in 1977 and created Cardinal by Pope John Paul II on the 30th June 1979, died 1990.

Cahal Daly: The present Archbishop of Armagh and ninth Irish Cardinal is His Eminence, Most Rev. Cahal Brendan Daly DD.

MEMBERSHIP OF MAIN IRISH CHURCHES

Irish Churches Membership

Religion	Members (000)		Ministers		Churches	
	1985	1993	1985	1993	1985	1993
Catholic	3,341,949	3,241,566	3,950	4,281	2,626	2,656
Anglican	221,200	220,570	605	514	1,186	1,000
Presbyterian	218,257	217,888	517	531	657	656
Methodist	24,284	22,146	137	141	282	248
Independent	16,627	16,828	86	116	356	402
Baptist	8,921	9,485	109	121	112	127
Pentecostal	5,225	7,630	75	95	80	92
Orthodox	475	522	3	3	3	3
Other Churches	6,157	6,589	95	102	106	110
Total	**3,843,095**	**3,743,224**	**5,577**	**5,904**	**5,408**	**5,294**

Church of Ireland Statistics

Diocese	Churches	No. of Clergy*
Armagh	89	50
Clogher	70	28
Derry & Raphoe	120	50
Down & Dromore	116	89
Connor	119	84
Kilmore etc.	107	22
Tuam etc.	15	9
Dublin & Glendalough	108	56
Meath & Kildare	66	18
Cashel etc.	151	28
Cork etc.	77	23
Limerick etc	68	14

*Clergy figures do not include the Archbishop/Bishop of each diocese or a number of auxiliary non-stipendiary clergy in each diocese.

Presbyterian Church in Ireland

Synod	Presbyteries	Congregations	Ministers
Armagh & Down	6	162	186
Ballymena & Coleraine	5	118	155
Belfast	3	71	139
Derry & Omagh	4	117	96
Dublin	3	89	63

Methodist Church in Ireland

District	Total Community	Number of Circuits*
Dublin	2,299	8
Midlands & Southern	1,964	10
Enniskillen & Sligo	3,324	9
Londonderry	3,594	6
North East	12,659	8
Belfast	18,480	15
Down	9,876	10
Portadown	7,473	11
Totals	59,669	77

*Circuits are groups of congregations which work together. In all there are are 246 congregations.
There are 199 Methodist ministers.

Catholic Parishes, Churches and Schools, 1995

	Parishes	Catholic Population	Churches	Primary Schools (No.)	Secondary Schools (No.)	Primary Schools Population	Secondary Schools Population
Armagh	61	197,446	150	169	30	28,834	20,715
Dublin	198	1,041,000	238	516	192		
Cashel	46	78,862	87	127	24	12,510	9,930
Tuam	56	116,201	131	240	38	29,433	9,500
Achonry	23	39,000	47	58	14	5,600	3,500
Ardagh	41	71,806	80	91	22	11,256	7,857
Clogher	37	84,286	86	99	20	12,984	8,494
Clonfert	24	32,600	47	51	8	6,800	3,200
Cloyne	46	119,714	106	125	31	17,155	13,176
Cork & Ross	68	215,500	124	186	53	41,000	
Derry	52	210,313	103	142	26		
Down & Connor	86	296,941	151	174	42	39,716	28,439
Dromore	23	63,300	48	51	14	10,874	9,506
Elphin	36	68,000	90	126	20	12,700	8,000
Ferns	49	98,170	101	97	20	17,000	10,000
Galway	40	78,639	71	90	22	12,302	7,399
Kerry	54	125,000	105	170	35		
Kildare & Leighlin	56	169,305	117	173	45	28,218	19,927
Killala	22	37,679	48	78	12	5,677	4,742
Killaloe	59	109,757	133	158	24	17,262	12,246
Kilmore	36	55,520	97	89	16	8,500	5,630
Limerick	60	141,514	97	114	34	22,000	18,500
Meath	69	185,000	149	186	36	30,000	16,000
Ossory	42	73,823	89	91	16	11,706	6,846
Raphoe	31	79,680	71	103	18	11,988	7,400
Waterford & Lismore	45	130,512	85	100	30	20,383	13,151
Estimated Total	**1,360**	**3,919,568**	**2,671**	**3,604**	**842**	**403,108**	**244,158**

Numbers of Catholic Priests and Religious

	Priests active in Diocese	Others	Religious Orders Clerical	Religious Orders Brothers	Sisters
Armagh	166	20	68	50	385
Dublin	603	78	975	505	2,736
Cashel	122	15	57	39	255
Tuam	152	23	28	48	393
Achonry	50	12	3	1	68
Ardagh	82	19	10	10	325
Clogher	93	15	7	5	164
Clonfert	53	15	39	0	176
Cloyne	140	18	6	28	291
Cork & Ross	156	28	166	99	822
Derry	139	16	5	3	168
Down & Connor	227	17	82	54	338
Dromore	67	11	21	9	167
Elphin	88	12	6	5	210
Ferns	118	40	14	16	275
Galway	68	23	49	29	232
Kerry	114	26	14	28	410
Kildare & Leighlin	109	25	91	70	382
Killala	46	16	1	3	82
Killaloe	124	21	26	25	320
Kilmore	95	4	14	0	85
Limerick	132	20	80	42	429
Meath	118	23	130	43	350
Ossory	82	25	23	39	288
Raphoe	76	20	12	7	76
Waterford & Lismore	120	6	149	65	532
Estimated Total	**3,287**	**548**	**2,076**	**1,223**	**9,881**

Active in Diocese includes priests who are active in voluntary, secondary and state schools.
Others are the priests of the diocese who are retired, sick, on study leave or working in other dioceses in Ireland and abroad.

Applicants and Entrants to Catholic Church, 1994

	Applicants	Entrants
Diocesan	193	98
Clerical Religious Orders	130	66
Sisters Orders	63	33
Brothers Orders	18	4
Total Number	**404**	**201**

Percentage of Irish Catholic Missionaries by Continent

Continent	%
Africa	47
Americas	22
Asia	14
Europe	9
India and the Middle East	8
Total Number	**5,571**

Personnel of Catholic Church, 1994

	Number
Sisters Orders	12,973
Clerical Religious Orders	4,437
Diocesan	3,714
Brothers Orders	1,024
Total Number	**22,148**

Nullity of Marriages in the Catholic Church

Year	Applications	Decrees
1987	882	209
1988	926	188
1989	915	212
1990	1,043	216
1991	402	215
1992	444	289
1993	347	282
1994	470	300

SELECTED BIOGRAPHIES OF RELIGIOUS FIGURES

Allen, Rev. Dr. David Henry (b. 1933, Down). Current Moderator of Presbyterian Church in Ireland. Installed as Moderator, June 1996.

Best, Rev. Kenneth President of Methodist Church in Ireland from June 1996 until June 1997. Instrumental in brokering Loyalist ceasefire in 1994.

Casey, Eamon (b. 1927). Former Bishop of Galway. Ordained 1951, in Limerick diocese. Was Bishop of Galway from1976, involved in Third World Charities. High media profile before falling from grace following revelations that he had a teenage son by American Annie Murphy. Now in exile in South America

Comiskey, Brendan (b. 1935). Bishop of Ferns. Educated in Monaghan, Washington D.C., Rome and Maynooth. First came to prominence in Dublin in 1971 as Auxiliary Bishop. In headlines during 1996 due to visit to United States for alcohol rehabilitation.

Connell, Desmond (b. 1926, Dublin). Archbishop of Dublin from 1988. Ordained in Dublin in 1951. Professor of Metaphysics, Dean of Philosophy, UCD, 1953-1988.

Daly, Cahal (b. 1917, Antrim). Roman Catholic Archbishop of Armagh and Primate of All-Ireland from 1990. Educated Belfast, Maynooth and Paris. Ordained in 1941. First Bishop in Longford in 1967. Outspoken on Northern Ireland situation, often drawing criticism from nationalists as well as unionists.

Eames, Dr. Robert (Robin) (b. 1937, Belfast). Church of Ireland Archbishop of Armagh, Primate of All-Ireland and Metropolitan. Moderate commentator on Northern situation.

McMullan, Gordon (b. 1934, Belfast). Ordained Church of Ireland Bishop of Clogher in 1980. Contributor of articles to theological publications.

EDUCATION

INTRODUCTION

Education is taken extremely seriously in Ireland. For the academic year 1993/1994 almost 27% of the population was engaged in full time education while third level institutions awarded almost 14,500 primary degrees and 4,500 post-graduate degrees.

In 1994/95 the British Government provided a block grant of £1.3bn. for the education sector in the North while the total expenditure from public funds on education in the Republic in 1993 was £1.6bn.

In the Republic, the Department of Education is the central administrative body for running the primary, secondary and third level systems. The Catholic Church is also deeply involved in schools, particularly at primary level, but in recent years its influence at secondary level has begun to significantly diminish.

The administrative system in the North is significantly different to that of the South. While the central administration, other than the universities, remains with Department of Education Northern Ireland (DENI) its powers are devolved at local level to five Education and Library Boards. However, a major shake up of these has been sought by the Northern Ireland Office and it is understood that at least one Board is to be abolished.

The Catholic Church is also very much involved in education in the North. In 1990 the Council for Catholic Maintained Schools was established to exercise certain responsibilities in relation to all Catholic maintained schools which are under the auspices of the diocesan authorities and of religious orders. The main objective, however, was to promote high standards in education in its schools.

The running costs of Catholic maintained schools are met in full while capital building costs are grant-aided up to 85 per cent by DENI.

In a country with the highest youth population in Europe competition for university places is extremely high, and each year the points required for third level college entry increase.

LIBRARIES

Public Libraries in Ireland

REPUBLIC OF IRELAND

Carlow County Library
Dublin Street, Carlow.
Cavan County Library
Farnham Street, Cavan.
Clare County Library
Mill Road, Ennis.
Cork Central Library
Grand Parade, Cork.
Cork County Library
Farranlea Road, Cork.
Donegal County Library
Letterkenny, Co. Donegal.
Dublin Public Library
Cumberland Hse., Fenian St., D2.
Dun Laoghaire / Rathdown County Library
Duncairn House, Blackrock.
Fingal County Library
11 Parnell Square, Dublin 2.
Galway County Library
Island Hse., Cathedral Sq., Galway.
Kerry County Library
Moyderwell, Tralee, Co. Kerry.
Kildare County Library
Athgarvan Rd.,, Newbridge, Kildare.
Kilkenny County Library
6 John's Quay, Kilkenny.
Laois County Library
County Hall, Portlaoise, Co. Laois.
Leitrim County Library
Ballinamore, Co. Leitrim.
Limerick City Library

The Granary, Michael St., Limerick.
Limerick County Library
58 O'Connell Street, Limerick.
Longford County Library
Annaly Carpark, Longford.
Louth County Library
Roden Place, Dundalk, Co. Louth.
Mayo County Library
Mountain View, Castlebar, Mayo.
Meath County Library
Railway Street, Navan, Co. Meath.
Monaghan County Library
The Diamond, Clones, Monaghan.
Offaly County Library
O'Connor Square, Tullamore, Offaly.
Roscommon County Library
Abbey Street, Roscommon.
Sligo County Library
The Courthouse, Sligo.
South Dublin County Library
Cumberland Hse., Fenian St., D2.
Tipperary (Joint) County Library
Castle Ave., Thurles, Co. Tipperary.
Waterford County Library
Lismore, Co. Waterford.
Waterford Municipal Library
Lady Lane, Waterford.
Westmeath County Library
Dublin Rd., Mullingar, Westmeath.
Wexford County Library
Abbey Street, Wexford.
Wicklow County Library
St. Fergal's Junior School,

Ballywaltrim, Bray, Co. Wicklow.

NORTHERN IRELAND
The Northern Ireland Education and Library Boards are currently under review (September 1996).

Central Library
1 Royal Avenue, Belfast, Co. Antrim.
Anderstown Branch Library
Slievegallion Drive, Belfast, Antrim.
Ardoyne Branch Library
446 Crumlin Rd., Belfast.
Ballyhackamore Branch Library
1 Eastleigh Drive, Belfast.
Ballymacarrett Branch Library
19 Templemore Avenue, Belfast.
Cairnmartin Branch Library
Cairnmartin Community High Schl., Lyndhurst Gardens, Belfast, Antrim.
Chichester Branch Library
Salisbury Ave., Belfast, Co. Antrim.
Falls Road Branch Library
49 Falls Road, Belfast, Co. Antrim.
Finaghy Branch Library
13 Sth. Finaghy Rd., Belfast, Antrim.
Holywood Road Branch Library
85 Holywood Rd., Belfast, Antrim.
Ligoniel Branch Library
53 Ligoniel Rd., Belfast, Co. Antrim.
Lisburn Road Branch Library
440 Lisburn Rd., Belfast, Co. Antrim.

Oldpark Branch Library
46 Oldpark Rd., Belfast, Antrim.
Ormeau Road Branch Library
Ormeau Rd. Embankment, Belfast.
Sandy Row Branch Library
127 Sandy Row, Belfast, Antrim.
Shankill Road Branch Library
298 Shankill Road, Belfast, Antrim.
Skegoniell Branch Library
Skegoniell Avenue, Belfast, Antrim.
Suffolk Branch Library
57 Stewartstown Road, Belfast.
Whiterock Branch Library
Whiterock Road, Belfast, Co. Antrim.
Whitewell Branch Library
17 Navarra Place, Newtownabbey,
Belfast, Co. Antrim.
Euston Street Library
Euston Street Primary School,
Euston Street, Belfast, Co. Antrim.
Rupert Stanley College Library
19 Templemore Ave., Belfast.
Donegall Road Library
121 Donegall Rd., Belfast, Antrim.

North East Board Area Library
County Hall, Coleraine, Co. Derry.
Demesne Avenue, Ahoghill.
Antrim Branch Library
41 Church Street, Co. Antrim.
Ballee Branch Library
2 Neighbourhood Centre, Ballee,
Ballymena, Co. Antrim.
Ballycastle Branch Library
41A Castle St., Ballycastle, Antrim.
Ballyclare Branch Library
School Street, Ballyclare, Antrim.
Ballymena Branch Library
Demesne Ave., Ballymena, Antrim.
Ballymoney Branch Library
Rodden Foot, Queen Street,
Ballymoney, Co. Antrim.
Bellaghy Branch Library
79 William Street, Bellaghy, Derry.
Broughshane Branch Library
Main Street, Broughshane, Antrim.
Bushmills Branch Library
44 Main St., Bushmills, Co. Antrim.
Carnlough Branch Library
Town Hall, Carnlough, Co. Antrim.
Carrickfergus Branch Library
Joymount Crescent, Carrickfergus,
Co. Antrim.
Castlerock Branch Library
57 Main Street, Castlerock, Derry.
Cloughmills Branch Library
Main Street, Cloughmills, Antrim.
Coleraine Branch Library
Queen Street, Coleraine, Co. Derry.
Crumlin Branch Library
Orchard Road, Crumlin, Co. Antrim.
Cushendall Branch Library
Mill Street, Cushendall, Co. Antrim.
Draperstown Branch Library
High Street, Draperstown, Co. Derry.
Garvagh Branch Library

Bridge Street, Garvagh, Co. Derry.
Glengormley Branch Library
40 Carnmoney Road, Glengormley,
Co. Antrim.
Greenisland Branch Library
17 Glassillan Grove, Whiteabbey,
Co. Antrim.
Greystone Branch Library -
Greystone Road, Antrim, Co. Antrim.
Kilrea Branch Library
52 Maghera Street, Kilrea, Derry.
Larne Branch Library
36 Pound Street, Larne, Co. Antrim.
Magherafelt Branch Library
43 Queen's Avenue, Magherafelt,
Co. Derry.
Maghera Branch Library
1 Main Street, Maghera, Co. Derry.
Monkstown Public Library
Bridge Road, Whiteabbey, Antrim.
Portglenone Branch Library
Townhill Road, Portglenone, Antrim.
Portrush Branch Library
Technical College, Dunluce Street,
Portrush, Co. Antrim.
Portstewart Branch Library
Town Hall, The Crescent,
Portstewart, Co. Derry.
Randalstown Branch Library
34 New Street, Randalstown, Antrim.
Rathcoole Branch Library
2 Rosslea Way, Whiteabbey, Antrim
Templepatrick Branch Library
23 The Village, Templepatrick,
Co. Antrim.
Whitehead Branch Library
17b Edward Rd., Whitehead, Antrim.
Library Headquarters
Demesne Ave., Ballymena, Antrim.

Library Headquarters
Main Street, Ballynahinch, Down.
Ballynahinch Branch Library
Main Street, Ballynahinch, Down.
Bangor Branch Library
Hamilton Road, Bangor, Down.
Belvoir Park Branch Library
Drumart Square, Belfast, Co. Antrim.
Braniel Branch Library
Glen Road, Belfast, Co. Antrim.
Carryduff Branch Library
Church Street, Carryduff, Co. Antrim.
Castlewellan Branch Library
Main Street, Castlewellan, Down.
Comber Branch Library
Newtownards Rd., Comber, Down.
Cregagh Branch Library
409 Cregagh Road, Belfast, Antrim.
Donaghadee Branch Library
Killaughey Rd., Donaghadee, Down.
Downpatrick Branch Library
Market Street, Downpatrick, Down.
Dundonald Branch Library
Church Rd., Dundonald, Co. Antrim.
Dunmurry Branch Library
Upper Dunmurry Lane, Dunmurry,

Co. Antrim.
Gilnahirk Branch Library
Gilnahirk Rise, Belfast, Co. Antrim.
Holywood Branch Library
Sullivan Place, 86 High St.,
Holywood, Belfast, Co. Antrim.
Killyleagh Branch Library
High Street, Killyleagh, Co. Antrim.
Lisburn Branch Library
29 Railway Street, Lisburn, Co.
Antrim.
Mount Oriel Branch Library
Saintfield Road, Belfast, Co. Antrim.
Newcastle Branch Library
Main Street, Newcastle, Co. Down.
Newtownards Branch Library
Regent Street, Newtownards, Down.
Poleglass Branch Library
Good Shepherd Rd., Poleglass,
Belfast, Antrim.
Portaferry Branch Library
High Street, Portaferry, Co. Down.
Saintfield Branch Library
Ballynahinch Road, Saintfield, Down.
Tullycarnet Branch Library
Kinross Avenue, Dundonald, Antrim.
Twinbrook Branch Library
Gardenmore Road, Belfast, Antrim.
Laurelhill Community Library
22 Laurelhill Road, Lisburn, Antrim.

Armagh Branch Library
Market Square, Armagh, Armagh.
Banbridge Branch Library
Scarva Street, Banbridge, Co. Down.
Bessbrook Branch Library
Church Rd, Bessbrook, Co. Armagh.
Brownlow Branch Library
Brownlow Road, Craigavon, Down.
Coalisland Branch Library
The Square, Coalisland, Co. Tyrone.
Crossmaglen Branch Library
The Square, Crossmaglen,
Co. Armagh.
Cookstown Branch Library
Burn Road, Cookstown, Co. Tyrone.
Dromore Branch Library
The Square, Dromore, Co. Down.
Dungannon Branch Library
Market Street, Dungannon, Tyrone.
Fivemiletown Branch Library
Main Street, Fivemiletown, Tyrone.
Gilford Branch Library
Main Street, Gilford, Co. Down.
Keady Branch Library
Market Street, Keady, Co. Armagh.
Kilkeel Branch Library
28 Greencastle St., Kilkeel, Down.
Lurgan Branch Library
Carnegie St., Lurgan, Armagh.
Moneymore Branch Library
8 Main Street, Moneymore, Derry.
Moy Branch Library
The Square, Moy, Co. Armagh.
Newry Public Library
Hill Street, Newry, Co. Down.

Portadown Branch Library
Edward Street, Portadown, Armagh.
Rathfriland Branch Library
John Street, Rathfriland, Co. Down.
Richhill Branch Library
Maynooth Rd., Richhill, Co. Armagh.
Tandragee Branch Library
Market Street, Tandragee, Armagh.
Waringstown Branch Library
1 Banbridge Road, Waringstown,
Co. Down.
Warrenpoint Branch Library
Summer Hill, Warrenpoint, Down.
Divisional Library (Headquarters)
113 Church Street, Craigavon,
Portadown, Co. Down.
Market Square, Dungannon,
Co. Tyrone.

Hill Street, Newry, Co. Down.
Omagh Library
1 Spillars Place, Omagh, Co. Tyrone
Castlederg Branch Library
Main Street, Castlederg, Co. Tyrone.
Central Library & Divisional HQ
35 Foyle Street, Derry
Creggan Branch Library
Central Drive, Creggan Estate, Derry
Divisional HQ (Enniskillen)
Hall's Lane, Enniskillen, Fermanagh
Dungiven Branch Library
25 Main Street, Dungiven, Co. Derry
Fintona Branch Library
112-114 Main Street, Fintona,
Omagh, Tyrone.
Irvinestown Branch Library
Main Street, Irvinestown, Enniskillen,

Co. Fermanagh.
Limavady Branch Library
5 Connell Street, Limavady, Derry.
Lisnaskea Branch Library
Lisnaskea, Enniskillen, Fermanagh.
Newtownstewart Branch Library
Main St., Newtownstewart, Tyrone.
Shantallow Branch Library
92 Racecourse Road, Derry.
Sion Mills Branch Library
The Square, Sion Mills, Strabane,
Co. Tyrone .
Strabane Branch Library
Butcher Street, Strabane, Tyrone.
Strathfoyle Branch Library
Claragh Crescent, Strathfoyle, Derry
Waterside Branch Library
137 Spencer Road, Waterside, Derry

Library Stocks (1993) in the Republic of Ireland

Local Authority County	Books			Non-book Items		
	Total in stock	Number added to stock	Number withdrawn from stock	Total in stock	Number added to stock	Number withdrawn from stock
CONNACHT	**940,979**	**36,951**	**18,455**	**27,059**	**1,079**	**86**
Galway	349,668	13,991	9,070	15,730	400	56
Leitrim	62,607	4,290	2,764	2,947	70	—
Mayo	236,939	8,727	5,115	803	34	—
Roscommon	197,233	4,965	110	6,428	541	22
Sligo	94,532	4,978	1,396	1,151	34	8
LEINSTER	**3,594,787**	**180,898**	**68,198**	**90,596**	**9,064**	**1,693**
Carlow	141,838	4,947	—	1,685	58	—
Dublin	844,552	39,915	23,588	46,527	2,267	1,048
Kildare	353,165	10,790	—	4,030	679	—
Kilkenny	253,963	12,127	10,028	5,146	698	477
Laois	167,812	20,915	3,999	3,501	1,916	5
Longford	87,558	3,753	1,396	1,597	269	25
Louth	227,270	45,512	493	5,897	1,782	25
Meath	281,397	3,554	7,987	2,178	343	60
Offaly	174,580	7,195	8,749	7,994	347	1
Westmeath	436,024	3,835	2,087	3,382		
Wexford	382,728	16,935	4,492	6,785	514	50
Wicklow	243,900	11,420	5,379	1,874	191	2
MUNSTER	**2,983,824**	**100,937**	**27,325**	**21,879**	**1,052**	**42**
Clare	310,160	20,515	11,489	6,618	106	13
Cork	1,068,968	37,740	—	2,389	148	—
Kerry	291,104	5,842	5,153	6,153	47	—
Limerick	698,158	21,601	5,589	2,114	437	12
Tipperary	528,629	13,603	4,263	4,605	314	17
Waterford	86,805	1,636	831	—	—	—
ULSTER (part of)	**534,071**	**19,947**	**8,271**	**7,071**	**591**	**69**
Cavan	116,974	6,317	824	1,821	116	18
Donegal	266,654	7,898	2,345	2,460	445	—
Monaghan	150,443	5,732	5,102	2,790	30	51
Total:	**8,053,661**	**338,733**	**122,249**	**146,605**	**11,786**	**1,890**
Municipal:						
Cork	426,177	7,577	17,356	23,063	965	250
Dublin	2,153,437	74,862	25,983	53,370	3,631	617
Dun Laoghaire	269,537	5,384	2,984	5,507	343	—
Limerick	176,142	6,277	2,662	2,540	93	—
Waterford	71,720	1,003	408	5,569	640	169
Total:	**3,097,013**	**95,103**	**49,393**	**90,049**	**5,672**	**1,036**
TOTAL STATE	**11,150,674**	**433,836**	**171,642**	**236,654**	**17,458**	**2,926**

Republic of Ireland RTC's and Colleges of Further Education

REGIONAL TECHNICAL COLLEGES

Athlone RTC
Dublin Road, Athlone, Westmeath.
Carlow RTC
Kilkenny Road, Carlow.
Cork RTC
Rossa Avenue, Bishopstown, Cork.
Dundalk RTC
Dundalk, Co. Louth.
Galway RTC
Dublin Road, Galway.
Letterkenny RTC
Port Road, Letterkenny, Donegal.
Limerick RTC
Moylish Park, Limerick.
Sligo RTC
Ballinode, Sligo.
Tallaght RTC
Tallaght, Dublin 24.
Tralee RTC
Clash, Tralee, Kerry.
Waterford RTC
Cork Road, Waterford.

COLLEGES OF EDUCATION

The Church of Ireland College of Education
96 Upper Rathmines Road, Dublin 6.
Froebel CoE
Mary Immaculate College of Education
South Circular Road, Limerick.
Mater Dei Institute of Education
Clonliffe Road, Dublin 3.
Sr. Angela's College of Education for Home Economics
Lough Gill, Co. Sligo.
St. Catherine's College of Education for Home Economics
Sion Hill, Blackrock, Co. Dublin.
St. Mary's College of Education
Griffith Avenue, Marino, Dublin 9.
St. Patrick's College of Education
Drumcondra, Dublin 9.
Dublin Institute of Technology
Fitzwilliam House, 30 Upper Pembroke Street, Dublin 2.

CONSTITUENT COLLEGES (DUBLIN INSTITUTE OF TECHNOLOGY)

Dublin Institute of Technology
Bolton Street, Dublin 1.
Dublin Institute of Technology
Kevin Street, Dublin 8.
Dublin Institute of Technology
Cathal Brugha Street, Dublin 1.
Dublin Institute of Technology
Mountjoy Square, 40-45 Mountjoy Square, Dublin 1.
Dublin Institute of Technology
Aungier Street, Dublin 2.

Dublin Institute of Technology
Adelaide Road, Dublin 2.

OTHER COLLEGES

Cork School of Music
13 Union Quay, Cork.
Crawford School of Art & Design
Sharman Crawford Street, Cork.
Dún Laoghaire College of Art and Design
Carriglea Park, Kill Avenue, Dún Laoghaire, Co. Dublin.
National College of Art and Design
100 Thomas Street, Dublin 8.
Royal College of Surgeons in Ireland
123 St. Stephen's Green, Dublin 2.
National College of Industrial Relations
Sandford Road, Dublin 6.
Garda Síochána College
Templemore, Co. Tipperary.
Institute of Public Administration
Lansdowne Road, Dublin 4.
Irish Management Institute
Sandyford, Dublin 16.
Military College
Curragh Camp, Co. Kildare.
All Hallows College
Grace Park Road, Dublin 9.
Burren College of Art
Newtown Castle, Ballyvaughan, Co. Clare.
Clonliffe (Holy Cross) College
Drumcondra, Dublin 3.
Holy Ghost College
Kimmage Manor, Dublin 12.
HSI College
The Crescent, Limerick.
Mid West Business Institute
Rutland Street, Limerick.
Milltown Institute of Theology and Philosophy
Milltown Park, Dublin 6.
Skerry's College
Wellington House, 9/11 Patrick's Hill, Cork City.
Shannon College of Hotel Management
Shannon Airport, Co. Clare.
The American College Dublin
2 Merrion Square, Dublin 2.
Accountancy and Business College (Ireland) Ltd.
ABC House, Little Longford Street, Dublin 2.
Griffith College - South Circular Road, Dublin 8.
LSB College Ltd.
Balfe Hse., 6-9 Balfe St., Dublin 2.
The Institute of Education, Business College
Portobello House, South Richmond Street, Dublin 2.

St. Patrick's College
Carlow.
St. Patrick's College
Thurles, Co. Tipperary.
St. Peter's College
Wexford.
St. John's College
John's Hill, Waterford.
Hotel Training College
Killybegs, Co. Donegal.

NORTHERN IRELAND

Armagh College of Further Education
Lonsdale Street, Armagh, Armagh
Belfast Institute of Further and Higher Education
Park House, Great Victoria Street, Belfast, Co. Antrim.
Causeway Institute of Further and Higher Education
Union Street, Coleraine, Co. Derry.
East Antrim Institute of Further and Higher Education
400 Shore Road, Newtownabbey, Co. Antrim.
East Down Institute of Further and Higher Education
Market Street, Downpatrick, Down.
Fermanagh College of Further Education
Fairview Avenue, 1 Dublin Road, Enniskillen, Co. Fermanagh.
Limavady College of Further Education
Main Street, Limavady, Co. Derry.
Lisburn College of Further Education
Castle Street, Lisburn, Co. Antrim
Newry and Kilkeel College of Further Education
Patrick Street, Newry, Co. Down
North East Institute of Further and Higher Education
Farm Lodge Avenue, Ballymena, Co. Antrim.
North Down and Ards Institute of Further and Higher Education
Castle Park Road, Bangor, Down.
North West institute of Further and Higher Education
Strand Road, Derry.
North West Institute of Further and Higher Education
(Strabane Centre)
Derry Road, Strabane, Co. Tyrone
NI Hotel and Catering College
Ballywillan Road, Portrush, Antrim.
Omagh College of Further Education
Mountjoy Road, Omagh, Co. Tyrone.
Upper Bann Institute of Further and Higher Education
(Portadown Campus), Lurgan Road, Portadown, Co. Armagh.

STUDENTS

Student Enrolment (1992-93)
Number of Students receiving full-time education in the Republic of Ireland

School / College	All Persons	Male	Female
TOTAL:	**976,181**	**494,144**	**482,037**
FIRST LEVEL:	**529,811**	**272,744**	**257,067**
Aided by Dept. of Education:			
National Schools:	521,531	268,449	253,082
Ordinary Classes	510,012	261,637	248,375
Special Schools	8,084	4,977	3,107
Special Classes	3,435	1,835	1,600
Non-Aided:			
Private Primary Schools	8,280	4,295	3,985
SECOND LEVEL:	**362,230**	**178,383**	**183,847**
Aided by Dept. of Education:			
Junior Cycle:	207,904	105,556	102,348
Secondary	132,150	59,823	72,327
Community & Comprehensive	27,924	15,636	12,288
Vocational	47,830	30,097	17,733
Senior Cycle (General)	128,777	62,884	65,893
Secondary	86,963	39,163	47,800
Community & Comprehensive	15,425	8,200	7,225
Vocational	26,358	15,518	10,840
Preparatory Colleges	31	3	28
Senior Cycle (Vocational)	21,728	7,813	13,915
Secondary	2,054	653	1,401
Community & Comprehensive	1,828	722	1,106
Vocational	17,846	6,438	11,408
Other Courses:	577	228	349
Regional Technical Colleges	577	228	349
Technology Colleges	-	-	-
Aided by other Departments:			
Agriculture / Defence	1,541	1,337	204
Non-Aided:			
Commercial	1,703	565	1,138
THIRD LEVEL: Aided by Dept. of Education:	84,140	43,017	41,123
HEA Institutions	48,124	22,933	25,191
Universities	46,540	22,164	24,376
Other HEA Institutions	1,584	769	815
Teacher Training	728	62	666
Primary	523	61	462
Home Economics	205	1	204
Vocational Technological	32,198	18,395	13,803
Regional Technical Colleges	22,364	12,990	9,374
Other Vocational Technological	9,834	5,405	4,429
Aided by Dept. of Defence:	63	53	10
Non-Aided:	3,027	1,574	1,453
Religious Institutions	915	574	341
Other	2,112	1,000	1,112

Students receiving full-time and part-time education in Northern Ireland

Particulars	1988-89	1989-90	1990-91	1991-92	1992-93	1993-94
GRAND TOTAL	412,428	414,371	357,303	441,324	450,930	452,694
Primary (incl. nursery) & Special Schools	192,895	194,493	194,813	195,094	196,154	196,511
Pupils on rolls:						
Primary	189,109	190,620	190,830	190,988	191,941	192,119
Special	3,786	3,873	3,983	4,106	4,213	4,392
Secondary Schools:	146,849	144,692	144,810	146,968	149,165	151,921
Pupils on rolls:						
Secondary	89,968	87,814	86,667	87,525	88,005	89,167
Grammar	56,881	56,878	58,143	59,443	61,160	62,754
Grant Aided Institutions of Further Education: (1)	56,708	58,684		80,021	84,808	81,523
Full-time	15,619	17,062		21,437	22,531	23,125
Part-time	41,089	41,622		58,584	62,277	58,398
Universities:	15,976	16,502	17,680	19,241	20,803	22,739
Full-time Students:						
Male	8,205	8,351	8,805	9,556	10,187	11,095
Female	7,771	8,151	8,875	9,685	10,616	11,644

(1) Excluding Ulster Polytechnic.

Attendance of National Schools in Republic of Ireland

Description	1991-92	1992-93	1993-94
TOTAL PUPILS	534,269	521,531	505,883
Number of Pupils not classified by standard:	11,472	11,519	11,561
Special Schools	8,163	8,084	8,059
Special Classes	3,309	3,435	3,502
Pupils on rolls according to standards:	522,797	510,012	494,322
Infants standards	123,378	120,224	114,711
First standard	61,190	60,350	59,617
Second standard	63,334	61,310	60,369
Third standard	66,367	63,081	61,188
Fourth standard	67,975	66,337	63,000
Fifth standard	69,711	68,049	66,676
Sixth standard	70,043	68,461	66,663
Other standards	799	2,200	2,098

Attendance at Secondary Schools in Republic of Ireland

Category	1991-92	1992-93	1993-94
TOTAL PUPILS ATTENDING:	348,917	358,347	367,645
Secondary Schools	216,740	221,167	224,035
Vocational Schools	88,655	92,003	94,760
Community Schools	34,546	35,959	39,487
Comprehensive Schools	8,976	9,218	9,363

Students receiving Higher Education in the Republic of Ireland

Type of Institution	Number of Students (1991-1992)		
	Male	Female	Total
Universities	20,583	22,029	42,612
Teacher Training: - Primary	105	734	839
Teacher Training: - Home Economics	1	220	221
Vocational Technological Colleges	6,640	5,105	11,745
Regional Technical Colleges	10,522	7,381	17,903
Other Institutions	1,876	2,012	3,888
Total	**39,727**	**37,481**	**77,208**
TOTAL, Less Students enrolled in more than one College	**39,694**	**37,115**	**76,809**

GRADUATION AND DROPOUT STATISTICS

Republic of Ireland:
Stage at which Leavers with no formal Qualifications left School (1995)

Year	Male	Female	Total
Estimated Number in Category	**1,400**	**800**	**2,100**
First Year Post-primary	17.2 %	16.8 %	17.0 %
Second Year	47.7 %	51.6 %	49.1 %
Third Year	32.8 %	28.4 %	31.2 %
Other	2.3 %	3.2 %	2.7 %

Republic of Ireland:
Economic Status of Second Level School Leavers, 1995.

Status	Male	Female	Total
Estimated Number in Category	**34,400**	**33,100**	**67,500**
Employed	43.6 %	37.0 %	40.4 %
Unemployed after loss of job	4.5 %	4.5 %	4.5 %
(of which on schemes)	(1.0 %)	(0.4 %)	(0.7 %)
Unemployed seeking first job	10.4 %	9.3 %	9.9 %
(of which on schemes)	(3.1 %)	(1.9 %)	(2.5 %)
Student (third level)	39.3 %	44.6 %	41.9 %
Unavailable for work	1.4 %	2.4 %	1.9 %
Emigrated	0.6 %	2.1 %	1.4 %
Total:	**100 %**	**100 %**	**100 %**

Republic of Ireland:
First Destination of all Sub-Degree Respondents

First Destination (1994)	Male	Female	Totals
TOTALS:	**3,453**	**3,019**	**6,472**
Further Studies - Ireland	1,641	1,327	2,968
Further Studies - Overseas	214	129	343
Work Experience - Ireland	110	112	222
Seeking employment - Ireland	181	155	336
Not available - Ireland	30	35	65
Gained Employment Full Time:			
- Ireland	1,105	1,035	2,140
- Overseas	98	133	231
Gained Employment Part Time:			
- Ireland	73	87	160
- Overseas	1	6	7

Number of Schools and Colleges in the Republic of Ireland

Description	1991-92	1992-93	1993-94
TOTAL: ALL LEVELS	4,287	4,268	4,262
First Level: Total	3,425	3,405	3,391
Aided by Dept. of Education:			
National Schools (ordinary)	3,224	3,209	3,202
Special Schools	117	117	115
Non-Aided:			
Private Primary Schools	84	79	74
Second Level: Total	825	823	820
Aided by Dept. of Education:			
Secondary Schools	474	467	461
Vocational Schools	249	248	248
Community Schools	52	54	57
Comprehensive Schools	16	16	16
Other (Horology & Preparatory Colleges)	2	2	2
Schools and Colleges aided by other Departments	17	17	17
Non-Aided Schools and Colleges	15	19	19
Third Level: Total:	37	40	51
Aided by Dept. of Education:			
Universities	4	4	7
Other H.E.A. Institutions	2	3	3
Teacher Training			
- Primary	5	4	3
- Domestic Science	2	2	2
Regional Technical Colleges	9	11	11
Other (including Dublin Institute of Technology)			4
Schools & Colleges aided by other Departments	1	1	2
Non-Aided:			
Miscellaneous Schools & Colleges	14	15	19

Northern Ireland: Number of Primary and Secondary Schools

Particulars	1988-89	1989-90	1990-91	1991-92	1992-93	1993-94
Primary (incl. nursery) and Special Schools	1,109	1,104	1,104	1,098	1,091	1,086
Total: Secondary Schools	245	240	239	236	234	232
Secondary	174	170	169	166	164	161
Grammar	71	70	70	70	70	71

TEACHERS

Republic of Ireland: Teachers employed in National Schools

Description	1993			1994		
	Total	Males	Females	Total	Males	Females
TOTAL	20,761	4,828	15,933	20,776	4,770	16,006
Qualified Teachers	20,744	4,828	15.916	20,751	4,767	15,984
Temporary Unqualified Teachers	17	-	17	25	3	22

Teachers employed in Second Level Education in Republic of Ireland

Category	1990-91	1991-92	1992-93	1993-94
TOTAL	20,223	21,038	21,885	22,457
Secondary: Total	11,550	12,034	12,474	12,784
- Full-time	11,550	11,895	12,250	12,514
- Part-time	-	139	224	270
Vocational: Total	6,129	6,383	6,676	6,542
- Full-time	4,836	4,912	5,005	5,126
- Part-time	1,293	1,471	1,671	1,416
Community/Comprehensive: Total	2,544	2,621	2,735	3,131
- Full-time	2,458	2,477	2,552	2,715
- Part-time	86	144	183	416

Republic of Ireland:
Number of Teachers Employed in Third Level Education

(Full-time) Description	1992-93			1993-94		
	R.T.C.'s	Other	Total	R.T.C.'s	Other	Total
TOTAL	1,480	695	2,175	1,562	693	2,255
College Teacher	79	45	124	82	44	126
Lecturer Scale I	810	317	1,127	843	308	1151
Lecturer Scale II	458	249	707	509	262	771
Senior Lecturer Scale I	76	53	129	72	50	122
Senior Lecturer Scale II	44	26	70	43	22	65
Principal	13	5	18	13	6	19
Others	-	-	-		1	1

Northern Ireland: Teachers employed Full-time in Primary, Secondary and Third Level Education

Particulars	1988-89	1989-90	1990-91	1991-92	1992-93	1993-94
TOTAL: ALL TEACHERS	22,256	22,277	22,438	22,378	22,770	23,003
Primary (incl. nursery) and Special Schools: Full-Time Teachers	8,437	8,527	8,634	8,722	8,924	9,022
Secondary Schools:Total:	9,596	9,498	9,539	9,422	9,586	9,735
Full-time Teachers:						
Secondary	6,200	6,072	6,052	5,935	6,013	6,024
Grammar	3,396	3,426	3,487	3,487	3,573	3,711
Grant-Aided Institutions of Further Education: Full-time Teachers	2,448	2,448	2,381	2,304	2,268	2,209
Universities: Total	1,775	1,804	1,884	1,930	1,992	2,037
Full-time Teaching Staff:						
Professors	162	163	167	186	201	216
Readers & Senior Lecturers	467	476	486	495	516	525
Lecturers, Assistant Lecturers, Demonstrators & Others	1,146	1,165	1,231	1,249	1,275	1,296

UNIVERSITIES

Universities in Ireland, North and South

REPUBLIC OF IRELAND
National University of Ireland
49 Merrion Square, Dublin 2.

CONSTITUENT COLLEGES
(National University of Ireland)
University College Dublin
Bellfield, Dublin 4.
Year Founded: 1854.
University College Galway
Galway.
Year Founded: 1845.
University College Cork
Cork.
Year Founded: 1845.

RECOGNISED COLLEGE
St. Patrick's College
Maynooth, Co. Kildare.
Year Founded: 1795.
University of Dublin, Trinity
College - Dublin 2.
Year Founded: 1592.
Dublin City University
Glasnevin, Dublin 9.
University of Limerick
Plassey Technological Pk., Limerick.

NORTHERN IRELAND
Queens University
Belfast, Co. Antrim BT7 1NN.

Year Founded: 1845.
University of Ulster at Belfast
York Street, Belfast, Co. Antrim
BT15 1ED. Year Founded: 1968.
University of Ulster at
Jordanstown
Shore Road, Newtownabbey,
Co. Antrim BT37 0QB.
Year Founded: 1968.
University of Ulster at Coleraine -
Cromore Road, Coleraine, Co. Derry
BT52 1SA. Year Founded: 1968.
University of Ulster, Magee
College
Northland Road, Derry, BT48 7JL.

University of Ulster: Northern Ireland
Total Student Population by Campus 1984/85 and 1994/95

	Belfast		Coleraine		Jordanstown		Magee College		Total	
	1984/85	1994/95	1984/85	1994/95	1984/85	1994/95	1984/85	1994/95	1984/85	1994/95
Full-time	380	849	2148	4180	4758	6077	172	1438	7458	12544
Part-time	177	38	283	625	2910	4324	354	1067	3724	6054
Total	557	887	2431	4805	7668	10401	526	2505	11182	18598

University of Ulster: Total Student Population by Faculty

Faculty	Full-Time	Part-Time	Total
Art and Design	895	38	933
Business and Management	2852	2069	4921
Engineering	1674	490	2164
Humanities	1779	235	2014
Informatics	1119	414	1533
Science	1433	301	1734
Social Health Services & Education	2735	1875	4610
Ulster Business School	57	632	689
Total	**12544**	**6054**	**18598**

Higher Education: Full Time Student Numbers in Republic of Ireland

Institution	1986/87	1987/88	1988/89	1989/90	1990/91	1991/92
University College Dublin	9339	9507	9904	10429	10706	12083
University College Cork	5560	5738	6108	6393	6777	7451
University College Galway	4298	4179	4219	4377	4913	5312
Trinity College Dublin	6555	6813	6945	7165	7625	8043
St. Patrick's College, Maynooth	1520	1706	1751	1877	2224	2571
Dublin City University	2090	2197	2530	2607	2679	2921
University of Limerick	2484	2623	2813	3084	3425	4251
National College of Art & Design	531	551	563	610	636	624
Thomond College of Education	656	674	562	494	391	0
Royal College of Surgeons in Ireland	863	872	884	885	893	904
TOTALS	**33896**	**34860**	**36279**	**37921**	**40269**	**44160**

The Higher Education Authority: Republic of Ireland
Student Numbers by Field of Study, 1991/92

Field of Study	Full-Time	Part-Time
Arts	13240	1737
Education	1703	508
Art & Design	581	1
Business, Economics & Social Studies	1057	151
Equestrian	10	-
European Studies	795	64
Social Science	592	40
Communications & Information Studies	894	87
Commerce	6054	1959
Law	1201	321
Science	6897	359
Engineering	5375	1291
Architecture	252	5
Medicine	3645	341
Dentistry	455	12
Veterinary Medicine	329	11
Agricultural Science & Forestry	649	13
Food Science & Technology	431	1
TOTALS	**44160**	**6901**

Qualifications of Northern Ireland School Leavers

	1990/1991	1991/1992	1992/1993	1993/1994
Males:	**12,080**	**12,034**	**11,320**	**11,955**
≥2 'A' levels	2,999	3,051	3,023	3,150
1 'A' level	380	321	318	339
≥ 5 GCSE higher grades	1,409	1,417	1,459	1,652
1-4 GCSE higher grades	2,989	3,146	3,255	3,356
Low grades	2,362	2,327	2,239	2,478
No GCSE/GCE qualifications	1,941	1,772	1,026	980
Females:	**11,613**	**11,447**	**10,996**	**11,400**
≥2 'A' levels	3,633	3,760	3,778	3,943
1 'A' level	497	431	397	410
≥ 5 GCSE higher grades	1,668	1,716	1,867	1,950
1-4 GCSE higher grades	2,910	2,943	2,829	3,006
Low grades	1,766	1,621	1,530	1,601
No GCSE/GCE qualifications	1,139	976	595	490
All School leavers:	**23,693**	**22,326**	**22,316**	**23,355**
≥2 'A' levels	6,632	6,811	6,801	7,093
1 'A' level	877	752	715	749
≥ 5 GCSE higher grades	3,077	3,133	3,326	3,602
1-4 GCSE higher grades	5,899	6,089	6,084	6,362
Low grades	4,128	3,948	3,769	4,079
No GCSE/GCE qualifications	3,080	2,748	1,621	1,470

University Degrees and Diplomas obtained in Northern Ireland

	1990/1991	1991/1992	1992/1993
First Degrees - honours	3,448	3,621	4,013
First Degrees - ordinary	499	593	406
Higher Degrees	1,070	1,290	1,548
All Degrees	5,017	5,504	5,967
Diplomas, Certs & other Qualifications	2,551	2,766	2,929

HEALTH

INTRODUCTION

The provision of a comprehensive health service for both parts of the island of Ireland is costly: in 1994, the total non capital expenditure in the Republic on health programmes and services was £1,097,451,000 while in the North public expenditure on "Health and Personal Social Services", for the year 1993/1994, was £1.3bn.

The health service is also a major contributor to the economy providing employment for almost 45,000 people in the Republic and 30,000 in North.

The ever increasing costs of the provision of services has resulted in major, and controversial, changes in the way health services have been provided. In Northern Ireland, the radical shake-up has seen the establishment of "Trust Status" hospitals which "purchase" services provided by the Health Boards, fund-holding G.P.'s. who administer the financial side of their own practices, and Competitive Compulsory Tendering for major hospital services such as catering where the service is privatised and awarded to the firm which meets an agreed criteria.

In the Republic, the structures have not changed so publicly but much of the day- to -day practice has. It is now illegal for a hospital to over-spend its budget. In addition, monitoring of hospital cost efficiencies, entitled the "Case-Mix" approach, was introduced in 1993 in an attempt to bring uniformity to the cost of care and treatment in hospitals which were deemed to have the same level of medical/ surgical activity.

The most major change in the psychiatric service in the Republic is that care in the community has replaced institutional care. The net result of this is that many of the old psychiatric hospitals are now virtually empty.

Health Boards

REPUBLIC OF IRELAND

Eastern Health Board - *Dublin City and County,* *Co. Kildare & Co. Wicklow.* Dr. Steeven's Hospital, John's Road, Dublin 8.

Midland Health Board - *Co. Laois, Co. Longford,* *Co. Offaly & Co. Westmeath.* Arden Road, Tullamore, Co. Offaly.

Mid-Western Health Board - *Co. Clare, Limerick City and County & Co. Tipperary (N.R).* 31/33 Catherine St., Limerick.

North Western Health Board - *Co. Donegal,* *Co. Leitrim & Co. Sligo.* Manorhamilton, Co. Leitrim.

South Eastern Health Board - *Co. Carlow, Co. Kilkenny, Co. Tipperary (S.R), Co. Waterford & Co. Wexford.* Lacken, Dublin Road, Kilkenny.

Southern Health Board - *Cork City and County & Co. Kerry.* Cork Farm Centre, Dennehy's Cross, Cork.

Western Health Board - *Co. Galway, Co. Mayo & Co. Roscommon.* Merlin Park Regional Hospital, Galway.

North Eastern Health Board - *Co. Cavan, Co. Louth, Co. Meath & Co. Monaghan.* Navan Road, Kells, Co. Meath.

NORTHERN IRELAND

Eastern Health & Social Services Board Linenhall Street, Belfast.

Northern Health & Social Services Board County Hall, Ballymena, Co. Antrim.

Southern Health & Social Services Board 20 Seagoe Industrial Area, Portadown, Co. Armagh.

Western Health & Social Services Board 15 Gransha Park, Campsie, Co. Derry.

HOSPITALS

Republic of Ireland:
Persons employed in Health Services, 1991

Occupation	Persons	Males	Females
Hospital & ward orderlies, hospital porters & attendants	11,215	3,340	7,875
Medical practitioners	6,418	4,434	1,984
Health inspectors, cardiographers, nutritionists, etc.	415	100	315
Nurses	34,863	2,963	31,900
Opticians, therapists, chiropodists, medical X-Ray personnel, etc.	3,088	540	2,548
TOTAL:	**55,999**	**11,377**	**44,622**

Northern Ireland: Persons employed in Health Services, 1991

Occupation	Persons	Males	Females
Health Professionals	5,141	3,457	1,684
Health Associate Professionals	20,081	1,916	18,165
Health and Related Occupations	11,792	1,489	10,303
TOTAL:	**37,014**	**6,862**	**30,152**

Publicly funded hospitals in the Republic of Ireland

(1993) Health Board Area	Number of Hospitals	Average no. of in-patient beds available	Patients discharged	Average number of day beds available	Average length of stay in days	Day Cases
Eastern	25	4,937	194,094	312	7.5	117,485
North-Eastern	5	964	39,630	12	6.6	5,984
South-Eastern	7	1,045	52,136	37	5.9	9,282
Western	5	1,208	55,999	26	6.7	8,762
Mid-Western	6	757	39,210	47	6.4	10,614
North-Western	3	658	33,381	15	5.4	12,698
Midland	3	485	24,902	24	5.6	4,804
Southern	9	1,755	82,705	43	6.3	17,213
TOTALS	**63**	**11,809**	**522,057**	**516**	**6.3**	**186,842**

Note: District Hospitals are not included in this table

Northern Ireland: Average Number of Beds Available, 1994

Provider	Available Beds
Trust Hospitals	3,797
Eastern Board	2,075
Southern Board	1,327
Northern Board	1,821
Western Board	1,858

TOTAL: (Average Beds available in wards open overnight) 10,878

Northern Ireland: Available Beds by Care Programme, 1994/95

Programme of Care	Available Beds
Acute Service	4,633
Maternity & Child Health	1,015
Elderly Care	2,354
Mental Health	1,489
Learning Disability	860

MORTALITY RATES

Deaths classified by cause in the Republic of Ireland (per 100,000), 1991-1994

Cause of Death	Number of Deaths				Death rates per 100,000			
	1991	1992(1)	1993(1)	1994(1)	1991	1992 (1)	1993(1)	1994(1)
Infectious and Parasitic diseases:	185	170	159	171	5.2	4.8	4.5	4.8
Malignant neoplasms:	7,262	7,494	7,538	7,343	205.9	211.2	211.5	205.6
Diseases of the circulatory system:	14,208	13,959	14,226	14,002	403.0	393.4	399.2	392.1
Injury and Poisoning:	1,431	1,368	1,372	1,304	37.0	38.6	38.5	36.5
Accidents & adverse effects:	1,049	1,000	1,012	919	29.8	28.2	28.4	25.7
TOTAL DEATHS	**31,305**	**30,780**	**31,656**	**30,744**	**894.0**	**867.5**	**888.4**	**861.0**

(1) Provisional.

Deaths classified by cause in Northern Ireland, 1992-1993

Causes of Death	Number of Deaths 1992	Number of Death 1993
Infectious and Parasitic diseases	41	55
Malignant neoplasms	3,554	3,624
Diseases of blood	145	185
Diseases of the nervous system	233	245
Heart disease	5,077	5,038
Diseases of the circulatory system	2,035	2,099
Diseases of the respiratory system	2,423	2,756
All other accidents and adverse effects	1,480	1,631
TOTAL DEATHS	**14,988**	**15,633**

Infant Mortality in the Republic of Ireland, 1988-1994

Description	1988	1989	1990	(Per 1,000 births) 1991(1)	1992(1)	1993(1)	1994(1)
Infant Mortality (i.e. deaths under one year of age)							
Ireland	9	8	8	8	7	6	6
County Boroughs	12	8	8	8	7	8	7
Dun Laoghaire, Rathdown, Municipal Boroughs and Urban Districts	8	8	8	8	8	5	6
Rural Districts	9	8	8	7	6	6	5
Neo-natal Mortality (i.e. deaths under 4 weeks of age):							
Ireland	5	5	5	5	4	4	4
County Boroughs	7	5	5	5	5	5	5
Dun Laoghaire, Rathdown, Municipal Boroughs and Urban Districts	4	4	5	5	5	4	4
Rural Districts	5	5	5	5	4	4	4

(1) Provisional.

Infant Mortality in Northern Ireland, 1988-1993

Description	1988	1989	1990	1991	1992	1993
Numbers:						
Deaths of infants under 1 year of age	248	180	198	194	153	176
Deaths of infants under 4 weeks of age	149	104	106	121	104	123
Rates:						
Deaths of infants under 1 year of age	8.9	6.9	7.5	7.4	6.0	7.1
Deaths of infants under 4 weeks of age	5.4	4.0	4.0	4.6	4.1	4.9

HEALTH SERVICE EMPLOYMENT & BUDGETS

Numbers employed in public health services in the Republic of Ireland

(1993) Health sector	Management - administration	Medical - dental	Nursing	Para- medical	Support services	Maintenance technical	Total
Health Boards:							
Eastern	1,192	535	3,151	681	2,486	257	8,303
Midland	298	172	1,232	191	1,035	83	3,010
Mid-Western	510	253	1,729	248	934	159	3,833
North-Eastern	348	176	1,277	153	1,146	61	3,161
North-Western	526	223	1,570	291	1,307	11	4,027
South-Eastern	550	320	2,277	272	1,431	127	4,977
Southern	740	461	2,905	407	1,724	219	6,455
Western	647	400	2,544	372	1,794	187	5,944
Total: Health Boards	**4,811**	**2,540**	**16,685**	**2,615**	**11,857**	**1,104**	**39,710**
Voluntary/Joint Board Hospitals	1,989	1,722	7,728	1,641	3,370	384	16,835
Mental Handicap Homes	443	45	1,890	371	2,416	100	5,264
GRAND TOTAL:	**7,243**	**4,307**	**26,303**	**4,627**	**17,643**	**1,588**	**61,809**

Source: Department of Health.

R.O.I. Capital expenditure allocated between health boards and voluntary bodies

1993 Programme (£m)	Voluntary boards	Health boards	Total
Community Health Services (incl. health centres)	-	1,127	1,127
Community welfare services (incl. welfare homes, child welfare (Task force), family aid)	-	105	105
Psychiatric services	928	1,974	2,902
Services for the Handicapped (incl. mental/ physical handicap, rehabilitation, deaf /blind)	1,333	693	2,026
General Hospital Services (incl. general, district, maternity, children's and orthopaedic hospitals, and county homes)	13,540	18,590	32,130
TOTAL:	**15,801**	**22,489**	**38,290**

Non-capital expenditure by programme in Republic of Ireland

Programme and Service	Expenditure (£ 000)		
	1991	1992	1993
Community Protection Programme	26,210	32,011	36,631
Community Health Service Programme	260,780	303,385	343,142
Community Welfare Programme	140,500(1)	157,590(1)	177,616(1)
Psychiatric Programme	183,390	197,253	209,381
Programme for the Handicapped	164,920	181,793	202,203
General Hospital Programme	897,060	993,821	1,097,451
General Support Programme	79,140	90,430	94,144
Gross Non-capital Total: All Programmes	1,752,000	1,956,283	2,160,568
Income (2)	121,000	126,600	143,966
Net Non-capital Total: All Programmes	1,631,000	1,829,683	2,016,602

(1) Incudes funds from the National Lottery
(2) Includes deductions from pay for emoluments and superannuation, retentions from pensions, other receipts such as canteen,
payments for agency services (health inspectors' etc.) and investment income (voluntary hospitals and homes).

R.O.I. Sources of funds for statutory non-capital health services, 1991-1993

Sources	£m		
	1991	1992	1993
Exchequer	1,441.7	1,604.2	1,767.1
Health Contributions etc.	147.4	175.0	193.4
Receipts under EC Regulations	41.9	50.5	56.1
Minor Income of Agencies	121.0	126.6	144.0
TOTAL	**1,752.0**	**1,956.3**	**2,160.6**

ACCIDENTS

Republic of Ireland: Number of Factories Accidents notified

Description	1990	1991	1992	1993	1994
Fatal Accidents	12	22	30	30	23
Non-Fatal Accidents	3,123	2,779	2,598	2,888	3,353
TOTAL:	**3,135**	**2,801**	**2,628**	**2,918**	**3,376**

Number of Railway Accidents (Republic of Ireland)

Description	1990	1991	1992	1993	1994
No. of Accidents:					
Fatal	14	11	11	3	11
Injury only	4	6	11	6	7
TOTAL:	**18**	**17**	**22**	**9**	**18**
Number of persons killed:					
Passengers	1	1	—	—	1
Railway employees	2	—	—	—	—
Others	11	10	11	3	10
TOTAL:	**14**	**11**	**11**	**3**	**11**
Number of persons injured:					
Passengers	—	—	4	28	1
Railway employees	7	1	2	2	1
Others	1	5	5	2	5
TOTAL:	**8**	**6**	**11**	**32**	**7**

Number of Fatal Road Accidents (Republic of Ireland), 1990-1994

Description	1990	1991	1992	1993	1994
TOTAL	432	402	384	394	371
of which: Dublin Metropolitan Area	79	70	76	76	68

All casualties in 1994 classified by road user type (Republic of Ireland)

Casualty Class	Killed	Serious Injury	Minor Injury	Total	%
Pedestrians	121	342	1,028	1,491	14.0
Pedal Cycle Users	26	95	572	693	6.5
Motor Cycle Users	55	263	686	1,004	9.4
Car Users	178	1,555	4,710	6,443	60.6
P.S.V. (Large) Users	2	17	113	132	1.2
Goods Vehicle Users	17	192	466	675	6.3
Other or Unknown	5	32	158	195	1.8
TOTAL:	**404**	**2,496**	**7,733**	**10,633**	**100.0**

All Road casualties classified by age and gender in Republic of Ireland

(1994) Age Groups	Male Killed	Male Injured	Male Total	Female Killed	Female Injured	Female Total	Persons Overall Total	%
0-5	2	178	180	2	127	129	309	3.0
6-9	5	179	184	1	122	123	307	2.9
10-14	10	329	339	5	198	203	542	5.2
15-17	11	217	228	9	145	154	382	3.7
18-20	23	633	656	7	319	326	982	9.4
21-24	51	785	836	14	309	323	1,159	11.1
25-34	54	1,285	1,339	10	809	819	2,158	20.7
35-44	34	783	817	12	585	597	1,414	13.6
45-54	22	548	570	9	355	364	934	9.0
55-64	25	316	341	11	245	256	597	5.7
65 and over	48	299	347	20	291	311	658	6.3
Unknown	10	550	560	4	423	427	987	9.5
TOTAL:	**295**	**6,102**	**6,397**	**104**	**3,928**	**4,032**	**10,429**	**100.0**

Road Accident Statistics (Northern Ireland), 1990-1994

	1990	1991	1992	1993	1994
Number of Injury Accidents	7,159	6,171	6,650	6,517	6,783
Casualties:					
Killed	185	185	150	143	157
Seriously Injured	1,993	1,648	1,841	1,725	1,648
Slightly Injured	9,583	8,481	9,273	9,232	10,289
All Casualties	11,761	10,314	11,264	11,100	12,094

Road Injury Accidents by Vehicle Type	1990	1991	1992	1993	1994
Motor Cars	10,323	9,084	9,904	9,805	10,293
Motor Cycles	470	393	359	274	265
Bicycles	408	356	393	291	324
Vans & Lorries	1,158	1,033	1,102	1,163	1,213
Omnibuses	221	226	265	252	224
Others	355	175	130	155	249
All Vehicles	**12,935**	**11,267**	**12,153**	**11,940**	**12,568**

LIST OF HOSPITALS IN IRELAND

REPUBLIC OF IRELAND

Eastern Health Board:
Dr. Steven's Hospital, Dublin 8.
Adelaide Hospital, Peter St., Dublin 8.
Beaumont Hospital, Beaumont Hospital, Dublin 9.
Cherry Orchard Hospital, Ballyfermot, Dublin 10.

Coombe Maternity Hospital, Dolphins Barn, Dublin 6.
District Hospital, Baltinglass, Co. Wicklow.
General Hospital, Naas, Co. Kildare.
Hume Street Hospital, Hume St., Dublin 2.
James Connolly Memorial Hospital, Blanchardstown.
Mater Misericordiae Hospital, Eccles St., Dublin 7.
Meath Hospital, Heytesbury St., Dublin 8.

Mount Carmel Hospital, Braemour Pk., Dublin 14.
National Maternity Hospital, Holles St., Dublin 2.
Our Lady's Hospital for Sick Children, Crumlin.
Peamount Hospital, Newcastle, Co. Dublin.
Rotunda Hospital, Parnell St., Dublin 1.
Royal Hospital, Donnybrook, Dublin 4.
Royal Victoria Eye & Ear Hospital, Adelaide Rd., D 2.
St. Anne's Hospital, Northbrook Rd., Dublin 6.
St. Brendan's Hospital, Upper Grangegorman, D 7.
St. Colman's Hospital, Rathdrum, Co. Wicklow.
St. Ita's Hospital, Portrane, Co. Dublin.
St. James' Hospital, James's St., Dublin 8.
St. Joseph's Hospital, Raheny, Dublin 5.
St. Loman's Hospital, Palmerstown, Dublin 20.
St. Luke's Hospital, Oaklands, Highfield Rd., Dublin 6.
St. Mary's Hospital, Phoenix Park, Dublin 20.
St. Columcille's Hospital, Loughlinstown, Co. Dublin.
St. Vincent's Hospital, Elm Park, Dublin 4.
St. Vincent's Hospital, Athy, Co. Kildare.
Vergemount Hospital, Clonskeagh, Dublin 6.

Midland Health Board:
Portlaoise General Hospital, Portlaoise, Co. Laois.
Tullamore General Hospital, Tullamore, Co. Offaly.
Mullingar General Hospital, Mullingar, Co. Westmeath.
Abbeyleix District Hospital, Abbeyleix, Co. Laois.
Birr District Hospital, Birr, Co. Offaly.
Mount Carmel/St. Joseph's Geriatric Hospital,
Longford.
St. Vincent's Geriatric Hospital, Mountmellick, Laois.
St. Mary's Geriatric Hospital, Mullingar, Westmeath.
St. Brigid's Geriatric Hospital, Portlaoise, Co. Laois.
St. Fintan's Psychiatric Hospital, Portlaoise, Laois.
St. Loman's Psychiatric Hospital, Co. Westmeath.

Mid-Western Health Board:
Regional Hospital, Dooradoyle, Limerick.
Regional Maternity Hospital, Limerick.
Regional Orthopaedic Hospital, Croom, Co. Limerick.
St. Camillus Hospital, Limerick.
St. Ita's Hospital, Newcastle West, Co. Limerick.
General Hospital, Ennis, Co. Clare.
Raheen District Hospital, Raheen, Co. Clare.
Ennistymon District Hospital, Ennistymon, Co. Clare.
St. Joseph's Geriatric Hospital, Ennis, Co. Clare.
General Hospital, Nenagh, Co. Tipperary.
Hospital of the Assumption, Thurles, Co. Tipperary.

North-Eastern Health Board:
Cavan General Hospital, Co. Cavan.
Monaghan General Hospital, Co. Monaghan.
Louth Hospital, Dundalk, Co. Louth.
Our Lady's Hospital, Navan, Co. Meath.
St. Felim's Hospital, Cavan, Co. Cavan.
St. Mary's Hospital, Castleblayney, Co. Monaghan.
St. Oliver Plunkett Hospital, Dundalk, Co. Louth.
St. Joseph's Hospital, Ardee, Co. Louth.
St. Mary's Hospital, Drogheda, Co. Louth.
Cottage Hospital, Drogheda, Co. Louth.
St. Joseph's Hospital, Trim, Co. Meath.

North Western Health Board:
Letterkenny General Hospital,
Letterkenny, Co. Donegal.
Sligo General Hospital, Sligo, Co. Sligo.
Manorhamilton Hospital, Manorhamilton, Co. Leitrim.

St. Joseph's Hospital, Stranorlar, Co. Donegal.
Sheil Hospital, Ballyshannon, Co. Donegal.
Donegal District Hospital, Co. Donegal.
Carndonagh District Hospital, Co. Donegal.
Dungloe District Hospital, Dungloe, Co. Donegal.
Lifford District Hospital, Lifford, Co. Donegal.
St. John's Hospital, Ballytivnan, Co. Sligo.
St. Patrick's Hospital, Carrick-on-Shannon, Co. Leitrim.
St. Conal's Psychiatric Hospital, Co. Donegal.

South Eastern Health Board:
Waterford Regional Hospital, Co. Waterford.
St. Luke's Hospital, Co. Kilkenny.
Lourdes Orthopaedic Hospital, Co. Kilkenny.
St. Joseph's County and Medical Hospital,
Clonmel, Co. Tipperary.
Our Lady's County Surgical Hospital, Co. Tipperary.
Wexford General Hospital, Co. Wexford.
Carlow District Hospital, Co. Carlow.
St. Brigid's District Hospital, Co. Tipperary.
District Hospital, Castlecomer, Co. Kilkenny.
St. Dympna's Psychiatric Hospital, Co. Carlow.
St. Canice's Psychiatric Hospital, Co. Kilkenny.
St. Luke's Psychiatric Hospital, Co. Tipperary.
St. Otteran's Psychiatric Hospital, Co. Waterford.
St. Senan's Psychiatric Hospital, Co. Wexford.
Sacred Heart Geriatric Hospital, Co. Carlow.
St. Patrick's Geriatric Hospital, Cashel, Co. Tipperary.
St. Joseph's Geriatric Hospital, Co. Waterford.
St. John's Geriatric Hospital, Enniscorthy, Wexford.
St. Columba's Geriatric Hospital,
Thomastown, Co. Kilkenny.
St. Patrick's Geriatric Hospital, Co. Waterford.
New Houghton Geriatric Hospital,
New Ross, Co. Waterford.

Southern Health Board:
Cork University Hospital, Wilton, Co. Cork.
Our Lady's Hospital, Lee Road, Co. Cork.
St. Mary's Orthopaedic Hospital, Co. Cork.
St. Steven's Hospital, Sarsfieldscourt, Co. Cork.
Erinville Hospital, Co. Cork.
St. Raphael's Auxiliary Mental Hospital,
Youghal, Co. Cork.
Mount Alvernia Hospital, Mallow, Co. Cork.
St. Joseph's Hospital, Bantry, Co. Cork.
Mallow General Hospital, Mallow, Co. Cork.
Bandon District Hospital, Bandon, Co. Cork.
St. Joseph's Hospital, Castletownbere, Co. Cork.
St. Anthony's Hospital, Dunmanway, Co. Cork.
St. Patrick's Hospital, Fermoy, Co. Cork.
Heatherside Hospital, Buttevant, Co. Cork.
St. Patrick's Hospital, Kanturk, Co. Cork.
Sacred Heart Hospital, Kinsale, Co. Cork.
Macroom District Hospital, Macroom, Co. Cork.
Our Lady of Lourdes Hospital, Midleton, Co. Cork.
St. Joseph's Hospital, Millstreet, Co. Cork.
St. Gabriel's Hospital, Schull, Co. Cork.
St. Anne's Hospital, Skibbereen, Co. Cork.
Youghal District Hospital, Youghal, Co. Cork.
Tralee General Hospital, Tralee, Co. Kerry.
Killarney District Hospital, Killarney, Co. Kerry.
Listowel District Hospital, Listowel, Co. Kerry.
Dingle District Hospital, Dingle, Co. Kerry.
Kenmare District Hospital, Kenmare, Co. Kerry.
Cahirciveen District Hospital, Cahirciveen, Co. Kerry.

St. Finan's Hospital, Killarney, Co. Kerry.

Western Health Board:
University College Regional Hospital, Co. Galway.
Merlin Park Regional Hospital, Co. Galway.
Castlebar General Hospital, Castlebar, Co. Mayo.
County Hospital, Co. Roscommon.
Ballina District Hospital, Ballina, Co. Mayo.
Belmullet District Hospital, Belmullet, Co. Mayo.
Clifden District Hospital, Clifden, Co. Galway.
St. Brigid's Hospital, Ballinasloe, Co. Galway.
St. Mary's Hospital, Castlebar, Co. Mayo.

NORTHERN IRELAND

Eastern Health & Social Services Board:
Albertbridge Road, Day Hospital, Belfast, Co. Antrim.
Alexandra Gardens, Day Hospital, Belfast, Co. Antrim.
Ards Hospital, Church Street, Newtownards, Co. Down.
Banbridge Hospital, Linenhall Street, Banbridge, Down.
Bangor Hospital, Bangor, Co. Down.
Belfast City Hospital, Belfast, Co. Antrim.
Belvoir Park Hospital, Belfast, Co. Antrim.
Cowan Heron Hospital, Dromore, Down.
Craigavon Area Hospital, Portadown, Co. Armagh.
Downe Hospital, Downpatrick, Co. Down.
Downpatrick Maternity Hospital, Downpatrick, Down.
Downshire Hospital, Downpatrick, Co. Down.
Forster Green Hospital, Saintfield Road, Belfast.
Jubilee Hospital (Trust Hospital).
Lagan Valley Hospital, Lisburn, Co. Antrim.
Lurgan Hospital, Sloan Street, Lurgan, Co. Armagh.
Mater Informium Hospital, Crumlin Road, Belfast.
Muckamore Abbey Hospital, Antrim, Co. Antrim.
Musgrave Park Hospital, Belfast, Co. Antrim.
Purdysburn Hospital, Saintfield Road, Belfast, Antrim.
Royal Belfast Hospital for Sick Children,
Falls Road, Belfast, Co. Antrim.
Royal Victoria Hospital, Belfast, Co. Antrim.
Shaftesbury Square Hospital, Belfast, Co. Antrim.
Spelga House Hospital (Trust Hospital).
Thompson House, Lisburn, Antrim.
Throne Hospital, Newtownabbey, Belfast, Co. Antrim.
Ulster Hospital, Dundonald, Co. Antrim.
Windsor House, Co. Antrim.

Southern Health & Social Services Board:
Armagh Community Hospital, Co. Armagh.
Daisy Hill Hospital, 5 Hospital Road, Newry. Co. Down.
Loan House Hospital, Co. Armagh.
Longstone Hospital, Co. Armagh.
Manor House Hospital,
Mourne Hospital, Newry Street, Kilkeel, Co. Down.
Mullinure Hospital.
St. Luke's Hospital, Co. Armagh.
South Tyrone Hospital, Dungannon, Co. Tyrone.
Tower Hill Hospital, Co. Armagh.

Northern Health & Social Services Board:
Ballymena Cottage Hospital, Ballymena, Co. Antrim.
Braid Valley Hospital, Ballymena, Co. Antrim.
Coleraine Hospital, Coleraine, Co. Derry.
Dalriada Hospital, Coleraine Road, Ballycastle, Antrim.
Greenisland Hospital, Whiteabbey, Co. Antrim.
Holywell Hospital, Antrim, Co. Antrim.
Massereene Hospital, Antrim, Co. Antrim.
Mid Ulster Hospital, Magherafelt, Co. Derry.
Moyle Hospital, Larne, Co. Antrim.
Robinson Memorial Hospital, Ballymoney, Co. Antrim.
Ross Thompson Hospital,
Waveney Hospital, Ballymena, Co. Antrim.
Whiteabbey Hospital, Newtownabbey, Co. Antrim.

Western Health & Social Services Board:
Altnagelvin Hospital, Derry.
Derg Valley Hospital, Castlederg, Co. Tyrone.
Erne Hospital, Enniskillen, Co. Fermanagh.
Gransha Hospital, Clooney Road, Campsie, Co. Derry.
Omagh General Hospital, Omagh, Co. Tyrone.
Roe Valley Hospital, Limavady, Co. Derry.
Strabane Hospital, Strabane, Co. Tyrone.
Stradreagh Hospital, Campsie, Co. Derry.
Tyrone County Hospital, Omagh, Co. Tyrone.
Tyrone and Fermanagh Hospital, Omagh, Co. Tyrone.
Waterside Hospital, Derry.

PSYCHIATRIC PATIENTS

Psychiatric patients (Republic of Ireland)

Patients in public psychiatric units and hospitals in each health board area, 1989-1992.

Health Board	1989	1990	1991	1992
Eastern Health Board	1,551	1,642	1,570	1,503
Midland Health Board	701	686	492	466
Mid-Western Health Board	766	705	620	520
North-Eastern Health Board	520	492	368	349
North-Western Health Board	527	536	375	321
South-Eastern Health Board	1,311	1,269	1,184	1,080
Southern Health Board	1,561	1,435	1,355	1,033
Western Health Board	1,459	1,042	957	858
TOTAL:	8,396	7,807	6,921	6,130

DICKSON & McNULTY
—— SOLICITORS ——

*Providing a Full Range
of Legal Services,
North and South.*

**MEMBER OF
THE HOME CHARTER SCHEME**
AUTHORISED TO CARRY ON INVESTMENT BUSINESS

50 SPENCER ROAD	6 CHURCH STREET
WATERSIDE	BUNCRANA
LONDONDERRY BT47 1AA	CO. DONEGAL
Telephone: 01504 41864 3 lines	Telephone: 077 61918
Fax: 01504 48837	Fax: 077 61385

LAW AND DEFENCE

INTRODUCTION

Despite the political divisions the legal system in both parts of Ireland is quite similar. Since the 17th century the system has been known as the "Common Law" system which has at its core the doctrine of precedent - that is, when a court/judge makes a ruling on a particular point of law it sets the "precedent" as the authority for what the law on that particular point is. However, the increasing introduction of legislation from both Europe and the Parliaments in London and Dublin has seen a significant decline in judge made law in recent years

There are also different structures in the systems as operated in the two jurisdictions

The Republic has a written Constitution which, under articles 20 to 27, gives Dáil Éireann powers to introduce, debate and pass legislation. The Constitution undertakes to protect the personal rights of all citizens, guarantees freedom of expression, assembly and association, subject to public order and morality. Most of the important cases, particularly in regard to controversial social issues, have been brought by private citizens in the past number of years on the basis that the either the courts or the Government has acted outside the terms of the Constitution.

While Britain does not have a written constitution, the legal system is not dramatically different.

During the years of the Stormont Parliament, Northern Ireland had authority to introduce "domestic" legislation as distinct from that being enacted at Westminster. Most of this was in the areas of local government, agriculture, education planning and certain sections of both the civil and criminal law.

The introduction of direct rule from Westminster in 1972 has, generally, resulted in a greater harmonisation of the N.I. legal system with that of England and Wales; Scotland has its own system. The three principal officers under this system are the Lord Chancellor, the Attorney General and the Secretary of State for N.I. Under their stewardship the legal professionals- Judges, public prosecutors, court clerks, etc. do the day-to-day work.

Defence and Security: The Garda Síochána is the civilian police force in the South of Ireland while the Royal Ulster Constabulary is its northern counterpart. Both forces owe their origins to the Royal Irish Constabulary which was disbanded with the division of Ireland in 1920.

The cost of security in Ireland is extremely high: £920m. was spent in the North on "Law, Order, Protective and Miscellaneous Services" in 1994/ 1995 while the costs for the Republic were in excess of £500m.

CONSTITUTION

The Constitution of Ireland, Bunreacht na hÉireann.

The Constitution of Ireland was approved by a Referendum on July 1st, 1937, the Dáil having already approved it on June 14th, 1937. It came into effect on December 29th 1937, replacing the Constitution of the Irish Free State (1922). The Taoiseach, Eamon de Valera played a large part in the drafting of the document which made the Free State a Republic in all but name.

Articles 20 to 27 deal with the introduction, debate of and passing of legislation. Government, which according to Article 6 derives all legislative, executive and judicial powers from the people is considered by Article 28, with reference to the exercising of that power, its responsibility to the Dáil, its powers during war or national emergency, the nomination and composition of the cabinet. Foreign Affairs and International Relations as conducted by the Government are provided for under Article 29 such as membership of the European Union.

Articles 34 to 39 deals with the Structure Organisation and Powers of the Courts. Articles 30 to 33 having been concerned with the establishment of the Offices of the Attorney General, Comptroller and Auditor General and the creation of a Council of State to advise the President.

Articles 40 to 44 are concerned with the fundamental rights of the Citizen under broad headings of: Personal Rights (Article 40); The Family and Education (Articles 41 to 42); Private Property (Article 43); Religion (Article 44). Other unenumerated Rights have been granted by the Courts. Under these Articles, all Citizens are equal before the law and the law undertakes to protect the personal rights of all Citizens. Freedom of expression, assembly and association are guaranteed, subject to Public Order and Morality.

The State will endeavour to educate its Citizens but recognises and respects that the family is the *"Primary and Natural Educator of the Child"* (Article 42.1). The right to own private property is guaranteed as is the Freedom of Religious Conscience and Practice and the State will not discriminate on grounds of Religious Belief (Article 44.2.3).

Republic of Ireland Court System

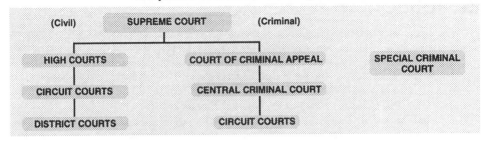

Judiciary of the Republic of Ireland

SUPREME COURT
Judges:
The Hon Mr. Justice Liam Hamilton, Chief Justice.
The Hon Mr. Justice Hugh James O'Flaherty.
The Hon Mr. Justice Séamus F. Egan.
The Hon Mr. Justice John Blayney.
The Hon Ms. Justice Susan Deneham.
The Hon Mr. Justice Ronan Keane.
The Hon Mr. Justice Kevin Lynch.
The Hon Mr. Justice Francis Murphy.
Ex-officio: The Hon Mr. Justice Declan Costello, President of the High Court.

HIGH COURT
Master of the High Court - Harry Hill, SC.
Judges:
The Hon Mr. Justice Declan Costello, President.
The Hon Miss. Justice Melia Carroll.
The Hon Mr. Justice Diarmuid O'Donovan.
The Hon Mr. Justice Henry Barron.
Ex-officio: The Hon Mr. Justice Liam Hamilton; Chief Justice.
The Hon Mr. Justice Robert Barr.
The Hon Mr. Justice Richard Johnson.
The Hon Mr. Justice Vivian Lavan.
The Hon Mr. Justice Frederick R. Morris.
The Hon Mr. Justice Paul J. P. Carney.
The Hon Mr. Justice Declan Budd.
The Hon Mr. Justice Feargus M. Flood.
The Hon Mr. Justice Brian McCracken.
The Hon Ms. Justice Mary Laffoy.
The Hon Mr. Justice Hugh Geoghegan.
The Hon Mr. Justice Dermot Kinlen.
The Hon. Mr. Justice Peter Shanley.
The Hon. Mr. Justice Michael Moriarty.
The Hon. Mr. Justice. Peter Kelly.
The Hon Mr. Justice Francis R. Spain, President of Circuit Court.

SPECIAL CRIMINAL COURT
Judges:
The Hon Mr. Justice Richard Johnson.
The Hon Mr. Justice Robert Barr.
The Hon Mr. Justice Frederick R. Morris.
His Hon Judge John G. Buchanan, the Circuit Court.

His Hon Judge Dominic Lynch, the Circuit Court.
His Hon Judge Matthew P. Smith, the Circuit Court.
Thomas J. Ballagh, Judge of the District Court.
Peter A. Smithwick, President of the District Court.
Michael C. Reilly, Judge of the District Court.
Registrars - Thomas Kelly; Patrick Morrissey.

CIRCUIT COURT
Judges:
The Hon Mr. Justice Francis R. Spain,
President of the Circuit Court, Dublin Circuit.
His Hon Judge Diarmuid P. Sheridan, South East Circuit.
His Hon Judge John G. Buchanan, Dublin Circuit.
His Hon Judge Dominic Lynch, Dublin Circuit.
His Hon Judge Matthew P. Smith, Eastern Circuit.
His Hon Judge Kevin C. O'Higgins, South West Circuit.
His Hon Judge James Carroll, Dublin Circuit.
His Hon Judge Michael Anthony Murphy, Cork Circuit.
His Hon Judge Michael A. Moriarty, Dublin Circuit.
His Hon Judge Matthew F. Deery, Northern Circuit.
His Hon Judge Patrick Joseph Moran, Cork Circuit.
His Hon Judge Kieran O'Connor, Dublin Circuit.
His Hon Judge Liam Devally, Dublin Circuit.
His Hon Judge Esmond Smyth.
His Hon Judge Cyril C. Kelly.
Her Hon Judge Catherine McGuinness, Dublin Circuit.
His Hon Judge Harvey Kenny, Midland Circuit.

Recently appointed to the Circuit Court:

His Hon Judge Anthony Kennedy.
Her Hon Judge Elizabeth Dunne
His Hon Judge Kevin Haugh.
His Hon Judge John Buckley.
Her Hon Judge Alison Lindsay.
His Hon Judge Frank O'Donnell.
His Hon Judge Michael White.
His Hon Judge Raymond Groarke.
Her Hon Judge Olive Buttimer.

CIRCUIT COURT
Higher Executive Officers:
Dublin - Brendan O'Donnell; Colm Gaffney; Michael

O'Donnell; Daniel Doyle; Brendan Scollan; Therese O'Rourke. Galway - Mary Shaughnessy. Kerry - Teresa Cotter. Kildare - Mary Flynn. Kilkenny - Liam Nolan. Limerick - Gerard McCague. Louth - Helen Lennon. Mayo - Marian E. Byrne. Meath - Seán Ó Cléircín. Tipperary - Gerard Connolly. Wicklow - Joseph Kelly.

DISTRICT COURT

President of the District Court - Peter A. Smithwick.
Dublin Metropolitan Judges: Peter A. Smithwick, Seán S. Delap, Maura Roche, Brian Kirby, Gillian M. Hussey, James Paul McDonnell, Desmond P.H. Windle, Timothy H. Crowley, Thelma King, Clare Leonard, John J. O'Neill, Michael O'Leary, David Riordan.

Chief Clerk - Diarmuid S. Mac Diarmada.

PROVINCIAL JUDGES OF THE DISTRICT COURT
Liam O McMenamin - (Ballybofey, Ballyshannon, Bunbeg, Buncrana, Carndonagh, Donegal, Dunfanaghy, Dungloe, Falcarragh, Glenties, Killybegs, Letterkenny, Lifford, Milford, Moville, Pettigo, Raphoe).

Oliver McGuiness - (Ballyfarnon, Ballymote, Boyle, Collooney, Dowra, Drumkeerin, Easky, Grange, Inniscrone, Manorhamilton, Riverstown, Skreen, Sligo, Tubbercurry).

Daniel G. Shields - (Achill, Balla, Ballina, Ballinrobe, Ballycastle, Ballycroy, Belmullet, Castlebar, Crossmolina, Foxford, Killala, Kiltimagh, Newport, Swinford, Westport).

Bernard M. Brennan - (Ballaghaderreen, Ballyhaunis, Castlerea, Charlestown, Claremorris, Dunmore, Elphin, Glenamaddy, Kilkelly, Roscommon, Ruskey, Strokestown, Williamstown).

Donal McArdle - (Arva, Bailieborough, Ballinamore, Ballyconnell, Ballyjamesduff, Belturbet, Cavan, Clones, Cootehill, Kingscourt, Mohill, Monaghan, Oldcastle, Virginia).

Flannan V. Brennan - (Ardee, Ballybay, Carlingford, Carrickmacross, Castleblayney, Drogheda, Dundalk, Dunleer).

John F. Garavan - (Carna, Clifden, Derreen, Derrynea, Galway, Headford, Kilronan, Letterfrack, Maam, Oughterard, Spiddal, Tuam).

James J. O'Sullivan - (Athlone, Ballinasloe, Ballyforan, Banagher, Birr, Borrisokane, Eyecourt, Kilcormac, Loughrea, Moate, Mount Bellew, Portumna, Woodford).

Aiden O'Donnell - (Ballymahon, Ballynacargy,

Castlepollard, Daingean, Delvin, Edenderry, Edgeworthstown, Granard, Kilbeggan, Kilucan, Longford, Mullingar, Tullamore).

John Patrick Brophy - (Athboy, Ceanannus Mór, Dunshaughlin, Kilcock, Navan, Trim).
District amalgamated with Dublin Metropolitan District.

Albert L. O'Dea - (Athenry, Corofin, Ennis, Ennistymon, Gort, Kildysart, Kilkee, Killaloe, Kilrush, Kinvara, Lisdoonvarna, Miltown Malbay, Scariff, Shannon, Sixmilebridge, Tulla).
Mary A. G. O'Halloran - (Abbeyfealel, Adare, Askeaton, Bruff, Drumcollogher, Kilfinane, Kilmallock, Listowel, Newcastlewest, Rathkeale, Rath Luirc, Shanagolden, Tarbert).

Michael C. Reilly -(Cappamore, Cappawhite, Limerick City, Nenagh, Newport, Thurles).

Mary H. Martin -(Abbeyleix, Athy, Ballyragget, Carlow, Castlecomer, Mountmellick, Mountrath, Portarlington, Portlaoise, Rathdowney, Roscrea, Templemore, Urlingford).

Thomas J. Ballagh - (Baltinglass, Blessington, Bray, Droichead Nua, Dunlavin, Hacketstown, Kildare, Naas).

Humphrey P. Kelleher - (Annascaul, Cahirciveen, Castlegregory, Castleisland, Dingle, Kenmare, Killarney, Killorglin, Sneem, Tralee, Waterville).

Brendan Wallace - (Bandon, Bantry, Castletownbere, Clonakilty, Coachford, Dunmanway, Glengariff, Kinsale, Macroom, Millstreet, Schull, Skibbereen).

Uinsin Mac Gruaic - (Cork City).

John P. Clifford - (Ballincollig, Buttevant, Carrigaline, Castlemartyr, Castletownroche, Cobh, Fermoy, Kanturk, Mallow, Middleton, Michelstown, Whitechurch).

Michael Pattwell - (Cahir, Cappoquin, Carrick-on-Suir, Cashel, Clogheen, Clonmel, Dungarvan, Killenaule, Lismore, Tallow, Tipperary, Youghal).

William Harnett - (Callan, Kilkenny, Kilmacthomas, Thomastown, Waterford).

Donnchadh Ó Buachalla - (Arklow, Bunclody, Enniscorthy, Gorey, Muine Bheag, New Ross, Rathdrum, Shillelagh, Tullow, Wexford, Wicklow).

Movable Judges of the District Court:
William G. J. Hamill, John F. Neilan, Joseph Mangan, Thomas A. Fitzpatrick, Desmond P. Hogan, Gerard John Haughton, J. W. Terence Finn, Murrough B. Connellan, Mary Fahy, Michael P. M. Connellan, William Early.

Northern Ireland Court System

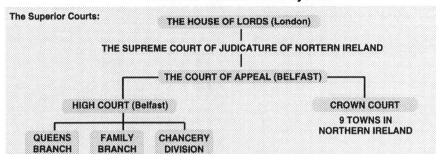

Judiciary of Northern Ireland

LORD CHIEF JUSTICE OF NORTHERN IRELAND -
The Right Hon. Sir James Brian Edward Hutton.

Judges:
The Right Honourable Lord Justice Kelly.
The Right Honourable Lord Justice MacDermott.
The Right Honourable Lord Justice Carswell.
The Honourable Mr. Justice Nicholson.
The Honourable Mr. Justice McCollum.
The Honourable Mr. Justice Campbell.
The Honourable Mr. Justice Sheil.
The Honourable Mr. Justice Pringle.
The Honourable Mr. Justice Kerr.
The Honourable Mr. Justice Higgins.

LORD CHIEF JUSTICE'S OFFICE
Principal Secretary to the Lord Chief Justice and
Clerk of the Crown - J. A. L. McLean   Esq. Q. C.

SUPREME COURT OFFICES
Queens Bench Appeals: Master - J. W. Wilson Esq.
Q. C. High Court Master - Mrs. D. M. Kennedy.
Office of Care and Protection: Master - F. B. Hall
Esq. LL.B.
Bankruptcy and Companies Office: Master - J. B. C.
Glass Esq. LL.B.
Probate and Matrimonial Office: Master - R. T. Millar
Esq. LL.B.
Taxing Office: Master - J. C. Napier Esq. B.A.
Court Funds Office: Accountant General - E. A.
Simpson Esq.

Official Solicitor: C. W. G. Redpath Esq. LL.B.

COUNTY COURT JUDGES
His Honour Judge Babington D.S.C., Q.C.
The Right Honourable Judge Sir Robert Porter Q.C.
His Honour Judge Russell Q.C.
His Honour Judge Curran Q.C.
His Honour Judge McKee Q.C.
His Honour Judge Gibson Q.C.
His Honour Judge Hart Q.C.
His Honour Judge Petrie Q.C.
His Honour Judge Smyth Q.C.
His Honour Judge Martin Q.C.
His Honour Judge Markey Q.C.
His Honour Judge McKay Q.C.

DISTRICT JUDGES
Division of Belfast - District Judge Kerr.
Division of Derry and Antrim - District Judge Keegan.
Division of Craigavon and Ards - District Judge
Wheeler.
District of Armagh, South Down, Fermanagh and
Tyrone - District Judge Rodgers.

OTHER OFFICERS
Director of Public Prosecutions - A. M. Fraser Esq.
Q.C.
Crown Solicitor - N. P. Roberts Esq.

Organisation and Location of Courts in Northern Ireland

Town/City	Circuit	County Court Division	Petty Sessions Division	Court Sittings
Derry	Northern	Derry	Derry	Crown, Recorder's, Magistrates
Limavady			Limavady	County, Magistrates
Magherafelt			Magherafelt	County, Magistrates
Strabane			Strabane	County, Magistrates
Castlederg			Strabane	Magistrates
Coleraine		N. Antrim	Coleraine	Crown, County, Magistrates
Ballymena			Ballymena	Crown, County, Magistrates
Ballymoney			Ballymoney	County, Magistrates
Ballycastle			Moyle	Magistrates

Antrim...Antrim...Magistrates

Armagh ....S. Western.....................Armagh.......................Armagh ....Crown, County, Magistrates
Lurgan...Craigavon ....County, Magistrates
Portadown...Craigavon..Magistrates
Omagh ....Fermanagh &.......................Omagh ....Crown, County, Magistrates
                                         South Tyrone
Cookstown..Cookstown ....County, Magistrates
Dungannon ....Dungannon ....County, Magistrates
Clogher ....Dungannon......................................Magistrates
Enniskillen..Fermanagh ....Crown, County, Magistrates
Newtownbutler ....Fermanagh ....Magistrates
Lisnaskea..Fermanagh ....Magistrates
Irvinestown..Fermanagh ....Magistrates
Derrygonnelly..Fermanagh ....Magistrates

Downpatrick .....S. Eastern.....................S. Down ....Down ....Crown, County, Magistrates
Newcastle...Down ....Magistrates
Banbridge...Banbridge ....County, Magistrates
Newry...Newry / Mourne ....County, Magistrates
Kilkeel ....Newry / Mourne................................Magistrates
Lisburn ....Ards.............Lisburn ....County, Magistrates
Hillsborough...Lisburn..Magistrates
Bangor ....N. Down...Magistrates
Newtownards ....Ards ....Crown, County, Magistrates
Newtownbreda ....Castlereagh ....Magistrates

Belfast ....Eastern ....Belfast ....Belfast ....Crown, Recorder's, Magistrates
Carrickfergus...Carrickfergus....................................Magistrates
Newtownabbey ....Newtownabbey ....Magistrates
Larne ....Larne ....Magistrates

SECURITY

Garda Personnel, Numbers and Ranks

Description	H.Q. 1993	H.Q. 1994	Templemore 1993	Templemore 1994	Dublin Met. 1993	Dublin Met. 1994	Others 1993	Others 1994	Total 1993	Total 1994
Divisions	—	—	—	—	5	5	18	18	23	23
Districts	—	—	—	—	17	17	90	90	107	107
Stations	—	—	—	—	45	45	659	659	704	704
Garda Síochána:										
Commissioner Ranks	9	8	—	—	1	1	—	—	10	9
Chief Superintendents	12	13	1	1	10	10	18	18	41	42
Superintendents	27	26	6	6	36	33	91	92	160	157
Inspectors	24	30	5	5	129	125	89	89	247	249
Sergeants	141	152	41	44	638	612	1,044	1,027	1,864	1,835
Gardaí	420	442	66	64	3,170	3,215	4,914	4,824	8,570	8,545
Total:	633	671	119	120	3,984	3,996	6,156	6,050	10,892	10,837

Garda Strength - by Rank, 1995

Rank	Number
Commissioner	1
Deputy Commissioner	2
Assistant Commissioner	6
Chief Superintendent	38
Superintendent	154
Inspector	224
Sergeant	1,603
Garda	8,472

Republic of Ireland Garda Stations

County / City	No. of Stations	County / City	No. of Stations
Carlow	9	Louth	13
Cavan	21	Mayo	37
Clare	28	Meath **	15
Cork (city)	18	Monaghan	13
Cork (county)	68	Offaly	16
Donegal	45	Roscommon	21
Dublin* (Metropolitan area)	58	Sligo	15
Galway	58	Tipperary	43
Kerry	39	Waterford	21
Kildare **	14	Westmeath	16
Kilkenny	20	Wexford	25
Laois	14	Wicklow **	16
Leitrim	15		
Limerick (city)	14		
Limerick (county)	23		
Longford	11		

* Dublin Metropolitan area includes Dublin, parts of Kildare, parts of Meath & parts of Wicklow.
** Does not include stations already accounted for in Dublin Metropolitan area.

Royal Ulster Constabulary, numbers and ranks - 1995

Rank	Establishment	Effective Strength	Vacancies	Over Established	Seconded to Central Services
Chief Constable	1	1	--	—	—
Deputy Chief Constable	2	1	1	—	—
Assistant Chief Constable	9	8	1	—	—
Chief Superintendent	42	34	8	—	1
Superintendent	120	122	—	2	1
Chief Inspector	167	162	5	—	1
Inspector	491	489	2	—	1
Sergeant	1,414	1,409	5	—	1
Constable	6,243	6,267	—	24	1
TOTALS:	8,489	8,493	—	4	6
RUC Reserve Full-Time	3,202	3,199	3	—	—
RUC Reserve Part-Time	1,765	1,491	274	—	—

Northern Ireland Police Stations

County / City	No. of Stations	Sub-stations	County / City	No. of Stations	Sub-stations
Belfast	22	—	Fermanagh	8	5
Antrim	13	12	Derry (city & county)	8	12
Armagh	11	5	Tyrone	10	14
Down	12	15			

Strength of Police Force and "Ulster Defence Regiment"/RIR

Force	1990	1991	1992	1993	1994
FORCE TOTAL:	**18,818**	**19,053**	**18,488**	**18,448**	**18,424**
Royal Ulster Constabulary: Total	**8,231**	**8,217**	**8,478**	**8,464**	**8,493**
Males	7,525	7,510	7,688	7,646	7,640
Females	706	707	790	818	853
RUC Reserve: Total	**4,544**	**4,560**	**4,593**	**4,572**	**4,690**
Males — part-time	1,150	1,089	1,014	964	996
Males — full-time	2,945	2,980	3,046	3,063	3,056
Females — part-time	404	429	419	424	495
Females — full-time	45	62	114	121	143
UDR / RIR: Total	**6,043**	**6,276**	**5,417**	**5,412**	**5,241**
Males — part-time	2,623	2,553	2,251	2,181	1,994
Males — full-time	2,686	2,998	2,526	2,608	2,675
Females — part-time	465	446	369	329	291
Females — full-time	269	279	271	294	281

CRIME

Republic of Ireland: Crime Rate per Garda Division:

Garda Division	1989 %	1990 %	1991 %	1992 %	1993 %
Outside Dublin (Metropolitan Area)	14.3	15.2	17.0	17.8	—
Carlow / Kildare	12.3	16.8	17.4	15.4	16.5
Cavan / Monaghan	7.1	8.4	9.0	10.4	9.6
Cork East	24.9	26.1	30.5	36.4	36.0
Cork West	7.4	7.1	11.4	11.2	9.5
Clare	9.4	8.7	8.8	7.9	10.3
Donegal	7.8	9.0	10.0	10.9	10.3
Galway West	16.6	16.5	19.1	19.8	21.8
Kerry	13.2	12.8	13.4	15.6	12.9
Laois / Offaly	8.2	10.3	11.2	10.7	11.4
Limerick	21.3	19.7	21.9	23.5	22.0
Longford / Westmeath	18.9	23.5	25.3	25.6	18.9
Louth / Meath	20.3	20.5	19.9	21.3	21.2
Mayo	4.5	5.7	7.4	7.5	7.4
Roscommon / Galway East	5.4	5.9	8.5	8.8	9.4
Sligo / Leitrim	10.7	11.2	11.8	10.2	11.2
Tipperary	12.7	14.8	17.3	16.4	14.5
Waterford / Kilkenny	14.5	13.9	15.4	14.0	15.8
Wexford	16.7	18.0	19.2	18.9	21.3
Dublin Metropolitan Area	49.0	47.6	49.9	49.9	53.6
State Total	**24.5**	**24.8**	**26.8**	**27.1**	**28.1**

Indictable Offences reported in Republic of Ireland, 1992 - 1994

Indictable Offences	1992	1993	1994
Offences against the Person:			
Murder (of persons aged above one year)	24	23	25
Murder (of infants aged one year and under)	1		
Infanticide			
Attempts to Murder	7	4	1
Threats, Conspiracy, or incitement to Murder	2	1	
Manslaughter (Traffic Fatalities)		4	1
Manslaughter (Fatalities other than Traffic)	17	5	7
Dangerous Driving (Causing Death)	12	8	16
Dangerous Driving (Causing serious bodily harm)	3	2	3
Wounding & Other Acts endangering life (Felonies)	73	76	98
Wounding & Other Acts endangering life (Gardaí on duty)	4		1
Assault, wounding & other like offences (Misdemeanours)	488	472	393
Assault, wounding & other like offences (Gardaí on duty)	70	48	40
Endangering Railway Passengers		1	1
Intimidation & Molestation	1	3	6
Intimidation by threatening letters, notices etc.	9	3	2
Cruelty to, or neglect of children (on indictment)	2	1	2
Abandoning Children under 2 years		1	
Child Stealing		1	
Procuring Abortion			
Concealment of Birth		1	1
Unnatural Offences	31	27	11
Rape of Females	127	143	193
Sexual Assault on Females or Males	300	368	381
Unlawful Carnal Knowledge under 15	23	17	12
Unlawful Carnal Knowledge 15 - 17	7	10	6
Incest	11	14	16

Indictable Offences	1992	1993	1994
Procuration			
Abduction	3		1
Bigamy		1	
Kidnapping			
False Imprisonment	21	31	36
Possession of Firearms with intent to endanger life	16	9	15
Use of Firearms to resist arrest or aid escape	1	1	
Possession of Firearms or Ammunition in suspicious circumstances	32	31	34
Carrying Firearms with Criminal Intent	13	8	25
Total: Offences against the Person	**1,298**	**1,314**	**1,327**

Offences against Property with violence:

	1992	1993	1994
Burglary	32,149	32,696	32,740
Aggravated Burglary	1,409	1,832	1,412
Robbery	2,473	2,194	2,128
Robbery with Arms	86	130	179
Assaults on Dwellings Houses using Firearms or explosives	8	12	4
Threatening to publish with intent to extort			
Arson	305	230	251
Killing & Maiming Cattle	2	1	3
Malicious damage to schools	232	316	392
Other Malicious injury to property	4,844	6,439	6,973
Causing an explosion likely to endanger life or damage property	2		3
Attempting to cause an explosion	1	2	3
Possession of explosive substances	5	7	3
Making of Explosives		1	
Interference with Railway	2	2	2
Unlawful seizure of Aircraft			
Unlawful seizure of Vehicles	24	31	23
Unlawful possession of house-breaking implements	194	238	197
Total: Offences against Property with Violence	**41,736**	**44,131**	**44,313**

Larcenies, Frauds etc.:

	1992	1993	1994
Larceny from the Person	5,691	6,575	6,722
Larceny of Motor Vehicles & Accessories	2,370	2,968	2,949
Larceny of Pedal Cycles	831	737	546
Larceny from unattended Vehicles	15,816	15,907	16,712
Other Larcenies	21,463	21,861	22,699
Embezzlement	48	31	31
Obtaining of Goods by false pretences	537	642	588
Other Frauds	484	300	375
Forgery & Uttering	3,370	2,368	2,706
Receiving Stolen Goods	1,430	1,771	1,710
Debtors Ireland Act 1872 - other			41
Offences against Post Office Act	16	14	21
Offences against Coinage Acts		1	
Extortion			14
Total: Larcenies, Frauds etc.	**52,026**	**53,175**	**55,114**

Other Indictable Offences:

	1992	1993	1994
Official Secrets Act			
Offences against Treason Act 1939			
Offences against the State Act 1939	1	1	1
Riot or unlawful Assembly	1	3	1
Indecent Exposure (Public Indecency)	25	9	26
Public Mischief	16	12	11
Conspiracy	24	4	3
Other Indictable Offences	264	330	240
Total: Other Indictable Offences	**331**	**359**	**282**

	1992	1993	1994
TOTAL: INDICTABLE OFFENCES	**95,391**	**98,979**	**101,036**

Non-indictable Offences reported in Republic of Ireland, 1992 - 1994

Non-indictable Offences	1992	1993	1994
Assaults	6,642	6,796	6,839
Assaults (Gardaí on Duty)	1,267	1,227	1,153
Cruelty to Animals:	160		
Badger Baiting		1	39
Cock Fighting			
Dog Fighting			15
Other Offences		296	353
Offences against Control of Dogs Act 1986	262		
Offences against School Attendance Act 1926	49		
Offences against Traffic Acts:			
Lighting Regulations - Pedal Cycles	2,304	2,126	1,654
Lighting Regulations M.P.V's	12,250	11,543	11,082
Not wearing Seat Belts		7,345	8,198
Not wearing Crash Helmet - Motor Cyclist		455	421
Lighting Regulations - Animal drawn Vehicles	60		
Licenses - Driving	52,411	56,304	54,330
Obstruction	1,135	1,058	874
Dangerous Parking	260	323	220
Road Traffic General Bye-Laws 1964	5,828	7,082	5,215
Local Bye-Laws	78,369	118,142	74,135
Dangerous & Careless Driving	11,225	9,793	9,094
Driving without reasonable consideration		2,541	2,816
Non-conformity with Traffic Lights		487	718
Compulsory Insurance	70,556		
No Insurance		36,198	35,068
Failing to produce		30,312	29,531
Insurance Disc Regulations		9,136	7,032
Other Offences		1,194	1,441
Drinking & Driving:			
Driving or attempting to drive M.P.V. while drunk	749	713	1,058
Being in charge of M.P.V. while drunk	209	95	86
Driving or attempting to drive M.P.V. - blood / urine /alcohol concentration above prescribed limit	5,284	4,707	4,152
Being in charge of M.P.V. blood / urine / alcohol concentration above prescribed limit	235	240	289
Refusing to provide preliminary specimen of breath	233	185	184
Refusing to provide or permit taking of blood / urine specimen at Garda Stations	664	628	574
Drinking or attempting to drive an animal-drawn vehicle while drunk	6		
Driving or attempting to drive / pedal / cycle while drunk	260		
Exceeding Speed Limit:			
Built-up Area	15,178	17,058	18,413
Special	3,126	4,150	3,551
Ordinary	2,012	1,692	2,097
General	10,011	12,045	12,778
Motorway		714	639
Driving dangerously defective M.P.V.	278	253	270
Other Offences	9,371	7,326	10,193
Construction Equipment & Use of Vehicles			
Regulations 1963:		32	
Defective Tyres	6,996	7,951	7,357
Defective steering	19	21	39
Defective brakes	517	495	415
Gross weights of Goods Vehicles	716	846	744
Axle weights of Goods Vehicles	14	29	14
Other Offences	14,156	10,313	8,168
EEC Regulations:			
Vehicle Testing	3,511	4,076	3,838
Tachograph	2,495	2,580	2,722
Taking M.P.V. without authority	1,731	1,923	2,257

Non-indictable Offences (continued)	1992	1993	1994
Unauthorised interference with mechanism of M.P.V.	1,328	1,247	1,192
Taking possession of pedal cycle with consent	96	66	122
Road Transport Acts	3,012	2,768	2,726
Roads Act & Finance Acts - Excise Duty	116,132	129,709	118,519
Offences against Intoxicating Liquor Laws:			
Illegally on Licensed Premises during closing hours	10,249	9,302	8,323
Simple Drunkenness	1,599	1,494	1,724
Drunkenness with aggravation	4,431	5,105	3,552
Offences by Licensed Persons against closing Regulations	5,269	5,247	5,152
Other Offences by Licensed Persons	224	248	301
Supplying or selling drink to persons under 18 years	83		
Offences by the Holders of On-Licenses		86	69
Offences by the Holders of Off-Licenses		16	27
Purchase of intoxicating liquor by Persons under 18 years		18	13
Consumption of intoxicating liquor by persons under 18 - years in any place other than private residence		25	17
Persons under 18 representing themselves to be over 18 for purpose of obtaining & consuming intoxicating liquor		18	1
Licensed Holders permitting persons under 18 years to be on licensed premises during period when exemption order is in force		8	7
Persons under 18 years illegally on licensed premises during period when exemption order is in force		4	2
Licensed Holders permitting person under 18 years (alone) to be on premises used for the sale of intoxicating liquor for consumption of the off the premises	55	3	9
Offences in connection with Registered Clubs	65	83	99
Other offences against Intoxicating Liquor Laws	562	456	731
Offences against Labour Laws	34		
Criminal Damage to Animals, Fences etc.	1,842	2,296	2,185
Offences against Police Regulations:			
Dublin Metropolitan Police Acts	2,533	3,547	2,268
Summary Jurisdiction (Ireland) Act 1851	477	865	608
Prostitution	4	1	13
Living on earnings of Prostitution	1		2
Offences against Revenue Laws	430	31	51
Stealing, Receiving or Possessing Stolen Property	348		
Offences against Street Trading Acts	1,692	2,350	2,101
Offences against Vagrancy Acts:			
Begging	132	121	115
Other Offences	53	150	148
Offences against Wireless Telegraphy Act 1926	162	49	26
Offences against Firearms Acts	295	576	531
Offences in relation to Explosives	2		1
Misuse of Drugs Act 1977 / 1984	3,160	4,154	4,498
Offences against Juries Act 1976	104	82	2,420
Other Offences	12,101	11,704	13,128
TOTAL: NON-INDICTABLE OFFENCES	**487,348**	**562,260**	**500,747**

Notable offences recorded by the Police in Northern Ireland, 1992 - 1994

Crime Category	1992	1993	1994
Violence against the Person:			
Murder	108	101	82
Manslaughter & Infanticide	3	5	4
Attempted Murder	311	416	255
Other Violence against the Person	3,680	4,075	4,452
Total: Violence against the Person	**4,102**	**4,597**	**4,793**
Sexual Offences:			
Rape	116	151	168
Incest	35	20	24

Crime Category (continued)	1992	1993	1994
Indecent Assault	493	597	698
Other sexual offences	329	419	443
Total: Sexual Offences	**973**	**1,187**	**1,333**
Burglary:			
Burglary in a dwelling	7,461	8,005	9,454
Burglary in a building other than a dwelling	8,677	6,675	6,480
Other burglary	979	1,055	968
Total: Burglary	**17,117**	**15,735**	**16,902**
Robbery:			
Armed Robbery	866	751	657
Hijacking	339	365	194
Other robbery	646	607	716
Total: Robbery	**1,851**	**1,723**	**1,567**
Theft:			
Theft from a Person	242	217	257
Theft in a dwelling	356	436	427
Theft from Motor Vehicles	7,117	6,729	6,555
Shoplifting	4,549	4,625	4,510
Theft or unauthorised taking of Motor Vehicles	9,376	9,011	8,974
Other thefts	12,616	12,143	12,510
Total: Theft	**34,256**	**33,161**	**33,233**
Fraud & Forgery:			
Frauds	4,991	4,922	4,127
Forgery	495	631	973
Total: Fraud & Forgery	**5,486**	**5,553**	**5,100**
Criminal Damage:			
Arson	860	901	940
Explosives offences	117	88	65
Other criminal damage	1,525	1,867	2,072
Total: Criminal Damage	**2,502**	**2,856**	**3,077**
Offences against the State:			
Offences under the N.I. Emergency Provisions Act	103	87	106
Firearms Offences	73	76	98
Other offences against the State	302	273	236
Total: Offences against the State	**478**	**436**	**440**
Other Notifiable offences	767	980	1,441
GRAND TOTAL:	**67,532**	**66,228**	**67,886**

Offences reported/known to the Police

	1990	1991	1992	1993	1994
Number	57,198	63,492	67,532	66,228	67,886
Rate per 1,000 population	36.0	40.4	42.4	40.6	41.3
Detection rate (%)	37.5	35.7	34.4	36.4	35.9

PRISONS

Republic of Ireland Prison Population

Description (No. committed during year)	1988	1989	1990	1991	1992
Total: On remand	2,118	2,848	2,199	2,466	3,755
Males	1,884	2,609	1,917	2,216	3,392
Females	234	239	282	250	363
Total: For Trial	161	407	199	374	509
Males	157	398	197	360	496
Females	4	9	2	14	13

Description (No. committed during year)	1988	1989	1990	1991	1992
Total: On conviction	3,484	2,475	2,537	2,491	3,536
Males	3,234	2,303	2,454	2,349	3,366
Females	250	172	83	142	170
Throughput of Prisoners during the years:					
Total: On remand	2,132	2,858	2,184	2,453	3,759
Males	1,899	2,622	1,900	2,205	3,397
Females	233	236	284	248	362
Total: For trial	166	419	196	378	509
Males	161	410	193	364	497
Females	5	9	3	14	12
Total: On conviction	3,674	2,323	2,348	2,435	3,421
Males	3,420	2,145	2,274	2,284	3,247
Females	254	178	74	151	174
Total: Daily Average Population	1,962	2,067	2,108	2,140	2,185
Males	1,918	2,025	2,062	2,100	2,146
Females	44	42	46	40	39

Northern Ireland Prison Population

Description of Prisoners	1989	1990	1991	1992	1993	1994
Male on remand: Aged under 21	82	87	79	93	96	106
Male on remand: Aged 21 or over	217	259	254	307	322	321
Total: On remand	299	346	333	400	418	427
Fine defaulter: Aged under 21	7	6	8	6	7	4
Fine defaulter: Aged 21 or over	28	23	23	27	23	23
Total: Fine defaulter	35	29	31	33	30	37
Immediate Custody: YOC	156	134	141	145	153	133
Immediate Custody: Young Prisoners	165	140	116	102	100	91
Immediate Custody: Adult Prisoners	1,129	1,105	1,136	1,088	1,192	1,179
Total: Immediate Custody	1,450	1,379	1,393	1,335	1,445	1,403
Non-criminal	6	1	1	1	1	1
TOTAL: MALE PRISONERS	**1,790**	**1,755**	**1,758**	**1,769**	**1,894**	**1,858**
Female on remand: Aged under 21	2	6	6	6	2	5
Female on remand: Aged 21 or over	6	8	10	7	6	7
Total: On remand	8	14	16	13	8	12
Fine defaulter: Aged under 21					1	1
Fine defaulter: Aged 21 or over	1	1	1	1	1	2
Total: Fine defaulter	1	1	1	1	2	3
Immediate Custody: YOC	3	2	2	4	3	4
Immediate Custody: Young Prisoners	1	1	1	2	3	3
Immediate Custody: Adult Prisoners	12	12	18	21	24	19
Total: Immediate Custody	16	15	21	27	30	26
Non-criminal						
TOTAL: FEMALE PRISONERS	**25**	**30**	**38**	**41**	**40**	**41**
All Prisoners: Remand	307	360	349	413	426	439
All Prisoners: Fine defaulter	36	30	32	34	32	30
All Prisoners: Immediate custody	1,466	1,394	1,414	1,362	1,475	1,429
Non-criminal	6	1	1	1	1	1
TOTAL:	**1,815**	**1,785**	**1,796**	**1,810**	**1,934**	**1,899**

SECURITY

Main Deaths and Injuries connected with the 'Troubles', 1969-1994

Year	DEATHS RUC	Regular Army	UDR/RIR	Civilians	Total People Killed	INJURIES RUC	Regular Army	UDR/RIR	Civilians	Total People Injured
1969	1	—	—	—	13	14	711	54	—	—	765
1970	2	—	—	—	23	25	191	620	—	—	811
1971	11	43	5	115	174	315	381	9	1,887	2,592
1972	17	105	26	322	470	485	542	36	3,813	4,876
1973	13	58	8	173	252	291	525	23	1,812	2,651
1974	15	30	7	168	220	235	453	30	1,680	2,398
1975	11	14	6	216	247	263	151	16	2,044	2,474
1976	23	14	15	245	297	303	242	22	2,162	2,729
1977	14	15	14	69	112	183	172	15	1,017	1,387
1978	10	14	7	50	81	302	127	8	548	985
1979	14	38	10	51	113	165	132	21	557	875
1980	9	8	9	50	76	194	53	24	530	801
1981	21	10	13	57	101	332	112	28	878	1,350
1982	12	21	7	57	97	99	80	18	328	525
1983	18	5	10	44	77	142	66	22	280	510
1984	9	9	10	36	64	267	64	22	513	866
1985	23	2	4	26	55	415	20	13	468	916
1986	12	4	8	37	61	622	45	10	773	1,450
1987	16	3	8	68	95	246	92	12	780	1,130
1988	6	21	12	55	94	218	211	18	600	1,047
1989	9	12	2	39	62	163	175	15	606	959
1990	12	7	8	49	76	214	190	24	478	906
1991	6	5	8	75	94	139	197	56	570	962
1992	3	4	2	76	85	148	302	18	598	1,066
1993	6	6	2	70	84	147	146	27	504	824
1994	3	1	2	54	60	170	120	6	529	825
1969-1994	296	449	203	2,238	3,186	6,960	5,272	493	23,955	36,680

Security incidents in Northern Ireland, 1969-1994

Year	Shooting incidents	Bomb explosions	Devices neutralised	Firearms found	Explosives found (kg)	Armed Robberies including attempts	Amount Stolen
1969	73	9	1	14	102	—	—
1970	213	153	17	324	305	—	—
1971	1,756	1,022	493	716	1,246	489	304,000
1972	10,631	1,382	471	1,259	18,819	1,931	795,000
1973	5,019	978	542	1,313	17,426	1,317	612,000
1974	3,208	685	428	1,236	11,848	1,353	576,000
1975	1,803	399	236	820	4,996	1,325	572,000
1976	1,908	766	426	736	9,849	889	545,000
1977	1,081	366	169	563	1,728	676	447,000
1978	755	455	178	393	956	493	233,000
1979	728	422	142	300	905	504	568,000
1980	642	280	120	203	821	467	497,000
1981	1,142	398	131	357	3,419	689	855,000
1982	547	219	113	288	2,298	693	1,392,000
1983	424	266	101	166	1,706	718	830,000
1984	334	193	55	187	3,871	710	702,000
1985	238	148	67	173	3,344	542	656,000
1986	392	172	82	174	2,443	839	1,207,000
1987	674	236	148	206	5,885	955	1,900,000
1988	538	253	205	489	4,728	742	1,389,000
1989	566	224	196	246	1,377	604	1,079,000
1990	557	166	120	179	1,969	492	1,729,000
1991	499	231	137	164	4,167	607	1,673,000
1992	506	222	149	194	2,167	739	1,666,000
1993	476	206	83	196	3,944	643	1,515,000
1994	348	123	99	178	1,285	555	1,709,000
1969-1994	35,058	9,974	4,909	11,074	111,604	18,972	23,451,000

REPUBLIC OF IRELAND DEFENCE FORCES

Defence Staff Breakdown, 1996

Rank	Name	Stationed
Minister of Defence	Mr. Sean Barrett, T.D.	
Minister of State for Defence	Mr. Jim Higgins, T. D.	
Chief of Staff	Lt. Gen. Gerry McMahon	Defence HQ, Dublin
Adjutant General	Maj. Gen. Bill Dwyer	Defence HQ, Dublin
Quartermaster General	Maj. Gen. Dave Stapleton	Defence HQ, Dublin
Assistant Chief of Staff	Brig. Gen. Patrick Nowlan	Defence HQ, Dublin
General Officer Commanding Eastern Command	Brig. Gen. Colm Mangan	Cathal Brugha Bks, Dublin
General Officer Commanding Western Command	Brig. Gen. John Martin	Custume Bks, Athlone
General Officer Commanding Southern Command	Brig. Gen. James Farrell	Collins Bks, Cork
General Officer Commanding Curragh Command	Brig. Gen. Frank Colclough	Ceannt Bks, Curragh
Commandant Military College	Brig. Gen. Pierce Redmond	Military College, Curragh
Flag Officer Commanding the Naval Service	Commodore John Kavanagh	Defence HQ, Dublin
General Officer Commanding the Air Corps	Brig. Gen. Pat Cranfield	Defence HQ, Dublin

Headquarters of the Irish Defence Forces

MAIN HEADQUARTERS

Defence Forces Headquarters, Parkgate, Dublin 8.
- Army Headquarters, Parkgate, Dublin 8.
- Air Corps Headquarters, Parkgate, Dublin 8.
- Naval Service Headquarters, Parkgate, Dublin 8.

COMMAND HEADQUARTERS

Eastern Command, Collins Barracks, Dublin 7.
Southern Command, Collins Barracks, Cork.
Western Command, Custume Barracks, Athlone, Co. Westmeath.
Curragh Command, Curragh, Co. Kildare.
Air Corps, Casement Aerodrome, Baldonnel, Dublin 22.
Naval Service, Haulbowline, Cobh, Co. Cork.

Republic of Ireland Defence Personnel, July 1996

Force	Male	Female	Total
Army	10,209	163	10,372
Air Corps	1,074	14	1,088
Naval Service	1,027	2	1,029
Total	**12,310**	**179**	**12,489**

Republic of Ireland Personnel on Overseas Duties, July 1996

Personnel	Total
Number of Overseas Missions	15
Total Numbers serving Overseas	784

Republic of Ireland Defence Personnel, 1960 - 1994

Year	Permanent Defence Force	Reserve Defence Force
1960	8,965	24,569
1965	8,199	21,946
1970	8,574	20,253
1975	12,059	17,221
1980	13,383	19,249
1985	13,778	16,358
1990	13,233	15,982
1994	12,606	16,334

CULTURE, ARTS AND ENTERTAINMENT

INTRODUCTION

Of all the developed countries in Western Europe Ireland is, probably, the most perfect place to examine the impact of where an ancient native culture clashes with modern day international multi-culturalism brought about by global mass communications.

There are many contradictions and contrasts: while turf is still cut by hand in many bogs in rural Ireland hi-tech computer companies have established a growing number of bases in many parts of the island; in a land where traditional music can be heard in public houses, rock stars U2, Van Morrison and the Cranberries sell millions of records internationally; in a country that still retains a deep affection for its native language, Gaelic, less than 10 per cent actually speak the language on a daily basis; and native games, Gaelic football and hurling, unique to the island of Ireland, not only exist but flourish side-by-side with international soccer games, horse-racing and greyhound racing

Ireland has had few internationally renowned scientists or sculptors but in a culture where conversation and debate are regarded as an art form it has produced an endless list of noted writers, many of whom have achieved international acclaim, from Swift, Goldsmith, Wilde, Yeats, Joyce, Behan, O'Connor, Beckett, O'Casey through to Seamus Heaney and Brian Friel. Their works appear on school syllabuses throughout the English speaking world.

The culture of Ireland has been shaped by many influences; its isolation as a island on the periphery of Europe resulted in many of the old ways surviving well into this century while the more recent overload of mass communications on Irish youth, the youngest population in Western Europe, has had a far reaching impact on many aspects of Irish life, from social attitudes to music tastes.

The old cultural imperialism of the British Empire has been replaced in more recent times by the international imperialism of mass communications - the Hollywood film, the Australian soap-opera, the videos of MTV.

Despite these influences much of the traditional culture remains, particularly in rural areas. Irish traditional music has undergone a real renaissance, writing remains a revered calling, community socialising remains strong particularly in the numerous Irish public houses, and church-going is still very much part of life.

There is a burgeoning film industry, a huge increase in book publishing, tremendous growth of interest in the arts and drama - many county councils have appointed Arts Officers- and theatres for the performing arts are no longer the exclusive preserve of the big cities.

Ireland remains rich in culture, in myths and legends, in language and folklore.

The Gaeltacht (Irish-Speaking Areas)

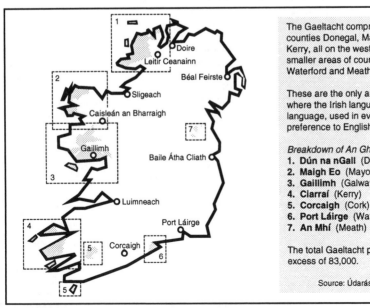

The Gaeltacht comprises large areas of counties Donegal, Mayo, Galway and Kerry, all on the west coast, as well as smaller areas of counties Cork, Waterford and Meath.

These are the only areas in Ireland where the Irish language is the preferred language, used in everyday life in preference to English.

Breakdown of An Ghaeltacht:
1. **Dún na nGall** (Donegal)
2. **Maigh Eo** (Mayo)
3. **Gaillimh** (Galway)
4. **Ciarraí** (Kerry)
5. **Corcaigh** (Cork)
6. **Port Láirge** (Waterford)
7. **An Mhí** (Meath)

The total Gaeltacht population is in excess of 83,000.

Source: Údarás na Gaeltachta

Glossary of Irish Words

Aerfort	Airport
Áiléar	Gallery
Aire	Government Minister
Airgead	Money
An Banc Ceannais	Central Bank
Amharclann	Theatre
Ard-Aighne	Attorney General
Ard-Rí	High King
Athair	Father
Aturnae	Solicitor
Bainisteoir	Manager
Banaltra	Nurse
Banc	Bank
Bórd	Board
Breitheamh	Judge
Bunreacht	Constitution
Bunreacht na hÉireann	Irish Constitution
Cathair	City
Cathaoirleach	Chairman
Ceannoifig	Head Office
Céim	Degree
Cigire	Inspector
Clann	Family
Clár	Agenda
Cláraitheoir	Registrar
Cléireach	Clerk
Coimisiún	Commission
Coiste	Committee
Coláiste	College
Comhairle	Council
Ceann Comhairle	Speaker (in Dáil Éireann)
Comhluadar	Company
Conradh	Contract
Córas	System
Cruinniú	Meeting
Cumann	Society, Club
Cumann Lúthchleas Gael	GAA
Cuntasóir	Accountant
Dáil Éireann	Irish Parliament
Dáilcheantar	Constituency
Daonra	Population
Déantóir	Manufacturer
Dlíodóir	Lawyer
Doctúir	Doctor
Dráma	Play
Drámaíocht	Drama
Eagarthóir	Editor
Ealaín	Art
Easpag	Bishop
Eitleán	Aeroplane

Eolaí	Directory
Fáilte	Welcome
Feirm	Farm
Focal	Word
Foclóir	Dictionary, Vocabulary
Fógra	Notice
Foras	Institute
Forbairt	Development
Fostóir	Employer
Gairm	Profession
Gaeilge	Irish Language
Gárda Síochána	Policeman
Iarnród	Railway
Innealtóir	Engineer
Iompar	Transport
Leabhar	Book
Leabharlann	Library
Léachtóir	Lecturer
Litríocht	Literature
Madadh	Dog
Mathair	Mother
Móin (móna)	Turf
Múnteoir	Teacher
Náisiún	Nation
Náisiúnta	National
Nuacht	News
Oideachas	Education
Oidhreacht	Heritage
Oifig	Office
Oifig an Phoist	Post Office
Oiliúint	Training
Oireachtas	Assembly, Dáil Éireann & Seanad Éireann combined
Oirmhinneach	Reverend
Ollamh	Professor
Ollscoil	University
Ospidéal / Otharlann	Hospital
Paipéar Nuachtán	Newspaper
Peil	Football
Pobal	Public
Poblacht	Republic
Reacht	Statute
Rialtas	Government
Roinn	Department
Rúnaí	Secretary

Rothar	Bicycle	Talamh (talún)	Land
		Tánaiste	Deputy Prime Minister
Sagart	Priest	Taoiseach	Leader, Prime Minister
Saoire	Holiday	Teachta Dála	Member of Parliament
Scoil	School	Teilifís	Television
Seanad	Senate	Teoranta	Limited
Seanadóir	Senator	Teo	Ltd
Seirbhís	Service		
Síocháin	Peace	Uachtarán	President
Sráid	Street	Udár	Author
Stát	State		
Stát-Seirbhis	Civil Service		
Stiúrthóir	Director		

Irish Speakers and non-Irish speakers in each province

	Total		Leinster		Munster		Connacht		Ulster (part of)	
Year	Irish	Non	Irish	Non	Irish	Non	Irish	Non	Irish	Non
Pop. of all ages										
1861	1,077,087	3,325,024	35,704	1,421,931	545,531	968,027	409,482	503,653	86,370	431,413
1871	804,547	3,248,640	16,247	1,323,204	386,494	1,006,991	330,211	516,002	71,595	402,443
1881	924,781	2,945,239	27,452	1,251,537	445,766	885,349	366,191	455,466	85,372	352,887
1891	664,387	2,804,307	13,677	1,174,083	307,633	864,769	274,783	449,991	68,294	315,464
1901	619,710	2,602,113	26,436	1,126,393	276,268	799,920	245,580	401,352	71,426	274,448
1911	553,717	2,585,971	40,225	1,121,819	228,694	806,801	217,087	393,897	67,771	263,454
1926	543,511	2,428,481	101,474	1,047,618	198,221	771,681	175,209	377,698	68,607	231,484
Pop. 3 yrs. plus										
1926	540,802	2,261,650	101,102	978,536	197,625	718,068	174,234	348,964	67,841	216,082
1936	666,601	2,140,324	183,378	966,434	224,805	668,030	183,082	315,322	75,336	190,538
1946	588,725	2,182,932	180,755	1,017,491	189,395	672,660	154,187	309,638	64,388	183,143
1961	716,420	1,919,398	274,644	964,383	228,726	576,613	148,708	246,592	64,342	140,810
1971	789,429	1,998,019	341,702	1,055,160	252,805	573,308	137,372	231,960	57,550	137,591
1981	1,018,413	2,208,054	473,225	1,202,292	323,704	612,526	155,134	244,264	66,350	148,972
1986	1,042,701	2,310,931	480,227	1,274,353	337,043	630,434	158,386	250,474	67,045	155,670
1991	1,095,830	2,271,176	511,639	1,264,188	352,177	612,988	162,680	242,091	69,334	151,909

Irish speakers in Gaeltacht areas

County	1981	1986	1991
Cork Gaeltacht	2,681	2,846	2,686
Donegal Gaeltacht	19,209	18,823	17,574
Galway Gaeltacht	19,819	20,873	21,533
Kerry Gaeltacht	6,264	6,142	5,945
Mayo Gaeltacht	8,457	8,071	7,096
Meath Gaeltacht	493	602	600
Waterford Gaeltacht	1,103	1,094	1,035
Total Gaeltacht Areas	**58,026**	**58,451**	**56,469**

FAMOUS IRISH WRITERS

Biographies of Famous Irish Writers

Allingham, William (b. 1824, Donegal) Poet of some note, best remembered by generations of schoolchildren for poem *The Fairies* which opens with "Up the airy mountains, down the rushy glen . . ." Died England, 1889.

Barrington, Sir Jonah (b. 1760, Laois) Lawyer and MP, writing deals with life as a member of the Anglo-Irish gentry. Best known for *Personal Sketches of His Own Time* (1827-32). Died France, 1834.

Beckett, Samuel (b. 1906, Dublin) Won Nobel Prize for Literature in 1969. Wrote in both English and French. Most famous work is play *Waiting for Godot* (1953). Also remembered for his novels *Murphy* (1938) and *Malone Dies* (1951). Died Paris, 1989.

Behan, Brendan (b. 1923, Dublin) Celebrated dramatist and wit, most famous plays were *The Quare Fellow* (1954) and *The Hostage* (1958). Also remembered for his controversial autobiography *The Borstal Boy* (1958). Died Dublin, 1964.

Binchy, Maeve (b. 1940, Dublin) Novelist, most famous works include *Light a Penny Candle, Echoes* and *Circle of Friends*.

Birmingham, George (b. 1865, Belfast) Novelist remembered for his satires on political events in Ireland. His autobiography is *Pleasant Places* (1934). Died London, 1950.

Boland , Eavan (b. 1944, Dublin) Poet whose work deals with the alienation felt by women. Published works include *The War Horse* and *Outside History*.

Brown, Christy (b. 1932, Dublin) Writer of immense courage, despite suffering from cerebral palsy he completed his autobiography *My Left Foot* (1964) and the autobiographical novel *Down all the Days* (1970). Died 1981.

Burke, Edmund (b. 1729, Dublin) Parliamentarian, best remembered for his *Reflections on the Revolution in France* (1790). Died England, 1797.

Carleton, William (b. 1794, Tyrone) Novelist, most famous works are two volumes of short stories *Traits and Stories of the Irish Peasantry* in 1830 and 1833. Died Dublin, 1869.

Colum, Patrick (b. 1881, Longford) Primarily a poet, wrote the famous *She Moved Through the Fair*, was also a playwright and novelist. Wrote a biography of Arthur Griffith, *Ourselves Alone* (1959) and a collection of anecdotes about James Joyce, *Our Friend James Joyce* (1958). Died Connecticut, 1972.

Deane, Seamus (b. 1940, Derry). Poet, *Rumours* (1977), *and History Lessons*. Also, *The Field Day Anthology of Irish Writing* (1989). Published his semi-autobiographical novel *Reading in the Dark* in 1996. Professor of Modern English and American Literature at University College Dublin and Professor of Anglo-Irish Literature at University of Notre Dame, Indiana.

Doyle, Roddy (b. 1958, Dublin) Novelist whose unique style captured the working class Dublin vernacular perfectly. Had major successes with comic novels such as *The Commitments* , the Booker Prize winning *Paddy Clarke Ha Ha Ha* and *The Woman who walked into Doors* . Three novels have been made into films and he has also written a T.V. series *'The Family'*.

Edgeworth, Maria (b. 1767, Oxfordshire) Novelist, her most famous book is *Castle Rackrent* (1800).

Lived most of her life at Edgeworthstown, Co. Longford. Died Edgeworthstown, 1849.

Ervine, St. John (b. 1883, Belfast) Playwright who largely dealt with Ulster themes. Famous plays include *Boyd's Shop* (1936) and *Friend and Relations* (1941). Wrote biographies of figures as diverse as Charles Stewart Parnell (1925), Sir James Craig (1949) and George Bernard Shaw (1956). Died England, 1971.

Friel, Brian (b. 1929, Tyrone) One of foremost English Language dramatists in the world. Most famous plays are *Philadelphia, Here I Come* (1964) *Translations* (1981) and *Dancing at Lughnasa* (1990).

Gogarty, Oliver St. John (b. 1878, Dublin) Poet and surgeon, major works include *An Offering of Swans* (1923) and *Elbow Room* (1939). Died New York, 1957.

Gregory, Lady (b. 1852, Galway) Dramatist and friend of Yeats. Director of Abbey Theatre, produced her own comedies *The Rising of the Moon* (1907) and *Spreading the News* (1904). Died Galway, 1932.

Heaney, Seamus (b. 1939, Derry) Considered one of finest poets writing in the English language. Won Nobel Prize for Literature in 1996. Works include *Wintering Out* (1972) and *Station Island* (1985).

Johnston, Jennifer (b. 1930). Author, novels include *Shadows on our Skin* and *The Christmas Tree*.

Joyce, James (b. 1882, Dublin) Leading novelist of early twentieth century. Best known works are *A Portrait of the Artist as a Young Man* (1916) and *Ulysses* (1922) which was censored until 1934. Other important works include *Dubliners* (1914) and *Finnegan's Wake* (1939). Died Zurich, 1941.

Kavanagh, Patrick (b. 1904, Monaghan) Primarily a poet, most famous poems are *The Great Hunger* (1942) and *Stony Grey Soil*. Also wrote the novel *Tarry Flynn* (1948). Died Dublin, 1967.

Keane, John B. (b. 1928, Kerry) Playwright, best works include *Sive, The Field* and *Big Maggie*. Screenplay of *The Field* starring Richard Harris was a major Box Office success.

Kickham, Charles (b. 1828, Tipperary) Fenian, journalist and novelist. Editor of Fenian newspaper *'The Irish People'*. Best known for novels *Sally Kavanagh* and *Knocknagow* (1879) and poems *Rory of the Hill*. Died Dublin, 1882.

Kinsella, Thomas (b. 1928, Dublin). Poet, published works include *'Another September'* and *'The Death of a Queen'*.

Lewis, Clive Staples (C. S.) (b. 1898, Belfast) Remembered for series of children's books known collectively as *The Chronicles of Narnia*. Professor of Medieval and Renaissance Literature at Cambridge University. Died 1963.

Macken, Walter (b. 1915, Galway) Novelist, remembered for historical trilogy *Seek the Fair Land* (1959), *The Silent People* (1962) and *The Scorching Wind* (1964). Died Galway, 1967.

Mangan, James Clarence (b. 1803, Dublin) Poet and contributor to *The Nation*. Best remembered for poems *Dark Rosaleen* and *The Woman of Three Cows*. Died Dublin, 1849.

McGill, Patrick (b. 1891, Donegal) Novelist and poet. Poetry collections include *Gleanings from a Navvy's Scrapbook* (1911) and *Songs of the Dead End*

(1912). Novels include *Children of the Dead End* (1914) and *The Rat Pit* (1915). Died United States, 1963.

McGuinness, Frank (b. 1953, Buncrana). Playwright who lectures at Maynooth. Director of Abbey Theatre since 1992. Plays include *Observe the Sons of Ulster Marching Towards the Somme* (1985), and *Someone Who'll Watch Over Me* (1992).

Merriman, Brian (b. 1749, Clare) Poet, most famous for epic *Cúirt an Mhéan Oíche*, 1780 (The Midnight Court) - most translated poem in the Irish language. Died Limerick, 1805.

Murphy, Dervla (b. 1931, Waterford). Author and literary critic. Publications include *Eight Feet in the Andes* (1983), *Transylvania and Beyond* (1992) and *The Ukimwi Road* (1993). Won many literary awards for her work.

Murphy, Tom (b. 1935, Galway). Playwright, whose plays include *She Stoops to Folly* (1995) and *The Morning After Optimism* (1971). One of country's foremost playwrights, was director of Abbey Theatre (1972-83).

Ní Chonaill, Eibhlin Dhubh (b. 1743, Kerry) Remembered for lament *Caoineadh Airt Uí Laoghaire* (1773) delivered in Irish over the body of her murdered husband. Died 1800.

O'Cadhain, Máirtín (b.1906, Galway Gaeltacht) Noted writer in the Irish language. Most famous for novel *Cré na Cille* (1949), which was translated into several European languages. First Irish-writer elected to the Irish Academy of Letters. Died Dublin, 1970.

O'Casey, Seán (b. 1880, Dublin) Dramatist, best remembered for plays dealing with the struggle for Irish Independence, *The Shadow of a Gunman* (1923), *Juno and the Paycock* (1924) and *The Plough and the Stars* (1926). Died England, 1964.

Ó'Cléirigh, Mícheál (b. 1575, Donegal) Compiled the Annals of the Four Masters, assisted by Cuigcoigriche Ó'Duigeanáin, Fearfeasa Ó'Maolconaire, and Cuigcoigriche Ó'Cléirigh. Wrote through the medium of Irish. Died Louvain, 1643.

Ó'Conaire, Pádraic (b. 1883, Galway) Writer of novels and short stories in Irish. Best known for *M'Asal Beag Dubh* and *Fearfasa MacFeasa* 1930. Died Dublin, 1928.

O'Connor, Frank (Pen name of Michael Francis O'Donovan). (b. 1903, Cork) Best known for short stories, collected in volumes such as *Guests of the Nation* (1931) and *Crab Apple Jelly* (1944). Died Dublin, 1966.

Ó'Criomhthain, Tomás (b. 1856, Great Blasket Island, off Kerry) Best known for his diary, *Allagar na h-Inise* (1928), regarded as a classic and his autobiography *An t-Oileánach* (1929). Died Great Blasket Island, 1937.

Ó'Doirnín, Peadar (b. 1682, Louth) Poet, best known for works as a political and humourous verse writer. Died Armagh, 1769.

O'Donnell, Peadar (b. 1893, Donegal) Revolutionary socialist and novelist. Famous novels are *Islanders* (1928) and *The Big Windows* (1955). Died Dublin, 1986.

O'Faolain, Sean (b. 1900, Cork) Novelist and short story writer. Most famous collections were "*Midsummer Night Madness*" (1932) and "*A Purse of Coppers*" (1937). Wrote biographies of many leading Irish figures including one on Daniel O'Connell *King of the Beggars* (1938). Died Dublin, 1991.

O'Flaherty, Liam (b. 1896, Inishmore) Novelist, best remembered for his works *The Neighbour's Wife* (1923), *The Informer* (1925), later filmed by John Ford in 1935, *Mr. Gilhooley* (1926), *The Assassin* (1928) and *Insurrection* (1950). Died Dublin, 1984.

O'Grady, Standish (b. 1846, Cork) Writer of historical novels such as *The Heroic Period* (1878) and *Red Hugh's Captivity* (1889). Died England, 1928.

Ó'Grianna, Séamus (b. 1891, Donegal) Known by the pen-name, "Máire" was a novelist and short story writer. Best known for *Cith is Dealain* (1926) and *Caislean Óir* (1924). Died Donegal, 1969.

Ó'Ríordáin, Séan (b. 1916, Cork) Poet. Best remembered for publications *Eireaball Spideóige* (1952) *Brosna* (1964) and *Línte Liombó* (1971). Irish Columnist in the Irish Times. Died Cork city, 1977.

Ó'Searcaigh, Cathal (b. 1956, Donegal) Irish language poet.

Ó'Súilleabháin, Eoghan Rua (b. 1748, Kerry) Poet. Wrote in Irish, about experiences as a school teacher, seaman and wandering labourer. Died Kerry, 1784.

Ó'Súilleabháin, Muiris (b. 1904, Great Blasket Island) Best remembered for autobiography *Fiche Blian ag Fás*, (Twenty Year a-Growing), 1933. Wrote in Irish. Died Galway, 1950.

Ó'Rathaille, Aodhagán (b. 1670, Kerry) Poet, whose poetry laments the end of the age of Gaelic chieftains. Wrote in Irish. Died Kerry, 1726.

Sayers, Peig (b. 1873, Kerry) Noted for her wealth of folklore and skill as a storyteller on the Great Blasket Island. Her tales and folksongs were recorded by the Irish Folklore Commission, and her classic dictated autobiography *Peig* was published in 1936. Died Kerry, 1958.

Shaw, George Bernard (b. 1856, Dublin) Won Nobel Prize for Literature in 1925. Most famous works include *Man and Superman* (1905) and *Saint Joan* (1923). Also noted essayist and music critic. Died Canada, 1950.

Stoker, Bram (b. 1847, Dublin) Best remembered for his novel *Dracula* (1897), which has inspired dozens of other works. Died London, 1912.

Swift, Jonathon (b. 1667, Dublin) Primarily, a Political Pamphleteer, published the satirical *Gulliver's Travels* in 1726. Died Dublin, 1745.

Synge, John Millington (b. 1871, Dublin) Dramatist, famous for his plays *The Shadow of the Glen* (1903) and *The Playboy of the Western World* (1907), controversial at the time for their portrayal of the Irish peasantry. Died Dublin, 1909.

Taylor, Alice (b. Cork). Writer. Best known for her book, *To School through the Fields*.

Wilde, Oscar Fingal O'Flahertie Wills (b. 1854, Dublin) Most famous wit and playwright of the Victorian era, most famous plays are *The Importance of Being Earnest* (1895) and *Salome* (1891) which was originally written in French. Also wrote the poem *The Ballad of Reading Gaol*. Died Paris, 1900.

Yeats, William Butler (b. 1865, Dublin) Poet and dramatist, was to the forefront of Irish Cultural Revival. Won Nobel Prize for Literature in 1923. Most famous play is *Cathleen Ni Houlihan* (1902), but is more famous for his poetry - *Lake Isle of Innisfree*, *September 1913*, *Easter 1916* and *The Circus Animal's Desertion*. Died France, 1939.

GALLERIES AND ART CENTRES

Galleries and Art Centres in Ireland

ANTRIM: Catalyst Arts Centre, Belfast; **Cavehill Gallery**, Belfast; **Clotworthy Arts Centre**, Antrim; **Crescent Arts Centre**, Belfast; **Harmony Hill Arts Centre**, Lisburn; **John Magee Ltd.**, Belfast; **Linen Hall Library**, Belfast; **Old Museum Arts Centre**, Belfast; **One Oxford Street**, Belfast; **Seymour Galleries**, Lisburn; **The Bell Gallery**, Belfast; **The Fenderesky Gallery** at Queen's, Belfast; **The Gallery**, Belfast; **Ulster Arts Club Gallery**, Belfast; **Ulster Museum**, Belfast.

ARMAGH: Adam Gallery, Armagh; **Armagh County Museum**, Armagh; **Hayloft Gallery**, Armagh; **Roy Edwards Fine Arts Ltd.**, Portadown; **The Peacock Gallery**, Craigavon.

CAVAN: Cavan County Arts Service, Cavan Town.

CARLOW: Pembroke Studio Gallery, Carlow Town.

CLARE: Dallán Gallery, Ballyvaughan; **De Valera Library**, Ennis; **Clare Branch Library**, Ennistymon; **Seán Lemass Library**, Shannon; **The Atlantis Gallery**, Kilshanny.

CORK: Bantry Library, Bantry; **Blackcoombe Art Gallery**, Cork; **Boole Library**, University College Cork; **Charleville Library**, Charleville; **Crawford Municipal Art Gallery**, Cork City; **Keane-on-Ceramics**, Kinsale; **Lavitt's Quay Gallery**, Cork City; **O'Kane's Green Gallery**, Bantry; **Sirius Commemoration Trust**, Cobh; **The Art Hive**, Cork City; **The Bandon Gallery**, Bandon; **Triskel Arts Centre**, Cork City; **Vangard Gallery**, Macroom; **West Cork Arts Centre**, Skibbereen.

DERRY: Context Gallery, Derry; **Flowerfield Arts Centre**, Portstewart; **Foyle Arts Centre**, Derry; **Gordon Galleries**, Derry; **Orchard Gallery**, Derry; **Riverside Gallery**, Coleraine; **Town House Gallery**, Coleraine.

DONEGAL: Cristeph Gallery, Letterkenny; **Donegal County Arts Service**, Letterkenny; **Donegal County Museum**, Letterkenny; **Glebe House & Gallery**, Churchill; **Port Gallery**, Letterkenny; **Ram's Head Gallery**, Kilcar; **Tullyarvan Mill Culture & Exhibition Centre**, Buncrana; **Ulster Cultural Institute**, Glencolumbkille.

DOWN: Ards Art Centre, Newtownards; **Castle Espie Gallery**, Comber; **Cleft Gallery**, Donaghadee; **Down Arts Centre**, Downpatrick; **Grant Fine Art**, Newcastle; **Newcastle Art Gallery**, Newcastle; **Newry & Mourne Arts Centre**, Newry; **North Down Visitors & Heritage Centre**, Bangor; **Priory Art Gallery**, Holywood; **Salem Gallery**, Comber; **Shambles Art Gallery**, Hillsborough.

DUBLIN: Andrew's Lane Theatre; City Arts Centre; Combridge Fine Arts Ltd.; Crafts Council Gallery; Davis Gallery; Designyard; Douglas Hyde Gallery; Dublin Photographic Centre; Dublin Public Libraries; Dublin Writers Museum; Dun Laoghaire - Rathdown Arts Centre; Gorry Gallery; Graphic Studio Dublin Gallery; Green on Red Gallery; Guinness Gallery; Guinness Hop Store; Hallward Gallery; Head Gallery; Howth Harbour Gallery; Hugh Lane Municipal Gallery of Modern Art; Irish Life Exhibition Centre; Irish Museum of Modern Art; Kennedy Gallery; Kerlin Gallery; Milmo-Penny Fine Art; New Appollo Gallery; Oisín Art Gallery; Oisín Art Gallery, Fairview; Old Bawn Community School, Tallaght; Oriel Gallery; Pantheon Gallery; Phoenix Art Studio, Lucan; Royal Dublin Society; RHA Gallagher Gallery; Rubicon Gallery; Swords Art & Craft Centre, Swords; Taylor Galleries; Temple Bar Gallery & Studios; The Architecture Centre; The Arts Council, Dublin; The Bobby Dawson Gallery, Dun Laoghaire; The Gallery of Photography; The James Gallery, Dalkey; The Mansion House; The National Gallery of Ireland; The Project Arts Centre; The Solomon Gallery; Village Art Gallery, Skerries; Wyvern Gallery.

FERMANAGH: Ardhowen Theatre & Arts Centre, Enniskillen; **Enniskillen Castle Heritage Centre**, Enniskillen.

GALWAY: An Dánlann, Casla; **Ballinasloe Library**, Ballinasloe; **Galway Arts Centre**, Galway; **The Grainstore Gallery**, Galway; **The Kenny Gallery**, Galway; **University College Galway**; **West Shore Gallery**, Oughterard.

KERRY: Bín Bán Gallery, Tralee; **Frank Lewis Gallery**, Killarney; **Iverni Gallery**, Kenmare; **Kerry Branch Library**, Killarney; **Sheeóg Art Gallery**, Killorglin; **Siamsa Tíre Theatre / Arts Centre**, Tralee; **Simple Pleasures Art Gallery**, Dingle; **St. John's Arts and Heritage Centre**, Listowel; **The Killarney Art Gallery**, Killarney; **Tralee Library**, Tralee; **The Wellspring Gallery**, Tralee.

KILDARE: Athy Community Library, Athy; **Crookstown Mill Heritage Centre**, Ballitore; **Kilcock Art Gallery**, Kilcock; **Kildare Branch Library**, Celbridge; **Kildare Branch Library**, Naas; **Maynooth Exhibition Centre**, Maynooth; **Tuckmill Gallery**, Naas.

KILKENNY: Butler Gallery, Kilkenny; **Kilkenny County Library**, Graiguenamanagh; **The Berkeley Gallery**, Thomastown.

LAOIS: Laois County Hall, Portlaoise.

LEITRIM: Fionn MacCumhaill Centre, Keshcarrigen; **Old Barrell Store Arts Centre**, Carrick-on-Shannon.

LIMERICK: AV Gallery, University of Limerick; **Belltable Arts Centre**, Limerick; **Chris Doswell's Gallery**, Limerick; **Dolmen Gallery**, Limerick; **Limerick Branch Library**, Foynes; **Limerick City Gallery of Art**; **Muse Gallery**, Limerick; **Newcastle West Library**.

LONGFORD: Carroll Gallery, Longford.

LOUTH: Artistic License,

Carlingford; **County Museum**. Dundalk; **Droichead Arts Centre**, Drogheda; **Holy Trinity Heritage Centre**, Carlingford; **Louth Branch Library**, Ardee; **The Basement Gallery**, Dundalk.

MAYO: Castlebar Public Library, Castlebar; **Claremorris Gallery**, Claremorris; **Foxford Exhibition Centre**, Foxford; **The Aimhirgin Gallery**, Louisburgh; **The Kirk Gallery**, Castlebar; **The Linenhall Arts Centre**, Castlebar; **Western Light Art Gallery**, Achill Island; **Westport Public Library**, Westport; **Yawl Gallery**, Achill Island.

MEATH: Navan Library, Navan; **Trim Library**, Trim.

MONAGHAN: Market House Gallery, Monaghan; **Monaghan County Museum**, Monaghan.

OFFALY: Offaly County Library Service, Tullamore.

SLIGO: Hawk's Well Theatre, Sligo; **Sligo Art Gallery**, Sligo; **Taylor's Art Gallery**, Riverstown; **The Model Arts Centre**, Sligo.

TIPPERARY: Carrick-on-Suir Heritage Centre, Carrick-on-Suir; **Nenagh District Heritage Centre**, Nenagh; **Roscrea Heritage Centre**, Roscrea; **Tipperary County Library Service**, Thurles; **Tipperary (SR) County Museum**, Clonmel; **The Lucy Erridge Gallery**, Birdhill.

WATERFORD: Garter Lane Arts Centre, Waterford; **Lismore Library**, Lismore.

WESTMEATH: Dolan Moore Gallery, Athlone; **Midland Arts Resource Centre**, Mullingar.

WEXFORD: Wexford Arts Centre, Wexford; **Woodland Arts & Crafts Gallery**, Gorey; **The Chantry Gallery**, Bunclody.

WICKLOW: Craft Art Gallery, Bray; **The Hangman Gallery**, Bray; **Renaissance III Gallery**, Wicklow; **Signal Art Centre**, Bray.

THEATRES

Irish Theatres, Theatre Companies & Receiving Venues

ANTRIM
Arts Theatre,
41 Botanic Ave., Belfast.
Castleward Opera,
61 Marlborough Pk. North, Belfast.
Clotworthy House Arts Centre,
Randalstown Rd., Co. Antrim.
DubbelJoint Productions,
351-353 Lisburn Rd., Belfast.
Golden Thread Theatre,
Brookfield Business Centre,
333 Crumlin Road, Belfast.
Grand Opera House,
Great Victoria St., Belfast.
Lyric Theatre,
55 Ridgeway St., Belfast.
Old Museum Arts Centre,
7 College Square North, Belfast.
Opera Northern Ireland,
Stranmillis Rd., Stranmillis, Belfast.
Point Fields Theatre Co. Ltd.,
Cathedral Buildings, 64 Donegall St.,
Belfast.
Tinderbox Theatre Co.,
Old Museum Buildings,
College Sq. North, Belfast.
Ulster Hall, Bedford St., Belfast.

ARMAGH
Gateway Theatre Co.,
57 Gilford Rd., Portadown, Armagh.

CARLOW
Bridewell Lane Theatre,
Bridewell Lane, Tullow St., Carlow.

CAVAN
Cornmill Theatre & Arts Centre,
Main St., Carrigallen, Co. Cavan.

CLARE
Theatre Omnibus Business Cent.,
Francis St., Ennis, Co. Clare.

CORK
Cork Opera House,
Emmet Place, Cork.
Everyman Palace,
15 McCurtain St., Cork.
Firkin Crane Centre,
Shandon, Cork.
New Granary Theatre,
University College, Mardyke, Cork.
Cork Arts & Theatre Club,
7 Knapps Sq., Cork.
Graffiti Theatre Co. Ltd.,
50 Popes Quay, Cork.
Kickstart Theatre, Community
Centre, Gurrahabraher Rd., Cork.

DERRY
Big Telly Theatre Co.,
Flowerfield Art Centre,
Coleraine Rd., Portstewart.
Field Day Theatre Company,
Foyle Arts Centre,
Lawrence Hill, Derry.
Minkey Hill Theatre Co.,
Foyle Arts Ct., Lawrence Hill, Derry.
O'Casey Theatre Co.,
The Playhouse,Artillery St., Derry.
Ridiculusmus,
The Playhouse, Artillery St., Derry.
Riverside Theatre,
Cromore Rd., Coleraine, Co. Derry.
Stage Beyond Theatre Co.,
Play Resource Centre.,
Artillery Street, Derry.
St. Columb's Theatre & Art Centre,
Orchard St., Derry.

DONEGAL
Balor Theatre, Ballybofey
Abbey Centre, Ballyshannon.

DUBLIN
Andrew's Lane Theatre,
Exchequer St., Dublin 2.
Crypt Art Centre Dublin Castle,
Dublin 2.
Ambassador Theatre,
Parnell St., Dublin 1.
Point Theatre,
Eastlink Bridge, Dublin 1.
Focus Theatre Co.,
6 Pembroke Place, Dublin 2.
Gaiety Theatre,
South King St., Dublin 2.
Gate Theatre,
8 Parnell Sq., Dublin 1.
Abbey & Peacock Theatre,
Lower Abbey St., Dublin 1.
Olympia Theatre,
72 Dame St., Dublin 2.
RDS, Simmonscourt Pavillion,
Ballsbridge, Dublin 4.
Second Age Ltd.
c/o 30 Dame St., Dublin 2.
Tivoli Theatre,
135-138 Francis St., Dublin 2.
Samuel Beckett Theatre,
Trinity College, Dublin 2.
Lambert Puppet Theatre & Museum, Clifton Lane,
Monkstown, Co. Dublin.
Down-to-Earth Theatre Co. Ltd.,
3 Beresford Place, Dublin 1.
Dublin Grand Opera Society,
John Player Hse., S C Rd., Dublin 8.
Dublin Theatre Festival Ltd.,
47 Nassau St, Dublin 2.

Dublin Youth Theatre,
23 Gardiner St. Upper, Dublin 1.
Gas Works Theatre Co.,
Iomha Ildanach Theatre Co. Ltd.,
6 Capel St., Dublin 1.
The Eblana Theatre,
Busaras, Store St., Dublin 1.
Passion Machine Theatre Co.,
30 Gardiner Place, Dublin 7.
Project Arts Centre,
39 East Essex St., Dublin 2.
Riverbank Studio / Theatre,
10 Merchants Quay, Dublin 8.
Rough Magic Ltd.,
11 East Essex St., Dublin 2.
St. Anthony's Theatres,
Merchants Quay, Dublin 8.
Team Theatre Co., 4 Marlborough
Place, Dublin 1.

FERMANAGH
Ardhowen Theatre,
Dublin Rd., Enniskillen.

GALWAY
Druid Theatre Co.,
Chapel Lane, Galway.
Mall Theatre,
The Mall, Tuam.
Punchbag Theatre Co.,
47 Dominick St., Galway.
Taibhdhearc na Gaillimhe,
Sráid Lár, Galway.
Glenamaddy Townhall Theatre,
Creggs Rd., Glenamaddy, Galway.

KERRY
Siamsa Tire Theatre, Tralee, Kerry.

KILKENNY
Cleere's Theatre,
28 Parliament St., Kilkenny.
Watergate Theatre Co.,
Parliament St., Kilkenny.

LEITRIM
Eggert Rodger,
Glenboy, Manorhamilton, Leitrim.

LIMERICK
The Belltable, 69 O'Connell St.
Theatre Royal, Upr. Cecil St.

LONGFORD
Backstage Theatre,
Farneyhoogan, Longford,
Bog Lane Theatre,
Bog Lane, Ballymahon, Longford.

LOUTH
Dundalk Town Hall,
Crowe St., Dundalk, Co. Louth.

MAYO
Yew Theatre Co., Cresent Hse.,
Casement St., Ballina.

MEATH
Duchas Folk Theatre,
Castle St., Trim, Co. Meath.

MONAGHAN
Garage Theatre,

St. Davnet's Complex, Armagh Rd.,
Monaghan.

SLIGO
Blue Raincoat Theatre Co.,
Lower Quay St., Sligo.
Hawk's Well Theatre,
Temple St., Sligo.

TIPPERARY
Magner's Theatre,
The Mall, Clonmel, Co. Tipperary.

WATERFORD
Forum Theatre,
The Glen, Waterford.
Theatre Royal,
The Mall, Waterford.
Garter Lane Theatre,
22A O'Connell St.
Red Kettle Theatre Co.,
33 O'Connell St.

WEXFORD
Gorey Little Theatre,
Pearse St., Gorey.
Theatre Royal, High St.
Razor Edge Arts Theatre Co. Ltd.,
Paul Quay, Wexford.
St. Michael's Theatre,
South St., New Ross.

WICKLOW
Dry Rain Performing Arts Centre,
An Lar Dargle Rd. Lower, Bray.

PUBLISHING HOUSES

Major Publishing Houses in Ireland

Appletree Press
19-21 Alfred St., Belfast.
Attic Press
29 Upper Mount Street, Dublin 2.
Blackstaff Press
3 Galway Park, Dundonald, Belfast.
Brandon
Brandon Book Publishers Ltd.,
Cooleen, Dingle, Kerry.
Butterworths
Butterworth Ireland Ltd., 26 Upper
Ormond Quay, Dublin 7.
Eason
Eason & Son Ltd., 66 Middle Abbey
Street, Dublin 1.
**Economic and Social Research
Institute**
4 Burlington Road, Dublin 4.
Educational Company of Ireland
Ballymount Road, Walkinstown,
Dublin 12.
C. J. Fallon
Lucan Road, Palmerstown,
Dublin 20.
Field Day Publications

Foyle Arts Centre, Old Foyle
College, Lawrence Hill, Derry.
Folens
Broomhill Business Park,
Tallaght, Dublin 24.
Gill & Macmillan
Goldenbridge, Dublin 8.
Institute of Irish Studies
The Queen's University of Belfast,
8 Fitzwilliam Street, Belfast.
Institute of Public Administration
Vergemount Hall, Clonskeagh,
Dublin 6.
Irish Academic Press
Kill Lane, Blackrock, Co. Dublin.
Lafferty Publications
IDA Tower, Pearse Street, Dublin 2.
The Lilliput Press
4 Rosemount Terrace, Arbour Hill,
Dublin 7.
Mentor Publications
43 Furze Road, Sandyford Industrial
Estate, Dublin 18.
Mercier Press
PO Box 5, 5 French Church Street,

Cork.
The O'Brien Press
20 Victoria Road, Rathgar, Dublin 6.
Oak Tree Press
4 Arran Quay, Dublin 7.
Poolbeg
Poolbeg Group Services Ltd.,
Knocksedan House, 123 Baldoyle
Industrial Estate, Dublin 13.
The Round Hall Press
Kill Lane Blackrock, Co. Dublin.
Sporting Books
4 Sycamore Road, Mount Merrion,
Co. Dublin.
Ulster Historical Foundation -
Balmoral Buildings, 12 College
Square East, Belfast.
Veritas
7-8 Lower Abbey Street, Dublin 1.
White Row Press
135 Cumberland Road, Dundonald,
Belfast BT16 0BB.
Wolfhound Press
68 Mountjoy Square, Dublin 1.

ARTS FUNDING

The Arts Council - Funding per Capita Expenditure (£m)

	1990-91	1991-92	1992-93	1993-94	1994-95	1995-96*
Britain (average)	3.15	3.46	3.93	4.00	3.94	4.04
England	3.09	3.39	3.85	3.91	3.83	3.92
Scotland	3.43	3.86	4.44	4.54	4.62	4.76
Wales	3.70	3.81	4.42	4.49	4.65	4.86
NORTHERN IRELAND	3.23	3.57	3.88	3.95	4.11	4.04

	1991	1992	1993	1994	1995 *
REPUBLIC OF IRELAND (IR£m)	2.84	2.90	3.30	3.80	4.64

*These figures are provisional.

Arts Attendances at Principal Venues and Festivals in Northern Ireland

	1990-91 (000)	1991-92 (000)	1992-93 (000)	1993-94 (000)	1994-95 (000)
Ardhowen	13	17	15	17	16
Arts Theatre	—	83	74	67	82
Cinemagic	6	8	10	12	13
Derry	—	—	75	37	28
Foyle Film Festival	5	6	7	7	8
Grand Opera House	190	87	173	115	221
Lyric Theatre	42	42	34	54	65
Queen's Festival	70	66	72	73	80
Riverside	19	22	19	17	22
Ulster Hall (Orchestra)	40	35	36	37	38
Totals	**385**	**366**	**515**	**436**	**565**

NOBEL PRIZE WINNERS

Irish Nobel Prize Winners

The Nobel Prizes have been awarded annually since 1901 in the fields of Physics, Chemistry, Physiology or Medicine, Peace and Literature. The awards were established under the will of Swedish Chemist Alfred Nobel, the interest of whose trust fund is divided among persons who have made outstanding contributions to the said fields. Ireland has had winners on seven occasions, they are :-

1923:	**William Butler Yeats**	(Literature)
1925:	**George Bernard Shaw**	(Literature)
1951:	**Ernest Thomas Sinton Walton** (Shared with Englishman Sir John Douglas Cockcroft)	(Physics)
1969:	**Samuel Beckett**	(Literature)
1974:	**Seán MacBride** (Shared with Eisaku Sato of Japan)	(Peace)
1976:	**Mairead Corrigan** and **Betty Williams**	(Peace)
1996:	**Seamus Heaney**	(Literature)

PAINTINGS

Top Five Paintings on Public Display in National Gallery of Ireland

These are five of the most important Irish Paintings in the National Gallery of Ireland in aesthetic terms. They date from the early eighteenth century to the end of the nineteenth century.

Artist	Painting Title
Nathaniel Hone the Elder	The Piping Boy
George Barret	Powerscourt Waterfall
Thomas Roberts	Lucan Castle
Francis Danby	The Opening of the Sixth Seal
Roderk O'Connor	La Ferme de Lezaver Finistére

TELEVISION AND RADIO

Television and Radio Broadcasting in Ireland

Ireland has had a long association with the broadcast media. Indeed, several authorative sources have claimed that the first real 'electronic" broadcast was made by the 1916 rebels holed up in the G.P.O. who attempted to send radio messages to an American ship to enable it to inform the world that revolution had broken out in Ireland.

Within eight years of that "broadcast" the BBC had established a radio service in N.I. while just two years later, in 1926, Radio Éireann came into being. Television broadcasting on the island of Ireland began with the BBC in the mid-fifties, and within four years Ulster Television (1959) and R.T.E. (1960) had entered the frame.

In the Ireland of the 1990, there are almost a million T.V. sets in the Republic alone while UTV can claim to be the most watched channel within Britain's I.T.V. network with a 42% share of its target audience. According to TAM ratings, Gay Byrne's "Late Late Show" , an agenda setting programme for many years, is still tops in the South while U.T.V's "Kelly" is the most viewed programme in the North. BBC N.I. has 28% share of its target market.

Without question, television and modern high-tech communications have totally changed much of the traditional way of life on the island. The peripherality and isolation of Ireland on the west coast of Europe has become, in communication terms, an irrelevance.

Number of Television Licences in Republic of Ireland per Province

County & Province	1994		
	Monochrome	Colour	Total
Connacht	7,322	94,554	101,876
Leinster	14,273	448,920	463,193
Munster	12,235	241,817	254,052
Ulster *	2,096	46,211	48,307
TOTAL STATE **	**35,926**	**831,502**	**867,428**

* Does not include six Counties in Northern Ireland.   ** Includes figures for Licences issued free.

Television Broadcasting by RTE (1993)

Programme	Home Produced	Programmes Purchased	Programmes (Repeats)	Total Hours
Advertising	839	—	—	839
Arts/Humanities/Sciences	261	85	58	404
Education	45	98	12	155
Fiction	127	3,391	427	3,945
Information	400	181	35	616
Light Entertainment	386	92	52	530
Music	181	283	53	517
News	710	22	2	734
Presentation & Promotion	412	—	—	412
Religious	72	11	8	91
Sport	483	208	52	743
Other Programmes	220	114	208	542
TOTAL	**4,136**	**4,485**	**907**	**9,528**

Radio Broadcasting by RTE (1993)

Programme	Hours Broadcast	%
Arts/Humanities/Sciences	336	1.5
Drama	363	1.7
Education	1	—
Information	1,365	6.3
Light Entertainment	1,247	5.7
Music	12,080	55.5
News	1,717	7.9
Religion	119	0.5
Sport	508	2.3
Other	4,048	18.6
TOTAL	**21,784**	**100.0**

Television Licences in Northern Ireland

	1990	1991	1992	1993	1994	1995
Monochrome	69,607	63,852	50,414	41,507	36,360	32,531
Colour	233,986	253,460	269,196	295,529	311,318	341,459
All Licences	**303,593**	**317,312**	**319,610**	**337,036**	**347,678**	**373,990**
Estimated number of Private households owning a television	508,000	514,000	523,000	532,000	543,000	554,000

50 Most Popular RTE 1 Programmes, 1995

Rank	Programme	Date	Number of Viewers
1	Eurovision Song Contest	May 13	1,325,000
2	The Late Late Show	Dec 8	1,313,000
3	Glenroe	Feb 26	1,298,000
4	The Rose of Tralee	Aug 30	1,110,000
5	Coronation Street	Dec 6	1,038,000
6	Fair City	Jan 31	1,029,000
7	Crimeline	Feb 13	964,000
8	Three Fugitives	Feb 12	963,000
9	Mr. Bean Goes to Town	Jan 17	952,000
10	Hot Shots	Jan 1	925,000
11	Millionaire	Sep 1	912,000
12	Murder in the Park	Nov 9	910,000
13	Winning Streak	Jan 28	909,000
14	Kenny Live	Apr 1	904,000
15	Four Weddings and a Funeral	Nov 14	901,000
16	A Desperate Affair	Nov 30	889,000
17	Keeping up Appearances	Nov 24	882,000
18	Eurosong	Mar 12	881,000
19	Father of the Bride	Jan 22	874,000
20	The Colleen Bawn	Dec 14	828,000
21	Sanctuary	Dec 7	826,000
22	Where in the World	Feb 19	820,000
23	Mystery at Marlhill	Nov 23	817,000
24	Summer Lemonade	Nov 16	811,000
25	Kindergarten Cop	Feb 26	801,000
26	Head to Toe	Jan 17	795,000
27	Check-Up	Jan 24	787,000
28	Riverdance - The Show	Dec 25	782,000
29	Sister Act	Dec 24	776,000
30	The Hand that Rocks the Cradle	Feb 21	758,000
31	Ear to the Ground	Mar 13	745,000
32	Lethal Weapon 3	May 2	717,000
33	Upwardly Mobile	Dec 25	698,000
34	Presumed Guilty	Oct 15	691,000
35	Ireland v Austria	Jun 11	690,000
36	The Hanging Gale	May 2	684,000
37	The Bodyguard	Sep 17	675,000
38	Strictly Ballroom	Dec 25	675,000
39	The Referendum	Nov 25	674,000
40	Home Alone 2	Dec 25	674,000
41	Cat Balou	Jan 1	670,000
42	Up for the Final	Sep 2	661,000
43	Terror on Highway 91	Dec 3	661,000
44	Dana - Some Kinds of Everything	May 6	661,000
45	Lifelines	May 7	659,000
46	Tuesday File	Feb 7	655,000
47	E. R.	Mar 6	651,000
48	The Lyrics Board	Feb 16	651,000
49	The Visit of the Prince of Wales	May 31	648,000
50	Prime Time	Feb 9	644,000

50 Most Popular Network 2 Programmes, 1995

Rank	Programme	Date	Number of Viewers
1	Ireland v England	Feb 15	1,167,000
2	Portugal v Ireland	Nov 15	1,110,000
3	Holland v Ireland	Dec 13	1,050,000
4	Ireland v Portugal	Apr 26	958,000
5	Ireland v Latvia	Oct 11	956,000
6	Coronation Street	Feb 22	939,000
7	Austria v Ireland	Sep 6	880,000
8	All Ireland Finals	Sep 17	760,000
9	Home & Away	Nov 27	688,000
10	Liechtenstein v Ireland	Jun 3	610,000
11	Ireland v Northern Ireland	Mar 29	577,000
12	Hot Shots	Nov 8	549,000
13	Million Dollar Babies	Jan 6	547,000
14	Coronation Street remembers Doris Speed	Jan 2	535,000
15	Blackboard Jungle	Jan 25	532,000
16	Fresh Prince of Bel Air	Feb 22	506,000
17	Rocky IV	Jan 3	478,000
18	All Ireland Semi-Finals	Aug 13	477,000
19	Home ALone	May 21	446,000
20	Die Hard	Sep 20	434,000
21	Children's Ward	Mar 17	414,000
22	Beetlejuice	Oct 4	411,000
23	Beyond 2000	Sep 3	406,000
24	European Champions League	Mar 15	405,000
25	Sweet Valley High	May 1	404,000
26	The X-Files	Oct 24	403,000
27	Movie Magic	Apr 26	401,000
28	The Sunday Game	Sep 3	393,000
29	National Lampoon's Christmas Vacation	Dec 28	389,000
30	Lois and Clarke	Jun 10	387,000
31	Rugby: The World Cup	May 27	384,000
32	My So-Called Life	Mar 9	380,000
33	Street Legal	Sep 6	377,000
34	Sword in the Stone	Mar 17	375,000
35	Baywatch	Dec 24	375,000
36	Sports Stadium	Aug 12	369,000
37	Diamonds are Forever	Nov 4	356,000
38	Golden Four Athletics	Sep 1	356,000
39	You Only Live Twice	Oct 21	356,000
40	Grace Under Fire	Feb 23	354,000
41	Batman	Dec 2	351,000
42	War of the Roses	Dec 24	333,000
43	A View to a Kill	Nov 25	333,000
44	Flintstones	Jan 20	333,000
45	Glenroe	Dec 28	330,000
46	Beetlejuice	Feb 15	329,000
47	Innerspace	Dec 9	328,000
48	European Cup Winners	May 10	325,000
49	Land before Time	Jan 4	325,000
50	Are You Afraid of the Dark?	May 1	325,000

FILM INDUSTRY

Irish Oscar Winners

The Motion Picture Academy Awards were instituted in 1928 for excellence in various aspects of cinema. Ireland has had numerous winners, they are :-

Cedric Gibbons (b. Dublin, 1893) ....won 12 Oscars between 1929 and 1956 for Art Direction
George Bernard Shaw (b. Dublin, 1856).. won Best Screen Play in1938
Greer Garson (b. Down, 1908)...won Best Actress for "Mrs. Miniver" in 1942
Barry Fitzgerald (b. Dublin, 1888)...won Best Supporting Actor for "Going my Way" in 1944
Shane Connaughton (b. Cavan)........................won an Oscar for 'Bottom Dollar' in the short film category in 1981
Michele Burke ....won Best Make-up in 1982
Josie McAvin (b. Dublin, 1923)...won an Oscar for Art Direction in 1985
Daniel Day Lewis (b. London, 1958)...won Best Actor for "My Left Foot" in 1989
Brenda Fricker (b. Dublin, 1945)...won Best Supporting Actress for "My Left Foot" in 1989
Neil Jordan (b. Sligo, 1951)...won Best Screenplay for "The Crying Game" in 1993

List of Irish Films, 1910-1996

The Lad from Old Ireland (1910); Director: Sidney Olcott; Starring: Gene Gauntier, Robert Vignola.

Rory O'Moore (1911); Director: Sidney Olcott; Starring: Gene Gauntier, Jack P. McGowan.

The Colleen Bawn (1912); Director: Sidney Olcott; Starring: Brian McGowan, Sidney Olcott.

Arragh-na-Pogue (1912); Director: Sidney Olcott; Starring: Jack P. McGowan, Robert Vignola.

The O'Neill (1912); Director: Sidney Olcott; Starring: Pat O'Malley, Gene Gauntier.

The Shaughran (1912); Director: Sidney Olcott; Starring: Gene Gauntier, Jack Clarke.

You'll Remember Ellen (1912); Director: Sidney Olcott; Starring: Gene Gauntier, Jack Clarke.

Shane the Post (1913); Director: Sidney Olcott; Starring: Jack Clarke, Pat O' Malley.

The Kerry Crow (1913); Director: Sidney Olcott; Starring: Gene Gauntier, Jack P. McGowan.

Ireland The Oppressed (1913); Director: Sidney Olcott; Starring: Robert Vignola, Jack Clarke.

The Kerry Dancer (1913); Director: Sidney Olcott; Starring: Gene Gauntier, Jack Clarke.

A Girl of Glenbeigh (1914); Director: Sidney Olcott; Starring: Gene Gauntier, Jack Clarke.

The Fishermaid of Ballydavid (1914); Director: Sidney Olcott; Starring: Gene Gauntier, Robert Vignola.

The Gypsies of Old Ireland (1914); Director: Sidney Olcott; Starring: Annie O'Sullivan, Valentine Grant.

Ireland A Nation (1914); Director: Walter MacNamara; Starring: Barry O'Brien.

Robert Emmet (1914); Director: Sidney Olcott; Starring: Jack Melville, Pat O'Malley.

Bunny Blarneyed (1914); Director: Larry Trimble; Starring: Johnny Bunny.

Broth of a Boy (1915).

Fun at Finglas Fair (1915); Director: F. J. McCormick; Starring: F. J. McCormick.

Puck Fair Romance (1916); Director: J. M. Kerrigan; Starring: J. M. Kerrigan, Kathleen Murphy.

Molly Bawn (1916); Director: Cecil M. Hepworth; Starring: Alma Taylor, Stewart Rome.

O'Neill of the Glen (1916); Director: J. M. Kerrigan; Starring: J. M. Kerrigan, Nora Clancy, Fred O'Donovan.

The Miser's Gift (1916); Director: J. M. Kerrigan;

Starring: J. M. Kerrigan, Kathleen Murphy, Fred O'Donovan.

An Unfair Love Affair (1916); Director: J. M. Kerrigan; Starring: Nora Clancy, Fred O'Donovan.

Widow Malone (1916); Director: J. M. Kerrigan; Starring: J. M. Kerrigan.

Food of Love (1916); Director: J. M. Kerrigan; Starring: Kathleen Murphy, Fred O'Donovan.

Woman's Wit (1916); Director: J. M. Kerrigan; Starring: Kathleen Murphy, Fred O'Donovan.

The Eleventh Hour (1917); Director: Fred O'Donovan; Starring: Brian MacGowan, Kathleen Murphy.

The Upstart (1917); J. M. Kerrigan; Starring: Kathleen Murphy, Fred O'Donovan.

Blarney (1917); Director: J. M. Kerrigan; Starring: Kathleen Murphy, J. M. Kerrigan.

The Byeways of Fate (1917); Director: J. M. Kerrigan; Starring: Nora Clancy.

The Irish Girl (1917); Director: J. M. Kerrigan; Starring: Kathleen Murphy.

In the Days of Saint Patrick (1917); Director: Norman Whitton; Starring: Ira Allen, Alice Cardinall, George Griffin.

Knocknagow (1916); Director: John McDonagh; Starring: Brian McGowan, J. McCarra, Alice Keating.

Rafferty's Rise (1918); Director: J. M. Kerrigan; Starring: Fred O'Donovan, Kathleen Murphy, Arthur Shields.

When Love Came to Gavin Burke (1918); Director: Fred O'Donovan; Starring: Brian Moore, Kathleen Murphy.

Willie Scouts While Jessie Pouts (1918); Director: William Power; Starring: William Power.

Rosaleen Dhu (1919); Director: William Power; Starring: William Power, Kitty Hart.

An Irish Vendetta (1920); Director: William Power; Starriing: William Power, Kitty Hart.

Willie Reilly and the Collen Bawn (1919); Director: John McDonagh; Starring: Brian McGowan, Kathleen Alexander.

The Life of Michael Dwyer (1919); Director: John McDonagh; Starring: F. J. McCormick.

The O'Casey Millions (1922); Director: John McDonagh; Starring: Jimmy O'Dea, Nan Fitzgerald.

Wicklow Gold (1922); Director: John McDonagh; Starring: Jimmy O'Dea.

Paying the Rent (1922); Director: John McDonagh; Starring: Jimmy O'Dea.

Land of her Fathers (1924); Director: John Hurley; Starring: Míchael MacLiammóir, Phyllis Wakeley.

Cruiskeen Lawn (1924); Director: John McDonagh; Starring: Tom Moran, Jimmy O'Dea, Fay Sargent.

Irish Destiny (1925); Director: I. J. Eppel; Starring: Dennis O'Dea, Una Shields, Daisy Campbell.

Ireland's Rough-Hewn Destiny (1929); Director: Victor Haddick; Starring: Gearóid O'Lochlinn.

Song of my Heart (1930); Director: Frank Borzage; Starring: John McCormick, Maureen O'Sullivan.

Some May Change (1933); Director: Michael Farrell; Starring: Sheila Fay.

Sweet Inniscarra (1934); Director: Emmet Moore; Starring: Sean Rodgers, Mae Ryan.

Guests of the Nation (1934); Director: Denis Johnson; Starring: Barry Fitzgerald, Shelagh Richards, Hilton Edwards.

General John Regan (1934); Director: Henry Edwards; Starring: Henry Edwards, Chrissie White, W. G. Fay.

Jimmy Boy (1934); Director: John Baxter; Starring: Jimmy O'Dea, Guy Middleton, Vera Sherburne.

Irish Hearts (1934); Director: Brian Desmond Hurst; Starring: Lester Matthews, Nancy Burne, Sara Allgood.

Riders to the Sea (1935); Director: Brian Desmond Hurst; Starring: Sara Allgood, Kevin Gutherie, Ria Mooney.

The Luck of the Irish (1935); Director: Donovan Pedeltry; Starring: Richard Hayward, Kay Walsh, Niall McGinnis.

The Informer (1935); Director: John Ford; Starring: Victor McLaglen, Heather Angel, J. M. Kerrigan.

Irish for Luck (1936); Director: Arthur Woods; Starring: Athene Seyler, Margaret Lockwood.

The Voice of Ireland (1936); Director: Victor Haddick; Starring: Richard Hayward, Victor Haddick, Barney O'Hara.

Wings of the Morning (1936); Director: Harold Schuster; Starring: Henry Fonda, John McCormack.

Irish and Proud of It (1936); Director: Donovan Pedelty; Starring: Richard Hayward, Dinah Sheridan, Liam Gaffney.

The Early Bird (1936); Director: Donovan Pedelty; Starring: Richard Hayward, Jimmy McGeean.

Man of Aran (1936); Director: Robert Flaherty; Starring: Tiger King, Maggie Dirrane, Aran Islanders.

The Dawn (1937); Director: Tom Cooper; Starring: Tom Cooper, Eileen Davis, Brian O'Sullivan.

Uncle Nick (1938); Director: Tom Cooper; Starring: Val Vousden.

Blarney (1938); Director: Harry O'Donovan; Starring: Jimmy O'Dea, Myrette Morven.

West of Kerry (1938); Director: Dick Bird; Starring: Eileen Curran, Cecil Ford.

The Islandman (1938); Director: Patrick Heale; Starring: Gabriel Fallon, Brian O'Sullivan.

Devil's Rock (1938); Director: Germaine Burger; Starring: Richard Heyward, Geraldine Mitchell.

Henry V (1943); Director: Laurence Olivier; Starring: Laurence Oliver, Robert Newton, Leslie Banks.

Hungry Hill (1946); Director: Brian Desmond Hurst; Starring: Margaret Lockwood, Dennis Price, F. J. McCormick.

Captain Boycott (1946); Director: Frank Launder; Starring: Stewart Granger, Cecil Parker, Kathleen Ryan.

Crime on the Irish Border (1946); Director: Maurice J. Wilson; Starring: Kieron Moore, Barbara White.

Odd Man Out (1946); Director: Carol Reed; Starring: James Mason, Kathleen Ryan, Robert Newton.

The Courtneys of Curzon Street (1947); Director: Herbert Wilcock; Starring: Anna Neagle, Michael Wilding.

Black Narcissus (1946); Director: Michael Powell, Emeric Pressburger; Starring: Deborah Kerr, Sabu, David Farrar.

I See a Dark Stranger (1946); Director: Frank Launder; Starring: Deborah Kerr, Trevor Howard.

Another Shore (1948); Director: Charles Crichton; Starring: Robert Beatty, Moira Lister, Stanley Holloway.

My Hands are Clay (1948); Director: Patrick McCrossan; Starring: Shelagh Richards, Bernadette Leahy, Cecil Brook.

The Greedy Boy (1948); Director: Richard Massingham; Starring: Joyce Sullivan, Jim Phelan.

Transatlantic Flight (1948); Director: Joseph Ryle; Starring: Gene Kelly, Betsy Blair.

At a Dublin Inn (1949); Director: Desmond Leslie; Starring: Valentine Dyall, Joseph O'Connor.

No Resting Place (1950); Director: Paul Rotha; Starring: Michael Gough, Eithne Dunne, Noel Purcell.

The Strangers Came (1950); Director: Alfred Travers; Starring: Seamus MacLocha, Gabriel Fallon.

Jack of All Maids (1951); Director: Tomas MacAnna; Starring: Jack McGowran.

The Promise of Barty O'Brien (1951); Director: George Freedland; Starring: Eric Doyle, Eileen Crowe, Harry Brogan.

The Gentle Gunman (1952); Director: Basil Dearden; Starring: John Mills, Dirk Bogarde, Gilbert Harding.

The Quiet Man (1952); Director: John Ford; Starring: John Wayne, Maureen O'Hara, Barry Fitzgerald.

Knights of the Round Table (1953); Director: Richard Thorpe; Starring: Robert Taylor, Ava Gardner, Mel Ferrer.

Captain Lightfoot (1954); Director: Douglas Sirk; Starring: Rock Hudson, Barbara Rush, Jeff Morrow.

Jacqueline (1955); Director: Roy Baker; Starring: John Gregson, Kathleen Ryan, Jacqueline Ryan.

Moby Dick (1955); Director: John Huston; Starring: Gregory Peck, Orson Welles, Richard Basehart.

The March Hare (1956); Director: George More O'Farrell; Starring: Terence Morgan, Peggy Cummins, Cyril Cusack.

Rising of the Moon (1956); Director: John Ford; Starring: Jimmy O'Dea, Noel Purcell, Cyril Cusack.

Boyd's Shop (1957); Director: Henry Cass; Starring: Geoffrey Golden, Eileen Crowe.

Professor Tim (1957); Director: Henry Cass; Starring: Ray McAnally, Márie O'Donnell.

Rooney (1957); Director: George Pollock; Starring: John Gregson, Murial Pavlow, Barry Fitzgerald.

Dublin Nightmare (1958); Director: John Pomeroy; Starring: William Sylvester, Marie Landi, Richard Leech.

Home is the Hero (1958); Director: Fielder Cooke; Starring: Arthur Kennedy, Máire O'Donnell, Walter

Macken.

Sally's Irish Rogue (1958); Director: George Pollock; Starring: Julie Harris, Tim Sheely, Harry Brogan.

The Big Birthday (1958); Director: George Pollock; Starring: Barry Fitzgerald, Tony Wright, June Thorburn.

Shake Hands with the Devil (1958); Director: Michael Anderson; Starring: James Cagney, Don Murray, Dana Wynter.

This Other Eden (1959); Director: Murial Box; Starring: Leslie Phillips, Audrey Dallton, Norman Roadway.

Darby O'Gill & the Little People (1959);

A Terrible Beauty (1960); Director: Tay Garnett; Starring: Robert Mitchum, Anne Heywood, Dan O'Herlihy.

Gorgo (1960); Director: Eugene Lourie; Starring: Bill Travers, William Sylvester, Barry Keegan.

Fr. Brown (1960); Director: Helmut Ashley; Starring: Heinz Ruhmann.

The Siege of Sidney Street (1960); Director: Roy Baker, Monty Berman; Starring: Donald Sinden, Nicole Berger, Kieron Moore.

Ambush in Leopard Street (1960); Director: J. H. Piperno; Starring: James Kenny, Michael Brennan, Bruce Seton.

Johnny Nobody (1960); Director: Nigel Patrick; Starring: Nigel Patrick, William Bendix, Aldo Ray.

The Big Gamble (1960); Director: Richard Fleischer; Starring: Stephen Boyd, Juliette Greco, David Wayne.

Sword of Sherwood Forest (1960); Director: Terence Fisher; Starring: Richard Greene, Peter Cushing, Nigel Greene.

Middle of Nowhere (1960); Director: Don Chaffy; Starring: John Cassavetes, Elizabeth Sellars, David Farrar.

Lies My Father Told Me (1960); Director: Don Chaffy; Starring: Betsy Blair, Harry Brogan.

The Mark (1961); Director: Guy Greene; Starring: Stuart Whitman, Rod Steiger, Maria Schell.

Murder in Eden (1961); Director: Max Varnell; Starring: Ray McAnally, Norman Rodway.

A Question of Suspense (1961); Director: Max Varnell; Starring: Peter Reynolds.

Enter Inspector Duval (1961); Director: Max Varnell; Starring: Anton Diffring.

Freedom to Die (1961); Director: Frances Searle; Starring: James Maxwell, T. P. McKenna.

Stork Talk (1961); Director: Michael Furlong; Starring: Tony Britton, Anne Heywood.

Term of Trial (1961); Director: Peter Grenville; Starring: Laurence Olivier, Simone Signoret, Sarah Miles.

The List of Adrian Messenger (1962); Director: John Huston; Starring: George C. Scott, Dana Wynter, Kirk Douglas.

The Quare Fellow (1962); Director: Arthur Dreyfuss; Starring: Patrick McGoohan, Walter Macken, Sylvia Syms.

The Very Edge (1962); Director: Cyril Frankfel; Starring: Richard Todd, Anne Heywood, Jack Hedley.

The Running Man (1962); Director: Carol Reed; Starring: Laurence Harvey, Lee Remick, Alan Bates.

Dead Man's Evidence (1962); Director: Frances Searle; Starring: Conrad Phillips, Jane Griffith.

A Guy Called Caesar (1962); Director: Frank Marshall; Starring: Conrad Philips, George Moon.

The Playboy of the Western World (1962); Director: Brian Desmond Hurst; Starring: Siobhan McKenna, Gary Raymond, Liam Redmond.

The Devil's Agent (1963); Director: John Paddy Carstairs; Starring: McDonald Carey, Peter Van Eyck, Christopher Lee.

Dementia 13 (1963); Director: Francis Ford Coppola; Starring: Patrick Magee, Eithne Dunne, William Campbell.

Of Human Bondage (1963); Director: Ken Hughes, Henry Hathaway; Starring: Laurence Harvey, Kim Novak, Robert Morley.

I Thank a Fool (1963); Director: Robert Stevens; Starring: Peter Finch, Susan Hayward, Diane Cilento.

Never Put It in Writing (1963); Director: Andrew Stone; Starring: Pat Boone, Milo O'Shea, Fidelma Murphy.

Girl With Green Eyes (1963); Director: Desmond Davis; Starring: Peter Finch, Rita Tushingham, Lynn Redgrave.

Ballad in Blue (1964); Director: Paul Henreid; Starring: Ray Charles, Mary Peach, Tom Bell.

The Spy Who Came in from the Cold (1964); Director: Martin Ritt; Starring: Richard Burton, Claire Bloom, Oscar Werner.

Finnegan's Wake (1964); Director: Mary Ellan Bute; Starring: Martin J. Kelly, Jane Reilly.

Face of Fu Manchu (1965); Director: Don Sharp; Starring: Christopher Lee, Senta Berger, Thorley Walters.

Sherlock Holmes and the Deadly Necklace (1964); Director: Terence Fisher; Starring: Christopher Lee, Senta Berger, Thorley Walters.

Ten Little Indians (1964); Director: George Pollock; Starring: Hugh O'Brien, Shirley Eaton, Stanley Holloway.

Young Cassidy (1965); Director: Jack Cardiff; Starring: Rod Taylor, Julie Christie, Maggie Smith.

The Blue Max (1965); Director: John Guillermin; Starring: George Peppard, James Mason, Ursula Andrews.

I Was Happy Here (1965); Director: Desmond Davis; Starring: Sarah Miles, Cyril Cusack, Julian Glover.

Rocket to the Moon (1966); Director: Don Sharp; Starring: Burl Ives, Troy Donoghue, Gert Frobe.

Robbery (1966); Director: Peter Yates; Starring: Stanley Baker, Joanne Pettet, James Booth.

The Viking Queen (1966); Director: Don Chaffy; Starring: Don Murray, Carita, Andrew Keir.

Casino Royale (1966); Director: John Huston, Val Guest, Ken Hughes, Joseph McGrath; Starring: David Niven, Deborah Kerr, Peter Sellers.

Ulysses (1966); Director: Joseph Strick; Starring: Milo O'Shea, Barbara Jefford, T. P. McKenna.

Sinful Davey (1967); Director: John Huston; Starring: John Hurt, Pamela Franklin, Nigel Davenport.

30 is a Dangerous Age, Cynthia (1967); Director: Joseph McGrath; Starring: Dudley Moore, Suzy Kendall, Patricia Routledge.

The Lion in Winter (1968); Director: Anthony Harvey; Starring: Peter O'Toole, Katherine Hepburn, Jane Merrow.

Lock Up Your Daughters (1968); Director: Peter Coe; Starring; Christopher Plummer, Susannah York, Glynis Johns.

Guns in the Heather (1968); Director: Robert Butler; Starring: Glenn Corbett, Kurt Russell, Alfred Burke.

Darling Lili (1968); Director: Blake Edwards; Starring: Julie Andrews, Rock Hudson, Jeremy Kemp.

The Prince and the Pauper (1968); Director: Elliott Geisinger.

Where's Jack? (1968); Director: Jack Clavell; Starring: Stanley Baker, Tommy Steele, Fiona Lewis.

The Italian Job (1968); Director: Peter Collinson; Starring: Michael Caine, Noel Coward.

Alfred the Great (1968); Director: Clive Donner; Starring: David Hemmings, Michael York, Prunella Ransome.

The Violent Enemy (1968); Director: Don Sharp; Starring: Tom Bell, Susan Hampshire, Ed Begley.

Wedding Night (1969); Director: Piers Haggard; Starring: Dennis Waterman, Tessa Wyatt, Eddie Byrne.

The Girl with the Paleface (1969); Director: Paul Gallico Jr.; Starring: Fidelma Murphy, Donal McCann, Lee Dunne.

McKenzie Break (1969); Director: Lamont Johnson; Starring: Brian Keith, Ian Hendry, Helmut Griem.

Underground (1969); Director: Arthur Nadel; Starring: Robert Goulet, Daneile Gaubert.

Paddy (1969); Director: Daniel Haller; Starring: Des Cave, Derbhla Molloy, Milo O'Shea.

Country Dance (1969); Director: J. Lee Thompson; Starring: Peter O'Toole, Susannah York, Michael Craig.

Ryan's Daughter (1969); Director: David Lean; Starring: Robert Mitchum, Sarah Miles, Trevor Howard.

Quackser Fortune has a Cousin in the Bronx (1969); Director: Warris Hussein; Starring: Gene Wilder, Margot Kidder, Seamus Forde.

Ace Eli and Rodgers of the Skies (1969); Director: Cliff Robertson; Starring: Cliff Robertson, Jack Watson.

Philadelphia Here I Come (1970); Director: John Quested; Starring: Donal McCann, Des Cave, Siobhan McKenna.

Flight of the Doves (1970); Director: Ralph Nelson; Starring: Ron Moody, Jack Wild, William Rushton.

Black Beauty (1970); Director: James Hill; Starring: Mark Lester, Walter Stezack, Patrick Mower.

The Red Baron (1970); Director: Roger Corman; Starring: John Philip Law, Don Stroud, Tom Adams.

Zeppelin (1970); Director: Etienne Perier; Starring: Michael York, Elke Sommer, Anton Diffring.

Act Without Words (1971)unfinished; Director: Tom Blevins; Starring: Rod Steiger.

Sitting Target (1971); Director: Douglas Hickox; Starring: Oliver Reed, Ian McShane, Jill St. John.

Images (1971); Director: Robert Altman; Starring: Susannah York, Rene Auberjonois, Hugh Millais.

A Fistful of Dynamite (1971); Director: Sergio Leone; Starring: Rod Steiger, James Coburn.

The Hebrew Lesson (1972); Director: Wolf Mankowitz; Starring: Milo O'Shea, Patrick Dawson, Alun Owen.

And No One Could Save Her (1972); Director: Kevin Billington; Starring: Lee Remick, Milo O'Shea, Frank Grimes.

A War of Children (1972); Director: George Schaffer; Starring: Jenny Agutter, Vivien Merchant, Aideen O'Kelly.

Catholics (1973); Director: Jack Gold; Starring: Trevor Howard, Cyril Cusack.

The Mackintosh Man (1973); Director: John Huston; Starring: Paul Newman, James Mason, Dominque Sanda.

Zardoz (1973); Director: John Boorman; Starring; Sean Connery, Charlotte Rampling, John Alderton.

A Quiet Day in Belfast (1973); Director: Milad Basada; Starring: Barry Foster, Margot Kidder.

Horowitz of Dublin Castle (1974); Director: William Kronick; Starring: Harvey Lembeck, Cyril Cusack, Sinead Cusack.

'Caoineadh' Art O' Laogharé (1974).

Barry Lyndon (1974); Director: Stanley Kubrick; Starring: Ryan O'Neal, Marisa Berenson.

The Next Man (1975); Director: Richard Sarafin; Starring: Sean Connery, Cornelia Sharpe;

Victor Frankenstein (1975); Director: Calvin Floyd; Starring: Per Oscarsson, Leon Vitali, Stacy Dorning.

Portrait of the Artist as a Young Man (1975); Director: Joseph Strick; Starring: Bosco Hogan, T. P. McKenna, John Gielgud.

The Last Remake of Beau Geste (1976); Director: Marty Feldman; Starring: Marty Feldman, Ann Margaret, Michael York.

The Purple Taxi (1976); Director: Yves Boisset; Starring: Peter Ustinov, Fred Astaire, Charlotte Rampling.

The Inn of the Flying Dragon (1977); Director: Calvin Floyd; Starring: Curt Jurgens, Niall Tóibín.

Down the Corner (1977); Director: Joe Comerford; Starring: Joe Keenan, Declan Cronin, Kevin Doyle.

The First Great Train Robbery (1978); Director: Michael Crichton; Starring: Sean Connery, Lesley Anne Down, Donald Sutherland.

The Outside (1978); Director: Tony Luraschi; Starring: Craig Wasson, Patricia Quinn, Sterling Hayden.

Cry of the Innocent (1978); Director: Michael O'Herlihy; Starring: Rod Taylor, Cyril Cusack.

Exposure (1978); Director: Kieran Hickey; Starring: Catherine Schell, T. P. McKenna, Bosco Hogan.

The Big Red One (1978); Director: Samuel Fuller; Starring: Lee Marvin, Mark Hamill.

Poitín (1978); Director: Bob Quinn; Starring: Cyril Cusack, Niall Tóibín, Donal McCann.

McVicar (1978); Director: Tom Clegg; Starring: Roger Daltry, Adam Faith.

North Sea Hijack (1979); Director: Andrew V. McLaglen; Starring: Roger Moore, James Mason, Anthony Perkins.

The Flame is Love (1979); Director: Michael O'Herlihy; Starring: Linda Purl, Timothy Dalton.

Tristan and Isolt (1979); Director: Tom Donovan; Starring: Richard Burton, Kate Mulgrew, Nicholas Clay.

The Hard Way (1979); Director: Michael Dryhurst; Starring: Patrick McGoohan, Lee Van Cleef, Edna O'Brien.

Excalibur (1980); Director: John Boorman; Starring: Nicol Williamson, Nigel Terry, Helen Mirren.

Inchon (1980); Director: Terence Young; Starring: Laurence Olivier, Jacqueline Bisset.

It's Handy When People Don't Die (1980); Director: Tom McArdle; Starring: Garret Keogh, Bob Carisle, Brendan Cauldwell.

Light Years Away (1980); Director: Alain Tanner; Starring: Trevor Howard, Mick Ford.

Wagner (1981); Director: Tony Palmer; Starring: Richard Burton, Vanessa Redgrave, Gemma Craven.

Fire and Sword (1981); Director: Keith Von Fuerstenberg; Starring: Peter Firth, Leigh Lawson.

Traveller (1981); Director: Joe Comerford; Starring: Judy O'Donovan, David Spillane.

Angel (1981); Director: Neil Jordan; Starring: Stephen Rea, Honor Heffernan, Ray McAnally.

Educating Rita (1982); Director: Lewis Gilbert; Starring: Michael Caine, Julie Walters.

The Outcasts (1982); Director: Robert Wynn Simmons; Starring: Cyril Cusack, Mary Ryan, Mick Lally.

Attracta (1982); Director: Kieran Hickey; Starring: Wendy Hiller, Kate Thompson;

State of Wonder (1983); Director: Martin Donovan; Starring: Anne Chaplin, Martin Donovan.

Pigs (1983); Director: Cathal Black; Starring: James Brennan, George Shane, Maurice O'Donoghue.

Anne Devlin (1983); Director: Pat Murphy; Starring: Brid Brennan, Bosco Hogan.

The Country Girls (1983); Director: Desmond Davis; Starring: Sam Neill, Maeve Germaine, Niall Tóibín.

Cal (1983); Director: Pat O'Connor; Starring: Helen Mirren, John Lynch, Ray McAnally.

Company of Wolves (1984); Director: Neil Jordan; Starring: Stephen Rea, Sarah Patterson, Angela Lansbury, David Warner.

Eat the Peach (1985); Director: Peter Ormrod; Starring: Stephen Brennan, Eamonn Morrissey, Catherine Byrne.

The Fantasist (1985); Director: Robin Hardy; Starring: Timothy Bottoms, Moira Harris, John Kavenagh.

Rawhead X (1986); Director: George Pavlov; Starring: David Dukes, Kelly Piper, Niall Tóibín.

Budawanny (1986); Director: Bob Quinn; Starring: Donal McCann, Margaret Fegan.

The Dead (1987); Director: John Huston; Starring: Anjelica Huston, Donal McCann, Dan O'Herlihy.

The Courier (1987); Director: Joe Lee, Frank Deasy; Starring: Gabriel Byrne, Padraig O'Loingsigh, Cait O'Riordain.

Reefer and the Model (1987); Director: Joe Comerford; Starring: Ian McElhinney, Carole Scanlan, Ray McBride.

The Lonely Passion of Judith Hearne (1987); Director: Jack Clayton; Starring: Bob Hoskins, Maggie Smith, Marie Kean.

Taffin (1987); Director: Francis Megahy; Starring: Pierce Brosnan, Alison Doody, Ray McAnally.

Clash of the Ash (1987).

Da (1987); Director: Matt Clark; Starring: Martin Sheen, Barnard Hughes, Doreen Hepburn.

The Dawning (1987); Director: Robert Knights, Starring: Anthony Hopkins, Jean Simmons, Trevor Howard.

Now I Know (1987); Director: Robert Pappas; Starring: Matthew Modine, Maeve Germaine.

High Spirits (1987); Director: Neil Jordan; Starring: Peter O'Toole, Daryl Hannah, Steve Guttenberg.

Joyriders (1988); Director: Aisling Walsh; Starring: Andrew Connolly, Patricia Kerrigan, Billie Whitlaw.

My Left Foot (1988); Director: Jim Sheridan; Starring: Daniel Day-Lewis, Brenda Fricker, Ray McAnally.

Fragments of Isabella (1989); Director: Ronan O'Leary; Starring: Gabrielle Reidy.

Hidden Agenda (1989); Director: Ken Loach; Starring: Brad Dourif, Brian Cox, Frances McDormand.

Fools of Fortune (1989); Director: Pat O'Connor; Starring: Julie Christie, Mary Elizabeth Mastrantonio, Ian Glen.

Hush-A-Bye-Baby (1989); Director: Margo Harkin; Starring: Emer McCourt, Sinead O'Connor.

The Field (1989); Director: John Sheridan; Starring: Richard Harris, John Hurt, Tom Berenger.

The Bargain Shop (1990);

December Bride (1990); Director: Thaddeus O'Sullivan; Starring: Donal McCann, Saskia Reeves, Ciaran Hinds.

The Miracle (1990); Director: Neil Jordan; Starring: Beverly D'Angelo, Donal McCann, Niall Byrne.

The Commitments (1990); Director: Alan Parker; Starring: Andrew Strong, Angeline Ball, Johnny Murphy.

Hear My Song (1990); Director: Peter Chelsom; Starring: Ned Beatty, Shirley Ann Field, Adrian Dunbar.

The Railway Station Man (1991); Director: Michael Whyte; Starring: Donald Sutherland, Julie Christie, John Lynch.

Far and Away (1991); Director: Ron Howard; Starring: Tom Cruise, Nicole Kidman, Colm Meaney.

Into the West (1991); Director: Mike Newell; Starring: Gabriel Byrne, Ellen Barkin, Ciarán Fitzgerald.

The Playboys (1991); Director: Gillies MacKinnon; Starring: Albert Finney, Aidan Quinn, Robin Wright.

The Crying Game (1992); Director: Neil Jordan; Starring: Stephen Rea, Adrian Dunbar, Jaye Davidson.

High Boot Benny (1992); Director: Joe Comerford; Starring: Mark O'Shea, Frances Tomelty, Alan Devlin.

The Bishop's Story (1992); Director: Bob Quinn; Starring: Donal McCann, Margaret Fegan.

The Snapper (1992); Director: Stephen Frears; Starring: Colm Meaney, Tina Kelleher, Ruth McCabe.

In the Name of the Father (1993); Director: Jim Sheridan; Starring: Daniel Day-Lewis, Emma Thompson, Pete Postlethwaite.

Broken Harvest (1993); Director: Maurice O'Callaghan; Starring: Colin Lane, Niall O'Brien, Marion Quinn.

Widow's Peak (1993); Director: John Irvine; Starring: Mia Farrow, Joan Plowright, Natasha Richardson.

All Things Bright and Beautiful (1993); Director: Barry Devlin; Starring: Gabriel Byrne, Tom Wilkinson, Ciarán Fitzgerald.

War of the Buttons (1993); Director: John Roberts; Starring: Colm Meaney, Johnny Murphy, John Coffey.

Moondance (1993); Director: Dagmar Hirtz; Starring: Ruaidhrí Conroy, Julia Brendler, Ian Shaw.

The Secret of Roan Inish (1993); Director: John Sayle; Starring: Mick Lally, Eileen Colgan, Jeni Courtney.

Aisla (1993); Director: Paddy Breathnach; Starring: Brendan Coyle, Andrea Irvine, Juliette Gruber.

An Awfully Big Adventure (1994); Director: Mike Newell; Starring: Alan Rickman, Hugh Grant, Peter Firth.

Braveheart (1994); Director: Mel Gibson; Starring: Mel Gibson, Sophie Marceau, Patrick McGoohan.

Words Upon the Window Pane (1994); Director: Mary McGuckian; Starring: Geraldine Chaplin, Geraldine James, Donal Donnelly.

Frankie Starlight (1994); Director: Michael Lindsay-Hogg; Starring: Ann Parillaud, Matt Dillon, Gabriel Byrne.

A Man of No Importance (1994); Director: Suri Krishnama; Starring: Albert Finney, Brenda Fricker, Tara Fitzgerald.

The Run of the Country (1994); Director: Peter Yates; Starring: Albert Finney, Matt Keeslar, Victoria Smurfit.

Circle of Friends (1994); Director: Pat O'Connor; Starring: Chris O'Donnell, Minnie Driver, Geraldine O'Rawe.
Korea (1994); Director: Cathal Black; Starring: Donal Donnelly, Andrew Scott, Fiona Molony.
Undercurrent (1994); Director: Brian O'Flaherty; Starring: Owen Roe, Stanley Townsend, Tina Kelleher.
Nothing Personal (1995); Director: Thaddeus O'Sullivan; Starring: Ian Hart, John Lynch, Michael Gambon.
The Disappearance of Finbar (1995); Director: Sue Clayton; Starring: Jonathon-Rhys-Myers, Luke Griffin, Fanny Risberg.
Driftwood (1995); Director: Ronan O'Leary; Starring: James Spader, Anne Brochet, Barry McGovern.
Guiltrip (1995); Director: Gerry Stembridge; Starring: Andrew Connolly, Jasmine Russell, Michelle Houlden.
Moll Flanders (1995); Director: Pen Densham; Starring: Robin Wright, Morgan Freeman, Stockard Channing.
Michael Collins (1995); Director: Neil Jordan; Starring: Liam Neeson, Julia Roberts, Alan Rickman.
The Last of the High Kings (1995); Director: David Keating; Starring: Gabriel Byrne, Colm Meaney, Christine Ricci.
This is the Sea (1995); Director: Mary McGuckian;

Starring: Gabriel Byrne, Richard Harris, John Lynch.
Joe My Friend (1995); Director: Chris Bould; Starring: John Cleese, Joel Grey, Schuyler Fox.
The Boy from Mercury (1995); Director: Martin Duffy; Starring: Tom Courtenay, Rita Tushingham, James Hickey.
The Van (1995); Director: Stephen Frears; Starring: Colm Meaney, Donal O'Kelly, Brendan O'Carroll.
Space Truckers (1995); Director: Stuart Gordon; Starring: Dennis Hopper, Stephen Dorff, Debi Mazar.
Some Mother's Son (1995); Director: Terry George; Starring: Helen Mirren, John Lynch, Fionnula Flanagan.
The Sun, The Moon and The Stars (1995); Director: Geraldine Creed; Starring: Angie Dickinson, Jason Donovan, Elaine Cassidy.
Spaghetti Slow (1995); Director: Valerie Jalango; Starring: Niamh O'Byrne, Guilio Di Marco, Brendan Gleeson.
Trojan Eddie (1995); Director: Gillies MacKinnon; Starring: Stephen Rea, Richard Harris, Angeline Ball.
A Further Gesture (1995); Director: Robert Dornhelm; Starring: Stephen Rea, Maria Doyle Kennedy, Brendan Gleeson.
Bloodfist VIII - Trained for Action (1995); Director: Rick Jacobson; Starring: Don Wilson, J. P. White.

REPUBLIC OF IRELAND NATIONAL LOTTERY

National Lottery has 3,500 Lotto agents around the country processing up to 820,000 combinations (lines) per hour. Agents' Commission and Bonus came to almost £19 million in 1995.

Biggest Ever Jackpot - 17 May 1995 - £4.43 m (6 roll overs), the winner remained anonymous having won using the 'quick pick'.

1995 had 61 Lotto Jackpot winning tickets (12 were 'quick pick').

In 1995, the number of Lotto millionaires increased to 50.

1987-1995 - £940m won in Lottery Prizes.

Two people won £250,000 on Winning Streak on Television.

Average of 35,000 Scratch Card Winners Daily.

National Lottery Results, 1995

Income ....£303,222,051 ....of which: £101,221,509 (Instant Games); £202,000,542 (Lotto).
Prizes ....£155,450,612 ....of which: £54,450,341 (Instant Games); £101,000,271 (Lotto).
Wages & Salaries.............£1,852,093 ....Number of Employees (78)

National Lottery Fund Expenditure

Group	1995 £m	%	1987-1995 £m	%
Youth, Sport, Recreation & Amenities	27.462	32.4	204.748	34
Arts, Culture, Natural Heritage	20.846	24.5	148.190	24
Health & Welfare	29.162	34.4	212.315	35
Irish Language	7.387	8.7	44.871	7

National Lottery Winning Tickets by Prize

Winning Tickets	Number
Over IR£4 million	1
IR£3 million to IR£4 million	2
IR£2 million to IR£3 million	3
IR£1 million to IR£2 million	21
IR£750,000 to IR£1 million	4
IR£500,000 to IR£750,000	12
IR£250,000 to IR£500,000	15
IR£100,000 to IR£250,000	3
Total: Winning Tickets	**61**

SELECTED BIOGRAPHIES OF ARTS AND ENTERTAINMENT PERSONALITIES

Aiken, Jim (b. 1932, Belfast). Concert promoter. Former national school teacher. Brings top acts from all over world to Dublin venues.

Allen, Darina (b. 1947, Laois) Cook. Proprietor of Ballymaloe Cookery School, Cork and presenter of RTE television cookery programme *Simply Delicious*.

Anderson, Gerry (b. Buncrana). Television Presenter. Professional musician with Irish showband *The Chessmen*. Journalist with community newspaper in Derry, took up post as broadcaster on BBC Radio Foyle. Presents television programmes on BBC Northern Ireland such as *Anderson on the Box* and *Anderson on the Road*.

Ballagh, Robert (b. 1943). Artist responsible for portraits of *Catherine McAuley, James Joyce, Daniel O'Connell* and *Douglas Hyde* which adorn Irish banknotes. Also involved in stage design.

Black, Mary Singer, released debut solo album in1983. Member of talented Black family from Dublin. Singer with *De Danann* from 1983-1986. Hugely successful solo album *No Frontiers* (1989). Part of *'A Woman's Heart'* album and tour success.

Brady, Paul (b. Tyrone) Singer-songwriter. Member of *The Johnstons* and *Planxty*. Songs have been recorded by likes of Tina Turner and Bonnie Rait. Enjoys much commercial and critical success.

Branagh, Kenneth (b. 1960, Belfast). Actor and Director. Directed and starred in *Dead Again*, (1990) and *Much Ado About Nothing*.

Brennan, Maire (b. 1952, Donegal). Singer with Clannad. Founded in Gweedore, 1970 by Maire, with twin brothers Paul and Kieran Brennan and uncles Noel and Pat Duggan. Massive following in Europe, but reached new level with acclaimed theme for television series *'Harry's Game'* in 1982.

Brosnan, Pierce (b. 1953, Meath). Actor. First became famous in American television series *Remington Steele*. Starred in films such as *Lawnmower Man* and *Mrs. Doubtfire*. Current James Bond, starred in *Goldeneye*, the latest Bond Film.

Byrne, Gabriel (b. 1950, Dublin). Actor. Starred in the R.T.E. production *The Riordans*. Films include *Miller's Crossing*, (1990), *Into the West*, (1991) and *The Usual Suspects*, (1995/6).

Byrne, Gay (b. 1934, Dublin). Ireland's best known television presenter and radio broadcaster. Worked with B.B.C. and various independent television stations in Britain and America before joining R.T.E. Presents Ireland's highest TAM rated television show *The Late Late Show*, on R.T.E. 1 (the world's longest running chat show) and *The Gay Byrne Show*, on R.T.E. Radio 1.

Colgan, Michael (b. 1950, Dublin). Director of the Gate Theatre in Dublin.

Davis, Derek (b. 1949, Down). Television presenter. Showband member. Joined BBC as journalist, also worked for American ABC news in Northern Ireland. Joined RTE as newscaster and presenter. Co-presents highly popular daytime magazine show *Live At Three* with Thelma Mansfield. Also presents hard-hitting chat show *Davis*.

Day Lewis, Daniel (b. 1958, London). Actor who won an Oscar for his performance as Christy Brown in *My Left Foot*, based on the life story of the Dublin writer. Also starred in *The Age of Innocence*, (1993) and *In the Name of the Father*, (1993).

De Burgh, Chris (b. 1948, Argentina). Singer whose major hits include *Lady in Red, Don't Pay the Ferryman* and *Blonde Hair Blue Jeans*.

Devlin, Barry (b. 1946). Film-maker. Played with famous Irish band *Horslips* in 1970's. Now a film maker.

Enya (b. Donegal) Singer who has sold millions of albums worldwide, including *Watermark* (1988) and *Shepherd Moons* (1991). Formerly a member of family group *Clannad*.

Evans, Dave a.k.a. Edge (b. 1961, London) Guitarist with rock band U2, enjoying phenomenal worldwide success with the Dublin quartet since their formation in the late 1970's.

Fanning, Dave (b. 1955, Dublin). Rock and film critic and Ireland's top rock broadcaster. Presents *The Movie Show* and *2TV* on R.T.E. television and his own radio show nightly on 2FM. Closely associated with U2.

Finnucane, Marian (b. 1950). Television and radio presenter with R.T.E. Presents her own chat show *Finnucane*, and co-presents Ireland's top Crime show *CrimeLine*.

Fricker, Brenda (b. 1945, Dublin). Actress who won an Oscar for her performance as Christy Brown's mother in *My Left Foot*, (1989). Also starred in *The Field*, (1990).

Galway, James (b. 1939, Belfast). World's most celebrated flautist. Played with London Symphony Orchestra and Royal Philharmonic Orchestra and Berlin Philharmonic Orchestra before embarking on successful solo career.

Geldoff, Bob (b. Dublin, 1952) Singer. Formed *The Boomtown Rats* in 1975. Had two British Number One's. Became a household name in 1984 as the organiser of the *Band Aid/Live Aid* project which raised millions of pounds for famine-struck Africa.

Gogan, Larry (b. Dublin). Legendary afternoon disc-jockey with 2FM. Presenter of various music programmes on RTE television.

Harris, Richard (b. 1932, Limerick). Actor. Starred in films such as *The Guns of Navarone*, (1961) and *The Field*, (1990).

Hewson, Paul a.k.a. Bono (b. 1960, Dublin). Lead vocalist of rock band U2. Writes most of lyrics for the bands songs. Major U2 albums include *War* (1983), *The Joshua Tree* (1987) and *Achtung Baby* (1991). Ireland's most commercially successful rock singer.

Hill, Derek (b. 1916). Artist, widely admired for his portraits. Has written books on North African Architecture and was influential in bringing the Tory Island painters to an international audience.

Hunniford, Gloria Television and radio presenter. Cabaret singer, before becoming presenter of main evening news and current affairs programme on Ulster Television in the mid-seventies. Now works in London for BBC, primarily on radio.

Jordan, Neil (b. 1951, Sligo). Film director who has also turned his hand to writing fiction such as *''Night in Tunisia and other Stories'*. Won an Oscar for the screenplay of *The Crying Game*, (1992). Also directed *We're no Angels*, (1989), *Interview With The Vampire*, (1995) and *Michael Collins*, (1996) which starred Liam Neeson.

Kelly, Gerry (b. 1948, Antrim). Television presenter. Began broadcasting career as G.A.A. correspondent with UTV, moved to feature items before getting his own show. Presents *"Kelly"*, Ulster Television's flagship chat show, which is now in its eighth series.

Kelly, Henry (b. 1946, Dublin) Former *Irish Times* journalist, Moved to London to present number of high profile quiz-game shows with the BBC. Currently presents afternoon quiz show *Going For Gold*.

Kenny, Pat (b. 1949). Television presenter. Joined R.T.E. in 1972, developed into one of the station's most high profile personalities, both on radio where he presents the daily *Pat Kenny Show* and on television where he presents the Saturday night prime time chat show *Kenny Live*.

Lally, Mick (b. 1945, Mayo). Actor, best known for portrayal of Miley in R.T.E.'s long running soap opera *'Glenroe'*. Has impressive reputation as a stage actor. Founding member of the Druid Theatre in 1975.

Lambert, Eugene (b. 1928, Sligo). Puppeteer whose show *'Wanderly Wagon'* ran for thirteen years on RTE. The Lambert Puppet Theatre and Museum is in Dublin.

Le Brocquy, Louis (b. 1916). Ireland's most internationally acclaimed living artist with instantly recognisable style. Specialises in portraits. First exhibited in 1937.

Leonard, Hugh (b. 1926, Dublin). Playwright, widely acclaimed freelance writer, script editor and newspaper columnist.

Mansfield, Thelma RTE presenter, best known as co-presenter with Derek Davis on popular daily magazine show *Live At Three*.

McGowan, Shane (b. London) Singer with famed London-Irish band *The Pogues* , which he formed in 1983. Acclaimed by critics and fans alike for his songwriting ability, including classics such as *'Summer In Siam'* and *'Fairytale Of New York"*. Left *The Pogues* in 1991 following internal differences.

McGuinness, Paul (b. 1951, Germany). Manager of rock group *U2* and Director of Principle Management Ltd. One of Ireland's wealthiest men thanks to his shrewd management of *U2*.

Moloney, Paddy (b. 1938, Dublin). Founding member of *The Chieftains* in 1961, Ireland's foremost traditional band. *The Chieftains* have enjoyed phenomenal album and film soundtrack success, with Paddy Moloney playing uilleann pipes and tin whistle. Spokesman for the group, *The Chieftains* have done more than anyone else to bring Irish music to a worldwide audience.

Moore, Christy Singer/songwriter. Founder of groundbreaking Irish folk group *Planxty* and the acclaimed *Moving Hearts*. Solo artist since 1982, renowned for his innovative song writing. Best known for *Ordinary Man* (1985) and *The Christy Moore Collection* (1991).

Morgan, Dermot (b. 1952). Comedian. Met with considerable success with his Channel Four irreverent comedy show *Father Ted*. At home in Ireland, his bitingly satirical radio show *Scrap Saturday* was highly rated by the critics, less so by the politicians.

Morrison, Van (b. 1945, Belfast). Singer. Legendary rock musician. Formed *Them* in 1963, enjoyed commercial success. Released debut solo album in 1967 and went on to enjoy phenomenally successful solo career. Raised to legendary status on strength of albums such as *Astral Weeks* (1968), *Moondance* (1969) and *No Guru, No Method, No Teacher* (1986).

Murphy, Mike (b. 1941, Dublin). Television and radio presenter, currently hosting *The Arts Show* on RTE Radio 1 and the National Lottery game show on

RTE television *Winning Streak*. Past television shows include *The Live Mike* and *Murphy's Micro Quiz-M*.

Murray, Brian (b. 1949, Dublin). Actor, who has starred in *The Irish RM* and *Strumpet City* as well as appearing on stage.

Neeson, Liam (b. Antrim). Actor. Starred in films such as *A Prayer for the Dying*, (1987), *Schindler's List*, (1993) and *"Michael Collins*, (1996). Oscar nominated for his powerful role as Oscar Schcindler.

O'Brien, Edna (b. Clare). Author. Won 1995 European Prize for Literature. Novels include: *Johnny I Hardly Knew You* (1977), *House of Splendid Isolation* (1994) and *Down By The River* (1996). Also writes poetry and short stories.

O'Connor, Sinead (b. 1966, Dublin). Ireland's most controversial entertainer, the 1990 Grammy Award Winner has met with considerable popular and critical acclaim with albums such as *Universal Mother* and *The Lion and the Cobra* and hits such as *Nothing Compares 2 U*.

O'Donnell, Daniel (b. 1961, Donegal). Ireland's leading country singer, also highly popular in Britain and world over. The clean cut entertainer has had a string of successful singles, albums, video's and television shows. Hit singles include *I Just Want to Dance with You* and *Destination Donegal*.

O'Riordan, Dolores (b. Limerick). Singer with *The Cranberries*. Signed to Island records, the Limerick band are Ireland's most successful musical export since U2. Enjoyed massive success with albums released to date.

O'Toole, Peter (b. 1932, Galway). Actor, whose films include *Lawrence of Arabia* (1960), *Goodbye Mr. Chips* (1969) and *The Last Emperor* (1986).

Patterson, Frank (b. 1941, Tipperary). Ireland's leading Tenor, has had many major tours in Europe and America, where he enjoys much success.

Potter, Maureen (b. Dublin). Actress, made debut at age of 7. Began long association at Olympia Theatre in 1935 with Jimmy O'Dea. Much loved Dubliner.

Roach, Hal (b. 1927, Waterford). Well known Cabaret entertainer.

Rock, Dickie (b. 1943, Dublin). Lead singer with *Miami Showband* from 1963-1972. Escaped death when members of band were killed by Loyalist terrorists.

Rodgers, Patsy Dan (b. Tory Island, Donegal). *King of Tory*. Member of acclaimed primitive painting school associated with British born artist, Derek Hill.

Ryan, Gerry (b. 1956). Broadcaster. Trained as a barrister. One of R.T.E. Radio's best known names. Has presented the popular *Gerry Ryan Show* on 2FM since 1988 and has presented a number of television shows such as *Ryantime* and *School around the Corner*.

Sheridan, Jim Film maker. Best known films to date have been *My Left Foot* (1988) in which Daniel Day Lewis won an Oscar; *The Field* (1989), and *In the Name of the Father* (1993) - all with Irish themes. His latest project *Some Mother's Son* (1996) is based on the Republican hunger strikes of the early 1980's.

Toibin, Niall (b. 1929, Cork). Comedian and actor. Has made many television appearances and currently starring in B.B.C's hugely popular comedy *Ballykissangel*.

Wogan, Terry (b. 1938, Limerick). Television Presenter and Radio Broadcaster. Worked briefly with R.T. E. before joining B.B.C. Became best known presenter on British Television hosting shows such as *Blankety Blank* and his own chat-show *Wogan*. Also long standing presenter of the Eurovision Song Contest for the B.B.C.

IRISH ALMANAC
YEARBOOK OF FACTS
1998

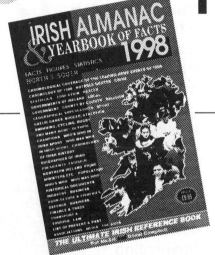

If <u>YOU</u> wish
to have your business
advertised in the
1998
IRISH ALMANAC &
YEARBOOK OF FACTS

Contact us at . . . .

16 HIGH STREET, DERRY, NORTHERN IRELAND.
TEL: 01504-45978   CODE FROM REPUBLIC OF IRELAND: 0801504-45978

IRISH ALMANAC
YEARBOOK OF FACTS
1998

The **1998 Irish Almanac and Yearbook of Facts** will be available from all good bookshops throughout Ireland in Autumn 1997. Alternatively, you can acquire same by filling in the coupon below and forwarding it to our office at **16 High Street, Derry, Northern Ireland** complete with payment of **£9.95** (P. & P. free).

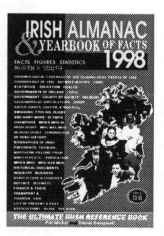

MEDIA IN IRELAND

Out of a total island population of 5.1 million, more than a million people north and south, buy a paper in Ireland on a daily basis. On a Sunday, newspaper sales increase to 1.2 million. In addition, 330,372 weekly papers are purchased in Northern Ireland with a further 233,949 "weeklies" sold in the Republic.

Ireland has one of the largest newspaper buying populations in Western Europe. As well as the domestically produced newspapers, English papers have always been popular in Ireland, with the tabloids having a very strong presence. Indeed many of the leading English papers, both tabloid and quality (broadsheet), now produce special "Irish editions" which are designed to increase sales in what seems to be a continually growing market. English papers, overall, have about a 10% share of that market.

In recent years there has been a remarkable growth in the broadcast media, particularly local radio. More than twenty regional stations were established in the Republic in the early 1990's to complement the existing national services provided by R.T.E. in Dublin.

Northern Ireland has had a strong regional broadcast service for many years, the B.B.C. establishing a radio facility in Belfast for the first time in 1924. A television service came into operation in 1953 while six years later, Ulster Television came into being.

Apart from the topical media, Ireland has undergone something of a revolution in book publishing in recent years with a considerable number of publishing houses being established on both sides of the border.

NEWSPAPERS

Most Popular Irish Daily Newspapers (1995)

Republic of Ireland (National) Newspaper	Average Circulation
The Examiner (Cork)	53,853
Evening Echo (Cork)	25,470
Evening Herald (Dublin)	121,216
Irish Independent (Dublin)	160,455
Irish Times (Dublin)	98,867
The Star (Dublin)	86,602

Northern Ireland (National) Newspapers	Average Circulation
Belfast Telegraph (Belfast)	133,132
Irish News (Belfast)	44,967
Ulster News Letter (Belfast)	33,753

Most Popular English Daily Newspapers (1995)
Bought in Ireland & UK

Newspaper	Ireland	UK	Total
Daily Mirror	62,313	2,427,606	2,489,919
Daily Record	2,209	741,131	743,340
Daily Star	0	655,576	655,576
The Sun	59,410	3,907,964	3,967,374
Daily Express	4,023	1,235,303	1,239,326
Daily Mail	4,004	1,844,745	1,848,749
Daily Telegraph	6,837	1,014,596	1,021,433
Financial Times	3,173	166,203	169,376
Guardian	2,258	360,725	362,983
Independent	4,859	273,767	278,626
Times	4,100	637,171	641,271
Racing Post	3,031	41,401	44,432
Sporting Life	5,885	59,686	65,571

Most Popular Sunday Newspapers (bought in Ireland 1995)

Newspaper	Ireland	UK	Total
News of the World	145,369	4,472,258	4,690,563
Sunday Mirror	70,376	2,415,938	2,534,566
The People	87,496	1,970,663	2,092,056
Mail on Sunday	9,128	2,001,846	2,040,758
Sunday Express	14,087	1,321,681	1,362,974
Independent on Sunday	14,933	295,063	326,675
Observer	8,795	425,740	463,301
Sunday Telegraph	8,256	641,702	674,031
Sunday Times	66,235	1,129,401	1,252,774
Sunday Business Post	33,010	***	33,010
Sunday Independent	339,061	***	339,061
Sunday Life	99,532	***	99,532
Sunday Tribune	82,569	***	82,569
Sunday World Group	299,698	***	299,698

*** Not available.

(Most Popular) Irish Provincial Newspapers (1995)

Northern Ireland (Provincial) Newspapers	Average Circulation	Republic of Ireland (Provincial) Newspapers	Average Circulation
Alpha Newspaper Group	29,956	Anglo Celt	15,818
Banbridge Chronicle	6,556	Anois	4,185
Carrickfergus Advertiser & East Antrim Gazette	2,954	The Argus	8,191
Coleraine Times	6,477	Clare Champion	20,196
County Down Spectator	12,640	Connacht Sentinel	6,598
Derry Journal (Tue)	25,842	Connacht Tribune Series	27,975
Derry Journal (Fri)	27,095	The Corkman	5,975
Derry Journal Group	73,788	Donegal Democrat	17,599
Down Recorder	12,697	Donegal People's Press	3,252
Dungannon News & Tyrone Courier	14,007	Drogheda Independent Series	13,865
Impartial Reporter	14,187	Enniscorthy Guardian Series	5,905
Larne Gazette Group	5,408	Irish Field	10,544
Larne Gazette Series	2,454	The Kerryman Series	28,437
Larne Times Series	13,770	Kilkenny People	16,649
Londonderry Sentinel Series	5,540	Limerick Leader (Weekend) Series	25,959
Lurgan Mail	9,818	Nationalist & Munster Advertiser	15,641
Mid Ulster Mail Series	12,318	Nenagh Guardian	7,557
Morton Newspaper Group	73,313	New Ross Standard	5,515
Mourne Observer Series	12,996	Tipperary Star	9,883
Newtownards Chronicle & County Down Observer	10,595	Wexford People	10,009
Newtownards Spectator	3,400	Wicklow People Series	15,796
Portadown Times	11,608		
Strabane Weekly News	2,266		
Tyrone Constitution & Strabane Weekly News Group	12,414		
Tyrone Constitution (Omagh)	10,148		
Ulster Gazette & Armagh Standard	10,541		
Ulster Star Series	13,782		

List of all Irish Newspapers

Anois
26-27 Cearnóg Mhuirfean, Baile Átha Cliath 2, Tel. (01) 6760268, Fax: (01) 6612438. Published weekly; 4,185 ABC. Editor: Bernard Harris.

Belfast Newsletter
Century Newspapers Ltd., 45-56 Boucher Crescent, Belfast BT12

6QY. Tel. (0801232) 680000. Published Weekdays except Sunday: 66,261. Free Circulation in Belfast. Editor: Geoff Martin.

Belfast Telegraph
Belfast Telegraph Newspapers Ltd., 124-144 Royal Avenue, Belfast BT1 1EB. Tel. (0801232) 321242. Fax.

(0801232) 554506. Published daily, evening: 133,132 ABC. Editor: Edmund Curran.

Examiner, The (1841) Cork Examiner Publications Ltd., P.O. Box 21, Academy Street, Cork. Tel. (021) 272722. Fax. (021) 275112. Published daily: 53,853 ABC. Editor: Brian Looney.

Evening Echo
Cork Examiner Publications Ltd., Academy Street, Cork. Tel. (021) 272722. Fax. (021) 275112. Published daily, evening: 25,470 ABC. Editor: Nigel O'Mahony.

Evening Herald
Independent Newspapers (Ireland) Ltd., Middle Abbey Street, Dublin 1. Tel. (01) 8731666. Fax. (01) 8731787. Published daily: 121,216 ABC. Editor: P. Drury.

Irish Family, The
P.O. Box 7, Mullingar, Co. Westmeath. Tel. (044) 42987. Fax. (044) 42987. Published weekly. Editor: Dick Hogan.

Irish Independent (1905)
Independent Newspapers (Ireland) Ltd., (01) 8731333 / 8731666. Fax. (01) 8731787 / 8720304. Published daily: 160,455 ABC. Editor. Vincent Doyle.

Irish News (1855)
113-117 Donegall Street, Belfast BT1 2GE. Tel. (0801232) 322226. Fax. (0801232) 337505. Published daily: 44,967 ABC. Editor: Tom Collins.

Irish Times, The (1859)
10-16 D'Olier Street, Dublin 2. Tel. (01) 6792022. Fax. (01) 6793910. Published daily: 98,867 ABC. Editor: Conor Brady.

Star, The
Independent Star Ltd., Star House, Terenure Road North, Dublin 6W. Tel. (01) 4901228. Fax. (01) 4902193 /4907425. Published daily: 86,602 ABC. Editor: Gerard O'Reagan.

Sunday Business Post
27-30 Merchants Quay, Dublin 8. Tel. (01) 6799777. Fax. (01) 6799496/6796498. Published weekly: 33,010 ABC. Editor: Damien Kiberd.

Sunday Independent (1906)
Independent Newspapers (Ireland) Ltd., Middle Abbey Street, Dublin 1. Tel. (01) 8731333/8731666. Fax. (01) 8731787/8720304. Published weekly: 339,061 ABC. Editor: Aengus Fanning.

Sunday Tribune
15 Lower Baggot Street, Dublin 2.

Tel. (01) 6615555. Fax. (01) 6615302. Published weekly: 82,569 ABC. Editor: Matt Cooper.

Sunday World (1973)
Sunday Newspapers Ltd., Newspaper House, Rathfarnham Road, Dublin 6. Tel. (01) 4901980. Fax. (01) 4901838. Published weekly: 299,698 ABC. Editor: Colm McGinty.

Anglo-Celt, The
Cavan. Tel. (049)31100 Fax. (049) 32280. Published weekly; 15,818 ABC. Editor: Johnny O'Hanlon.

Antrim Guardian (1970)
1A Railway Street, Antrim. Tel. (0801849) 462624. Fax. (0801849) 465551. Localised edition of Ballymena Guardian. Published weekly, Wednesday: 23,500 combined circulation. Editor: Liam Heffron.

Argus, The
Jocelyn Street, Dundalk, Co. Louth. Tel. (042) 34632 / 31500. Fax (042) 31643. Published weekly; 8,191 ABC. Editor: Kevin Mulligan.

Armagh-Down Observer
Irish Street, Dungannon, Co. Tyrone. Tel. (0801868) 722557. Fax. (0801868) 727334. Published weekly. Editor: Maurice O'Neill.

Armagh Observer
26 English Street, Armagh. Tel. (0801868) 722557. Fax. (0801868) 727334. Published weekly. Editor: D. Mallon.

Athlone Topic
The Crescent, Ballymahon Road, Athlone, Co. Westmeath. Tel. (0902) 73180. Fax. (0902) 75521. Published weekly. Editor: Oliver Heaney.

Ballymena Chronicle and Antrim Observer
Irish Street, Dungannon, Co. Tyrone. Tel. (0801868) 722557. Fax. (0801868) 727334. Published weekly. Editor: D. Mallon.

Ballymena Guardian (1970)
Northern Newspaper Group, Railway Road, Coleraine. Tel. (0801265)

41221/2/3/4/5/6. Fax. (0801265) 653920. Published weekly; 24,000. Editor: Maurice O'Neill.

Banbridge Chronicle (1870)
The Banbridge Chronicle Press Ltd., 14 Bridge Street, Banbridge, Co. Down. Tel. (08018206) 62332. Fax. (08018206) 24397. Published weekly; 6,556 ABC. Editor: Bryan Hooks.

Carrickfergus Advertiser
31A High Street, Carrickfergus, Co. Antrim. Tel. (0801960) 363651. Fax. (0801960) 3363092 Published weekly; 14,000. Editor: Gary Kelly.

Clare Champion
Barrack Street, Ennis, Co. Clare. Tel. (065) 28105. Fax. (065) 20374. Published weekly: 20,196 ABC. Editor: J. F. O'Dea.

Coleraine Chronicle (1844)
Northern Newspaper Group, Railway Road, Coleraine, Co. Derry. Tel. (0801265) 43344. 23,000. Published weekly. Editor: Grant Cameron.

Connacht Sentinel, The (1925)
The Connacht Tribune Ltd., 15 Market Street, Galway. Tel. (091) 67251. Fax. (091) 67970. Published weekly; 6,598 ABC. Editor: Brendan O'Carroll.

Connacht Tribune, The (1909)
The Connacht Tribune Ltd., 15 Market Street, Galway. Tel. (091) 67251. fax. (091) 67970. Published weekly; 27,975 ABC. Editor: John Cunningham.

Connaught Telegraph
Castlebar, Co. Mayo. Tel. (094) 21711 / 21403 / 21108. Fax. (094) 24007. Published weekly: 16,000. Editor: Tom Courell.

County Down Spectator (1904)
109 Main Street, Bangor, Co. Down. Tel. (0801247) 270270. Fax. (0801247) 271544. Published weekly:12,640 ABC. Editor: Paul Flowers.

Craigavon Echo
14A Church Street, Portadown, Co. Armagh. Tel. (0801762) 350041. Fax. (0801762) 350203. Published weekly, distributed free; 22,919. Editor: David Armstrong.

Democrat, The
Ann Street, Dungannon, Co. Tyrone
Tel. (0801868) 722557. Fax.
(0801868) 727334. Editor: D. J.
Mallon.

Derry Journal (1772)
Buncrana Road, Derry. Tel.
(0801504) 2722000 Fax. (0801504)
272260. Church Street, Letterkenny,
Co. Donegal. Tel. (074) 26240. Fax.
(074) 26329. Published twice
weekly; Tuesday (25,842 ABC) and
Friday (27,095 ABC). Editor: Pat
McArt.

Derry People and Donegal News
(1932) Crossview House,
Letterkenny, Co. Donegal. Tel. (074)
21014 / 21491 / 26301/2. Fax. (074)
22881. Published weekly, Friday;
Editor: John McCrory.

Donegal Democrat (1919)
Donegal Democrat Ltd., Donegal
Road, Ballyshannon, Co. Donegal.
Tel. (072) 51201.   Fax. (072)
51945. Published weekly; 17,599
ABC. Editor: John Bromley.

Donegal Peoples Press(1932)
Port Road, Letterkenny, Co.
Donegal. Tel. (074) 28000.
Published weekly; 3,252 ABC.
Editor: Paddy Walsh.

Down Recorder
Church Street, Downpatrick, Co.
Down.   Tel. (0801396) 613711.
Fax: (0801396) 614624. Published
weekly;   12,697 ABC. Editor: Paul
Symington.

Drogheda Independent
9 Shop Street, Drogheda, Co. Louth.
Tel. (041) 38658. Fax. (041) 34271.
Published weekly; 13,865 ABC.
Editor: Paul Murphy.

Dundalk Democrat (1849)
3 Earl Street, Dundalk. Tel. (042)
34058 / 36976. Fax. (042) 31399.
Published weekly;   16,000. Editor:
T. P. Roe.

**Dungannon News and Tyrone
Courier**
58 Scotch Street, Dungannon, Co.
Tyrone. Tel. (0801868) 722271.
Fax. (0801868) 726171. Published
weekly;   14,007 ABC. Editor: R. G.
Montgomery.

Dungannon Observer
Irish Street, Dungannon, Co. Tyrone.
Tel. (0801868) 722557.   Fax.

(0801868) 727334. Published
weekly. Editor: D. Mallon.

**Dungarvan Leader and Southern
Democrat** (1938)
78 O'Connell Street, Dungarvan, Co.
Waterford. Tel. (058) 41203. Fax.
(058) 41203. Published weekly,
Wednesday;   12,800. Editor: Colm
J. Nagle.

**Dungarvan Observer and Munster
Industrial Advocate**
Shandon,   Dungarvan,   Co.
Waterford. Tel. (058) 41205 /
42042.   Fax. (058) 41559.
Published weekly;   10,500. Editor:
P. Lynch.

Echo Newspapers Group, The
*(weekly publishers of The Echo,
Wexford Echo, Gorey Echo, New
Ross Echo and monthly publishers
of Farming Echo, Property Echo)*
Mill Park Road, Enniscorthy, Co.
Wexford. Tel. (054) 33231. Fax.
(054) 33506. Editor-in-Chief: James
Gahan.

Fermanagh Herald
30 Belmore Street, Enniskillen, Co.
Fermanagh. Tel. (0801365) 322066.
Fax. (0801365) 325521. Published
weekly, Wednesday;   10,500.
Editor: Dominic McClements.

Fermanagh News
Irish Street, Dungannon, Co. Tyrone.
Tel. (0801868) 722557.   Fax.
(0801868) 727334. Published
weekly. Editor: D. Mallon.

Galway Advertiser (1970)
2-3 Church Lane, Galway.   Tel.
(091) 67077. Fax. (091) 67079.
Published weekly, Thursday;
36,000. Managing Editor: Ronnie
O'Gorman.

Herald and Post Newspapers
*(weekly publishers of east Belfast
Herald and Post, South Belfast
Herald and Post, North and
Newtownabbey Herald and Post and
North Down Herald and Post).*
124 Royal Avenue, Belfast BT1 1EB.
Tel. (0801232) 239049 / 439993.
Fax. (0801232)239050. Combined
circulation 158,999. Editor: Nigel
Tilson.

Inner City News
51 Amiens Street, Dublin 1. Tel.
(01) 8363832. Fax. (01) 8787403.
Published monthly, distributed free;

10,000. Editor: John Hedges.

Kerryman, The, / Corkman, The
Clash Industrial Estate, Tralee, Co.
Kerry. Tel. (066)21666. Fax. (066)
21608. Published weekly;   33,544
ABC. Editor: Gerard Colleran.

Kerry's Eye (1974)
Kenno Ltd., 22 Ashe Street, Tralee,
Co. Kerry. Tel. (066) 23199. Fax.
(066) 23163. Published weekly;
17,500. Editor: Padraig Kennelly.

Kildare Nationalist
Liffey House, Edward Street,
Newbridge, Co. Kildare. Tel. (045)
432147. Fax. (045) 433720. Editor:
Eddie Coffey.

Kilkenny People (1892)
34 High Street, Kilkenny. Tel. (056)
21015.   Fax. (056) 21414.
Published weekly;   16,649 ABC.
Editor: John Kerry Keane.

Leader, The
The Square, Dromore, Co. Down.
Tel. (0801846) 692217 / 692217.
Fax. (0801846) 699260. Published
weekly: 7,500. Editor: Carlton
Baxtor.

Leinster Express (1831)
Leinster Express Newspapers Ltd.,
Dublin Road, Portlaoise, Co. Laois.
Tel. (0502) 21666. Fax. (0502)
20491. Published weekly;   17,368.
Editor:Teddy Fennelly.

Leinster Leader
18 South Main Street, Naas, Co.
Kildare. Tel. (045) 897302. Fax.
(045)897647. Published weekly;
15,250. Editor: Vicky Weller.

Leitrim Observer (1889)
Leitrim Observer Ltd., St. Georges
Terrace, Carrick-on-Shannon, Co.
Leitrim. Tel. (078) 20025 / 20299.
Fax. (078) 20112.   Published
weekly: 10,000. Editor: Anthony
Hickey.

Liffey Champion
3 Captain's Hill, Leixlip, Co. Kildare.
Tel. (01) 6245533.   Fax. (01)
6243013. Published fortnightly.
Editor: V. Sutton.

Limerick Chronicle (1766)
The Limerick Leader Ltd., O'Connell
Street, Limerick. Tel. (061) 315233.
Fax. (061) 314804. Published
weekly, Tuesday;   8,000. Editor:
Brendan Halligan.

Limerick Leader (1889)
The Limerick Leader Ltd., O'Connell Street, Limerick. Tel. (061) 315233. Fax. (061) 314804. Published four times weekly: 25,959 ABC weekend edition. Editor: Brendan Halligan.

Lisburn Echo
12A Bow Street, Lisburn Co. Antrim. Tel. (0801846) 679111. Fax. (0801846) 602904. Published weekly, distributed free; 22,955. Editor: Joe Fitzpatrick.

Local News Publication
Rosehill House, Main Street, Finglas, Dublin 11. Tel. (01) 8361666. Fax. (01) 8342079. 9 Lower Kevin Street, Dublin 8. Tel. (01) 4757132. Fax. (01) 8342079. Tel. (088) 524064. Circulation 28,000.

Londonderry / Limavady Sentinel
Suite 3, Spencer House, Spencer Road, Derry. Tel. (0801504) 48889. Fax. (0801504) 41175. Published weekly; 10,971 ABC. Editor: James Cadden.

Longford Leader, The
Longford Leader Ltd., Market Square, Longford. Tel. (043) 45241. Fax. (043) 41489. Published weekly, Wednesday; 25,000. Editor: Eugene McGee.

Longford News (1936)
Five County News, The Longford News, Earl Street, Longford. Tel. (043) 46342 / 45627 / 41147. Fax. (043) 41549. Published weekly, Wednesday: 23,840. Editor: Joe Flaherty.

Lurgan and Portadown Examiner
Irish Street, Dungannon, Co. Tyrone. Tel. (0801868) 722557. Fax. (0801868) 727334. Published weekly. Editor: D. Mallon.

Lurgan Mail
4A High Street, Lurgan, Co. Armagh. Tel. (0801762) 327777. Fax. (0801762) 325271. Published weekly; 9,818 ABC. Editor: Richard Elliott.

Mayo News
The Fairgreen, Westport, Co. Mayo. Tel. (098) 25311. Fax. (098) 26108. Published weekly: 12,000. Managing Editor: Seán Staunton.

Meath Chronicle and Cavan & Westmeath Herald (1897)

Market Square, Navan, Co. Meath. Tel. (046) 21442. Fax. (046) 23565. Published weekly: 19,635. Editor: Ken Davis.

Meath Topic
Combined circulation with Westmeath Topic and Offaly Topic. Part of the Topic Newspapers Ltd. Group.

The Roundabout, 6 Dominick Street, Mullingar. Tel. (044) 48868. Fax. (044) 43777. Published weekly. Editor: Dick Hogan.

Midland Tribune, The (1881)
Emmet Street, Birr, Co. Offaly. Tel. (0509) 20003 / 20132. Fax. (0509) 20588. Published weekly: 16,000. Editor: John O'Callaghan.

Mid-Ulster Observer
Irish Street, Dungannon, Co. Tyrone. Tel. (0801868) 722557. Fax. (0801868) 727334. Published weekly. Editor: D. Mallon.

Morton Newspapers Ltd.,
(Publishers of Coleraine/Ballymoney Times, Ballymena/Antrim Times, Ballymena Observer, Larne/Carrickfergus/Newtownabbey Times, Londonderry/Roe Valley Sentinel, Lurgan Mail, Portadown Times, Ulster Star (Lisburn), Dromore Star, The Leader (Dromore), Banbridge Leader, Mid-Ulster Mail, South Derry edition (Magherafelt), Craigavon Echo, Lisburn Echo, North-West Echo, Mid-Ulster Echo, East Antrim Advertiser, Tyrone Times, Specialist Publications)

Head Office, 21-35 Windsor Avenue, Lurgan, Craigavon, Co. Armagh. BT67 9BG Tel. (0801762) 326161. Fax. (0801762) 343618. Combined circulation 73,313 ABC.

Mourne Observer (1949)
Newcastle, Co. Down. Tel. (08013967) 22666. Fax. (08013967) 24566. Published weekly: 12,996 ABC. Editor: Terence Bowman.

Munster Express, The (1859)
37 The Quay, Waterford. 1-3 Hanover Street, Waterford. Tel. (051) 72141/3. Fax. (051) 73452. Published twice weekly; 18,500. Editor: K. J. Walsh.

Nationalist and Leinster Times (1883). Carlow. Tel. (0503) 31731.

Published weekly; 17,170 ABC. Editor: Thomas Mooney.

Nationalist Newspaper
Queen Street, Clonmel, Co. Tipperary. Tel. (052) 22211. Fax. (052) 25248. Published weekly; 15,641 ABC. Editor: Tom Corr.

Nenagh Guardian Ltd.,
13 Summerhill, Nenagh, Co. Tipperary. Tel. (067) 31214. Fax. (067) 33401. Published weekly; 7,608. Editor: Gerry Slevin.

Newry Reporter, The (1867)
4 Market Street, Newry, Co. Down. Tel. (0801693) 67633. Fax. (0801693) 63157. Published weekly; 16,370. Editor: D. O'Donnell.

Newtownards Spectator
109 Main Street, Bangor, Co. Down. Tel. (0801247) 270270. Fax. (0801247) 271544. Published weekly; 3,400 ABC. Editor: Paul Flowers.

Northern Constitution (1876)
Northern Newspaper Group, Coleraine, Co. Derry. Tel. (0801265) 43344. Published weekly; 8,790. Editor: Grant Cameron.

Northern Newspaper Group (1970)
(Publishers of Coleraine Chronicle, Ballymena Guardian, Antrim Guardian, Newtownabbey Guardian, The Leader, Northern Constitution) Head Office, Railway Road, Coleraine, Co. Derry. Tel. (0801265) 43344. Combined circulation 79,592. Group Editor: Maurice O'Neill.

Northern Standard
The Diamond, Monaghan. Tel. (047) 81867 / 82188. Fax. (047) 84070. Published weekly; 14,500. Editor: Martin Smyth.

Offaly Express
(Combined circulation with Leinster Express)
Bridge Street, Tullamore, Co. Offaly. Tel. (0506) 21744. Fax. (0506) 51930. Published weekly, distributed free. Editor: Teddy Fennelly.

Offaly Topic
(Combined circulation with the Westmeath Topic and Meath Topic, part of the Topic Newspapers Ltd.,).
The Roundabout, 6 Dominick Street, Mullingar. Tel. (0506) 41182; (044) 48868. Fax. (044) 43777.

Published weekly.

Outlook, The
Castle Street, Rathfriland, Co. Down. Tel. (08018206) 30202. Fax. (08018206) 31022. Published weekly; 7,500. Editor: Ken Purdy.

People Newspapers
(*Publishers of five regional newspapers and Irelands Own*).
Bray People, Main Street, Bray, Co. Wicklow. Tel. (01) 2867393.

The Guardian, Court Street, Enniscorthy. Tel. (054) 33833; Thomas Street, Gorey, Co. Wexford. Tel. (055) 21423.

New Ross Standard, South Street, New Ross, Co. Wexford. Tel. (051) 21184.

The People, 1A North Main Street, Wexford. Tel. (053) 22155.

Wicklow People, Main Street, Wicklow. Tel. (0404) 67198. Fax. (0404) 69937; Main Street, Arklow. Tel. (0402) 32130. Fax. (0402) 39309. Published weekly. Combined circulation 35,800. Editor: Gerard Walsh.

Portadown Times
14A Church Street, Portadown, Co. Armagh. Tel. (0801762) 336111. Fax. (0801762) 350203. Published weekly; 11,608 ABC. Editor: David Armstrong.

Roscommon Champion (1927)
Abbey Street, Roscommon. Tel. (0903) 25051/2. Fax. (0903) 25053. Published weekly: 10,417. Editor: Paul Healy.

Roscommon Herald (1859)
Boyle, Co. Roscommon. Tel. (079) 62622 / 62004 / 62052. Fax. (079) 62926. Published weekly: 16,550. Editor: Christina McHugh.

Sligo Champion (1836)
The Champion Publications Ltd., Wine Street, Sligo. Tel. (071) 69222 / 69133. Fax. (071) 69040. Published weekly: 16,500. Editor: Seamus Finn.

Sligo Weekender (1983)
Castle Street, Sligo. Tel. (071) 42140. Fax. (071) 42255. Circulation 12,100. Editor: Brian McHugh.

South News
Unit 5, Wood Park, Glenageary, Co. Dublin. Tel. (01) 2840266. Fax. (01) 2840860. Circulation 51,000. Editor: Ken Finlay.

Southern Star
Skibbereen, Co. Cork. Tel. (028) 21200. Fax. (028) 21071. Published weekly: 16,000. Editor: L. O'Regan.

Strabane Chronicle
Ulster Herald Series, John Street, Omagh, Co. Tyrone. Tel. (0801662) 243444/5. Fax. (0801662) 242206. Published weekly, Thursday; 4,034. Editor: Paddy Cullen.

Strabane Weekly News (1908)
The Tyrone Constitution Ltd., 25-27 High Street, Omagh, Co. Tyrone. Tel. (0801662) 242721. Fax. (0801662) 243549. Published weekly: 2,266 ABC. Editor: Wesley Atchison.

Tipperary Star (1909)
Friar Street, Thurles, Co. Tipperary. Tel. (0504) 21122 / 21639. Fax. (0504) 21110. Published weekly; 9,883 ABC. Editor: Michael Dundon.

Topic Newspapers Ltd.,
(weekly publishers of Westmeath Topic, Offaly Topic, Meath Topic and monthly magazine Ireland's Eye, circulating in Westmeath, Offaly, Meath, Kildare and Longford).

The Roundabout, 6 Dominick Street, Mullingar, Co. Westmeath. Tel. (044) 48868. Fax. (044) 43777. Editor: Dick Hogan.

Tuam Herald (1837)
Dublin Road, Tuam, Co. Galway. Tel. (093) 24183. Fax. (093) 24478. Published weekly, Wednesday: 11,000. Editor: David Burke.

Tullamore Tribune, The (1978)
Church Street, Tullamore, Co. Offaly. Tel. (0506) 21152 / 21058 / 21927. Fax. (0506) 21927. Published weekly: 6,000. Editor: G. J. Scully.

Tyrone Constitution, The (1844)
25-27 High Street, Omagh, Co. Tyrone. Tel. (0801662) 242721. Fax. (0801662) 243549. Published weekly: 10,148 ABC. Editor: Wesley Atchison.

Ulster Farmer (1990)
Irish Street, Dungannon, Co. Tyrone. Tel. (0801868) 722557. Fax. (0801868) 727334. Published weekly.

Ulster Gazette and Armagh Standard (1844)
56 Scotch Street, Armagh. Tel. (0801861) 522639. Fax. (0801861) 527029. Published weekly; 10,541 ABC. Editor: Karen Bushby.

Ulster Herald (1901)
John Street, Omagh, Co. Tyrone. Tel. (0801662) 243444/5. Fax. (0801662) 242206. Published weekly, Thursday; 10,907. Editor: Paddy Cullen.

Ulster Star
12A Bow Street, Lisburn, Co. Antrim. BT28 1BN Tel. (0801846) 679111. Fax. (0801846) 602904. Published weekly; 13,782 ABC. Editor: David Fletcher.

Waterford News & Star (1848)
25 Michael Street, Waterford. Tel. (051) 74951/2. Fax. (051) 55281. Published weekly; 16,000. Editor: Peter Doyle.

Western People, The (1883)
Francis Street, Ballina, Co. Mayo. Tel. (096) 21188. Fax. (096) 70208. Published weekly; 28,001. Editor: Terry Reilly.

Westmeath Examiner, The (1882)
19 Dominick Street, Mullingar. Tel. (044) 48426. Fax. (044) 40640. Published weekly; 13,327. Editor: N. J. Nally.

Westmeath Topic
The Roundabout, 6 Dominick Street, Mullingar, Co. Westmeath. Tel. (044) 48868. Fax. (044) 43777. Published weekly. Editor: Dick Hogan.

BROADCASTING MEDIA

National & Local Radio Listenership Ratings

Station Name	Listenership % Home/Local	Listenership in 000's	Listenership % Reach	Peak Listenership Time
NATIONAL				
Any Local	51%	1,362,210	N/A	N/A
Home Local	46%	1,228,660	26	09.00-11.00 Reach
R.T.E. Radio 1	35%	934,850	21%	08.00-09.15 Reach
2FM	29%	774,590	14%	09.00-12.00 Reach
LOCAL				
C.K.R.	41%	49,200	24%	09.00-11.00 Reach
L.M.F.M.	42%	61,320	24%	09.00-11.00 Reach
Radio Kilkenny	61%	33,550	32%	11.00-14.00 Reach
Radio 3	40%	50,000	21%	11.00-14.00 Reach
South East Radio	57%	43,320	31%	09.00-11.00 Reach
East Coast Radio	25%	18,500	11%	11.00-14.00 Reach
Radio Limerick 95FM	60%	73,900	31%	09.00-11.00 Reach
Tipp FM	50%	40,500	24%	11.00-14.00 Reach
Tipp Mid West	37%	6,290	18%	09.00-11.00 Reach
W.L.R. FM	55%	38,500	32%	11.00-14.00 Reach
Clare FM	49%	33,320	29%	09.00-14.00 Reach
Radio Kerry	57%	53,010	33%	09.00-11.00 Reach
Galway Bay FM	34%	49,940	17%	11.00-14.00 Reach
M.W.R.	59%	47,790	35%	09.00-11.00 Reach
Shannonside/Northern Sound	43%	64,500	24%	09.00-11.00 Reach
N.W.R.	67%	45,560	36%	09.00-11.00 Reach
Donegal Highland Radio	60%	43,800	38%	11.00-14.00 Reach
96FM/County Sound	*54%	*167,400	31%	11.00-14.00 Reach
Classic Hits 98FM	*27%	*216,000	12%	15.00-18.00 Reach
FM 104	*23%	*184,000	7%	10.00-14.00 Reach

* Data based on statistics for 6 months

National Radio & Television Stations

TELEVISION STATIONS

British Broadcasting Corporation (Northern Ireland)
Broadcasting House, Ormeau Avenue, Belfast BT2 8HQ. Tel. (0801232) 338000; Fax. (0801232) 338800; Founded: 1924. Northern Ireland Controller: Pat Loughrey; Head of Programmes: Anna Kelleher.

Radio Telefís Éireann:
Donnybrook, Dublin 4. Tel. (01) 2083111; Fax. (01) 2083080; Founded: 1961; Director General: Joe Barry; Director of Television Programmes: David Blake; Regional Studios: 10; Output: 200 hours per week.

Ulster Television PLC.:
Havelock House, Ormeau Road, Belfast BT7 1EB. Tel. (0801232) 328122; Fax. (0801232) 246695; Founded: 1959; Managing Director: J. D. Smyth; Controller of Programming: Alan Bremner; Regional Studios: 1; Output: 12 hours of home produced programmes per week.

RADIO STATIONS

British Broadcasting Corporation (Northern Ireland):
Broadcasting House, Ormeau Avenue, Belfast BT2 8HQ. Tel. (0801232) 338000; Fax. (0801232) 338800; Radio Ulster and Radio Foyle are branches of BBC Northern Ireland; Founded: 1924. Controller: Pat Loughrey.

Radio Telefís Éireann:
Donnybrook, Dublin 4. Tel. (01) 2083111; Fax. (01) 2083080; RTE operates five radio stations nationwide Radio 1, 2FM, FM3, Raidió na Gaeltachta & RTE Radio Cork; Founded: 1926; Director of Radio Programming: Kevin Healy; Output: 24 hours a day, seven days a week.

Raidió na Gaeltachta:
Casla, Co. na Gaillimhe. Tel.: (091) 506677; Fax: (091) 506688. Founded: 1972. Ceannaire: Pól Ó Gallchóir.

Local Radio Stations

Anna Livia 103.8 FM:
3 Grafton Street, Dublin 2. Tel. (01) 6778103; Fax. (01) 6778150; Chairman: Tom Walsh; Station Manager: John Furlong; Broadcasting Area: Dublin City and County.

Atlantic 252:
Radio Tara Ltd., Morningtion House, Trim, Co. Meath; Tel. (046) 36655; Fax. (046) 36704; Chairman: G. Thorn; Managing Director: T. Baxter; Broadcasting Area: Directed mainly at the British market plus Ireland.

Carlow Kildare Radio Limited:
Lismard House, Tullow Street, Carlow. Tel. (0503) 41044 / 41048; Fax. (0503) 41047; ACC House, 51 South Main Street, Naas, Co. Kildare. Tel. (045) 879666; Fax. (045) 897611; Station Manager: Tom Dowling; Broadcasting Area: Leinster;

Clare FM:
The Abbeyfield Centre, Francis Street, Ennis, Co. Clare. Tel. (065) 28888; Fax. (065) 29392; Executive Chairman: Michael Evans; Broadcasting Area: Clare.

Classic Hits 98 FM:
8 Upper Mount Street; Dublin 2. Tel. (01) 6765800; Fax. (01) 6765252; Station Manager: Ken Hutton; Broadcasting Area: Dublin.

Cool FM:
PO Box 974, Belfast BT1 1RT. Tel. (0801247) 817181; Fax. (0801247) 814974; Managing Director: David Sloan; Broadcasting Area: Greater Belfast Area.

Highland Radio:
Pinehill, Letterkenny, Co. Donegal. Tel. (074) 25000; Fax. (074) 25344; Station Manager: Charlie Collins; Broadcasting Area: Donegal, Derry & Tyrone.

Downtown Radio:
Newtownards, Co. Down, BT23 4ES. Tel. (0801247) 815555; Fax. (0801247) 818913; Managing Director: David Sloan; Broadcasting Area: Northern Ireland.

East Coast Radio:
9 Prince of Wales Terrace, Quinsboro Road, Bray, Co. Wicklow. Tel. (01) 2866414; Fax. (01) 2861219; Chairman: Blaise Treacy; Broadcasting Area: Wicklow, Dublin;

FM 104:
Ballast Office, O'Connell Bridge, Dublin 2. Tel. (01) 6777111; Fax. (01) 6711797 / 6772286; Chairman: M. Cassidy; Chief Executive: D. Hanrahan; Broadcasting Area: Dublin City and County.

Galway Bay FM:
Sandy Road, Galway. Tel. (091) 770000 / 770077; Fax. (091) 752689; Chief Executive: Keith Finnagan; Broadcasting Area: Galway.

Ireland Radio News:
8 Upper Mount Street, Dublin 2. Tel. (01) 6618186; Fax. (01) 6616536; Chief Executive & Chairman: Denis O'Brien; Broadcasting Area: Dublin.

LM FM Radio:
(Independent Broadcasting Corporation Ltd.), Boyne Centre, Drogheda, Co. Louth. Tel. (041) 32000; Fax. (041) 32957; Chairman: E. Caulfield; Chief Executive: Gavin Duffy; General Manager: Michael Crawley; Broadcasting Area: North-East.

Mid and North West Radio:
Regional Advertising Office, Abbey Street, Ballyhaunis, Co. Mayo. Tel. (0907) 30553; Fax. (0907) 30285; Chairman (MWR): M. Hughes; Chairman (NRW): D. O'Shea; Broadcasting Area: Connaught and Donegal.

96 FM:
Broadcasting House, Patrick's Place, Cork. Tel. (021) 551596; Fax. (021) 551500; Managing Director: Colm O'Conaill; Broadcasting Area: Cork City and County.

103 FM:
Mallow, Co. Cork. Tel. (022) 42103; Fax. (022) 42488; Bandon, Co. Cork. Tel. (023) 43103; Fax. (023) 44294; Managing Director: Colm O'Conaill; Broadcasting Area: Cork City and County.

Radio Kerry:
Maine Street, Tralee, Co. Kerry. Tel. (066) 23666; Fax. (066) 22282; Chief Executive & Programme Controller: Dan Collins; Chairman: Joe McGarry; Broadcasting Area: Kerry and South- West region.

Radio Kilkenny:
Hebron Road, Kilkenny. Tel. (056) 61577; Fax. (056) 63586; Chief Executive: John Purcell; Chairman: Michael O'Reilly; Broadcasting Area: Kilkenny City and County.

Radio Limerick 95 FM:
100 O'Connell Street, Limerick. Tel. (061) 319595; Fax. (061) 419890. Chief Executive: Jerry Madden; Station Manager: Frank Carberry; Broadcasting Area: Limerick.

Radio 3:
The Mall, William Street, Tullamore, Co. Offaly. Tel. (0506) 51333; Fax. (0506) 52546; Chief Executive: Joe Yerkes; Broadcasting Area: Offaly, Laois and Westmeath.

Raidió na Life 102FM:
7 Cearnóg Mhuirfean, Baile Átha Cliath 2. Tel. (01) 6616333; Fax. (01) 6763966 / 6790214; Chairman: Seosamh Ó Murchú; Station Manager: Fionnuala Mac Aodha; Broadcasting Area: Dublin.

Shannonside / Northern Sound:
Minard House, Sligo Road, Longford. Tel. (043) 46669 / 46581; Fax. (043) 46591 / 47726; Chief Executive: Owen Purcell; Broadcasting Area: Cavan, Galway, Leitrim, Longford, Monaghan, Roscommon, Westmeath, and areas of Armagh, Fermanagh, Louth, Meath, Tyrone.

South East Radio:
Custom House Quay, Wexford. Tel. (053) 45200; Fax. (053) 45295; Managing Director: Eamonn Butler;

Tipp FM:
Co Tipperary Radio Limited, Whitbridge House, Old Waterford Road, Clonmel, Co. Tipperary; Tel. (052) 25299; Fax. (052) 25447; Managing Director: John O'Connell; Broadcasting Area: Tipperary;

Tipperary Mid-West Radio:
St. Michael's Street, Tipperary Town. Tel. (062) 52555; Fax. (062) 52671; Chairman & Managing Director: Sean Kelly; Controller of Programmes: Martin Quinn; Broadcasting Area: Tipperary.

WLR FM:
The Radio Centre, George's Street, Waterford. Tel. (051) 72248/77471/ 77592; Fax. (051) 77420; Chairman: Gerry Sheridan; Managing Director: Des Whelan.

PERIODICALS, MAGAZINES & JOURNALS

Irish Periodicals, Magazines & Business Journals (1996)

Accountancy Ireland (1969) 87-89 Pembroke Road, Ballsbridge, Dublin 4. Tel. (01) 6680400; Fax. (01) 6680842; Published twice monthly: 16,835 ABC; Editor: Charles O'Rourke.

Administration (1953) Institute of Public Administration, 57-61 Lansdowne Road, Dublin 4. Tel. (01) 2697011; Fax. (01) 2698644; Published quarterly; 2,200; Editor: Tony McNamara.

Administration Yearbook & Diary (1966) Institute of Public Administration, 57-61 Lansdowne Road, Dublin 4. Tel. (01) 2697011; Fax. (01) 2698644; Published yearly; 9,025 ABC; Editor-in Chief: Jim O'Donnell.

Afloat Magazine 2 Lower Glenageary Road, Dún Laoghaire, Co. Dublin. Tel. (01) 2846161; Fax. (01) 2846192; Published monthly; 9,000; Editor: W. M. Nixon.

Africa (1938) St. Patrick's Missionary Society, Kiltegan, Co. Wicklow. Tel. (0508) 73233; Fax. (0508) 73281; Published monthly; Editor: Revd. Gary Howley.

Aisling Magazine, The Eochaill, Inis Mór, Árainn, Co na Gaillimhe. Tel. (099) 61245; Fax. (099) 61245; Published quarterly; 1,500; Editors: Dara Molloy & Tess Harper.

Amnesty International (1974) 48 Fleet Street, Dublin 2. Tel. (01) 6776361; Fax. (01) 6776392; Published twice monthly; 12,000; Editor: Morina O'Neill.

AMT Magazine (1979) Computer House, 66 Patrick Street, Dún Laoghaire, Co. Dublin. Tel. (01) 2800424; Fax. (01) 2808468; Published monthly; 4,450; Editor: John McDonald.

Angling Holidays in Ireland (1986) Libra House Ltd., 4 St. Kevin's Terrace, Dublin 8. Tel. (01) 4542717; 10,640; Editor: Cathal Tyrrell.

Apple Report Computerscope Ltd., Prospect House, 1 Prospect Road, Glasnevin, Dublin 9. Tel. (01) 8303455; Fax. (01) 2808468; Published quarterly; 6,000; Editor: Frank Quinn.

Archaeology Ireland PO Box 69, Bray, Co. Wicklow. Tel. (01) 2862649; Fax. (01) 2864215; Editor: Dr. Gabriel Cooney.

Aspect (1982) 7 Mount Street Crescent, Dublin 2. Tel. (01) 6760774; Fax. (01) 6760773; Annual Publishers of Aspect Premier 2,000 Irish Companies & The Irish Stock Market Annual; Editor: John O'Neill.

Astronomy & Space (1994) Astronomy Ireland, PO Box 2888, Dublin 1. Tel. (01) 4598883; Fax. (01) 4599933; Published monthly.

AudIT (1980) Cork Publishing. 19 Rutland Street, Cork. Tel. (021) 313855; Fax. (021) 313496; Published six times a year; Editor: Ken Ebbage.

Bakery World Jemma Publications Ltd., Marino House, 52 Glasthule Road, Sandycove, Co. Dublin. Tel. (01) 2800000; Fax. (01) 2801818; Published every two months; 2,500; Editor: Natasha Swords.

Béaloideas Department of Irish Folklore, University College Dublin, Dublin 4. Published Annually; 1000; Editor: Pádraig Ó Héalaí.

Big Issues Magazine, The Ormond Multi-Media Centre, 16-18 Lower Ormond Quay, Dublin 1. Tel. (01) 8723500; Fax. (01) 8723348; Directors: Niall Skelly, Ronan Skelly, Ger Egan.

Blueprint Home Plans Oisín Publications, 4 Iona Drive, Dublin 9. Tel. (01) 8305236; Fax. (01) 8307860; Published annually; 7,000; Editor: Liam Ó hOisín.

Books Ireland (1976) 11 Newgrove Avenue, Dublin 4.

Tel. (01) 2692185; Fax. (01) 2692185; Published monthly (except January, July & August); 3,500; Features Editor: Shirley Kelly.

Bord Altranais News, An 31-32 Fitzwilliam Square, Dublin 2. Tel. (01) 6760226; Fax. (01) 6763348; Published quarterly; 50,000; Editor: Eugene Donoghue.

Bride & Groom and First Home 28-32 Exchequer Street, Dublin 2. Tel. (01) 6774186 / 6774279; Fax. (01) 6774516; Published six times a year; Editor: Leanne de Cerbo.

Build Belenos Publications, 32 Upper Fitzwilliam Street, Dublin 2. Tel. (01) 6619222; Fax. (01) 6612417; Published monthly; 4,000 ABC; Editor: John Low.

Bulletin (1956) Society of St. Vincent de Paul, 8 New Cabra Road, Dublin 7. Tel. (01) 8384164 / 8384167'; Fax. (01) 8387355; Published quarterly; 12,000; Editor: Tom McSweeney.

Business and Exporting (1994) Jude Publications Ltd., Tara House, Tara Street, Dublin 2. Tel. (01) 6713500; Fax. (01) 6713074; Published monthly; Editor: Neil Whoriskey.

Business and Finance (1964) Belenos Publications, 50 Fitzwilliam Square, Dublin 2. Tel. (01) 6764587; Fax. (01) 6619781; Published weekly; 11,000; Editor: Dan White.

Business Contact (1988) Dyflin Publications Ltd., 58 North Great Charles Street, Dublin 1. Tel. (01) 8550477; Fax. (01) 8550473; Published monthly; 4,500; Editorial Director: Karen Hesse.

Business Ulster Ulster Journals Ltd., 39 Boucher Road, Belfast. Tel. (0801232) 681371; Fax. (0801232) 381915; Published monthly; Editor: Patricia Rainey.

Cara
Smurfit Publications, 126 Lr. Baggot Street, Dublin 2. Tel. (01) 6623158; Fax. (01) 6619757; Published twice monthly; Editor: Vincent DeVeau.

Car Driver
7 Cranford Centre, Montrose, Dublin 4. Tel. (01) 2600899; Fax. (01) 2600911; Published monthly; 9,000 ABC; Editor: Karl Tsigdinos.

Catering and Licensing Review
(1975) Greer Publications, 151 University Street, Belfast BT7 1HR. Tel. (0801232) 231634; Fax. (0801232) 325736; Published monthly; Editor: Kathy Jensen.

Catholic Standard
55 Lower Gardiner Street, Dublin 1. Tel. (01) 8747538; Fax. (01) 8364805; Published weekly; 8,000; Editor: Cristina Odone.

Celtic Journey
MAC Publishing Ltd., Taney Hall, Eglinton Terrace, Dundrum, Dublin 14. Tel. (01) 2960000; Fax. (01) 2960383; Published annually; 35,000; Editor: Rosemary Delaney.

Certified Accountant (1908)
Cork Publishing, 19 Rutland Street, Cork. Tel. (021) 313855; Fax. (021) 313496; Published monthly; 55,000; Editor: Brian O'Kane.

Checkout Magazine (1966)
Checkout Publications Ltd., 22 Crofton Road, Dún Laoghaire, Co. Dublin. Tel. (01) 2808415; Published monthly; 6,500; Editor: Mary Brophy.

Church of Ireland Gazette
36 Bachelor's Walk, Lisburn, Co. Antrim. Tel. (0801846) 675743; Fax. (0801846) 675743; Published weekly; 6,500; Editor: Canon C. W. M. Cooper.

Clár na Nóg
National Youth Council of Ireland, 3 Montague Street, Dublin 2. Tel. (01) 4784122; Fax. (01) 4783974; Published monthly.

CIF Blue Pages
Cedar Media and Communications Ltd., 12 Upper Mount Street, Dublin 2. Tel. (01) 6619322; Fax. (01) 6619326; Editor: Jim Sherlock.

CIF Directory and Diary (1975)
Cedar Media and Communications

Ltd., 12 Upper Mount Street, Dublin 2. Tel. (01) 6619322; Fax. (01) 6619326; Publisher: Jim Sherlock.

CIS Report
Newmarket Information (Publications) Ltd., Unit 3, Argyle Square, Morehampton Road, Donnybrook, Dublin 4. Tel. (01) 6689494; Fax. (01) 6689649; Published weekly; Managing Editor: Karl Glynn- Finnegan.

Circa Art Magazine
58 Fitzwilliam Square, Dublin 2. Tel. (01) 6765035; Fax. (01) 6613881; Published quarterly; 7,000; Editor: Tanya Kiang.

Cois Coiribe (1981)
University College, Galway. Tel. (091) 750339; Fax. (091) 526388; Published annually; distributed free; 22,000; Editor: Kathleen O'Connell.

Comhar (1942)
4 Rae Mhuirfean, Baile Átha Cliath 2. Tel. (01) 6785443; Fax. (01) 6785443; Published monthly; 2,500; Editor: Vivian Uíbh Eachach.

Commercial Law Practitioner
(1994) Brehon Publishing, Brehon House, 4 Upper Ormond Quay, Dublin 7. Tel. (01) 8730101; Fax. (01) 8730939; Published monthly; Editor: Thomas B. Courtney.

Communications Today
CPG Group Publication, Computer House, 66 Patrick Street, Dun Laoghaire, Co. Dublin. Tel. (01) 2800424; Fax. (01) 2808468; 6,500; Editor: Felicity Hogan.

Communications Worker (1989)
Communications Workers' Union, 575 North Circular Road, Dublin 1. Tel. (01) 8366388; Fax. (01) 8365582; Published twice monthly; 18,000; Editor: David T. Begg.

ComputerScope (1985)
Prospect House, 1 Prospect Road, Glasnevin, Dublin 9. Tel. (01) 8303455; Fax. (01) 8300888; Published ten times a year; distributed free; 7,800; Editor: Paul Healy.

Constabulary Gazette
Ulster Journals Ltd., 39 Boucher Road, Belfast. Tel. (0801232) 681371; Fax. (0801232) 381915; Published monthly; 11,000; Editor: Martin Williams.

Construction
Tara Publishing Co. Ltd., Poolbeg House, 1-2 Poolbeg Street, Dublin 2. Tel. (01) 6719244; Fax. (01) 6719263; Published monthly; 4,148 ABC; Managing Director: Fergus Farrell.

Construction and Property News
175 North Strand Road, Dublin 1. Tel. (01) 8742265; Fax. (01) 8741242; Published fortnightly; 5,208 ABC; Editor: Barry McCall.

Consultant, The
Jude Publications Ltd., Tara House, Tara Street, Dublin 2. Tel. (01) 6713500; Fax. (01) 6713074; Published monthly; Publisher: Kate Tammemagi.

Consumer Choice
Consumers' Association Of Ireland, 45 Upper Mount Street, Dublin 2. Tel. (01) 6612442; Fax. (01) 6612464; Published monthly; 10,000; Editor: Kieran Doherty.

Cosantóir, An (1940)
Department of Defence, Parkgate Street, Dublin 8. Tel. (01) 8379911; Fax. (01) 6779018; Published ten times a year; Editor: Terry McLaughlin.

CPA Journal of Accountancy
The Institute of Certified Public Accountants in Ireland, 9 Ely Place, Dublin 2. Tel. (01) 6767353; Fax. (01) 6612367; Published quarterly; 3,000; Editor: Denis Hevey.

Cuba Today
15 Merrion Square, Dublin 2. Tel. (01) 6761213 / 8436448; Published 6 times a year, plus updates; Editor: Joyce Williams.

Cyphers
3 Selskar Terrace, Ranelagh, Dublin 6. Tel. (01) 4978866; Fax. (01) 4978866; Published two or three times a year; 800;

Dairy Executive, The
Dairy Executives' Association, 33 Kildare Street, Dublin 2 Tel. (01) 6761989; Fax. (01) 6767162; Published quarterly; 1,650; Editor: Kyran Lynch.

Dance News Ireland
65 Fitzwilliam Square, Dublin 2. Tel. (01) 6762677; Fax. (01) 6610392; Published quarterly; 2,000.

Directory and Diary of the Association of Consulting Engineers of Ireland, The
Oisín Publications, 4 Iona Drive, Dublin 9. Tel. (01) 8305236; Fax. (01) 8307860; Published annually; 1,000; Editor: Anne Potter.

Doctor Desk Book
M.P. House, 49 Wainsfort Park, Terenure, Dublin 6W. Tel. (01) 4924034; Fax. (01) 4924035; 4,500; Editor: Troy Gogan.

Doctrine and Life
Dominican Publications, 42 Parnell Square, Dublin 1. Tel. (01) 8721611; Fax. (01) 8731760; Published monthly; 3,000; Editor: Bernard Treacy OP.

d'Side
The Factory, 35A Barrow Street, Dublin 4. Tel. (01) 6684966; Fax. (01) 6684157; Published monthly; 15.000; Editor: Melanie Morris.

Dublin Corporation Yearbook and Diary
Oisín Publications, 4 Iona Drive, Dublin 9. Tel. (01) 8305236; Fax. (01) 8307860;Published annually; 2,500; (pocket edition 2,000);

Dublin Event Guide
7 Eustace Street, Dublin 2. Tel. (01) 6713377; Fax. (01) 6710502; Published fortnightly; 13,000; Editor: Michael Beirne.

Dublin Historical Record (1934)
Old Dublin Society, City Assembly House, 58 South William Street, Dublin 2; Published half yearly; 1,000; Editor: Robin Simmons (Honorary).

Dublin Port & Docks Yearbook
Tara Publishing Co. Ltd., Poolbeg House, 1-2 Poolbeg Street, Dublin 2. Tel. (01) 6719244; Fax. (01) 6719263; Published annually; 2,500; Managing Director: Fergus Farrell.

Dublin's Evening Classes
Oisín Publications, 4 Iona Drive, Dublin 9; Tel. (01) 8305236; Fax. (01) 8307860; Published annually; 15,000; Editor: Liam Ó Oisín.

Economic and Social Review
(1969) Economic & Social Studies, 4 Burlington Road, Dublin 4. Tel. (01) 6671525; Published quarterly; Editors: G. Boyle & C. T. Whelan.

Economic Series
Government Supplies Agency, 4-5 Harcourt Road, Dublin 2. Tel. (01) 6613111; Published monthly; Publications Manager: Con Lucey.

Education Magazine
Tara Publishing Co. Ltd., Poolbeg House, 1-2 Poolbeg Street, Dublin 2. Tel. (01) 6719244; Fax. (01) 6719263; Published monthly; 3,000; Managing Director: Fergus Farrell.

Education Directory / Diary
Tara Publishing Co. Ltd., Poolbeg House, 1-2 Poolbeg Street, Dublin 2. Tel. (01) 6719244; Fax. (01) 6719263; Published annually; 3,000; Managing Director: Fergus Farrell.

Education Today
35 Parnell Square, Dublin 1. Tel. (01) 8722533; Fax. (01) 8722462; Published three times a year; 25,000; Editor: Sinead Shannon.

Eighteenth Century Ireland / Iris an dá chultúr (1986)
English Department, Trinity College Dublin, Dublin 2. Tel. (01) 6081111 / 6081104; Modern Irish Department, University College Dublin, Dublin 4. Tel. (01) 2693244   ext. 8140; Published annually;   Editors: Ian Campbell Ross & Alan Harrison.

Element
2 Upper Mount Street, Dublin 2; Published annually; Editor: Mariaymone Djeribi.

Employment Law Reports (1990)
The Round Hall Press, Kill Lane, Blackrock, Co. Dublin. Tel. (01) 2892922; Fax. (01) 2893072; Published quarterly; Editor: Eilis Barry.

Engineers Journal
Dyflin Publications, 58 North Great Charles Street, Dublin 1; Tel. (01) 8550477; Fax. (01) 8550473; Published monthly; 10,000; Editor: Hugh Kane.

Entertainer, The
5 Lower Abbey Street, Dublin 1. Tel. (01) 8787894; Editor: Martin Thomas.

Environmental Health Officers Association Yearbook
Tara Publishing Co. Ltd., Poolbeg House, 1-2 Poolbeg Street, Dublin 2.

Tel. (01) 6719244;   Fax. (01) 6719263; Published annually; 2,000; Managing Director: Fergus Farrell.

Environmental Management Ireland
Nestron Ltd., 58 Middle Abbey Street, Dublin 1. Tel. / Fax: (01) 8720734 / 8720084 / 8720030; Published twice monthly; distributed free of charge; Editor: Annette O'Riordan.

Fáilte / Welcome
MAC Publishing Ltd., Taney Hall, Eglinton Terrace, Dundrum, Dublin 14; Tel. (01) 2960000; Fax. (01) 2960383; Published annually; 200,000; Editor: Rosemary Delaney.

Faith Today
Domincan Publications, 42 Parnell Square, Dublin 1; Tel. (01) 8721611; Fax. (01) 8731760; Editor: Bernard Treacy.

Far East, The
St. Columban's, Navan, Co. Meath. Tel. (046) 21525; Published nine times a year; 185,000 inc. England; Editor: Revd. Alo Connaughton.

Farm Holidays in Ireland (1970)
Head Office, 2 Michael Street, Limerick. Tel. (061) 400700; Published annually; 90,355; Chairman: Eileen McDonagh.

Farm Week
14 Church Street, Portadown, Craigavon, Co. Armagh BT62 3LN. Tel. (0801762) 339421; Fax. (0801762) 350203; Published weekly; 11,165 ABC; Editor: Hal Crowe.

Feasta (1948)
13 Paráid na Díge, Corcaigh. Tel. (021) 307579; Published monthly; 2,500; Editor: Séamus Ruiséal.

Finance Magazine
162 Pembroke Road, Ballsbridge, Dublin 4. Tel. (01) 6606222; Fax. (01) 6606830; Published monthly; 3,000; Editor: Ken O'Brien.

Flaming Arrows
County Sligo VEC, Riverside, Sligo. Tel. (071) 45844; Fax. (071) 43093; Published annually; 500; Editor: Leo Regan.

Fleet Management Magazine
13 Ranelagh Village, Dublin 6. Tel.

(01) 4976050; Fax. (4967408; Published monthly; 5,300; Editor: Phil O'Kelly.

Focus
Maxwell Publicity Ltd., M.P. House, 49 Wainsfort Park, Terenure, Dublin 6W. Tel. (01) 4924034; Fax. (01) 4924035; Published twice monthly; 900; Editor: Ronnie Norton.

Focus on Ireland in the Wider World
c/o Comhlámh, 10 Upper Camden Street, Dublin 2. Tel. (01) 4783490; Fax. (01) 4783738; Published twice yearly; 2,500.

Fold, The (1953)
Diocesan Communications Office, St. Maries of the Isle, Cork; Tel. (021) 312330; Fax. (021) 965209; Published ten times a year; 7,500; Editor: Father Bernard Cotter.

Food Ireland
Tara Publishing Co. Ltd., Poolbeg House, 1-2 Poolbeg Street, Dublin 2. Tel. (01) 6719244; Fax. (01) 6719263; Published monthly; 2,958 ABC; Managing Director: Fergus Farrell.

Fortnight (1970)
7 Lower Crescent, Belfast BT7 1NR. Tel. (0801232) 232353/311337/ 324141; Fax. (0801232) 232650; Published eleven times a year; 3,000; Editor: John O'Farrell.

Forum
Alma House, Alma Place, Carrickbrennan Road, Monkstown Co. Dublin; Tel. (01) 2803967; Fax. (01) 2807076; Published monthly; 2,500; Editor: Geraldine Meagan.

Friendly Word, The
40 College Park Avenue, Belfast BT7 1LR; Tel. (0801232) 247982; Published twice monthly; 400; Editor: Rachel Kirk-Smith.

Furrow, The
St. Patrick's College, Maynooth, Co. Kildare; Tel. (01) 6286215; Fax. (01) 7083908; Published monthly; 8,000; Editor: Ronan Drury.

Futura
Unit 9, Sandyford Office Park, Sandyford, Dublin 18; Tel. (01) 2958119; Fax. (01) 2958065; Published monthly; 3,500; Editor: Pat Lehane.

Gaelic Sport (1958)
139A Lower Drumcondra Road, Dublin 9; Tel. (01) 8374311; Published monthly; 41,117; Editor: T. McQuaid.

Gaelic World
10 Burgh Quay, Dublin 2; Tel. (01) 6798655; Fax. (01) 6798655; Published monthly; Editor: Mick Dunne.

Gaelsport Magazine
6-7 Camden Place, Dublin 2. Tel. (01) 4784322; Fax. (01) 4781055; Published monthly; 15,000; Editor: Owen McCann.

GALAPS Directory
Bracetown Business Park, Clonee, Co. Meath. Tel. (01) 8251355; Fax. (01) 8252082; Published annually; Managing Director: Colm O'Callaghan.

Garda Journal, The (1994)
Jude Publications Ltd., Tara House, Tara Street, Dublin 2; Tel. (01) 6713500; Fax. (01) 6713074; Published monthly; Editor: Brendan K. Colvert.

Garda News
6th Floor, Phibsboro Tower, Dublin 7.Tel. (01) 8303166; Fax. (01) 8306396; Published monthly; 4,000; Editor: Austin Kenny.

Garda Review (1923)
Floor 5, Phibsboro Tower, Dublin 7. Tel. (01) 8303533; Fax. (01) 8303331; Published monthly; 7,000; Editor: Catherine Fox.

Gay Community News (1988)
The Hirschfeld Centre,10 Fownes Street Upper, Dublin 2 Tel. (01) 6719076/6710939; Fax. (01) 6713549; Published monthly; 8,000; Editor: Cathal Kelly.

Gazette of Law Society in Ireland
Blackhall Place, Dublin 7; Tel. (01) 6710711; Fax. (01) 6710704; Published ten times a year; 6,200; Editor: Catherine Dolan.

Genuine Irish Old Moore's Almanac, The
MAC Publishing, Taney Hall, Eglinton Terrace, Dundrum, Dublin 14; Tel. (01) 2960000; Fax. (01) 2960383; Published annually; Publisher: John O' Connell.

Go Direct
Ryan Media, The Basemount, 12 Hume Street, Dublin 2; Tel. (01) 6769538; Fax. (01) 6769538; Published five times a year; 4,411; Editor: Damian Ryan.

Golden Pages
Golden Pages Ltd., St. Martin's House, Waterloo Road, Dublin 4; Tel. (01) 6608488; Fax. (01) 6688527; 26-27 South Mall, Cork; Published annually; 1,495,000; Chief Executive: David A. McGonigle.

Greats of Gaelic Games Book
Costar Associates Ltd., 10 Burgh Quay, Dublin 2; Tel. (01) 6798655; Fax. (01) 6792016; Published every three years; Managing Director: Michael Wright.

Guideline
14 Cherry Drive, Castleknock, Dublin 15; Tel. (01) 8204501; Fax. (01) 8204501; Published five times a year; 700; Editors: Loretta Jennings & Rita Wall.

Health and Safety
Jude Publications Ltd., Tara House, Tara Street, Dublin 2; Tel. (01) 6713500; Fax. (01) 6713074; Published monthly; Publisher: Kate Tammemagi.

Health Services News (1989)
Vergemount Hall, Clonskeagh, Dublin 6; Tel. (01) 2697011; Fax. (01) 2698644; Published quarterly; 3,000; Editor: Tim O'Sullivan.

History Ireland
PO Box 695, James' Street Post Office, Dublin 8; Tel. (01) 4535730; Fax. (01) 4535730; Published quarterly; 6,000; Editors: Hiram Morgan & Tommy Graham.

Hot Press
13 Trinity Street, Dublin 2; Tel. (01) 6795077; Fax. (01) 6795097; Published fortnightly; 21,008 ABC (Ireland), 5,000 (UK); Editor: Niall Stokes.

Hotel and Catering Review (1974)
Jemma Publications Ltd., Marino House, 52 Glasthule Road, Sandycove, Co. Dublin; Tel. (01) 2800000; Fax. (01) 2801818; Published monthly; Editor: Frank Corr.

IBAR - Irish Business and Administration Research (1979)

Department of Business Administration, University College Dublin; Published annually; Editors: Aidan Kelly, UCD; Nial Cairns, University of Ulster; Patrick Flood.

Image (1975)
Image Publications Ltd., 22 Crofton Road, Dún Laoghaire, Co. Dublin; Tel. (01) 2808415; Fax. (01) 2808309; Published monthly; 24,060 ABC; Editor: Jane McDonnell.

IMPACT News
Bradán Media Sales Ltd., 1 Eglinton Road, Bray, Co. Wicklow; Tel. (01) 2869111; Fax. (01) 2869074; Editor: Bernard Harbor.

In Dublin (1976)
6-7 Camden Place, Dublin 2; Tel. (01) 4784322; Fax. (01) 4781055; Published fortnightly; 15,750; Editor: Siobhán Cronin.

Industrial Relations News Report
121-123 Ranelagh, Dublin 6; Tel. (01) 4972711; Fax. (01) 4781055; Published weekly; Editor: Brian Sheehan.

Industry and Commerce
Jude Publications, Tara House, Tara Street, Dublin 2; Tel. (01) 6713500; Fax. (01) 6713074; Published monthly; 8,500; Editor: Neil Whoriskey.

Innti
32 Albany Road, Ranelagh, D 6. Tel. (01) 4972353; Published annually; 1,000; Editor: Michael Davitt.

Inside Business (1991)
Dyflin Publications Ltd., 58 North Great Charles Street, Dublin 1; Tel. (01) 8550477; Fax. (01) 8550473; Published twice monthly; 10,000; Editor: Claire Reilly.

Inside Ireland (1978)
PO Box 1886, Dublin 16; Tel. (01) 4931906; Fax. (01) 4934538; Published quarterly; 10,000; Editor: Brenda Weir.

Insight Magazine
Harmony Publications Ltd., Roslyn Park, Sandymount, Dublin 4; Tel. (01) 2698422; Fax. (01) 2830163; Published quarterly; Editor: John Cunningham.

Intercom
Veritas, 7-8 Lower Abbey Street,

Dublin 1; Tel. (01) 8788177; Fax. (01) 8786507; Published monthly; 8,000.

IPU Review (1976)
Irish Pharmaceutical Union, Butterfield House, Butterfield Avenue, Dublin 14; Tel. (01) 4931801; Fax. (01) 4936407; Published monthly; 1,600; Editor: David Butler.

Ireland Series, The
Euro Lingua Publishing Ltd., 12 Parliament Street, Dublin 2; Tel. (01) 6794291; Fax. (01) 6794386; Published annually; Editor: Steve White.

Ireland of the Welcomes (1952)
Bord Fáilte, Baggot Street, Dublin 2; Tel. (01) 6024000; Fax. (01) 6615775; Published every two months; 100,000; Editor: Dr. Peter Harbison.

Ireland's Eye
Lynn Industrial Estate, The Roundabout, 6 Dominick Street, Mullingar, Co. Westmeath; Tel. (044) 48868; Fax. (044) 43777; Published monthly.

Ireland's Own (1902)
The People Newspaper Ltd., North Main Street, Wexford; Tel. (053) 22155; Published weekly; 52,000 ABC; Editors: Austin Channing & Margaret Galvin.

Iris Oifigiúil
Government Supplies Agency, 4-5 Harcourt Road, Dublin 2; Tel. (01) 6613111; Fax. (01) 4780645; Published twice weekly; Publications Manager: Con Lucey.

Irish Architect
CPG Group Publication, Computer House, 66 Patrick Street, Dún Laoghaire, Co. Dublin; Tel. (01) 2800424; Fax. (01) 2808468; Published ten times a year; Editor: Tomás O'Beirne.

Irish Banking Review, The
Irish Bankers' Federation, Nassau House, Nassau Street, Dublin 2; Tel. (01) 6715311; Fax. (01) 6796680; Published quarterly; Editor: Stewart MacKinnon.

Irish Birds (1977)
Irish Wildbird Conservancy, Ruttledge House, 8 Longford Place, Monkstown, Co. Dublin; Tel. (01)

2804322; Fax. (01) 2844407; Published annually; 1,000; Editor: Hugh Brazier.

Irish Brides and Homes Magazines
Crannagh House, 198 Rathfarnham Road, Dublin 14; Tel. (01) 4905504 / 4900550; Fax. (01) 4906763; Published quarterly; 10,000; Editor: Ruth Kelly.

Irish Building Services News
Pressline, 5-7 Main Street, Blackrock, Co. Dublin; Tel. (01) 2885001; Fax. (01) 2886966; Published ten times a year; 2,500; Editor: Pat Lehane.

Irish Catholic, The
55 Lower Gardiner Street, Dublin 1; Tel. (01) 8742795 / 8742795; Fax. (01) 8364805; Published weekly; 37,000; Editor: Bridget Anne Ryan.

Irish Chemical and Processing Journal (1985)
CPG Group Publication, 66 Patrick Street, Dún Laoghaire, Co. Dublin; Tel. (01) 2800424; Fax. (01) 2808468; Published ten times a year; 2,800; Editor: John McDonald.

Irish Competition Law Reports
Baikonur, Delgany Post Office, Co. Wicklow; Tel. (088) 557584; Fax. (088) 557584; Published ten times a year; Editor: Peter Byrne.

Irish Computer (1977)
CPG Group Publication, Computer House, 66 Patrick Street, Dún Laoghaire, Co. Dublin; Tel. (01) 2800424; Fax. (01) 2808468; Published monthly; 7,000; Editor: Donald McDonald.

Irish Computer Directory and Diary (1978)
CPG Group Publication, Computer House, 66 Patrick Street, Dún Laoghaire, Co. Dublin; Tel. (01) 2800424; Fax. (01) 2808468; Published annually; 2,500; Editor: Donald McDonald.

Irish Criminal Law Journal (1991)
Round Hall Press, Kill Lane, Blackrock, Co. Dublin; Tel. (01) 2892922; Fax. (01) 2893072; Published every six months; 450; Editor: Shane Murphy.

Irish Current Law Monthly (1995)
Brehon Publishing, Brehon House, 4 Upper Ormond Quay, Dublin 7; Tel.

(01) 8730101; Fax. (01) 8730939; Published monthly.

Irish Dental Association, Journal of the (1946)
10 Richview Office Park, Clonskeagh Road, Dublin 14; Tel. (01) 2830496; Fax. (01) 2830515; Published quarterly; Editor: Dr. Frank Quinn.

Irish Doctor
Medical Press, Tara House, Tara Street, Dublin 2; Tel. (01) 6713500; Fax. (01) 6713074; Published monthly; Editor: Dr. Bridget Maher.

Irish Economic and Social History (1974)
c/o Dublin Diocesan Library, Clonliffe Road, Dublin 3; Tel. (01) 8741680; Fax. (01) 8368920; Published annually; Editor: Neal Garnham.

Irish Education Studies
Educational Studies Association of Ireland, Education Department, University College Cork; Published annually; 600; Editor: Áine Hyland.

Irish Electrical Review
Unit 9, Sandyford Office Park, Dublin 18; Tel. (01) 2958069; Fax. (01) 2958065; Published monthly; 3,000; Publisher: Patrick J. Codyre.

Irish Exporter Yearbook and Diary, The
Jude Publications Ltd., Tara House, Tara Street, Dublin 2; Tel. (01) 6713500; Fax. (01) 6713074; Published annually; Publisher: Kate Tammemagi.

Irish Family Law Reports
Balkonur, Delgany Post Office, Co. Wicklow; Tel. (088) 557584; Fax. (088) 557584; Published ten times a year; Editor: Peter Byrne.

Irish Farmers' Journal (1948)
Irish Farm Centre, Bluebell, Dublin 12; Tel. (01) 4501166; Fax. (01) 4520876; Published weekly; 71,218 ABC; Editor: Matt Dempsey.

Irish Farmers Monthly
31 Deansgrange Road, Blackrock, Co. Dublin; Tel. (01) 2893305; Fax. (01) 2896406; Published monthly; 22,000; Editor: Brian Gilsenan.

Irish Farmers Yearbook and Diary, The
Kevin Street House, 9 Lower Kevin Street, Dublin 2; Tel. (01) 4757132;

Published annually; 5,000; Contact: Frank Bambrick.

Irish Field, The
Irish Times Ltd., PO Box 74, 11-15 D'Olier Street, Dublin 2; Tel. (01) 6792022; Fax. (01) 6793029; Published weekly; 10,223 ABC; Editor: Vincent Lamb.

Irish Food
31 Deansgrange Road, Blackrock, Co. Dublin; Tel. (01) 2893305; Fax. (01) 2896406; Published weekly; 10,000; Editor: Brian Gilsenan.

Irish Forestry (1942)
Society of Irish Foresters, 2 Lower Kilmacud Road, Stillorgan, Co. Dublin; Tel. (01) 2781874; Fax. (01) 2835890; Published twice a year; 600; Editor: Donal Magner.

Irish Geography (1944)
Department of Geography, Trinity College, Dublin 2; Tel. (01) 7021143; Fax. (01) 6713397; Published twice a year; Secretary: Joe Brady.

Irish Hardware Magazine
Jemma Publications, Marino House, 52 Glasthule Road, Sandycove, Co. Dublin; Tel. (01) 2800000; Fax. (01) 2801818; Published monthly; 1,000 ABC; Editor: Sandra O'Connell.

Irish Health Professional
Maxwell Publicity, 49 Wainsfort Park, Dublin 6W; Tel. (01) 4924034; Fax. (01) 2801818; Published twice monthly; 5,000; Editor: Terry Gogan.

Irish Historical Studies
Department of Modern History, Trinity College, Dublin 2; Tel. (01) 7021578; Published twice a year; 1,000; Editors: Ciaran Brady & Keith Jeffery.

Irish Homes Magazine
48 North Great Georges Street, Dublin 1; Tel. (01) 8721414 / 8721636; Published quarterly; 27,000; Editor: Bernice Brindley.

Irish Journal of Education (1967)
Educational Research Centre, St. Patrick's College, Dublin 9; Tel. (01) 8373789; Fax. (01) 8378997; Published annually; 1,000; Editor: Thomas Kellaghan.

Irish Journal of European Law (1991)
The Round Hall Press, Kill Lane,

Blackrock, Co. Dublin; Tel. (01) 2892922; Fax. (01) 2893072; Published twice a year; Editors: James O'Reilly & Anthony Collins.

Irish Journal of Medical Science (1832)
6 Kildare Street, Dublin 2; Tel. (01) 6767650; Fax. (01) 6611684; Published quarterly; 8,000; Editor: Thomas F. Gorey.

Irish Journal of Psychology, The
13 Adelaide Road, Dublin 2; Published four times a year; Editors: Professor Ken Brown & Dr. Carol McGuinness; Tel. (0801232) 245133; Fax. (0801232) 664144.

Irish Jurist (1966)
Jurist Publishing Co., University College Dublin, Dublin 4 Published annually; Editor: W. N. Osborough.

Irish Law Log (1995)
Brehon Publishing, Brehon House, 4 Upper Ormond Quay, Dublin 7; Tel. (01) 8730101; Fax. (01) 8730939; Published weekly; Editors: Bart D. Daly & Nevil Lloyd Blood.

Irish Law Reports Monthly (1981)
The Round Hall Press, Kill Lane, Blackrock, Co. Dublin; Tel. (01) 2892922; Fax. (01) 2893072; Published fourteen times a year; Editor: Hilary Delany.

Irish Law Times and Solicitors' Journal (1983)
The Round Hall Press, Kill Lane, Blackrock, Co. Dublin; Tel. (01) 2892922; Fax. (01) 2893072; Published monthly; Editor: Raymond Byrne.

Irish Laws (Statutes)
Baikonur, Delgany Post Office, Co. Wicklow; Tel. (088) 557584; Fax. (088) 557584; Published ten times a year; Editor: Peter Byrne.

Irish Literary Review
15 St. Stephen's Green, Dublin 2; Editor: Richard Pyne.

Irish Marketing Journal
Unit T31, Stillorgan Industrial Park, Stillorgan, Co. Dublin; Tel. (01) 2950088; Fax. (01) 2950089 Published monthly; 4,500; Editor: Dr. Norman Barry.

Irish Medical Directory
Medical Information Systems, 7 Castlefield Grove, Dublin 16; Tel.

(01) 4936853; Fax. (01) 4936853; Published annually; 2,000; Editor: Dr. Maurice Guéret.

Irish Medical Journal
10 Fitzwilliam Place, Dublin 2; Tel. (01) 6767273; Fax. (01) 6622818; Published twice monthly; 5,761; Editor: Dr.John Murphy.

Irish Medical News
MAC Publishing, Taney Hall, Eglinton Terrace, Dundrum, Dublin 14; Tel. (01) 2960000; Fax. (01) 2960383; Published weekly; 6,395; Editor: Niall Hunter.

Irish Medical Times (1967)
Medical Publications (Ireland) Ltd., 15 Harcourt Street, Dublin 2; Tel. (01) 4757461; Fax. (01) 4757467; 6,909; Editor: Dr. John O'Connell.

Irish Motor Industry
Jude Publications, Tara House, Tara Street, Dublin 2; Tel. (01) 6713500; Fax. (01) 6713074; Published monthly; Editor: Maura Henderson.

Irish Pharmacy Journal (1923)
Kenlis Publication Ltd., 37 Northumberland Road, Dublin 4; Tel. (01) 6600551; Fax. (01) 6681461; Published monthly; 2,100; Editor: Val Harte.

Irish Planning and Environmental Law Journal (1994)
Brehon Publishing, Brehon House, 4 Upper Ormond Quay, Dublin 7; Tel. (01) 8730101; Fax. (01) 8730939; Published quarterly; Editor: Eamon Galligan.

Irish Political Studies (1986)
PSAI Press, College of Humanities, University of Limerick, Limerick; Published annually; 600; Editors: Vincent Geoghegan & Richard English; Department of Politics, Queen's University, Belfast.

Irish Post (1970)
Irish Post Ltd., Uxbridge House, 464 Uxbridge Road, Hayes, Middlesex UB4 0SP; Tel. (0044181) 5610059; Fax. (0044181) 5613047; Editor: Donal Mooney.

Irish Printer
Jemma Publications Ltd., Marino House, 52 Glasthule Road, Sandycove, Co. Dublin; Tel. (01) 2800000; Fax. (01) 2801818; Published monthly; 1,939 ABC; Editor: Frank Corr.

Irish Psychologist, The (1974)
The Psychology Society of Ireland, 13 Adelaide Road, Dublin 2; Tel. (01) 4783916; Fax. (01) 4783916; Published monthly; Editor: Chris Morris.

Irish Racing Calendar (1970)
The Stewards of the Turf Club, The Curragh, Co. Kildare Tel. (045) 441599; Fax. (045) 441478 / 441116; Published weekly.

Irish Racingform Race Ratings
Irish Racingform Ltd., 10 Merrion Square, Dublin 2; Tel. (01) 6766495; Fax. (01) 6766496; Directors: Tony Sweeney & Annie Sweeney.

Irish Reporter, The
PO Box 3195, Dublin 6; Tel. (01) 8745158; Editor: Anthony O'Keefe.

Irish Review, The (1986)
The Institute of Irish Studies, Queen's University, Belfast; Tel. (0801232) 439238; Fax. (0801232) 439238; Editors:Kevin Barry, Tom Dunne, Edna Longley, Clare O'Halloran, Brian Walker & Caoimhín Mac Giolla Léith.

Irish Roots
Belgrave Publications, Belgrave Avenue, Cork; Tel. (021) 5000067; Fax. (021) 5000067; Published quarterly; Editor: Tony McCarthy.

Irish Skipper, The (1964)
MAC Publishing Ltd., Taney Hall, Eglinton Terrace, Dundrum, Dublin 14; Tel. (01) 2960000; Fax. (01) 2960383; Published monthly; Editor: Niall Fallon.

Irish Social Worker
114-116 Pearse Street, Dublin 2; Tel. (01) 6774838; Fax. (01) 6715734; Published quarterly; Editor: Loretto Reilly.

Irish Stamp News
27 Upper Mount Street, Dublin 2; Tel. (01) 6767228; Fax. (01) 6767229; Published quarterly; 5,000; Editor: Ian Whyte.

Irish Sword, The (1949)
c/o Newman House, 86 St. Stephen's green, Dublin 2; Published twice yearly; Editor: Dr. Harman Murtagh.

Irish Tatler
Smurfit Publications Ltd., 126 Lower Baggot Street, Dublin 2; Tel. (01)

6623158; Fax. (01) 6619757; Published monthly; 156,000; Editor: Sarah Foot.

Irish Theological Quarterly (1906)
St. Patrick's College, Maynooth, Co. Kildare; Tel. (01) 6285222; Published quarterly; 1,000; Editors: Patrick McGoldrick & Patrick Hannon.

Irish Travel Trade News
9 Western Parkway Business Centre, Ballymount Road, Dublin 12; Tel. (01) 4502422; Fax. (01) 4502954; Published monthly; 2,050; Editor: Michael Flood.

Irish University Review
Room K203, University College, Belfield, Dublin 4; Published twice yearly; Editor: Christopher Murray.

Irish Veterinary Journal
Jude Publication Ltd., Tara House, Tara Street, Dublin 2; Tel. (01) 6713500; Fax. (01) 6713074; Published monthly; Editor: Pat O'Mahony.

Irish Woman
An Grianan, Termonfeckin, Co. Louth; Tel. (041) 22119 / 22635; Fax. (041) 22690; Published quarterly; 5,000; Editor: James Creed.

Irish YouthWork Scene
National Youth Federation, 20 Lower Dominick Street, Dublin 1; Tel. (01) 8729933; Published five times a year; Editor: Louise Hurley.

IWC News (1974)
Irish Wildbird Conservancy, Ruttedge House, 8 Longford Place, Monkstown, Co. Dublin; Tel. (01) 2804322; Fax. (01) 2844407; Editor: C. MacLochlainn.

Journal, The
EETPU Section, 5 Whitefriars, Aungier Street, Dublin 2; Tel. (01) 4784141; Fax. (01) 4750131; Published twice monthly; Editor: James Wims.

Journal of Industrial and Commercial Property
Government Supplies Agency, 4-5 Harcourt Road, Dublin 2; Tel. (01) 6613111; Fax. (01) 4752760; Published fortnightly; Publications Manager: Con Lucey.

Krino
PO Box 65, Dún Laoghaire, Co. Dublin; Tel. (01) 2300304; Fax. (01) 2300304; Published twice yearly; Editor: Gerald Dawe.

LAMA Yearbook / Diary
Nestron Ltd., 68 Middle Abbey Street, Dublin 1; Tel / Fax. (01) 8720734/8720084/8720030; Published annually; Editor: Annette O'Riordan.

LAN - Local Authority News
Nestron Ltd., 68 Middle Abbey Street, Dublin 1; Tel / Fax. (01) 8720734 / 8720084 / 8720030; Published monthly; Editor: Annette O'Riordan.

Lawyer's Desk Diary
Oisín Publications, 4 Iona Drive, Dublin 9; Tel. (01) 8305236; Fax. (01) 8307860; Published annually; 2,000; Editor: Liam Ó hOisín.

Leabharlann, An / The Irish Library
Cumberland House, Fenian Street, Dublin 2; Editors: Fionnuala Hanrahan & Kevin Quinn.

Licensed and Catering News (1994) Ulster Magazine Ltd., Crescent House, 58 Rugby Road, Belfast BT7 1PT; Tel. (0801232) 230425; Fax. (0801232) 243595; Published monthly; 4,154 ABC; Publisher: Conor Kelly.

Licensed Vintners Association Directory and Diary
Tara Publishing Co. Ltd., Poolbeg House, 1-2 Poolbeg Street, Dublin 2; Tel. (01) 6719244; Fax. (01) 6719263; Published annually; 2,000; Managing Director: Fergus Farrell.

Licensing World (1942)
Marino House, 52 Glasthule Road, Sandycove, Co. Dublin; Tel. (01) 2800000; Fax. (01) 2801818; Published monthly; 4,000; Editor: Pat Nolan.

Lifeboats Ireland (1947)
15 Windsor Terrace, Dún Laoghaire, Co. Dublin; Tel. (01) 2845050; Fax. (01) 2845052; Published annually; 6,000; Editor: Dermot Desmond.

Linen Hall Review
c/o Linen Hall Library, 17 Donegall Square North, Belfast BT1 5GD; Tel. (0801232) 321707; Fax. (0801232)

438586; Published three times a year; 6,000; Editors: John Gray & Paul Campbell.

Local Authority Times (1986)
57-61 Lansdowne Road, Dublin 4; Tel. (01) 6686233; Fax. (01)6689135; Published quarterly; 3,000; Editor: Ellen MacCafferty.

Management (1954)
Jemma Publications Ltd., Marino House, 52 Glasthule Road, Sandycove, Co. Dublin; Tel. (01) 2800000; Fax. (01) 2801818; Published monthly; 7,320 ABC; Editor: Frank Dillon.

MAPS (Marketing, Advertising, Promotions and Sponsorship)
MAC Publishing Ltd., Taney Hall, Eglinton Terrace, Dundrum, Dublin 14; Tel. (01) 2960000; Fax. (01) 2960383; Published annually; 2,000; Publisher: John O'Connell.

Marketing
1 Albert Park, Sandycove, Co. Dublin; Tel. (01) 2807735; Fax. (01) 2807735; Published monthly; Editor: Michael Cullen.

Medical Missionaries of Mary Magazines
MMM Communications, Rosemount, Booterstown, Blackrock, Co. Dublin; Tel. (01) 2887180; Fax. (01) 2834626; Published quarterly; 15,000; Editor: Sr. Isabelle Smyth.

Medico-Legal Journal of Ireland (1995)
Brehon Publishing , Brehon House, 4 Upper Ormond Quay, Dublin 7; Tel. (01) 8730101; Fax. (01) 8730939; Published three times a year; Editor: Dr. Denis Cusack.

Micléinn Le Chéile
16 North Great Georges Street, Dublin 1; Tel. (01) 8786366; Fax. (01) 8786020; Published six times a year; Editor: Colm Keaveney.

Milltown Studies (1978)
Milltown Institute of Theology & Philosophy, Milltown Park, Dublin 6; Tel. (01) 2698802; Fax. (01) 2692528; Published two times a year; Editor: Gervase Corcoran.

MIMS Ireland (1960)
Medical Publications Ltd., 15 Harcourt Street, Dublin 2; Tel. (01) 4757461; Fax. (01) 4757467; 3,964 ABC; Editor: Andrea Letoha.

Modern Woman
Meath Chronicle Group of Publications, Market Square, Navan, Co. Meath; Tel. (046) 21442; Fax. (046) 23565; Published monthly; Supplement with Meath Chronicle; Editor: Margot Davis.

Motor Business
Jude Publications Ltd., Jude House, Tara Street, Dublin 2; Tel. (01) 6713500; Fax. (01) 6713074; Published monthly; Editor: Simon Rowe.

Motoring Life (1946)
Cyndale Enterprises Ltd., 48 North Great Georges Street, Dublin 1; Tel. (01) 8721636 / 8721414; Published monthly; 9,500; Editor: Fergal K. Herbert.

New Music News
The Contemporary Music Centre, 95 Lower Baggot Street, Dublin 2; Tel. (01) 6612105; Fax. (01) 6762639; Published three times a year; 3,500; Editor: Eve O'Kelly.

Newmarket Business Report
Newmarket Information Ltd., Unit 3, Argyle Square, Morehampton Road, Donnybrook, Dublin 4; Tel. (01) 6689494; Fax. (01) 6689649; Published fortnightly; Editor: Karl Glynn-Finnegan.

NODE News
c/o Comhlámh, 10 Upper Camden Street, Dublin 2; Tel. (01) 4781998; Fax. (01) 4783738; Published five times a year.

North County Leader
23-25 Main Street, Swords, Co. Dublin; Tel. (01) 8400200; Fax. (01) 8400550; Editor: Fergal Maddock.

Northern Ireland Legal Quarterly (1964) SLS Legal Publications (NI), Faculty of Law, Queen's University, Belfast BT7 1NN; Tel. (0801232) 245133; Fax. (0801232) 325590; Published quarterly; 700; Editor: Dr. Peter Ingram.

Oblate Missionary Record (1891)
Oblate Fathers, Inchicore, Dublin 8; Tel. (01) 4542417; Published five times a year; 8,000; Editor: Fr. J. Archbold.

Off Licence
Jemma Publications Ltd., Marino House, 52 Glasthule Road, Sandycove, Co. Dublin; Tel. (01)

2800000; Fax. (01) 2801818; Published twice monthly; Editor: Natasha Swords.

Oghma
38 Faiche Steach Póilín, Baile Dúill, Baile Átha Cliath 13; Tel. (01) 8325672; Published annually; Editor: Seosamh Ó Murchú.

Oideas
An Roinn Oideachais, Sráid Mhaoilbhríde, Baile Átha Cliath; Tel. (01) 8734700; Editor: E. Mac Aonghusa.

Outlook
Holy Ghost Missions, Booterstown Avenue, Co. Dublin; Tel. (01) 2881789; Fax. (01) 2834307; Published twice monthly; Editor: Rev. Brian Gogan.

PC Live!
ComputerScope Ltd., Prospect House, 1 Prospect Road, Glasnevin, Dublin 9; Tel. (01) 8303455; Fax. (01) 8300888; Published twice monthly; 10,000; Publisher: Frank Quinn.

Phoblacht, An / Republican News
58 Parnell Square, Dublin 1; Tel. (01) 8733611 / 8733839; Fax. (01) 8733074; 2A Monagh Crescent, Turf Lodge, Belfast 12; Tel. (0801232) 624421; Fax. (0801232) 622112; Published weekly; 28,000; Editor: Micheál Mac Donncha.

Phoenix (1983)
Penfield Enterprises Ltd., 44 Lower Baggot Street, Dublin 2; Tel. (01) 6611062; Fax. (01) 6682697; Published fortnightly; 20,018 ABC; Editor: Paddy Prendiville.

Pioneer (1948)
27 Upper Sherrand Street, Dublin 1; Tel. (01) 8746464; Fax. (01) 8748485; Published monthly; 18,000; Information Officer: Maureen Manning.

Plan-Architectural Review
Plan Magazines Ltd., 8-9 Sandyford Office Park, Sandyford, Dublin 18; Tel. (01) 2958115; Fax. (01) 2959350; Published monthly; 3,011 ABC; Editor: Emer Hughes.

Plantman
1 The Green, Kingsway Heights, Dublin 24; Tel. (01) 4520898; Published monthly; 3,960; Editor: Patrick Murphy.

Poetry Ireland Review
Bermingham Tower, Upper Yard, Dublin Castle, Dublin 2 Tel. (01) 6714632; Fax. (01) 6714634; Published quarterly; Editor: Theo Dorgan.

Presbyterian Herald (1942)
Church House, Fisherwick Place, Belfast BT1 6DW; Tel. (0801232) 322284; Fax. (0801232) 248377; Published monthly; 17,000; Editor: Rev. Arthur Clarke.

Private Research Ltd. (1992)
7-8 Mount Street Crescent, Dublin 2; Tel. (01) 6760774; Fax. (01) 6760773; Published monthly; Publisher: John O'Neill.

Provincial Farmer
Market Square, Navan, Co. Meath; Tel. (046) 21442; Fax. (046) 23565; Published monthly; Supplement to Meath Chronicle; Editor: Ken Davis.

Public Sector Times
Bradán Publishing, 1 Eglinton Road, Bray, Co. Wicklow; Tel. (01) 2869111; Fax. (01) 2869074; Published monthly; 20,000; Editor: James D. Fitzmaurice.

Public Service Review
30 Merrion Square, Dublin 2; Tel. (01) 6767271 / 6767272; Fax. (01) 6615777; Published every two months; 6,000; Editor: Tom McKevitt.

Reality (1935)
Redemptorist Publications, 75 Orwell Road, Rathgar, Dublin 6; Tel. (01) 4922488 / 4922688; Published monthly; 20,000; Editor: Gerard R. Moloney.

Recover (1968)
St. Camillus, South Hill Avenue, Blackrock, Co. Dublin; Tel. (01) 2882873; Fax. (01) 2833380; Published quarterly; 6,500; Editor: Fr. G. Price.

Religious Life Review
Dominican Publications, 42 Parnell Square, Dublin 1; Tel. (01) 8731355; Fax. (01) 8731760; Published six times a year; Editor: Austin Flannery.

Retail Grocer
Ulster Magazines Ltd., Crescent House, 58 Rugby Road, Belfast Bt7 1PT; Tel. (0801232) 230425; Fax. (0801232) 243595; Published monthly; 4,441 ABC; Editor: Larry

Nixon.

Retail News
Tara Publishing Co. Ltd., Poolbeg House, 1-2 Poolbeg Street, Dublin 2; Tel. (01) 6719244; Fax. (01) 6719263; Published monthly; 3,858 ABC; Managing Director: Fergus Farrell.

Retail News Directory / Buyer's Guide
Tara Publishing Co. Ltd., Poolbeg House, 1-2 Poolbeg Street, Dublin 2; Tel. (01) 6719244; Fax. (01) 6719263; Published annually; Managing Director: Fergus Farrell.

RIAI Yearbook & Directory
CPG Group Publication, Computer House, 66 Patrick Street, Dún Laoghaire, Co. Dublin; Tel. (01) 2800424; Fax. (01) 2808468; Published annually; Editor: Thomas O'Beirne.

Riverine
Laurel Cottage, Dowlin, Piltown, Co. Kilkenny; Published annually; Editor: Edward Power.

RTE Guide (1961)
Commercial Enterprises Ltd., R.T.E., Donnybrook, Dublin 4; Tel. (01) 2083111; Fax. (01) 2083085; Published weekly; 182,133 ABC; Editor: Heather Parsons.

Running Your Business
Firsthand Publishing Ltd., Landscape House, Landscape Road, Churchtown Dublin 14; Tel. (01) 2962244; Published twice monthly; 30,000; Managing Director: Donal McAuliffe.

Runway Airports (1970)
Aer Rianta cpt., Level 4, terminal Building, Dublin Airport, Tel. (01) 7044170 / 7044273; Fax. (01) 7044663; Published monthly; 5,000; Editor: Brian McCabe.

Sacred Heart Messenger, The (1988) Messenger Publications, 37 Lower Leeson Street, Dublin 2; Tel. (01) 6767491 / 6767492; Fax. (01) 6611606; Published monthly; Editor: Brendan Murray.

Salesian Bulletin, The (1939) Salesian House, St. Teresa's Road, Dublin 12; Tel. (01) 4555605; Fax. (01) 4558781; Published quarterly; 20,000; Editor: Eddie Fitzgerald.

Science
Mount Temple School, Malahide Road, Dublin 3; Published three times a year; Editor: Randal L. Henly.

Scripture in Church
Dominican Publications, 42 Parnell Square, Dublin 1; Tel. (01) 8721611; Fax. (01)8731760; Published quarterly; Editor-in-Chief: Martin McNamara.

Search
RE Resource Centre, Holy Trinity Church, Rathmines, Dublin 6; Tel. (01) 4972821; Fax. (01) 4972821; Published twice yearly; Editor: Rev. M. A. J. Burrows.

Seirbhís Phoiblí
Lansdowne House, Lansdowne Road, Dublin 4; Tel. (01) 6767571; Published every four months; 3,300; Editor: Breda Byrne.

Shelflife (1975)
CPG Group Publication, Computer House, 66 Patrick Street, Dún Laoghaire, Co. Dublin; Tel. (01) 2800424; Fax. (01)2808468; Published monthly; 7,625 ABC; Editor: Colette O'Connor.

SMA Magazine - The African Missionary (1914)
Society of African Missionaries, Blackrock Road, Cork; Published five times a year; 43,000; Editor: Fr. Peter McCawille.

Social and Personal
27 Lower Baggot Street, Dublin 2; Tel. (01) 66200500; Fax. (01) 6616153; Published monthly; 18,000' Editor: Nell Stewart-Liberty.

Socialist Voice
James Connolly House, 43 East Essex Street, Temple Bar, Dublin 2; Tel. (01) 6711943; Fax. (01) 6711943; Published fortnightly.

Specify (1979)
Greer Publications, 151 University Street, Belfast BT7 1HR; Tel. (0801232) 231634; Fax. (0801232) 325736; Published twice monthly; 4,700; Editor: Brian Russell.

Sporting Press
Davis Road, Clonmel, Co. Tipperary; Tel. (052) 21422 / 21634; Fax. (052) 25018; Published weekly; 8,000; Editor: J. L. Desmond.

Sportsworld
48 North Great Georges Street, Dublin 1; Tel. (01) 8721414/ 8721636; Published monthly; 23,000; Editor: Liam Nolan.

Statistical Bulletin
Government Supplies Agency, 4-5 Harcourt Road, Dublin 2; Tel. (01) 6613111; Published quarterly; Publications Manager: Con Lucey.

Student Yearbook and Career Directory
'Shancroft', O'Hanlon's Lane, Malahide, Co. Dublin; Tel. (01) 8452470; Fax. (01) 8454759; Published annually; 27,277; Editors: J. Duddy & R. Keane.

Studia Hibernica (1961)
St. Patricks College, Dublin 9; Tel. (01) 8376191; Fax. (01) 8376197; Published annually; Editor: L. Mac Mathúna.

Studies
35 Lower Leeson Street, Dublin 2; Tel. (01) 6766785; Fax. (01) 6762984; Published quarterly; Editor: Noel Barber.

Studies in Accounting and Finance (1993)
Cork Publishing, 19 Rutland Street, Cork; Tel. (021) 313855; Fax. (021) 313496; Published four times a year; Editor: Conal O'Boyle.

Taxi News
48 Summerhill Parade, Dublin 1; Tel. (01) 4747578 / 8367578; Fax. (01) 8364415; Published annually; 3,000 ABC; Editor: Martin J. Morris.

Technology Ireland
Glasnevin, Dublin 9; Tel. (01) 8370101; Fax. (01) 8367122; Published ten times a year; Editors: Tom Kennedy & Mary Mulvihill.

Tillage Farmer, The
Athy Road, Carlow; Tel. (0503) 31487; Fax. (0503) 43087; Published six times a year.

Today's Farm (1990)
Teagasc, 19 Sandymount Avenue, Dublin 4; Tel. (01) 6688188; 35,000; Editor: John Keating.

Trade-Links Journal (1979)
Libra House, 4 ST. Kevin's Terrace, Dublin 8; Tel. (01) 4542717; Published every two months; 3,344; Editor: Cathal Tyrrell.

Trade Statistics
Government Supplies Agency, 4-5 Harcourt Road, Dublin 2; Tel. (01) 6613111; Published monthly; Publications Manager: Con Lucey.

Tuarascáil
35 Parnell Square, Dublin 1; Tel. (01) 8722533; Fax. (01) 8722462; Published monthly (except July & August); Editor: Billy Sheehan.

U Magazine (1979)
Smurfit Publications, 126 Lower Baggot Street, Dublin 2; Tel. (01) 6608264; Fax. (01) 6619757; Published monthly; 24,100; Editor: Maura O'Kiely.

Ulster Business (1987)
Greer Publications, 151 University Street, Belfast BT7 1HR; Tel. (0801232) 231634; Fax. (0801232) 325736; Published monthly; 7,700; Editor: Richard Buckley.

Ulster Countywoman
209-211 Upper Lisburn Road, Belfast BT10 0LL; Tel. (0801232) 301506; Fax. (0801232) 431127; Published monthly; 6,500; Editor: Mrs. Mildred Brown.

Ulster Farmer
Ann Street, Dungannon, Co. Tyrone; Tel. (0801868) 722557; Fax. (0801868) 727334; Published weekly; Editor: D. Mallon.

Ulster Grocer (1972)
Greer Publications, 151 University Street, Belfast BT7 1HR; Tel. (0801232) 231634; Fax. (0801232) 325736; Published monthly; Editor: Brian McCalden.

Ulster Medicine
Carrick Publications Ltd., River House, 41 The Mall, Newry, Co. Down, BT34 1AN; Tel. (0801693) 61107; Published weekly.

Ulster Tatler
39 Boucher Road, Belfast BT12 6UT; Tel. (0801232) 681371; Published monthly; 11,000; Editor: R. M. Sherry.

Unity
James Connolly House, 43 East Essex Street, Dublin 2; Tel. (01) 6711943; Fax. (01) 6711943; Published weekly; Editor: James Stewart.

Updata
Kompass House, Parnell Court, 1 Granby Row, Parnell Square North, Dublin 1; Tel. (01) 8728800; Fax. (01) 8733711; Published annually; 10,000; Manager: Frances Buggy.

Visitor
MAC Publishing Co. Ltd., Taney Hall, Eglinton Terrace, Dundrum, Dublin 14; Tel. (01) 2960000; Fax. (01) 2960383; Published annually; 250,000; Editor: Rosemary Delaney.

Walking World Ireland
109 Old Country Road, Dublin 12; Tel. (01) 4545135; Fax. (01) 4545141; Published quarterly; 12,000; Editor: Frank Greally.

WHERE Killarney
Frank Lewis Public Relations, 6 Bridgewell Lane, Killarney, Co. Kerry; Tel. (064) 31108; Fax. (064) 31570; Published six times a year; 100,000.

Wicklow Times
North Wicklow Times Ltd., 1 Eglinton Road, Bray, Co. Wicklow; Tel. (01) 2869111; Fax. (01) 2869074; Published fortnightly; 30,500; Editor: Shay Fitzmaurice.

Woman's Way
Smurfit Publications, 126 Lower Baggot Street, Dublin 2; Tel. (01) 6623158; Fax. (01) 6619757; Published weekly; 66,500 ABC; Editor: Celine Naughton.

Women's Clubs Magazine
Maxwell Publicity Ltd., M.P. House, 49 Wainsfort Park, Terenure, Dublin 6W; Tel. (01) 4924034; Fax. (01) 4924035; Editor: June Cooke.

Word, The (1953)
Divine Word Missionaries, Moyglare Road, Maynooth, Co. Kildare; Tel. (01) 6289564; Fax. (01) 6289184; Published monthly; 35,000; Editor: Rev. Thomas Cahill.

Writings
PO Box 3707, Dublin 6; Published five times a year; 5,000; Editor: Edward Browne.

Xchange (1995)
Telecom Éireann, St. Stephen's Green West, Dublin 2; Tel. (01) 6714444; Fax. (01) 4781211; Published monthly (except January & August).

Youth in Print
National Youth Council of Ireland, 3 Montague Street, Dublin 2; Tel. (01) 4784122; Fax. (01) 4783974; Published four times a year; 5,000.

COPYRIGHT

Irish Copyright Law

Under Irish law neither facts nor information can be copyright. However, the right to copy - be that in print, publishing, performance, or broadcasting - belongs to the person who created the work.

The only deviation from this is where the work created is done so on commission for someone else for a fee paid, or written as part of a writer's work for an employer and thus the copyright belongs to the commissioner or employer.

While facts and information cannot be copyrighted the form of the words used to convey them can be.

Copyright can be sold, assigned or leased.

In regard to the written word, copyright remains "active" until the end of seventieth year after the death of the writer/author (or after first publication if the author died first). After that works are deemed to be in the "public domain" and can be copied and/or published freely.

Those who wish to quote from a copyright work should first obtain permission from the copyright owner who can usually be contacted via his/her publisher.

SELECTED BIOGRAPHIES OF MEDIA PERSONALITIES IN IRELAND

Brady, Conor Patrick (b. 1949, Dublin). Editor of *The Irish Times* since 1986, having previously worked with R.T.E. Radio News. Former Editor of *The Sunday Tribune*.

Browne, Vincent (b. 1944, Limerick). Journalist. Joined RTE as researcher for *The Late Late Show* in late 60's. Former Editor of *The Sunday Tribune*, Previously worked with R.T.E. and *The Irish Independent*. Founded now defunct current affairs magazine *Magill*. Now contributes to the *Irish Times*.

Coogan, Tim Pat (b. 1935). Writer. Worked with *'Evening Press'* and *'Irish Press'*. In 1968 became Editor of the *Irish Press*. Much sought after

commentator on Northern Ireland situation. Has written extensively on modern Irish history - *'Ireland Since the Rising'*, *'Long Fellow, Long Shadow'*, *'Secret Army'* and *'The Troubles'*.

Cronin, Anthony (b. 1926). Poet, critic, novelist. Has extensively published his poems and writings. Was contributor to the *Irish Times, Sunday Tribune* and various literary journals.

Dunphy, Eamon Journalist with weekly column in *The Sunday Independent*. Formerly professional soccer player in England. Controversial figure in print and on television, has written books such as *The Unforgettable Fire* (1987) and *A Strange Kind of Glory* (1976).

Finn, Vincent (b. 1930, Dublin). Joined R.T.E. in 1961, he is the current Director General. Heavily involved in European Broadcasting Union of which R.T.E. is a member. Chairman of European Broadcasting Union Finance Group.

Holland, Mary (b. 1936). Journalist. Worked with *Vogue, The Observer, New Statesman, Sunday Press* and now *The Irish Times*. Well known face on RTE as contributor to current affairs programmes.

Kennedy, Geraldine (b. 1951). Political journalist, worked with *Cork Examiner* in 1970, before joining *The Irish Times* and *Sunday Tribune*. Her telephone, and that of fellow journalist Bruce Arnold, was tapped during her employment with the *Sunday Tribune*, sparking a political crisis. Former Progressive Democrats T.D.

Kiberd, Damien (b. 1945). Journalist. Worked with the *Irish Press* and *The Sunday Tribune*, he is the current editor of *The Sunday Business Post*.

Myers, Kevin (b. 1947). Journalist. Joined the *Irish Times* in 1980 and regularly contributes to *An Irishman's Diary*. Also presents the university quiz show *Challenging Times* on RTE.

O'Herlihy, Bill (b. 1938, Cork). Public Relations Executive and broadcaster. Joined RTE in 1972. Anchor man on many of their major sporting coverages, i.e., the Olympics, athletics, soccer internationals.

Quinn, Peter (b. Fermanagh). Proprietor of Sunday sporting newspaper *The Title*, launched in the summer of 1996. Former President of the GAA from 1991 to 1994.

Stokes, Niall (b. 1951). Founder and Editor of Ireland's most popular Rock magazine, *Hot Press* in 1977. Worked freelance for the *Irish Times* and the *Irish Independent*. Current Chairman of the *Independent Radio and Television Commission*.

Fanning, Aengus (b. 1943, Kerry). Editor of *The Sunday Independent* since 1984 having come through ranks in *Independent Newspapers* which he joined in 1969. Former inter-county Gaelic footballer with native Kerry.

O'Leary, Olivia (b. 1949). One of R.T.E.'s leading current affairs presenters. Worked with B.B.C. and Yorkshire T.V. Presented programmes such as *Today Tonight* and *Questions and Answers* on R.T.E. and *Newsnight* on B.B.C. Reporter for the *Irish Times* in the early 1980's.

O'Reilly, Dr. Tony (b. 1936, Dublin). Chairman and majority stockholder of *Independent Newspapers*. Has interests in Fitzwilton and Arcon as well as a stake in the Australian newspaper group *APN*. President, Chairman and Chief Executive Officer of the *H. J. Heinz Company*. Won 28 caps for Ireland in international rugby and played 10 times for the Lions.

First Trust Bank is the result of a vision. A vision that not only establishes a major financial force but brings a fresh new approach right across banking in Northern Ireland. A vision that will reflect and respond to the needs of the unique business community in Northern Ireland and offer inward investors an International Bank with real hands-on experience.

All corporate and commercial banking services are now located at First Trust's new headquarters in the heart of Belfast's Laganside Development - an investment which demonstrates the

A BETTER
VISION
FOR
BUSINESS

Bank's commitment to take a leading role in the future growth of business in Northern Ireland.

FIRST TRUST Bank

CORPORATE AND COMMERCIAL BANKING

Corporate and Commercial Banking, First Trust Centre, 92 Ann Street, Belfast BT1 3HH.
Telephone 01232 325599. Facsimile 01232 439592.
International Telephone +44 1232 325599. International Facsimile +44 1232 439592.

First Trust Bank is a trade mark of AIB Group (UK) p.l.c., incorporated in Northern Ireland,
Registered Office 4 Queen's Square, Belfast BT1 3DJ, Registered Number NI 18800.

SPORT IN IRELAND

Ireland has a whole new pantheon of sporting heroes who have achieved worldwide success in recent years. Billy Bingham's Northern Ireland squad shook the major soccer powers in the 1982 World Cup; some years later, Barry McGuigan (boxing) won a World Title; Jack Charlton (soccer) took the Republic to two World Cup Finals; Sean Kelly (cycling) dominated the world rankings throughout most of the 1980's; Stephen Roche (cycling) won the Tour de France, the Tour d'Italia and the World Championship in one remarkable, never to be forgotten year, 1987; Eamonn Coughlin and John Tracey (athletics) put Ireland on World Class standard with the former winning numerous Indoor titles, setting World indoor records plus winning the 5,000 metres World Title at Helsinki in 1983 while the diminutive Tracey took two world Cross-Country titles and a brilliant Olympic Silver medal in the marathon in the 1984 games in Los Angeles; Sonia O'Sullivan (athletics) has dominated women's world middle distance running for a number of years, winning a World Title in 1995 while Michelle Smith (swimming) dominated the world scene with three gold medals and a bronze at the 1996 Olympic Games in Atlanta.

Other international success stories have been Wayne McCullough (boxing) whose world title was won against all the odds in Japan; Dave "Boy" McAuley (boxing) the only Irish or British boxer to fight in eight world title fights; Joey Dunlop (motor cycling) the greatest road racer of them all; and Michael Carruth (boxing) who won Olympic Gold in the 1992 games at Barcelona, the first Irish Gold medallist for thirty-six years.

The most popular sporting code on the island, Gaelic Games, has shown remarkable growth in recent years with major developments at both national and local level particularly in regard to the provision of facilities. The key development on the field of play, however, has been the emergence of the Ulster counties who have totally dominated football, winning more All-Ireland titles in the early 1990's than in any previous decade.

Domestic soccer, north and south, has also witnessed sustained growth. In the Irish League, Linfield's dominance has been broken with a host of clubs now regularly challenging for the top spot.

League of Ireland football introduced a second division in 1985 thereby increasing league representation over a more widespread geographical area. Large sums of money have been spent improving facilities and standards.

In the other major sports, rugby at international level has been in the doldrums though the introduction of an All-Ireland League has given the domestic game a new edge.

The emergence of Paul McGinley, Darren Clarke and Padraig Harrington has boosted Irish Golf in recent times, these players being recognised as among the top new talent at international level.

In world terms, Irish sporting achievement in the past twenty years has never been higher.

THE OLYMPIC GAMES

Irish Olympic Games Medalists, 1896-1996

Games	Name	Event	Medal
Amsterdam 1928	Dr. Pat O'Callaghan	Hammer	Gold
Los Angeles 1932	Dr. Pat O'Callaghan	Hammer	Gold
	Bob Tisdall	400m Hurdles	Gold
Helsinki 1952	John McNally	Boxing (Bantam)	Silver
Melbourne 1956	Ron Delaney	1500m	Gold
	Fred Tiedt	Boxing (Welter)	Silver
	Freddie Gilroy	Boxing (Bantam)	Bronze
	John Caldwell	Boxing (Fly)	Bronze
	Tony Byrne	Boxing (Light)	Bronze
Tokyo 1964	Jim McCourt	Boxing (Light)	Bronze
Moscow 1980	David Wilkins & Jamie Wilkinson	Yachting (Flying Dutchman)	Silver
Moscow 1980	Hugh Russell	Boxing (Fly)	Bronze
Los Angeles 1984	John Treacy	Marathon	Silver
Barcelona 1992	Michael Carruth	Boxing (Welter)	Gold
	Wayne McCullagh	Boxing (Bantam)	Silver
Atlanta 1996	Michelle Smith	Swimming (400 Individual Medley)	Gold
	Michelle Smith	Swimming (400 Freestyle)	Gold
	Michelle Smith	Swimming (200 Individual Medley)	Gold
	Michelle Smith	Swimming (200 Butterfly)	Bronze

Irish Olympians, 1924 - 1996

1924 PARIS: *(Athletics):* John Kelly, W. J. Lowe, Sean Lavan, Norman McEachern, J. O'Connor, John O'Grady, Larry Stanley, J. J. Ryan. *(Boxing):* M. Doyle, Sgt. P. Dwyer, Pte. J. Flaherty, R. M. Hilliard, Pte. J. Kelleher, Pte. J. Kidley, Pte. M. McDonagh, W. J. Murphy. *(Lawn Tennis):* W. G. Ireland, E. D. McCrea, H. Wallis, P. Blair-White. *(Water Polo):* S. Barrett, J. Beckett, J. S. Brady, P. Convery, C. Fagan, M. A. O'Connor, N. M. Purcell.

1928 AMSTERDAM: *(Athletics):* Pat Anglim, Alister F. Clarke, G. N. Coughlan, L. D. E. Cullen, Denis Cussen, Sean Lavan, Norman McEachern, Dr. Pat O'Callaghan, Con O'Callaghan, Theo Phelan. *(Cycling):* Bertie Donnelly, J. B. Woodcock. *(Boxing):* Garda J. Chase, Gda. Matt Flanagan, G. Kelly, P. J. Lenihan, Cpl. M. McDonagh, Gda. W. J. Murphy, Pte. W. O'Shea, Edward Traynor. *(Swimming):* J. S. Brady, W. D. Broderick, M. Dockrell, T. H. Dockrell, H. B. Ellerker, C. Fagan, N. Judd, T. McClure, J. A. O'Connor, M. A. O'Connor.

1932 LOS ANGELES: *(Athletics):* Eamonn Fitzgerald, M. J. Murphy, Bob Tisdall, Dr. Pat O'Callaghan. *(Boxing):* John Flood, Patrick Hughes, James Murphy, Ernest Smith.

1948 LONDON: *(Athletics):* J. J. Barry, Cummin Clancy, Dan Coyle, Charles Denroche, Paul Dolan, Pat Fahy, Dave Guiney, Jimmy Reardon, Frank Mulvihill, Reggie Myles. *(Basketball):* H. Boland, Lt. P. Crehan, Lt. J. Flynn, Sgt. W. Jackson, Pte. T. Keenan, G. McLaughlin, Cadet J. R. McGee, Cpl. T. Malone, Cdt. F. B. O'Connor, Lt. D. O'Donovan, Sgt. D. Reddin, Pte. D. Sheriff, Pte. P. Sheriff, Sgt. C. Walsh. *(Boxing):* William E. Barnes, Peter Foran, Willie Lenihan, Maxie McCullagh, Mick McKeon, Kevin Martin, Gearoid O'Colmain, Hugh O'Hagan. *(Equestrian):* Cmdt. Fred Ahern, Cmdt. Dan J. Corry, Lt. Col. John J. Lewis. *(Fencing):* Dorothy Dermody, Patrick Duffy, T. Smith, Nick Thuillier, Owen Tuohy. *(Football):* W. Barry, W. Brennan, J. Cleary, F. Glennon, P Kavanagh, P. Lawlor, P. McDonald, Lt. P. McGonagle, E. McLoughlin, W. O'Grady, B. O'Kelly, W. Richardson, R. Smith. *(Rowing):* H. R. Chantler, P.G. Dooley, T. G. Dowdall, S. Hanley, P. D. Harrold, D. Lambert-Sugrue, B. McDonnell, E. M. A. McElligott, J. Nolan, W. J Stevens, R. W. R. Tamplin, D. B. C. Taylor. *(Yachting):* R.H. Allen, A.J. Mooney.

1952 HELSINKI: *(Athletics):* Paul Dolan, Joe West. *(Boxing):* Peter Crotty, William Duggan, John Lyttle, John McNally, Kevin Martin, Terry Milligan, Andrew Reddy, Thomas Reddy. *(Equestrian):* Capt. Mark Darley, Harry Freeman-Jackson, Ian Hume-Dudgeon. *(Fencing):* George Carpenter, Paddy Duffy, Harry Thuillier, Tom Rafter. *(Wrestling):* Jack Vard. *(Yachting):* Dr. Alf Delaney.

1956 MELBOURNE: *(Athletics):* Ronnie Delany, Eamonn Kinsella, Maeve Kyle. *(Boxing):* Anthony Byrne, John Caldwell, Freddie Gilroy, Harry Perry, Patrick Sharkey, Martin Smyth, Fred Tiedt. *(Equestrian):* Capt. Kevin Barry, Harry Freeman-Jackson, Ian Hume-Dudgeon, Lt. Patrick Kiernan, William Mullin, Lt. William Ringrose. *(Wrestling):* Gerald Martina. *(Yachting):* John Somers-Payne.

1960 ROME: *(Athletics):* Ronnie Delany, Willie Dunne, Michael Hoey, Maeve Kyle, John Lawlor, Patrick Lowry, Gerald McIntyre, Bertie Messitt, Frank O'Reilly. *(Boxing):* Joseph Casey, Patrick Kenny, Adam McClean, Colm McCoy, Eamonn McKeon, Bernard Meli, Danny O'Brien, Harry Perry, Ando Reddy, Michael Reid. *(Cycling):* Peter Crinion, Anthony Cullen, Seamus Herron, Michael Horgan, Martin McKay. *(Equestrian):* Lt. John Daly, Lt. Edward O'Donohoe, Capt. William Ringrose. *(Eventing):* Anthony Cameron, Ian Hume Dudgeon, Harry Freeman-Jackson, Edward Harty. *(Fencing):* Shirley Armstrong, Chris Bland, George Carpenter, Brian Hamilton, Tom Kearney, Harry Thuillier. *(Weightlifting):* Sammy Dalzell, Tommy Hayden. *(Wrestling):* Dermot Dunne, Joseph Feeney, Gerry Martina, Sean O'Connor. *(Yachting):* Dr R. G. Benson, Charles Gray, Jimmy Hooper, Dr A. J. Mooney, Dr D. A. Ryder, John Somers-Payne.

1964 TOKYO: *(Athletics):* Noel Carroll, Basil Clifford, Jim Hogan, Maeve Kyle, John Lawlor, Derek McCleane, Tom O'Riordan. *(Boxing):* Brian Anderson, Paddy Fitzsimons, Sean McCafferty, Jim McCourt, Chris Rafter. *(Fencing):* John Bouchier-Hayes, Michael Ryan. *(Judo):* John Ryan. *(Wrestling):* Joseph Feeney, Sean O'Connor. *(Yachting):* Robin D'Alton, Johnny Hooper, Eddie Kelliher, Harry Maguire. *(Equestrian):* Tommy Brennan, Tony Cameron, John Harty, Harry Freeman-Jackson.

1968 MEXICO: *(Athletics):* Noel Carroll, John Kelly, Pat McMahon, Mick Molloy, Frank Murphy. *(Boxing):* Mick Dowling, Brendan McCarthy, Jim McCourt, Eamonn McCusker, Martin Quinn, Eddie Tracey. *(Cycling):* Peter Doyle, Morrison Foster, Liam Horner. *(Fencing):* John Bouchier-Hayes, Finbarr Farrell, Colm O'Brien, Michael Ryan. *(Shooting):* Dr. Gerry Brady, Dermot Kelly, Arthur McMahon. *(Swimming):* Liam Ball, Anne O'Connor, Donnacha O'Dea, Vivienne Smith. *(Equestrian):* Tommy Brennan, Capt. Ned Campion, Diana Conolly-Carew, Juliet Jobling-Purser, Ada Matheson, Penny Moreton, Diana Wilson.

1972 MUNICH: *(Athletics):* Phil Conway, Neil Cusack, John Hartnett, Mike Keogh, Eddie Leddy, Danny McDaid, Dessie McGann, Fanahan McSweeney, Frank Murphy, Margaret Murphy, Mary Tracey, Claire Walsh, Donie Walsh. *(Boxing):* Mick Dowling, Christy Elliott, Neil McLaughlin, James Montague, Charlie Nash, John Rodgers. *(Canoeing):* Gerry Collins, Ann McQuaid, Brendan O'Connell, Howard Watkins. *(Cycling):* Peter Doyle, Liam Horner, Kieran McQuaid, Noel Taggart. *(Equestrian):* Bill Butler, Patrick Conolly-Carew, Juliet Jobling-Purser, Bill McLernon, Ronnie McMahon. *(Fencing):* John Bouchier-Hayes. *(Judo):* Anto Clarke, Liam Carroll, Matthew Folan, Patrick Murphy, Terry Watt. *(Rowing):* Sean Drea. *(Clay Pigeon Shooting):* Dr. Gerry Brady, William Campbell, Arthur

McMahon, Dermot Kelly. *(Swimming):* Liam Ball, Brian Clifford, Christine Fulcher, Andrew Hunter, Brenda McGrory, Ann O'Connor, Aisling O'Leary. *(Weighlifting):* Frank Rothwell. *(Yachting):* Harry Byrne, Harold Cudmore, Owen Delaney, Robert Hennessy, Kevin McLaverty, Richard O'Shea, David Wilkins, Sean Whittaker.

1976 MONTREAL: *(Archery):* Jim Conroy. *(Athletics):* Eamonn Coghlan, Neil Cusack, Eddie Leddy, Danny McDaid, Jim McNamara, Niall O'Shaughnessy, Mary Purcell. (Boxing): Brian Byrne, Brendan Dunne, Gerry Hammill, Dave Larmour, Christy McLaughlin. *(Canoeing):* Declan Burns, Ian Pringle, Brendan O'Connell, Howard Watkins. *(Cycling):* Alan McCormack, Oliver McQuaid. *(Equestrian):* Eric Horgan, Ronnie McMahon, Gerry Sinnott, Norman Van der Vater. *(Rowing):* Sean Drea, Martin Feeley, Ian Kennedy, Andrew McDonough, James Muldoon, Christopher O'Brien, Liam Redmond, James Renehan, Michael Ryan, William Ryan. *(Clay Pigeon Shooting):* Richard Flynn. *(Swimming):* Miriam Hopkins, Robert Howard, Deirdre Sheehan, Kevin Williamson. *(Yachting):* Robert Dix, Peter Dix, Derek Jago, Barry O'Neill, James Wilkinson, David Wilkins.

1980 MOSCOW: *(Archery):* Jim Conroy, Hazel Greene, Willie Swords. *(Athletics):* Eamonn Coghlan, Sean Egan, Ray Flynn, Pat Hooper, Dick Hooper, Mick O'Shea, John Treacy. *(Boxing):* Martin Brerton, P. J. Davitt, Sean Doylelt, Gerry Hawkins, Barry McGuigan, Hugh Russell, Phil Sutcliffe. *(Canoeing):* Declan Burns, Ian Pringle. *(Clay Pigeon Shooting):* Nicholas Cooney, Thomas Hewitt, Albert Thompson. *(Rifle & Pistol Shooting):* Ken Stanford. *(Cycling):* Billy Kerr, Tony Lally, Stephen Roche. *(Judo):* Alonzo Henderson, Dave McManus. *(Modern Pentathlon):* Mark Hartigan, Jerome Hartigan, Sackville Curry. *(Rowing):* Christy O'Brien, Frances Cryan, Noel Graham, Pat Gannon, David Gray, Iain Kennedy, Pat McDonagh, Willie Ryan, Ted Ryan, Denis Rice, Liam Williams. *(Swimming):* David Cummins, Catherine Bohan, Kevin Williamson. *(Yachting):* David Wilkins, James Wilkinson.

1984 LOS ANGELES: *(Archery):* Hazel Greene, Mary Vaughan. *(Athletics):* Ray Flynn, Declan Hegarty, Dick Hooper, Monica Joyce, Regina Joyce, Jerry Kiernan, Conor McCullough, Carey May, Caroline O'Shea, Marcus O'Sullivan, Frank O'Mara, Paul Donovan, Liam O'Brien, Mary Parr, Roisin Smith, John Treacy, Patricia Walsh. *(Boxing):* Tommy Corr, Paul Fitzgerald, Gerry Hawkins, Kieran Joyce, Sam Storey, Phil Sutcliffe. *(Canoeing):* Ian Pringle. *(Cycling):* Philip Cassidy, Seamus Downey, Martin Earley, Paul Kimmage, Gary Thompson. *(Equestrian):* Capt. David Foster, Sarah Gordon, Margaret Tolerton, Fiona Wentges, Capt. Gerry Mullins. *(Judo):* Kieran Foley. *(Clay Pigeon Shooting):* Roy Magowen, Albert Thompson. *(Swimming):* Carol-Anne Heavey, Julie Parkes. *(Yachting):* Bill O'Hara.

1988 SEOUL: *(Archery):* Noel Lynch, Joe Malone, Hazel Greene-Pereira. *(Athletics):* Marcus O'Sullivan, Gerry O'Reilly , Ann Keenan-Buckley, Brendan Quinn, Eamonn Coghlan, Frank O'Mara, John Doherty, John Treacy, John Woods, Dick Hooper, Marie Murphy-Rollins, Ailish Smyth, Conor McCullough, Terry McHugh, Carlos O'Connell, Jimmy McDonald, T. J. Kearns , Barbara Johnson. *(Boxing):* Wayne McCullough, Joe Lawlor, Paul Fitzgerald, John Lowey, Michael Carruth, Billy Walsh, Kieran Joyce. *(Canoeing):* Alan Carey, Pat Holmes, Pete Connor, Declan Bums. *(Cycling):* Phil Cassidy, Cormac McCann, Paul McCormack, John McQuaid, Stephen Spratt. *(Equestrian):* Cmdt. Gerry Mullins, Capt John Ledingham, Paul Darragh, Jack Doyle, Capt. David Foster, John Watson, Shea Walsh. *(Judo):* Eugene McManus. *(Rowing):* Frank Moore, Pat McDonagh, Liam Williams. *(Swimming):* Michelle Smith, Stephen Cullen, Aileen Convery, Richard Gheel, Gary O'Toole. *(Tennis):* Owen Casey, Eoin Collins. *(Wrestling):* David Harmon. *(Yachting):* Bill O'Hara, David Wilkins, Peter Kennedy, Cathy McAleavy, Aisling Byrne.

1992 BARCELONA: *(Archery):* Noel Lynch. *(Athletics):* Sonia O'Sullivan, Catherina McKiernan, Marcus O'Sullivan, Paul Donovan, John Doherty, Frank O'Mara, Noel Berkeley, Sean Dollman, John Treacy, Andy Ronan, Tommy Hughes, Victor Costello, Paul Quirke, Terry McHugh, Nicky Sweeney, Perri Williams, Bobby O'Leary, Jimmy McDonald, T. J. Kearns. *(Boxing):* Paul Buttimer, Wayne McCullough, Paul Griffin, Michael Carruth, Paul Douglas, Kevin McBride. *(Canoeing):* Ian Wiley, Mike Corcoran, Pat Holmes, Conor Holmes, Alan Carey. *(Cycling):* Paul Slane, Mark Kane, Kevin Kimmage, Robert Power, Conor Henry. *(Equestrian):* Mairead Curran, Melanie Duff, Olivia Holohan, Eric Smiley, Anna Merveldt, Peter Charles, Francis Connors, Paul Darragh, James Kernan, Eddie Macken. *(Fencing):* Michael O'Brien. *(Judo):* Keith Gough, Ciaran Ward. *(Rowing):* Niall O'Toole. *(Swimming):* Gary O'Toole, Michelle Smith. *(Tennis):* Owen Casey, Eoin Collins. *(Yachting):* David Wilkins, Peter Kennedy, Mark Mansfield, Tom McWilliams, Denise Lyttle.

1996 ATLANTA: *(Athletics):* Neil Ryan, Gary Ryan, Eugene Farrell, David Matthews, Niall Bruton, Shane Healy, Marcus O'Sullivan, Cormac Finnerty, Sean Dollman, T.J. Kearns, Sean Cahill, Tom McGuirk, Jimmy McDonald, Mark Mandy, Nicky Sweeney,Terry McHugh, Roman Linscheid, Sinead Delahunty, Sonia O'Sullivan, Kathy McCandless, Marie McMahon, Catherina McKiernan, Susan Smith, Deirdre Gallagher. *(Boxing):* Damaen Kelly, Brian Magee, Francis Barrett, Cathal O'Grady. *(Canoeing):* Ian Wiley, Michael Corcoran, Andrew Boland, Stephen O'Flaherty, Conor Moloney, Gary Mawer. *(Clay Pigeon Shoot):* Thomas Allen. *(Cycling):* Declan Lonergan, Philip Collins, Martin Earley, Alister Martin, David McCann. *(Equestrian):* Jessica Chesney, Capt John Ledingham, Eddie Macken, Peter Charles. *(Three Day Event):* Mick Barry, Alfie Buller, David Foster, Virginia McGrath, Eric Smiley. *(Dressage):* Heike Holstein. *(Gymnastics):* Barry McDonald. *(Rowing):* Brendan Dolan, Niall O'Toole, John Holland, Neville Maxwell, Tony O'Connor, Sam Lynch, Derek Holland. *(Yachting):* Mark Lyttle, Mark Mansfield, David Burrows, Marshall King, Dan O'Grady, Garrett Connolly, Denise Lyttle, Louise Cole, Aisling Bowman, John Driscoll. *(Judo):* Kieran Ward. *(Swimming):* Marion Madine, Michelle Smith, Earl McCarthy, Adrian O'Connor, Nick O'Hare. *(Shooting):* Gary Duff, Ronagh Barry. *(Tennis):* Eoin Casey, Scott Barron

GAELIC GAMES

All-Ireland Senior Hurling Winners, 1887 - 1996

Year	Winner	Year	Winner	Year	Winner	Year	Winner
1887	Tipperary	1915	Laois	1943	Cork	1971	Tipperary
1888	C'ship unfinished	1916	Tipperary	1944	Cork	1972	Kilkenny
1889	Dublin	1917	Dublin	1945	Tipperary	1973	Limerick
1890	Cork	1918	Limerick	1946	Cork	1974	Kilkenny
1891	Kerry	1919	Cork	1947	Kilkenny	1975	Kilkenny
1892	Cork	1920	Dublin	1948	Waterford	1976	Cork
1893	Cork	1921	Limerick	1949	Tipperary	1977	Cork
1894	Cork	1922	Kilkenny	1950	Tipperary	1978	Cork
1895	Tipperary	1923	Galway	1951	Tipperary	1979	Kilkenny
1896	Tipperary	1924	Dublin	1952	Cork	1980	Galway
1897	Limerick	1925	Tipperary	1953	Cork	1981	Offaly
1898	Tipperary	1926	Cork	1954	Cork	1982	Kilkenny
1899	Tipperary	1927	Dublin	1955	Wexford	1983	Kilkenny
1900	Tipperary	1928	Cork	1956	Wexford	1984	Cork
1901	London	1929	Cork	1957	Kilkenny	1985	Offaly
1902	Cork	1930	Tipperary	1958	Tipperary	1986	Cork
1903	Cork	1931	Cork	1959	Waterford	1987	Galway
1904	Kilkenny	1932	Kilkenny	1960	Wexford	1988	Galway
1905	Kilkenny	1933	Kilkenny	1961	Tipperary	1989	Tipperary
1906	Tipperary	1934	Limerick	1962	Tipperary	1990	Cork
1907	Kilkenny	1935	Kilkenny	1963	Kilkenny	1991	Tipperary
1908	Tipperary	1936	Limerick	1964	Tipperary	1992	Kilkenny
1909	Kilkenny	1937	Tipperary	1965	Tipperary	1993	Kilkenny
1910	Wexford	1938	Dublin	1966	Cork	1994	Offaly
1911	Kilkenny	1939	Kilkenny	1967	Kilkenny	1995	Clare
1912	Kilkenny	1940	Limerick	1968	Wexford	1996	Wexford
1913	Kilkenny	1941	Cork	1969	Kilkenny		
1914	Clare	1942	Cork	1970	Cork		

All-Ireland Senior Football Winners, 1887 - 1996

Year	Winner	Year	Winner	Year	Winner	Year	Winner
1887	Limerick	1915	Wexford	1943	Roscommon	1971	Offaly
1888	No C'ship	1916	Wexford	1944	Roscommon	1972	Offaly
1889	Tipperary	1917	Wexford	1945	Cork	1973	Cork
1890	Cork	1918	Wexford	1946	Kerry	1974	Dublin
1891	Dublin	1919	Kildare	1947	Cavan	1975	Kerry
1892	Dublin	1920	Tipperary	1948	Cavan	1976	Dublin
1893	Wexford	1921	Dublin	1949	Meath	1977	Dublin
1894	Dublin	1922	Dublin	1950	Mayo	1978	Kerry
1895	Tipperary	1923	Dublin	1951	Mayo	1979	Kerry
1896	Limerick	1924	Kerry	1952	Cavan	1980	Kerry
1897	Dublin	1925	Galway	1953	Kerry	1981	Kerry
1898	Dublin	1926	Kerry	1954	Meath	1982	Offaly
1899	Dublin	1927	Kildare	1955	Kerry	1983	Dublin
1900	Tipperary	1928	Kildare	1956	Galway	1984	Kerry
1901	Dublin	1929	Kerry	1957	Louth	1985	Kerry
1902	Dublin	1930	Kerry	1958	Dublin	1986	Kerry
1903	Kerry	1931	Kerry	1959	Kerry	1987	Meath
1904	Kerry	1932	Kerry	1960	Down	1988	Meath
1905	Kildare	1933	Cavan	1961	Down	1989	Cork
1906	Dublin	1934	Galway	1962	Kerry	1990	Cork
1907	Dublin	1935	Cavan	1963	Dublin	1991	Down
1908	Dublin	1936	Mayo	1964	Galway	1992	Donegal
1909	Kerry	1937	Kerry	1965	Galway	1993	Derry
1910	Louth	1938	Galway	1966	Galway	1994	Down
1911	Cork	1939	Kerry	1967	Meath	1995	Dublin
1912	Louth	1940	Kerry	1968	Down	1996	Meath
1913	Kerry	1941	Kerry	1969	Kerry		
1914	Kerry	1942	Dublin	1970	Kerry		

Holders of Most All-Ireland Senior Medals, hurling and football

Hurling
Noel Skehan (Kilkenny) 9
John Doyle (Tipperary) 8
Christy Ring (Cork) 8

Frank Cummins (Kilkenny) 8
Jimmy Doyle (Tipperary)...............6
Football
Pat Spillane (Kerry).......................8

Mike Sheehy (Kerry)......................8
Paidi O'Shea (Kerry)......................8
Ogie Moran (Kerry).......................8
Ger Power (Kerry)..........................8

Main G.A.A. Statistics, county by county

County	Main Stadium & capacity (approx.)	Colours	All Ireland S.F.C (F)	All Ireland S.H.C (H)	N.F.L. Titles	N.H.L. Titles
ULSTER...........St. Tighearnach's Park, Clones			12	0	10	0
Tyrone.....................Healy Park (23,000)	White & red		0	0	0	0
Cavan.................................Breffni Park	Blue & white		5	0	1	0
Down.....................Pairc an Iúir, Newry	Red & black		5	0	4	0
Antrim........Casement Park, Belfast (40,000)	Saffron & white		0	0	0	0
Armagh............Athletic Grounds, Armagh (14,000)	Orange & white		0	0	0	0
Derry.....................Celtic Park, Derry city	Red & white		1	0	4	0
Donegal...............McCumhaill Park, Ballybofey	Green & gold		1	0	0	0
Fermanagh.........Michael Brewster Park, Eniskillen	Green & white		0	0	0	0
Monaghan..St. Tighearnach's Park, Clones (33,000)	White & blue		0	0	1	0
CONNACHT.....................Castlebar (30,000)			12	4	15	6
Galway.....................Tuam Park (22,000)	Maroon & white		7	4	4	6
Letrim...............Pairc MacDiarmada (12,000)	Green & gold		0	0	0	0
Mayo.....................McHale Park (30,000)	Green & red		3	0	10	0
Roscommon...............Dr. Hyde Park (30,000)	Gold & blue		2	0	1	0
Sligo.....................Markievicz Park (13,000)	White & black		0	0	0	0
LEINSTER...............Croke Park, Dublin (68,000)			42	41	18	16
Westmeath.............................Mullingar	Maroon & white		0	0	0	0
Longford..............Pearse Park, Longford	Blue & gold		0	0	1	0
Louth.............................Drogheda	Red & white		3	0	0	0
Meath...............Pairc Tailteann, Navan	Green & gold		6	0	7	0
Dublin............Parnell Park, and Croke Park	Navy & sky blue		22	6	8	2
Carlow.............................Dr. Cullen Park	Red & green & yellow		0	0	0	0
Kilkenny...............Nowlan Park (30,000)	Black & Amber		0	25	0	9
Kildare.............................Newbridge	White		4	0	0	0
Wicklow.............................Aughrim (10,000)	Blue & gold		0	0	0	0
Laois...............Ó'Moore Park, Portlaoise (25,000)	Blue & white		0	1	2	0
Wexford...............Wexford Park, Wexford	Purple & gold		5	6	0	4
Offaly............Pairc Úi Conchuir, Tullamore	Green & white & gold		3	3	0	1
MUNSTER.........Semple Stadium/Páirc Úi Chaoimh			42	63	19	43
Clare...............Cusack Park, Ennis (25,000)	Saffron & blue		0	2	0	3
Kerry............Fitzgerald Stadium, Killarney (50,000)	Green & gold		30	1	15	0
Cork...............Páirc Úi Chaoimh, Cork (50,000)	Red & white		6	27	4	13
Limerick............Gaelic Grounds, Limerick (55,000)	Green & white		2	7	0	10
Waterford.............................Walsh Park, Waterford	White & blue		0	2	0	1
Tipperary............Semple Stadium, Thurles (59,000)	Blue & gold		4	24	0	16

Presidents of the Gaelic Athletic Association

Maurice Davin (Tipperary)....................................1884
Eamonn Bennet (Clare)....................................1887
Maurice Davin (Tipperary)....................................1888
Peter Kelly (Galway)....................................1889
Frank Dineen (Limerick)....................................1895
Michael Deering (Cork)....................................1898
James Nowlan (Kilkenny)....................................1901
Daniel McCarthy (Dublin)....................................1921
Patrick Breen (Wexford)....................................1924
William Clifford (Limerick)....................................1926
Seán Ryan (Dublin)....................................1928
Seán McCarthy (Cork)....................................1932
Bob O'Keffe (Laois)....................................1935
Pádraig McNamee (Antrim)....................................1938
Seamus Gardiner (Tipperary)....................................1943
Dan O'Rourke (Roscommon)....................................1946
Michael Kehoe (Wexford)....................................1949

Michael O'Donoghue (Waterford)....................................1952
Seamus McFerran (Antrim)....................................1955
Dr. J.J. Stuart (Dublin)....................................1958
Hugh Byrne (Wicklow)....................................1961
Alf Murray (Armagh)....................................1964
Seamus Ó Riain (Tipperary)....................................1967
Pat Fanning (Waterford)....................................1970
Dr. Donal Keenan (Roscommon)....................................1973
Con Murphy (Cork)....................................1976
Paddy McFlynn (Down)....................................1979
Paddy Buggy (Kilkenny)....................................1982
Dr. Mick Loftus (Mayo)....................................1985
John Dowling (Offaly)....................................1988
Peter Quinn (Fermanagh)....................................1991
Jack Boothman (Wicklow)....................................1994

Note: Easter 1997 sees Mattie McDonagh (Galway) take over as President for a three-year term.

Gaelic Athletic Association Players' All-Stars, 1995

FOOTBALL AWARDS	HURLING AWARDS

FOOTBALL AWARDS

John O'Leary
(Dublin)

Tony Scullion	Mark O'Connor	Fay Devlin
(Derry)	(Cork)	(Tyrone)

Paul Curran	Keith Barr	Steven O'Brien
(Dublin)	(Dublin)	(Cork)

Brian Stynes	Anthony Tohill
(Dublin)	(Derry)

Jarlath Fallon	Dessie Farrell	Paul Clarke
(Galway)	(Dublin)	(Dublin)

Tommy Dowd	Peter Canavan	Charlie Redmond
(Meath)	(Tyrone)	(Dublin)

Footballer of the Year: Peter Canavan (Tyrone)

HURLING AWARDS

David Fitzgerald
(Clare)

Kevin Kinahan	Brian Lohan	Liam Doyle
(Offaly)	(Clare)	(Clare)

Brian Whelehan	Seán McMahon	Anthony Daly
(Offaly)	(Clare)	(Clare)

Michael Coleman	Ollie Baker
(Galway)	(Clare)

Johnny Dooley	Gary Kirby	James O'Connor
(Offaly)	(Limerick)	(Clare)

Billy Dooley	DJ Carey	Ger O'Loughlin
(Offaly)	(Kilkenny)	(Clare)

Hurler of the Year: Brian Lohan (Clare)

1996 All-Ireland Hurling Final Statistics

Wexford 1-13, Limerick 0-14.

Wexford - D Fitzhenry; C Kehoe, G Cushe, J O'Connor (0-1); R Guiney, L Dunne, L O'Gorman (0-2); A Felon, G O'Connor; R McCarthy, M Storey (0-2), L Murphy (0-1); E Scallan (0-1), G Laffan (0-3), T Dempsey (1-3). *Subs:* B Byrne for L Murphy (66 mins); P Finn for R Guiney (69 mins); P Codd for G Laffan (71 mins).

Limerick - J Quaid; S McDonagh, M Nash, D Nash; D Clarke (0-1), C Carey (0-3), M Foley; M Galligan, Seán O'Neill; F Carroll (0-1), G Kirby (0-2), B Foley (0-4); O O'Neill (0-1), D Quigley (0-1), TJ Ryan (0-1). *Subs:* P Tobin for O O'Neill (49 mins); B Tobin for TJ Ryan (55 mins); T Herbert for B Foley (64 mins).

Referee: P Horan (Offaly). *Attendance:* 65,847. *Number of first-half scores:* 19. *Number of second-half scores:* 9. *Number of players sent off:* One - E Scallan, Wexford (34 mins). *Number of players booked:* Five - J O'Connor, Wexford (17 mins); M Houlihan, Limerick (17 mins); O O'Neill, Limerick (17 mins); A Fenlon, Wexford (33 mins); C Carey, Limerick (33 mins).

1996 All-Ireland Football Final (Replay) Statistics

Meath 2-9, Mayo 1-11

Meath - C Martin; M O'Reilly, D Fay, M O'Connell; C Coyle, E McManus, P Reynolds; J McGuinness, J McDermott; T Giles (1-4), T Dowd (1-3), G Geraghty; C Brady, B Reilly (0-1), B Callaghan (0-1). *Subs:* J Devine for B Callaghan (66 mins); O Murphy for B Reilly (71 mins).

Mayo - J Madden; D Flanagan, K Cahil, K Mortimer; P Holmes, J Nallen, N Connelly; L McHale, D Brady; J Horan (0-5), C McManamon, M Sheridan (0-5); R Dempsey, J Casey (0-1), A Finnerty. *Subs:* PJ Loftus (1-0) for Dempsey (26 mins); P Fallon for D Flanagan (45 mins); T Reilly for A Finnerty (69 mins).

Referee: P McEnaney (Monaghan). *Number of first-half scores:* 10. *Number of second-half scores:* 13. *Number of players sent off:* Two - Liam McHale, Mayo; Colm Coyle, Meath. *Number of players booked:* Five.

General Secretary/Director Generals' of the Gaelic Athletic Association

Michael Cusack (Clare)	1884-85	Patrick Tobin (Dublin)	1891-94
John McKay (Cork)	1884-85	David Walsh (Cork)	1894-95
John W. Power (Kildare)	1884-87	Richard Blake (Meath)	1895-98
J.B. O'Reilly (Dublin)	1885-87	Frank Dineen (Limerick)	1898-1901
Timothy O'Riordan (Cork)	1885-89	Luke O'Toole (Dublin)	1901-09
James Moore (Louth)	1887-88	Pádraic Ó Caoimh (Cork)	1929-64
William Prendergast (Tipperary)	1888-89	Seán Ó Síocháin (Cork)	1964-79
P.R. Cleary (Limerick)	1889-90	Liam Mulvihill (Longford)	1979-
Maurice Moynihan (Kerry)	1890-92		

ASSOCIATION FOOTBALL

Republic of Ireland Football Team Fact File

Name	Age	Club	Caps	Goals	First Cap	World Cup Appearances
John Aldridge	38	Tranmere Rovers	68	19	26/03/86	25
Phil Babb	25	Liverpool	20	0	23/03/94	4
Packie Bonner	36	Glasgow Celtic	80	0	24/05/81	29
Gary Breen	22	Birmingham City	7	1	-	1
Tony Cascarino	34	Marseille	66	12	11/09/85	25
David Connolly	19	Watford	4	2	-	1
Tommy Coyne	33	Motherwell	21	6	25/03/92	6
Shay Given	20	Blackburn Rovers	8	0	-	1
Ian Harte	19	Leeds United	5	2	-	1
Ray Houghton	34	Crystal Palace	67	*7	26/03/86	29
Denis Irwin	30	Manchester United	41	1	12/09/90	15
Roy Keane	25	Manchester United	30	1	22/05/91	16
Alan Kelly	28	Sheffield United	14	0	17/02/93	0
David Kelly	30	Sunderland	20	8	10/11/87	2
Gary Kelly	22	Leeds United	18	1	23/03/94	2
Jeff Kenna	26	Blackburn Rovers	13	0	26/04/95	1
Mark Kennedy	20	Liverpool	5	0	06/09/95	0
Alan Kernaghan	29	Manchester City	17	1	09/09/92	9
Jason McAteer	25	Liverpool	18	0	23/03/94	4
Paul McGrath	36	Aston Villa	82	8	05/02/85	28
Eddie McGoldrick	31	Arsenal	15	0	25/03/92	4
Alan McLoughlin	29	Portsmouth	26	1	03/06/90	4
Keith O'Neill	20	Norwich City	7	4	-	1
Terry Phelan	29	Chelsea	35	1	11/10/95	13
Niall Quinn	29	Sunderland	61	17	25/05/86	19
John Sheridan	32	Sheffield Wednesday	34	5	23/03/88	8
Steve Staunton	27	Aston Villa	63	6	19/10/88	26
Andy Townsend	33	Aston Villa	61	7	07/02/89	26

FAI/Opel International Soccer Senior Player Awards

Year	Name
1989	Kevin Moran
1990	Paul McGrath
1991	Paul McGrath
1992	John Aldridge
1993	Steve Staunton
1994	Ray Houghton
1995	Andy Townsend

Top Ten International Scorers

Name	No. of Goals
Frank Stapleton	20
John Aldridge	19
Don Givens	19
Niall Quinn	17
Noel Cantwell	14
Gerry Daly	13
Tony Cascarino	12
Jimmy Dunne	12
Liam Brady	9
Kevin Sheedy	9

F.A.I. Cup Winners

Year	Winners	Year	Winners	Year	Winners
1922	St. James Gate	1936	Shamrock Rovers	1951	Cork Athletic
1923	Alton United	1937	Waterford	1952	Dundalk
1924	Athlone Town	1938	St. James Gate	1953	Cork Athletic
1925	Shamrock Rovers	1939	Shelbourne	1954	Drumcondra
1926	Fordsons	1940	Shamrock Rovers	1955	Shamrock Rovers
1927	Drumcondra	1941	Cork United	1956	Shamrock Rovers
1928	Bohemians	1942	Dundalk	1957	Drumcondra
1929	Shamrock Rovers	1943	Drumcondra	1958	Dundalk
1930	Shamrock Rovers	1944	Shamrock Rovers	1959	St. Patrick's Athletic
1931	Shamrock Rovers	1945	Shamrock Rovers	1960	Shelbourne
1932	Shamrock Rovers	1946	Drumcondra	1961	St. Patrick's Athletic
1933	Shamrock Rovers	1947	Cork United	1962	Shamrock Rovers
1934	Cork	1948	Shamrock Rovers	1963	Shelbourne
1935	Bohemians	1949	Dundalk	1964	Shamrock Rovers
		1950	Transport	1965	Shamrock Rovers

1966 ....Shamrock Rovers	1977..............................Dundalk	1988................................Dundalk
1967 ....Shamrock Rovers	1978 ....Shamrock Rovers	1989................................Derry City
1968 ....Shamrock Rovers	1979................................Dundalk	1990........................Bray Wanderers
1969 ....Shamrock Rovers	1980 ....Waterford	1991 ....Galway United
1970..............................Bohemians	1981..............................Dundalk	1992..............................Bohemians
1971 ....Limerick	1982 ....Limerick United	1993 ....Shelbourne
1972..................Cork Hibernians	1983 ....Sligo Rovers	1994 ....Sligo Rovers
1973..................Cork Hibernians	1984 ..................................U.C.D.	1995................................Derry City
1974........................Finn Harps	1985 ....Shamrock Rovers	1996 ....Shelbourne
1975..........................Home Farm	1986 ....Shamrock Rovers	
1976..............................Bohemians	1987 ....Shamrock Rovers	

League of Ireland Championship Winners

Season Winners	1951-52...........St. Patrick's Athletic	1982-83....................Athlone Town
1921-22 ....St. James's Gate	1952-53 ....Shelbourne	1983-84..............Shamrock Rovers
1922-23 ....Shamrock Rovers	1953-54 ....Shamrock Rovers	1984-85 ....Shamrock Rovers
1923-24.........................Bohemians	1954-55...........St. Patrick's Athletic	**Premier Division**
1924-25 ....Shamrock Rovers	1955-56...........St. Patrick's Athletic	1985-86 ....Shamrock Rovers
1925-26 ....Shelbourne	1956-57..............Shamrock Rovers	1986-87 ....Shamrock Rovers
1926-27 ....Shamrock Rovers	1957-58......................Drumcondra	1987-88 ....Dundalk
1927-28..........................Bohemians	1958-59..............Shamrock Rovers	1988-89.............................Derry City
1928-29 ....Shelbourne	1959-60 ....Limerick	1989-90...........St. Patrick's Athletic
1929-30..........................Bohemians	1960-61 ....Drumcondra	1990-91 ....Dundalk
1930-31 ....Shelbourne	1961-62 ....Shelbourne	1991-92 ....Shelbourne
1931-32 ....Shamrock Rovers	1962-63 ....Dundalk	1992-93..............................Cork City
1932-33 ....Dundalk	1963-64 ....Shamrock Rovers	1993-94 ....Shamrock Rovers
1933-34..........................Bohemians	1964-65 ....Drumcondra	1994-95 ....Dundalk
1934-35 ....Dolphin	1965-66.........................Waterford	1995-96...........St. Patrick's Athletic
1935-36..........................Bohemians	1966-67 ....Dundalk	**1st Division**
1936-37 ....Sligo Rovers	1967-68.........................Waterford	1985-86.................Bray Wanderers
1937-38 ....Shamrock Rovers	1968-69.........................Waterford	1986-87.............................Derry City
1938-39 ....Shamrock Rovers	1969-70.........................Waterford	1987-88.....................Athlone Town
1939-40 ....St. James's Gate	1970-71 ....Cork Hibernians	1988-89 ....Drogheda United
1940-41 ....Cork United	1971-72.........................Waterford	1989-90 ....Waterford United
1941-42.........................Cork United	1972-73.........................Waterford	1990-91 ....Drogheda United
1942-43.........................Cork United	1973-74 ....Cork Celtic	1991-92 ....Limerick City
1943-44 ....Shelbourne	1974-75.........................Bohemians	1992-93 ....Galway United
1944-45.........................Cork United	1975-76 ....Dundalk	1993-94 ....Sligo Rovers
1945-46.........................Cork United	1976-77 ....Sligo Rovers	1994-95.................................U.C.D.
1946-47 ....Shelbourne	1977-78.........................Bohemians	1995-96.................Bray Wanderers
1947-48 ....Drumcondra	1978-79 ....Dundalk	
1948-49 ....Drumcondra	1979-80................Limerick United	
1949-50 ....Cork Athletic	1980-81 ....Athlone Town	
1950-51 ....Cork Athletic	1981-82 ....Dundalk	

League of Ireland all time top scorers

Goals Player	156......................Johnny Matthews	135.........................Sean McCarthy
235.....................Brendan Bradley	153 ....Alfie Hale	132................................Mick Leech
178 ....Turlough O'Connor	143 ....Paul McGee	130..........................Jack Fitzgerald
162.........................Donal Leahy	141 ....Eric Barber	130 ....Eugene Davis

Current League of Ireland Football Club Statistics

Club	Founded	Ground & capacity	Colours	F.A.I. Cup	League Champ.	League Cup
St. Patrick's Athletic	1929	Richmond Park (7,000)	Red & White	2	5	0
Bohemians	1890	Dalymount Park (18,000)	Red & Black	5	7	2
Sligo Rovers	1928	The Showgrounds (7,000)	Red	2	2	0
Shelbourne	1895	Tolka Park (9,000)	Red	5	8	1
Shamrock Rovers	1901	RDS, Dublin (14,000)	Green & White	24	15	1
Derry City	1928	Brandywell Stadium (8,500)	Red & White	2	1	4
Dundalk	1922	Oriel Park (20,000)	White & Black	8	9	5
U.C.D.	1895	Belfield Park (4,000)	Navy Blue	1	0	0
Cork City	1984	Turner's Cross (12,000)	Green, White & Red	0	1	1
Athlone Town	1887	St. Mel's Park (10,000)	Blue & Black	1	2	3
Drogheda Utd	1919	United Park (6,000)	Maroon & Blue	0	0	1
Galway United	1977	Terryland Park (8,000)	Maroon & Blue	1	0	1

Club	Founded	Ground	Colours	F.A.I. Cup	League Champ.	League Cup
Bray Wanderers	1942	Carlisle Ground (3,000)	Green & White	1	0	0
Finn Harps	1954	Finn Park (8,000)	White & Blue	1	0	0
Home Farm Everton	1928	Whitehall (3,500)	Blue & White	1	0	0
Cobh Ramblers	1922	St. Colmans Park (10,000)	Claret & Blue	0	0	0
St. James's Gate	1902	Iveagh Grounds (3,000)	Red & Green	2	2	0
Limerick	1983	Hogan Park (10,000)	Blue & White	0	0	1
Kilkenny City	1966	Buckley Park (7,000)	Amber & Black	0	0	0
Waterford Utd	1982	Waterford Sports Ct. (8,000)	Blue & White	0	0	1
Longford Town	1924	Connaught Road (10,000)	Red & Black	0	0	0
Monaghan Utd	1979	Gortakeegan (5,000)	Blue & White	0	0	0

Northern Ireland Irish League Championship Winners (1891-1996)

Year	Winner
1891	Linfield
1892	Linfield
1893	Linfield
1894	Glentoran
1895	Linfield
1896	Distillery
1897	Glentoran
1898	Linfield
1899	Distillery
1900	Belfast Celtic
1901	Distillery
1902	Linfied
1903	Distillery
1904	Linfield
1905	Glentoran
1906	Cliftonville/Distillery
1907	Linfield
1908	Linfield
1909	Linfield
1910	Cliftonville
1911	Linfield
1912	Glentoran
1913	Glentoran
1914	Linfield
1915	Belfast Celtic
1920	Belfast Celtic
1921	Glentoran
1922	Linfield
1923	Linfield
1924	Queen's Island
1925	Glentoran
1926	Belfast Celtic
1927	Belfast Celtic
1928	Belfast Celtic
1929	Belfast Celtic
1930	Linfield
1931	Glentoran
1932	Linfield
1933	Belfast Celtic
1934	Linfield
1935	Linfield
1936	Belfast Celtic
1937	Belfast Celtic
1938	Belfast Celtic
1939	Belfast Celtic
1940	Belfast Celtic
1948	Belfast Celtic
1949	Linfield
1950	Linfield
1951	Glentoran
1952	Glentoran
1953	Glentoran
1954	Linfield
1955	Linfield
1956	Linfield
1957	Glentoran
1958	Ards
1959	Linfield
1960	Glenavon
1961	Linfield
1962	Linfield
1963	Distillery
1964	Glentoran
1965	Derry City
1966	Linfield
1967	Glentoran
1968	Glentoran
1969	Linfield
1970	Glentoran
1971	Linfield
1972	Glentoran
1973	Crusaders
1974	Coleraine
1975	Linfield
1976	Crusaders
1977	Glentoran
1978	Linfield
1979	Linfield
1980	Linfield
1981	Glentoran
1982	Linfield
1983	Linfield
1984	Linfield
1985	Linfield
1986	Linfield
1987	Linfield
1988	Glentoran
1989	Linfield
1990	Portadown
1991	Portadown
1992	Glentoran
1993	Linfield
1994	Linfield
1995	Crusaders
1996	Portadown

Northern Ireland Irish Cup Final Winners (1946/47-1995/96)

Year	Winner
1946/47	Belfast Celtic
1947/48	Linfield
1948/49	Derry City
1949/50	Linfield
1950/51	Glentoran
1951/52	Ards
1952/53	Linfield
1953/54	Derry City
1954/55	Dundela
1955/56	Distillery
1956/57	Glenavon
1957/58	Ballymena United
1958/59	Glenavon
1959/60	Linfield
1960/61	Glenavon
1961/62	Linfield
1962/63	Linfield
1963/64	Derry City
1964/65	Coleraine
1965/66	Glentoran
1966/67	Crusaders
1967/68	Crudasers
1968/69	Ards
1969/70	Linfield
1970/71	Distillery
1971/72	Coleraine
1972/73	Glentoran
1973/74	Ards
1974/75	Coleraine
1975/76	Carrick Rangers
1976/77	Coleraine
1977/78	Linfield
1978/79	Cliftonville
1979/80	Linfield
1980/81	Ballymena United
1981/82	Linfield
1982/83	Glentoran
1983/84	Ballymena United
1984/85	Glentoran
1985/86	Glentoran
1986/87	Glentoran
1987/88	Glentoran
1988/89	Ballymena United
1989/90	Glentoran
1990/91	Portadown
1991/92	Glenavon
1992/93	Bangor
1993/94	Linfield
1994/95	Linfield
1995/96	Glentoran

Northern Ireland Irish League Football Club Statistics

Club	Founded	Ground	Colours	Irish League titles	Irish Cup titles
Portadown	1924	Shamrock Park (15,000)	Red	3	1
Crusaders	1898	Seaview (9,000)	Red & black	3	2
Glentoran	1882	The Oval (30,000)	Green, black & red	19	16
Glenavon	1889	Mourneview Park (11,000)	Royal blue & white	3	4
Linfield	1886	Windsor Park (29,000)	Ryal blue & white	42	35
Cliftonville	1879	Solitude (8,000)	Red & white	2	8
Ards	1902	Castlereagh Park (10,000)	Red and blue	1	4
Bangor	1918	Clandeboye Park (5,000)	Gold & royal blue	0	1
Coleraine	1927	The Showgrounds (12,500)	Blue & white	1	4
Ballymena United	1928	The Showgrounds (8,000)	Sky blue & white	0	6
Omagh Town	1964	St. Julian's Road (8,000)	White & black	0	0
Distillery	1879	New Grosvenor Stad. (7,000)	White & blue	6	12
Ballyclare Comrades	1919	Dixon Park (4,500)	Red & white	0	0
Carrick Rangers	1939	Taylors Avenue (5,000)	Tan & black	0	1
Larne	1900	Inver Park (12,000)	Red & white	0	0
Newry Town	1923	The Showgrounds (5,000)	Blue & white	0	0

Republic of Ireland Bord Gáis FAI Premier Division Final League Table 1995/96

Club	P	W	D	L	F	A	P
St. Patrick's Athletic	33	19	10	4	53	34	67
Bohemians	33	18	8	7	60	29	62
Sligo Rovers	33	16	7	10	45	38	55
Shelbourne	33	15	9	9	45	33	54
Shamrock Rovers	33	14	8	11	32	32	50
Derry City	33	11	13	9	50	38	46
Dundalk	33	11	9	13	38	39	42
UCD	33	12	6	15	38	40	42
Cork City *	33	12	8	13	37	41	41
Athlone Town	33	8	7	18	38	59	31
Drogheda United	33	7	9	17	39	51	30
Galway United	33	5	6	22	26	67	21

Champions: St. Patrick's Athletic. *Relegated:* Drogheda Utd., Galway Utd., Athlone Town. * 3 points deducted.

Republic of Ireland Bord Gáis FAI First Division Final League Table 1995/96

Club	P	W	D	L	F	A	P
Bray Wanderers	27	16	7	4	53	21	55
Finn Harps	27	14	7	6	50	25	49
Home Farm-Everton	27	14	4	9	42	34	46
Cobh Ramblers	27	10	13	4	30	15	43
St. Jame's Gate	27	9	11	7	35	30	38
Limerick	27	10	6	11	37	34	36
Kilkenny City	27	9	8	10	33	38	35
Waterford United	27	9	7	11	37	40	34
Longford Town	27	5	6	16	26	46	21
Monaghan United	27	2	5	20	10	70	11

Champions: Bray Wanderers. *Also Promoted:* Finn Harps and Home Farm-Everton.

Northern Ireland Smirnoff Premier Division Final League Table 1995/96

Club	P	W	D	L	F	A	P
Portadown	28	16	8	4	61	40	56
Crusaders	28	15	7	6	45	32	52
Glentoran	28	13	7	8	56	39	46
Glenavon	28	13	5	10	47	32	44
Linfield	28	11	8	9	32	33	41
Cliftonville	28	6	11	11	27	48	29
Ards	28	6	7	15	29	43	25
Bangor	28	3	5	20	23	54	14

Champions: Portadown. *Relegated:* Bangor

Northern Ireland Smirnoff First Division Final League Table 1995/96

Club	P	W	D	L	F	A	P
Coleraine	28	21	4	3	82	27	67
Ballymena United	28	13	10	5	38	25	49
Omagh Town	28	12	7	9	50	43	43
Distillery	28	10	7	11	35	34	37
Ballyclare Comrades	28	10	3	15	29	48	33
Carrick Rangers	28	9	3	16	32	46	30
Larne	28	7	7	14	30	35	28
Newry Town	28	7	5	16	31	58	26

Champions: Coleraine (Promoted)

BOXING

Irish Amateur Boxing Statistics

President...Mr. Nicholas White
Main venue ....The National Stadium (capacity 2,000)
Number of clubs affiliated to the Association 330

Irish Boxers who have won medals at Olympic and European level

Name	Olympic Games	Venue	Medal	Weight
John McNally	1952	Finland	Silver	54kg
Fred Tiedt	1956	Australia	Silver	67kg
Fred Gilroy	1956	Australia	Bronze	54kg
Tony Byrne	1956	Australia	Bronze	60kg
John Caldwell	1956	Australia	Bronze	51kg
Jim McCourt	1964	Tokyo	Bronze	60kg
Hugh Russell	1980	Moscow	Bronze	51kg
Michael Carruth	1992	Barcelona	Gold	67kg
Wayne McCullough	1992	Barcelona	Silver	54kg

Name	European C'ships	Venue	Medal	Weight
Jim Ingle	1939	Ireland	Gold	51kg
Paddy Dowdal	1939	Ireland	Gold	60kg
Maxie McCullough	1949	Norway	Gold	60kg
Paul Griffin	1991	Sweden	Gold	57kg
Gerry O' Colmain	1947	Ireland	Gold	91kg
Peter Maguire	1947	Ireland	Silver	57kg
John Kelly	1951		Silver	54kg
David Connell	1949-51		Bronze	60kg
Terry Milligan	1951		Bronze	63.5kg
Terry Milligan	1953		Silver	63.5kg
Fred Tiedt	1957	Prague	Bronze	67kg
Harry Perry	1959	Lucerne	Bronze	67kg
Colm McCoy	1959	Lucerne	Bronze	75kg
Jim McCourt	1965		Bronze	60kg
Mick Dowling	1965-71		Bronze	54kg
Niall McLoughlin	1971		Bronze	51kg
Phil Sutcliffe	1977-79		Bronze	48 + 51kg
Gerry Hawkins	1981		Bronze	48kg
Kieran Joyce	1983		Bronze	71kg
Sean Casey	1985		Bronze	51kg

Irish Amateur Boxing Senior Champions 1996

Weight	Boxer's Name & Club
48 Kg Light Flyweight	Jim Prior (Darndale)
51 Kg Flyweight	Damaen Kelly (Holy Trinity)
54 Kg Bantamweight	Damien McKenna (Holy Family, Drogheda)
57 Kg Featherweight	Adrian Patterson (St. Pat's, Newry)
60 Kg Lightweight	Martin Reneghan (Keady)
63.50 Kg Light Welterweight	Francis Barrett (Olympic)
67 Kg Welterweight	Neil Gough (St. Paul's, Waterford)
71 Kg Light Middleweight	Declan Higgins (Fermoy/Defence Forces)
75 Kg Middleweight	Brian Magee (Holy Trinity)
81 Kg Light Heavyweight	Stephen Kirk (Cairn Lodge)
91 Kg Heavyweight	Cathal O'Grady (St. Saviours)
91+ Kg Super Heavyweight	Sean Murphy (St. Michael's New Ross)

RUGBY

International Championship Winners (Five Nations)

1883 England	1909 Wales	& Wales	1956 Wales	1977 France
1884 England	1910 England	& Ireland	1957 England	1978 Wales
1886 England	1911 Wales	1933 Scotland	1958 England	1979 Wales
& Scotland	1912 England	1934 England	1959 France	1980 England
1887 Scotland	& Ireland	1935 Ireland	1960 France	1981 France
1890 England	1913 England	1936 Wales	& England	1982 Ireland
& Scotland	1914 England	1937 England	1961 France	1983 France
1891 Scotland	1920 England	1938 Scotland	1962 France	& Ireland
1892 England	& Scotland	1939 England	1963 England	1984 Scotland
1893 Wales	& Wales	& Wales	1964 Scotland	1985 Ireland
1894 Ireland	1921 England	& Ireland	& Wales	1986 France
1895 Scotland	1922 Wales	1947 Wales	1965 Wales	& Scotland
1896 Ireland	1923 England	& England	1966 Wales	1987 France
1899 Ireland	1924 England	1948 Ireland	1967 France	1988 Wales
1900 Wales	1925 Scotland	1949 Ireland	1968 France	& France
1901 Scotland	1926 Scotland	1950 Wales	1969 Wales	1989 France
1902 Wales	& Ireland	1951 Ireland	1970 France	1990 Scotland
1903 Scotland	1927 Scotland	1952 Wales	& Wales	1991 England
1904 Scotland	& Ireland	1953 England	1971 Wales	1992 England
1905 Wales	1928 England	1954 England	1973 Quintuple Tie	1993 France
1906 Ireland	1929 Scotland	& France	incl...... Ireland	1994 Wales
& Wales	1930 England	& Wales	1974 Ireland	1995 England
1907 Scotland	1931 Wales	1955 France	1975 Wales	1996 England
1908 Wales	1932 England	& Wales	1976 Wales	

Irish Rugby Football Statistics

Founded (as I.R.F.U.)	1879
President	Dr. S. Millar
Number of rugby players in Ireland	50,000
Number of National league clubs	19
Number of senior graded clubs	28
Main Stadium	Lansdowne Road
Biggest crowd at a rugby fixture	50,000 (full capacity of Lansdowne Road) 25,900 seated
Provincial champions	Leinster
First rugby football club founded in Ireland	Dublin University R.C. (1854)
Oldest six clubs in operation for over 100 years	NIFC (1868)
	Wanderers (1869), Queen's University (1869)
	Lansdowne (1872), Dungannon (1873)

....UCC (1874), Ballinasloe (1875)
First International match played...February 1875 (Versus England)
First fifteen a side match..1877
Best World Cup performance...Quarter-finals 1987, 1991 and 1995
Grand Slam 1 (1948)
Triple Crown 6 (1894, 1899, 1948, 1949, 1982, 1985)
International Championship wins ....18 (10 outright)

Rugby: Number of Clubs, Commercial Clubs and Schools

	Clubs	Commercial Clubs	Schools
Ulster	57	17	91
Munster	59	5	34
Leinster	71	8	62
Connacht	21	0	16
London Irish (affiliated to IRFU)	1		
	209	**30**	**203**

Top Ten most capped Irish Rugby players

Player	Number of Caps	Player	Number of Caps
C. M. H. Gibson (1964-79)	69	D. G. Lenihan	52
W. J. McBride	63	M. I. Keane	51
J. F. Slattery	61	J. W. Kyle	46
P. A. Orr	58	K. W. Kennedy	45
T. J. Kiernan	54	B. I. Mullin	45

SWIMMING

Association founded:..1893
Current President.. Peter Brennan
Total number of clubs 135
Leinster 51
Munster 21
Ulster...45
Connacht..18
I.A.S.A. registered swimmers nationwide 6,000
Number of swimming pools nationwide 219
Largest crowd at swimming fixture.................................500 (Leisureland International Swim Meet, Galway) annually

Womens Individual National Swimming Champions / Irish Record Holders

Race	1996 Champion	Club	Time	Irish Recrd Holder (club)	Time
50m Freestyle	Chantal Gibney	Trojan	26.39	Michelle Smith (Kings Hos.)	25.85
100m Freestyle	Chantal Gibney	Trojan	58.55	Michelle Smith (Kings Hos.)	54.87
200m Freestyle	Chantal Gibney	Trojan	2:07.98	Marion Madine (Leander)	2:01.65
400m Freestyle	Niamh Hennessy	Glenalbyn	4:35.24	Marion Madine (Leander)	4:15.77
800 Freestyle	Rachael Lee	Coolmine	9:23.85	Michelle Smith (Kings Hos.)	8:44.06
50m Backstroke	Lee Kelleher	City of Cork	31.29	Niamh O'Connor (New Ross)	29.44
100m Backstroke	Claire Hogan	St. Paul's	1:05.24	Michelle Smith (Kings Hos.)	1:02.36
200m Backstroke	Niamh Cawley	Claremorris	2:19.82	Michelle Smith (Kings Hos.)	2:10.76
50m Breaststroke	Gina Galligan	Trojan	32.94	Gina Galligan (Trojan)	32.47
100m Breaststroke	Louise Robinson	Coleraine	1:13.43	Siobhan Doyle (Glenalbyn)	1:10.71
200m Breaststroke	Mary Corless	Tuam	2:36.94	Sharlene Brown (Lisburn)	2:32.26
50m Butterfly	Lee Kelleher	City of Cork	29.31	Michelle Smith (Kings Hos.)	28.15
100m Butterfly	Lee Kelleher	City of Cork	1:04.14	Michelle Smith (Kings Hos.)	59.99
200m Butterfly	Lee Kelleher	City of Cork	2:20.54	Michelle Smith (Kings Hos.)	2:07.61

100m Indvidual Medley ....Lee Kelleher .....City of Cork....1:07.39 ....Michelle Smith (Kings Hos.) 1:02.70
200m Individual Medley..........Lee Kelleher .....City of Cork....2:24.42 ....Michelle Smith (Kings Hos.) 2:13.46
400m Individual Medley ......Sally O'Herlihy.............Trojan....5:05.70 ....Michelle Smith (Kings Hos.) 4:36.84

Mens Individual National Swimming Champions and Irish Record Holders

Race	1996 Champion	Club	Time	Irish Recrd Holder (club)	Time
50m Freestyle	Michael Giles	Coolmine	23.58	Nick O'Hare (Coolmine)	22.79
100m Freestyle	Michael Giles	Coolmine	51.70	Earl McCarthy (Aer Lingus)	50.18
200m Freestyle	Colin Louth	Cormorant	1:53.67	Ken Turner (C.R.C.)	1:49.38
400m Freestyle	Colin Louth	Cormorant	4:04.23	Ken Turner (Glenalbyn)	3:53.82
1500m Freestyle	Ciaran Kearney	Limerick	16:00.97	Ken Turner (Aer Lingus)	15:33.57
50m Backstroke	Hugh O'Connor	New Ross	26.81	Adrian O'Connor (New Ross)	25.80
100m Backstroke	Hugh O'Connor	New Ross	56.51	Adrian O'Connor (New Ross)	55.23
200m Backstroke	Julian Dooley	Terenure Col	2:06.07	Adrian O'Connor (New Ross)	1:59.71
50m Breaststroke	Michael Giles	Coolmine	29.58	Gary O'Toole (Trojan)	28.59
100m Breaststroke	Michael Giles	Coolmine	1:03.53	Gary O'Toole (Triton)	1:01.87
200m Breaststroke	Daragh Sharkey	Trojan	2:16.48	Gary O'Toole (Trojan)	2:11.35
50m Butterfly	Donncha Redmond	Trojan	25.95	Gary O'Toole (Triton)	25.48
100m Butterfly	Donncha Redmond	Templeogue	56.66	Declan Byrne (Trojan)	55.41
200m Butterfly	Colin Louth	Cormorant	2:03.49	Colin Louth (Cormorant)	2:02.51
100m Indvidual Medley	Daragh Sharkey	Trojan	58.74	Standard	57.39
200m Individual Medley	Julian Dooley	Terenure Col	2:07.44	Gary O'Toole (Trojan)	2:02.23
400m Individual Medley	Daragh Sharkey	Trojan	4:27.71	Gary O'Toole (Triton)	4:22.97

Relay: National Swimming Champions and Irish Record Holders

Race	1996 Champions	Time	Irish Recrd Holders	Time
MEN				
4 x 200m Free Relay	Trojan	7:45.82	Glenalbyn	7:34.35
4 x 100m Med. Relay	Trojan	3:54.79	Trojan	3:51.30
4 x 100m Free Relay	Trojan	3:31.18	Coolmine	3:25.47
WOMEN				
4 x 100 Med. Relay	Glenalbyn	4:37.46	Glenalbyn	4:22.99
4 x 100 Free Relay	Trojan	4.00.19	Leander	3:59.74

PARALYMPICS

Irish Medal Winners at 1996 Paralympic Games (Atlanta, U.S.A.)

GOLD
Bridie Lynch (Blindsports) ....Discus

SILVER
Michael Barry (Cerebral Palsy) ....Swimming - 50m Backstroke
David Malone (Wheelchair Association) .... Swimming - 100m backstroke
Tom Leahy (Cerebral Palsy) ....Boccia

BRONZE
Bridie Lynch (Blindsports) ....Shot Putt
Joan Salmon (Blindsports)...Equestrian
Sean O'Grady (Wheelchair Association)..Discus
Grainne Barrett Condron (Wheelchair Association) ....Shot Putt
Sharon Rice (Cerebral Palsy) ....Shot Putt
Mary Rice (Cerebral Palsy)...200 Metres

ATHLETICS

Number of senior athletic clubs in Ireland...144
Number of juvenile athletic clubs in Ireland 135
National registered membership of all athletic clubs..16,495
Main stadia and capacity ....Morton Stadium, Dublin (10,000)
Mardyke Stadium, Cork (8,000)
Tullamore Harriers A.C. (5,000)
Biggest crowd at an athletics meeting ....25,000 - 30,000 (World Cross Country Championship), Limerick 1979

IRISH ATHLETES WHO HAVE WON EUROPEAN CHAMPIONSHIP MEDALS

1967, 1968, 1969...Noel Carroll (800m indoor) - gold
1969...Frank Murphy (1,500m outdoor) - silver
1975 ....John Treacy (5,000m Junior outdoor) - silver
1978 ....Eamon Coghlan (1,500m outdoor) - silver
1979...Eamon Coghlan (1,500m indoor) - gold
1981 ....Ray Flynn(1,500m indoor) - silver
1981 ....Mary Purcell (1,500m indoor) - bronze
1985 ....Marcus O'Sullivan (1,500m indoor) - silver
1985 ....Nick O'Brien (3,000m Junior outdoor) - gold
1991 ....Mark Carroll (5,000m Junior outdoor) - gold
1994 ....Sonia O'Sullivan (3,000m outdoor) - gold
1994...Catherina McKiernan (Cross-Country) - gold

IRISH ATHLETES WHO HAVE WON WORLD CHAMPIONSHIP MEDALS

1970...John Hartnett (World Junior Cross Country) - gold
1978, 1979 ....John Treacy (World Cross Country Championship) - gold
1979...Irish Cross Country team (World Cross Country Championship) - silver
1983..Eamon Coghlan (5,000m outdoor) - gold
1987, 1989, 1993 ....Marcus O'Sullivan (1,500m outdoor) - gold
1987, 1991..Frank O'Mara (3,000m indoor) - gold
1992, 1993, 1994 and 1995...................................Catherina McKiernan (World Cross Country Championship) - silver
1995 ....Sonia O'Sullivan (5,000m outdoor) - gold

CURRENT IRISH TRACK AND FIELD CHAMPIONS

Men	Women
100m ....Neil Ryan (10.74)	100m ....Lea Barry (12.35)
200m...Gary Ryan (21.10)	200m...................................Jacqui Stokes (24.46)
400m ....Eugene Farrell (47.56)	400m ....Emma Nicholson (54.79)
800m ....David Matthews (1.48.10)	800m ....Freda Davorish (2.05.65)
1,500m ....Niall Bruton (3.41.68)	1,500m...................................Sonia O'Sullivan (4.15.24)
5,000m ....John Daly (14.34.82)	5,000m ....Catherina McKiernan (15.27.10)
10,000m ....Sean Dollman (29.17.49)	100m Hurdles.......................Patricia Naughton (14.44)
3,000m Steeplechase ....John Murray (8.39.24)	400m Hurdles ....Susan Smith (56.01)
110m Hurdles............................Peter Coghlan (14.08)	High Jump ....Breda Brown (1.73)
400m Hurdles...............................Tom McGuirk (50.61)	Long Jump ....Jacqui Stokes (5.97)
High Jump ....Mark Mandy (2.23)	Triple Jump ....Siobhan Hoey (11.95)
Pole Vault ....Dylan McDermott (4.50)	Shot ....Emma Gavin (12.45)
Long Jump ....Ciaran McDonagh (7.74)	Discus ....Ailish O'Brien (41.06)
Triple Jump ....Michael McDonald (15.04)	Hammer ....Julie Kirkpatrick (48.90)
Shot ....John Farrrelly (15.12)	Javelin ....Alison Moffit (49.10)
Discus ....Nick Sweeney (60.66)	5,000m Walk....................Deirdre Gallagher (22.00.05)
Hammer ....Roman Linscheid (72.88)	
Javelin ....Terry McHugh (73.92)	
10,000m Walk ....Jimmy McDonald (41.02.52)	

Current Irish World Record Holders

Name	Event	Time	Date
Eamonn Coghlan.............................1 mile indoor ....3 mins 49.78 secs.................................27/02/83
Sonia O'Sullivan ....2,000m outdoor ....5 mins 25.36 secs 08/07/94

CYCLING

Federation founded:..1988
Current President... Pat McQuaid
Total number of clubs 124
Total membership (1995)..2,330
- Northern (Ulster Cycling Federation) membership 720
- Western membership 180
- Southern membership 390
- South-Eastern membership 225
- Eastern membership 240
- Mid-Eastern membership 575
Annual Budget £275,000

Irish Cycling Champions

Senior Road Race
Michael Fitzgerald ....Carrick Cidona CC

Junior Road Race
Robert Moore ....Stamullen RC

Senior 3 Road race
Martin Cronin....................................Corrib Wheelers

Veterans Road Race
Michael Carroll ....Bann Valley/Clarke Bros.

Ladies Road Race
Claire Moore.......................................Dungannon Whs.

Senior 25ml TT
Philip Collins ....Amev I.R.C.

Junior 25ml TT
Kirk Sloan ....Ards CC

Ladies 25ml TT
Claire Moore.......................................Dungannon Whs.

Senior 10ml TT
Philip Collins ....Amev I R.C.

Junior 10ml TT
Raymond Corbett ....Cork CC

Ladies 10ml TT
Claire Moore.......................................Dungannon Whs.

Senior 50ml TT
Scott Hamilton ....Banbridge CC

Hill Climb
William Byrne ....Sorrento CC

Senior Cyclo Cross 1994
Robin Seymour...No club

Junior Cyclo Cross 1994
Ciaran Steed................................Hillcrest Hire Kilcullen

Points Championship
Paul Giles.................................Bann Valley RC

MTB Championship (Expert)
Robin Seymour ....No club

Junior
Sean Herlihy...E.L.M.A.

Ladies
Tarja Owens ....Bray Whs.

Veterans
Alan Cranston..................................Team Madigan

FBD Milk RÁS
Paul McQuaid ....Ireland Lee Strand

Irish League of Credit Unions Junior Tour
Anthony Aspel..Britain

GOLF

President ....Eamon Curran
Number of Golf Clubs affiliated to G.U.I...349
Number of golfers in Ireland...97,000
Biggest crowd at a golfing championship ....50,000 (Irish Open Professional Championship) annually
Number of Dunhill Cup victories...2 (1988 and 1990)
Number of Private Courses...257
Number of Public Courses...5
Oldest club with continuous experience ....Royal Belfast (1881)

Carroll's Irish Open Winners and Venues

Venue	Year	Winner	Venue	Year	Winner
Woodbrook (Bray)	1963	B.J. Hunt	Woodbrook (Bray)	1970	B. Huggett
Woodbrook (Bray)	1964	C. O'Connor	Woodbrook (Bray)	1971	N.C. Coles
Cork (Little Island)	1965	N.C. Coles	Woodbrook (Bray)	1972	C. O'Connor
Royal Dublin (Bull Island)	1966	C. O'Connor	Woodbrook (Bray)	1973	P. McGuirk
Woodbrook (Bray)	1967	C. O'Connor	Woodbrook (Bray)	1974	B. Gallagher
Woodbrook (Bray)	1968	J. Martin	Woodbrook (Bray)	1975	C. O'Connor Jnr.
Woodbrook (Bray)	1969	R.D. Shade	Portmarnock (Dublin)	1976	B. Crenshaw

Venue	Year	Winner	Venue	Year	Winner
Portmarnock (Dublin)	1977	H. Green	Portmarnock (Dublin)	1987	B. Langer
Portmarnock (Dublin)	1978	K. Brown	Portmarnock (Dublin)	1988	I. Woosnam
Portmarnock (Dublin)	1979	M. James	Portmarnock (Dublin)	1989	I. Woosnam
Portmarnock (Dublin)	1980	M. James	Portmarnock (Dublin)	1990	J.M. Olazabal
Portmarnock (Dublin)	1981	S. Torrance	Killarney (Kerry)	1991	N. Faldo
Portmarnock (Dublin)	1982	J. O'Leary	Killarney (Kerry)	1992	N. Faldo
Royal Dublin (Bull Island)	1983	S. Ballesteros	Mount Juliet (Kilkenny)	1993	N. Faldo
Royal Dublin (Bull Island)	1984	B. Langer	Mount Juliet (Kilkenny)	1994	B. Langer
Royal Dublin (Bull Island)	1985	S. Ballesteros	Mount Juliet (Kilkenny)	1995	S. Torrance
Portmarnock (Dublin)	1986	S. Ballesteros	Druids Glen (Wicklow)	1996	C. Montgomerie

CRICKET

Biggest attendance at international fixture..4,000 (v West Indies 1995)
Number of clubs...160
Number of registered players...7,500
Number of provincial unions ....4 (Munster, Leinster, North, and North-West)
President ....AJ O'Riordan
Chairman...G Craig
Honourary Secretary...D Scott
National Coach..M Hendrick
Most capped player...SJS Warke (1981-1994)
Most runs...4003 (SJS Warke)
Most wickets...326 (JD Monteith)
Highest score..198 (IJ Anderson v Canadian XI 1973)
Best bowling analyses...9-26 (F Fee v Scotland 1957)
Most catches ....57 (AJ O'Riordan)
Quickest century ....51 mins (JA Prior v Warwickshire 1982)
Most centuries ....7 (IJ Anderson)
International matches played 1946-April 1995...273
Players used 181
Appearances...3,003
Average number of caps per player...16
1994 All Ireland Cup Winners...Limavady (v Strabane)
Northern Cricket Union 1994 League Winners ....Downpatrick
Munster Cricket Union 1994 League Winners...Church of Ireland
North-West Cricket Union 1994 League Winners..Limavady
Leinster Cricket Union 1994 League Winners ....Pembroke
Principal Grounds ....Malahide, Leinster, Clontarf, Downpatrick, Eglinton, and North of Ireland Cricket Clubs

LADIES CRICKET

Number of provincial unions...3 (North Leinster, South Leinster, Ulster)
Honourary Secretary..Judy Cohen
Number of branches of Irish Women's Cricket Union..2 (Leinster and Ulster)
Current provincial champions ....South Leinster
Number of players...1,235
Rank of Irish senior ladies team...No. 2 in Europe, No. 5 in World
Largest attendance ....300 (July 1995, European Cup Final)
President...Mary Hackett

TUG OF WAR

Founded..1967
Current chairman ....Jim Curtis
Main venue..Varies from year to year
Biggest crowd ever recorded...4,000 (Ferns, Co. Wexford)
Number of clubs affiliated 30
Number of members ....1,125 approx.
Number of medals won by Ireland's national team at 1995 European C'ships................4 (2 gold, 2 bronze)

SAILING

President Irish Sailing Association...W.P. Rodger Bannon
Number of Category 1 clubs...42
Number of Category 2 clubs...3
Number of Category 3 clubs...39
Total number of affiliated clubs...84

Sailing: Presidents Awards 1995

Junior Sailing...Laura Dillon
Cruising..W.M. Nixon
International Sailing Achievement...John Lavery & David O'Brien
Domestic Sailing Achievements..Ruan O'Tiarnaigh
Overall Award for Special Services to Sailing..Ken Ryan

SEA ANGLING

Irish Federation of Sea Anglers founded...1953
President..Captain Christy O'Toole
Number of clubs in Ulster...58
Number of clubs in Munster...41
Number of clubs in Leinster...73
Number of clubs in Connaught..18
Total number of clubs in Ireland...190

Selected Irish Record weights for various specimen

Brill...9lb 8oz
Cod...42lb
Herring...425 kilos
Mackerel..4lb 2oz
Monkfish...73lb
Plaice..8lb 23oz
Pollack...19lb 3oz
Ray - Sting...51lb
Shark - Blue...206lb

SURFING

Association founded:...1967
Current President...Brian Britton
Number of people employed by the Irish Surfing Association...6
Number of clubs affiliated to the Association...10
Total number of active registered members...983
Total female..183
Total male..800
Total estimated number participating in the sport in Ireland...3,000
Major championships hosted in Ireland......................................1972 European Championships (Lahinch, Co. Clare)
1985 European Championships (Rossnowlagh, Co. Donegal)
1997 European Championships (Bundoran, Co. Donegal)

FENCING

NORTHERN IRELAND

NIAFU affiliated adult clubs...4
NIAFU affiliated school clubs..8
Number of members...140
Largest fencing competition in Ireland..Northern Ireland Open
Men's Foil Champion..C. Kelly
Ladies Foil Champion...M. O'Reilly
Men's Epee Champion..R. Date
Ladies Epee Champion...H. Clarke
Men's Sabre Champion..D. McCusker

TENNIS

Association founded:..1895
Current President ....Mrs. Kay Stanton
Number of people playing tennis in Ireland ....Approx. 90,000
Number of clubs...220
Members affiliated to Tennis Ireland...40,000
Top world-ranked Irish male player...Owen Casey (302)
Top world-ranked Irish ladies player..Gina Niland (606)
Top world-ranked under-18 boy ....George McGill (320)
Top world-ranked under 18 girl ....Claire Curran (93)
Number of senior competitions held in Ireland in 1996..67
Number of registered coaches in Ireland (Level 1, 2, 3, and 4) 140

HOCKEY

(Men)

Association founded:..1893
Current President ....Marius Gallagher
Number of players...Approx. 15,000 in all of Ireland
Biggest recorded crowd.........................4,000 (European Nations' Cup Final) 27th Aug. 1995 at UCD, Belfield, Dublin
Current Provincial Champions.......................*Under 16 level*...Leinster
                                              Under 18 level..Leinster
                                              Under 21 level ....Ulster
                                              Junior...Ulster
                                              Senior ....Ulster
Irish Senior Cup Champions...Avoca Hockey Club
Irish Hockey Union Club Champions ....Instonians Hockey Club

(Ladies)

Association founded:..1894
Current President..Mrs. Anita Manning
Number of clubs affiliated 127
Number of schools available..187
Number of women playing hockey in Ireland ....Approx. 17,000 in all of Ireland
Number of schoolgirls playing hockey in Ireland ....Approx. 10,000
Biggest recorded crowd..........5,000 (8th Women's Hockey World Cup Final) 24th July 1994 at UCD, Belfield, Dublin
Current Irish Senior Cup Champions..Pegasus H.C., Belfast
Current Irish Senior League Champions...Muckross H.C., Dublin
Ireland's world ranking 11

ICE HOCKEY

Ice Hockey (Northern Ireland) Statistics

Current number of senior teams 1
Name of team...Castlereagh Knights Ice Hockey Club
Main stadium & capacity...Dundonald International Ice Bowl (1,500)
Largest recorded crowd ....2,000 (Castlereagh Flames vs Paisley Pirates) at Dundonald (06.03.1993)

ROWING

Founded..1899
1st National championships 1912
First overseas competition ....1870 (Trinity travelled to Henley)
Current L.A.R.U. President...Dermot Henihan
Number of clubs..65

Irish Rowing World Championship Medalists

Niall O'Toole (Gold) ....(Vienna, 1991) Lightweight Single Sculls
Sean Drea (Silver) ....(Nottingham, 1975) Lightweight Single Sculls
Niall O'Toole (Silver)..(Indianapolis, 1994) Lightweight Single Sculls
Neville Maxwell and Tony O'Connor (Bronze) ....(Indianapolis, 1994) Lightweight Coxless Pairs
Neville Maxwell and Tony O'Connor (Silver)........................(Strathclyde, 1996) Lightweight Coxless Pairs

MOTOR SPORT

R.I.A.C. National Rally Champions

Year	Driver				
1965/66	Noel Smith	1976	Sean Campbell	1987	Vincent Bonner
1966/67	Noel Smith	1977	John Coyne	1988	Ken Colbert
1967/68	Not awarded	1978	Mick O'Connell	1989	George Robinson
1968/69	Noel Smith	1979	Jer Buckley	1990	Richard Smyth
1969/70	Noel Smith	1980	Jer Buckley	1991	Donie Keating
1970/71	Eamonn Cotter	1981	Donie Keating	1992	Peadar Hurson
1972	Eamonn Cotter	1982	Eddie Colten	1993	Ian Greer
1973	Arnie Poole	1983	Bertie Law	1994	Micheal Farrell
1974	Sean Campbell	1984	Bertie Law	1995	Stephen Murphy
1975	Sean Campbell	1985	James Doherty		
		1986	Frank Meagher		

Analysis of Selected Motor Sport Events, 1990 - 1996

Year	'90	'91	'92	'93	'94	'95	'96
Car Race Meetings	13	13	12	13	12	13	13
Hill Climb/Sprints	7	6	10	9	8	8	9
Rallycross Meetings	8	8	7	7	9	7	7
Rallysprints	4	4	1	1	3	5	4
Kart Races	20	18	21	22	20	21	21
Tarmac Special Stage Rallies	20	22	19	20	20	20	21
Tarmac Single Stage Rallies	1	1	4	3	3	3	3
Forestry Stage Rallies	5	8	7	8	5	6	5

MOTOR CYCLING

Current President ....Mr. Frank Semple
Total number of clubs affiliated to M.C.U.I. 57
  - Ulster Centre 27
  - Southern Centre..30
Oldest event license holder..79 years
Best attended event..International North-West 200 road races
Approximate biggest crowd..100,000
1st Irish Motorcycle World Champion...Ralph Bryans (Belfast), 1965 c.c title
Most successful Irish rider ....Joey Dunlop (Ballymoney)
  - Winner of: ....19 Isle of Man TTs, 5 Formula One motorcycle World Championships

Current Motorcycle National Champions

Road Racing
125 c.c. ....Dennis McCullough
200 c.c. ....Brian Campbell
250 c.c. ....James Courtney
Junior..R.J. Hazelton
600 c.c. ....Chris Richardson
Senior ....James Courtney
Support 201-400 c.c. ....Nigel Watt
Support 401-750 c.c. ....Kenny Allen

Classic Classes
250 c.c. ....Derek Whalley
350 c.c. ....Norman Jamison
500 c.c. ....Danny Shimmin
1000 c.c. ....Billy Keenan

Irish Motorcross Championships
Open Class ....Philip McCullough
Support Class......................................Edward Allingham
125 c.c. ....Mark Norton

Irish Trials Champions
Grade A ....Paul McLoughlin
Grade B..Philip Harris
Grade C ....Alan Claffey
Junior..Gareth Andrews

Irish Enduro Championship
....Adrian Lappin

CAMOGIE

Number of clubs affiliated to the Association (Ireland) 470
Number of clubs affiliated to the Association (Abroad) 28
Total number of active registered members 74,290
Total female 72,929
Total male 1,361
Total estimated number playing camogie in Ireland 67,734
1995 Senior All-Ireland Champions...Cork
1995 Junior All-Ireland Champions ....Limerick
1995 Intermediate All-Ireland Champions...Clare
1995 Minor All Ireland Champions ....Wexford
Most All-Ireland Senior titles (county)..Dublin (26)
Most all Ireland Senior medals (player) ....Angela Downey, Kilkenny (12)

INDOOR BOWLING

Men's Bowling

President...Howard Mullan
Number of clubs in Ireland...1,100
Number of above clubs based in the North...950
Biggest Crowd recorded ....450 (National Championships at Antrim Forum, 1980)
Estimated number of members...5,000

Ladies Bowling

Association founded...1966
Main Stadiums and membership ....Belfast Indoor Bowling Stadium (2,570)
....County Antrim Indoor Bowling Stadium (1,170)
....Provincial Town's Indoor Bowling Club, Ballymoney (632)
Total number of registered lady bowlers 1996...668
Largest crowd ....700 daily (Ballymoney Stadium) International Series and British Isles Championships (Mar '95)
Current Singles Champion..Geraldine Law
Current Pairs Champions..................................Mary Jane Campbell & Nan Montgomery
Current Triples Champions.......................Mary Tosh, Margaret Boyd and Winnie Miller
Current Fours Champions....................Evelyn Smyth, Ena Smith, Daisy Frazer and Nan Allelly
President 1995 - 1996 ....Mabel Crawford
President 1996 - 1997 ....Gladys White
President 1997 - 1998 ....Beth Bailie

STADIA

Selected Sports Stadia in Ireland

Stadium	Capacity (approx.)
Croke Park, Dublin (Gaelic Games)	68,000
Semple Stadium, Thurles (Gaelic Games)	59,000
Lansdowne Road, Dublin (Rugby & Soccer internationals)	50,000
Pairc Ui Chaoimh, Cork (Gaelic Games)	50,000
Tighearnach's Park, Clones (Gaelic Games)	33,000
McHale Park, Mayo (Gaelic Games)	30,000
The Oval, Glentoran (Soccer)	30,000
Windsor Park, Linfield (Soccer)	29,000
Dalymount Park, Dublin (Soccer)	25,000
Oriel Park, Dundalk (Soccer)	20,000
Solitude, Cliftonville (Soccer)	17,000
The Showgrounds, Newry Town (Soccer)	15,000
New Grosvenor Stadium, Distillery (Soccer)	14,000
Bishopstown, Cork (Soccer)	13,000
Morton Stadium, Dublin (Athletics)	10,000
The Brandywell, Derry (Soccer)	10,000
King's Hall, Belfast (Boxing)	7,000
UCD, Belfield, Dublin (Hockey)	4,000
National Stadium, Dublin (Boxing)	2,000
Dundonald International Ice Bowl, Belfast (Ice hockey)	1,500
Leisureland, Galway (Swimming)	500

IRELAND'S MOST POPULAR SPORTS

Membership of Selected Sports in Ireland

Sport	Membership - Players
Athletics	16,495
Camogie	74,290
Cricket (Men)	7,500
Cricket (Women)	1,335
Cycling	2,330
Fencing	140
Gaelic Games	750,000
Golf	97,000
Hockey (Men)	15,000
Hockey (Ladies)	17,000
Indoor Bowling (Men)	5,000
Indoor Bowling (Ladies)	668
Rugby	50,000
Surfing	983
Tennis	40,000
Tug of War	1,125

IRISH SPORTING DIRECTORY

Sports Organisations in the Republic of Ireland, 1996

Angling Irish Federation of Sea Anglers, 67 Windsor Drive, Monkstown, Co. Dublin.

Irish Trout Fly Fishing Association Cullies, Co. Cavan.

National Coarse Fishing Fed. of Ire. "Blathin", Dublin Road, Cavan.

Athletics Bord Lúthchleas na hÉireann, 11 Prospect Rd., Glasnevin, Dublin 9.

National Athletic & Cultural Assoc. Claremont Stadium,, Commons Road, Navan, Co. Meath.

Irish Schools Athletic Association, 35 Bettyglen, Raheny, Dublin 5.

Archery Irish Amateur Archery Association, 61 Ashwood Road, Clondalkin, Dublin 22.

Aviation Irish Aviation Council, c/o 38 Pembroke Road, Dublin 4.

Irish Hang Gliding Association, House of Sport, Long Mile Road, Walkinstown, Dublin 12.

Parachute Association of Ireland, House of Sport, Long Mile Road, Walkinstown, Dublin 12.

Balloon and Airship Assoc. of Ireland 5 Cill Cais, Old Bawn, Tallaght,

Dublin 24.

Irish Micro-Light Aircraft Association, 6 Wilfield Park, Ballsbridge, Dublin 4.

Badminton Badminton Union of Ireland, Baldoyle Badminton Centre, Baldoyle Ind. Est., Grange Rd., Baldoyle, Dublin 13.

Baseball Irish Baseball & Softball Association, 14 Inishmaan Road, Whitehall, Dublin 9.

Basketball Irish Basketball Association, Tymon Park, Dublin 24.

Schoolgirls Basketball Assoc. of Ire., St. Paul's Secondary School, Monastervin, Co. Kildare.

Bowling Bowling League of Ireland, "Dookinelly", 13 Glenabbey Road, Mount Merrion, Dublin.

Ból Chumann na hÉireann, 22A Westcliffe, Ballincollig, Co. Cork.

Irish Ten Pin Bowling Association, 40 Cabinteely Green, Cabinteely, Dublin 18.

Boxing Irish Amateur Boxing Association, South Circular Road, Dublin 8.

Canoeing Irish Canoe Union,

House of Sport, Long Mile Rd., Walkinstown, Dublin 12.

Camogie Cumann Camógaíochta na nGael, Páirc an Chrócaigh, Dublin 3.

Community Games National Community Games, 22 Store Street, Dublin 1.

Cricket Irish Cricket Union, 45 Foxrock Park, Foxrock, Dublin 18.

Irish Womens Cricket Union, 50 St. Alban's Park, Dublin 4.

Croquet Croquet Association of Ireland, Flat 13, 65 Grosvenor Road, Rathgar, Dublin 6.

Cycling Federation of Irish Cyclists, 619 North Circular Road, Dublin 1.

Equestrian Sport Equestrian Federation of Ireland, Ashton House, Castleknock, Dublin 15.

Fencing Irish Amateur Fencing Federation, Branksome Dene, Frankfort Park, Dundrum, Dublin 14.

Gaelic Games Cumann Lúthchleas Gael, Páirc an Chrócaigh, Baile Átha Cliath 3.

Ladies Gaelic Football Association,

Rahugh, Kilbeggan, Co. Westmeath.

Golf Golfing Union of Ireland, Glencar House, 81 Eglinton Road, Donnybrook, Dublin 4.

Irish Ladies Golf Union, 1 Clonskeagh Square, Clonskeagh Road, Dublin 14.

Gymnastics
Irish Amateur Gymnastics, House of Sport, Long Mile Road, Walkinstown, Dublin 14.

Handball
Comhairle Liathróid Láimhe na hÉireann, Páirc an Chrócaigh, Baile Átha Cliath 3.

Irish Olympic Handball Association, Tymon Bawn Community Centre, Firhouse Road West, Old Bawn, Tallagh, Dublin 24.

Hockey Irish Hockey Union, 6A Woodbine Park, Blackrock, Co. Dublin.

Irish Ladies Hockey Union, 95 Sandymount Road, Dublin 4.

Horseshoe Pitching Horseshoe Pitchers Assoc. of Ire. Ballyroe, Grangemellon, Athy, Co. Kildare.

Judo Irish Judo Association, 79 Upper Dorset Street, Dublin 1.

Mini Sport Irish Mini Sport Movement, House of Sport, Long Mile Road, Walkinstown, Dublin 12.

Motor Cycling Motor Cycle Union

of Ireland, 94 Drogheda Street, Balbriggan, Co. Dublin.

Motor Rallying R.I.A.C., 34 Dawson Street, Dublin 2.

Mountaineering Mountaineering Council of Ireland, House of Sport, Long Mile Road, Walkinstown, Dublin 12.

Netball Republic of Ireland Netball Assoc., Tower Business Centre, Enterprise Centre, Pearse St., Dublin 2.

Orienteering Irish Orienteering Association, House of Sport, Long Mile Road, Walkinstown, Dublin 12.

Pitch and Putt Pitch & Putt Union of Ireland, House of Sport, Long Mile Road, Walkinstown, Dublin 12.

Racquetball Racquetball Association of Ireland, 29 Calderwood Road, Drumcondra, Dublin 9.

Rowing Irish Amateur Rowing Union, House of Sport, Long Mile Road, Walkinstown, Dublin 12.

Table Tennis Irish Table-Tennis Association, 46 Lorcan Villas, Santry, Dublin 9.

Tennis Tennis Ireland, Argyle Square, off Morehampton Rd. Donnybrook, Dublin 4.

Triathlon Irish Triathlon Association 202 St. Donagh's Road, Donaghmede, Dublin 13.

Tug-Of-War Irish Tug-Of-War Association, Omeath, Dundalk, Co. Louth.

Volleyball Volleyball Association of Ireland, Dublin Executive Offices, Red Cow, Naas Road, Dublin 12.

Water Polo Irish Water-Polo Association, 3 Strand Mews, Lea Road, Sandymount, Dublin 4.

Water-Skiing Irish Waterski Federation, 91 South Mall, Cork.

Weightlifting Irish Amateur Weightlifting Assoc., 27 O'Connell Gardens, Bath Avenue, Dublin 4.

Windsurfing Irish Windsurfing Association, 48 Marlfield Gardens, Cabinteely, Co. Dublin.

Wrestling Irish Amateur Wrestling Assoc., 32F Macken St., Dublin 2.

Disabled Sports Organisations
Irish Deaf Sports Organisation, 8 Dun Emer Dr, Dundrum, Dublin 16.

Irish Wheelchair Association, Sports Section, Aras Chuchuláin, Blackheath Drive, Clontarf, Dublin 3.

Special Olympics Ireland, House of Sport, Long Mile Road, Walkinstown, Dublin 12.

Irish Blindsports, 25 Turvey Close, Donabate, Dublin.

Cerebral Palsy Sport Ireland, Sandymount Avenue, Dublin 4.

Sports Organisations in Northern Ireland, 1996

Archery NI Archery Society, 17 Bridge Road, Kilmore, Lurgan BT67 9LA.

Athletics NI Amateur Athletic Federation, 106 Cumberland Road, Dundonald, Belfast, BT16 0BB.

Badminton Badminton Union of Ireland, House of Sport, Upper Malone Road, Belfast, BT9 5LA.

Basketball Ulster Basketball Association, 49 Glengoland Avenue, Dunmurry, Belfast.

Billiards NI Billiards & Snooker Control Co., 105 Glenburn Road, Dunmurry, Belfast.

Bowling Irish Bowling Association, 55 Beechgrove Park, Belfast BT6 0NQ.

Irish Indoor Bowling Association, 7 Cherryvalley Park West, Belfast BT5 6PU.

Irish Womens Indoor Bowling Assoc., 101 Skyline Drive, Lambeg, Lisburn, Antrim BT27 4HW.

Irish Womens Bowling Association, 102 Downview Park West, Belfast BT15 5HZ.

Boxing Ulster Provincial Council, Irish Amateur Boxing Assoc., 10 Tonagh Heights, Draperstown.

Camogie Ulster Camogie Council, 288 Falls Road, Belfast, BT12 6AN.

Canoeing Canoe Association of NI, 5 Edenderry Village, Belfast.

Cricket NI Cricket Association, House of Sport, Upper Malone Rd., Belfast, BT9 5LA.

NI Womens Cricket Union of Ireland, 18 Belvedere Park, Stranmillis Belfast BT9 5GS.

Cycling Ulster Cycling Federation, 108 Moneymore Road, Cookstown, Co. Tyrone BT80 9UU.

Fencing NI Amateur Fencing Union,

40 Groomsport Road, Bangor, Co Down BT20 5LR.

Football Irish Football Association, 20 Windsor Ave., Belfast BT9 6EG.

NI Boys Football Association, 15 Beechgrv. Rise, Belfast BT6 ONH.

NI Schools Football Association, 6 Prince Edward Drive, Belfast BT9 5GB.

NI Womens Football Association, 11 Ravenhill Gardens, Belfast.

Gaelic Games Gaelic Athletic Association, Ulster Council, Glenfield House, Ballybay, Co. Monaghan.

Gliding Ulster Gliding Club Ltd., Ardnagie House, Seacoast Road, Limavady, Co. Derry.

Golf Golfing Union of Ireland, UB, 58a High Street, Holywood, Co. Down BT18 9AE.

Irish Ladies Golf Union , Northern Executive, The Rock, Drumbo, BT27 5LB

Gymnastics NI Amateur Gymnastics Association, 58 Castlemore Avenue, Belfast.

Handball Ulster Handball Council, 19 Pinevalley Road, Rostrevor, Newry, Co. Down.

Hockey Ulster Branch Irish Hockey Union, House of Sport, Upper Malone Rd., Belfast, BT9 5LA.

Ulster Women's Hockey Union, 41 The Meadow, Antrim, Co. Antrim BT41 1EY.

NI Ice Hockey Association, Dundonald International Ice Bowl, 111 Old Dundonald Road, Belfast.

Ice Skating NI Ice Skating Association, 49 Moyne Park, Gilnahirk, Belfast BT5 7QT.

Jiu Jitsu NI Jiu Jitsu Association, 279 Coalisland Road, Dungannon, Co. Tyrone BT71 6ET.

Judo NI Judo Federation, 22 Drumcashel Court, Newry.

Karate NI Karate Board, 33 Corrina Park, Upper Dunmurry Lane, Belfast.

Karting NI Karting Association, 92

New Mills Rd., Coleraine, Co. Derry.

Martial Arts NI Martial Arts Commission, House of Sport, Upper Malone Rd., Belfast.

Mountaineering Mountaineering Council of Ireland, AFAS Office, House of Sport, Longmile Road, Dublin 12.

Netball NI Netball Association, 19 Ailsbury Road, Belfast.

Orienteering NI Orienteering Association, 42 The Gables, Randalstown, Co. Antrim BT41 3JY.

Racquetball Ulster Council, Racquetball Assoc., 13 Tullymore Gardens, Belfast BT11 8ND.

Rambling Ulster Federation of Rambling Clubs, 27 Slievegallion Drive, Belfast BT11 8JN.

Horse British Horse Society (NI Region) House of Sport, Upper Malone Rd., Belfast, BT9 5LA.

Rowing UB, Irish Amateur Rowing Union, 330 Stranmillis Rd., Belfast.

Rugby Irish Rugby Football Union (Ulster) 36 Donegal Park Avenue, Belfast BT15.

Shooting (All disciplines) The Sports Council for NI, House of Sport, Upper Malone Rd., Belfast.

Skiing NI Ski Council Ltd, 43 Ballymaconnel Road, Bangor, Co. Down BT20 5PS.

Squash Ulster Squash Rackets Association, 37 Ferris Bay Road, Islandmagee, Co. Antrim BT40 3RT.

Ulster Womens Squash Racket Association, 18 Onslow Gardens, Bangor.

Sub Aqua NI Federation of Sub Aqua Clubs, 13 Pinley Park, Banbridge, Co. Down, BT32 3TX.

Surfing NI Surfing Association, 24 Breandrum Court, Tempo Road, Enniskillen, Co. Fermanagh.

Swimming UB Irish Amateur Swimming Assoc., House of Sport, Upper Malone Rd., Belfast.

Table Tennis UB Ulster Table Tennis Assoc., 29 Knockgreenan

Avenue, Omagh, Co. Tyrone.

Taekwondo Taekwondo Association of NI, 20 Lester Avenue, Lisburn, Co. Antrim, BT28 3QD.

Tennis Ulster Branch, Tennis Ireland, 67 Dundela Street, Belfast.

Ten Pin Bowling NI Ten Pin Bowling Association, 172 Orritor Road, Cookstown, Co. Tyrone.

Trampoline NI Trampoline Association, Fir Tree Grove, 40 Monlough Road, Ballygowan.

Triathlon UB, Irish Triathlon Association 32 Sefton Drive, Belfast.

Tug Of War NI Tug Of War Association, 22 Annahugh Road, Loughgall, Co. Armagh BT61 8PQ.

Volleyball NI Volleyball Association, 29a Cranmore Gardens, Belfast.

Water Skiing Irish Water Ski Fed., NI Sub Comm., Craigavon Leisure Centre, Brownlow Road, Craigavon.

Water Polo Irish Water Polo Association, UB, 8 Hampton Gardens, Belfast.

Weightlifting NI Amateur Weightlifters Association, 71 Beechgrove Avenue, Belfast BT6.

Wrestling NI Olympic Wrestling Association, 62 Glenkeen Drive, Greenisland, Co. Antrim BT38 8XG.

Yachting Royal Yachting Association (NIC), House of Sport, Upper Malone Rd., Belfast.

Yoga Yoga Fellowship of NI, 13 Wynchurch Avenue, BT6 0JP.

Sports Organisations for the Disabled

NI Blind Sports 12 Sandford Avenue, Belfast, BT5 5NW.

Ulster Deaf Sports Council 11 Bute Park, Dundonald, Belfast.

NI Sports Association for People with a Mental Handicap 55 Main Street, Moira, Craigavon, Co. Armagh.

NI Paraplegic Association 45 Knightsbridge Court, Ballycrochan Road, Bangor.

WHO'S WHO IN IRISH SPORT

G.A.A.

Boothman, Jack: (born Wicklow) President of the Gaelic Athletic Association (1994-97) A veterinary surgeon by profession, he is the first Protestant to achieve the highest office within the organisation.

Canavan, Peter: (born Tyrone, 1971) Most feared forward in gaelic football. Deadly accurate from play and from frees, All-Star Canavan was the lynchpin of the Tyrone team who put two Ulster Senior Football titles back to back in 1995 and 1996. All-Ireland U-21 medalist with Tyrone.

Carey, Ciaran: (born Limerick, 1970). Centre half back and captain of the 1996 Munster hurling champions, Limerick, Carey was a member of the 1992 National Hurling League winning team. Made his debut for Limerick in 1988, has unsuccessfully competed in two All-Ireland finals.

Carey, D.J.: (born Kilkenny, 1971). The top scoring member of the Kilkenny side which won back-to-back All-Ireland hurling titles in 1992 and 1993. Holds All-Ireland medals at minor and U-21 and is an accomplished handballer and winner of many national titles in that sport.

Dowd, Tommy: (b. 1969, Leicester, England) Captain of the Meath team in 1996. Made his senior debut in 1990. All-Star award winner on three occasions, he has won 3 Leinster S.F.C. medals, 2 National League medals and 1 Railway Cup medal.

English, Nicky: (born Tipperary, 1962). The 1989 Texaco Hurling Sportstar of the Year, English has won two All Ireland hurling medals and a National hurling league medal. A winner of six All Star awards between 1983 and 1989 he is one of the most revered forwards in the game.

Griffin, Liam: Manager of the Wexford Hurling team, steering the county in 1996 to a first All-Ireland success since 1968. Griffin took on the job, having failed to get the post of minor manager, in October 1994.

McCartan, James: (born Down, 1971) Winner of two All-Ireland medals with Down in 1991 and 1994, and an All-Star in the same years, won an All-Ireland Minor medal with Down in 1987. Became household name in G.A.A. circles playing with Ireland in the

Compromise Rules series against Australia in 1990.

McCarthy, Teddy: (born Cork, 1965). Holder of four All Ireland medals, two in each code. Made history in 1990 when he became the first man to win All Ireland medals in both football and hurling in the one year. Also holds a National football league and a National hurling league winners medal.

McHugh, Martin: (born Donegal, 1961). Cavan football manager and analyst on RTE. Made senior debut with Donegal in 1980 aged 18, won an All-Ireland U-21 medal in 1982, 3 Ulster S.F.C. medals, an All-Ireland medal in 1992, and was awarded an All-Star in 1982 and 1992.

Mulvihill, Liam: (b. 1946). Formerly a national school teacher, has been the Director General of the GAA since 1979. Presided over the modernisation of the GAA through the ongoing development of Croke Park and various provincial grounds and a better marketing of the game in general.

Pilkington, Johnny: (born Offaly, 1969). All Ireland Senior Hurling Championship winner when a last gasp effort by Offaly overcame Limerick in the 1994 decider. The Birr player has also won a National hurling league medal and saw his club team beaten in the 1992 All Ireland club championship final.

Redmond, Charlie: (born Dublin, 1964). The darling of Hill 16, Charlie won an All Ireland Football medal in 1995 in his fourth final appearance. Dublin's best place kicker had the unhappy distinction of missing penalties in important games but that hoodoo now seems laid to rest.

Storey, Martin: (born Wexford, 1964). Captain of the Wexford hurling team who won All-Ireland title in 1996, defeating Limerick in the final. An All Star winner in 1993, made his senior debut in 1985.

Tohill, Anthony: (born Derry, 1971). Regarded as one of countries top gaelic footballers, won an All-Ireland medal with Derry in 1993, and an All-Star in 1992 and 1993. Played Australian Rules football in Melbourne, and has played soccer for Derry City in the League of Ireland.

SOCCER

Aldridge, John: (born Liverpool, 1958). Currently player-manager of

Tranmere Rovers, in a phenomenal goal scoring career has also played for Oxford, Liverpool, and Real Sociedad. Holder of the all time goal scoring record in the English league, has been capped 68 times for the Republic of Ireland between 1986 and 1996 and has found the net on 19 occasions.

Bonner, Packie: (Born, Donegal 1960). Legendary goalkeeper for both Glasgow Celtic and Republic of Ireland. Played in two World Cup final stages, in Italy in 1990 and in the U.S.A. in 1994. Played 80 times for Republic of Ireland.

Charlton, Jack: (born Newcastle, 1935). Manager of the Republic of Ireland soccer team from 1986 until 1995, during which time the team enjoyed unprecedented success qualifying for two World Cups and a European Championship. Holds a World Cup Winners medal from the 1966 English success.

Dowie, Ian: (born Hatfield, 1965). Northern Ireland international Joined West Ham for 1995/96 season, having previously played for Crystal Palace, Southampton and Luton.

Gillespie, Keith: (born Larne, 1975). Northern Ireland international. Joined Newcastle United from Manchester United in January 1995 as part of the £7m deal which brought Andy Cole to Manchester United. One of the most naturally gifted players in the English Premiership.

Houghton, Ray: (born Glasgow, 1962). Scorer of the Republic's most famous international goal when he headed the ball into the English net at the 1988 European Championships. Now a Crystal Palace clubman Houghton - who has won 67 caps - previously played with Oxford, Liverpool, and Aston Villa. Has two FA Cup and two League Championship medals.

Hughes, Michael: (born Larne, 1971). Northern Ireland International player. Has Played for West Ham since 1994/95 season, having joined Manchester City in 1988. Moved to Strasbourg (France) at end of 1991/92 season until signing for West Ham.

Irwin, Denis: (born Cork, 1965). A permanent fixture on the Manchester United team since 1990 (he previously played with Leeds United and Oldham). An excellent defender he has played in two World Cups (1990 and 1994) with the Republic of Ireland and has won 41 caps.

Keane, Roy: (born Cork, 1971). Currently playing with Manchester United (he transferred from Nottingham Forest in 1993) he holds FA Cup and League Championship medals. A central player for United he is also central to the Republic of Ireland team, with whom he has won 30 caps, despite initial difficulties in his relationship with newly appointed manager, Mick McCarthy.

McCarthy, Mick: (born Barnsley, 1959). The former Manchester City and Glasgow Celtic player has managed the Republic of Ireland team since January of 1996. As a player he won 56 caps for the Republic and captained the side during the World Cup finals in 1990.

McGrath, Paul: (born London, 1959). Capped 82 times for the Republic of Ireland, scoring 8 goals during that time, is the team's most capped player. Overcoming serious knee problems he has proven himself to be one of the outstanding defenders in European football . Former Manchester United player he now plays with Aston Villa. Has an FA Cup medal. Named Player's Player of the Year in 1993 by his Premiership colleagues.

Morrow, Steve: (born Belfast, 1970). Northern Ireland international player. Joined Arsenal for 1992/93 season, having played for Barnet, Reading, and Watford.

Quinn, Niall: (born Dublin, 1966). First capped in 1986 Quinn has a total of 61 Irish appearances scoring 17 goals. Former hurler and gaelic footballer, Quinn plays with Sunderland in the English Premiership, after his transfer from Manchester City earlier this season.

Staunton, Steve: (born Drogheda, 1969). The former Liverpool player now plys his trade with Aston Villa. An FA Cup and League medal winner with Liverpool. Has played with the Republic since 1989 playing in two World Cups, 'Stan' has won 63 caps and scored 6 goals.

Townsend, Andy: (born Maidstone, 1963) The captain of the Republic of Ireland team (with whom he has won 61 caps) he is an integral part of the midfield. Having previously played with Norwich and Chelsea he now captains the Aston Villa team.

Worthington, Nigel: (born Ballymena, 1961). Began career in 1981/82 with Nottingham County. In February 1984 joined Sheffield Wednesday before moving to Leeds United for 1994/95 season. Currently with Stoke City. Regular in the Northern Ireland shirt.

ATHLETICS

McHugh, Terry: (born Tipperary, 1963). The only Irish athlete to compete in both Summer and Winter Olympics (Javelin and Bobsleigh). Competed in the Javelin in the Atlanta Olympics. His best result was finishing a very credible tenth in the 1993 World Championship. Holds the Irish Javelin record. Captain of the Irish team at the 1996 Olympics.

McKiernan, Catherina: (born Cavan, 1969). 10,000m Irish record holder McKiernan competed in the 1996 Olympic 10,000m finishing out of the medals. Better known as a cross-country runner she won the World Cross Country Grand-Prix series on four consecutive occasions between 1992 and 1995 and has won four silver medals at the World Cross Country Championships.

O'Sullivan, Marcus: (born Cork, 1961). After posting a personal best time for the 1500m in early 1996, O'Sullivan competed in his fourth Olympic games at Atlanta. Supremely successful as an indoor athlete he won back-to-back World Indoor Championship gold medals in 1987 and 1989 and again in 1993 (all in the 1,500m) and was considered the best indoor miler in the world in his prime winning six Wannamaker Miles.

O'Sullivan, Sonia: (born Cork, 1969). Ireland's top female athlete Sonia holds the Irish records for all track events from 800m to 5,000m. Unbeaten on the European Grand Prix circuit in 1996 prior to the Atlanta Olympics. Current European and World 5,000m champion, silver medallist in the 1,500m at the 1993 World Championships. Holds the world 2,000m record and the European 3,000m record. Had a disappointing time at 1996 Olympic games in Atlanta, where she was odds on favourite for two gold medals but lost out totally due to viral illness.

SWIMMING

O'Toole, Gary: (born Wicklow, 1968). First Irish swimmer to win any kind of medal in top international competition when he won silver in the 200m breaststroke at the 1989 European Championships. In 1991 won gold in the 200m breaststroke at the World Student Games. Competed in two Olympics (1988 and 1992) and broke national records with apparent ease. Acclaimed for his role as swimming analyst for RTE during Atlanta Olympics.

Smith, Michelle: (born Dublin, 1969). Ireland's golden girl from the pool at the Atlanta Olympics winning gold in the 400m Individual Medley, 400m freestyle, 200m individual medley, and bronze in the 200m butterfly, becoming Ireland's first female Olympic medallist. She set national records in each event and has won more Olympic medals than any other Irish person. Smith also won double gold in the 1995 European Championships in the 200m medley and 200m butterfly.

BOXING

Barrett, Francis: (born Galway, 1977). The first member of the travelling community to represent Ireland at the Olympic Games where he fought in the welterweight division, reaching the second round. Had the honour of leading the Irish team into the Olympic stadium and carrying the Tricolour.

Carruth, Michael: (born Dublin, 1967). Will be forever remembered for his Olympic welterweight gold medal winning performance at the Barcelona Olympics in 1992. The former army sergeant has since turned professional.

Collins, Steve: (born Dublin, 1964). W.B.O. Super-Middleweight Champion of the world, a title he won in 1995 by defeating Britain's Chris Eubank. Has since defended his title against both Eubank and Nigel Benn. Collins had suffered two world title fight defeats before finally winning his title.

Kelly, Damean: (born Belfast) Represented Ireland in the flyweight division at the Atlanta Olympics, reaching the quarter final. His previous international tournament bests were winning bronze at the 1993 World Senior Championship and bronze again at this year's European Seniors.

Loughran, Eamonn: (born Antrim, 1970). Former Welterweight World Champion, lost his title in May 1996. Had a much lower profile than other Irish world champions. Injury worries may force a premature end to his career.

McCullough, Wayne: (born Belfast, 1970). The WBC Featherweight World Champion, he has defended the title successfully. Before turning professional in 1993 he won a silver medal in the Bantamweight division at the Barcelona Olympics in 1992 and a Commonwealth Games gold medal at Fly-weight in 1990.

SNOOKER

Doherty, Ken: (born Dublin, 1969). World Amateur Champion in 1989 he turned professional in 1990, enjoying some success in reaching the latter stages of major world ranking tournaments. Has suffered a slump in form in recent times.

Higgins, Alex: (born Belfast, 1949). A snooker professional since 1971, has been World Champion twice, 1972 and 1982. The most popular -and controversial - snooker player ever to grace the green baize he won two Benson & Hedges titles, a UK Championship, and the Benson & Hedges Irish Masters among others.

Taylor, Denis: (born Tyrone, 1949). 1985 Embassy World Champion after an epic 18-17 frame victory over Steve Davis. Turned professional in 1971, winning the Benson & Hedges Masters and the Rothman's Grand Prix in the 1980s. Has also made his mark as a snooker commentator.

GOLF

D'Arcy, Eamon: (born Delgany, 1952). Turned professional as a 17 year old, D'Arcy has won numerous titles and captained the 1988 Irish Dunhill Cup team to victory. Has represented Europe in Four Ryder Cups between 1975 and 1987.

Harrington, Padraig: (born Dublin, 1971). A new professional, Harrington won the Spanish Open in 1996, and by July 1996 was seventh in the European order of merit with prize winnings of £194,363. As an amateur he played in the Walker Cup twice.

McGinley, Paul: (born Dublin, 1967). After a knee injury ended a promising gaelic football career, McGinley concentrated on golf and turned professional in 1991. Has proved to be one of the finest young golfers on the current European circuit. Winner of Austrian Open in

August 1996.

Rafferty, Ronan: (born Down, 1964). An outstanding amateur golfer, Rafferty turned professional in 1981 and has won numerous tournaments including the Scandinavian Open (1989), the Volvo Masters (1989), and the 1993 Austrian Open. Twice a member of Irish Dunhill Cup winning teams and a member of the 1989 Ryder Cup team (he finished top of golf's order of merit that year). One of Ireland's highest profile golfers.

Walton, Philip: (born Dublin, 1962). After a successful amateur career Walton turned professional in 1983. A member of the victorious Irish Dunhill Cup team in 1990, he played an important part in Europe's 1995 Ryder Cup victory in America. Has won many titles including the French Open.

RUGBY

Bradley, Michael: (born Cork, 1962). Former scrum half and captain of the Irish international team. A Cork Constitution player, captained them to their 1991 All Ireland league victory.

Clohessy, Peter: (born Limerick, 1966). Plays his club rugby with Young Munster, with whom he has won All Ireland League medals. Recognised as a tough player he won his first cap for Ireland in the 1992 Five Nations championship. Played a significant part in Munster's famous 1992 victory over Australia. Received a suspension and much adverse publicity for dangerous play in this years Five Nations.

Costello, Victor: (born Dublin, 1970). A former Irish Olympian (he represented Ireland in the shot putt in 1992 at Barcelona) has since concentrated on rugby.

Geoghegan, Simon: (born Herefordshire, 1968). Currently playing with Wasps in England Geoghegan used to play for London Irish. The most exciting player on the Irish team, scorer of numerous breathtaking tries for club and country, he recently underwent an operation for a leg injury.

Mullins, Brendan: (born Israel, 1963). The only remaining link with the Triple Crown winning team of 1985 Mullins had a prolific scoretrying international career. Currently playing with Blackrock in the All Ireland league. A talented athlete he has represented Ireland internationally in the 110m hurdles.

Popplewell, Nick: (born Dublin, 1964) Prop forward on the Irish international team 'Poppy' plays his club rugby in England, having previously played with Greystones. He has also played with the Lions.

HORSE RACING

Bolger, Jim: (b. 1941). One of Ireland's foremost racehorse trainers and bloodstock breeder. Has had many prestigious winners in a relatively short time since becoming a trainer in 1976.

Dunwoody, Richard: (born Down, 1964). National Hunt jockey who has won, among others, two Aintree Grand Nationals, two King George V's and the Cheltenham Gold Cups. He is considered one of the finest jockeys in Britain and Ireland.

Eddery, Pat: (born Dublin, 1952). Has been champion jockey (on the flat) in Britain nine times between 1974 and 1991. Has rode in excess of 3,500 winners including numerous classics in both England and Ireland.

Kinane, Mick: (born Tipperary, 1959). Irish champion jockey (on the flat) a record nine times between 1984 and 1993. He has had classic wins in Ireland, England, France, Italy, America, and Australia. Perhaps most famously he won the Melbourne Gold Cup on Vintage Crop in 1993.

Maguire, Adrian: (b. 1971). Champion point-to-point rider in 1990/91. Youngest ever winning jockey of Irish Grand National in 1991. Rode 71 winners in 1991/92 season, including the Cheltenham Gold Cup. Rode 124 winners the following season, and just lost out to Richard Dunwoody for jockeys championship in 1993/94, earning £1,193,917 en-route. Enjoys a huge reputation for a young jockey.

O'Brien, Vincent: (b. 1917). Irish racehorse trainer of international repute. An amateur jockey in his youth, he obtained his training license in 1943. Has won innumerable major Irish and English steeplechases and classics. One of a handful of Irish sporting personalities to be rightly labelled - "a legend in his own lifetime".

O'Neill, Jonjo: (born Cork, 1952). As a jockey he had over 900 winners between 1972 and 1986. Along with Dawn Run he completed a unique Cheltenham double of the Champion Hurdle in 1984 and the Gold Cup in 1986. Since retiring from the saddle he has concentrated on training.

Weld, Dermot: (born Surrey, 1948). Ireland's most successful trainer on the flat he has trained over 2,000 winners including eight classic winners (in both England and Ireland) and was the trainer of Vintage Crop who won the 1993 Melbourne Cup. A former champion jockey in the late 1960's, early 1970's. He has been the Texaco Horse Racing Sportstar of the Year on two occasions.

OTHER SPORTS

Dunlop, Joey : (born Antrim, 1952). The greatest T.T. racer ever. From the road racing motorcycling Dunlop family, Joey has been the outstanding racer of the 1980s and early 1990s. Five times World T.T. Champion between 1982 and 1986 he has also won an endless list of races in Ireland and the Isle of Man.

Fisher, Bertie: (born Fermanagh, 1950). One of the most popular rally drivers in the country Fisher has won numerous rallies including multiple Donegal, Killarney, and Ulster rallies. Has won the Irish Tarmac Driver's Championship three times.

Irvine, Eddie: (born Down) Formula One racing driver who currently drives with Ferrari. Previously was a member of the Irish Jordan Peugeot team. Despite a few podium finishes he has yet to win his first Grand Prix.

Lynch, Bridie: (born Donegal, 1965) 1996 Paralympic gold and bronze medalist. Partially sighted discus thrower and shot putter. Competes at club level in Ireland with Finn Valley. Came to prominence winning bronze at European championships in 1983.

O'Toole, Niall: (born Dublin, 1970). Competed at Atlanta (in his second Olympics) in the single sculls. In 1991 O'Toole won gold and in 1994 silver at the World Championships over the 2000m course.

Stelfox, Dawson (b. 1959, Belfast). First Irishman to reach summit of Mount Everest, on 27 May 1993.

WHO WAS WHO OF IRISH SPORT

GAA

Barry-Murphy, Jimmy: (born Cork, 1954). Outstanding dual player who won six All-Ireland medals, one in football (1973) and five in hurling (between 1976 and 1986). His other achievements are almost as breathtaking, two All-Ireland Hurling Club Championships, two All-Ireland Football Club Championships, two National Hurling League titles, one National Football League title and four Railway Cup medals in Hurling. An All-Star winner on seven occasions, five in Hurling and two in Football. Retired in 1987. Regarded as the greatest dual player of the modern game.

Brady, Phil (born Cavan) Winner of three All-Ireland Football medals between 1947 and 1952. This Cavan midfielder has also won a National Football League medal (1948) and a Railway Cup medal (1950). Known in G.A.A. circles as The Gunner Brady.

Connolly, John: (born Galway , 1948). Eldest of the Hurling Connolly brothers, won an All-Ireland Hurling medal in 1980 with his brothers Michael, Padraic and Joe. Twice an All-Star Winner, was the the 1980 Texaco Hurler of the Year.

Cregan, Eamon: (born Limerick, 1946). Hurler who won an All-Ireland medal (1973), three Railway Cup medals and a National Hurling League Medal (1971). Won three All-Star awards. Former Offaly manager, steering them to victory over his native Limerick in 1994.

Doran, Tony: (born Wexford, 1946). One of Wexford's best known hurlers, played in twenty inter-county campaigns, winning an All-Ireland medal in 1968, two National Hurling League medals and seven Railway Cup medals (two of these as Captain). Won a Hurling All-Star at full forward, was Texaco Hurler of the Year in 1976. Retired from intercounty hurling in 1984 but led his club, Buffer's Alley to an All-Ireland Club Championship in 1989.

Doyle, Jimmy: (born Tipperary, 1939). Hurler, who in his sixteen years senior inter-county career won 6 All-Ireland medals between 1958 and 1971, when he came out of retirement, captaining his county in 1962 and 1965. He also won eight Railway Cup medals (a Tipperary record) and six National Hurling League medals. Texaco Hurler of the Year in 1965.

Earley, Dermot: (born Mayo, 1948). In a twenty-three year inter-county career was Roscommon's most outstanding player. All-Star Winner in 1974 and 1979, won two Railway Cup medals. Despite winning five Connacht Senior Football Championship titles between 1972 and 1980 he and Roscommon never won an All-Ireland title, he does however, hold a National Football League medal from 1979.

Heffernan, Kevin: (born Dublin, 1938). Football forward who captained Dublin to their 1958 All-Ireland win. Won three National Football League titles between 1953 and 1958 and seven Railway Cup medals (captaining Leinster in 1959). Went on to train the great Dublin team of the 1970's, steering them to three All-Ireland Senior Football titles.

Keating, Babs: (born Tipperary, 1944). Dual player who met with much success in hurling, winning three All-Ireland medals between 1964 and 1971, two Railway Cup Hurling medals and one Railway Cup Football (1972). Both an All-Star and Texaco Hurling Sportstar in 1971. Remembered for playing barefoot, later managed Tipperary to two All-Ireland Senior Hurling Championship titles and is current Laois Hurling manager.

Keaveney, Jimmy: (born Dublin, 1945). Dual player best remembered for his football exploits winning three All-Ireland Titles in 1974, 1976 and 1977 (coming out of retirement to do so). An excellent full forward, also won two National Football League medals, three All-Star Awards and two Texaco Gaelic Footballer of the Year Awards (1976 and 1977).

Keher, Eddie: (born Kilkenny, 1941). Deadly Kilkenny hurling marksman, made senior championship debut as seventeen year old in the 1959 All-Ireland Final Replay and played until 1977, winning six All-Ireland Senior Hurling Championship medals, nine Railway Cup medals and three National Hurling League medals along the way. Texaco Hurler of the Year in 1972 and an All-Star Winner on five successive occasions between 1971 and

1975.

Lynch, Jack: (born Cork, 1917). Dual player who won a record six consecutive All-Ireland medals between 1941 and 1946, five in hurling and one in football. Having made his debut in 1935, he retired in 1951 winning three National Hurling League medals and three Railway Cup medals. Entered the Dáil in 1948 and went on to become Taoiseach from 1966 to 1973 and from 1977 to 1979.

McCartan Snr., James: (born Down). Down midfielder who won All-Ireland Football medals in 1960 and 1961. Won three Railway Cup medals in 1964, 1965 and 1969 (as captain). His brother Dan, won three All-Ireland medals and his son James is the holder of two All-Ireland medals.

McCarthy, Liam: (born London, 1853). Born of Irish parents, McCarthy was the first treasurer of the London G.A.A. County Board. The cup which All-Ireland Hurling winning captains now receive bears his name. He presented the cup which was first awarded in 1923 (for the 1921 championship). Bob McConkey captained Limerick to victory on that occasion. In 1922, Kilkenny's Liam Fennelly was the first captain to be presented with the new Liam McCarthy cup.

McDonagh, Mattie: (born Galway, 1935). President Elect of the Gaelic Athletic Association, due to take office in Easter 1997. Holds four All-Ireland Football medals between 1956 and 1966 (was part of famous Galway three-in-a-row team of the mid 1960's). Won a Railway Cup medal in 1958, was Texaco Footballer of the Year in 1966.

McEniff, Brian: (born Donegal, 1943). Donegal footballer who won a National Football League medal with New York in 1964. An All-Star in 1972, won two Railway Cup medals with Ulster and is current manager of the Ulster Railway Cup team. As manager of Donegal, guided them to their first All-Ireland Senior Football Championship in 1992. Has managed the Ulster Railway Cup side since 1982, leading them to nine titles.

Mackey, Mick: (born Limerick, 1912; died 1982). Another legendary name in the annals of hurling. Won three All-Ireland Hurling medals with Limerick (1934, 1936 & 1940) captaining the team on two occasions, eight Railway Cup medals between 1934 and 1945 and five National Hurling League medals. It has been said that Mackey was to Hurling what Babe Ruth was to baseball.

Maguire, Sam: (born Cork, 1879; died, 1927). Gaelic footballer who played championship football for London in the early 1900's. Maguire had the distinction of swearing Michael Collins into the IRB and the cup which All-Ireland Football winning captains now receive bears his name. It was presented for the first time in 1928 (to Bill 'Squires' Gannon of Kildare).

Mullins, Brian: (born Dublin, 1954) Outstanding Gaelic football midfielder, won four All-Ireland Football medals between 1974 and 1983 (coming back from severe injury to win in 1983), contested a further five All-Ireland Finals but Kerry defeated Dublin in each of those. Won two National Football League medals and captained Leinster to Railway Cup success in 1985. Winner of two All-Star Awards, is the current Derry manager and brought the National Football League title to Derry in 1996.

O'Connell, Mick: (born Kerry, 1937). One of Gaelic

football's most famous names, won four All-Ireland Football medals with Kerry between 1959 (when he captained the team) and 1970, six National Football League medals and one Railway Cup medal. Won an All-Star award (1972) and was Texaco Footballer of the Year in 1962. O'Connell's high fielding was renowned and he is generally regarded as Gaelic Football's best ever midfielder.

O'Connor, Matt: (born Offaly, 1959). Won an All-Ireland Senior Football Championship medal in 1982, when Offaly put an end to Kerry's dream of five-in-a-row. The country's leading scorer for a record 5 years he won three All-Star awards in the early 80's. A serious car accident in 1984, cruelly ended his career.

O'Dwyer, Mick: (born Kerry, 1936). Winner of four All-Ireland Football medals between 1959 and 1970. His impressive collection also includes eight National Football League winners medals (between 1959 and 1974), a Railway Cup medal and Texaco Footballer of the Year 1969. Shortly after retiring, he became manager of the Kerry senior team and guided them to eight All-Ireland Senior Football Championship titles between 1975 and 1986.

O'Hehir, Michael (b. 1920, Dublin). Retired broadcaster. Worked with *Irish Independent* until 1960. Began his commentary on gaelic football and hurling in 1938. Also covered racing for RTE and BBC. First RTE Head of Sport (1960-72). Penned a weekly column with the *Irish Press*. Was most widely known and celebrated voice in Ireland up until his retirement due to a stroke.

O'Rourke, Colm: (born Meath, 1957). Inspiring Meath Gaelic Football football full forward who won two All-Ireland medals in 1987 and 1988 and two National Football League medals. Holds two All-Stars and in 1991 was the Texaco Footballer of the Year. Retired from inter-county football in 1995. Gaelic football analyst on R.T.E.'s Sunday Game.

O'Shea, Jack: (born Kerry, 1957). Finest Gaelic footballer of his era. Won seven All-Ireland Football medals from 1978 to 1986. Winner of six consecutive midfield All-Star Awards (1980 - 1985) and a record four Texaco Awards. 'Jacko' captained the Irish compromise rules teams against Australia in 1984 and 1986. Was manager of the Mayo team for a time and guided them to Connacht success in 1993.

Rackard, Nicky, Bobby & Billy: (born 1922, 1929 & 1930 respectively). Brothers who formed a formidable backbone in the Wexford Senior Hurling team of the 1950's. All three played in Wexford's All-Ireland Hurling Final successes of 1955 and 1956, while Billy also won an All-Ireland medal in 1960. Between them they also won six Railway Cup medals and three National Hurling medals. In 1992, both Billy and Bobby became All-Time All-Stars.

Ring, Christy: (born Cork, 1920; died 1979). Recognised as one of the all time greats in hurling. Won eight All-Ireland Hurling medals (three as captain) between 1941 and 1954, eighteen Railway Cup medals between 1942 and 1963, and four National Hurling League medals. Ring played with Cork from just after his nineteenth birthday until the age of forty-two.

Sheehy, Mikey: (born Kerry, 1954). Gaelic Footballer who won eight All-Ireland Football medals between 1975 and 1986. Won seven All-Star awards in an illustrious career.

Skehan, Noel: (born Kilkenny, 1946). Former

Kilkenny Hurling goalkeeper holds a record nine All-Ireland Senior Hurling Championship medals won between 1963 and 1983. Holds four Railway Cup medals. All-Star goalkeeper on seven occasions and Texaco Award Winner in 1982. Retiring from inter-county hurling at the age of thirty-nine, he went on to become an accomplished squash player.

SOCCER

Bambrick, Joe: (born Belfast, 1905). On Feb. 1st 1930 at Celtic Park, Belfast, scored a record six goals in a home international match against Wales making him the first British player to score a double hat-trick in a full international match. Scored twelve goals in only eleven international matches which was a N.I. record until surpassed by Colin Clarke in 1992. His nine goals for the Irish League is still a record

Best, George: (born 1946, Belfast). Regarded by most as the finest ever player born in Ireland, North or South. Joined Manchester Utd. in 1961, making senior debut in 1964. Won a European Cup winners medal in 1968 when United became the first English club to lift the trophy. Also won two English League Championship medals (in 1964-65 and 1967-68), a Fairs Cup medal in 1964-65. Was named European Player of the Year in 1968, the only Irish born player to receive the award.

Blanchflower, Danny: (born Belfast, 1925). Joined Tottenham Hotspur in December 1954 and had unprecedented success with the club. Played 337 league matches for Spurs, skippering them to the "double" of F.A. Cup and League championship victories in the 1960-61 season. Captained them to F.A. cup success the following year while the next year was a member of the side which became the first British club to lift a European trophy, the Cup Winners Cup. Played for N.I. 56 times captaining them to the last eight of the 1958 World Cup in Sweden. Voted "Footballer of the Year" in 1958 and 1961. Went on to manage N.I. from 1976 to 1979.

Bingham, Billy: (born Belfast, 1931). After a very successful career in English League soccer, during which he scored more than 100 goals, became one of the "greats" of Irish soccer when he managed the N.I. side to two World Cup final stages, in 1982 and 1986.

Bradley, Brendan: (born Derry, 1949). The League of Ireland"s all time leading goal scorer with 235 goals, 181 of which were scored for Donegal side, Finn Harps.

Brady, Liam: (born Dublin, 1956). Regarded as one of the greats of Irish soccer. Played 225 top flight games with Arsenal in the English League winning an F.A. Cup medal in 1979 and runners-up medals in 1978 and 1980. In 1979 was voted Player of the Year by both the Soccer Writers Association and his fellow professionals. Moved to Italy in the season 1980/81 and helped Juventus win two league titles in 1981 and 1982. Later played for Sampdoria, Inter Milan and Ascoli. Capped by Ireland when only 18 and subsequently played 71 times for his country. Managed Glasgow Celtic for a short period in the early '90s.

Brennan, Shay: (born Manchester, 1937). Capped 19 times by the Republic, was a member of the Manchester United side that lifted the European Cup in 1968.

Cantwell, Noel: (born Cork, 1932). Played 245 matches with West Ham between 1952 and 1960 before transferring to Manchester United where he was to

captain their F.A. Cup winning team of 1963. Club captain of the Man Utd side which won the League title in 1967. Capped 36 times for the Republic between 1954 and 1967 scoring ten goals. Later managed Coventry City. Also played as a cricket international, being capped five times by Ireland.

Carey, Jackie: (born Dublin, 1919). Played for Manchester United between 1936 and 1953 during which he played 306 games. Captained the side which won the F.A. Cup in 1948 (the club's first success in cup for 40 years) and won a championship medal in 1951-52. Was capped 29 times for the Republic and seven times for the North. Captained a Rest of Europe side against a Great Britain side in 1947. Was awarded the Footballer of the Year accolade for the season 1948-49.

Clarke, Colin: (born Newry, 1962). In 1992 broke the N.I. goal scoring record in internationals when he scored his 13th against Albania in a World Cup qualifying game.

Doherty, Peter: (born Magherafelt, 1913). Known as "Peter the Great" he won a League Championship medal with Manchester City in 1936-37. Later won a F.A. Cup medal with Derby County. Northern Ireland's first international team manager holding the post from 1951 to 1962, the highlight of which was bringing his side through, against all the odds, to the quarter-finals of the World Cup in Sweden in 1958.

Dougan, Derek: (born Belfast, 1938). His twelve goals in European competition remain a record for a N.I. player. Won 43 caps for Northern Ireland and was chairman of the Professional Footballers Association from 1970 until 1978.

Dunne, Jimmy: (born Dublin, 1905). "Snowy" Dunne joined Sheffield United in 1926 and within a few years was regarded as a great centre-forward. In the season 1929-30 he scored 36 goals in 39 games and 41 goals in 41 games the following season. On moving to Arsenal, won a First Division Championship medal in 1933-34 and later played for Southampton. In all scored 170 English League goals. Returned to League of Ireland football after his English career and recorded a further 52 senior goals with Shamrock Rovers. Capped fifteen times, scoring 12 international goals.

Dunne, Tony: (born Dublin, 1941). Played 529 at full back for Manchester United winning a European Cup medal in 1968. Regarded as possibly the best left back in Europe at that time, played 32 times for the Republic.

Farrell, Peter: (born Dublin, 1922). Scored the winning goal at Goodison Park, Everton, in 1949, for Ireland when they became the first team to defeat England on home soil. Capped 28 times for the Republic and seven times by the North.

Finucane, Al: (born Limerick, 1944). Oldest player to ever play in a European Cup tie, turning out for Limerick at the age of 44. Won eleven international caps.

Gallagher, Patsy: (born Donegal, 1894). One of the all time "Irish" soccer greats in Scottish football. Won six Scottish League championship medals with Glasgow Celtic in addition to his four Scottish Cup medals. Scored 184 goals for Celtic in 436 matches. Played eleven times for Northern Ireland.

Giles, Johnny: (born Dublin, 1940). In a great career in English soccer, played for Manchester United in the early part of career and won a F.A. Cup medal in 1963 with the "Reds". But his career was to blossom with the great Leeds United side he was to join shortly after that

F.A. cup win. At Leeds he played 380 times, scored 115 goals, won two championship medals, an F.A. Cup medal (1972), played in a further three losing finals and was capped sixty times by the Republic. Also won a Fairs Cup medal with Leeds in 1967-68.

Gregg, Harry: (born Derry, 1932). Northern Ireland international goalkeeper, capped 24 times. Voted "Goalkeeper of the Tournament" in the 1958 World Cup. Signed for a world record fee for a 'keeper, £24,000, when he moved from Doncaster Rovers to Manchester United in 1957. Survived the Munich air disaster in 1958.

Heighway, Steve: (born Dublin, 1947) One of the top Irish players of the 'Seventies winning five league championship medals with Liverpool and scoring a goal for the Liverpool team which defeated Newcastle United in the 1974 F.A. Cup final. Was a member of the Liverpool side which won three European Cups, 1976-77, 1977-78, and 1980-81, and two UEFA cup wins, 1972-73 and 1975-76. Played 34 times for the Republic.

Hughton, Chris: (born London, 1958). Recorded a notable first when, in 1980, he became the first black player to play for the Republic. Went on to play 52 internationals.

Hurley, Charlie: (born Cork, 1936). At the height of his career, in the early 1960's, while playing for Sunderland, was regarded as the finest centre-half in English soccer. Capped 40 times for the Republic he was honoured by the F.A.I. when he was named as the first player to be installed into their Hall of Fame.

Irvine, Sammy: (born Belfast, 1894). Had the distinction of playing for Cardiff City in their F.A. Cup final win of 1927, the one and only occasion that the famous cup was won by a team from outside England.

Jennings, Pat: (born Newry, 1945). Won his 119th cap, then a world record, on his 41st birthday while playing for N.I. against Brazil in the World Cup in Mexico in 1986. Played 758 English League games and was universally regarded as one of the top goalkeepers in the world at his peak. With Spurs he won an F.A. Cup medal, two League cup medals, a European Cup-Winners cup, and a UEFA cup medal. Joining Arsenal in 1977 he won a further F.A. Cup medal in 1979. The only Irish born player to receive both the Football Writers' Association "Player of the Year" (1972-73) and the Professional Footballers Association Player of the Year (1976).

Kelly, Jimmy: (born Donegal, 1912). Kelly, who played for Derry City, had the unique distinction of scoring all three goals when the Irish League scored a famous victory over the English League at Windsor Park in 1936.

Lawrenson, Mark: (born Preston, 1957). One of the most distinguished careers in English League soccer, Lawrenson won four League Championships with Liverpool, an F.A.Cup medal in 1986, three League cup medals and a European Cup medal in 1984. Capped 38 times for the Republic.

Martin, Con: (born Dublin, 1923). On his debut in 1946, against Portugal, Martin became the first substitute to be used by the Republic of Ireland. He was one of a number of players of that period to have gained international caps for both North and South of Ireland.

McElhinney, Gerry: (born Derry 1956). As well as playing six times for Northern Ireland at soccer, McElhinney gained international honours when he boxed for Ireland and, for good measure, he gained a G.A.A.

All-Star Award in 1975, an award the G.A.A. equates to being of International standard for their sport. Thus it could be claimed that he was of "international" standard in three different sports.

McEvoy, Andy: (born Dublin, 1938). McEvoy's 29 goals for Blackburn Rovers in the season 1964-65 made him joint top scorer in the English League that year, the only player from the Republic to achieve this status in the post-war years. Capped 17 times.

McGee, Paul: (born Sligo 1954). As a professional footballer, it is believed McGee holds the unofficial British and Irish soccer record for club changes, playing for twenty seven different clubs between 1969-91. Had no less than eight different spells with his home town club, Sligo Rovers.

McIlroy, Jimmy: (born Antrim, 1931). Capped 55 times for N.I. McIlroy's high standing as a quality player was confirmed when he was selected, in 1955, for a full Great Britain side which took on the rest of Europe. He and Danny Blanchflower were regarded as the finest N.I. players of that era.

McMahon, Johnny: (born Belfast). The only League of Ireland player to be capped by Northern Ireland, playing against Scotland in 1934. Played for Dublin side, Bohemians,

Moran, Kevin: (born Dublin, 1954). Still the only player to have won both a senior All-Ireland Gaelic Football medal and an F.A. Cup winners medal. Moran, in fact, holds two of each, his Gaelic medals coming with Dublin in 1976 and 1977, and his soccer medals with Manchester United in 1983 and 1985. Had the unique "distinction" of being the first, and still the only, player to be sent off in a F.A. Cup final (1985 V Everton).

Neill, Terry: (born Belfast, 1942). Capped 59 times for N.I. Had a very successful career in soccer, both on and off the field. Played for Arsenal on 275 occasions and left them to become, at the age of 28, manager of Hull City, the youngest manager in the League in 1970. Was later to manage both Arsenal and Spurs, taking the former to three successive F.A. cup finals, winning in 1979. He was also elected chairman of the Professional Footballers Association in the early Seventies. Managed the N.I. side for a period in 1970's.

O'Leary, David: (born London, 1958). Despite his numerous successes and honours as a player David O'Leary will always be remembered for one thing by Irish fans: his penalty score against Romania in the 1990 World Cup finals which brought Ireland through to the last sixteen for the first time ever. With Arsenal for almost twenty years, he won two League championship medals, two F.A. cup medals, two League Cup medals while making a record 723 appearances for the club. Capped 68 times for the Republic.

Reynolds, John: First player to be capped for two different countries. Reynolds played for Belfast club Distillery and was capped five times by the I.F.A. in 1890/1891. Was subsequently transferred to England and on joining West Bromwich Albion it was discovered he had been born in England and was eligible to play for their international side. On his debut, against Scotland, in 1892 he became the first soccer player to turn out for two countries.

Rice, Pat: (born Belfast, 1949). In a honours laden career with Arsenal, Rice was a member of the side which did the double (League and Cup victory) in 1971 and also captained the Arsenal side which won the cup in 1979. Captained the sides which lost on two cup final occasions, 1978 and 1980. In fact, Rice holds Arsenal records for most F.A. cup games played (67) and most games in Europe (27).

Roberts, Fred: In the 1930-31 season this now largely forgotten player created a record unlikely ever to be broken in senior soccer in either Britain or Ireland: he scored an aggregate of 96 cup and league goals in a single season for Glentoran.

Scott, Elisha: (born Antrim, 1894). Legendary Liverpool goalkeeper, spent 22 years with the Merseyside club where he won two successive League Championship medals, in 1921-22 and 1922-23. Regarded by many as the finest goalkeeper of his era, he was capped 31 times by Northern Ireland.

Stapleton, Frank: (born Dublin, 1956). Created history in 1983 when he became the first player to score for two different winning teams in F.A. Cup finals. Stapleton first F.A. cup win was with Arsenal in 1979 when he scored against Manchester United. His goal against Brighton in 1983, while playing for Manchester United, gave him his second cup medal. Also scored a record 20 goals for the Republic during his 71 caps. At his peak was regarded as the best centre forward in Britain.

Stevenson, Alex: (born Dublin, 1912). Capped seven times for the then Irish Free State between 1932 and 1949. However, his fourteen year "wait" between first and second caps is believed to be the longest recorded in international football.

Vernon, Jackie: (born Belfast, 1918). Selected at Centre-half for the Great Britain team which played at Hampden Park, Glasgow in 1947 and later captained the Rest of Britain team at Cardiff when the Welsh F.A. celebrated their 75th anniversary. Won 17 caps for N.I. and two for the Republic.

Whelan, Ronnie: (born Dublin, 1961). The most successful Irish born player of all time in English soccer. Six League Championship medals (between 1981-1990), two F.A. cup wins (1986,and 1989 as captain), a European Cup medal (1983/84), five Charity Shields, and three League Cups - all with Liverpool. Collected 54 caps for the Republic.

Whiteside, Norman: (born Belfast, 1965). On the 17th June,1982 entered the history books when he became the youngest player ever to play in the World Cup finals. Was 17 years and 42 days old when he made his debut for N.I. in the finals in Spain. Added to his achievements in less than year when he became the youngest player to score in an F.A.Cup final (18 years and 19 days). Won another F.A. cup medal with United in 1985. Played 36 times for N.I. before injury finally ended his career in 1990.

GOLF

Bradshaw, Harry: (born Wicklow, 1913). After turning professional in 1934 , won ten Irish titles in a sixteen year period. In addition won the Irish Open twice, the Irish Dunlop once, the British Dunlop twice, the P.G.A. Close as well as playing in three Ryder Cups. Member of the team which achieved the famous Ryder Cup victory in 1957.

Bruen, Jimmy: (born Antrim, 1920). Bruen successes are legendary in Irish golf - at 16, British Boys Champion, at 17 he won the Irish Close Championship for the first time, and a year later was Irish Amateur Open Champion. His outstanding ability was recognised internationally the same year when he was selected for Ryder Cup duty, the then youngest player ever selected, and the team won the Cup for the first time ever. World War II significantly interrupted his career but in 1946 he took up where he left off winning the British Amateur title. During the course of his career he played 24 home internationals.

Carr, Joe: (born Dublin, 1922). Without question Ireland's most successful amateur golfer. Won the Irish amateur title four times, the British title four times, the Irish close title six times, the East of Ireland a record 12 times, the West a record 12 times in addition to having the distinction of never being beaten in a final. Won the South title three times, and was on the Walker Cup team a record ten times. Holds the Irish record of having played in 138 Home International matches (over 23 years from 1947 to 1969) and was on the side which won the title outright in 1955. Won a number of international golfing awards for his sportsmanship and services to golf.

Daly, Fred: (born Derry, 1911). Professional golfer, won the Irish Open in 1946, the first native born player to win the title. To date is the only Irish man to win the British Open, winning in 1947. In the same year he also won the British Professional matchplay title, the first player in 42 years to do the "double". Attained Ryder Cup honours three times. Other honours included eleven Ulster Professional titles, Irish Professional title three times plus many other titles and accolades.

O'Connor Snr., Christy: (born Galway, 1924). List of achievements is enormous - Irish Professional title winner ten times, the Irish Dunlop four times, the Carroll's International four times, two Dunlop Masters, the Martini two times, the P.G.A. Matchplay (1957), ten successive Ryder Cup appearances, the World Senior's title in 1976 and 1977, the British Senior's P.G.A. title six times plus various other lesser titles.

ATHLETICS

Ahearne, Tim: (born Co. Limerick). Representing Britain in the triple jump at the 1908 games in London Ahearne won the gold medal. Until Lynn Davis won a field gold 56 years later this was to be Britain only success away from the track.. His jump of 14.91 was a world record at that time. However, his brother, Dan, was to better this jump two years later to set a new world best.

Barry, John Joe: (born Illinois, 1924). When he was two Barry's family moved to Ballincurra, Co. Tipperary. His talent as an athlete was spotted in his late teens and he became the first Irish athlete to gain what was really a U.S. scholarship to attend Villanova University. Broke the Irish record over three miles, two miles and one mile and was Irish Champion over these distances. Also broke the world record for two miles and represented Ireland at the 1948 Olympic Games in both the mile and the three miles.

Bull, Mike: (born Antrim, 1946). Bull was the leading British pole-vaulter for almost ten years, winning no less than thirteen titles while representing Northern Ireland. Won eight indoor titles, five outdoors and, in 1972, became the first British athlete to jump over 17ft. Capped almost seventy times for Britain.

Carroll, Michelle: (born Dublin, 1961). Born Michelle Walshe, Carroll was never selected to represent her country at international level but her dominance of domestic athletics was total. In a sixteen year career she won twenty eight national titles, fourteen 100 metres titles, eleven 200 titles and three four hundred metres. Also the national record holder of both the 100 and 200 for a long number of years.

Carroll, Noel: (born Louth, 1941). Carroll's outstanding talent became evident very early in his career when, on going to Villanova University in the U.S.A., he became the world's fastest under-20 runner for both the half mile and the 800 metres. Was a member of the All-American teams of 1963 and 1965. Carroll also became the first Irishman to receive a World Record Holder citation when he and his Villanova team mates set a world record for the 4x880 metres relay. Won a total of 14 Irish titles, at 440 and 880 yards, three British AAA titles, three European Indoor titles and, in 1963, set a European record for 880 yards.

Coughlan, Eamonn: (born Dublin, 1952). In terms of achievement Couglan was Ireland's most successful athlete of the modern era. The crowing glory was his World Championship win at the inaugural championships in Helsinki in 1983. In addition, he was an indoor runner without equal , winning 52 out of 70 races over 14 years including seven Wannamaker Miles at Madison Square Garden in New York. Broke the World Indoor record for the mile on two occasions (3.49,78) and also the World Indoor 2,000 metres (4.54.07). At European level, he won the 1500 indoor title in 1979. Was a member of the Irish team that broke the 4x1 mile outdoor record in 1985 and in 1993 he twice broke the world mile record for an over-40's athlete. During his career he also won eleven Irish titles, at 800/1500/ and 5,000, and held 14 outdoor national records. Despite being one of the main favourites lost out on an Olympic title in 1976 to New Zealander, John Walker - Coughlan could only finish fourth - and the same fate befell him in the 1980 Olympics in Moscow when Britain's Steve Ovett won.

Courtney, A.C: Little is known about this middle distance runner other than his 2.23.4 for the 1,000 yards at Trinity College Races in 1873 is acknowledged as the first World Record recorded by an Irishman. It was also accepted as the first world record for a race.

Davins, Tom, Maurice and Pat: (born Tipperary). These sporting brothers had amazing success. Tom, the eldest, set a world record for the high jump in 1873 and seven years later his youngest brother, Pat, bettered it to set the new mark. Pat was the first man to be officially recorded as jumping over six feet in height and, being a athlete of considerable talent, held six world records - including the 100 yards flat and hurdles. While not quite achieving the same eminence as his brothers, Maurice secured a British shot-putt title in 1881.

Delaney, Ronnie: (born Wicklow, 1935). Only just scraped into the Ireland team for the 1956 Olympics in Melbourne after a very disappointing season at home. Qualified for the Olympic final after an uninspiring race in the semi-final which saw him come in third. In the final he was in tenth place at the bell for the last lap but a scorching finish saw him set a new Olympic record of 3.41.2 (only 0.6 secs. outside the world record) to take the gold. He was only 21 years old. Delaney, like his successor, Eamon Coughlan, was a superb indoor athlete winning forty consecutive races indoor in the U.S., breaking the world record on three occasions. He

has been the recipient of numerous awards and honours both in Ireland and the U.S.

Flanagan, John J.: (born Limerick, 1873). After emigrating to the U.SA Flanagan became a three time gold medal winner at three different Olympics, all in the hammer: in Paris in 1900, St. Louis in 1904, and 1908 at London. Also won an Olympic silver medal in 1904 for throwing the 56lb weight.

Flynn, Ray: (born Longford, 1957). During his career, which was predominantly American based, became the first Irishman to break 3 mins 50 seconds barrier for the mile. Also held the Irish record for 1,500 three times, and the Irish mile and 2,000 metres titles twice.

Healion, Bert: (born Dublin, 1919). In 1943 set a world's best throw in the hammer at a meeting in Milltown in Dublin. His throw of 192' 11" broke the world record by three feet.

Hooper, Dick: (born Dublin, 1957). Won four national marathon titles. Won the Dublin Marathon three times and competed in the Olympic marathon on three occasions.

Hopkins, Thelma: (born Hull 1936). Won a silver medal for Britain in the 1956 Melbourne Games in the high jump. Spent her childhood in Northern Ireland, winning a total of 33 N.I. titles from 1951 on. Her British record for the high jump, a world record when set, was not dislodged until 1964. Won a European High jump gold medal at the Berne Games of 1954 and won the European cup the same year. A quality athlete, she won 45 caps for Ireland at hockey and was later chosen to play squash for Ireland.

Kerr, Bobbie: (born Co. Fermanagh 1882) Only seven when his family emigrated to Canada, he went on to win gold in the 200metres in 1908 in London.

Kiely, Tom: (born Co Tipperary 1869) Winner of no less than 53 Irish titles, 18 of them in the hammer, 16 British Crown Gold Medals and five British AAA titles he set a world record in the hammer, in 1899, with a throw of 162 feet, the first person ever to get the hammer over the 160 ft. mark. Told he would get a free trip to the Olympic Games of 1904 if he declared for Britain, Kiely declared for Ireland, paid his own fare, and won the gold medal for the All-Round Championship, the fore-runner to the modern day decathlon.

Leahy, Con (born Co. Cork 1876) An Irishman, Leahy represented Britain and won for that country three Olympic medals though his gold medal, for the high jump, in the 1906 games in St. Louis, U.S.A. is somewhat in doubt as the games were unofficial.

McDonald, Pat (born Co. Clare 1878) New York based policeman won a gold medal in the 1912 Olympic Games in Stockholm in the shot putt. Throw of 50' 4" was an Olympic record and was not beaten until 1928. The Great War interrupted his career but McDonald returned in glory in 1920 with another gold medal, this time in the 56lb. shot at the Antwerp Games. Being 42 years and 26 days this made him one of the oldest Olympic gold medal winner in history.

Mitchell, James (born Co. Tipperary 1864). An amazing record of 76 national championships in a variety of countries including Ireland (17 titles), England, Canada and U. S. A. in hammer throwing. Broke the world record four times. Having emigrated to America, where he too became a New York policeman, he won ten American Athletic Union titles.

O'Callaghan, Dr. Pat (born Co. Cork 1905) Became

the first athlete from the newly created "Free State" to win Olympic gold when in Amsterdam in 1928 he took the hammer title. In Los Angeles, four years later, he retained the title and thus became the first Irishman, representing Ireland, to win successive Olympic gold medals. Won many titles in the States and at home.

O'Connor, Peter J. (born Co. Wicklow 1874). Holds the distinction of being the first athlete affiliated to the Irish Amateur Athletics Federation to have a world record ratified when his long jump of 24' 11" in Dublin (1901) was deemed a world's best. This world record was to stand for more than twenty years and remained an Irish record for a further 89 years. An Irish All-Comers record for 67 years, the first Briton to exceed it was Lynn Davis who was to become an Olympic champion. O'Connor won a gold medal in the unofficial games of 1906 in the triple jump.

Peters, Mary: (born Lancashire, 1939). After an honours laden career, Mary Elizabeth Peters was 33 years old in 1972 when she went to Munich to compete in her 45th international pentathlon. In one of the closest finishes possible she beat her nearest challenger by only ten points when setting her own new world record score of 4801. Had she been one-tenth of a second slower in her final event, the 200 metres, she would have only received silver. Thus she became N.I.'s first Olympic Gold medal winner, and only the third British woman athlete at that time to do so. Roll of honour includes winning two Commonwealth Pentathlon titles, a Commonwealth gold in the shot, eight British womens AAA titles in the pentathlon, five British shot putt titles and a 100metres hurdles title. Has been the recipient of numerous awards and honours, and has held high office on a number of occasions at the top level of British athletics.

Purcell, Mary: (born Dublin, 1952). The first Irish woman athlete to win seven B.L.E. titles, Mary Purcell (nee Tracey) also won four British womens AAA titles. Her titles were won over 800 metres to 3,000m. In 1982 in her debut marathon she won the Irish National Championship.

Ryan, Paddy: (born Limerick, 1882). Another of the great Irish hammer throwers of the early 1900s, Paddy Ryan emigrated to the U.S.A. in 1910 and in 1913 was to set a world record throw, of 189' 6", that was to last for 25 years. It stood as an American record for 40 years. In 1920, representing the U.S., he won the gold medal at the Antwerp Olympic Games, his victory margin of 15 feet being the biggest ever recorded in the competition. Won a silver medal in the 56lb. shot behind his countryman, Pat McDonald. In 1919 he returned to Ireland and won yet another title, bringing his total to 12.

Sheridan, Marty: (born Mayo, 1881). In an amazing career Sheridan set 16 world records and was regarded as the finest athlete in the world at his peak. He emigrated to the U.S. and, like so many others, became a New York cop. Won three American All-Round titles (forerunner to the decathlon)which were universally accepted at that time as being the unofficial equivalent of a world title, as well as three American discus titles. In 1902 he became the first man to reach 40 metres for the discus, holding the world record for ten years, breaking it eight times himself until he reached his all-time best of 43.69 metres. Representing the U.S.A. in three successive Olympic games, between 1904 and 1908, he won five gold, three silver and a bronze thus

becoming one of the most successful American olympians ever. He died in 1918 at 37 years of age.

Tisdall, Bob: (born Ceylon, 1907). A truly international athlete Tisdall, the son of Irish parents, won international titles in both South Africa and Canada in 1929. In 1932, while a student at Cambridge, he won a place on the Irish Olympic team with a time of 54.2 seconds in only his third championship race over the distance. In the Olympic final, his seventh race over the 440 yards hurdles, he took the gold and bettered the world record but it was denied him as he had knocked down a hurdle. Won his gold in the same hour as Dr. Pat 'O Callaghan won his thus making it Irish athletics' finest ever hour.

Tracey, John: (born, Waterford 1957). During a star studded career Tracey was to win the World Cross Country championship on two successive occasions, in 1978 in Scotland and in Limerick the following year. Winner of numerous Irish titles (five times 5,000 metres champ, three 10,000) he also won the AAA 10,000 metres title in 1979. Perhaps his finest ever run was taking the silver medal in the stifling heat of Los Angeles in the Olympic marathon of 1984 won by Carlos Lopes of Portugal. Having represented Ireland four times at the Olympics, Tracey also had the distinction of winning an International Marathon in Los Angeles in 1992 with a time of 2hrs. 12ms. 28sec.

CYCLING

Eliott, Shay: (born Dublin, 1934). Shay Eliott was, without question, Ireland's finest cyclist prior to the Sean Kelly- Stephen Roche era. As a raw 17 year old he stunned the Irish cycling world with a win in the Grand Prix of Ireland race. In 1955 he went to the continent to become a professional with the St. Raphael-Gitane team, where he was expected to fill the role of one of the teams "domestiques", the riders who are expected to do the work for the team's main star. Eliott had other ideas, winning three Grand Prix in 1956, four the next year, two in 1958, six in 1959, four in 1960, and two in 1961. Also has another unique distinction; he was the first Irish man to wear the Yellow Jersey as leader of the Tour de France when, in 1963, he led the race for three stages. He went on to win many more races on the continent before his tragically early death at 36.

Kelly, Sean: (born Tipperary, 1956). Sean Kelly dominated world cycling in the 1980's. From 1984 until 1988 he was the awarded the World Number One slot for all five years. His list of other achievements is enormous: Nissan Classic (4 wins), Giro de Lombardi(3), Paris -Roubaix (2), Paris-Nice (seven years in row, and once winning coming from last place after an incident resulted in him being placed there as a result of a disciplinary decision), overall victory in the Tour of Spain (1980), Tour of Switzerland (2), plus four green jerseys in the Tour of France for most points won. Also won the first ever World Cup event in 1989. In all won eleven classic races.

McCormack, J.J.: (born Offaly, 1926). One of the outstanding father figures of Irish cycling, McCormack won 26 Irish championships titles, participated in six world championships and represented Ireland 21 times.

McQuaid, Jim: (born Waterford, 1921). Won the Grand Prix of Ireland Road Race six times between 1949 and 1960, took part in four world championships and was denied participation in Olympic Games of 1948 because of a political row in regard to the affiliations of the various cycling organisations in the country at that time. His son, Pat, won the Tour of Ireland twice, in 1975 and '76, and won a number of other quality races in Britain.

O'Hanlon, Shay: (born , Dublin 1942). Winner of the Ras Tailteann on no less than four occasions, O'Hanlon 's hat-trick of victories between 1965 and 1967 has yet to be surpassed. His total of 26 stage wins in the Ras has not been equalled either. Such was his dominance of domestic cycling that during his 1967 Ras victory he held the leader's jersey from start to finish. A rider of immense natural talent, he went to the Continent in 1963 and despite five race victories came home after a short spell.

Roche, Stephen: (born Dublin, 1959). In an amazing career Roche had one absolutely amazing year: 1987. That year he won the ultimate: the Tour de France, the Giro d'Italia (the Tour of Italy) and to cap it all off, the World Championship in Austria. Roche's talent was evident from early in his career winning the Ras Tailteann when only 19. In 1980, while still an amateur, he won the Paris- Roubaix and in 1983 in his first Tour de France was awarded the white jersey for best newcomer. In all Roche won 57 professional races.

RUGBY

Campbell, Ollie: (born Dublin, 1954). The holder of 22 caps, Seamus Oliver Campbell scored all 21 points when Ireland defeated Scotland to take the Triple Crown in 1982. Went on tour with the British and Irish Lions on two occasions; in South Africa (1980) he was the Lions' top scorer with 60 points, and a record 19 penalty conversions; and in New Zealand (1983) he was again the highest scorer with 124 points. He scored, in all, 217 points for Ireland, and holds quite a number of records for his scoring feats for his country.

Dawson, Ronnie: (born Dublin, 1932). Capped 27 times by Ireland, he was honoured by being chosen as captain of the Barbarians in 1960 when they defeated the South African Springboks, Became only the fifth Irishman to captain the Lions when, in 1959, he led the team on tour to Australia, New Zealand and Canada. The Lions won 27 of their 33 matches.

Fitzgerald, Ciaran: (born Galway, 1952). One of the greatest ever captains in Irish sport leading his teams, of 1982 and 1985, to Triple Crown wins and to the International Championship of 1983. Captain of the British and Irish Lions in 1983 also, but they lost the test series 4-0 against New Zealand.

Gallagher, Dave: (born Donegal, 1873). Deserves inclusion for one reason: his family left the little village of Ramelton and emigrated to New Zealand where, in 1903, he was appointed as the first ever All-Blacks captain for their first international match, against Australia.

Gibson, Mike: (born Belfast, 1942). Capped 69 times for Ireland and 12 times for the British Lions, which makes him the most capped rugby player ever. Regarded as one of the world's truly great players at his peak, Gibson played in a variety of positions for Ireland and was outstanding in all of them. Goes down in rugby history as being the first international replacement coming on as a replacement for the Welsh great, Barry John during the Lions tour of South Africa in 1968.

Kiernan, Michael: (born Cork, 1961). In 1991 Kiernan

became Ireland's all time highest points scorer with 308 points. Remembered also for a dramatic last minute drop goal in the game against England which gave Ireland victory in their Triple Crown decider. A noted athlete, he once held the Irish 200m. title.

Kiernan, Tom: (born Cork, 1939). Kiernan is an Irish rugby legend, winning a world record 54 caps for a fullback. He also captained Ireland for a record 24 times and was the world's most capped player until surpassed by Willie John McBride in 1974. Also captained the British and Irish Lions touring side to South Africa in 1966 and holds the distinction of being the only Lions player to score all his side's points in three test matches.

Kyle, Jackie: (born Belfast, 1926). Ireland's most capped out-half, with 46 caps, Kyle was the world's most capped player from 1958 to 1971. Also had a great success rate being on twenty two winning Irish sides. It was on the Lions tour of Australia and New Zealand in 1950 that he established his reputation as one of the game's greats with some outstanding displays, being selected for all six test matches. Was the mastermind of numerous Irish victories but particularly the Grand Slam win of 1948, the Triple Crown of 1949 and the International Championship in 1951.

Mc Bride, Willie John: (born Antrim, 1940). McBride is the all-time most successful Lions captain ever. In 1974, he led his side to three test victories against New Zealand, drawing one and winning all other 18 matches on the tour. He is the world's most capped forward, 63 caps, and holds the record for most Lions tours, five. While on tour he played in 17 test matches, 15 consecutively - a feat unlikely to be equalled. Has been awarded a host of domestic accolades.

McLoughlin, Ray: (born Galway, 1939). A man of prodigious strength, McLoughlin is credited with introducing the modern era of forward play to Irish rugby. One of the world's great prop forwards at his peak, had the honour of being the first Irish captain, in 1965, to defeat a touring Springboks team. He is also the most capped Connacht player in Irish rugby history with 40 caps.

Miller, Syd: (born Antrim, 1934). Miller had a liking for doing things in threes: he was the first Irish player to play international rugby in three different decades (being capped first in 1958 and gaining his last in 1970) and being the first Irishman to go on three British and Irish Lions tours. Was later appointed manager of the Lions, in 1980, for their tour of S. Africa.

Mullen, Dr. Karl: (born Wexford 1926). Regarded as the finest hooker in the world at his peak, Mullen was capped 25 times. A brilliant tactician, he led Ireland as captain on 16 occasions and was at the helm for what many still regard as the "golden era " of Irish rugby, 1948-1949, when this country won the Grand Slam and Triple Crown in successive years.

O'Flanagan, Kevin and Mick: (born Dublin, 1919/ 1922). These brothers were unique: they played both rugby and soccer for Ireland at international level. The only time they played international rugby together was in 1947, against England.

O'Reilly, Tony: (born Dublin, 1928). O'Reilly was only 18 when he won his first cap for his country. His international reputation was earned during his tours with the Lions, scoring 16 tries on his record breaking tour of South Africa in 1955. Four years later on the Lions tour to New Zealand and Australia he scored a record 22 tries in 23 appearances. His total of 38 tour tries is regarded as one of the great achievements in rugby.

Ward, Tony: (born Dublin, 1954). Hugely talented rugby player Ward was voted "European Player of the Year" in 1979. Despite this, he was frequently overlooked by the Irish selectors. Capped only 19 times during an international career that began in 1978 and ended in 1987, in his first season at this level he scored a then record of 38 points. Touring with the Lions in South Africa in 1980 he only won one test place but managed to again break a record, scoring 18 points and equalling another, five penalties for the most penalties scored in an international match. A noted athlete, he played League of Ireland soccer at senior level winning an F.A.I. cup winners medal with Limerick in 1980.

BOXING

Caldwell, Johnny: (born Belfast, 1938). After winning a bronze medal at the Melbourne Games of 1956, when only 18, Caldwell turned professional two years later. Just three years later he was World Bantamweight champion after beating Alphonse Halimi, of France. He subsequently lost the title to Eder Jofre, of Brazil, in 1962. However, what he is probably best remembered in these islands for was his famous British and Commonwealth title fight with Freddie Gilroy in Belfast when he lost in an epic contest.

Dempsey, Jack: (born Kildare, 1862). Born John Kelly, Dempsey held the World Middleweight title for seven years, from 1884. Fighting in America, he defended his title successfully on five occasions. So greatly was he admired as a boxer, a certain William Dempsey took the name Jack and subsequently went on to become the world heavyweight champion.

Dowling, Mick: (born Kilkenny, 1948). Has a unique record in Irish domestic boxing, winning the National Senior title at bantamweight for eight successive years from 1968.

Doyle, Jack: (born Cork, 1903). A legend in Irish boxing, 6ft. 5" Jack Doyle won each of his first six fights as a professional heavyweight boxer inside two rounds. But his remarkable good looks - he was known as the "Gorgeous Gael " - attracted all sorts of offers outside the ring and his career as boxer declined very quickly.

Gilroy, Freddie: (born Belfast, 1936). His name and that of John Caldwell have almost become synonymous, Gilroy, a hard hitting bantamweight, won a bronze medal in the 1956 Olympics and turned pro the following year. Two years later he won the European title by beating the Italian, Piero Rollo. He fought the French world champion, Alphonse Halimi, for the title in 1960 and despite the opinion of most neutrals that he had won, Halimi got the decision. In his last fight he beat Johnny Caldwell for the British and Commonwealth title.

Ingle, Jimmy: (born Dublin, 1921). Ingle has the distinction of being the first Irish boxer to win a European title, winning the flyweight title in 1939. He was only 17 at the time.

Kelly, Jimmy (born Derry, 1912) Won the British Empire title in 1938. His career spanned a remarkable 21 years.

Kelly, Billy: (born Derry, 1932). Son of Jimmy Kelly. Billy won his father's old title in 1954 when beating Roy Ankrah of Ghana. His most controversial fight was for the European title against Ray Famechon which resulted

in a riot after the verdict was awarded to Famechon. This fight was held in Dublin.

Kelly, John: (born Belfast, 1932). Kelly held the European Bantamweight title as a professional in 1953-54, and only lost three times in his 31 fight career.

McAlinden, Danny: (born Down, 1947). When he knocked out Jack Bodell in Birmingham in 1972 McAlinden became the first Irishman to hold both the British and Commonwealth heavyweight titles. Lost both titles in his first defence.

McAuley, Dave: (born Antrim, 1961). Dave "Boy" McAuley made two attempts at winning the world flyweight title, losing to Fidel Bassa in both 1987 and 1988, before finally gaining a world title belt when defeating Britain's Duke McKenzie. Subsequently successfully defended his title five times and is the only British or Irish boxer to fight in eight world title bouts.

McCormack, John: (born Dublin, 1944). Became British light-heavyweight champion in 1967, holding the title for two years

McCormack, Pat: (born Dublin, 1946). Brother of John, he too became a British champion when he won the light-welterweight title in 1974. He only held it for eight months.

McCormick, Tom: (born Louth, 1890) Became World Welterweight Champion in 1914 in Melbourne, Australia. Lost the title later the same year.

McCourt, Jim: (born Belfast, 1945). Had a distinguished amateur career, winning seven Irish senior titles. In 1964 he won a bronze medal at the Tokyo Olympic Games. Won a bronze the following year at the European Championships and boxed in his second Olympics in 1968. Took the gold medal in the Commonwealth Games in Jamaica while fighting at light-welterweight.

McGuigan, Barry: (born Monaghan, 1961). Showed early on that he was a special talent when, aged just 17, he won a gold medal at the Commonwealth Games. Turned professional in 1980, and by 1983 he had both the British and European bantamweight titles under his belt. The highlight of a great career came on June 8th, 1985 when he outpointed Eusebio Pedrosa, the reigning world champion, to take the world title in front of a huge outdoor crowd at Loftus Road, the home of Queen's Park Rangers Football club. Defended his title twice before losing it to Steve Cruz of Mexico in the burning heat of the Las Vegas desert in Nevada.

McLarnin, Jimmy: (born Down, 1906). The only Irishman of the modern era included in Ring magazine's Hall of Fame, McLarnin was a phenomenon of his era winning 63 of 77 contests, twice holding the World Welterweight title.

McNally, John: (born Antrim). In 1952, Belfast born McNally took a silver medal at the Helsinki Games, thus becoming the first Irish boxer to win an Olympic medal. In fact, his was the only medal won by Ireland at those games.

McTigue, Mike: (born Clare, 1892). On St. Patrick's Day 1923 in the La Scala Opera House in Dublin McTigue won the World Light-heavyweight title beating Battling Siki, of Senagal, on points in a 20 round contest. It proved to be the last world title fight at any weight to go more than fifteen rounds. He held the title for two years.

Monaghan, Rinty: (born Belfast, 1920). In March, 1948 Rinty Monaghan became undisputed flyweight champion of the world when he defeated Scotland's

Jackie Patterson in the King's Hall, Belfast. In a great career Monaghan won Irish, British and European titles. Because of various medical ailments he was forced to retire in early 1950 thus ending his career on a high as undefeated World title holder.

Nash, Charlie: (born Derry, 1951). After a very successful amateur career during which he won five senior Irish titles, turned professional and earned both British and European titles as a light-weight. Became British champion in 1978 and European Champion in 1979, winning the latter title in his home city when he defeated French man, Andre Holyk for the vacant title. Biggest disappointment was his fourth round defeat in 1980 by Scotsman, Jim Watt for the world title.

O'Colmain, Gerry: (born Dublin, 1924). In a very successful amateur career, won two light-heavyweight titles and seven heavyweight titles in a row (from 1946). The undoubted highlight of his career was the winning of the European heavyweight gold medal at the European games held in Dublin in 1947.

O'Sullivan, Jim: (born Wexford, 1959). O'Sullivan entered the record books of Irish boxing in 1990 when he became the first and, so far, the only boxer to win ten national senior titles. He won his championships at four different weights, beginning in 1980 at light-middleweight (1), light-heavyweight (1) heavyweight (4) and Super-Heavyweight (4)

Roche, Jem: (born Wexford, 1878). Despite having little professional boxing experience, Roche, a blacksmith, challenged Tommy Burns of Canada to a match for the World Heavyweight title. The contest took place on St. Patrick's Day 1908 at the Theatre Royal, Dublin. It lasted 88 seconds of the first round when Burns knocked Roche out cold. It is one of the shortest world title fights on record.

Russell, Hugh: (born Belfast, 1959). In 1980 at the Moscow Olympics, Russell won a bronze medal in the flyweight division, being beaten by the eventual winner of the gold. The following year he turned professional and became British bantamweight champion in 1984. Successfully defended the title three times and is one of the few Irish boxers to be awarded a Lonsdale belt outright. Now a noted photographer with a Belfast newspaper.

Sharkey, Tom: (born Louth, 1873). While never a world champion, Sharkey defeated two world heavyweight champions - Gentleman Jim Corbett and Bob Fitzsimmons - and actually fought for the world title against James J. Jeffries, of America. In an epic contest that went 25 rounds Sharkey eventually lost out.

Sullivan, David: (born Cork, 1877). In only his fifth fight O'Sullivan, who had emigrated to America as a young boy, became world flyweight champion when, against all predictions, he managed to break the arm of the champion, Sol Smith, and the fight had to be stopped. In what was to be the shortest reign of any world featherweight champion he lost the title in his first defence just 6 weeks later.

Tiedt, Freddie: (born Dublin, 1939). Tiedt is still remembered in Irish boxing as the man who "won" an Olympic title but didn't get the gold medal. In 1956 at the Melbourne Olympics he received more points than his Romanian opponent but he lost the decision by three votes to two, despite the fact that two judges had marked it a draw but "gave" the verdict to the Romanian. He did, however, come away with an Olympic silver medal

OTHER SPORTS

Armstrong, Reg: (born Dublin, 1930). In a four year period between 1952-'56 Armstrong recorded seven World Championship Grand Prix victories in motor cycling. He finished runner-up in the world championships on no less than five occasions.

Barnville, Geraldine: (born Offaly, 1942). One of Ireland's most successful squash players ever, Barnville was also an international tennis player. At squash, she was capped more than 70 times making her one of the most capped players in the world.

Barrington, Jonah: (born Cornwall, 1944). World class squash player Barrington played eighteen times for Ireland. Between 1967 and 1973, he won the British Open on six occasions, this being ranked as the premier tournament in world squash.

Bryans, Ralph: (born, Antrim 1941). In 1965 he won the World Championship 50c.c. motor-cycling title, the first Irish man to do so. In all he recorded ten Grand Prix victories.

DeLacy, Stan (born Limerick 1915). Had success as an Irish hockey player, winning five triple crowns in a career that spanned 17 years (1937-'54). Also had the unusual distinction for an Irish international sportsman, of any code, of being on the winning side in each of his first twenty games for his country.

Doyle, Matt: (born California, 1955). In the 1980's Matt Doyle brought a degree of credibility to Ireland's standing in world tennis when he was the driving force behind the climb to Division One of the Davis Cup competition. The highlight of his individual career was a win in a Grand Prix in 1983, in Cologne. Also won the Irish Open six times.

Drea, Sean: Ireland's most successful sculler ever, Drea won numerous international class sculling races but the highlight of a great career was a silver medal placing in the 1975 World Championships held in England.

Gill, James: (born Dublin, 1911). As a cricket international Gill played only once for Ireland - in one innings he scored a century, in the second he was out for a duck. His record in annals of world cricket is believed to be unique.

Gilmartin, John Joe: (born Kilkenny, 1916). His record of 24 All-Ireland senior titles in handball was only surpassed in the mid-1990's. His elevated status in this widely played sport in Ireland was such that up until he retired in 1947 he had not lost a singles match in more than ten years.

Gregg, Terry: (born Antrim, 1950). One of the "greats" of Irish hockey, Gregg played a record 103 times for Ireland and 42 times for the Great Britain team. A prolific goal-getter, he brilliantly led Ireland to the final of the Inter-Continental Cup in Rome 1977, their best ever performance at international level.

Herron, Tommy: (born Down, 1950). Died tragically at the age of 30, Herron was regarded as one of the top motorcycle riders in the world in the 1970's. Won three Isle of Man T.T.s, and at the North-West 200 in 1978 he averaged 127.6 m.p.h. to record the fastest time for any racer in either Britain or Ireland.

Hopkirk, Paddy: (born Antrim, 1933). The highlight of a great international rally-driving career came in 1964 when he won the Monte-Carlo rally. Five years later, when rallying was at its most popular, he came second in the London -to-Sydney race. Hopkirk also won the Circuit of Ireland five times.

Judge, David: (born Dublin, 1936). In a twenty one year international career (1957- 1978) Judge played a then record 124 times for Ireland, and a further 15 times for Britain. His career was leaden with both representative and domestic honours.

Kirby, Pat: (born Clare, 1936): In terms of achievement few handballers will ever equal Kirby. The highlight of a spectacular career was achieved when he was crowned World Champion in 1972. Won two further world titles, in 1971 and 1972. In addition to his world title victories, Kirby, who had emigrated to America in the late 1950's, won national titles there as well as in Canada and in Ireland. A fitness fanatic, Kirby won six over-40 world titles in the 1980's and added the World Over-55 title to the roll of honour in 1991. In all he won ten Irish singles titles.

Kyle, Maeve: (born Kilkenny, 1928). Kyle concentrated her interests on hockey in her early sporting career winning 58 caps for Ireland, the highlight of which was the 1950 winning of the Triple Crown. She then switched to athletics and represented Ireland on three occasions at the Olympic Games (Melbourne, Rome and Tokyo). A winner of numerous titles, she set several world best times for indoor running but was never officially accredited with a world record.

Langan, Jimmy: (born Dublin, 1951). An outstanding table tennis player from early childhood, became the youngest player to represent Ireland in senior sport when at 12 years of age he was called for international duty. Went on to play in excess of 200 matches for his country and was Irish senior champion ten times.

Langrishe, May: (born Dublin). When she won Irish Ladies Singles tennis title in 1879 she became the world's first national women's singles title winner, as the Irish were the first to hold a women's national competition. Won the title on two further occasions.

Maher, Joey: (born Louth, 1934). After winning numerous Irish handball titles at both junior and senior level, Maher emigrated to Canada in 1965 and during his three years there won the Canadian title three times. Highlight of his career was winning the World Handball title in 1967 while representing Canada.

McConnell, Billy : (born Down, 1956). Ireland's most capped hockey player with 135 caps, McConnell won a further 51 caps for Britain. At the Olympic Games of 1984, in Los Angeles, was a member of the British squad which won the Bronze medal.

Miller, Sammy (born Antrim, 1933). As a motor cycle trialist, Miller's record will probably stand forever - more than 900 victories in twenty years(1950-1970), British champion for eleven years in a row, five gold medals in team trialing with the British international team, and European champion twice.

Monteith, Dermott: (born Antrim, 1943). Probably Ireland's most successful cricketer, Monteith took 326 international wickets, for an average of just over 17 runs per wicket. On 27 occasions in test cricket he took five or more wickets, while his scoring total of 1,712 runs with the bat places him in the top twenty Irish batsmen of all time.

O'Dea, Donnacha (born Dublin, 1945) O'Dea smashed all kinds of swimming records when winning more than 90 Irish titles. His greatest achievement was recorded in 1965 when he became the first Irishman to break the 60 sec. barrier for the 100 metres free-style.

O'Kelly, Con (born Cork, 1886). The only Irish born person to win an Olympic wrestling gold, Kelly took the title in the heavyweight division at the 1908 Games in London while representing Britain.

Pim, Joshua (born Wicklow, 1869). In 1893 he created history by becoming the first Irish man, and the last, to win the Wimbledon Singles tennis title. He retained it the following year.

Potter, Jacqui (born 1963). Held the world record for most capped woman hockey player when she retired in the early 1990's with 83 caps.

Pratt, Don (born Dublin, 1935). Between 1956 and 1972 Pratt was capped 52 times for Ireland at Squash., a then world record for a Squash player. Won the Irish title for a record ten times and lost out on four other occasions. Also a cricket international.

Pringle, Ian (born Dublin, 1953). One of Ireland's finest oarsmen ever, Pringle represented his country at three Olympic Games. During a great career he won the Spanish Open (1986), won the British 10,000 metres title (1978) plus a host of domestic titles.

Robb, Tommy (born Antrim, 1934). After winning the Irish 500 c.c. championship in 1961, won the 250 road racing Grand Prix championship two years later. He had two other great Grand Prix victories. Despite many victories Robb won only one T.T., that win coming in 1973.

Thompson, Syd (born Antrim, 1912). In a career spanning more than a quarter of a century (1947-73), Thompson set a then world record for an outdoor bowls player when he represented Ireland 78 times.

Tyrell-Smith, Harry (born Dublin, 1907). Motor cyclist par excellence, Tyrell-Smith was European Champion twice, in 1931 and 1936. Took part in numerous Isle of Man T.T.s but only won one.

Watson, John (born Antrim, 1946). The first Irish born racing driver to win a Formula One Grand Prix, made history in 1976 when winning the Austrian championship. One of the most satisfying wins of his career was his victory in the British G.P. of 1981, which was only his second. In all he was to win five Grand Prix races, the last of which, the Long Beach Grand Prix, saw him bring his car from 22nd place on the grid right through to victory and thus creating what many feel was one of the most amazing pieces of driving history.

White, Francis (born Dublin, 1965). The highlight of a superb career which saw him win numerous domestic swimming titles, came in the 1975 European Championships when he won the 1,500 metres freestyle. Later in his career, in the early 1990s, White recorded some great wins in the veterans swimming circuit.

Wilkins, David (born Dublin, 1950). At the 1980 Olympic Games in Moscow, Wilkins and his sailing partner, James Wilkinson, took the silver medal in the Flying Dutchman class. Wilkins has won numerous British and Irish sailing honours and has represented Ireland at five different Olympics, the only person to achieve that distinction.

Woods, Stanley (born Dublin, 1903). Until the advent of Dunlop brothers, Woods was the most successful motor-cyclist the island of Ireland had produced. Won five 500c.c. T.T. titles, five junior T.T. titles, 22 Continental Grand Prix victories, and more than forty international titles in all.

USEFUL INFORMATION

PASSPORTS

Passport Requirements (Republic of Ireland)

Requirements:
2 Passport Size Photographs (35mm x 45mm)
Long form of Birth Certificate/most recent Irish Passport.

Application forms are available at all Garda Stations and at selected Post Offices in the Republic of Ireland. Passports can be obtained by post (via the 'Passport Express') or by travelling in person to the Passport Office.

Completed application forms must be signed in the presence of a Garda. The Garda must also sign the photograph after first ensuring the likeness to the applicant.

Irish Passports are available to anyone born in the thirty-two counties and to anyone who can produce evidence of an entitlement to Irish Citizenship.

Children under 16 can be included on their parent's passport.

Passports are usually valid for ten years, exceptions being those issued to those who are under 18 or over 65. Such passports are valid for 3 years.

Passport Fees:
Standard Passport (valid for 10 years): £45
Large Passport (valid for 10 years): £55
Three Year Passport: £10

Address:
Passport Office, Molesworth Street, Dublin 2.

DIPLOMATIC REPRESENTATION

Republic of Ireland Diplomatic Representation

There are 70 embassies accredited to Ireland: 37 embassies are resident in Ireland and 33 are non-resident. In addition, 28 countries are represented by Honorary Consulates in various parts of Ireland.

EMBASSIES

(The date in brackets refers to the year in which the embassy was founded or raised to the status of embassy)

Algeria (1983). Chancery: 54 Holland Park, London. Tel: (0044174) 221 7800/4.

Argentina (1964). Chancery: 15 Ailesbury Drive, Dublin 4. Tel: (01) 269 1546.

Australia (1946). Chancery: 2nd Floor, Fitzwilton House, Wilton Terrace, Dublin 2. Tel: (01) 676 1517.

Austria (1966). Chancery: 15 Ailesbury Court, 93 Ailesbury Road, Dublin 4. Tel: (01) 269 4577.

Bahrain (1981). Chancery: 98 Gloucester Road, London. Tel: (0044171) 370 5132.

Belgium (1958). Chancery: 2 Shrewsbury Road, Dublin 4. Tel: (01) 269 2082.

Brazil (1974). Chancery: Europa House, Harcourt Street, Dublin 2. Tel: (01) 475 6000.

Brunei (1987). Chancery: The Brunei Darussalam Embassy, 20 Belgrave Square, London. Tel: (0044171) 581 0521.

Bulgaria (1991). Chancery: Embassy of the Republic of Bulgaria, 186-188 Queen's Gate, London. Tel: (0044171) 584 9400.

Canada (1940). Chancery: 65-68 St. Stephen's Green, Dublin 2. Tel: (01) 478 1988.

Chile (1992). Chancery: Embassy of Chile, 12 Devonshire Street, London. Tel: (0044171) 580 6392.

China, People's Republic of (1980). Chancery: 40 Ailesbury Road, Dublin 4. Tel: (01) 269 1707.

Cyprus (1980). Chancery: 2 Square Ambiorix, 1040 Brussels, Belgium. Tel: (00322) 735 3510.

Czech Republic (1993). Chancery: 57 Northumberland Road, Ballsbridge, Dublin 4. Tel: (01) 668 1135.

Denmark (1973). Chancery: 121-122 St. Stephen's Green, Dublin 2. Tel: (01) 475 6404.

Egypt (1975). Chancery: 12 Clyde Rd, Ballsbridge, Dublin 4. (01) 6606566.

Estonia, Republic of (1994). Chancery: 16 Hyde Park Gate, Kensington, London. Tel: (0044171) 589 3428.

Ethiopia (1994). Chancery: 17 Prince's Gate, London. Tel: (0044171) 589 7212.

Federal Republic of Germany (1951). Chancery: 31 Trimleston Avenue, Booterstown, Blackrock, Co. Dublin. Tel: (01) 269 3011.

Finland (1962). Chancery: Russell House, Stokes Place, St. Stephen's Green, Dublin 2. Tel: (01) 478 1344.

France (1930). Chancery: 36 Ailesbury Road, Dublin 4. Tel: (01) 260 1666.

Greece (1977). Chancery: 1 Upper Pembroke Street, Dublin 2. Tel: (01) 676 7254.

Holy See (1929). Apostolic Nunciature, 183 Navan Road, Dublin 7. Tel: (01) 838 0577.

Hungary (1977). Chancery: Embassy of the Republic of Hungary, 2 Fitzwilliam Place, Dublin 2. Tel: (01) 661 2902.

Iceland (1951). Chancery: 1 Eaton Terrace, London. Tel: (0044171) 730 5131.

India (1951). Chancery: 6 Leeson Park, Dublin 6. Tel: (01) 497 0843.

Indonesia (1984). Chancery: 38 Grosvenor Square, London. Tel: (0044171) 499 7661.

Iran (1976). Chancery: Embassy of the Islamic Republic of Iran, 72 Mount Merrion Ave., Blackrock, Co. Dublin. Tel: (01) 288 0252.

Israel (1994). P.O. Box 3021, Dublin 6. Tel: (01) 668 0303.

Italy (1937). Chancery: 63-65 Northumberland Road, Dublin 4. Tel: (01) 660 1744.

Japan (1964). Chancery: Nutley Building, Merrion Centre, Nutley Lane, Dublin 4. Tel: (01) 269 4244.

Jordan (1984). Chancery: Embassy of the Hashemite Kingdom of Jordan, 6 Upper Philimore Gardens, Kensington, London. Tel: (0044171) 937 3685.

Kenya (1984). Chancery: 45 Portland Place, London. Tel: (0044171) 636 2371.

Korea, Republic of (1983). Chancery: 20 Clyde Road, Ballsbridge, Dublin 4. Tel: (01) 660 8800.

Latvia, Republic of (1994). Chancery: 45 Nottingham Place, London. Tel: (0044171) 312 0040.

Lebanon (1974). Chancery: 15-21 Palace Gardens Mews, London. Tel: (0044171) 229 7265.

Luxembourg (1973). Chancery: 27 Wilton Crescent, London. Tel: (0044171) 235 6961.

Malaysia (1969). Chancery: 45-46 Belgrave Square, London. Tel: (0044171) 235 8033.

Malta (1990). Chancery: Embassy of Malta, Malta House, 36-38 Piccadilly, London. (0044171) 292 4800.

Mexico (1980). Chancery: 43 Ailesbury Road, Dublin 4. Tel: (01) 260 0699.

Morocco (1959). Chancery: The Embassy of the Kingdom of Morocco, 53 Raglan Road, Ballsbridge, Dublin 4. Tel: (01) 660 9449.

Netherlands (1956). Chancery: 160 Merrion Road, Ballsbridge, Dublin 4. Tel: (01) 269 3444.

New Zealand (1966). Chancery: New Zealand House, Haymarket, London. Tel: (0044171) 930 8422.

Nigeria, Federal Republic of (1963). Chancery: 56 Leeson Park, Dublin 6. Tel: (01) 660 4366

Norway (1950). Chancery: 34 Molesworth Street, Dublin 2. Tel: (01) 662 1800.

Oman, Sultanate of (1988). Embassy: 167 Queen's Gate, London. Tel: (0044171) 225 0001.

Pakistan (1962). Embassy: 18 Rue Lord Byron, 75008-Paris. Tel: (00331) 45622332.

Philippines (1984). Chancery: 9A Palace Green, London. Tel: (0044171) 937 1600.

Poland (1990). Chancery: 5 Ailesbury Road, Dublin 4. Tel: (01) 283 0855.

Portugal (1965). Chancery: Knocksinna House, Knocksinna, Foxrock, Dublin 18. Tel: (01) 289 4416.

Qatar (1976). Chancery: 1 South Audley Street, London. Tel: (0044171) 493 2200.

Romania (1995). Chancery: 60 Merrion Road, Ballsbridge, Dublin 4. Tel: (01) 668 1336.

Russian Federation (1974). Chancery: 186 Orwell Road, Rathgar, Dublin 14. Tel: (01) 492 2048.

Saudi Arabia (1981). Chancery: 30 Charles Street, London. Tel: (0044171) 917 3000.

Singapore (1975). Chancery: 9 Wilton Crescent, London. Tel: (0044171) 235 8315.

Slovak Republic (1993). Chancery: 25 Kensington Palace Gardens, London. Tel: (0044171) 243 0803.

Spain (1950). Chancery: 17A Merlyn Park, Dublin 4. Tel: (01) 269 1640.

Sudan Chancery: 3 Cleeveland Row, St. James's, London. Tel: (0044171) 839 8080.

Sweden (1959). Chancery: Sun Alliance House, 13-17 Dawson Street, Dublin 2. Tel: (01) 671 5822.

Switzerland (1939). Chancery: 6 Ailesbury Road, Dublin 4. Tel: (01) 269 2515.

Tanzania (1979). Chancery: 43 Hertford Street, London. Tel: (0044171) 499 8951.

Thailand (1976). Chancery: 29-30 Queen's Gate, London. Tel: (0044171) 589 0173.

Tunisia (1978). Chancery: 29 Prince's Gate, London . Tel: (0044171) 584 8117.

Turkey (1972). Chancery: 11 Clyde Road, Ballsbridge, Dublin 4. Tel: (01) 668 5240.

United Arab Emirates (1990). Chancery: Embassy of the United Arab Emirates, 30 Prince's Gate, London . Tel: (0044171) 581 1281.

United Kingdom (1939). Chancery: 29 Merrion Road, Dublin 4. Tel: (01) 205 3700.

United States of America (1950). Chancery: 42 Elgin Road, Ballsbridge, Dublin 4. Tel: (01) 668 7122.

Venezuela (1981). Chancery: 1 Cromwell Road, London. Tel: (0044171) 5898887.

Zambia (1983). Chancery: 2 Palace Gate, London. Tel: (0044171) 589 6655.

Zimbabwe (1984). Chancery: Zimbabwe House, 429 Strand, London. Tel: (0044171) 836 7755.

REPRESENTATIVES ABROAD

Algeria see Spain

Argentina - Ambassador Bernard Davenport. Embassy of Ireland, Suipacha 1380, Second Floor, 1011 Buenos Aires. Tel: (00541) 3258588.

Australia - Ambassador Richard O'Brien. Embassy of Ireland, 20 Arkana Street, Yarraiumia, ACT 2600. Tel: (00616) 2733022.

Austria - Ambassador Thelma Doran. Embassy of Ireland, Hilton Centre, 1030 Vienna, Landstresse Hauptstrasse 2A, 1030 Vienna. Tel: (00431) 7154246/7.

Bahrain see Saudi Arabia
Belarus see Russian Federation

Belgium - Ambassador Patrick Cradock. Embassy of Ireland, 19 Rue du Luxembourg, B-1040 Brussels. Tel: (00322) 5136633.

Brazil see Portugal
Brunei see India

Bulgaria see Russian Federation

Canada - Ambassador Paul Dempsey. Embassy of Ireland, 130 Albert St, Ottawa, KIP5G4, Ontario. Tel: (001613) 2336281.

Chile see Argentina

China, People's Republic of: Ambassador Joe Hayes. Embassy of Ireland, Ritan Donglu 3, Beijing 100600. Tel: (008610) 5322691.

Council of Europe - Ambassador Geraldine Skinner. Strasbourg.

Cyprus see Iraq

Czech Republic - Ambassador Marie Cross. Embassy of Ireland, c/o Hotel Inter-Continental, Namesti Curieovych 43/5, 110 00 Praha 1. Tel: (00422) 2488 1111.

Denmark - Ambassador Andrew O'Rourke. Embassy of Ireland, Ostbanegade 21.1.Th.DK-2100, Copenhagen. Tel: (0045) 31423233.

Egypt - Ambassador Hugh Swift. Embassy of Ireland, Abu-El-Fida Building, Zamalek, Cairo. Tel: (00202) 3408264.

Estonia see Sweden.

Ethopia - First Secretary: David Barry. Embassy of Ireland, Dev. Co-operation Office, House No. 413, Higher 24, Kebele 13. Tel: (002511) 710835.

European Union
Permanent Representative: Denis O'Leary. Avenue Galilée 5, bte 22, 1030 Brussels. Tel: (00322) 2180605.

FAO of the Union see Italy

Finland - Ambassador Dáithí Ó Ceallaigh. Embassy of Ireland, Erottajankatu, 7A, 00130 Helsinki. Tel: (003580) 646006

France - Ambassador Patrick O'Connor. Embassy of Ireland, 12 Avenue Foch, 75116 Paris. Tel: (00331) 44176700.

Germany, Federal Republic of
Ambassador Padraig Murphy. Embassy of Ireland, Godesberger Allee 119, 53175 Bonn. Tel: (0049228) 959290

Ghana see Nigeria

Greece - Ambassador Liam Rigney. Embassy of Ireland, 7 Leoforos Vasileos Konstantinov, GR 10674 Athens. Tel: (00301) 7232771/2

Holy See - Ambassador Gearóid Ó Broin.
Embassy of Ireland, Villa Spada, Via Giacomo Medici 1,
00153 Rome. Tel: (00396) 5810777

Hungary - Ambassador Declan Connolly.

IAEA - see Austria
Iceland - see Denmark

India - Ambassador Jim Flavin. Embassy of Ireland,
13 Jor Bagh, New Delhi 110003. Tel: (009111) 4617435

Indonesia - see Australia

Iran - Ambassador Anthony Mannix.
Embassy of Ireland, Avenue Mirdamad, Khiaban
Razane Shomali No. 8, Tehran. Tel: (009821) 2227627

Iraq - Embassy temporarily relocated.

Israel see Greece.

Italy - Ambassador Joseph Small.
Embassy of Ireland, Piazza di Campitelli, 00186 Rome.
Tel: (00396) 6979121

Japan - Ambassador Declan O'Donovan.
Embassy of Ireland, Ireland House 5F,
2-10-7 Kojimachi Chiyoda-Ku, Tokyo 102.
Tel: (00813) 3263 0695

Jordan - see Iraq
Kazahkstan see Russian Federation.
Kenya see Egypt

Korea, Republic of - Ambassador Brendan Moran.
Embassy of Ireland, Daehan Fire and Marine Insurance
Building, 51-1 Namchang-Dong, Chung-Ku,
100-778 Seoul. Tel: (00822) 7746455

Kuwait - see Saudi Arabia
Latvia - see Poland
Lebanon - see Iraq

Lesotho - Consul General Fintan Farrelly.
Development Co-operation Office of Ireland, Christie
House, Plot No. 856, Maseru. Tel: (00266) 314068

Libya - see Italy
Liechtenstein - see Switzerland
Lithuania - see Poland

Luxembourg - Ambassador Geraldine Skinner.
Embassy of Ireland, 28 Route D'Arlon,
L-1140 Luxembourg. Tel: (00352) 450610

Malaysia - Ambassador Brendan Lyons.
Embassy of Ireland, Room 1808, Shangri-la Hotel,
11 Jalan Sultan Ismail, 50250, Kuala Lumpur.
Tel: (00603) 232 2385

Malta see Italy

Mexico see USA
Morocco see France

The Netherlands - Ambassador John Swift.
Embassy of Ireland, 9 Dr. Kuyperstraat, 2514 BA,
The Hague. Tel: (003170) 3630993/4

New Zealand - see Australia

Nigeria, Federation of -
Chargé d'Affaires Brendan McMahon.
Embassy of Ireland, PO Box 2421, 34 Koto Abayomi
Street, Victoria Island, Lagos. Tel: (002341) 2617567

Norway see Denmark

OECD see France
Oman see Saudi Arabia

OSCE - Head of Delegation Justin Harman.
Hilton Centre, Landstrasse Haupstrasse,
1030 Vienna. Tel: (00431) 7157698

Pakistan see China
Philippines see China

Poland Ambassador Patrick McCabe.
Embassy of Ireland, Ul Humanska 10, 00-789 Warsaw.
Tel: (004822) 4966331

Portugal Ambassador Eamon Ryan.
Embassy of Ireland, Rua da Imprensa 1-4, 1200 Lisbon.
Tel: (003511) 3961569

Qatar see Saudi Arabia

Romania see Greece

Russian Federation - Ambassador Ronan Murphy.
Embassy of Ireland, Grokhoiski Pereulok 5,
Moscow, 129010. Tel: (007095) 2884101

Saudi Arabia - Ambassador Michael Collins.
Embassy of Ireland, Diplomatic Quarter, Riyadh.
Tel: (009661) 4882300

Singapore see India

Slovak Republic, The see Austria

South Africa - Ambassador Eamon Ó Tuathail.
Embassy of Ireland, Delheim Suite, Tubach Centre,
1234 Church Street, 0083 Colbyn, Pretoria.
Tel: (002712) 3425062

Spain - Ambassador Richard Ryan.
Embassy of Ireland, Claudio Coello 73, Madrid 28001.
Tel: (00341) 5763500

Sudan Co-ordinator of Irish Projects: Seán Courtney.
Irish Aid, P.O. Box 299, Wad Medani, Sudan.
Tel: (00249) 512279

Sweden - Ambassador Martin Burke.
Embassy of Ireland, Ostermalmsgatan 97 (IV), PO Box 10326, 10055 Stockholm. Tel: (00468) 6618005

Switzerland - Ambassador Gearoid Ó Cléirigh.
Embassy of Ireland, Kirchenfeidstrasse 68, CH. 3005 Berne. Tel: (004131) 3521442

Syria see Saudi Arabia

Tanzania see Egypt
Thailand see India
Tunisia see Spain
Turkey see Italy

Ukraine see Russian Federation
UNESCO see France
UNIDO see Austria
United Arab Emirates see Saudi Arabia

United Kingdom - Ambassador Ted Barrington.
Embassy of Ireland, 17 Grosvenor Place, London. Tel: (0044171) 2352171

United Nations - *Geneva*
Ambassador Anne Anderson.
Permanent Mission of Ireland to the United Nations, 45-47 Rue de Lausanne, 1202 Geneva 2, Cornavin. Tel: (004122) 7328550

United Nations - *New York*
Ambassador John Campbell.
Permanent Mission of Ireland to the United Nations, 1 Dag Hammarskjold Plaza, 885 Second Avenue, 19th Floor, New York, NY 10017. Tel: (001212) 4216934

UNRWA see Austria

United States of America -
Ambassador Dermot Gallagher.
Embassy of Ireland, 2234 Massachusetts Avenue,

NW Washington, DC 20008.
Tel: (001202) 4623939

New York
Consul General Donal Hamill
Consulate General of Ireland, Ireland House, 345 Park Avenue, 17th Floor, New York 10154-0037
Tel: (001212) 3192555

Boston
Consul General Conor O'Riordan
Consulate General of Ireland, Chase Building, 535 Boylston Street, Boston, Massachusetts 02116
Tel: (001617) 2679330

Chicago
Consul General Frank Sheridan
Consulate General of Ireland, 400 North Michigan Avenue, Chicago, Illinois 60611.
Tel: (001312) 3371868

San Francisco
Consul General Declan Kelly.
Consulate General of Ireland, 44 Montgomery Street, Suite 3830, San Francisco, California 94104
Tel: (001415) 3924214

Uganda - Chargé d'Affaires Patrick Curran.
Embassy of Ireland, Plot 12, Acacia Avenue, Kampala.

Venezuela see Argentina

Zambia - 1st Secretary Brendan Rogers.
Development Co-operation Office of Ireland, 6663 Katima Mulilo Road, Po Box 34923, 10101 Lusaka.
Tel: (002601) 290650

Zimbabwe see Nigeria

POSTAL & TELECOMMUNICATIONS

Republic of Ireland and Northern Ireland

Post:	Republic of Ireland	Northern Ireland
First class (inland)	32p	25p
Air Mail (within EU)	32p	25p
Courier: *		
Package to London (10 kg)	£35	£25
Package to Paris (10 kg)	£63	£63

* VAT is charged on Courier Services in Republic of Ireland and Northern Ireland at 21% and 17.5% respectively.

Telecommunications: based on a 3 minute call	Republic of Ireland	Northern Ireland
Local Calls	0.115p	15p
UK	£1.08p	30p
United States	£2.49p	£1.19p
Germany	£1.29p	£1.06p

TELEPHONE CODES

Direct Telephone Codes within Republic of Ireland and Northern Ireland

A

Abbeydorney	066
Abbeyfeale	068
Abbeyleix	0502
Achill Sound	098
Adare	061
Aghadowey	0801265
Aghalee	0801846
Ahoghill	0801266
Annaghmore	0801762
Annagry	075
Annalong	08013967
Antrim	0801849
Ardara	075
Ardee	041
Ardglass	0801396
Ardmore (Waterford)	024
Arklow	0402
Armagh	0801861
Armoy	08012657
Ashford	0404
Askeaton	061
Athboy	046
Athenry	091
Athlone	0902
Athy	0507
Aughafatten	0801266
Aughnacloy	08016625

B

Bailieborough	042
Bailie's Mills	0801846
Balla	094
Ballaghaderreen	0907
Ballina	096
Ballinamallard	0801365
Ballinamore	078
Ballinasloe	0905
Ballinaskeagh	08018206
Ballincollig	021
Ballingarry (Limerick)	069
Ballingarry (Nenagh)	067
Ballingarry (Waterford)	052
Ballingeary	026
Ballinrobe	092
Ballybay	042
Ballybofey	074
Ballybunion	068
Ballycastle (Antrim)	08012657
Ballyclare	0801960
Ballinconneely	095
Ballycotton	021
Ballycumber	0506
Ballydehob	028
Ballydesmond	064
Ballyferriter	066
Ballygally	0801574
Ballygar	0903
Ballygawley	08016625
Ballygowan	0801238
Ballyheigue	066

Ballyjamesduff	049
Ballykinler	0801396
Ballymahon	0902
Ballymakeera	026
Ballymena	0801266
Ballymoney (Antrim)	08012656
Ballymore	044
Ballymore Eustace	045
Ballymote	071
Ballynahinch	0801238
Ballynoe	058
Ballyporeen	052
Ballyronan	0801648
Ballyshannon	072
Ballyvaughan	065
Ballywalter	08012477
Ballyward	08018206
Baltinglass	0508
Banagher	0509
Banbridge	08018206
Bandon	023
Bangor (Down)	0801247
Bangor Erris	097
Bantry	027
Bawnboy	049
Belcoo	0801365
Belfast	0801232
Bellaghy	0801648
Bellarena	08015047
Belleek	08013656
Bellewstown	041
Belmullet	097
Belturbet	049
Benburb	0801861
Beragh	08016627
Bessbrook	0801693
Birr	0509
Blackwater	053
Blarney	021
Blessington	045
Borris (Carlow)	0503
Borris-in-Ossory	0505
Borrisokane	067
Borrisoleigh	0504
Boyle	079
Bready	0801504
Brittas Bay	0404
Brookeborough	08013655
Broughshane	0801266
Bruree	063
Bunbeg	075
Bunclody	054
Buncrana	077
Bundoran	072
Burrin	065
Burtonport	075
Bushmills	08012657

C

Cahir	052
Cahirciveen	066

Caledon	0801861
Callan	056
Campsie	0801504
Cappamore	061
Cappawhite	062
Cappoquin	058
Carbury	0405
Carlingford	042
Carlow	0503
Carnlough	0801574
Carrickfergus	0801960
Carrickmacross	042
Carrickmore	08016627
Carrick-on-Shannon	078
Carrick-on-Suir	051
Carrigaline	021
Carrigart	074
Carryduff	0801232
Cashel (Tipperary)	062
Castlebar	094
Castleblayney	042
Castlecomer	056
Castledawson	0801648
Castlederg	08016626
Castledermot	0503
Castlegregory	066
Castleisland	066
Castlemahon	069
Castlepollard	044
Castlerea	0907
Castlereagh	0801232
Castlerock	0801265
Castletownbere	027
Castlewellan	08013967
Cavan	049
Charlestown	094
Charleville	063
Clane	045
Clara	0506
Clare Island	098
Claremorris	094
Claudy	0801504
Clear Island	028
Clifden	095
Clogher (Tyrone)	08016625
Clonakilty	023
Clones	047
Clonmany	077
Clonmel	052
Cloughjordan	0505
Cloughmills	08012656
Coachford	021
Coagh	08016487
Coalisland	0801868
Cobh	021
Coleraine	0801265
Collooney	071
Comber	0801247
Cong	092
Cookstown	08016487
Cootehill	049

Cork..................................021
Corofin..............................065
Courtown Harbour................055
Craigavon........................0801762
Craughwell 091
Cross (Derry)..................0801504
Crossgar........................0801396
Crosshaven.........................021
Crossmaglen 0801693
Crossmolina 096
Crumlin (Antrim).............0801849
Cullybackey....................0801266
Curragh..............................045
Cushendall 08012667
Cushendun...................08012667

D

Daingean..........................0506
Derry 0801504
Derryard 0801762
Derrygonnelly................08013656
Derrylin........................08013657
Dervock........................08012657
Dingle...............................066
Donaghadee 0801247
Donaghmore 0801868
Donard 045
Donegal.............................073
Downpatrick 0801396
Draperstown...................0801648
Drogheda 041
Dromara 0801238
Dromard............................071
Dromore (Down)..........0801846
Dromore (Tyrone)...........0801662
Dromore West....................096
Drumbo 0801232
Drumlish............................043
Drumquin.......................0801662
Drumshanbo......................078
Dublin..............................01
Dunamanagh 0801504
Dundalk...........................042
Dundonald.....................0801232
Dundrod 0801232
Dundrum (Down)..........08013967
Dungannon 0801868
Dungarvan..........................058
Dungiven......................08015047
Dungloe............................075
Dunlavin...........................045
Dunleer............................041
Dunloy (Antrim) 08012656
Dunmanway 023
Dunmore East 051
Durrow............................0502

E

Edenderry..........................0405
Edgeworthstown...............043
Edmondstown 041
Eglinton 0801504
Elphin..............................078
Enfield 0405
Ennis................................065
Enniscorthy 054

Enniskillen.....................0801365
Ennistymon 065

F

Feakle 061
Feeny...........................08015047
Ferbane...........................0902
Fermoy...........................025
Ferns...............................054
Fethard (Tipperary) 052
Fethard (Wexford)............051
Fintona 0801662
Fivemiletown 08013655
Florencecourt 0801365
Forkhill..........................0801693
Foulksmills 051
Foxford..............................094
Freshford..........................056

G

Galway 091
Garvagh 08012665
Gilford (Armagh).............0801762
Glarryford 0801266
Glaslough.........................047
Glenbeigh.........................066
Glencar.............................066
Glendalough 0404
Glenanne 0801861
Glenarm 0801574
Glengarriff........................027
Glengormley..................0801232
Glenties 075
Glenwherry 0801266
Gorey 055
Gort 091
Gortin 08016626
Gowran............................056
Graiguenamanagh 0503
Granard............................043
Greyabbey 08012477

H

Hacketstown.......................0508
Headford (Galway)............093
Headford (Kerry) 064
Helen's Bay 0801247
Hillsborough 0801846
Holywood 0801232
Holycross 0504

I

Inniskeen..........................042
Irvinestown...................08013656
Islandmagee 0801960

J

Jerrettspass...................0801693
Johnstown 056

K

Kanturk...........................029
Katesbridge.................08018206
Keady.........................0801861
Kells (Meath)..................046
Kells (Antrim)...............0801266

Kenagh...........................043
Kenmare..........................064
Kerrykeel.........................074
Kesh............................08013656
Kilbeggan 0506
Kildare 045
Kilfinnan 063
Kilkee 065
Kilkeel.........................08016937
Kilkelly 094
Kilkenny..........................056
Kill 045
Killala..............................096
Killaloe............................061
Killarney 064
Killeavy.........................0801693
Killenaule.........................052
Killeshandra 049
Killinchy.......................0801238
Killorglin..........................066
Killucan...........................044
Killybegs..........................073
Killyleagh.....................0801396
Kilmacthomas....................051
Kilmallock 063
Kilmihill 065
Kilmore Quay 053
Kilrea..........................08012665
Kilronan...........................099
Kilrush............................065
Kingscourt 042
Kinnegad..........................044
Kinsale 021
Kinvara 091
Kircubbin 08012477
Knock (Mayo)...................094
Knocknagoshel 068

L

Lahinch............................065
Lanesboro 043
Larne...........................0801574
Letterkenny 074
Lifford 074
Limavady.....................08015047
Limerick 061
Lisbellew 0801365
Lisburn 0801846
Lisdoonvarna.....................065
Lismore 058
Lisnaskea 08013657
Listowel 068
Longford 043
Loughgall 0801762
Loughgiel.....................08012656
Loughrea..........................091
Louisburgh 098
Louth 042
Lurgan.........................0801762

M

Macroom 026
Maghera.......................0801648
Magherafelt...................0801648
Mallow............................022
Manorcunningham 074

Manorhamilton 072
Markethill.....................0801861
Martinstown (Antrim) 08012667
Mayobridge 0801693
Maze 0801846
Midleton..............................021
Millisle 0801247
Millstreet.............................029
Miltown Malbay 065
Mitchelstown 025
Moate 0902
Mohill..................................078
Moira 0801846
Monaghan 047
Monasterevin......................045
Moneymore 08016487
Moone 0507
Mostrim 043
Mount Bellew.....................0905
Mountfield...................08016627
Mountmellick 0502
Mountrath 0502
Moville 077
Moy 0801868
Moycullen 091
Moyglass...........................0509
Moynalty.............................046
Moyvore 044
Muine Bheag 0503
Mullingar............................044
Mulrany 098
Multyfarnham 044

N
Naas...................................045
Navan.................................046
Nenagh...............................067
Newbridge..........................045
Newcastle (Down).........08013967
Newcastle West 069
New Inn (Galway).................052
New Inn (Tipperary) 052
Newmarket..........................029
Newmarket-on-Fergus 061
Newport (Mayo)....................098
Newport (Tipperary) 061
New Ross.............................051
Newry..........................0801693
Newtownards 0801247
Newtownbutler 08013657
Newtowngore 049
Newtownhamilton...........0801693
Newtownstewart...........08016626
Nobber 046

O

Oldcastle 049
Omagh 0801662
Oranmore............................091
Oughterard.........................091

P
Patrickswell 061
Pomeroy.......................0801868
Portadown.....................0801762
Portaferry 08012477
Portarlington....................0502
Portavogie....................08012477
Portglenone..................0801266
Portlaoise 0502
Portrush......................0801265
Portstewart..................0801265
Portumna..........................0509
Poyntzpass 0801762

R
Ramelton............................074
Randalstown 0801849
Raphoe...............................074
Rasharkin....................08012665
Rathangan..........................045
Rathdowney.......................0505
Rathfriland...................08018206
Rathkeale...........................069
Rathlin........................08012657
Rathmore...........................064
Recess 095
Rhode................................0405
Richhill.........................0801762
Rochford Bridge 044
Rooskey 078
Roscommon 0903
Roscrea.............................0505
Roslea........................08013657
Rosscarbery.......................023
Rosses Point......................071
Rosslare 053
Rostrevor....................08016937

S
Saintfield 0801238
Scarriff...............................061
Scotstown...........................047
Seaforde (Down).............0801396
Shannon.............................061
Sion Mills.................. 08016626
Slane 041
Skibbereen.........................028
Sligo 071
Sneem...............................064
Spiddal 091
Springfield 0801365

Stewartstown..................0801868
Stoneyford....................0801846
Strabane 0801504
Stradbally (Laois) 0502
Stradbally (Waterford).............051
Strandhill 071
Strangford 0801396
Strokestown 078
Summerhill 0405
Swanlinbar 049
Swatragh 0801648
Swinford 094

T
Tandragee...................0801762
Tarbert...............................068
Templemore 0504
Templepatrick.................0801849
Tempo 08013655
Thomastown.......................056
Thurles 0504
Tinahely............................0402
Tipperary 062
Toomebridge..................0801648
Tory Island 074
Tralee 066
Tramore...............................051
Trillick.........................08013655
Trim....................................046
Tuam.................................093
Tubbercurry........................071
Tullamore 0506
Tullow 0503
Tulnacross..................08016487
Tyrrellspass........................044

V
Valentia 066
Virginia 049

W
Waringstown 0801762
Warrenpoint...................08016937
Waterford 051
Waterville 066
Wellington Bridge 051
Westport.............................098
Wexford..............................053
Whiteabbey 0801232
White Gate 021
Whitehead......................0801960
Wicklow............................0404
Woodford...........................0509

Y
Youghal..............................024

Temperatures

°C	°F	°C	°F	°C	°F	
0	32	30	86	70	158	°C = 5/9 (°F-32)
5	41	40	104	80	176	°F = 9/5 (°C+32)
15	59	50	122	90	194	
20	68	60	140	100	212	

International Telephone Codes

Country	Access Code	Country Code	Country	Access Code	Country Code
Australia	00	61	Malta	00	356
Austria	00	43	Mexico	00	52
Bahrain	00	973	Morocco	00	212
Belgium	00	32	Netherlands	00	31
Brazil	00	55	New Zealand	00	64
Canada	00	1	Nigeria	00	234
China	00	86	Norway	00	47
Czech Republic	00	42	Pakistan	00	92
Denmark	00	45	Poland	00	48
Egypt	00	20	Portugal	00	351
Finland	00	358	Russian Federation	00	7
France	00	33	Saudi Arabia	00	966
Germany	00	49	Singapore	00	65
Greece	00	30	Slovak Republic	00	42
Hong Kong	00	852	South Africa	00	27
Hungary	00	36	Spain	00	34
India	00	91	Sweden	00	46
Iran	00	98	Switzerland	00	41
IRELAND	00	353	Taiwan	00	886
Israel	00	972	Trinidad & Tobago	00	1809
Italy	00	39	Tunisia	00	216
Japan	00	81	Turkey	00	90
Kuwait	00	965	UK	00	44
Luxembourg	00	352	USA	00	1

WEIGHTS, MEASURES & FORMULAE

LENGTH
1 centimetre (cm)	= 10 millimetres	= 0.3937 inch
1 metre (m)	= 100 centimetres	= 1.0936 yards
1 kilometre (km)	= 1000 metres	= 0.6214 mile
1 inch	= 2.54 centimetres	
1 foot (ft)	= 12 inches	= 30.48 cm
1 yard (yd)	= 36 inches	= 0.9144 metre
1 mile	= 1760 yards	= 1.6093 km

WEIGHT
1 gram	= 1000 milligrams	= 0.0353 ounce
1 kilogram	= 1000 grams	= 2.2046 pounds
1 tonne	= 1000 kilograms	= 0.9842 ton
1 ounce	= 437.5 grains	= 28.350 grams
1 pound	= 16 ounces	= 0.4536 kg
1 stone	= 14 pounds	= 6.35 kilograms
1 ton	= 2240 pounds	= 1.016 tonnes

SURFACE / AREA
1 sq centimetre	= 100 sq millimetres	= 0.1550 sq inch
1 sq metre	= 10,000 sq cm	= 1.196 sq yards
1 hectare	= 10,000 sq metres	= 2.4711 acres
1 sq kilometre	= 100 hectares	= 0.3861 sq mile
1 sq foot	= 144 sq inches	= 0.0929 sq m
1 sq inch	= 6.4516 sq miles	
1 sq yard	= 9 sq feet	= 0.8361 sq m
1 sq mile	= 640 acres	= 2.59 sq km
1 acre	= 4840 sq yards	= 4046.9 sq m

VOLUME / CAPACITY
1 cu decimetre (dm)	= 1000 cu cm	= 0.0353 cu foot
1 cu centimetre	= 0.0610 cu inch	
1 cu metre	= 1000 cu dm	= 1.3080 cu yd
1 litre	= 1 cu decimetre	= 0.22 gallon
1 hectolitre	= 100 litres	= 21.997 gal.s
1 cu inch	= 16.387 cu cm	
1 cu yard	= 27 cu feet	= 0.7646 cu m
1 pint	= 20 fluid ounces	= 0.5683 litre
1 gallon	= 8 pints	= 4.5461 litres

CONVERSION TABLE
To Convert	Multiply by
Length:	
Inches to Centimetres	2.540
Centimetres to Inches	0.3937
Feet to Metres	0.3048
Metres to Feet	3.281
Yards to Metres	0.9144
Metres to Yards	1.094
Miles to Kilometres	1.609
Kilometres to Miles	0.6214
Area:	
Sq inches to sq Centimetres	6.452
Sq Centimetres to sq Inches	0.1550
Sq Metres to sq Feet	10.764
Sq Feet to sq Metres	0.0929
Sq Yards to sq Metres	0.8361
Sq Metres to sq Yards	1.196
Sq Miles to sq Kilometres	2.590

To Convert	Multiply by	To Convert	Multiply by
Sq Kilometres to sq Miles	0.3861	**Weight:**	
Acres to Hectares	0.404678	Grains to Grams	0.0648
Hectares to Acres	2.47101	Grams to Grains	15.43
		Ounces to Grams	28.35
Capacity:		Grams to Ounces	0.03527
Cu Inches to cu Centimetres	16.387	Pounds to Grams	453.6
Cu Centimetres to cu Inches	0.061	Grams to Pounds	0.002205
Cu Feet to cu Metres	0.02832	Pounds to Kilograms	0.4536
Cu Metres to cu Feet	35.31	Kilograms to Pounds	2.205
Cu Yards to cu Metres	0.7646	Tons to Kilograms	1016.00
Cu Metres to cu Yards	1.308	Kilograms to Tons	0.0009842
Cu Inches to Litres	0.01639		
Litres to cu Inches	61.03		
Gallons to Litres	4.546		
Litres to Gallons	0.22		

LIST OF ASSOCIATIONS   *(Abbreviation 'D' = Dublin)*

ACCORD - All Hallows, Gracepark Rd., Drumcondra, D 9.

Alcoholics Anonymous 109 South Circular Rd., Leonard's Corner, D 8.

ALONE 1 Willie Bermingham Place, Kilmainham Lane, D 8.

Alzheimer Society of Ireland St. John of God Hospital, Stillorgan, Co. Dublin.

Amalgamated Transport & General Workers Union (ATGWU) 29a William St., Portadown, Co. Armagh.

Amnesty International (Irish Section), Sean MacBride Hse., 48 Fleet St., D 2.

An Taisce, The National Trust for Ireland The Tailor's Hall, Black Lane, D 8.

Arthritis Foundation of Ireland 1 Clanwilliam Sq., Grand Canal Quay, D 2.

Arts Council for N. I. 185 Stranmillis Rd., Belfast.

Association of Local Authorities 123 York St., Belfast.

Association of Secondary Teachers, Ireland (ASTI) ASTI Hse., Winetavern St., D 8.

Association of Advertisers in Ireland Ltd. (AAI) Rock Hse., Main St., Blackrock, Co. Dublin.

Association of Independent Radio Stations Rock Court, 40 Main St.,

Blackrock, Co. Dublin.

Association of Irish Grocery & Confectionery Distributors 18 Rowan Hall, Milbrook Court, D 6.

Association for Children & Adults with Learning Disabilities 1 Suffolk St., D 2.

Asthma Society of Ireland Eden Hse., 15-17 Eden Quay, D 1.

Astronomy Ireland PO Box 2888, D1.

Automobile Association (A.A) 23 Rock Hill, Blackrock, Co. Dublin. 108/110 Great Victoria St., Belfast.

AWARE, Helping to Defeat Depression 147 Phibsboro Rd., D 7.

Bar Council, The P.O. Box 4460, 158-159 Church St., D 7.

Belfast Zoological Gardens Antrim Rd., Newtownabbey, Co. Antrim.

Booksellers Association of Great Britain & Ireland (Irish Branch), 54 Middle Abbey St., D 1.

Bord Fáilte Éireann Baggot St. Bridge, D 2.

BRAINWAVE, The Irish Epilepsy Association 249 Crumlin Rd., D 12.

British Dental Association 131 Ballygowan Rd., Banbridge, Co. Down.

British Medical Association 61 Malone Rd., Belfast.

British Wool Marketing Board 20 Tigracey Rd., Muckamore, Co. Antrim.

CAIRDE 25 St. Mary's Abbey, (Off Capel St.,) D 7.

Carers Association Ltd. St. Mary's Community Centre, Richmond Hill, Rathmines, D 6.

Cerebral Palsy Ireland Head Office, Sandymount Ave., D 4.

Chartered Association of Chartered Institute of Journalists (Irish Office), EETPU Section, 5 Whitefriars, Aungier St., D 2.

Chartered Institute of Management Accountants (CIMA) (Irish Division), 44 Upper Mount St, D 2.

Chartered Institute of Public Finance & Accountancy (Irish Branch), c/o IPA, 57-61 Lansdowne Rd., D 4.

Chartered Institute of Transport in Ireland 1 Fitzwilliam Place, D 2.

Cherish 2 Lower Pembroke St., D2.
Civil & Public Service Union (CPSU) 72 Lower Leeson St., D 2.

Conradh na Gaeilge Áras an Chonartha, 6 Sráid Fhearchair, D 2.

Coeliac Society of Ireland Carmichael Hse., 4 North Brunswick St., D 7.

Comhaltas Ceoltóirí Éireann Cearnóg Belgrave, Baile na Manach, Co. Bhaile Átha Cliath.

CONCERN Camden St., D 2.

Consumers' Association of Ireland Ltd. 45 Upr Mount St., D 2.

Co-Operation North 37 Upr. Fitzwilliam St., D 2. 7 Botanic Ave., Belfast BT7 1JG.

COPE Foundation Bonnington, Montenotte, Cork.

Cumann Lúthchleas Gael (GAA) Croke Pk., D 3.

Cystic Fibrosis Association of Ireland 24 Lower Rathmines Rd., D 6.

Disability Federation of Ireland 2 Sandyford Office Pk, D 18.

Disabled Drivers' Association of Ireland & The Irish Association of Physically Handicapped People Ballindine, Co. Mayo.

Down's Syndrome Association of Ireland 5 Fitzwilliam Place, D 2.

EARTHWATCH, Friends of the Earth Ireland Harbour View, Bantry, Co. Cork.

Electrical & Electronic Retailers Association of Ireland Temple Hall, Blackrock, Co. Dublin.

Electrical Contractors Association 17 Farm Lodge Drive., Greenisland, Whiteabbey, Co. Antrim.

Encounter c/o Mary Clear, IPA, 57-61 Lansdowne Rd., D 4.

Enterprise Ulster (Job Creation & Training) Armagh Hse., Ormeau Avenue, Belfast.

Equal Opportunities Commission for N. I. - Andras Hse., 60 Great Victoria St., Belfast.

Fair Employment Agency for N. I. Andras Hse., 60 Great Victoria St., Belfast.

Farm Tractor & Machinery Association Ltd. Irish Farm Centre, Bluebell, D 12.

Federation of Irish Scout Associations 19 Herbert Place, D 2.

Federation of Small Businesses 3 Farrier Court, Newtownabbey,

Glengormley, Co. Antrim.

Feis Ceoil Association 37 Molesworth St., D 2.

Film Institute of Ireland Irish Film Centre, 6 Eustace St., Temple Bar, D 2.

Film Makers Ireland 6 Eustace St., D 2.

Financial & Business Information Group c/o Business Information Centre, KPMG Stokes Kennedy Crowley, 1 Stokes Place, St. Stephen's Green, D 2.

Folk Music Society of Ireland 15 Henrietta St., D 1.

Football Association of Ireland (FAI) 80 Merrion Sq., D 2.

Foróige (National Youth Development Organisation), Irish Farm Centre, Bluebell, D 12.

Freight Transport Association Ltd. 187 Bangor Rd., Holywood, Belfast.

Friedreich's Ataxia Society of Ireland San Martino Mart Lane, D 18.

Gael-Linn 26-27 Cearnóg Mhuirfean, D 2.

Gay & Lesbian Equality Network (GLEN) Hirschfeld Centre, 10 Fownes St., D 2.

Geographical Society of Ireland c/o Dept. of Geography, UCD, Belfield, D 4.

Gingerbread Ireland 29-30 Dame St., D 2.

Girls' Brigade Ireland Brigade Hse., 5 Upper Sherrard St., D 1.

Grand Orange Lodge of Ireland 65 Dublin Rd., Belfast.

Greenpeace 44 Upper Mount St., D 2.

Guaranteed Irish Ltd. 1 Fitzwilliam Place, Dublin 2.

Hospitality Association of N. I. 108-110 Midland Building, Whitla St., Belfast.

Huntington's Disease Association of Ireland Carmichael Hse., North Brunswick St., D 7.

Industrial Development Board (IDB) 64 Chichester St., Belfast.

Institute for Numerical Computation & Analysis (INCA) 26 Temple Lane, D 2.

Institute of Accounting Technicians in Ireland (IATA) Chartered Accountants Hse., 87-89 Pembroke Rd., Ballsbridge, D 4.

Institute of Advertising Practitioners in Ireland (IAPI) 36 Upper Fitzwilliam St., D 2.

Institute of Bankers in Ireland Nassau Hse., Nassau St., D 2.

Institute of Certified Public Accountants in Ireland 9 Ely Place, D 2. 41 Fitzwilliam St., Belfast BT9 6AW.

Institute of Chartered Accountants in Ireland 87-89 Pembroke Rd., Ballsbridge, D 4. 11 Donegall Sq., Belfast BT1 5JE.

Institute of Foreign Trade c/o The Irish Exporters Association, Holbrook Hse., Holles St., D 2.

Institute of Professional Auctioneers & Valuers 36 Upper Fitzwilliam St., D 2.

Institute of Public Administration 57-61 Lansdowne Rd., D 4.

Institute of Taxation in Ireland 19 Sandymount Ave., D 4.

Insurance Institution of Ireland 32 Nassau St., D 2. **Interaid** 27 Wyattville Close, Ballybrack, Co. Dublin.

Irish Agriculture Association, The Irish Farm Centre, Naas Rd., Bluebell, D 12.

Irish Association of Non-Smokers PO Box 1024, Sheriff St., D 1.

Irish Association for Spina Bifida & Hydrocephalus Old Nangor Road, Clondalkin, D 22.

Irish Auctioneers & Valuers Institute 38 Merrion Sq., D 2.

Irish Bankers' Federation Nassau Hse., Nassau St., D 2.

Irish Banking Foundation 5 Lucerne Court, 39 Castle Ave.,

Clontarf, D 3.

**Irish Book Publishers'
Association (CLÉ)** The Irish
Writers Centre, 19 Parnell Sq., D 1.

**Irish Building Societies
Association** Heritage Hse.,
23 St. Stephen's Green, D 2.

**Irish Business & Employers
Confederation (IBEC)**
Confederation Hse., 84-86 Lower
Baggot St., D 2.

Irish Cancer Society
5 Northumberland Rd., D 4.

**Irish College of General
Practitioners**
Corrigan Hse., Fenian St., D 2.

Irish Computer Society
17 Earlsfort Terrace, D 2.

**Irish Congress of Trade Unions
(ICTU)**19 Raglan Rd., Ballsbridge,
D 4.   3 Wellington Pk., Belfast.

Irish Council for Acupuncture
87 North Circular Rd., D 7.

**Irish Council against Blood
Sports**   PO Box 147, Cork.

Irish Council for Civil Liberties
35 Arran Quay, D 7.

**Irish Countrywomen's
Association (ICA)**
58 Merrion Rd., D 4.

Irish Deaf Society Carmichael
Hse., North Brunswick St., D 7.

Irish Dental Association
10 Richview Office Pk.,
Clonskeagh Rd., D 14.

Irish Diabetic Association
76 Lower Gardiner St., D 1.

**Irish Detergent & Allied Products
Association**
c/o 1 Kincora Rd., Clontarf, D 3.

**Irish Educational Publishers
Association** c/o Gill & Macmillan
Ltd., Goldenbridge Industrial Estate,
Inchicore, D 8.

Irish Exporters Association
Holbrook Hse., Holles St., D 2.

Irish Farmers' Association (IFA)
Irish Farm Centre, Bluebell, D 12.

**Irish Family Planning Association
(IFPA)** Halfpenny Court, 36-37
Lower Ormond Quay, D 1.

Irish Family History Society
PO Box 36, Naas, Co. Kildare.

Irish Fight for Sight Campaign
4 Parnell St., Waterford.

**Irish Fish Producers'
Organisation** 11 Elgin Rd., D 4.

**Irish Fishermen's Organisation
Ltd.** Cumberland Hse., Fenian St.,
Dublin 2.

Irish Football Association (IFA)
20 Windsor Ave., Belfast.

Irish Gas Association
c/o Bord Gais Éireann, PO Box 51,
Inchera, Little Island, Co. Cork.

Irish Girl Guides
27 Pembroke Pk., D 4.

Irish Haemophilia Society
4-5 Eustace St., D 2.

Irish Heart Foundation
4 Clyde Rd., Ballsbridge, D 4.

Irish Hospice Foundation
9 Fitzwilliam Plc., D 2.

**Irish Hospital Consultants
Association** Lowell Hse.,
Herbert Ave., Merrion Rd., D 4.

**Irish Hotel & Catering
Association**
Mespil Hse., Sussex Rd., D 4.

Irish Hotels Federation
13 Northbrook Rd., D 6.

Irish Institute for Brain Injuries
Kilnacourt Hse., Portarlington,
Co. Laois.

Irish Insurance Federation
Russell Hse., Russell Court, St.
Stephen's Green, D 2.

Irish Kidney Association Donor
Hse., 156 Pembroke Rd., D 4.

Irish League of Credit Unions
Castleside Drive, Rathfarnham, D 14.

**Irish Meat Processors
Association**   11 Merrion Sq., D 2.

Irish Mensa PO Box 3647, D 1.

**Irish Motor Neurone Disease
Association** Carmichael Hse.,
North Brunswick St., D 7.

Irish Museums Association c/o
National Archives, Bishop St., D 8.

**Irish Municipal, Public & Civil
Trade Union (IMPACT)**
Nerney's Court, D 1.

**Irish Music Rights Organisation
Ltd. (IMRO)**
Copyright Hse., Pembroke Row,
Lower Baggot St., D 2.

**Irish National Teachers'
Organisation (INTO)**
35 Parnell Sq., D 1.
23 College Gardens, Belfast

**Irish Nurses' Organisation &
National Council of Nurses of
Ireland (INO)**
11 Fitzwilliam Place, D 2.

**Irish Organic Farmers & Growers
Association (IOFGA)**
56 Blessington Rd., D 7.

Irish Pharmaceutical Union
Butterfield Hse., Butterfield Ave.,
Rathfarnham, D 14.

Irish Planning Institute
8 Merrion Sq., D 2.

Irish Printing Federation
Baggot Bridge Hse., 84-86 Lower
Baggot Street, D 2.

Irish Quality Association (IQA)
Merrion Hall, Strand Rd.,
Sandymount, D 4.

Irish Red Cross Society
16 Merrion Sq., D 2.

**Irish Retail Newsagents
Association (IRNA)** 21 Priory Hall,
Stillorgan, Co. Dublin.

Irish Road Haulage Association
40 Lower Leeson St., D 2.

Irish Rugby Football Union
62 Lansdowne Rd., D 4.
85 Ravenhill Pk., Belfast.

**Irish Society of Chartered
Physiotherapists** Royal College of
Surgeons, St Stephen's Green, D 2.

Irish Society for Autism
Unity Buildings, 16 Lower O'Connell
St., D 1.

Irish Society for the Prevention of Cruelty to Animals (ISPCA)
300 Lower Rathmines Rd., D 6.

Irish Society for the Prevention of Cruelty to Children (ISPCC)
20 Molesworth St., D 2.

Irish Sudden Infant Death Association   Carmichael Hse., 4 North Brunswick St., D 7.

Irish Taxi Federation
48 Summerhill Parade, D 1.

Irish Tourist Industry Confederation (ITIC)
Alliance Hse., Adelaide St., Dún Laoghaire, Co. Dublin.

Irish Travel Agents Association
3rd Floor, Heaton Hse., 32 South William St., D 2.

Irish Traveller Movement
4-5 Eustace St., D 2.

Irish Veterinary Association 53 Lansdowne Rd., Ballsbridge, D 4.

Irish Vocational Education Association   McCann Hse., 99 Marlborough Rd., Donnybrook, D 4.

Irish Wildlife Federation
39 Fitzwilliam St., D 2.

Irish Wheelchair Association - Áras Chuchulain, Blackheath Drive, Clontarf, D 3.

Irish Writers' Centre
19 Parnell Sq., D 1.

Irish Youth Foundation
Sandyford Rd., Dundrum, D 16.

Labour Relations Agency
Windsor Hse., Bedford St., Belfast.

Library Association of Ireland
53 Upper Mount Street, D 2.

Licensed Vintners' Association
Anglesea Hse., Anglesea Rd., Ballsbridge, D 4.

Livestock Marketing Commission
57 Malone Rd., Belfast.

Macra na Feirme
Irish Farm Centre, Bluebell, D 12.

Mental Health Association of Ireland   Mensana Hse., 6 Adelaide St., Dún Laoghaire, Co. Dublin.

Milk Marketing Board
456 Antrim Rd., Belfast.

Minus One
68 Lower Leeson St., D 2.

Multiple Sclerosis Society of Ireland 2 Sandymount Green, D 4.

Muscular Dystrophy Ireland
Carmichael Hse., North Brunswick St., D 7.

Music Association of Ireland Ltd.
5 North Frederick St., D 1.

National Association for the Deaf
35 North North Frederick St., D 1.

National Association for the Mentally Handicapped of Ireland (NAMHI) 5 Fitzwilliam Place, D 2.

National Association of Head Teachers   31 Church Rd., Holywood, Co. Down.

National Association of Independent Retailers
1 Main St., Rathfarnham, D 14.

National Association of Shopkeepers
338a Beersbridge Rd., Belfast.

National Council for the Blind of Ireland   PV Doyle Hse., Whitworth Rd., Drumcondra, D 9.

National Council of YMCA's of Ireland Ltd.   Great Island Enterprise Pk, Ballincollig, Co. Cork.

National Youth Council of Ireland
3 Montague St., D 2.

National Community Games
22 Store St., D 1.

National Council of Y.M.C.A.'s in Ireland - 37-41 High St., Belfast.

National Dairy Council, The (NDC)
Grattan Hse., Lower Mount St., D2.

National Eczema Society
Carmichael Hse., North Brunswick St., D 7.

National Federation of Self Employment & Small Business Ltd.
3 Farrier Court, Newtownabbey, Glengormley, Co. Antrim.

National Federation of Retail Newsagents 17 Greenmount Hse.,

Greenmount Office Pk., Harold's Cross Rd., D 6

National Irish Safety Organisation (NISO) 10 Hogan Place, D 2.

National Newspapers of Ireland
Clyde Lodge, 15 Clyde Rd., D 4.

National Womens Council of Ireland 32 Upr. Fitzwilliam St., D 2.

National Trust
86 Botanic Ave., Belfast.

N. I. Agricultural Producers' Association
15 Molesworth St., Belfast.

N. I. Bakers Union
80 High St., Belfast.

N. I. Bankers Association
Stokes House, 17-25 College Sq. East, Belfast.

N. I. Chamber of Commerce & Industry   Chamber of Commerce Hse., Great Victoria St., Belfast.

N. I. Chamber of Trade
3rd Floor, Brands Arcade, Belfast.

N. I. Economic Council
Bulloch Hse., 2 Linenhall St., Belfast.

N. I. Hotels & Caterers Association 73 May St., Belfast.

N. I. Housing Executive
The Housing Centre, 2 Adelaide St., Belfast.

N. I. Musicians Association
Unit 4 Fortwilliam Business Pk., Dargan Rd., Belfast.

N. I. Public Service Alliance
54 Wellington Pk., Belfast BT9 6DP.

Northern Ireland Tourist Board
16 Nassau St., D 2.
St. Annes Court, 59 North St., Belfast BT1 1 NB.

N. I. Trade Association Ltd.
10 Arthur St., Belfast.

N. I. Wholesale Merchants & Manufacturers Association
10 Arthur St., Belfast.

Olympic Council of Ireland
27 Mespil Rd., D 14.

Parentline Carmichael Centre,

North Brunswick St., D 7.

Peace Train Organisation
90 Georges Ave., Blackrock,
Co. Dublin.
Peace Hse., 224 Lisburn Rd.,
Belfast BT9 6GE.

Pharmaceutical Society
73 University St., Belfast.

Polio Fellowship of Ireland
Park Hse. Vocational & Residential
Training Centre, Stillorgan Grove,
Stillorgan, Co. Dublin.

Poster Advertising Association
7 Sweetmount Dr., Dundrum, D 14.

**Provincial Newspapers
Association of Ireland**
33 Parkgate St., D 8.

**Psychiatric Nurses Association
of Ireland** - 2 Gardiner Place, D 1.

Psychological Society of Ireland
13 Adelaide Rd., D 2.

Rape Crisis Centre
70 Lower Leeson St., D 2.

Restaurateurs Association of N. I.
3 University St., Belfast.

Retail Motor Industry Federation
107a Shore Rd., Belfast.

Royal Automobile Club (R.A.C)
65 Chichester St., Belfast.

Royal College of Nursing
17 Windsor Ave., Belfast.

Royal Dublin Society
Ballsbridge, D 4.

Royal Ulster Agricultural Society
The King's Hall, Balmoral, Belfast.

Reading Association of Ireland
Blackrock Teachers' Centre,
Carysfort Ave., Blackrock,
Co. Dublin.

**Regional Newspaper Advertising
Bureau (RNAB Ireland)**
33 Parkgate St., D 8.

Rehab Group
Roslyn Pk., Sandymount, D 4.

**Restaurants Association of
Ireland**
11 Bridge Court, City Gate, St.
Augustine St., D 8.

**Retail, Grocery, Dairy & Allied
Trades' Association (RGDATA)**
Rock Hse., Main St., Blackrock,
Co. Dublin.

**Royal Academy of Medicine in
Ireland** 6 Kildare St., D 2.

**Royal Horticultural Society of
Ireland** Swanbrook Hse.,
Bloomfield Ave., Morehampton Rd.,
Dublin 4.

**Royal Institute of the Architects
of Ireland** 8 Merrion Sq., D 2.

Royal Life Saving Society
(Ireland Branch), PO Box 71,
Dún Laoghaire, Co. Dublin.

**Royal National Lifeboat
Institution** (Ireland Branch),
15 Windsor Terrace,
Dún Laoghaire, Co. Dublin.

Samaritans 20 Barington St.,
Limerick. 112 Marlborough St., D 1.

Separated Persons Association
Carmichael Hse., Brunswick St.,
North, D 7.

Simon Community St. Andrew's
Hse., 28-30 Exchequer St., D 2.

**Schizophrenia Association of
Ireland** 4 Fitzwilliam Place, D 2.

Scout Association of Ireland
Morrisson Chambers, 32 Nassau
St., D 2.

**Services Industrial Professional
Technical Union (SIPTU)**
Liberty Hall, D 1.
3 Antrim Rd., Belfast, BT15 2BE.

Society of St. Vincent de Paul
8 New Cabra Rd., Phibsborough,
Dublin 7.

Sports Council for N. I. Hse. of
Sport, Upper Malone Rd., Belfast.

**Standing Conference of Youth
Organisations**
50 University St., Belfast.

Small Firms Association (SFA)
Confederation Hse., 84-86 Lower
Baggot St., D 2.

**Society of Chiropodists /
Podiatrists** (Ireland Branch),
The Medical Centre, Drogheda St.,
Balbriggan, Co. Dublin.

**Society of the Irish Motor
Industry**
5 Upper Pembroke St., Dublin 2.

**Soft Drink & Beer Bottlers'
Association Ltd.** 13 Adelaide
Street , Dún Laoghaire, Co. Dublin.

**Trade & Professional Publishers
Association** 31 Deansgrange Rd.,
Blackrock, Co. Dublin.

Teachers' Union of Ireland
73 Orwell Rd., Rathgar, D 6.

Trust Bride Road., D 8.

Ulster Chemists Association
73 University St., Belfast.

Ulster Farmers Union
475 Antrim Rd., Belfast.

Ulster Teachers' Union
94 Malone Rd., Belfast.

U.N.I.C.E.F. 4 St. Andrew St., D 2.

Union of Students in Ireland (USI)
National Student Centre, 1-2 Aston
Place, Temple Bar, D 2.
Belfast Regional Office, 34 Botanic
Ave., Belfast.

USIT
Aston Quay, O'Connell Bridge, D 2.

Vegetarian Society of Ireland
PO Box 3010, D 4.

Vegetarian Society of Ulster
66 Ravenhill Gardens, Belfast.

Victim Support
29-30 Dame St., D 2.

Video Retailers Association
19 Sandyford Office Pk., D 18.

Vintner's Federation of Ireland
52 Upper Mount St., D 2.

Well Woman Centre
73 Lower Leeson St., D 2.

**Wine & Spirit Association of
Ireland** 33 Clarinda Pk. West,
Dún Laoghaire, Co. Dublin.

Women's Aid - PO Box 791, D 7.

Zoological Society of Ireland
Phoenix Pk., D 8.

IRISH ALMANAC
YEARBOOK OF FACTS
1998

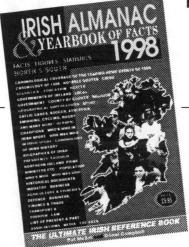

If <u>YOU</u> wish
to have your business
advertised in the
1998
IRISH ALMANAC &
YEARBOOK OF FACTS

Contact us at . . . .

16 HIGH STREET, DERRY, NORTHERN IRELAND.
TEL: 01504-45978   CODE FROM REPUBLIC OF IRELAND: 0801504-45978

IRISH ALMANAC
&YEARBOOK OF FACTS
1998

The 1998 Irish Almanac and Yearbook of Facts will be available from all good bookshops throughout Ireland in Autumn 1997. Alternatively, you can acquire same by filling in the coupon below and forwarding it to our office at **16 High Street, Derry, Northern Ireland** complete with payment of £9.95 (P. & P. free).

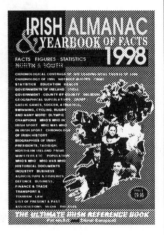